The Prehistoric
Archaeology of Ireland

The Prehistoric Archaeology of Ireland

Revised edition

John Waddell

well

THIS BOOK IS DEDICATED TO ALL WHO FOUGHT FOR THE TARA LANDSCAPE

First published 1998 by Galway University Press Ltd

This edition 2010 by Wordwell Ltd, Leopardstown, Dublin

British Library Cataloguing-in-Publication Data.
A catalogue record for this book is available from the British Library.

Printed in Ireland by Gemini International

ISBN 978 1 905569 47 5

Contents

Preface   vi

Acknowledgements   x

List of illustrations   xiii

1   Postglacial Ireland: the first colonists   1

2   Farmers of the fourth millennium   25

3   The cult of the dead   63

4   Sacred circles and new technology   115

5   Enigmatic monuments   173

6   Bronze and gold and power: 1600–1000 BC   187

7   The consolidation of wealth and status: 1000–600 BC   233

8   From bronze to iron   291

9   Elusive settlements and ritual sites   333

10   Protohistory   395

Bibliography   403

Index   437

Preface

When *The prehistoric archaeology of Ireland* was first published in 1998, it was intended to be simultaneously an introduction to the subject, a work of reference and a synthesis placing Irish archaeology in its wider British and Continental context. Because a detailed radiocarbon chronology was emerging, allowing the extensive use of absolute dates, I also attempted to dispense with the antiquated Three-Age system born in the nineteenth century and tried to abandon the terms Mesolithic, Neolithic, Bronze Age and Iron Age. I was not the first to make an effort to do this, of course. Colin Burgess, for example, in his *Age of Stonehenge* in 1980 recognised the inadequacies of this terminology in his study of a period spanning part of the Neolithic and the Bronze Age and employed terms such as the 'Meldon Bridge' period for the late Neolithic and the 'Knighton Heath' period for the Middle Bronze Age. Others have expressed their disenchantment with this Three-Age arrangement as well, but it stubbornly refuses to die. Over the last decade, a host of publications in Ireland and abroad testify to its enduring popularity as a convenient labelling system—as titles such as *Landscapes of Neolithic Ireland* (Cooney 2000) and *The Bronze Age landscapes of the Pipeline to the West* (Grogan *et al.* 2007) indicate. It may be time to capitulate and accept the inevitable. Thus, with some reluctance, the following traditional broad periodisation is adopted here and the traditional but antiquated terminology used as sparingly as possible:

Mesolithic:	Early Mesolithic	8000–6500 BC
	Late Mesolithic	6500–4000 BC
Neolithic	Earlier Neolithic	4000–3100 BC
	Later Neolithic	3100–2500 BC
Bronze Age	Early Bronze Age	2500–1600 BC
	Middle Bronze Age	1600–1000 BC
	Late Bronze Age	1000–600 BC
Iron Age		600 BC–AD 400

As before, in discussing some artefact types, attention is paid to typological niceties; this is not unnecessary tedious detail for it serves to demonstrate the value these studies sometimes have and how they may illuminate certain archaeological questions. Whatever about typologies, chronological labels and book titles, publications such as *Landscapes of Neolithic Ireland* and *Bronze Age landscapes of the Pipeline to the West* illustrate something far more important. They form part of a significant body of research over the past decade that has advanced our understanding of several aspects of Ireland's prehistory.

This advance has been on a number of fronts. To mention just a few major studies in the last ten years, Peter Woodman's excavation at the important Mesolithic site at Ferriter's Cove was published in 1999 (Woodman *et al.* 1999), Eamon Cody's *Survey of the megalithic tombs of County Donegal* was published in 2002 and Billy O'Brien's 1999 monograph *Sacred ground—megalithic tombs in coastal south-west Ireland* was another valuable contribution to megalithic tomb studies. The monumental report on his programme of excavation and research on early copper-mining at Ross Island, Co. Kerry, *Ross Island. Mining, metal and society in early Ireland,* appeared in 2004. Muiris O'Sullivan's welcome account of the 50-year-old excavations initiated by Seán P. Ó Ríordáin at the Mound of the Hostages at Tara was published in 2005 and followed by Eoin Grogan's 2008 summary of Ó Ríordáin's work at the Rath of the Synods. Important artefact studies include Gabriel Cooney and Steven Mandal's *The Irish stone axe project* (1998), George Eogan's *The socketed bronze axes in Ireland* (1999) and Anna Brindley's *The dating of food vessels and urns in Ireland* (2007). Some of the more important artefacts noted in the following pages are well illustrated in *Treasures of the National Museum of Ireland* (Wallace and Ó Floinn 2002).

Significant results are emerging from the work of the Discovery Programme. In a range of publications—such as the series of studies in *The kingship and landscape of Tara* edited by Edel Bhreathnach (2005)—our understanding of the Tara landscape has been altered forever, and one of its greatest discoveries must be the huge double pit and ditch circle on that famous hill revealed by Joe Fenwick and Conor Newman's geophysical survey (2002). If, as seems likely, this was once an enormous late Neolithic timber circle, it was four or five times the size of its celebrated stone counterpart, Stonehenge.

Also noteworthy is the appearance of the results of its North Munster Project in Eoin Grogan's two-volume study (2005) and Martin Doody's volume on his Ballyhoura Hills Project (2008), both significant contributions to our understanding of Bronze Age settlement. A number of major studies have emerged from the commercial sector, including that *Bronze Age landscapes of the Pipeline to the West* mentioned above and *The Lisheen Mine Archaeological Project* (Gowen *et al.* 2005). The National Roads Authority, established in 1993, has begun to publish some of the findings made in the course of road development, including Ed Danaher's *Monumental beginnings: the archaeology of the N4 Sligo Inner Relief Road* (2007), *The archaeology of life and death in the Boyne floodplain: the linear landscape of the M4, Kinnegad–Enfield–Kilcock motorway* (Carlin *et al.* 2008), and *Near the bend of the river. The archaeology of the N25 Kilmacthomas realignment* (Johnston *et al.* 2008).

Various scientific techniques commonly employed in Irish archaeology, such as radiocarbon dating, dendrochronology or tree-ring dating, animal and human osteoarchaeology and pollen analysis, are described in *Environmental archaeology in Ireland* (edited by E. M. Murphy and N. J. Whitehouse 2007). Radiocarbon dates cited in the text are given in calibrated calendar years BC or AD as calculated by the authors cited (at two sigma).

The economic expansion and infrastructural development of the last decade have had a major impact on archaeology. As successive issues of the *Excavations Bulletin* edited by Isabel Bennett demonstrate, the number of excavation licences issued trebled over this time-span. Important discoveries have been made: there have been considerable advances in our knowledge of Neolithic rectangular houses and Bronze Age round houses; Mesolithic cremated burials and fish-traps have come to light. But in some quarters the price has been too high. Geophysical survey has not been the only activity to alter our appreciation of the Tara landscape forever.

The routing of a new motorway, the M3, through the valley between the Hill of Tara and Skreen prompted an international controversy and brought out the best and worst in politics and archaeology. Faced with an intransigent government that seemed to believe that sustainable development meant sustaining development at all costs, some archaeologists studiously positioned themselves on neutral ground, but others refused to accept a bad planning decision and an act of cultural vandalism on a par with that demolition of a block of houses in Fitzwilliam Street in 1965 that destroyed Dublin's longest expanse of intact Georgian architecture. The Tara debacle, to 2005, has been documented by Conor Newman (2007a).

The pressures of development caused other archaeological problems as well. While an enormous amount of archaeological excavation and other work was carried out to a high standard, a lack of coherent quality control and strategic planning produced a situation where self-regulation was considered acceptable practice, where publication became the exception rather than the rule, and where the need for adequate curation of archaeological material and archives went unmet (Gowen 2007; Cooney *et al.* 2006). Maggie Ronayne (2008) has voiced her concern about the pressures that the commercial sector has exercised on the archaeological profession in general and on the universities in particular, and I offered some comments on this theme in the pages of *Archaeology Ireland* in 2005. I noted that the university world in Ireland was still some distance from the enormous pressures apparent in some areas of the life sciences. In biotechnical research, for instance, collaboration with major corporations, and with the pharmaceutical industry in particular, has meant that normal academic scepticism and caution as well as research directions have had to give way to the demands of the market-place. We have also been spared—so far—the 'grade inflation' that has plagued some American universities. When an institution needs to attract and retain students in a competitive market, intellectual standards are likely to be compromised. The production of high grades because of market forces is a form of academic prostitution and neatly illustrates the fact that these forces are not always a benign influence. In this commodification of knowledge the market can decide what is scholarship. Just as the traditional universities' collegial approach to management is often perceived as alien to industry and government, the traditional pursuit of truth and knowledge as an essential contribution to contemporary society is often considered an expensive luxury today. The agenda of scholarship is increasingly set not by the collegiate academy but by the political establishment (and their academic supporters) in the name of the market-place. In this situation fundamental principles are easily forgotten, and that essential balance between scholarship within the university and engagement with economic and social forces without is not easily maintained.

Even though it has been claimed that 'archaeology [in Ireland] is predominantly a business domain, operating in a competitive economic climate radically different from the research ethos which characterised earlier decades' (Cooney *et al.* 2006), I would argue that the practice of archaeology, whether it takes place in the commercial sector, in the university, in museums or in other milieux, can never be just a business or a service. Indeed, if there are those who see archaeology as a service industry, then we must ask them the question, 'In whose service?'

It is necessary to reiterate some of those fundamental principles. Archaeology is an intellectual discipline that studies the evidence of past human behaviour. It attempts to understand the processes that determined this activity, using a variety of approaches, methodologies and theoretical perceptions. Its more immediate roots lie in the philosophical liberation of the Enlightenment, and its theoretical and methodological elements began to develop, along with those of many other disciplines, in the nineteenth century. Archaeology still has the goal of illuminating aspects of our common humanity. This objective is just one of many links between its various practitioners, whether in the library or in the field. Though rarely articulated, it is shared by archaeologists in both the university world and the commercial sphere. One important strand in these linkages is the fact that most archaeologists share a university education which, one hopes, has alerted them to the philosophical significance and scholarly limitations of what they do. Whatever mechanisms they use, whatever theoretical stance they adopt, they share an appreciation that they are in the special position of being able to investigate a socially constructed past. They share a commitment to undertake this work of advancing knowledge in a responsible and professional fashion with a determination to achieve the best interpretative results.

Therefore the dumbing down of archaeological practice does everyone a disservice. This happens when university teaching and research fail to attain the highest standards, or when academic fatalism produces an unquestioning acceptance of the contemporary condition. It happens when professional independence is compromised or when the State regulatory body decides that the assessment of academic qualifications should no longer be a part of the excavation licensing process and thereby reduces the complex challenge of systematic excavation to a routine craft. Excavation is not just the acquisition of data; it is—or should be—an analytical programme that from beginning to end is part of a considered research strategy. There is no way that an individual's competence to formulate this sort of strategy—from the identification of initial research problems to the interpretation and dissemination of the results—can be assessed without analysing the calibre of their professional education. This diminution also happens when archaeologists adopt the euphemism 'preservation by record' for rescue excavation, even though they know that there is no such thing and that excavation is controlled clinical destruction and not a mere recording exercise. This nonsensical phrase is a reminder that the extinct Dodo might be considered a good example of preservation by taxidermy. The pressures of the market-place cannot be ignored, of course, and archaeological practice has to accept some limitations. These limitations, however, should be defined by independent professional archaeologists, not by developers or road-builders. A strong professional ethic and a clear understanding of the intellectual basis of the discipline are needed to counter the perception that archaeology is just another service industry with malleable principles. This is required in both the commercial and university sectors, for both face pressures undreamt of a decade ago. While some may argue that professional archaeologists have no privileged authority when it comes to interpreting ancient remains, it is necessary to remember the special responsibility they do have; the study of archaeology has a unique capacity to reach the very depths of antiquity, and their reconstruction of this past gives form and meaning to the present.

John Waddell

Acknowledgements

I am deeply grateful for the help and advice of Stefan Bergh, Joe Fenwick, Angela Gallagher, Carleton Jones, Conor Newman, Máirín Ní Dhonnchadha, Michael O'Connell and Maggie Ronayne, all of whom, of course, bear no responsibility for what transpired. Jane Conroy deserves special thanks, and George Eogan and Barry Raftery have always been particularly generous in their permission to use illustrations from their many publications.

The sources of the various figures are as follows, and this list offers a good indication of the measure of my debt to the work of many other friends and colleagues in the field of Irish prehistoric archaeology: Figs 1.1–1.2 after Woodman 1985 (Crown copyright; reproduced with the permission of the Controller of Her Majesty's Stationery Office); 1.3–1.4 after Woodman 1978a; 1.5 after Clark 1975; 1.6 after Woodman 1978a; 1.7 after Movius 1953, Woodman 1977 and 1978b, and Woodman *et al.* 1999; 1.8–1.9 after Woodman *et al.* 1999; 1.10 after Fry 2000; 1.11 after Pedersen 1995 and FitzGerald 2007b; 1.12 after Woodman 2003a; 1.13 after Collins and Coyne 2003.

Fig. 2.1 after O'Connell 1994; 2.2 after Glob 1951; 2.3 after S. P. Ó Ríordáin 1954; 2.4 after ApSimon 1969a and Gowen 1988 (reconstruction by Eoin Grogan); 2.5 after Ó Nualláin 1972, and Simpson 1995 and 1996b; 2.6 after Purcell 2002a; 2.7 after O'Donovan 2004; 2.8 after Eogan and Roche 1997, and after Grogan 1996 modified by G. Mulligan; 2.9 after Caulfield 1992; 2.10 after Danaher 2007; 2.11 after Case 1973; 2.12 from Case 1961, after Kilbride-Jones 1939 and Eogan 1984;

2.13 after Lucas 1967; 2.14–2.15 after Sheridan *et al.* 1992; 2.16 after Knowles 1886 and 1909; 2.17 after Lucas 1964, Eogan 1963, Collins and Seaby 1960, and Collins 1966; 2.18 after J. Raftery 1970 and Lucas 1966.

Fig. 3.1 after Ó Nualláin 1989, Herity 1974 and Burenhult 1980; 3.2 after Shee Twohig 1981 by permission of Oxford University Press; 3.3 after C. O'Kelly 1971; 3.4 after O'Kelly 1982; 3.5 after Eogan 1986; 3.6 after Eogan and Richardson 1982; 3.7–3.8 after Shee Twohig 1981 by permission of Oxford University Press; 3.9 after M. O'Sullivan 2005; 3.10 after Shee Twohig 1981 by permission of Oxford University Press; 3.11 after Eogan 1986 and Bergh 1995; 3.12 after Herity 1974; 3.13 after Shee Twohig 1981 by permission of Oxford University Press; 3.14 after Ó Nualláin 1989 and Waterman 1978; 3.15 after Waterman 1965, and Ó Nualláin 1972 and 1976; 3.16 after de Valera 1960 and 1965; 3.17 after Ó Nualláin 1989 and Topp 1962; 3.18 after Borlase 1897; 3.19 after Ó Nualláin 1989, P. Walsh 1995, Herring and May 1937, and Davies 1939c; 3.20 after O'Kelly 1958b; 3.21 after J. Raftery 1973.

Fig. 4.1 after Lynn 1988 (Crown copyright; reproduced with the permission of the Controller of Her Majesty's Stationery Office); 4.2 after Collins 1957b (Crown copyright; reproduced with the permission of the Controller of Her Majesty's Stationery Office) and Hartwell 1994; 4.3 after Fenwick and Newman 2002, reconstruction in inset by kind permission of Colm Crowley and RTE Cork; 4.4 after O'Kelly *et al.* 1983, Sweetman 1987, Brennan *et al.* 1978, Earwood 1992, and various authors redrawn by Case 1995a; 4.5 courtesy of Carleton Jones; 4.6 after Harbison 1976 and 1978, Flanagan 1970, Lucas 1971 and Rynne 1972b; 4.7 after W. O'Brien 2004a; 4.9 after Harbison 1968 and O'Kelly 1970; 4.10 after Harbison 1968, Lucas 1966 and Rynne 1963; 4.11 after Harbison 1969a, J. Raftery 1951, Ramsey et al. 1992, Lucas 1970, Coghlan and Raftery 1961, and Coffey 1894; 4.12 after Armstrong 1933, and Butler 1963 after Paton; 4.13 after Coffey 1909, Harding 1993 and Eogan 1994; 4.14 after W. O'Brien 1994; 4.15 after B. Ó Ríordáin and Waddell 1993; 4.16 after Mount 1995, and B. Ó Ríordáin and Waddell 1993; 4.17 after B. Ó Ríordáin and Waddell 1993, and O'Kelly from Waddell 1990; 4.18 after O'Kelly and Shee 1974; 4.19 after Rynne 1964, Ryan 1975 and Longworth 1984; 4.20 after Kavanagh 1976, B. Ó Ríordáin 1967 and Williams et al. 1992; 4.21 after Hartnett from Waddell 1990, Waterman 1968 and Grogan 1990; 4.22 after Hencken 1935, Brindley and Lanting 1992b, and Hencken and Movius 1934.

Fig. 5.1 after Coffey 1911, and Ann O'Sullivan and Sheehan 1996; 5.2 after Fahy 1960 and Pilcher 1969; 5.3 after O'Kelly 1954.

Fig. 6.1 after Coghlan and Raftery 1961; 6.2 after Evans and Mitchell 1954; 6.3 after Ramsey 1995; 6.4 after Burgess 1974, and Burgess and Gerloff 1981; 6.5 after Armstrong 1917 and Eogan 1983; 6.6 after Burgess 1974; 6.7–6.8 after Eogan 1983; 6.9 after Eogan 1994; 6.10 after Eogan 1994 and Armstrong 1933; 6.11–6.16 from Eogan 1983; 6.17 after Eogan 1965, and Colquhoun and Burgess 1988; 6.18 after Conway 2005; 6.19 after Gowen et al. 2005; 6.20 after Doody 1987; 6.21 after Doody 2008; 6.22 after O'Kelly 1989; 6.23–6.24 after Moloney 1993; 6.25 after Mallory 1995; 6.26–6.27 after Cotter 1993, 1995 and 1996.

Fig. 7.1 after Eogan 1983; 7.2 after Briggs 1987; 7.3 after Patay 1990, J. Evans 1881 and Corcoran 1965; 7.4 after Warner 2006; 7.5 after Briggs 1987 and Gerloff 1986; 7.6 after Lucas 1968 and Briggs 1987; 7.7 after R. A. Smith 1920; 7.8 after B. Raftery 1983; 7.9 after Eogan 1964 and Desnoyers 1876; 7.10 after J. M. Coles 1963; 7.11 after Eogan 1964 and Lucas 1961; 7.12 after Eogan 1983; 7.13 after Coffey 1913, Ruiz-Gálvez Priego 1995 and J. M. Coles 1971; 7.14 after J. M. Coles 1962 and Almagro 1966; 7.15 after Ryan 1983, J. M. Coles 1962 and B. Raftery 1982; 7.16 from Armstrong 1933; 7.17 after Eogan 1983; 7.18, 1 after J. Raftery

1967, 2 inspired by Cahill 2001, 3–4 after Müller-Karpe 1980; 7.19 from Armstrong 1933; 7.20 from Hawkes and Clarke 1963; 7.21–7.22 from Eogan 1994; 7.23 from Eogan 1994 and Wilde 1862; 7.24 after Armstrong 1933 and Eogan 1983; 7.25 after Eogan 1983; 7.26 after Eogan 1994; 7.27 after Herity and Eogan 1977; 7.28 after Eogan 1983; 7.29 from Wilde 1862 and after Gerloff 1995; 7.30 after J. Raftery 1971; 7.31 after Eogan 1974; 7.32 after Eogan 1983; 7.33 after Fox 1939, Eogan 1983, Eogan 1964 and Burgess 1982; 7.34 after Eogan 1964, Pryor 1980, Wilde 1861, and Mallory et al. 1996; 7.35 after Collins and Seaby 1960 and Williams 1978; 7.36 after Hencken 1942 and Newman 1997a; 7.37 after Grogan 1993; 7.38–7.39 after B. Raftery 1976a, 1975 and 1987, and after Raftery from O'Kelly 1989; 7.40 after Lucas 1972, Rynne 1962 and Lucas 1968.

Fig. 8.1 after Eogan 1965, Coffey 1906 and Lucas 1960; 8.2 after Eogan 1965, and Colquhoun and Burgess 1988; 8.3 after Jope 1962 and Eogan 1983; 8.4–8.5 after Scott 1974 and B. Raftery 1983; 8.6 after Scott 1977 and B. Raftery 1983; 8.7 after Carlin et al. 2008; 8.8 after Scott 1990; 8.9–8.10 after B. Raftery 1983; 8.11 after B. Raftery 1983 and Warner 1982; 8.12 after Haworth 1971 and B. Raftery 1983; 8.13 after B. Raftery 1983; 8.16 after B. Raftery 1983 and Pryor 1980; 8.17 after B. Raftery 1983; 8.18 after B. Raftery 1983, and B. Raftery 1984 after Duval; 8.19 after B. Raftery 1983; 8.20 after B. Raftery 1983 and C. Bourke 1993; 8.21–8.22 after B. Raftery 1983; 8.23 after B. Raftery 1983 and Sprockhoff 1955.

Fig. 9.1 after B. Raftery 1983; 9.2 after Caulfield 1977 and B. Raftery 1994a; 9.3 after Earwood 1989 and B. Raftery 1983; 9.4 after Halpin and Newman 2006; 9.5 after Corns et al. 2008; 9.6 from Bhreathnach and Newman 1995; 9.7 from Bhreathnach and Newman 1995 and Grogan 2008; 9.8 from Newman 1993, renumbered according to Newman 1997b; 9.9 from Warner 1994a; 9.10 from Lynn 1997 (Crown copyright; reproduced with the permission of the Controller of Her Majesty's Stationery Office) and Mallory 1985; 9.11–9.12 after Lynn 1986; 9.13 after Lynn 2002; 9.14 from Lynn 1986 and Mallory 1985; 9.15 after Raftery 1987; 9.16–9.17 after Johnston and Wailes 2007; 9.18 after Lynn 2003b; 9.19 after Johnston and Wailes 2007, and Lynn 1991 and 1992a; 9.26 after Newman et al. 2007; 9.27 after Doody 2008; 9.28

after Masterson 1999; 9.29 after Condit 1992; 9.30 after Lynn 1989a; 9.31 from the Ordnance Survey Memoranda, courtesy of the Royal Irish Academy, after a photograph from the National Museum of Ireland, after Rynne 1972a, and after a photograph from the Ulster Museum; 9.32 after Duignan 1976 and B. Raftery 1983; 9.33 after Ó Floinn 1995; 9.34 from Newman 1997b; 9.35 after Lacy 1983, Cuppage 1986 and B. Raftery 1981.

Fig. 10.1 after Warner 1991; 10.2 after E. Bourke 1989 and Ó hEailidhe 1992; 10.3 after Ó Floinn 2001 and Kilbride-Jones 1980.

Illustrations

Fig. 1.1. Plan of Mount Sandel hut sites.

Fig. 1.2. Mount Sandel territory.

Fig. 1.3. Early flint assemblage.

Fig. 1.4. Core, flake and partly polished stone axes.

Fig. 1.5. Adzes in antler sleeves and microliths mounted as arrow tip and barb.

Fig. 1.6. Sequence of deposits at Newferry, Co. Antrim.

Fig. 1.7. Late flint assemblage.

Fig. 1.8. Greenstone flakes from Ferriter's Cove.

Fig. 1.9. Cache of polished stone axeheads from Ferriter's Cove.

Fig. 1.10. Part of a log boat from Lough Neagh.

Fig. 1.11. Reconstruction of a fish weir, and a wooden basket from Clowanstown, Co. Meath.

Fig. 1.12. Rate of discovery of Mesolithic material in Ireland from 1870 to 2000.

Fig. 1.13. Burial pit and cremation found at Hermitage, Castleconnell, Co. Limerick.

Fig. 2.1. Pollen diagram from Lough Sheeauns, Connemara, Co. Galway.

Fig. 2.2. Engraving of a prehistoric crook-ard.

Fig. 2.3. Houses at Lough Gur, Co. Limerick.

Fig. 2.4. Plan of house at Ballynagilly, Co. Tyrone, and plan and reconstruction of house 1 at Tankardstown, Co. Limerick.

Fig. 2.5. Plan of house at Ballyglass, Co. Mayo, and simplified plan of house at Ballygalley, Co. Antrim, and reconstruction.

Fig. 2.6. Plans of houses at Corbally, Co. Kildare.

Fig. 2.7. Plan and reconstruction of a rectangular house at Kishoge, Co. Dublin.

Fig. 2.8. Plans of three possible circular stake-built houses at Knowth, Co. Meath, and plan of a circular house at Slieve Breagh, Co. Meath.

Fig. 2.9. General interim plan of the Céide Fields, Co. Mayo.

Fig. 2.10. Reconstruction of a segmented ditch enclosure with timber palisade at Magheraboy, Co. Sligo, and plan of ditch segments and palisade on north-east.

Fig. 2.11. Plan of ritual site at Goodland, Co. Antrim.

Fig. 2.12. Neolithic pottery styles.

Fig. 2.13. Polished stone axehead with haft from Edercloon, Co. Longford.

Fig. 2.14. Stone axes.

Fig. 2.15. Distribution of porcellanite axes and other artefacts in Ireland and Britain.

Fig. 2.16. Flint arrowheads.

Fig. 2.17. Flint artefacts.

Fig. 2.18. A basketry bag from Twyford, Co. Westmeath, and a wooden bowl from Timoney, Co. Tipperary.

Fig. 3.1. General distribution of passage tombs.

Fig. 3.2. Map of the Boyne cemetery.

Fig. 3.3.   Plan and section of Newgrange passage tomb.

Fig. 3.4.   The decorated entrance stone at Newgrange.

Fig. 3.5.   Plan of the Knowth cemetery.

Fig. 3.6.   Carved flint macehead from Knowth.

Fig. 3.7.   Fourknocks I, Co. Meath.

Fig. 3.8.   Decorated stones from Fourknocks I, Co. Meath.

Fig. 3.9.   Passage tomb in the Mound of the Hostages, Tara.

Fig. 3.10.   Map of passage tomb cemetery at Loughcrew, Co. Meath.

Fig. 3.11.   Map of the Carrowmore and Knocknarea passage tomb cemeteries in County Sligo.

Fig. 3.12.   Finds from passage tombs.

Fig. 3.13.   Passage tomb art motifs.

Fig. 3.14.   General distribution of court tombs and plan of Tully, Co. Fermanagh.

Fig. 3.15.   Court tomb plans and distribution of central and full court tombs.

Fig. 3.16.   Court tomb plans.

Fig. 3.17.   General distribution of portal tombs and plan and section of Drumanone, Co. Roscommon.

Fig. 3.18.   Portal tomb, Kernanstown, Brownshill, Co. Carlow.

Fig. 3.19.   General distribution of wedge tombs and plans.

Fig. 3.20.   Wedge tomb at Island, Co. Cork.

Fig. 3.21.   Linkardstown-type grave from Ballintruer More, Co. Wicklow.

Fig. 4.1.   Plan of penannular ring-ditch at Scotch Street, Armagh.

Fig. 4.2.   Giant's Ring, Ballynahatty, Co. Down, and timber circle.

Fig. 4.3.   Gradiometry image of the ditch and pit circle on the Hill of Tara.

Fig. 4.4.   Beaker pottery.

Fig. 4.5.   Plan of settlement enclosures on Roughan Hill, Co. Clare.

Fig. 4.6.   Wrist-guards, barbed and tanged flint arrowhead, V-perforated buttons, stone battleaxe, tanged copper knives.

Fig. 4.7.   Artist's reconstruction of the Beaker period copper-mining settlement at Ross Island, Killarney, Co. Kerry.

Fig. 4.8.   Metalwork phases of the earlier Bronze Age.

Fig. 4.9.   Copper axes.

Fig. 4.10.   Bronze axes.

Fig. 4.11.   Halberds, daggers and spearheads.

Fig. 4.12.   Beaker period goldwork.

Fig. 4.13.   Gold lunulae.

Fig. 4.14.   Mount Gabriel copper mines.

Fig. 4.15.   Pottery of the Bowl Tradition.

Fig. 4.16.   Cist grave in a cemetery at Keenoge, Co. Meath, and general distribution of pottery of the Bowl Tradition.

Fig. 4.17.   Vases of the Vase Tradition.

Fig. 4.18.   Urns of the Vase Tradition.

Fig. 4.19.   Biconical cup and collared urn.

Fig. 4.20.   The Cordoned Urn Tradition.

Fig. 4.21.   Plans of flat cemetery at Edmondstown, Co. Dublin, ring-ditch at Urbalreagh, Co. Antrim, and cist grave at Carrig, Co. Wicklow.

Fig. 4.22.   Cemetery mounds at Poulawack, Co. Clare, and Knockast, Co. Westmeath.

Fig. 5.1.   Rock art.

Fig. 5.2.   Stone circles at Drombeg, Co. Cork, and Beaghmore, Co. Tyrone.

Fig. 5.3.   Burnt mound at Ballyvourney, Co. Cork.

Fig. 6.1.   Stone moulds from Killymaddy, Co. Antrim.

Fig. 6.2.   Spearheads from Tattenamona, Co. Fermanagh.

Fig. 6.3.   Bronze spearheads.

Fig. 6.4.   Dirks and rapiers.

Fig. 6.5.   Short-flanged axes.

Fig. 6.6.   The Irish palstave series.

Fig. 6.7.   The Bishopsland hoard, Co. Kildare.

Fig. 6.8.   The Annesborough hoard, Co. Armagh.

Fig. 6.9.   General distribution of gold bar torcs.

Fig. 6.10.   Gold bar torcs.

Fig. 6.11.   Flange-twisted gold torcs from Tara, Co. Meath.

Fig. 6.12.   Hoard from Coolmanagh, Co. Carlow.

Fig. 6.13.   Gold earrings.

Fig. 6.14.   Gold hoards from Downpatrick, Co. Down.

Fig. 6.15.   Gold hoard from Saintjohns, Co. Kildare.

Fig. 6.16.   The Roscommon hoard.

Fig. 6.17.   Sword from Ballintober, Co. Mayo, and general distribution.

Fig. 6.18.   Settlement at Corrstown, Co. Derry.

Fig. 6.19.   Circular houses at Killoran, Co. Tipperary.

Fig. 6.20.   Ballyveelish, Co. Tipperary.

Fig. 6.21.   Chancellorsland, Co. Tipperary.

Fig. 6.22.   Carrigillihy, Co. Cork.

Fig. 6.23.   Palisaded enclosure at Clonfinlough, Co. Offaly, with reconstruction.

Fig. 6.24.   Finds from Clonfinlough, Co. Offaly.

Fig. 6.25.   Schematic plan of Haughey's Fort, Co. Armagh.

Fig. 6.26.   General plan of Dún Aonghasa, Aran, Co. Galway.

Fig. 6.27.   Excavation and finds: Dún Aonghasa.

Fig. 7.1.   The Dowris hoard.

Fig. 7.2.   General distribution of buckets and cauldrons in Britain and Ireland.

Fig. 7.3.   Bronze buckets.

Fig. 7.4.   General distribution of the types of bronze vessels found in the Tamlaght hoard, Co. Armagh.

Fig. 7.5.   Early bronze cauldrons.

Fig. 7.6.   Class B cauldrons.

Fig. 7.7.   Bronze flesh-hook from Dunaverney, Co. Antrim.

Fig. 7.8.   Wooden idol from Ralaghan, Co. Cavan.

Fig. 7.9.   Bronze horns or trumpets.

Fig. 7.10.   General distribution of bronze horns in Ireland.

Fig. 7.11.   Bronze swords.

Fig. 7.12.   Weapon hoards from Blackhills, Co. Laois, and Tempo, Co. Fermanagh.

Fig. 7.13.   Spearheads with lunate openings in the blade.

Fig. 7.14.   Shields with V-shaped notches.

Fig. 7.15.   Bronze shields.

Fig. 7.16.   Gold gorgets.

Fig. 7.17.   Hoard of gold ornaments from Gorteenreagh, Co. Clare.

Fig. 7.18.   Suggested manner of use of some gold ornaments.

Fig. 7.19.   Gold hoard from Lattoon, Co. Cavan.

Fig. 7.20.   Possible method of attachment of a dress-fastener.

Fig. 7.21.   Distribution of lock-rings in Ireland, Britain and France and distribution of gorgets and other goldwork.

Fig. 7.22.   Distribution of dress-fasteners, sleeve-fasteners, bullae, etc.

Fig. 7.23.   Hair-rings and larger penannular rings.

Fig. 7.24.   Gold bullae.

Fig. 7.25.   Hoards from Drissoge, Co. Meath, and Mount Rivers, Co. Cork.

Fig. 7.26.   General distribution of penannular bracelets of Irish type.

Fig. 7.27.   Two regional groups of Dowris Phase metalwork as depicted in 1974.

Fig. 7.28.   A selection of gold neck-rings, collars and penannular bracelets from 'the great Clare find' near Mooghaun.

Fig. 7.29.   Gold objects: decorative ear-spools and hats or crowns.

Fig. 7.30.   Hoard from Ballytegan, Co. Laois.

Fig. 7.31.   General distribution of disc- and cup-headed pins and a cup-headed pin from Arboe, Co. Tyrone.

Fig. 7.32.   Hoards of tools and other bronzes from Crossna, near Boyle, Co. Roscommon, and Ballinderry, Co. Westmeath.

Fig. 7.33.   Bronze sickles and bronze knives.

Fig. 7.34.   Bronze socketed axeheads.

Fig. 7.35.   Lough Eskragh, Co. Tyrone.

Fig. 7.36.   Ballinderry, Co. Offaly.

Fig. 7.37.   Schematic plan of Mooghaun hillfort, Co. Clare.

Fig. 7.38.   Rathgall, Co. Wicklow.

Fig. 7.39.   Rathgall, Co. Wicklow.

Fig. 7.40.   Block wheel from Doogarymore, Co. Roscommon, rattle-pendants from Lissanode, Co. Westmeath, and bronze ferrule from Moynalty Lough, Co. Monaghan.

Fig. 8.1.   Gündlingen swords and chapes.

Fig. 8.2.   General distribution of Gündlingen swords.

Fig. 8.3.   Fibula from Ireland and hoard from Kilmurry, Co. Kerry.

Fig. 8.4.   Iron axes.

Fig. 8.5.   Iron axe from Feerwore, Co. Galway.

Fig. 8.6.   Shaft-hole axe from Kilbeg, Co. Westmeath.

Fig. 8.7.   Reconstruction of an early iron-smelting furnace.

Fig. 8.8.   Distribution of iron ores in Ireland.

Fig. 8.9.   Gold hoard found in Knock townland, Co. Roscommon.

Fig. 8.10. The Somerset, Co. Galway, hoard.

Fig. 8.11. The Broighter, Co. Derry, hoard.

Fig. 8.12. Bronze horse-bits.

Fig. 8.13. Fragmentary bronze bit.

Fig. 8.14. Bronze pendants.

Fig. 8.15. Hoard found near Attymon, Co. Galway.

Fig. 8.16. Yoke mounts, wooden yoke and bronze linchpin.

Fig. 8.17. Iron swords and hilt of bronze anthropoid sword from Ballyshannon Bay, Co. Donegal.

Fig. 8.18. Bronze scabbards.

Fig. 8.19. Decorated bronze scabbard plates.

Fig. 8.20. Iron and bronze spearheads, bronze ferrule and spearbutts, shield of leather and wood and two-piece bronze ring.

Fig. 8.21. Fibulae.

Fig. 8.22. Ring-headed pins.

Fig. 8.23. The Bann disc, the Petrie crown, the Cork horns, and bronze disc of Monasterevin type with solar imagery.

Fig. 9.1.   Beehive querns.

Fig. 9.2.   General distribution maps of beehive querns and other artefacts.

Fig. 9.3.   Drinking vessels and cauldrons.

Fig. 9.4.   General plan of the Hill of Tara.

Fig. 9.5.   Computer model of the Hill of Tara obtained by aerial LiDAR survey.

Fig. 9.6.   The Forrad and Teach Cormaic.

Fig. 9.7.   The Rath of the Synods.

Fig. 9.8.   Ráth Gráinne and associated monuments.

Fig. 9.9.   The Navan complex.

Fig. 9.10. Navan Fort.

Fig. 9.11. Navan sites A and B.

Fig. 9.12. Navan phase 3ii.

Fig. 9.13. Schematic plan of Navan site C.

Fig. 9.14. Plan of Navan phase 4: the 40m structure.

Fig. 9.15. The Loughnashade horn.

Fig. 9.16. Plan of Knockaulin, Co. Kildare.

Fig. 9.17. Plan of the summit area of Knockaulin.

Fig. 9.18. Navan phase 3ii and the Knockaulin 'rose' phase.

Fig. 9.19. Reconstruction of the Knockaulin 'mauve' phase structure.

Fig. 9.20. General plan of Rathcroghan, Co. Roscommon.

Fig. 9.21. Contour plan of Rathcroghan Mound.

Fig. 9.22. Magnetic gradiometry survey of Rathcroghan Mound and its vicinity.

Fig. 9.23. Avenues at Rathcroghan, Navan and Knockaulin.

Fig. 9.24. Magnetic gradiometry image of Rathcroghan Mound.

Fig. 9.25. Magnetic susceptibility survey of Rathcroghan Mound.

Fig. 9.26. Raffin, Co. Meath.

Fig. 9.27. Carn Tigherna hillfort, Co. Cork.

Fig. 9.28. The Grianán of Aileach, Co. Donegal.

Fig. 9.29. Hillfort complex at Baltinglass, Co. Wicklow, and Spinan's Hill, Co. Wicklow.

Fig. 9.30. The Dorsey, Co. Armagh.

Fig. 9.31. Wooden idol found at Ballybritain, Co. Derry, the Corleck head, Co. Cavan, stone head from Beltany, Co. Donegal, and the Tandragee idol, Co. Armagh.

Fig. 9.32. Iron Age decorated stones.

Fig. 9.33. Bog body found at Gallagh, Co. Galway.

Fig. 9.34. Types of Iron Age burial monuments.

Fig. 9.35. Ring-barrows and embanked ring-ditches.

Fig. 10.1. Ptolemy's map of Ireland of the second century AD.

Fig. 10.2. Finds from a Roman burial at Stonyford, Co. Kilkenny, and a carvel-built wooden boat from Lough Lene, Co. Westmeath.

Fig. 10.3. General distribution of Hiberno-Roman penannular brooches.

1

POSTGLACIAL IRELAND: THE FIRST COLONISTS

Half a million years ago, when Britain was a peninsula of continental Europe, a small hunting group of early humans occupied the area around Boxgrove, near Chichester in west Sussex, in southern England. A shin bone and two teeth of an adult individual, an exceptional find at such an early date, show that these people belonged to a species named *Homo heidelbergensis* who were the ancestors of both *Homo sapiens*, anatomically modern humans, and *Homo neanderthalensis*, the Neanderthals. The faunal remains indicate a temperate climate, and this grassy coastal area supported wolf, bear, wild cat, lion, elephant, rhinoceros, wild horse, red deer, roe deer, and many smaller animals and birds. Many of the large mammal bones showed butchery marks, the results of skinning, dismemberment or breakage for marrow extraction. Whether some or all of these animals were hunted or were scavenged in competition with other predators is uncertain, but one horse scapula has a puncture in it that could have been made by a spear-like object. Flint tools were manufactured, the local chalk cliffs offering an abundant supply of fine-grained raw material. Neatly flaked oval-shaped hand-held bifaces or handaxes were used, probably in the butchering of large animals (Roberts and Parfitt 1999; Pitts and Roberts 1998).

Boxgrove is one of a number of Lower Palaeolithic sites in southern Britain variously assigned to different cold (glacial) or temperate (interglacial) climatic phases. Study of the oxygen stable isotope content of plankton remains preserved in deep sea cores has allowed the identification of a whole series of glaciations in Britain during the period termed the Pleistocene, and some thirteen glacials and interglacials in the last 500,000 years. Long cold periods, perhaps lasting 100,000 years, were interspersed with shorter warm periods of about 10,000 to 15,000 years' duration. These have been numbered downwards from the present and, apart from a few fixed points, are not always readily correlated with terrestrial evidence. A major Ice Age (traditionally known as the Anglian Glaciation or Oxygen Isotope Stage 12) around 470,000 years ago would have forced the abandonment of Boxgrove and other early sites. This was followed by the Hoxnian Interglacial (OIS 11—named after Hoxne in Suffolk, another well-known Palaeolithic site), which in turn was followed by a further sequence of glacial–interglacial cycles (OIS 10–OIS 1) over the ensuing 350,000 years. Throughout all of this long timespan, embracing the Lower, Middle and Upper Palaeolithic periods in Britain, there is no evidence at all that Ireland was ever occupied by early humans.

It is possible that some early hominids of the Boxgrove kind ventured further west, even successfully traversing that body of water of variable width later to become the Irish Sea, but no traces of them, no butchered animal bones or any stone tools, have been found in Ireland. Various claims for the presence of such Palaeolithic or 'Old Stone Age' people are now discounted. What were thought to be primitive stone implements from north-eastern Ireland and from County Sligo are now known to be flakes of natural origin. Two stone handaxes, one found near the fort of Dún Aonghasa on Inis Mór, Aran, Co. Galway (Murphy 1977), the other a casual find in a garden in County Cork (Woodman 1998), are genuine artefacts but are modern discards. Human bones found in Kilgreany Cave, north-west of Dungarvan, Co. Waterford, were associated with the remains of giant deer, but deposits in the cave were greatly disturbed by a fluctuating water-table and radiocarbon dating of some of the human bones has indicated that these are of more recent, fourth-millennium BC, date (Dowd 2002). A small but relatively thick flint flake found in Mell townland, near Drogheda, Co. Louth, apparently came from a deposit of glacial gravel. It has a broad striking platform and prominent bulb of percussion, indicating that it was struck from its parent core by direct percussion with a hard hammer, a technique found in the Palaeolithic stone industries of southern England. The Drogheda flake is a genuine piece of flint-worker's waste and it is slightly rolled or blunted by water action, so it may have been collected somewhere in the Irish Sea area, along with other debris, by glacial action (Mitchell and de G. Sieveking 1972). Another flint flake from Ballycullen, near Newtownards, Co. Down, may have been transported there in a similar way (Stirland 2008). They cannot be taken to demonstrate very early human activity in Ireland, however, and, at present, the earliest evidence for a human presence is of postglacial date.

The relatively warm climate that we are experiencing at present is known as the Holocene and follows that series of Pleistocene glacial and interglacial climatic fluctuations. We know that the greater part of Ireland was covered, at least twice, by extensive ice sheets of considerable thickness during this Pleistocene period. The movement of these masses of ice scoured the surface of the land and numerous geomorphological features testify to their passing, but as they ground their way across the land they would easily have erased any evidence of human occupation. Two main glaciations occurred but many questions remain about their extent and their timing. The older is the Munsterian (OIS 6–8), possibly dating from about 300,000–130,000 years ago and correlated with the Wolstonian glaciation in Britain. The Midlandian (OIS 2–5d) extended from about 120,000 years ago to its maximum *c.* 20,000 years ago and is correlated with the British Devensian period. They are separated by

an unnamed interglacial (OIS 5e) coeval with the British Ipswichian (Knight *et al.* 2004).

The Munsterian glaciation engulfed the whole of Ireland at one time or another, with the possible exception of some mountainous areas in the south-west. The last or Midlandian glaciation covered the northern and central parts of the country and at its height may have engulfed most of the island. Many drumlins, such as those in Leitrim, Cavan, Monaghan, the Clew Bay area, and north of Ennis in County Clare, and the long esker ridges that are such a prominent feature of the midlands were a product of the dissolution of these ice sheets during the late Midlandian. During the long timespan of this glaciation there were several cold (stadial) and warmer (interstadial) phases, which allowed the establishment of a rich and diverse mammalian fauna.

A programme of radiocarbon dating of animal bone samples from Irish caves has shown that animals such as woolly mammoth, brown bear, giant deer, reindeer, wolf, wild horse, red deer, spotted hyena, arctic fox, hare and lemming were present before the maximum advance of the last, Midlandian, ice sheet (Woodman, *et al.* 1997). The presence of these animals demonstrates that the waters of the area of what later became the Irish Sea were not an insurmountable barrier to beast or even man at that time. Nevertheless, with most, if not all, of the south of Ireland covered with ice at the height of this glaciation, even the Arctic lemming and mammoth may have had to retreat before the bitter cold. Some mammalian recolonisation occurred before Ireland became separated from Britain probably around 16,000 years ago.

A rise in temperature around this time marks the commencement of the well-defined Woodgrange interstadial of the late glacial period and heralds the end of the last Ice Age. An arctic or subarctic grassy tundra had been gradually established and species of dock (*Rumex*) were prominent. Such a Gramineae–*Rumex* pollen zone is clearly identifiable in a pollen record from Woodgrange, Co. Down, and elsewhere and is followed, as temperatures continued to rise, by the appearance and strong expansion of juniper and some birch (*Betula*) copses in suitably sheltered areas. The improvement in climate did not continue uninterrupted; there was a return to cold conditions, and juniper and birch were largely replaced by grasslands that provided rich grazing for herds of reindeer and giant Irish deer. It is conceivable that, as elsewhere in western Europe, these herds of herbivores could have attracted the attention of late Palaeolithic hunting groups, but, as already mentioned, no evidence has yet been found. There are, for example, no indications that the giant deer or their antlers were ever exploited (Woodman 2003b). This cold spell, *c.* 10,000 years ago, is known as the Nahanagan stadial, named after Lough Nahanagan, Co. Wicklow. Animals such as the giant deer, reindeer and red deer did not survive this icy interlude, but as the ice finally retreated and the climate improved various plants and animals again colonised the country. Whether there were temporary land-bridges with Britain or whether some narrow stretches of a narrower Irish Sea were easily traversable remains uncertain. The warming climate and the melting of the great ice sheets produced dramatic changes in sea level and coastal topography (Edwards and Brooks 2008). The same rising seas may well have inundated early coastal habitation sites. This is also one of the reasons given for Ireland's considerably more limited range of plant and animal types compared with Britain. Ireland has only about fourteen native species of mammal, including wild pig, wild cat, brown bear, hare and wolf. Rising sea levels may have combined with other factors, both climatic and geographical, to contribute to a floral and faunal impoverishment that left a smaller variety of mammals for the earliest settlers to hunt (Woodman *et al.* 1997; McCormick 2007; McCormick and Murray 2007).

The rise in temperature in postglacial times continued until the fourth millennium BC, and from about 6000 BC there was a climatic optimum that lasted for several thousand years. This was a period of increased summer and winter warmth, the mean annual temperature being one or two degrees centigrade higher than that of today. The changing climate had, of course, a considerable effect on the composition of the vegetation. In general, extensive birch woods were eventually supplanted by forests of pine and hazel, and these in turn were replaced to varying degrees by oak and elm. There was considerable variation in Britain and Ireland, and, not surprisingly, local variations occurred too. Pine, for example, continued to be of considerable importance in parts of the west of Ireland, including the Burren in County Clare and

parts of Connemara and Mayo. Indeed, it is known to have survived into the medieval period on the Aran Islands. Broad generalisations are possible, and several authorities have divided the history of vegetation development in late and postglacial times into various phases. A sequence proposed for Scandinavia at the turn of the century has been modified for Ireland by several writers, including G. F. Mitchell. Pollen analyses and radiocarbon determinations are now giving us an increasingly detailed picture of the changing environment and regional variations in Ireland in the last 10,000 years (Mitchell and Ryan 1997).

The postglacial vegetation sequence commences with Zone IV, in which climatic amelioration and a rapid rise in temperature saw juniper and willow (*Salix*) quickly overshadowed by the expansion of birch (*Betula*) woodlands. With increasing temperatures, hazel (*Corylus*) quickly expanded to form the dominant woodland cover throughout the country in Zone V. This early dominance of hazel is characteristic of early vegetation development throughout Europe but was particularly marked in Ireland. Hazel soon had to compete with tall-canopy trees, and the first of these was Scots pine (*Pinus sylvestris*) and then elm (*Ulmus*) and oak (*Quercus*), which eventually expand rapidly at the expense of birch in Zone VI. The boundary between Zone VI (Boreal) and Zone VII (Atlantic) is marked by the appearance and expansion of alder (*Alnus*).

This brief sketch, of course, obscures the fact that there was considerable regional diversity in this forested landscape. Oak and elm dominated the midlands, with pine probably confined to the margins of the developing raised bogs. Hazel was probably the main tall shrub in most areas. Pine remained important in the north and in the west, even in the Burren, and continued to be significant in woodlands and on peat until about 2000 BC, after which it declined rapidly and was extinct in most (though not all) areas by the end of the last millennium BC. It now seems likely that these great primeval woodlands were not as closed as was once thought; local soil conditions and other factors may have dictated a degree of variability in composition and development. In the Boreal period, for instance, an expansion of cold-tolerant species such as pine, birch and juniper at the expense of hazel indicates a cold spell around 6250 BC, coinciding with an oscillation in the oxygen isotope ratios recorded in ocean cores and in Greenland ice cores (O'Connell and Molloy 2005). The nature of the Boreal forest cover is debated, however; given the likely absence of large herbivores like red deer, it has been suggested that the Irish forest may have been dense and impenetrable, and relatively inhospitable, for early colonists. Such a belief in an almost hostile relationship between foragers and their forested landscape is, as Graeme Warren (2003) has remarked, an attitude very redolent of an agriculturalist's perspective. It seems unlikely that the forest environment was an ecological barrier that early hunters and foragers were unable to penetrate. Indeed, the postglacial forest may have comprised a series of woodland areas with different levels of closed and open growth (J. Moore 2003). It is very likely that there was human interference with the woodlands too, but it seems not to have been extensive: the fluctuations so far detected in the pollen record could be due to natural causes. In general, there seems to have been little significant impact on early woodlands until they were assailed by early farmers around 4000 BC. Nonetheless, it seems equally unlikely that there was no woodland management whatever. Suitable wood must have been harvested on a regular basis for the manufacture of baskets, fish-traps and fish weirs, for example, and the coppicing of trees to produce the desired type of growth for this sort of craftwork was probably practised at an early date; it is certainly known from an early sixth-millennium BC context in the estuary of the River Liffey in Dublin.

The improved postglacial climate and the woodland cover favoured wild fauna such as pig, wolf, fox and bear. Wild pig and a variety of birds and fish were to become the main prey of groups of hunters and food-gatherers moving westwards from Britain, though how these early colonists came is unclear. The history of land and sea relationships at this time is a complex one, still imperfectly understood. Late and postglacial changes in the Irish coastline occurred at different times in different places and for various reasons. The story is not simply one of continuous eustatic inundation; isostatic changes (namely changes in the level of the land in relation to the sea) also took place. With the disappearance of the great weight of Midlandian ice, which had covered the north of Ireland in particular, the land rose and its rise, in some areas,

exceeded the eustatic rise in sea level. Some of the submerged peat deposits and forests around the Irish coast, and indeed some drowned archaeological sites, are testimony to the latter phenomenon. Some old submerged forests near Bray, Co. Wicklow, and at Roddansport, Co. Down, were presumably drowned by the sea as it rose to its maximum. Other drowned peaty deposits and trees may be of more recent, prehistoric, date. In Boreal and Atlantic times the rising sea also deposited marine clays in sheltered lagoons in parts of the north-east of Ireland and elsewhere. At Cushendun, Co. Antrim, for example, the rising waves deposited several metres of silts and gravels on a layer of freshwater peat, and the flint implements of hunting and foraging groups were incorporated in these deposits as the sites of their camps were washed away by the slowly rising sea. The maximum marine transgression, when the sea had risen to as much as 4m above present level, occurred around 4000 BC in many coastal parts, but in the northern half of Ireland, as in parts of Scotland, the isostatic rise of the land continued or resumed. It raised shorelines above the level of the high-tide mark, producing postglacial raised beaches. These are deposits of shingle or wave-cut platforms, several metres above present sea level, which are to be seen today from Donegal to Drogheda. These ancient shorelines were seasonally frequented by hunters and foragers (Woodman 2004b).

EARLY HUNTERS AND FORAGERS: 8000–6500 BC

An early settlement at Mount Sandel (Upper), Co. Derry, was situated south of Coleraine on a bluff overlooking the valley of the River Bann. Excavation by Peter Woodman from 1973 to 1977 explored a relatively large area of almost 700 square metres (Woodman 1985). While traces of activity, such as pits and hearths, were scattered over the site, the most significant discovery was an occupation area measuring about 10m by 7m containing the remains of huts. Though the site had been eroded and had been disturbed by post-medieval agriculture, a charcoal-flecked occupation soil with a maximum depth of 10cm and pits, hearths and other features did survive in places. A small, artificially enlarged hollow in the ground contained

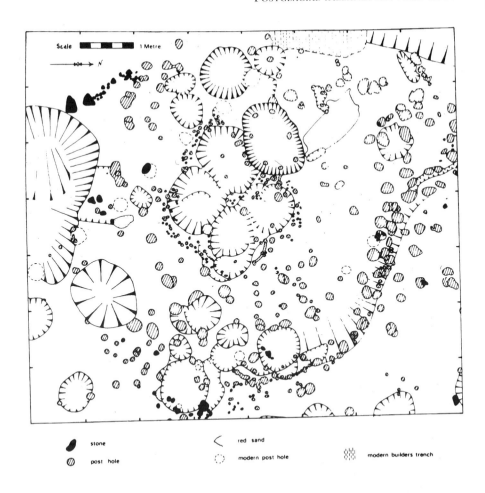

stone

post hole

red sand

modern post hole

modern builders trench

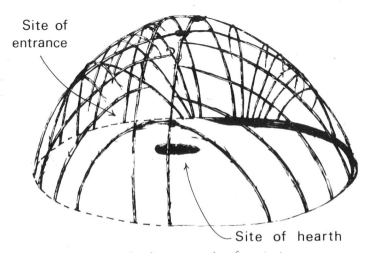

Fig. 1.1—Plan of Mount Sandel hut sites and outline reconstruction of one structure.

a large number of post-holes and stake-holes, some of which could be identified as the remains of several circular huts. These had been constructed, as some sloping post-holes (placed in the ground at an angle of 60°) suggested, with saplings bent over and tied together to produce a more-or-less circular tent-like structure, presumably roofed with hides or other materials which left no trace (Fig. 1.1). It is possible that sods were used at least in the lower part of the roof structure. The huts were of fairly substantial construction: the saplings were up to 20cm in diameter. Some hearths cut through the remains of post-holes, and several arcs of these holes interrupted another arc of stake- and post-holes constructed with its edge around the rim of the hollow. Four slightly egg-shaped huts could be identified; each was about 6m across and had a hearth near the centre. These represent a series of reoccupations of the site, and the larger mass of post-holes might represent as many as ten huts altogether. Assuming one hut per occupation, it was estimated that at any one time the Mount Sandel site would have been occupied by fewer than ten people. The hearths were broad and shallow, about 1m across, cut into the compact subsoil, and several had a line of burnt earth around their edges; two were recut. A hut of similar size and date that was rebuilt twice has been found at Howick in north-eastern England (Waddington 2007) and another substantial structure has been excavated at East Barns, near Dunbar, in Scotland (Gooder 2007).

Numerous pits of various sizes, some presumably storage pits, also occurred in the Mount Sandel hollow, and both these features and the hearths were filled with dark occupation soil, rich in organic material, some also containing layers with burnt hazelnut shells and sometimes layers of soil containing fragments of burnt bone. Erosion and later disturbance made analysis of the site organisation difficult, but specific activity areas were identified. The distribution of some flint artefacts in the hut area suggested that hut entrances may have been on the south-west and, judging from a small concentration of flakes, there may have been a chipping area, perhaps for axe-manufacturing, just north of the hearth. A number of pits with burnt hazelnuts and flints appeared to contain distinct groups of particular microlith types, perhaps reflecting a measure of individual stylistic variation. Several large pits, some distance from the huts, may

have been for rubbish disposal, and a number of small pits filled with burnt stones represented another activity on the margins of the site; perhaps hot stones were used to heat liquids in skin containers. To the west of the huts there was a second area of occupation soil with no pits or post-holes but which contained large quantities of waste flint material, the result of extensive flint-working or knapping on site, water-rolled nodules of flint being brought to the site for this purpose.

Acidic soil conditions did not favour the preservation of unburnt bone; the surviving faunal remains consisted entirely of burnt bone fragments. Judging from this evidence, wild pig and fish were the principal sources of food. Of the identifiable remains 15% were from mammals, 4% from birds and 81% from fish. Pig bones represented 98% of the mammal remains recovered, however, and analysis revealed substantial numbers of young pig. One bone of a wolf or a dog was found, and since the domesticated dog is known elsewhere in Europe at this time it is not impossible that it was present here. Bones of hare also occurred. Bird bones included woodpigeon, woodcock, capercaillie and grouse, as well as ducks and divers such as mallard, teal, wigeon and the red-throated diver. Fish bones, which were common, included salmon (41% of the bones recovered), trout (32%) and eel (7%), as well as some sea bass and flounder.

Winter occupation was demonstrated by certain features of the pig bones recovered: the pattern of bone fusion implied young animals less than two years old, probably butchered in late winter. Winter occupation was also suggested by the presence of foetal pig bones (sows bear their young in April or May). The presence of quantities of hazelnut shells among the charred plant remains denoted at least autumnal occupation (though they could have been collected at this time and stored for consumption later). If salmon runs (which are dictated by water temperature) occurred at the same time of the year as they do today, summer occupation is also a possibility. The hazelnuts and the recovery of water-lily seeds as well as seeds of wild pear or crab-apple are a reminder that the foraging of wild edible plants played a significant role in the subsistence economy, and this is also the sort of evidence that survives only in exceptional circumstances. Hazelnuts are high in protein and have the advantage that they can be easily stored,

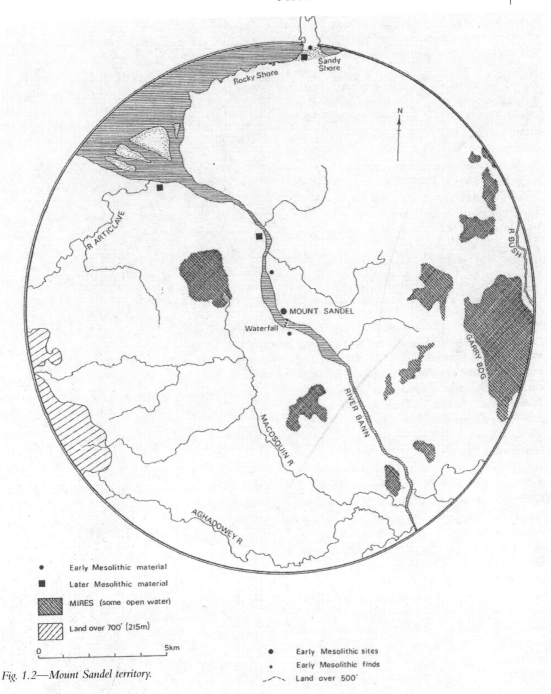

Fig. 1.2—Mount Sandel territory.

Legend:
- Early Mesolithic material
- Later Mesolithic material
- MIRES (some open water)
- Land over 700' (215m)

0   5km

- Early Mesolithic sites
- Early Mesolithic finds
- Land over 500'

and as a concentrated dietary resource they may have been particularly important. Indeed, they may have been the most abundant and nutritious vegetable food available (McComb and Simpson 1999). There was no evidence to show that the water-lily seeds were processed but they could have been boiled as a soup or even fried in fat to make a sort of popcorn.

The site evidently served as a winter camp, but the salmon remains also suggest spring and summer occupation, while eel would probably have been fished in autumn when eel migration took place in the River Bann. Mount Sandel was probably occupied throughout much of the year, but the number of hunters and food-gatherers present may well have varied from time to time and they may have been part of a larger community who occupied several sites in the wider region of the Bann estuary. It may have been a base camp occupied for a major part of the year at least, its inhabitants exploiting a range of resources within a 10km radius or two hours' walking distance. In addition to large tracts of Boreal hazel forest, attractive for wild pig, this catchment area would have included coast, estuary and river (Fig. 1.2). Several radiocarbon dates were obtained from samples of charcoal and hazelnut shells and they suggest that occupation occurred around 8000 BC and spanned several centuries though the period of hut construction may have been quite short (Bayliss and Woodman 2009).

Over 44,000 stone artefacts were recovered, mostly flint. By far the greater part of this material was the product of flint-working on site, consisting of flint debris or debitage, cores, and unretouched blades and flakes. The retouched flint material included over 1,100 small narrow blades or microliths, on average about 4cm long; these formed the largest group of retouched pieces from the site. The principal types of microlith were scalene triangles, rods and points. Flake axes, core axes and two polished stone axes were also found. The main features of this early stone industry are summarised below.

Drainage of the modern Lough Boora, near Birr, Co. Offaly, resulted in the discovery of another important site broadly contemporary with Mount Sandel. The Lough Boora campsite was situated on a gravel ridge on the shore of a large lake and was, in time, sealed by peat and subsequently inundated by the modern lake (Ryan 1980; O'Connell 1980; van Wijngaarden-Bakker 1985). Excavation revealed several hearths but no traces of structures were found. Burned bone recovered from these hearths provided the only faunal data: the remains were those of mammals (23%), birds (8%) and fish (68%). The mammal bones were mainly wild pig (98%) and a few other smaller animals, such as wolf or dog and wild cat. The absence of red deer here and at Mount Sandel is noteworthy given how common this animal was in Britain and on the Continent at this time. Assuming that its absence on such sites is not due to some dietary prohibition, it may be—as has been suggested—that deer was a later immigrant or introduction to Ireland (Woodman and McCarthy 2003). Woodpigeon was

common among the bird bones, with jay, teal, mallard and grouse also present. The large quantity of fish remains comprised bones of brown trout and eel. Hazelnuts suggest autumnal use of the site, and the eel bones here probably imply fishing in the lake in the summer months. The stone assemblage comprised chert microliths including rods, points and some scalene triangles, as well as cores and three complete axes of partly polished stone and fragments of others. Charcoal from hearths provided several radiocarbon dates indicating contemporaneity with Mount Sandel, and pollen analysis and further radiocarbon dates from peat samples indicate that the peat, which sealed the habitation site, had begun to form there quite rapidly shortly before 6000 BC. Mount Sandel and Lough Boora have produced a stone assemblage which is a narrow blade industry, and these flint and chert types are characteristic of the period 8000–6500 BC.

Stone assemblage

Cores (Fig. 1.3, 1–2): flint or chert cores with a single striking platform for the production of narrow blades are most common, though dual-platformed and multi-platformed cores also occur. Blades were struck from these cores by direct percussion using a hammer possibly made of a soft stone such as sandstone, mudstone or schist (Costa et al. 2005; Woodman et al. 2006). The blades produced are usually 4–6cm in length and about 1cm wide, with a small striking platform.

Microliths (Fig. 1.3, 3–14): a microlith is a retouched piece of flint or chert, usually a fragment of a blade and usually less than 5cm in length. It is, in itself, not an implement; microliths served as part of a composite tool or weapon of bone or wood, such as arrow-tips, barbs in an arrowshaft, or as the cutting edges of a knife. The retouching is usually abrupt and, with the exception of points, is confined to the edges. The principal types of microliths found in Ireland include points, scalene triangles and rods, a more limited range of forms compared with Britain and continental Europe. Points or 'needle points' (Fig. 1.3, 3–4) are narrow blades trimmed to a sharp point with the usual abrupt retouch; some surface retouching occurs, usually at tip and butt. They are usually more than 3cm long and 4mm or less in width. The scalene triangle (Fig. 1.3, 5) is a microlith which

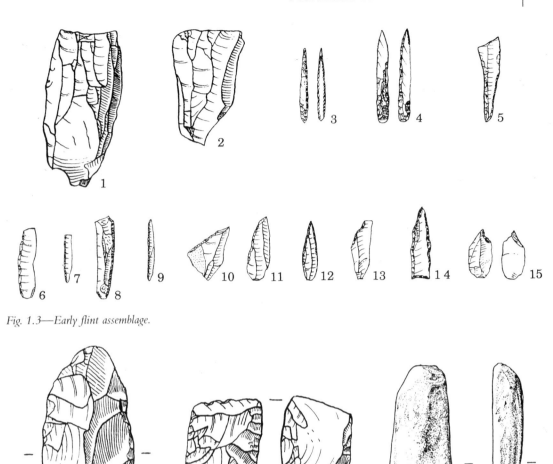

Fig. 1.3—Early flint assemblage.

Fig. 1.4—Core, flake and partly polished stone axes.

approximates, as its name implies, to an unequal-sided triangle of narrow, elongated form; both short edges are retouched and the short edge of the triangle may be concave, convex or straight. Rods (Fig. 1.3, 6–9) are small blades that are heavily trimmed down one edge only for more than half their length; they are usually 1cm or less in width and are sometimes called 'backed blades'. Other microlith forms include small obliquely trimmed types (Fig. 1.3, 10–13) and hollow-based points

(Fig. 1.3, 14).

Axes (Fig. 1.4): several types of flint and chert axes are recorded. Core axes are fashioned from a flint nodule or large flakes; they vary in size and shape and usually have a diamond- or lozenge-shaped cross-section. Sometimes called 'tranchet axes', these implements have a comparatively narrow cutting edge, produced by a transverse blow, and are sometimes trimmed to an almost pointed butt. In some instances the butt is so carefully

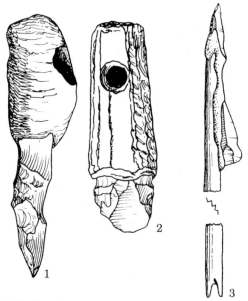

Fig. 1.5—Scandinavian adzes in antler sleeves and microliths mounted as arrow-tip and barb.

pointed as to suggest that it too may have been functional. Flake axes, a type seemingly confined to the north-east, were struck from a prepared core, their cutting edge being an unretouched edge of the primary flake; the rest of the flake was trimmed to a triangular or almost parallel-sided shape up to about 10cm in length. Axes of partly polished stone from the Lough Boora site, a finely polished example from an early Mesolithic burial at Hermitage, Co. Limerick (Fig. 1.13), and similar implements from Mount Sandel (Fig. 1.4, 3) clearly demonstrate that implements of this type were in use from the early Mesolithic onwards.

Other implement types include trimmed bladelets, burins and scrapers. While artefacts such as blades and scrapers were presumably used for a variety of cutting and scraping tasks, including the preparation of edible plants and roots, the preparation of animal hides and the dismembering of carcasses, there is still little evidence in Ireland as to the function and method of use of these various flint and chert types. A study of the microscopic traces of wear on some of the Mount Sandel material revealed polish on various tool types which could be due to use on wood, bone and hides. There is evidence from Britain and Scandinavia to show that microliths were sometimes used as arrowheads and as barbs in arrowshafts; for example,

an arrow of pine wood from Scania in Sweden (Fig. 1.5, 3) has a microlithic tip held in a notch in the wood by a resinous substance, and a microlithic barb is similarly glued into the shaft—a resin or pitch obtained from birch bark was probably used. Scrapers and blades may have been mounted in various ways in wooden or bone hafts, and objects such as flint points may have been used as awls or drills. Axes may, like their north European counterparts, have been mounted in bone or wooden sleeves, which in turn were mounted on a wooden haft. Indeed, the flake axes may have been mounted in adze fashion at right angles to the haft (as in Fig. 1.5, 2) and used as a planing rather than a chopping implement.

LATER HUNTERS AND FORAGERS: 6500–4000 BC

There is an intriguing difference between the stone industry of what has been called the 'earlier Mesolithic' and that of the 'later Mesolithic'. The narrow blade industry was replaced some time before 6500 BC by an industry characterised by heavy blades produced by direct percussion with a hard stone hammer, a development without parallel in Britain or western Europe. The development of this later broad blade tradition is to be seen at one of several sites at Newferry, in the floodplains of the River Bann just north of Lough Beg. The site in question is site 3 on the eastern side of the river in County Antrim (Woodman 1977), where several occupation levels, evidence of a long history of intermittent habitation on the site, were found in deposits of sand, gravel, silt and diatomite laid down by fluctuations of the river over a period of some 2,000 years. The rising of the level of the river had, of course, considerably disturbed the archaeological material. Only a few burnt fragments of fish bones (of eel and salmon or trout) were found, and in some cases the washed-out remains of hearths were detected spread over an area about 5m across; some flints were slightly rolled, their edges smoothed by water action. A series of radiocarbon dates, mainly from charcoal, confirmed the general validity of the vertical stratigraphy that revealed the developments in the stone industry over a long period of time. Woodman divided the complex sequence of deposits into nine zones, each containing one or

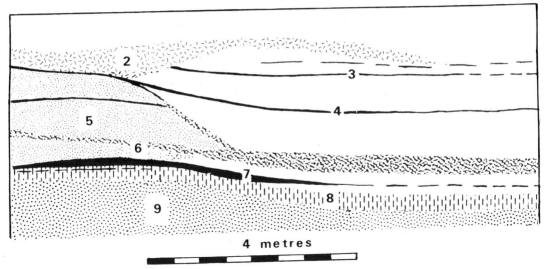

Fig. 1.6—Sequence of deposits at Newferry, Co. Antrim.

more layers (Fig. 1.6).

The basal deposit at Newferry (zone 9) was a sandbank with a couple of flint flakes indicating a little human activity. This was overlain by zone 8, a layer of peat and layers of microscopic shells of diatoms deposited by the rising river; a small scatter of flint and stone was found. Zone 7 comprised several layers of occupation debris, silt and sand, covered in part by a layer of diatomite also containing some traces of occupation. The only substantial traces of human activity survived in this zone where stones and pieces of wood were thrown down to stabilise the edge of the sandbank. Zone 6 was a layer of silt and diatomite that produced some flint and stonework. The superimposed zone 5 was a complex series of deposits: at one end of the area excavated it consisted of a sandbank containing several occupation layers and with traces of activity on its surface; at the other end the sandbank gradually tailed off into a layer of silt that merged with the silt of zone 6. Large quantities of flint and fragments of three bone points were recovered. Zones 4 and 3 consisted of deposits of diatomite containing a certain amount of stone and flint. Zone 2 comprised coarse silts and gravel and represented a phase of erosion and redeposition when a stream of water ran across the site; some flint and stone and fragments of Neolithic pottery were found. Above this was a layer of diatomite (zone 1) and topsoil.

The range of flint implements found at Newferry is very different to that uncovered at Mount Sandel. In addition to flint cores and waste material, zone 8 and the main levels of zone 7 at Newferry produced a variety of blades and flakes; only one microlith and a micro-awl were found, and small fine blades were absent. Blades were fairly elongated; a quarter of the complete examples were over 7.5cm in length and some were slightly trimmed at the butt. Flint cores and waste material were noticeably rarer from upper zone 7 onwards, suggesting that after zone 7 the bulk of the flintwork was manufactured elsewhere and brought to the site. Thereafter, too, there was a general tendency towards the production of a shorter, broader type of flint flake, though elongated narrower forms continued to be used. Radiocarbon dates suggested a timespan from 5500 BC for zone 8 to about the middle of the fifth millennium for zone 3. Aside from various forms of butt-trimmed flakes, other flint implements from various levels included backed knives, distally trimmed blades, blade points and bar forms; other flint types are rare and include spokeshaves, borers and a few scrapers and burins.

Polished stone axes of schist and mudstone were more common, and polishing stones of sandstone also occurred. Except for polished stone axes, these and other implements characteristic of this later stone industry (Fig. 1.7) are known from a considerable number of sites in various parts of the country. Much of this late assemblage comes from

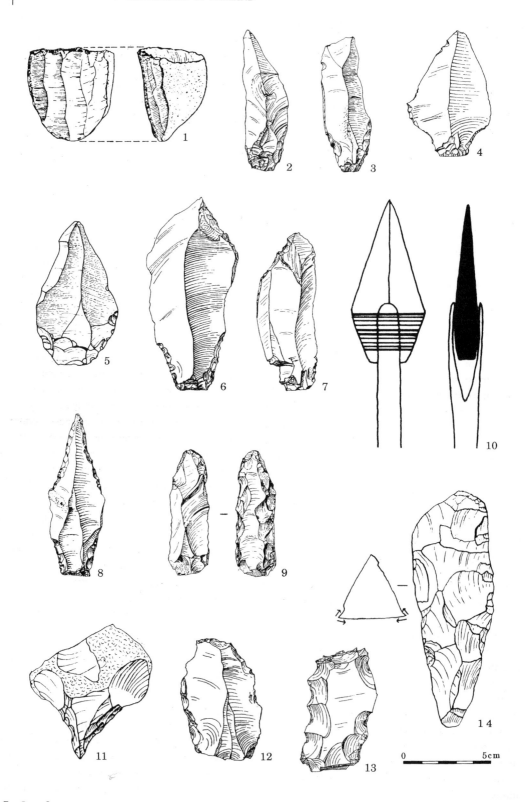

Fig. 1.7—Late flint assemblage.

surface collections or old explorations of coastal sandhills and raised beaches. Of those sites which have been scientifically excavated many have produced stone and flintwork in secondary position, they having been, in varying degrees, disturbed by the action of river or sea with a consequent loss of archaeological information and the destruction of faunal and other organic remains.

At Cushendun, Co. Antrim, excavations in 1934 in the raised beach on the western bank of the River Dun revealed that freshwater peat of Boreal age was covered with estuarine silt when the eustatic rise in sea level overtook the isostatic rise of the land (Movius 1940a). The rising waves continued to deposit gravels and silts up to a thickness of about 5m, and flint implements were incorporated in various deposits. The lower silt (horizon 1) was dated to the later sixth millennium BC and along with the lower gravel (horizon 2) produced flint flakes and blades, rolled by wave action and undamaged; this was a mixed collection of blades of various sizes, possibly from several sites of differing dates, and included elongated blades as in the basal levels at Newferry. The upper gravel or raised beach (horizon 3) contained a few water-rolled flints, and later scrapers and a hearth were found in the surface accumulation on this beach (horizon 4).

Raised beach gravels at Larne, Co. Antrim, are prolific in flint implements, and for many years the term 'Larnian Culture' was applied to this material (Movius 1942). Excavations at Curran Point, near Larne, in a pebbly storm beach overlying beds of gravel and sand, produced some late material and an abundance of rolled flint, most of it waste (Movius 1953). Excavations undertaken in raised beaches in different parts of the north of Ireland have also produced typical later flint assemblages: Glenarm, Co. Antrim (Movius 1937), Dunaff, Co. Donegal (Addyman and Vernon 1966), Ringneill, Co. Down (Stephens and Collins 1960), and Rough Island, Co. Down (Movius 1940b). Two chipping floors were found at Bay Farm, near Carnlough, Co. Antrim, and quantities of flint cores, flakes, unretouched blades and quartzite hammer stones were excavated. This seems to have been a coastal location repeatedly visited for flint-knapping purposes close to the source of the raw material (Woodman and Johnson 1996).

Shell middens of various dates are known around much of the Irish coast, and several of these deposits of molluscs and occupation debris are of similar late Mesolithic date. A midden at Sutton, Co. Dublin, measured some 100m in length but had a general depth of only 30cm. It had been formed at a time when Howth was an island and the shell layer proper was composed of over twenty varieties of shellfish, including limpets, whelks, cockles, scallops, periwinkles, oysters and mussels; it rested on a mixture of clay and shell that overlay glacial deposits. Excavations in 1949 and 1970 produced artefacts of flint, chert and stone, including cores (mainly single-platformed), butt-trimmed flakes, two fragmentary axes of polished schist, and several round and elongated hammer stones. Bone was scanty but the remains of wild pig, hare, wolf and fish were identified. Radiocarbon dates for the wild pig and another animal bone suggest a sixth-millennium date; a later hearth in the midden is dated to 4340–3810 BC (Mitchell 1956; 1972; Woodman et al. 1997).

Two middens at the western end of Dalkey Island, Co. Dublin, seem to have accumulated over a long period of time (Liversage 1968; Leon 2005). A sample of shells from one (site V) was analysed and revealed a very limited range of types, limpet accounting for 70% and periwinkle for 20%. Flint cores and flakes were found, as well as hammer stones, polished stone axes and (from site II) sherds of pottery. Animal bones from both middens included domestic ox, sheep or goat, wild pig, brown bear, grey seal, bones of various seabirds and remains of tope, mullet and possibly cod. Seal bone from site V has been radiocarbon-dated to 5970–5560 BC but other dates indicate intermittent hunting and foraging occupation to the end of the fifth millennium, and later activity with domesticates in the fourth millennium and thereafter.

At Rockmarshall, Co. Louth, two middens (I and II) were situated on a morainic ridge on the southern side of the Cooley peninsula, while a third midden occurred higher up on the ridge above the other two (Mitchell 1947; 1949; 1971). Midden I was situated on the highest point of the raised beach and was rich in charcoal and shells, notably oyster, periwinkle, limpet, whelk, mussel and cockle; claws of crab and fish bones were common. Middens II and III contained a similar mixture of shell and charcoal. Flints were few from the three sites:

mainly blades and flakes and a number of cores. Some charcoal from midden III provided a radiocarbon date of 4570–4040 BC and a human femur from the same midden was dated to 4774–4366 BC. The measurement of the stable isotopes of carbon and nitrogen in human bone collagen can provide information about the protein portion of an adult individual's diet for the previous five to ten years. The relative importance of a marine or a terrestrial protein-based diet can be determined: a $\partial^{13}C$ value of −12% or thereabouts would suggest that almost all of the diet came from the sea, while values of about −20% imply a land-based diet. The Rockmarshall femur with a $\partial^{13}C$ value of −18.1% suggests that this was a community for whom coastal resources were just a part of the resource exploitation of a larger territory that included inland locations (Woodman and McCarthy 2003).

Relatively slight traces of occupation were found associated with midden material at Ferriter's Cove, near Ballyferriter, Co. Kerry. The excavations undertaken by Peter Woodman over a dozen years from 1983 were significant, however, because they demonstrated late Mesolithic activity in the south-west at the westernmost end of the Dingle peninsula, they revealed an idiosyncratic stone industry exploiting a range of local rocks and they produced some unburnt animal bones (a rare find on Irish sites of the period). Equally significantly, this excavation produced evidence of hunter-gatherer interaction with a community with domesticated animals (Woodman et al. 1999).

The traces of occupation lay beneath 4m of sand on a low, coastal wave-cut platform cut into local gravels. Some 400 square metres were excavated, an area over 40m in length and varying in width from a few metres to 15m. Small concentrations of shells, fish remains, deposits of animal bones, burnt stones and evidence of burning, shallow pits, stake-holes and stone implements and pieces of struck stone were found. The stake-holes formed no coherent pattern but probably represent the remains of structures such as windbreaks or fish-drying racks.

The shellfish, fish and animal remains have provided a significant contribution to our limited knowledge of later Mesolithic food-gathering and hunting. Among the commonest shellfish were periwinkle, dog-whelk and limpet; cockles and mussels were represented but were limited in quantity (though poor preservation of mussel shells might mean that they were under-represented). Shells were sometimes found with fish remains, crab claws, charcoal and burnt stones—all suggesting brief eating episodes. In contrast to the large shell heaps found in other middens, the small deposits on this site are the result of a number of different activities. Some larger concentrations of shells might reflect the preparation of bait for fishing.

Over 80% of the identifiable fish bones were burnt, suggesting cooked food. Fifteen species were identified, and it is interesting to note that only five of these would have been recorded in the absence of sieving. Whiting and wrasse were the most common, with ling, cod, saithe, tope and ray also occurring in limited numbers. Most of the remains were of young individuals that, like whiting generally, would be found close to shore. Presumably fishing close to shore involved hooks, lines and nets, though no traces of these were found. Judging from the small size of some of the species caught, this activity took place in summer and autumn.

The sample of identifiable animal remains was too small to allow a reliable evaluation of the mammalian contribution to diet. Wild pig represented 82% and was presumably hunted in nearby woodland. Some bones of sea birds such as gull and gannet were found but these were of minor importance. No red deer and no dog occurred. Of particular interest, however, was the discovery of seven bones of cattle and one sheep incisor. One interpretation of these domesticated animal remains is that they are evidence of interaction between this hunter-gatherer community and early farmers in the locality c. 4500 BC. Other organic finds included burnt hazelnuts and a small scatter of unburnt human remains. The large quantity of fire-cracked stones found was noteworthy and, while some stones may have been accidentally burnt, it seemed probable that many had been heated for roasting or boiling purposes.

The greater part of the lithic assemblage consisted of material derived from a diverse range of beach pebbles and local rocks. The large quantity of debitage or debris (and the small quantity of retouched tools) suggests that the knapping of the locally available material was one of the reasons for visiting the site. The general term 'greenstone' was

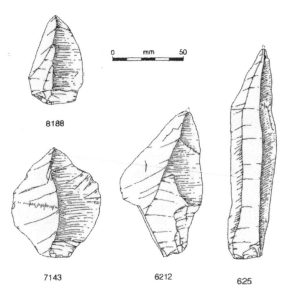

Fig. 1.8—Greenstone flakes from Ferriter's Cove.

used to cover a range of rhyolites and siltstones, the commonest stone type used (84%). Volcanic tuffs (9%) and flint derived from beach pebbles (9%) were exploited to a lesser extent. Chert and quartz, so common in the midlands, for instance, were virtually absent. Rocks such as rhyolite, tuff and siltstone are difficult to work; they fracture in unpredictable ways and often produce a diverse range of undiagnostic forms. Small flint pebbles were worked and produced short flakes and blades, usually 2–3cm in length, while greenstone usage produced larger blades and sometimes shattered into unrecognisable fragments. It was clearly knapped on site, leaving large chunks, flakes and debitage behind. A small number of greenstone butt-trimmed forms were found, but a larger number of unretouched leaf-shaped flakes occurred and these may have had a similar purpose (Fig. 1.8). Points and picks were produced as well, along with a number of slender blades. Limited wear-trace analysis was inconclusive. Apart from very slight traces of wear on a few pieces, most may have been used only for very brief periods, if used at all.

Some rounded beach pebbles showed signs of use and probably served as hand-held hammers; some had flakes removed, perhaps to produce an edged implement. One pebble had been used as a grindstone or polishing stone. Over a dozen polished stone axes, or fragments, were recovered.

Made of shale beach pebbles with little modification, most were quite small, being just under 8cm or just over 10cm in length, but an exceptional example was over 25cm long. A small cache of five shale axes rested on a thin layer of silt just above the underlying terrace and evidently was a deliberate deposition at some stage during the continuing occupation of the site (Fig. 1.9). A 17cm-long siltstone point displayed some wear near the butt and may have been hafted. Ground stone points have also been found at Moynagh Lough, near Nobber, Co. Meath.

An extensive series of radiocarbon dates indicate that several phases of occupation occurred at Ferriter's Cove between 5000 and 4000 BC, with a main phase of activity taking place around 4500 BC. Dates for the human remains suggest that this deposition took place towards the end of the fifth millennium BC, while two dates for cattle bone suggest an exceptionally early date for these domesticates of *c.* 4500 BC. The site has been interpreted as a temporary camp exploited in the summer and autumn months for fishing and for producing raw materials to make stone tools. It was the coastal component of the territory of a hunting and foraging community who perhaps had other sites in the general area where inland resources were significant. At Ferriter's Cove, analysis of a human femur and tooth revealed $\partial^{13}C$ values of −14% that indicate a very heavy reliance, perhaps 78%, on marine resources. This might suggest that here was a community who mainly exploited coastal environments around the Dingle peninsula and perhaps further afield. The shellfish from this site has provided important data about early prehistoric middens. Earlier work at sites like Sutton and Rockmarshall was very limited, though it did demonstrate that these were large and complex middens displaying a very varied spectrum of molluscan exploitation, with oysters and limpets as important components. The preference for dog-whelk and periwinkle at Ferriter's Cove has shown the importance of these species at an early date in the south-west of Ireland, where, at least at this location, some of the smaller deposits may reflect what the excavator has described as 'dinnertime camp activities'.

Late Mesolithic occupation has also been found at Moynagh Lough, Co. Meath, where parts of three brushwood platforms were examined

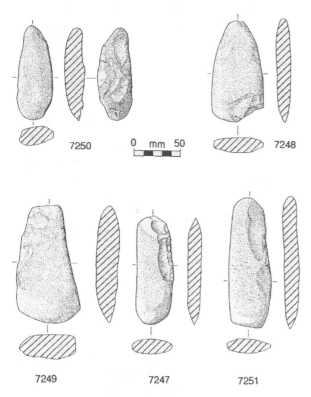

7250   0   mm   50   7248

7249   7247   7251

Fig. 1.9—Cache of five polished stone axeheads from Ferriter's Cove.

(Bradley 1999). A bone point, the ground stone points already mentioned, and chert and flint blades were recovered. There was little evidence of on-site stone-working. A small quantity of unburnt animal bone was preserved thanks to the wet conditions. Hare, bear and otter were represented but most of the bones were those of wild pig and, since only bones of adult males and young pigs were present, there may have been a deliberate strategy of not killing females. As there was no evidence of wetland birds or fish at this lakeside location, it may have been a specialised site for hunting wild pig (McCormick 2004). A radiocarbon date from charcoal of 4313–3980 BC suggests a date at the Mesolithic–Neolithic transition.

Stone assemblage

The stonework of the period 6500–4000 BC differs from that of the earlier period in so far as microliths are conspicuous by their absence and instead there is an emphasis on the production of relatively large

and often butt-trimmed flakes by direct percussion with a hard stone hammer. This novel macrolithic industry is not just radically different from what went before but, as already mentioned, is also different from the contemporary lithic technology in Britain and continental Europe. While flint and chert were the common raw materials in the early Mesolithic and were often transported to settlements for working, in the later period a greater range of stone types were exploited (in addition to flint and chert) and included quartz, mudstone, rhyolites and siltstones. Lithic production strategy took a different form in the later period too: blanks were often made near the source of the raw material (like Bay Farm, Co. Antrim, with its numerous cores and knapping debris) and then taken to the occupation site (as at Newferry, Co. Antrim, where tools and blanks occurred but few cores).

Cores (Fig. 1.7, 1): the majority of cores are single-platformed, although dual- and multi-platformed examples are known. The single-platformed cores differ from their earlier counterparts in the extent to which they were worked; earlier examples were worked in a circular fashion (Fig. 1.3, 1–2), sometimes right around the striking platform, but most later cores were worked to a roughly flat surface, with at least half their surface still covered by cortex.

Flakes and blades (Fig. 1.7, 2–7): various types of flakes and blades are particularly frequent, ranging from elongated narrow to short broad forms. Smooth striking platforms, well-defined bulbs of percussion and lengths of 6–8cm are common. Several forms have been identified. Butt-trimmed flakes (Fig. 1.7, 2–3) are approximately parallel-sided flakes more than 4cm in length; trimmed at the butt along at least one lateral edge for about 1.5cm, they have a thin and pointed distal end. On the classic form retouch should occur on both proximal lateral edges; tanged forms also occur. Bann flakes (Fig. 1.7, 4–5) are flakes 4cm or more in width with light retouch on the proximal (butt) end. In the past, the term 'Bann Flake' has been more loosely used of any leaf-shaped flake. Both tanged flakes and Bann flakes were apparently contemporary in zone 5 at Newferry, where tanged forms are also earlier. Distally trimmed flakes (Fig. 1.7, 6–7) are trimmed at the distal end for less than half their length; trimming may or may not occur on the proximal (butt) end. Backed flakes have a steep retouch for more than half the length, producing a straight back. Points (Fig. 1.7, 8) are flakes and blades trimmed to a definite point, with the retouch often confined to the distal end; butts are occasionally trimmed. The term 'bar-form' (Fig. 1.7, 9) is applied to narrow flakes trimmed along both edges and with a rough point.

The function of these various types of flakes is uncertain. It has been suggested that Bann flakes and similar forms were mounted in wooden shafts as the prongs of fish-spears, but the thick butts of many examples make this an unlikely hypothesis. These different forms may have served a variety of purposes, and even morphologically similar flakes may have had various uses; some could conceivably have been used as projectile tips (Fig. 1.7, 10), others may have been mounted in wooden or bone sleeves and used as knives and scrapers, and some may have been used as woodworking tools. These simple flake forms and their relative ease of manufacture even in difficult stones such as greenstone (Fig. 1.8) have prompted the suggestion that they represent an expedient technology in which tools are formed quickly for immediate use and then discarded. The identification of at least fourteen hoards or caches of these flakes (ranging in size from three to 158 pieces) demonstrates, however, that some had a special significance and were curated and disposed of in a particular way. A puzzling aspect of these caches is an evident tendency for groups of three to occur (Finlay 2003). Some ritual explanation is likely and they may conceivably reflect some form of ceremonial gift exchange.

Heavy flakes or so-called 'spokeshaves' are large, crude, notched flakes (Fig. 1.7, 13); some heavy, thick flakes with rough retouch, occasionally on bulbar and dorsal surfaces (Fig. 1.7, 12), are similar. Picks (Fig. 1.7, 14) are elongated implements with a rounded butt and a narrow point or a working end sometimes formed by a transverse blow producing an edge less than 1cm wide. Borers (Fig. 1.7, 11) are crude, irregularly shaped implements worked to a point. Flake axes were not used to any extent and core axes are rare. Polished stone axes are now more frequent and are known from Newferry (where examples of schist were predominant up to zone 5, with mudstone more common thereafter) and from Ferriter's Cove (Fig. 1.9).

Other implement types include a few scrapers and burins, and a series of pebbles showing signs of wear: some may have been used as polishing and grinding tools, others as light hammers. Some elongated pebbles from Rockmarshall, Dalkey Island and Ferriter's Cove have slightly bevelled ends and may have been used for the removal of limpets from rocks. The siltstone point from Ferriter's Cove and six examples of a ground or polished version in slate or sandstone from Moynagh Lough suggest that a series of ground stone points may be another implement type of this period.

Organic remains

It is certain that much of the hunting, fishing and foraging equipment was of organic material. Fragments of three simple bone points were found in zone 5 at Newferry and one bone point was discovered at Moynagh Lough; these serve as a reminder that a wide range of implements of bone and wood were used but survive only in exceptional circumstances. Fragments of bone, trimmed and ground to a slender point, could have been used for a variety of purposes, some perhaps as fish-spears. Similar bone points found in the Cutts area of the River Bann are of uncertain date; such simple artefacts could have been used over long periods of time (Whelan 1952). Wood was no doubt worked extensively; remains of a log boat have been found on the western shore of Lough Neagh, fish-traps have been found in the estuary of the River Liffey, and some wooden pieces associated with a hearth at Toome Bay, in the north-west corner of Lough Neagh, included a small flat piece of hazel wood with three rough holes pierced in it and three narrow pieces of pine wood showing signs of working (Mitchell 1955).

The rarity of settlement sites with organic remains makes it very difficult to assess the economic patterns of these early hunters and foragers or to gauge the relative importance of hunting, fishing and food-gathering. Only a small number of sites have produced faunal remains (about thirteen out of more than 180). The range of stone implements that survives provides few clues and the investigated coastal middens are mostly imprecisely dated, and some, such as Ferriter's Cove, Co. Kerry, are contemporary with communities who practised animal husbandry. The remains from the three inland sites that have produced faunal evidence, Mount Sandel, Lough Boora and Newferry, are therefore of great interest. Wild pig was evidently an important source of meat. Other animals seem to have been of less consequence: wild cat, hare and dog or wolf have been identified. Some animals, however, may just have been hunted for their hides and pelts, their carcasses rarely finding their way to the campsite. While in some cases archaeological evidence is lacking, it is possible that animals such as fox, squirrel, badger, otter, pine marten, brown bear and lynx were all hunted or trapped. The absence of red deer on early sites is surprising: the earliest securely dated examples come from fourth-millennium contexts. The scarcity of burins (with small chisel-like edges) and scrapers suitable for working deer carcasses, and the apparent absence of early upland sites, might suggest that red deer is a genuine absentee in the Boreal period, in contrast to Britain and continental Europe.

Campsites situated close to rivers or lakes would not only allow the exploitation of the fauna of the surrounding forests but would also offer the opportunity for fowling and fishing. The fish remains from Mount Sandel and Lough Boora indicate the importance of this food source, and dugout canoes, fish-spears, bone hooks, wooden fish-traps and nets may all have been used in this pursuit. Part of the base of an oak dugout log boat found during a period of low water on the western shore of Lough Neagh in Brookend, Co. Tyrone

(Fry 2000), has been dated to the late sixth millennium BC (Fig. 1.10). Irish evidence is limited, but Boreal fisherfolk on the Continent used simple bone hooks, barbed bone and antler points, as well as log boats; the remains of fish weirs, conical fish-traps of twisted willow rods and fishing nets (including a seine-net of double-threaded cord made from the fibrous bark of the willow) have all been found. Intensive fishing was possibly a seasonal occupation when migratory shoals of fish such as salmon, eel or bream were available. The discovery of the remnants of up to five fish-traps of different sorts dating from the early sixth millennium BC in the estuary of the River Liffey in Dublin offers a significant insight into what was probably a very widespread practice (McQuade and O'Donnell 2006; McQuade 2008). The fragmentary wooden structures were found on an ancient shoreline preserved over 6m beneath present mean sea level when deep basement excavations were required at North Wall Quay. One construction, dated to 6090–5890 BC, consisted of two wattle fences of hazel wood that were probably part of a roughly V-shaped fish weir leading to a trap (Fig. 1.11). The purpose of a structure like this was to guide fish into a narrow area where they could be captured in a net, basket or trap; this was an ebb weir designed to catch fish moving downstream with the ebbing tide. A C-shaped arrangement of hazel stakes and some woven wattlework that opened out towards the estuary was another form of fish-trap and was

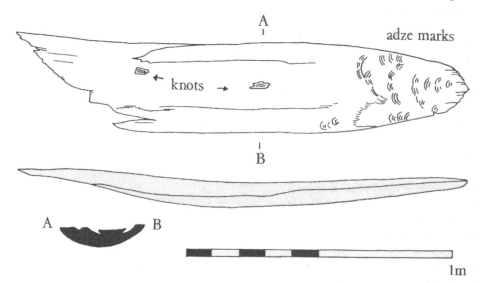

Fig. 1.10—Lower part of a log boat from Lough Neagh.

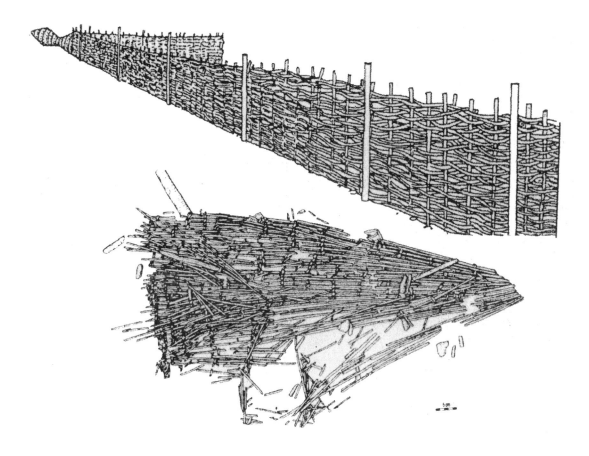

Fig. 1.11—Above: reconstruction of a fish weir based on a Danish example (no scale); the flow of the ebbing tide would enter the weir from the right. Below: wooden basket over 1m in length from Clowanstown, Co. Meath.

dated to 6080–5840 BC. Some hazel stakes and rods were probably part of a basket trap, and this feature was dated to 5930–5740 BC. It seems that this part of the ancient Liffey estuary was intermittently used over a timespan of about two centuries. The hazel rods and round wood used in these structures were of consistent sizes, stakes usually 10–45mm in diameter, wattle 5–15mm. There was a distinct clustering of stakes aged 7–10 years, and this age grouping indicates that the hazel was harvested on a coppice rotation cycle of 8–9 years.

Several wooden baskets have been found at Clowanstown, near Dunshaughlin, Co. Meath, and dated to the sixth millennium BC. Woven from slender rods of materials such as alder and birch, these conical containers were probably fishing baskets (FitzGerald 2007a; Mossop 2009). Such

organic survivals are quite exceptional in an Irish context and provide a rare insight into both fishing practice and woodland exploitation (Smart 2000).

It is difficult at present to estimate the extent to which birds may have contributed to the diet, and the same is true of edible plants and roots. The occasional discovery of hazelnuts has been noted; these are an easily stored and valuable source of fat, protein and other elements. In general, the evidence for the exploitation of plant food and nuts, roots and fungi is exceptionally meagre, yet these food sources may have been as important or even more important than meat or fish. Because the evidence is so hard to come by, it is still a widespread assumption that hunting was the most important subsistence activity, with men being the principal participants. Certainly substantial quantities of

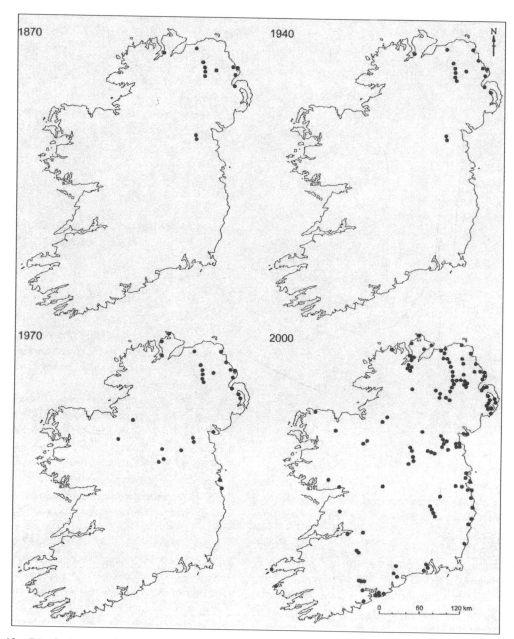

Fig. 1.12—Distribution maps showing the increasing rate of discovery of Mesolithic material in Ireland from 1870 to 2000.

potential plant foods were available at any time of the year, and these could actually have been supplemented by fungi, fish, molluscs and animals (Clarke 1976; Zvelebil 1994; MacLean 1993). Equally significantly, the evidence from some modern foraging societies suggests that women may have been the principal providers, since their food-gathering could have produced up to 60–70% of the diet by weight. Thus their status in prehistoric hunting and foraging groups may have been rather better than in later agricultural communities (Ehrenberg 1989a; Janik 2005).

Hunting and foraging communities probably had a shifting, seasonal pattern of settlement and subsistence, some or all of a group exploiting different resources at different times of the year, one site perhaps serving as a base camp for more prolonged settlement. So little is known, however, about the settlements of this period that it is still difficult to determine with any degree of confidence the possible migratory cycle of a hunting and gathering group. The degree of mobility and the possible networks of communication are just some of the unanswered questions. The evidence from Lough Boora not only demonstrates that the midlands had been penetrated by about 7000 BC but also suggests that other early sites may await discovery beneath the raised bogs of the region.

Typical broad-bladed chert implements of late date are also known from other lakeside sites in this area, for example from Lough Kinale and Lough Derravaragh, Co. Westmeath, and from Lough Allen, Co. Leitrim (O'Sullivan 1998). A possible chert quarry has been identified on Knockeyon hill on the shores of Lake Derravaragh and this may have been one source of the midland material (O'Sullivan *et al.* 2007). Western finds, also of late date, include large quantities of worked chert, including butt-trimmed flakes, from Lough Gara, Co. Sligo, where small stone platforms may have been built to mark special places on the lakeshore for fishing and for tool-making (Fredengren 2002). The distribution of both early and late material has been expanded significantly in recent years; some 400 locations are now recorded (Fig. 1.12), but this is still much the same number of find-spots as on the much smaller land mass of the Isle of Man. Nonetheless it is clear that most of the island was colonised (Woodman 2003a; 2004a). Extensive field survey has recovered later stone implements in the south-east in the Waterford area and in the Barrow valley (Zvelebil *et al.* 1987; 1996; Green and Zvelebil 1990; 1993) and in Donegal (Kimball 2000a; 2000b).

To complicate matters, an absence of diagnostic stone artefacts may not indicate an absence of settlement: a brushwood platform at Mitchelstowndown East, Co. Limerick, and a stone platform on Valencia Island, Co. Kerry, produced no finds but were radiocarbon-dated to about 4900 BC and to the sixth millennium BC respectively (Mitchell 1989; Woodman and Anderson 1990). A poorly recorded trackway, 1.8m wide and constructed of transversely laid and radially split pine planks, found in Lullymore Bog, Co. Kildare,

has also been dated to the sixth millennium BC (Brindley and Lanting 1998).

The identification of further settlements is clearly one of the important tasks of the future. Their investigation would not only increase our understanding of subsistence strategies but also possibly explain the difference between the early and later stone industries and clarify the relationship between these industries and those of Britain. The material from Mount Sandel differs in several respects from contemporary British industries, notably in the occurrence of flake axes and needle points. Such regional features suggest that an earlier Irish industry may await discovery. Flint implements such as core axes, micro-awls and the remainder of the Irish microlith types are, however, represented in northern England, whence the first hunting and foraging communities presumably came. In contrast, the later Irish material finds no parallels across the Irish Sea and, apart from some evidence from the Isle of Man, there is little indication of cross-channel contact (McCartan 2003) and surprisingly little evidence from south-west Scotland (Saville 2003).

That striking change in character between the early and late stone assemblages is not easily explained. A shift in procurement strategies may be part of the explanation. At sites like Mount Sandel flint nodules were collected on the coast several kilometres away. This collection process may have been an integrated strategy, part and parcel of the normal round of excursions to the coast for fish or other purposes. Judging from the evidence in the north-east of the country, at least, where some large caches of flint blades have been found, the heavy-bladed later assemblage may reflect a more organised strategy involving the scheduled procurement of flint by small and specific groups of people. The evidence is inconclusive, and whether this change is part of a broader shift in subsistence strategies from expedient hunting and foraging to more intensive resource exploitation remains to be seen.

We know very little about the ritual activities of these hunters and foragers, but ethnographic analogies suggest that there was probably no great distinction between the sacred and the secular (Zvelebil 2003). Belief systems no doubt encompassed seasonal food procurement strategies in which animals, fish and birds were more than

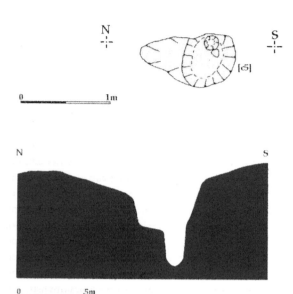

Fig. 1.13—Schematic plan and section of a burial pit containing cremated human bones and a post-hole for a timber grave-marker found at Hermitage, Castleconnell, Co. Limerick.

mere objects of the food quest but had complex symbolic relationships with their human pursuers. Given the significance of wild pig in the hunt, for instance, the boar—a large, strong animal with sharp tusks—may have been a special prize and its remains may have been the object of special treatment. It may have played a special role in myth and legend. Hunting trails and a host of natural features such as rivers, lakes and rock formations may have had supernatural associations. In a world where ritual concerns pervaded all aspects of daily life, the landscape was much more than an economic resource to be exploited. Some of those caches of stone tools may have marked special places.

The disposal of the dead may have been a particularly complex process, but the Irish evidence is still very limited. Two cremations found close to the River Shannon in the townland of Hermitage, just south-west of Castleconnell, Co. Limerick, are exceptional finds. One (A) was in a subcircular pit 60cm in diameter and 30cm deep and consisted of the cremated bones of an adult, probably male. A post-hole, 20cm in diameter, was found in the base of the pit and the bones had evidently been placed

around this feature, which may have been a grave-marker (Fig. 1.13). A polished stone axehead, showing signs of burning, had been placed at the centre of the pit by the post, and two burnt microliths were discovered in the pit fill. The second cremation (B) was found 100m away and consisted of a small amount of burnt bone representing an adult of indeterminate sex. This was a token deposit in a large pit measuring 2.3m by 1.5m and 65cm deep. The pit also contained some heat-shattered stone and pieces of burnt and baked clay. A series of radiocarbon dates from both charcoal and bone indicate that burial A dates from about 7400 BC while burial B is a little later, dating from around 7000 BC. A third pit (C) was also found but is later still and contained a few minute fragments of unidentifiable burnt bone (Collins and Coyne 2003; 2006; Collins 2009). The burial with the axe, placed by the river, must surely have demarcated a place of special importance, perhaps because the locality was just downstream of a major fording place at Castleconnell. The burials were discovered when a 10m-wide strip of land was being excavated in advance of pipe-laying and may well be part of a larger group of features. The cremations at Hermitage provide a glimpse of one aspect of a complex ritual where death and water may have had some association.

Different treatment of unburnt human remains is recorded from a few sites. Some scattered unburnt human bones, including part of a femur, were found in the shell midden at Rockmarshall, Co. Louth, and some fragments of long bones (again mainly of lower limbs) and seven teeth of a minimum of one individual were scattered close together at Ferriter's Cove. Here we may have the placing of certain parts of the human skeleton among animal bones and shellfish, perhaps to deliberately treat all in the same way. This sort of similar treatment of human and animal bones has been interpreted as suggesting the absence of any fundamental distinction between the human and animal worlds (Bradley 1998a). Some human bones have also been found in Killuragh cave, south-east of Cappamore, Co. Limerick, where, however, a taphonomic explanation may be appropriate—the bones having been washed into the cave. These remains have been radiocarbon-dated to 7000–6546 BC and 7194–6658 BC and could possibly indicate ritual activity in the vicinity of the cave mouth (Woodman 1997; 2004b; Conneller 2006). In any event, the production of disarticulated human bone may have involved complex treatment of the corpse, perhaps through exposure to the elements to allow the flesh to decay or to facilitate its removal by animals or carrion birds. This sort of fragmentation of the human skeleton may imply that some bones were stored and then circulated among some members of the community as treasured items.

While excavations at sites such as Mount Sandel and Ferriter's Cove have added considerably to our knowledge of the Mesolithic, a great number of fundamental questions remain about a period of Irish prehistory that spanned some 4,000 years. When and how initial colonisation occurred is unknown. The degree of sedentism in base camps like Mount Sandel and the nature of mobile subsistence strategies remain unclear. We have little understanding as to how groups of hunters and foragers moved around the landscape or how they exploited it and related to it. An explanation for the emergence of the exceptional and peculiarly insular heavy-bladed later stone industry has yet to be found and it seems to imply a significant degree of cultural isolation. In general, the limited data offer little opportunity for exploring questions such as regional variation and social complexity. Both early and late stone artefacts now have an impressively wide distribution but there are still many significant and unexplained gaps, not least in the west of the country. Some favoured places such as coast, lakeshore and riverine locations may have been regularly exploited, but some dense woodlands and upland areas may have been more rarely frequented. In these circumstances population estimates based on the densities of modern hunters and foragers (of 0.02–0.09 persons per square kilometre), suggesting a population of about 7,000 for the whole island, are inevitably educated guesswork (Cooney and Grogan 1999). Ferriter's Cove has provided evidence of interaction between a hunting and foraging community and early agriculturalists, but this is a reminder that how and why such indigenous hunter-gatherers acquired novel agricultural characteristics like domesticated animals remains obscure.

2

FARMERS OF THE FOURTH MILLENNIUM

There was a decisive change in the economy of prehistoric Ireland shortly after 4000 BC, a change that has been traditionally considered one of the characteristic features of the Neolithic period. The transition from a hunting and foraging lifestyle to an economy based on stock-raising and cereal cultivation was a radical development with major social consequences. Agriculture would become the fundamental economic activity in pre-industrial society and a crucial factor in shaping the physical and mental landscape. With the advent of domesticated animals and grain cultivation, the fourth millennium saw significant forest clearance, more permanent settlement, a greater concern with territoriality and the construction of large communal ritual monuments. Since the wild ancestors of cereals like wheat and barley and animals such as cattle and sheep did not exist in postglacial Ireland, they had to be introduced. It is commonly believed that these changes were initiated by the arrival of pioneering farming communities who brought with them not just the new domesticated plant and animal species but also new artefact types and adopted new ritual practices such as the building of stone tombs as well. The Neolithic period is thus defined economically, artefactually and monumentally. It has been divided by some writers such as Gabriel Cooney (2000) into three phases, an Early Neolithic (4000–3600 BC), a Middle Neolithic (3600–3100 BC) and a Late Neolithic (3100–2500 BC). It has also been thought that this transition from hunting and foraging to farming was relatively sudden, but it now seems that this process may have been more complicated and even quite prolonged, with tentative beginnings centuries earlier in the fifth millennium BC.

Archaeological and other evidence for this important transitional phase from a hunting and foraging economy to an agricultural one is scarce, and what precisely happened in Ireland is still quite unclear. The forager–farmer interface (Kimball 2000a) is indistinct to say the least. There is no certain evidence for continuity between late Mesolithic and Neolithic settlement, there are significant differences in stone technology and there are problems in evaluating the available radiocarbon-dating evidence (Woodman 2000). Because the timing of the transition and the duration of the process are so uncertain, and because of the lack of informative settlement sites, the role that hunting and foraging might have played alongside crop cultivation and animal husbandry in a long-drawn-out period of change is unknown. Because human skeletal remains from this crucial early period are rare, the opportunities for stable isotope analysis in Ireland are limited. The $\partial^{13}C$ values studied to date from a number of coastal locations are too few to demonstrate a rapid dietary change from a marine-based to a terrestrial-based subsistence economy (Woodman 2004a). In western Scotland, however, isotopic analysis combined with good radiocarbon-dating evidence suggests a speedy and fairly complete change to a protein-rich dietary regime, but how widespread this was is uncertain. Such a change in subsistence nevertheless raises the possibility that some form of colonisation by early farming groups was responsible for the introduction of this and other elements characteristic of the Neolithic, such as material culture and monumental architecture, early in the fourth millennium BC (Schulting and Richards 2002). Of course, it does not follow that this was the process elsewhere.

While colonisation by groups of pioneering farmers remains a possibility as far as Ireland is concerned, it is also possible that the introduction of innovations such as plant cultivation, domestic animals, new forms of stone implements or ceramic production was not a simultaneous event and that different Neolithic elements were introduced at different times (Thomas 1996). The introduction of farming was, of course, a profoundly important development, but the appearance of pottery would have altered aspects of the domestic world as well, and the production of some finely made stone tools demonstrates an appreciation of the aesthetic qualities of certain materials. Assuming a reasonably sized population of hunters and foragers in Ireland, it is difficult to imagine that they were completely supplanted by newcomers and had no role whatever in the adoption of what we call Neolithic practices.

There may be some evidence, both archaeological and palynological, for a pioneering phase of early agricultural activity in the fifth millennium BC but much of this evidence is tenuous and the subject of debate. Directly dated domesticated animal bones, however, though still few in number, are important indicators. The two dates for cattle bone at Ferriter's Cove, Co. Kerry, suggest an early date for these domesticates, *c.* 4500 BC. A sheep bone from Dalkey Island, Co. Dublin, has also provided quite an early date, *c.* 4000 BC (Leon 2005). This evidence and the late radiocarbon date, *c.* 4000 BC, for the Mesolithic hunting activity at Moynagh Lough, Co. Meath, suggest a transitional Mesolithic–Neolithic phase of some duration.

At Ballynagilly, north-west of Cookstown, Co. Tyrone, a number of radiocarbon determinations suggest the possibility of an early date for the presence of farmers with their characteristic pottery, flint and stonework. Here, an occupation area with post- and stake-holes and a hearth yielded flint artefacts and sherds of pottery and charcoal that produced a radiocarbon date with a range of 4770–4490 BC, and pits containing pottery and charcoal provided dates with ranges of 4670–4360

BC. These early dates have been questioned, however, and it may be that the samples dated are from old wood and thus several centuries earlier than the associated archaeological material (Woodman 2000). But they are not impossible, and if they do date the typical pottery and some typical flints, then these occupants were farmers who left only scanty traces of their passing. Pollen-sampling in an adjacent bog has shown that widespread clearance of the primeval forest of birch, pine, oak, elm and hazel did not occur there for several centuries, but this very early activity, if it only involved the clearance of a hectare or so of woodland, would leave little or no trace in the pollen record.

Some early dates associated with a number of megalithic tombs in County Sligo are also debated. Charcoal from a post-hole found dug into the natural surface below a tomb at Carrowmore, Co. Sligo (no. 7), provided a radiocarbon date of *c.* 4100 BC and probably relates to some pre-tomb structure. Charcoal from beneath and between the stones of the lowest level of stone packing around another tomb at Carrowmore (no. 27) has also provided a series of early radiocarbon dates *c.* 3900 BC. This charcoal could indicate an early date for the construction of this tomb but it has also been suggested that the burnt material could be derived from earlier settlement in the locality. Two early dates of 5640–5490 BC and 4675–4460 BC have also been obtained from charcoal associated with cremated bones from a small subrectangular megalithic tomb in a cairn on the summit of Croghaun Mountain, south of Ballysadare Bay, Co. Sligo, but here it is possible that contamination has occurred since monuments like this are sometimes open to disturbance.

Palynological evidence for agricultural activity of possibly early date has been found in Cashelkeelty, near Lauragh, Co. Kerry. Cereal pollen grains (two of wheat and one of barley) have been identified near the base of a 3m peat core (at a depth of 276–291cm), and a noteworthy drop in tree pollen was observed at the same level. A peat sample (from a depth of 291–294cm in the core) provided a radiocarbon date of 4950–4470 BC. One wheat pollen grain was found at 291cm and was associated with a first clearance phase that may have lasted for some 400 years. Given the moist nature of the core at these depths, it is conceivable that some downward displacement of cereal pollen had occurred, but since this initial clearance of pine and birch wood coincided with the appearance of weed pollen, a phase of both clearance and cereal cultivation is possible. One wheat and one barley grain at a depth of 276cm may be associated with a second bout of clearance and agricultural activity lasting 300–400 years (Lynch 1981; Monk 1993).

Early clearance has also been detected in a pollen diagram from a raised bog at Ballyscullion, Co. Antrim (Smith 1975), dated to sometime in the fifth millennium BC and possibly contemporary with the supposed primary activity at Ballynagilly. While the Ballyscullion land clearance could be the work of early farmers, in the absence of any clear indication of cereal cultivation, interference with the forest cover may have other explanations. For instance, a significant increase in the pollen of ribwort plantain (*Plantago lanceolata*) dated to *c.* 4500 BC in a diagram from Inis Oírr, Aran, Co. Galway, indicates an opening up of woodland and an expansion of herbaceous vegetation at this time. A climatic cause is possible, however, because this event may coincide with a series of narrow tree-rings identified in the Irish tree-ring record denoting a deterioration in climate owing to volcanic activity dated to 4370 BC (Molloy and O'Connell 2007). A number of such Atlantic period episodes of woodland instability are now known (O'Connell and Molloy 2001). The existence of a pioneering early farming phase in the fifth millennium BC, however, and the role, if any, of indigenous hunters and foragers in the adoption of agriculture are questions that are still unresolved.

There is unambiguous evidence for early farming in the fourth millennium BC, from shortly after 4000 BC. The pollen diagram from Ballynagilly shows a noticeable decline in the pollen of elm and pine and a corresponding increase in grass pollen with some cereal and plantain pollen at about 3900 BC (Pilcher and Smith 1979). These fluctuations in the pollen record and the presence of charcoal reflect more extensive human interference with the forest vegetation and indicate the creation of open ground with the clearing by fire of a mixed forest of elm, pine and some oak. Some cereal pollen was encountered at this clearance stage, suggesting some arable farming, but its relative scarcity thereafter prompted the suggestion that pastoral farming may have become predominant.

A marked decline in elm (*Ulmus*) in the pollen record is a widespread phenomenon around 3900 BC. In Ireland this decline is well dated but the reasons for it are debated. The term *landnam*, a German word for 'land-winning', has been applied to this phenomenon, where a drop in tree pollen such as elm is often accompanied by the appearance of pollen of plants which even today are recognised as weeds of cultivation, such as ribwort plantain, dock and nettle. The reduction in elm pollen occurs so consistently, not only in Ireland but also in Britain and parts of western Europe, that it is considered to mark the Zone VII–Zone VIII (Atlantic–Sub-Boreal) transition in the pollen record. Various explanations have been offered for this remarkably widespread and apparently synchronous decline, and these include factors such as climatic change, disease and human interference. The latter anthropogenic explanation was favoured in the past particularly because, as already mentioned, the elm decline at several sites appears to coincide not only with an increase in the pollen of grasses and weeds of cultivation but, occasionally, with the appearance of cereal pollen as well. It is possible that a reduction in elm pollen could be due to the utilisation of elm leaves for cattle fodder by early farmers without any necessary reduction in the number of trees, but it has also been suggested that in Ireland elm was concentrated in pure stands on patches of light soils and that, since such soils are more easily cultivated, early farmers would have been quick to appreciate their value. It has also been argued that freely ranging cattle may have been encouraged to winter in woodland when herbage became scarce and where elm bark could be readily stripped and eaten. This too could have been a significant contributory factor in the decline of elm, but since elm also declines in various localities where it was clearly a minor component in the wooded landscape, and was thus unlikely to be targeted by farmers or their cattle, it is now widely accepted, as we shall see, that an elm disease was the main cause.

At Fallahogy, near Kilrea, Co. Derry, detailed pollen analysis combined with radiocarbon dating has provided a general picture of the impact of early farmers on the Atlantic (Zone VII) oak, elder, hazel and elm forest (Smith and Willis 1962). About 3800 BC in this area, a sharp decline in elm and a slight

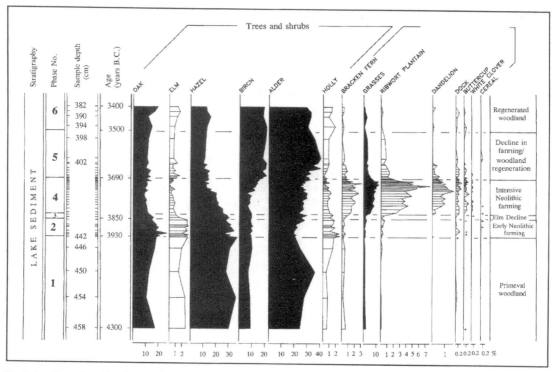

Fig. 2.1—Part of a pollen diagram from lake sediment at Lough Sheeauns, Connemara, Co. Galway, showing the vegetation history over one millennium and the changes in percentage pollen when farming was introduced shortly after 4000 BC.

decline in hazel coincide with an abrupt rise in grass pollen, which represents a clearance stage. This was followed by a rise in weeds of cultivation and bracken, denoting a farming stage. After a period of agriculture, which presumably drew to a close as the natural fertility of the cleared patches of soil was reduced, the abandoned land was recolonised first by hazel and then by other trees which gradually repressed the grasses and weeds. Following this period of secondary woodland, during which the soil regained much of its lost fertility, further clearance and farming took place around 3100 BC. No cereal pollen was encountered at Fallahogy but was found, for example, at Beaghmore, Co. Tyrone, where three stages of land clearance and management were also recognised, commencing around 3800 BC (Pilcher 1969). A period of land clearance and some cereal cultivation, which lasted for several centuries and probably included at least 100 years of continual clearing of new ground, was followed by a phase of possible pastoral activity. This was a shorter phase in which cereal pollen was absent but which did produce grass and plantain pollen, often considered as evidence of pastoralism;

a sharp rise in hazel pollen (noted too at Fallahogy) would also be consistent with grazing since cattle find the leaves of this tree unpalatable, thus increasing its representation in the pollen diagram. The third phase was marked by regeneration of the woodland. The scarcity of cereal pollen is not surprising because it has poor dispersal qualities and is invariably under-represented in the pollen record. Caution is necessary, therefore, but it may be that grazing and cattle-raising were the more important part of the economy.

Lough Sheeauns, near Cleggan in north Connemara, has provided detailed palynological evidence of the landscape changes wrought by early farmers there (O'Connell and Molloy 2001). Two cores, one from a small lake and the other from adjacent peat, revealed the existence in the fifth millennium BC of forest dominated by oak, hazel, alder and birch with only a little elm and pine (Fig. 2.1). A rise in holly pollen *c.* 4400 BC combined with the appearance of plantain indicates limited opening of the woodland, though whether through human or natural agency is uncertain. The first cereal-type pollens appear *c.* 3900 BC, shortly before the elm decline occurs, and indicate cereal cultivation near the lake. These first agriculturalists made little impact on the natural environment. Even though elm may not have been present in any quantity, the classic elm decline is recorded at about 3800 BC but obviously does not coincide with the appearance of pioneering farmers, who had arrived a century before, or with a decrease in other tree pollens, or indeed with an increase in herbaceous pollen, all lending some support to the argument that a fungal disease may have been the cause. The occurrence of pre-elm decline cereal is significant and suggests that the occasional discovery of large grass pollen grains of possible cereal type in similar pre-elm decline contexts elsewhere may also denote small-scale early farming episodes.

The elm decline at Lough Sheeauns is followed immediately by major woodland clearances involving the more or less complete disappearance of oak and the creation of pasture, demonstrated not only by an increase in grass and plantain pollen but by a rise in pollen of species such as dandelion, buttercup and chickweed as well. Only the occasional cereal pollen occurs and the emphasis seems to have been on pastoral farming. This intensive agricultural phase lasted for about 150 years and was followed by a phase of diminishing farming activity of about the same duration accompanied by a regeneration of woodland.

At Redbog, Co. Louth, elm initially declined around 3800 BC from 18% to 3%; oak also declined, with a corresponding rise in grasses and plantain, all suggesting land clearance (Weir 1995). At Céide, Co. Mayo, where pine was probably the dominant species on the relatively poorer mineral soils of the region, the elm decline is recorded about 3900 BC and precedes almost 500 years of pastoral farming with a small cereal-growing element; an extensive field system was probably built in the period of most intensive pastoral activity from about 3700 to 3200 BC (O'Connell and Molloy 2001). In Scragh Bog, near Mullingar, Co. Westmeath, a significant reduction in elm (from about 30% of the total pollen to 3%) was accompanied by a rise in grass and plantain pollen. Cereal pollen occurred here at the beginning of the elm decline before the expansion of grasses and this may suggest that arable farming was important at first. This phase of cereal-growing was followed by

a period of pastoral activity suggested by substantial increases in grass and plantain pollen (and further forest clearance, including that of oak, is indicated). Thereafter the land was abandoned and recolonised by woodland. Prior to the *landnam* at Scragh Bog, fluctuations in elm and hazel pollen there, if anthropogenic, might have been due to the activities of pioneering farmers (O'Connell 1990).

It has often been claimed that early agriculturalists elsewhere in Europe cleared the land of trees with axe and fire—the 'slash-and-burn' method—but at present there is little evidence for the use of this method in Britain or Ireland. Charcoal in pre-elm decline levels at Redbog was considered to represent natural, non-anthropogenic fires on a relatively dry bogland, and abundant charcoal found pre-dating the *landnam* at the Céide Fields, Co. Mayo, may be due to burning quite unconnected with the early farmers there. Charcoal occurred in the later Cashelkeelty record *c*. 3700 BC, and at Ballynagilly abundant charcoal in the old soil suggested the possibility of some local clearance in this fashion, but other methods may have been used and more often than not trees may have been killed by ring-barking.

Today's landscape, with its large tracts of pasture, bog and tree-less land, presents an utterly different picture to that which confronted early farming groups. In the fourth millennium BC, for instance, much of the lowland landscape would have consisted of extensive virgin forest and secondary woodland in various stages of regeneration, the tree cover being broken by occasional tillage patches and areas of rough pasture which might be abandoned when the fertility of the soil was exhausted. There was probably some regional and chronological variation in this general picture of shifting agriculture, with varying emphasis on arable and pastoral farming, and there were some areas which were more or less permanently cleared of woodland and, as in the Céide Fields in County Mayo, enclosed by field systems.

It is also worth remembering that the Atlantic period probably witnessed climatic amelioration, with an increase in both summer and winter temperatures; an average improvement on present temperatures in this and the following Sub-Boreal period of 1.0° to 2.0°C is thought possible. This climatic improvement would also permit a tree line

200–300m higher than that of the present day and means that uplands that are marginal today, like Ballynagilly and Beaghmore, at about 200m or more above OD, were suitable for agriculture. There is even slight evidence for agricultural activity at higher altitudes, including possible cereal pollen grains (found in blanket peat dated to the second half of the fourth millennium) at about 450m OD on Slieve Croob, Co. Down (Kirk 1974). That other activities occurred at such locations is well known: a flint-knapping site on Nappan Mountain, near Carnlough, Co. Antrim, at 250m OD, produced some pottery and porcellanite flakes and may have been a temporary occupation site for flint-working and the production of porcellanite artefacts (Sheridan 1987), and a site, also near Carnlough at Windy Ridge, at an altitude of 300m may have been an upland site associated with the seasonal grazing of cattle or sheep (Woodman *et al.* 1992). Extensive traces of flint-working were found at Goodland, in north-east Antrim, about 240m above sea level (Case 1973). Some circular structures with occasional rectangular hearths found at an altitude of about 360m at Piperstown in the Dublin mountains may also reflect some particular upland activity (Rynne and Ó hÉailidhe 1965).

As in the rest of north-western Europe, early farming in Ireland was in all probability mixed, being based both on the cultivation of cereals and on animal husbandry. Although the limited evidence is not easy to evaluate, it does seem that a pastoral economy may have been predominant, with cereal cultivation playing a lesser role. Wheat (emmer with some einkorn—both sturdy primitive types) and barley were the principal cereal crops, but information is still limited. As we have seen, wheat pollen has been identified from time to time in palynological studies of various lake sediment or bog samples. It has also been recorded in a layer of turves beneath the great cairn at Newgrange, Co. Meath. Cereal impressions are occasionally preserved on pottery surfaces and occur when a grain accidentally sticks to the clay as it is being worked; the grain disintegrates on firing but often leaves a detailed impression. It is now recognised that such accidental inclusions in a confined domestic context are not a reliable guide to the wider picture of crop cultivation. Impressions of grains of both wheat and barley have been recognised on pottery sherds from various localities (Monk 1986).

Cereal grains, however, are direct and unambiguous evidence and have been recovered from a significant number of settlement and other sites: carbonised wheat grains were found beneath the passage tomb cairn on Baltinglass Hill, Co. Wicklow, beneath the mound of a satellite tomb at Knowth, Co. Meath, on a small habitation site at Townleyhall, Co. Louth, and on other settlements such as Ballyharry and Ballygalley, Co. Antrim, Tankardstown, Co. Limerick, and Cloghers, near Tralee, Co. Kerry. Charred barley is reported from a tumulus at Drimnagh, Co. Dublin, and from settlements such as Ballyharry, Ballygalley, Lyles Hill and Donegore, Co. Antrim, and Cloghers (Monk 1986; 2000). A small group of three houses excavated at Monanny, near Carrickmacross, Co. Monaghan, produced grains of both wheat and barley, hazelnuts and some unidentifiable burnt mammal bone (Walsh 2006).

Hazelnuts have been recovered at a number of sites and may have been valued because they are high in fats and rich in certain vitamins. Sloe seeds, a blackberry seed and an apple pip and core found at Ballyharry (J. Moore 2003), an apple core from a rectangular house at Gortore, just north of Fermoy, Co. Cork (Kiely 2006), a crab-apple pip from Pepperhill, Co. Cork, and crab-apple pips and charred fragments of dried apples from Tankardstown, Co. Limerick, are all important indicators that berries and fruit may have been significant dietary supplements, apples possibly being stored and dried for winter consumption (Monk 1988).

The unidentifiable burnt mammal bone from Monanny is, unfortunately, fairly typical. As McCormick and Murray (2007) point out, little is known about the animals exploited at this time. In part this is due to the absence on settlement sites of enclosing ditches or rubbish pits that might contain domestic refuse. Small amounts of burnt animal bone simply reveal the exploitation of cattle, pig and sheep or goat. No firm conclusions can be drawn about the relative importance of cattle and pig, for instance, or indeed about the wild animals that may have been hunted; fishing and fowling were probably quite important, but the scarcity of evidence means that the significance of these resources is still impossible to assess. Animal bones also come from burial contexts, where they are sometimes considered to be the remains of funeral

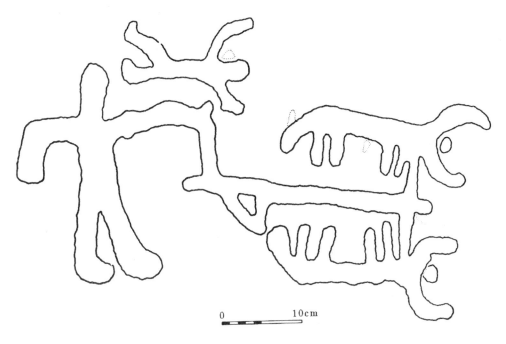

Fig. 2.2—A rock engraving of a prehistoric crook-ard at Finntorp, southern Sweden.

feasts, but such samples may be biased—possibly reflecting ritual imperatives rather than the animal population as a whole. This may be the case at Newgrange, Co. Meath, where an assemblage of bone found outside the tomb (with a high proportion of pig) may reflect feasting episodes in the later third millennium BC (Chapter 4). Red deer and horse make an appearance here at Newgrange as well, and it is possible that both were introduced at some stage in the Neolithic period (Woodman and McCarthy 2003).

Cereals, ground with rubbing stones on saddle querns (Connolly 1994), were possibly used for both bread and gruel, and maybe even for fermented drinks. While simple agricultural implements such as wooden hoes, spades and digging sticks were probably used by these early cultivators, evidence from Britain, where plough marks or lynchets (banks produced by ploughing) have been found beneath several long barrows, indicates the use of a light plough by the fourth millennium BC. Plough marks of possibly early date have been found at the Céide Fields. A simple ard-type plough may have been used just to break the soil; the simplest form of ard, the crook-ard (Fig.

2.2), basically consists of a forked branch, one short prong of which acts as a share, the other as a beam. More complicated types of ard had their various wooden elements mortised together or had stone shares; a point of an ard is reported from a house site at Ballyharry, Co. Antrim. Such ploughs could have been pulled by manpower but the use of oxen for traction is also a possibility.

SETTLEMENTS

A great variety of fourth- and third-millennium settlements have been identified and a considerable number have revealed traces of substantial timber houses, indicating a degree of permanent settlement and shedding some light on domestic activities. The evidence has been reviewed by Eoin Grogan (1996; 2002; 2004), Sarah Cross (2003) and Jessica Smyth (2006). In those that had a domestic function, food preparation (including grinding grain and cooking), food storage and possibly spinning and weaving may have occurred in or near the house, while pottery-making and stone tool manufacture may have been undertaken nearby. The term settlement

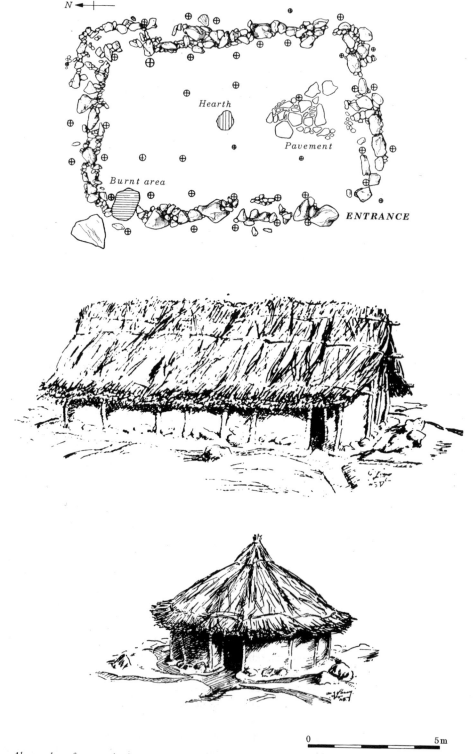

Fig. 2.3—Above: plan of rectangular house at site A, Lough Gur, Co. Limerick, with reconstruction. Below: a reconstruction of one of the circular houses at site C.

should of course encompass an even greater range of activities and probably include such features as associated garden plots and fields, managed woodland, water sources and burial and ritual areas; significant structures may not always have been present. At present the available data usually consist of traces of occupation and structural remains in a relatively confined area.

Evidence of habitation of various dates has been found on Knockadoon, a rocky peninsula in Lough Gur, Co. Limerick, a majority of house sites being located on south- and south-west-facing slopes, a tendency noted elsewhere as well. Site A there was excavated in 1939 and it is interesting to note that this site, the first early prehistoric house to be investigated in Ireland, was visible before excavation, with the tops of the stones that marked the position of the walls protruding above the turf; all the other early sites to be considered here had no surface expression and were accidentally revealed in the course of development work such as gravel-digging, pipe-laying or road-building. Site A proved to be a large rectangular structure; its remains consisted of six rows of post-holes, the outer pair forming the walls, which had an irregular stone foundation (Fig. 2.3), with two internal rows supporting the roof. It measured about 10m by 5m internally. Part of the beaten clay floor of the house was paved with stones; there was a central hearth, and a gap in the stony wall foundation on the south-west was believed to be the entrance. A considerable amount of charcoal in the soil, particularly in the area of the wall, and traces of burning (as at the north-west corner) suggested that the house had been burnt down. It has been proposed that the pairs of wall posts may have retained a wall about 1m thick with an organic fill, perhaps of sods, brushwood or rushes, standing on the stone footing, which would have acted as a damp-proof course, an unusual form of cavity wall construction also found at a partly excavated house at Curraghatoor, Co. Tipperary (Doody 2007). The posts could themselves have supported rafters, but they may have been attached to horizontal timbers, wall-plates, which would have allowed greater freedom in the positioning of roof timbers. The roof was probably thatched. Sherds of pottery were found, along with several flint and chert implements, including a leaf-shaped arrowhead, several scrapers, a polished stone axe and a fragment

of what may have been a slate spearhead (Ó Ríordáin 1954).

The burnt remains of a rectangular timber house were revealed when blanket bog was removed by bulldozer at Ballynagilly, Co. Tyrone, on a low gravel hill about 200m above OD about 8km north-west of Cookstown (ApSimon 1969a; 1976). The house measured 39 square metres in area, being 6.5m in length and almost 6m in width; the side walls on the north and south were constructed of oak planks, 45–50cm wide, vertically set in a narrow trench up to 30cm deep (Fig. 2.4). Post-holes found on the west and east may indicate end walls, though these were not clearly defined. If these were the end walls of the house, the posts presumably supported panels of wickerwork or wattle and daub, but it is also possible that the ground-plan is incomplete and what survives is just a central room. Two posts in the middle of the house were probably roof supports. A roughly circular hearth and an area of burnt clay, possibly the site of an oven, were found within the house, as was a shallow pit containing sherds of pottery. Three leaf-shaped flint arrowheads were also found in the house and three more just outside it. Charcoal from the northern wall-trench provided two radiocarbon determinations with date ranges of 4340–3790 BC and 4222–3814 BC, which suggest that the construction of the house was contemporary with the forest clearance indicated in the nearby pollen record. Two other pits in the vicinity with similar date ranges probably belong to this phase of activity. Later occupation may be attested by a hearth and two pits with dates ranging from about 3900 to about 3400 BC, and this may coincide with a phase of possible pastoral activity suggested by pollen analysis.

Finds included narrow flint flakes with secondary trimming of the edges, the flint arrowheads already mentioned, and fragments of polished stone axes; fragments of pottery represented plain, round-bottomed shouldered vessels, an early pottery style called Lyles Hill ware. Because the soil was not conducive to the preservation of unburnt bone, only a few small fragments of burnt animal bone survived, as did some burnt hazelnut shells.

A similar rectangular plank-built house was discovered and excavated during construction work on a natural gas pipeline at Tankardstown, near Kilmallock, Co. Limerick. This (house 1) was one of

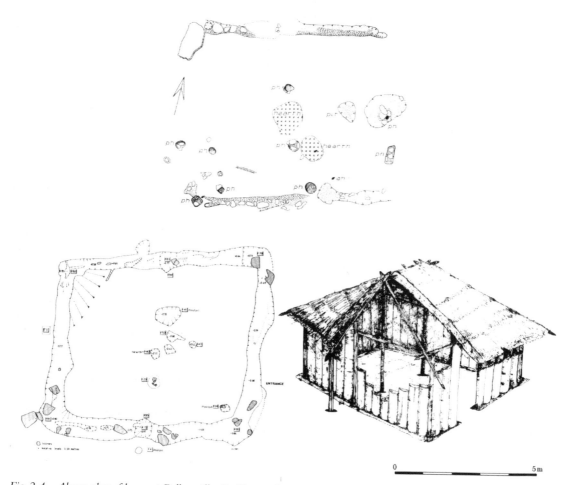

0   5m

Fig. 2.4—Above: plan of house at Ballynagilly, Co. Tyrone, showing post-holes (ph), positions of flint arrowheads (ah) and foundation trenches for plank walling. Below: plan and one possible reconstruction of house 1 at Tankardstown, Co. Limerick.

two houses excavated on this site; with an area of 47.3 square metres, it was almost square, measuring 7.4m by 6.4m, and was also built of split oak timbers set in foundation trenches up to 69cm deep (Fig. 2.4). In contrast to Ballynagilly, however, this example was built entirely of oak planking, with corner posts, a post in the centre of each of the longer sides, two internal and two external posts all giving added support to the roof and walls. Concentrated deposits of burnt animal bone were found in the fill of the foundation trench, usually near the bases of the packing stones for the posts, and may indicate some ritual practice in the course of construction. No occupation floor survived; ploughing had effectively destroyed everything except those features dug into the subsoil. There

was no clear indication of a doorway but, since the house had been destroyed by fire, the absence of burning in a section of the foundation trench on the north-east side may denote the position of a door. An area of oxidised clay with an adjacent post-hole just north of centre may be the site of a hearth. Finds included pottery sherds and a leaf-shaped flint arrowhead. Charred cereal grains of wheat were identified and radiocarbon-dated to 3938–3378 BC. Fragments of hazelnuts and seeds of crab-apple were also found, a reminder that food-gathering had some role in the economy. A second house, truncated by ploughing, was found 20m to the north-west; of different plan with maximum dimensions of about 15.2m by 7.4m, it had a large central room, 9.2m long, apparently flanked by smaller, 2m-wide rooms or annexes at either end, with a total area of about 112.5 square metres. It too had been destroyed by fire. These gas pipeline investigations also revealed traces of another burnt structure at Pepperhill, near Buttevant, Co. Cork, but only limited excavation was undertaken. Both Tankardstown and Pepperhill were located on south-west-facing slopes (Gowen 1988; Gowen and Tarbett 1988; 1990). A small settlement of three rectangular and probably plank-built houses at Ballintaggart, near Loughbrickland, Co. Down, was also located on a sheltered south-facing slope (Chapple *et al.* 2009).

Lough Gur (site A), Ballynagilly and Tankardstown (house 1) are examples of one-roomed houses, but more complex interiors occur. One of two houses (house 1) found at Ballygalley, Co. Antrim, was a subrectangular structure 13m long and 4.5m wide, with a foundation trench for the external walls and three pairs of internal posts that possibly supported walls dividing the interior into three areas; there was a possible entrance on the south-west and an extension or annexe (with a shallower foundation trench) at the other, north-eastern end (Fig. 2.5). No traces of timber walling survived and it was assumed that the house might have been deliberately dismantled. A saddle quern was found in the annexe and six others were also recovered on the site. A considerable quantity of carbonised cereal grains was found (mostly einkorn) and clearly cereal cultivation was probably important, but the soil conditions did not favour the preservation of unburnt bone, though a few cattle teeth and a little burnt bone were recovered nearby. Large numbers of potsherds, flints and stone axes were recovered, including axe roughouts made of Tievebulliagh and Rathlin porcellanite. A quantity of Arran pitchstone was imported from Scotland, and other imported material included two stone axes from Great Langdale, Cumbria, and an axe of possible Cornish greenstone. Situated some 500m inland from Ballygalley Bay, north of Larne, this settlement may have been a redistribution centre of some importance for local and imported material. The foundation trench of what seems to have been a second rectangular house (house 2) was partly exposed some 35m to the south (Simpson 1995; 1996b). Like house 1, a rectangular house at Cloghers, Co. Kerry, may have had a tripartite

interior but it had been severely damaged by later agricultural activity (Kiely 2003).

Part of a long rectangular house with a clearly defined internal dividing wall, and measuring at least 10m in length and 6.9m in width, has been found during construction work on a natural gas pipeline at Newtown, Co. Meath. Situated on the northern side of a gently sloping hill, this house had a row of three posts on its central long axis and a gap in the internal wall has been plausibly interpreted as a doorway; an external entrance probably existed at the north-east corner. Radiocarbon determinations indicate a probable date in the first half of the fourth millennium BC (Gowen and Halpin 1992).

Another large, compartmented house with an annexe at one end was revealed beneath part of a megalithic tomb at Ballyglass, Co. Mayo (Ó Nualláin 1972; 1976). This structure was rectangular, measuring about 13m by 6m, and its remains consisted of surprisingly shallow foundation trenches about 20cm deep and a number of stout post-holes up to 70cm in depth (Fig. 2.5). The entrance was possibly at the north-western end, where the excavator thought that three post-holes and a short foundation trench might represent some sort of porch and entrance passage. There was a narrow compartment or annexe at the south-eastern end, and while part of its wall was, like most of the house, probably built of timbers embedded in a foundation trench, the south-eastern corner was represented by only a shallow depression in the subsoil and was, it seems, of less substantial construction. Two internal lines of post-holes may have been load-bearing and denote divisions of the house interior. Both the end compartment and the main part of the house contained areas of fire-reddened clay; these possible hearths and the wall-trenches and post-holes contained sherds of pottery akin to that from Ballynagilly. Flint implements were few but some leaf-shaped arrowheads and concave scrapers may be associated with this occupation. Charcoal from the wall-trenches of the house produced a series of radiocarbon determinations indicating occupation in the second half of the fourth millennium, but the nature of this activity is debated. This and some other large rectangular structures could have had a purpose other than a domestic one—ritual assemblies or feasting halls are just two possibilities

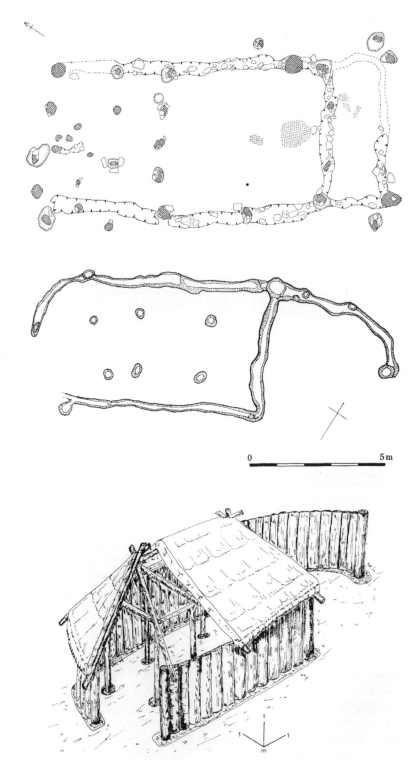

Fig. 2.5—Above: plan of house at Ballyglass, Co. Mayo, with annexe. Below: simplified plan of house with annexe at Ballygalley, Co. Antrim, and reconstruction.

(Topping 1996; Cross 2003).

One phase of a complex sequence of structures at Ballyharry, Co. Antrim, was a rectangular post- and plank-built house measuring 6.5m by 5m, with traces of part of an attached rectilinear structure of lighter construction, perhaps wattlework, giving the whole edifice an overall length of some 23m. The house interior had a narrow rectangular area in its south-eastern corner defined by a thin foundation slot measuring 3m by 1.5m, which the excavator thought might be a bedding area. Part of the main structure was burnt, and the presence of numerous arrowheads suggested that it had been attacked (D. Moore

2003). The material evidence, which included charred grain, pottery sherds, flint and stone implements, saddle querns and the ard point already mentioned, suggests domestic activity. Part of a second rectangular house some 300m to the south-east was also excavated.

Three subrectangular post- and plank-built houses in Corbally, near Kilcullen, Co. Kildare, were of very similar construction and, if not contemporary, were certainly built within a short timespan in the earlier fourth millennium BC (Purcell 2002a). They were internally divided in two, the larger room (roughly on the north-west) containing traces of one or more hearths (Fig. 2.6).

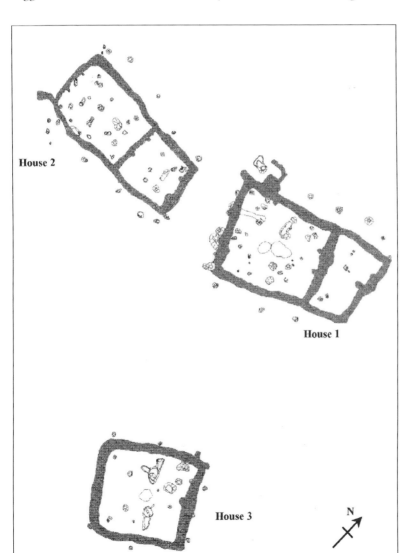

Fig. 2.6—Plans of three houses at Corbally, Co. Kildare.

House 2

House 1

House 3

N

0   3m

Entrances appeared to be on the south-east. The largest example measured 11m by 6.7m and had an internal area of 52.8 square metres. It was a substantial structure with foundation trenches up to 1m deep. Its floor level did not survive, but two slot-trenches in the northern corner of the large room suggested a further subdivision of this area and traces of two large hearths were found in the centre of the room. Though smaller, the two other houses also had hearths in the larger room. Cereal grains (both wheat and barley), hazelnuts, pottery sherds and flint implements including scrapers and leaf-shaped arrowheads were recovered, as well as polished stone axes, a slate spearhead and part of a saddle quern. Animal bone was virtually absent. A series of radiocarbon dates indicate occupation in the first half of the fourth millennium from about 3700 BC to 3600 BC. Another cluster of at least three or four houses was found 60–100m to the south (Tobin 2003).

Whether or not that small internal space in Ballyharry and the small subdivision in the large room in the larger Corbally house were bedding areas is impossible to say; evidence for internal activities is invariably lacking and the destruction of house floors is always a significant loss (whether owing to agricultural activities or the deplorable practice of over-rigorous topsoil-stripping in advance of development). The beaten clay floor at Lough Gur (site A) and a compacted floor in an almost square house at Granny, Co. Kilkenny (just north of Waterford), are rare examples. Only slight traces of a central hearth survived at Granny, prompting the suggestion that it may have been raised or suspended in some way (Hughes 2005). The scarcity of floor deposits makes correlation between spatial organisation and material culture very difficult. Nonetheless, it is clear that in some cases these buildings were domestic dwellings and certain parts of the house were differentiated; some may indeed have been sleeping areas, others set apart for specific tasks. Activities were probably carefully structured, and the configuration of space almost certainly had a role in determining and maintaining social relations. Some spaces, or indeed some houses, may have been the preserve of males or females or others kin. While doors on the east or south-east are common and might well have a functional explanation (to optimise natural lighting in the interior, for instance), other symbolic factors

may have influenced their positioning here or at other points of the compass. The door in a house at Enagh, Co. Derry, may have faced the River Foyle and—possibly—another settlement at Thornhill, 1km away across the river to the north-west (McSparron 2003; Logue 2003). As Gabriel Cooney (2000) notes in his study of these houses, their interior was a complex architectural space.

The substantial nature of some timber structures—like those at Corbally, for instance—suggests that they were architecturally imposing and were probably at the very least statements of identity. Because there were rituals associated with the domestic world, they should be considered to be both domestic and ceremonial monuments. Some houses may have been deliberately burnt (Smyth 2006) or dismantled in part or in whole; the latter seems to have been the case at one of the houses at Ballygalley and at Corbally, for example. While there may be a functional explanation, large timber planks and posts being valuable items, it is also possible that their reuse maintained important links with past lives and events. The equally deliberate deposition of material in pits, post-holes and foundation trenches has been noted as well. A pit in the Ballynagilly house contained many pottery sherds, and a phase of rebuilding at Ballyharry included the placing of a complete stone axehead and a leaf-shaped arrowhead, blade and point downwards, in the central post-holes of the western and eastern wall foundation trenches. A stone axehead was also placed blade downwards in a post-hole, possibly during the construction process, in one of the Monanny houses. A flint arrowhead was placed in a post-hole in one of two houses excavated at Granny, Co. Kilkenny, and a chert arrowhead was deposited in a post-hole in the other.

While many of these houses seem to have been domestic dwellings, the purpose of some is sometimes not so clear. Cross (2003) has suggested that competitive feasting may have been a feature of the earlier Neolithic, and the regularity of the rectangular form may imply that some of these buildings had a particular social role and may have been feasting halls. As far as a non-domestic function is concerned, a structure excavated at Kishoge, near Clondalkin, Co. Dublin (O'Donovan 2004), raises interesting questions. Like so many of these houses, it was more or less rectangular, though

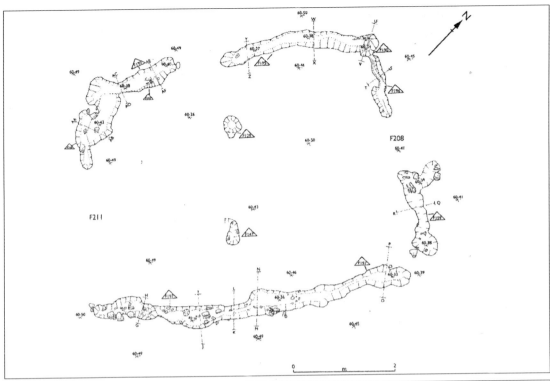

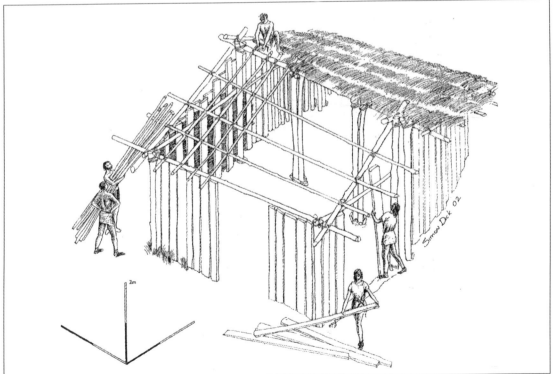

Fig. 2.7—Plan and reconstruction of a rectangular house at Kishoge, Co. Dublin, with two possible entrances, one on the north-east and the other on the south-west.

the walls curved slightly on the south-west; it measured about 6m north-east/south-west and 4.5m north-west/south-east (Fig. 2.7). The foundation trenches for the walls survived as very shallow features; plough furrows across the site testified to the fact that the remains had been severely truncated by agriculture in the past. Nonetheless, excavation demonstrated that the walls had been built mainly of upright oak planking, though in several places other techniques such as posts and horizontal planking had been used. Two internal post-holes suggested subdivision into two areas. A gap just over 1m wide in the north-east wall was identified as an entrance, and a larger gap just over 2m wide in the opposite south-western end was thought to be another. Given the degree of agricultural disturbance, it was not surprising that neither floor nor hearth survived. What was surprising, however, was that careful excavation uncovered no pottery sherds and few flints, while botanical analysis of over 50 samples from almost all the archaeological deposits produced not a single charred seed nor any cereal remains. It seems unlikely that the later disturbance could have removed all traces of domestic activity so completely, so it is possible that the Kishoge building served some other purpose.

Though the evidence is limited, the belief that a pattern of isolated single farmsteads with associated tillage plots and grazing land was the Neolithic norm is no longer tenable. Scattered groups of houses as at Corbally and Ballyharry now imply that dispersed clusters of houses may have been more common, perhaps a reflection of kinship ties, a desire to reinforce communal identity and the need for cooperative labour posed by early agriculture. A bucolic picture of scattered, self-sufficient farmsteads, rather than settlement clusters, is probably due to limited investigation. The correlation of some megalithic tombs and good soils also suggests a keen awareness of the agricultural potential of certain areas and this must have influenced settlement location in a significant way.

These large rectilinear buildings seem to have been a relatively short-lived phenomenon of the earlier fourth millennium BC. A series of radiocarbon dates indicate that they were mainly constructed in a narrow time-frame in the period 3800–3500 BC (McSparron 2003; 2008; Smyth 2006) and that they were an architectural form eventually replaced by a much longer-lived tradition of circular houses. Though the division into rectangular and circular is a convenient simplification, it should be remembered that the use of the term rectangular is an over-simplification. There is considerable variability in plan, and the rectilinear category embraces a range of rectangular, subrectangular, trapezoidal, almost square, and structures with rounded corners, as Grogan (2004) has noted. The circular group is equally varied in ground-plan. The rectilinear timber structures were a relatively short-lived monumental expression that should probably be seen as a deviation from a tradition of flimsier round houses, easily built and easily replaced, that was at least as old as the Mesolithic.

The early excavations at Lough Gur yielded the remains of three small, approximately circular houses, possibly of third-millennium BC date but not certainly contemporary; their average diameter was about 6m (Fig. 2.3). Two (at site C) were built of a double ring of posts, as at site A, and also possibly had an organic fill retained by facings supported on the timber uprights; an irregular scatter of posts within supported the roof. It is interesting that the round houses should be built in the same manner as the rectangular one. Each of these circular houses contained a hearth and one or more pits up to 60cm deep that the excavator, Seán P. Ó Ríordáin, thought might be for rubbish. They apparently contained quantities of pottery fragments and may not have been entirely utilitarian. It is possible that, as instances of structured deposition, some of these pits and their contents, like the pottery in the Ballynagilly pit and the stone axeheads already mentioned, may have had some particular social or ritual significance. A third structure there apparently consisted of a single circle of posts that may have supported a wattle-and-daub wall. Two circular houses just under 5m in diameter are also reported from Slieve Breagh, near Slane, Co. Meath; though excavated from 1960 to 1962 no report has been published, but one had an internal ring of roof supports, a centrally placed rectangular hearth and an entrance on the south-west with a projecting porch-like feature (Fig. 2.8).

A sequence of occupation has been identified at Knowth, Co. Meath, pre-dating the construction

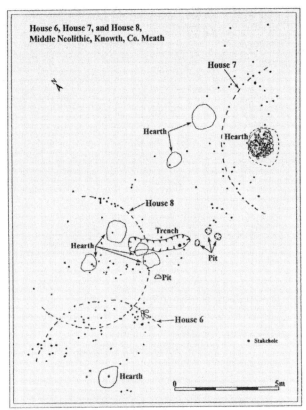

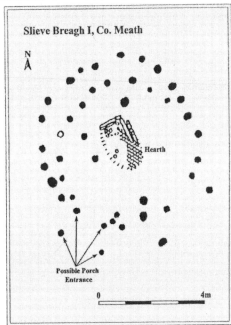

House 6, House 7, and House 8,
Middle Neolithic, Knowth, Co. Meath

House 7

Hearth

Hearth

House 8

Trench

Hearth

Pit

Pit

House 6

Stakehole

Hearth

0   5m

Slieve Breagh I, Co. Meath

N

Hearth

Possible Porch
Entrance

0   4m

Fig. 2.8—Above: plans of three possible circular stake-built houses (nos 6, 7 and 8) at Knowth, Co. Meath. Below: plan of a circular house with a possible porch-like entrance at Slieve Breagh, Co. Meath.

of the great passage tomb mound (Eogan 1984; Eogan and Roche 1997). A number of foundation trenches on the north-east may be the remains of rectangular structures and have been interpreted as the earliest phase of settlement there (named Early Neolithic 1 in Cooney 2000). Two roughly rectangular houses were found on the western side of the mound (Early Neolithic 2). One lay beneath one of the small satellite tombs and was subrectangular with rounded corners. Among the larger examples recorded, it measured 10.7m by 9.1m internally and had an entrance on the north-east. The foundation trench for the walls was deepest on the west (up to 97cm) and this section contained a line of eleven post-holes. Traces of burning and ash may represent an internal hearth just north of centre. Seven pits were also found in the interior but one (no. 4) was clearly earlier, being cut by the wall-trench. Each was filled with soft dark earth and one (no. 6) also contained some pottery sherds of early undecorated type and pieces of flint. A second, slightly smaller house was discovered some 7m to the east but was only partly excavated because it lay beneath the outer section of the passage of the western tomb in the great mound (Eogan and Roche 1998). A series of stake-built structures revealed on the north-east and east of the mound are considered to represent Middle Neolithic occupation; hearths, animal bones and decorated pottery were also found. Though hundreds of stake-holes were found in several areas, no complete house plans could be identified with certainty; in many instances the evidence was obscured by later passage tomb construction and early medieval activity. A number of arcs or partial circles of stake-holes, and the occasional hearth in what may have been a central or near-central position in a possible circle, have led to suggestions that at least nine round stake-built houses with diameters ranging from 3.75m to 7m may have been present (Fig. 2.8).

A scatter of some sixteen hearths found beside the mound at Newgrange has also been interpreted as a settlement cluster of round houses there (Cooney and Grogan 1999), but the excavator, noting the limited number of associated stake- or post-holes, saw them as evidence of more transient Late Neolithic squatting activities (O'Kelly *et al.* 1983). Indeed, many Neolithic dwellings may have been relatively flimsy structures, frequently replaced and leaving little archaeological trace. Evidence of temporary occupation was found beneath a megalithic tomb at Townleyhall, Co. Louth, where an occupation layer had a maximum thickness of 15cm and extended over a roughly oval area about 15m by 11m. A scatter of over 140 small stake-holes (with no coherent plan) and nine hearths were revealed. Since some stake-holes were found beneath hearths and one hearth was superimposed on another, it seems likely that the site was occupied on several occasions. Finds included numerous pottery fragments and flint scrapers, as well as carbonised grains of wheat and charred hazelnut shells. The fact that the bulk of the flints were either concave scrapers or convex scrapers suggests that some specialised activity occasioned this intermittent occupation, which, judging from a radiocarbon date obtained from charcoal, may date from the earlier third millennium BC (Eogan 1963). Another site at Townleyhall, called Townleyhall I and situated 1.8km to the east, may have been similar. It consisted of a mound that covered a large scatter of over 90 stake-holes, again associated with convex and concave flint scrapers; this occupation area was partly enclosed by a low penannular bank with external ditch (Liversage 1960).

Grogan (2002; 2004) suggests that there was a shift from rectangular to circular house forms in the Neolithic and that this marks a reduction in the range of activities that took place within them, as well as a slightly smaller number of occupants. The circular houses at Mount Sandel are a reminder, however, that a tradition of round house construction may go back to the Mesolithic. As already mentioned, the rectangular timber buildings that are such a striking feature of a part of the fourth millennium may be a relatively short-lived innovative departure from a long-lived and persistent but much more ephemeral round house tradition. There is an assumption in prehistoric studies generally that because contemporary Western houses are substantial permanent structures, early settlements should have an identifiable house as well (Brück 1999). The large rectangular timber house may have been a brief monumental fashion.

There are instances of temporary encampments, and some communities may have been less sedentary than others; the practice of transhumance—the movement of livestock to summer hill-pastures—may have involved the construction of temporary huts, as may seasonal visits to the coast for fishing, shellfish-collecting or perhaps salt production. Coastal settlement is certainly attested in marshland at Bay Farm II, near Carnlough, Co. Antrim (Mallory 1992a), and coastal activity of some description by numerous finds of pottery and flints in sand-dunes notably in north-eastern Ireland such as Whitepark Bay, Co. Antrim, Portstewart, Co. Derry, and Dundrum, Co. Down. Artefacts from these northern sandhills range in date from the fourth millennium BC to the medieval era; shells and bones have been found, and dark layers in the dunes are interpreted as old land surfaces and deposits of organic refuse. Hearths represented by concentrations of charcoal and burnt stones have been noted from time to time. Few of these sandhills sites have been scientifically excavated, but it is clear that because of wind erosion, for example, and for other reasons, material of widely different dates may sometimes occur in association.

In the White Rocks sandhills, near Portrush, Co. Antrim, part of a polished stone axe, various flints, a late prehistoric brooch, pottery of the early medieval period and a medieval coin were all found in or on the same old land surface (Collins 1977). Several sites on the Murlough peninsula at Dundrum, Co. Down, have been excavated and have produced evidence of activity in prehistoric and early medieval times. Fourth-millennium finds comprised pottery sherds and crude flints, and in one area (site 6) traces of fires were found in the form of charcoal and burnt stones, a rough semicircle of five stake-holes may have been the remains of a shelter or windbreak, and a pair of post-holes some metres away may also have supported a flimsy structure of some sort. Charcoal from a pebble-floored hearth (at site 12) associated with plain, shouldered pottery and some flintwork has provided radiocarbon dates with ranges spanning the fourth millennium (Collins 1952; 1959a). If the reasons for the brief and possibly seasonal visits to Dundrum are obscure, it is evident that the collecting of shellfish was of importance elsewhere. At Culleenamore, Co. Sligo, a shell midden contained a hearth that produced a fourth-millennium radiocarbon date; shells were mainly oyster, with some cockle, mussel, periwinkle, scallop and limpet, and it has been suggested that this and other coastal middens in the area were one of a series of food sources seasonally exploited by the builders of the nearby megalithic tombs on Knocknarea and at Carrowmore (Burenhult 1980; 1984). A shallow oyster midden just over 21cm deep at Rough Island overlooking Strangford Lough, Co. Down, with associated pottery and stake-holes, seems to have been a temporary camp associated with shellfish-gathering and perhaps fishing (O'Neill *et al.* 2003). A log boat, radiocarbon-dated to 3499–3032 BC, found on the foreshore of Greyabbey Bay on the far side of Strangford Lough, is the sort of craft probably widely used in the Neolithic in this sea lough (McErlean *et al.* 2002; Forsythe and Gregory 2007).

A different type of seasonal activity may have taken place on Geroid Island in Lough Gur. Limited excavations there revealed a third-millennium occupation layer: charcoal, burnt stones, animal bones, pottery sherds and flints were found, and pollen analysis suggested that the island supported oak trees at this time. The small number of animal bones recovered were mainly of cattle and pig but, in contrast to nearby Knockadoon, where cattle was predominant, almost 50% of the island bones were those of pig. Since pig is a woodland animal, this small wooded island may have provided seasonal grazing for both pig and cattle (Liversage 1958).

Not surprisingly, both the identification and the explanation of temporary occupation sites present problems. That house found beneath the megalithic tomb at Ballyglass, Co. Mayo, was evidently a substantial structure even if its purpose is uncertain, but hearths, spreads of charcoal, pottery sherds and stone implements found beneath other tombs such as Ballybriest, Co. Derry (Evans 1939), Ballymarlagh, Co. Antrim (Davies 1949), and Baltinglass, Co. Wicklow (Walshe 1941), are equally difficult to interpret. While these finds may be the remains of some temporary habitation on the site prior to the construction of the monument, it is also possible that they could represent ritual activity. At Knockiveagh, Co. Down, a layer of black earth beneath a hilltop cairn was up to 10cm thick and contained charcoal, pottery sherds and carbonised hazelnuts. This was considered to be an artificial accumulation scraped up from an area of occupation and intentionally dumped on the site; charcoal provided a radiocarbon determination

suggesting a fourth-millennium date (Collins 1957a). Occupation found beneath one of the small mounds at Newgrange, Co. Meath (site L), was clearly earlier than the superimposed monument. A few small pits, a hollow containing broken pottery, a few small areas of burning, and some flint scrapers and waste flakes were all that remained, and no traces of structures were found. The hollow containing pottery had silted up and a thin grass line had formed before the mound was built, suggesting some period of time between the two phases of activity. A possible hearth and a few scattered post-holes were found beneath site Z and indicate pre-tomb activity there, though what form this took is impossible to identify (O'Kelly *et al.* 1978). The purpose of two irregularly C-shaped structures represented by shallow foundation trenches and post- or stake-holes discovered close to and pre-dating a second court tomb at Ballyglass is difficult to determine, though one was thought to have possibly been a workshop of some sort (Ó Nualláin 1998).

Some house sites were enclosed, though this may not have been common. A rectangular house at Russellstown, near Carlow town, seems to have been surrounded by a subrectangular ditch delimiting an area about 60m by 70m (Logan 2007). An oval enclosure in Glenulra townland, near Ballycastle, Co. Mayo, may possibly be of late fourth-millennium date. It was formed by a low, poorly built stone wall demarcating an oval area 25m by 22m. Stake-holes perhaps representing some sort of structure, pottery sherds, a few chert and flint implements, and the stone tip or share of a primitive plough were found. Charcoal from a hearth provided a radiocarbon date of 3500–2890 BC (Caulfield *et al.* 1998). It is one of several enclosures and megalithic tombs associated with an extensive field system extending over several townlands and now known as the Céide Fields. Several stretches of foundation trenches for substantial timber palisades, two over 20m in length, were found on the settlement at Thornhill, Co. Derry, where they may have served to demarcate its south-western limits. Part of one of these was burnt (Logue 2003). Two long, curving and parallel palisades at Knowth do not seem to have been a part of a large enclosure and they may have been built to delimit an area of activity some 10m wide between them (Eogan 1984). A curving segment of

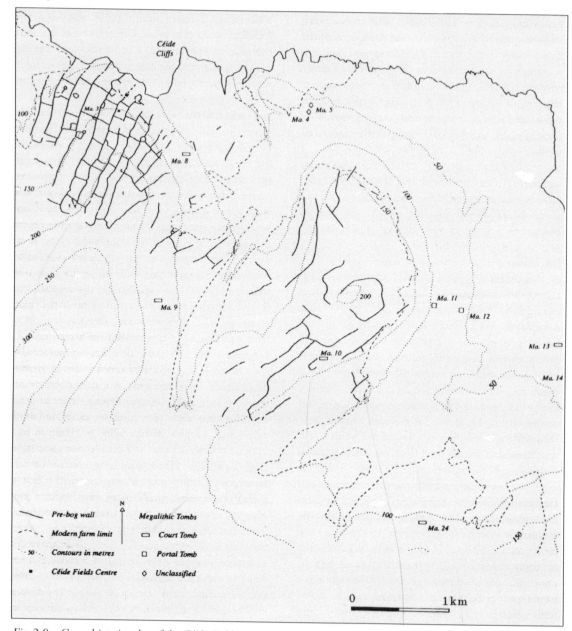

Fig. 2.9—General interim plan of the Céide Fields, Co. Mayo. The tomb marked Mayo 13 on the east is the court tomb and house at Ballyglass; Mayo 14 is the small court tomb with associated C-shaped structures.

ditch is the earliest identified feature on the Hill of Tara, possibly part of an enclosure, and has been radiocarbon-dated to 3500–3000 BC (O'Sullivan 2005).

The Céide Fields, a complex system of contemporary fields in Glenulra, Behy and neighbouring townlands, demonstrate that early farmers, in this region at least, had an integrated agricultural system on a considerable scale. Long parallel stone walls, some up to 2km in length and 150–200m apart, form long rectangles which are divided by cross-walls into large rectangular fields up to 7ha in area (Fig. 2.9). The field system, preserved beneath blanket bog up to 4m in depth, has been traced by probing over an area of over 1,000ha, but only a very small portion of it has been exposed and, regrettably, only brief preliminary reports have been published to date (Caulfield 1978; 1983; 1988; 1992). The surviving walls are surprisingly low, usually 50–70cm high, rarely exceeding 80cm. In Seamas Caulfield's opinion, the large fields were designed for stock-raising rather than tillage, though some smaller ones may have been used for growing wheat and barley, a picture supported by pollen analysis.

This sort of coaxial field system, possibly planned and certainly laid out with one dominant axis, contrasts with the commoner aggregate field system, where an irregular pattern has developed by piecemeal land enclosure. Whether the whole complex was planned and laid out by one or more farming communities to allow easier management of stock and grassland is not certain. Caulfield believes the clearance of this large area of its forest cover and the division of the landscape into stone-walled fields demanded the cooperative effort of a very sizeable settled community, and the presence of a dozen megalithic tombs in the general area might give weight to this suggestion. Communal effort is very probable, but the numbers involved are difficult to estimate. Both tomb construction and the development of the field complex may have spanned several centuries. What prompted wall construction and the coaxial rectilinear plan is also obscure; it may be that the long rectangles represent some piecemeal land clearance in long rectangular swathes, and that the low stone walls were a means of resolving the problem of disposing of cleared stones and even provided the foundation for some form of fencing or thorn hedge. Molloy and O'Connell (1995) point out that the exposed low linear rows have a lateral spread of about 2.5m and, since peat is absent from beneath the stones, collapse may have been minimal; in other words, the rows were deliberately built in this low wide fashion and, while they evidently served to demarcate specific areas, they could have been due to field clearance. It is also possible that these fields were a social statement asserting ownership and control: the construction of fields, like the building of houses and tombs, is a way of laying claim to place. Pollen analysis indicates that the period of intensive farming here spanned some 500 years from about 3700 to 3200 BC and was at its most intensive for about 250 years. It is possible that a series of severe storms *c.*

3200 BC, reflected in silt deposits in peat profiles on Achill, Co. Mayo (Caseldine, Thompson *et al.* 2005), may have contributed to the abandonment of the field system. The spread of the blanket bog, which was to envelop the complex, was under way by 2700 BC.

A much smaller group of pre-bog stone walls forming small irregular fields has been identified just 7km to the west of the Céide Fields in the townland of Belderg Beg (Caulfield 1978). A series of radiocarbon dates from pine and oak trees growing on a thin layer of peat formed just as the blanket bog commenced to grow suggests that this aggregate field system dates from some time before the early third millennium BC, a date supported by the discovery of some pottery, flints and a polished stone axe. Other evidence of early pre-bog settlement, including field systems, house sites and megalithic tombs, has been found at Rathlackan, east of Ballycastle (Byrne 1991; 1994).

Hilltop settlement has also been recorded. At Lyles Hill, Co. Antrim, the picture is complicated by later activity. Excavations by Estyn Evans at various times from 1937 to 1951 on this conspicuous 250m-high hill north-west of Belfast concentrated on a low cairn near the summit, which proved to be a burial monument of the second millennium BC. It overlay a hearth and occupation area measuring over 4m by 2m that produced numerous flints and hundreds of fragments of characteristic pottery soon to be widely known as Lyles Hill pottery. This material was assumed to be a ritual accumulation derived from nearby settlement; no house foundations were found, but the excavator suggested that the quantity of pottery argued for more than brief occupation in the vicinity. Similar pottery was found in an earthen bank that surrounded the hilltop and enclosed an area about 380m by 210m, or some 6.25ha. It was tentatively suggested that the occupation and the large enclosure were contemporary, but such an early date for a hilltop enclosure was disputed. Further limited excavation in 1987 and 1988 demonstrated that the enclosing bank was indeed a later feature but also revealed two approximately parallel stone-packed palisade trenches, set 3–6m apart, which were traced for at least 25m around the contours of the hill. A hearth produced some carbonised barley and was radiocarbon-dated to the fourth millennium BC. The palisade trenches yielded typical Lyles Hill pottery, and charcoal from both indicated dates in the third millennium. Even though only relatively short stretches of palisade have been uncovered, it seems possible that the hilltop was enclosed by two timber palisades rather than an earthwork at this time; the inner palisade dated from about 3000 BC, the other from about 2800–2300 BC (Gibson and Simpson 1987; Simpson and Gibson 1989).

Evidence of extensive hilltop activity has also been found on Donegore Hill, Co. Antrim, 8km to the north of Lyles Hill (Mallory 1986; Mallory and Hartwell 1984). Field survey recovered large quantities of pottery and flints in a ploughed field on the summit of this 234m hill. Excavation demonstrated that ploughing had destroyed all but the last traces of various structures but some pits did contain potsherds. Carbonised hazelnut shells and many thousands of pottery sherds were found. The lithic assemblage, comprising almost 25,000 pieces, was dominated by scraping and cutting tools, suggesting a domestic function for the site, and concave scrapers were all but absent. Waste flint material indicated flint-working on site (Nelis 2003). Aerial photography after a particularly dry spell of weather revealed that the hilltop had been partly enclosed by a parallel pair of ditches that delimited an area about 200m by 150m. Further excavation showed that the ditches were rock-cut, being dug through the glacial till into the basalt below; they were about 1–2m deep and 3m wide and produced more pottery. There were gaps in both at several places, recalling the similar interrupted (segmented or causewayed) ditches of enclosures in England and on the Continent, where discontinuous stretches of ditches seem to be a means of symbolically defining areas of special significance. An inner palisade trench is also reported. A series of radiocarbon dates indicates prolonged occupation from about 4000 to 2700 BC.

While enclosing ditches or palisades may have been expressions of special or higher status, in some cases such measures may well have been defensive too and indicative of some warlike activity. There is some rather tenuous evidence for violent skirmishing at least. While evidence of burning at some house sites and the presence of numbers of arrowheads might suggest aggression, symbolic destruction is a possibility too. The flint arrowheads

found in and near the burnt house at Ballynagilly may indicate a violent end to that homestead, while the evidence from Ballyharry and the burnt stretch of palisade at Thornhill with associated calcined flint arrowheads have been considered as indications of violent activity with fire and bow and arrow (Moore 2004). The discovery in a megalithic tomb at Poulnabrone, Co. Clare, of an adult male with the tip of a flint or chert arrowhead embedded in a hip bone (with no evidence of subsequent healing) shows how lethal such weapons might be; another male skull displayed a healed fracture (Lynch 1988; Lynch and Ó Donnabháin 1994). It seems likely that warfare was an occasional early prehistoric pastime. It may, however, have been a small-scale and even a symbolic activity initiated at particular times of the year or prompted by various causes, including the collapse of exchange mechanisms, for instance. Evidence from Britain indicates that men and women are equally represented in cases of healed and unhealed cranial trauma (Schulting and Wysocki 2005).

Some enclosure clearly had a significant ritual dimension. Excavation in Magheraboy, just south of Sligo town, has revealed a portion of a segmented ditch or causewayed enclosure (Fig. 2.10). Only a limited area of this monument has been investigated (Danaher 2007) but it seems that a wooden palisade with irregular ditch segments outside it may have partly enclosed an elliptical area of some 2ha (5 acres). No enclosing element was found on the east within the excavated area. The palisade was of fairly uniform construction and may have been a timber fence of posts and planks some 1.5m high. The ditch segments varied considerably, from shallow elongated pits to ditches of U-shaped profile over 12m in length, some 1.5m wide and up to 70cm deep. They were not all contemporary and some were evidently dug sequentially; judging from radiocarbon dates, some were dug as early as 4100–3950 BC, while others were as late as *c.* 3600 BC. A series of pits were found in the interior but, apart from a rectangular timber structure that abutted the palisade on the south and some post-holes associated with a nearby causeway between ditch segments, the interior of the enclosure seems to have been mainly an empty space. Acidic soil did not favour the preservation of unburnt bone but the ditches contained a range of deposited matter, including occupation material

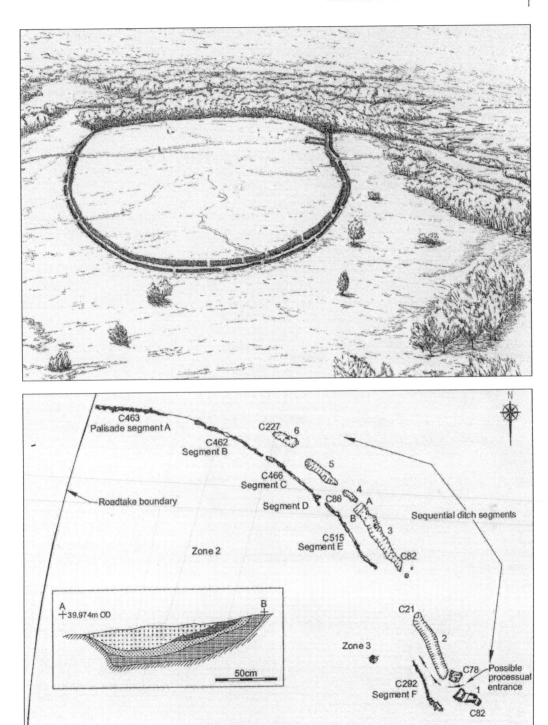

Fig. 2.10—Above: reconstruction of a segmented ditch enclosure with timber palisade at Magheraboy, Co. Sligo. Below: plan of ditch segments and palisade on north-east.

comprising dark soil and charcoal, remains of burnt oak planks, chert and flint implements, Carinated Bowl sherds and fragments of stone axes, one deliberately broken. Some ditch segments had been recut for further depositional episodes. While most of the pottery came from the ditches, the pits in the interior contained deposits of similar material as well as chert and flint and some charred cereal grains, including barley. Ed Danaher believed that Magheraboy was probably a multifunctional site where a range of activities might have occurred, including ceremonies associated with both private and communal offerings, rites of passage, feasting and exchange of goods, as in many of its English counterparts. There is also no shortage of ethnographical evidence to remind us that enclosures such as this may have been arenas for ritual activities that might leave little or no archaeological trace, such as dance, music and song.

Smaller enclosures were constructed as well: an oval ditched enclosure (37m by 27m) at Kilshane, Co. Dublin, was formed of intersecting and overlapping ditch segments that contained Neolithic pottery and a large quantity of animal bone; early Bronze Age pottery indicated intermittent later activity (FitzGerald 2006). Excavations in Goodland townland, just over 3km south-east of Fair Head, Co. Antrim, revealed a

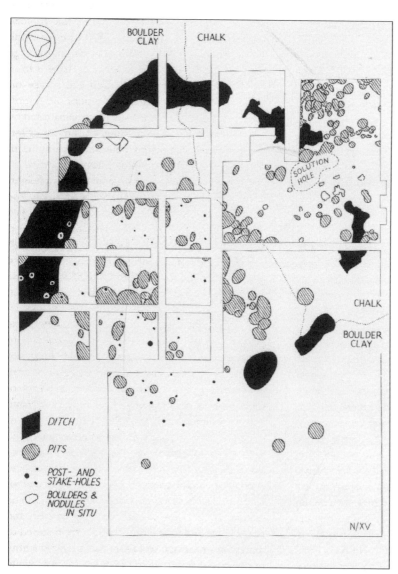

Fig. 2.11—Plan of ritual site at Goodland, Co. Antrim.

complex of pits, ditches and other features in the subsoil beneath an area of blanket bog. A series of irregular segments of shallow ditches of varying lengths with gaps of different sizes between them appear to have delimited an oval area about 14m by 12m (Fig. 2.11). The segments of ditch were formed by pulling out weathered blocks of rock, which accounted for their very irregular shapes; depths varied from 20cm to 65cm and it seemed that they were quickly and deliberately filled with soil. Boulders with pottery sherds packed around them or deposits of potsherds and flints were either incorporated in or inserted into the fill of these ditches. Numerous shallow pits were found both inside and outside the enclosed area, none deeper than 40cm, and post-holes and stake-holes were found for the most part within the ditch system. Many of the pits contained identical deposits to those found in the ditches: boulders packed round with sherds and flints. Some pits contained little except soil, and these occurred mainly outside the enclosure to the east. There was clearly a sequence of activity: at least one pit was earlier than a segment of the ditch, and pits sometimes intersected each other.

The pottery included Decorated Bowls and Goodland bowls. Flint implements included leaf-shaped arrowheads and convex and concave scrapers. The ditched area, the contents of the pits within it and the absence of hearths or other traces of habitation all suggested to the excavator, Humphrey Case, that 'it is hardly possible rationally to look beyond a ritual explanation for the enclosure and many of its associated pits'. There was evidence for flint-knapping to the east and to the south-west of the site: large quantities of struck flint were found, and it seems that nodules of flint were dug out of the boulder clay and the upper few centimetres of the underlying chalk. Judging from the waste material present, knapped pieces of flint were removed to be worked elsewhere. It seems that this activity had begun before the digging of the ditch and its enclosed pits, and it continued during the use of the enclosure (Case 1973). Judging from one radiocarbon date obtained from charcoal in a pit, the ritual activity at Goodland may have begun in the later fourth millennium and involved the deposition in pits of material such as potsherds, flints, scraps of animal bone and phosphate-enriched dark soil which was derived

from settlement debris. He suggested that the contribution such material might make to the fertility of the land would have been fully appreciated by prehistoric farmers and it thus might be deliberately buried as part of some fertility ritual. This recalls the depositional evidence identified within the much larger segmented ditched enclosure at Magheraboy, and at Goodland the purpose may have been to encourage the land to continue to produce nodules of flint for the nearby flint-knapping.

Some upland activity probably had a strong ritual dimension too. The conspicuous mountain of Knocknarea in County Sligo is a very characteristic landmark, its visual impact enhanced by the huge passage tomb cairn of Miosgán Meabha (Queen Maeve's cairn) on its flat summit. There are some five smaller passage tombs there as well, but only the great central monument seems to have had a substantial cairn. Some excavation and survey on Knocknarea have revealed that, besides the tombs, the eastern side of the mountain was demarcated by a complex system of stone-built walls more or less following the 250–260m contours (about 100m downhill from the summit). The walls varied in width from 2m to 5m and were up to 1m in height. Several parallel lines of banks occur on the north-east and some of these are segmented. Linked to the wall complex, which has a total length of *c.* 2.4km, are a number of hut sites.

More than twenty hut sites have been identified around the 250m contour. Two of these on the north-east were excavated in 1980 (Bengtsson and Bergh 1984): one consisted of an oval penannular stony bank enclosing an area some 7m by 4m. An external ditch had been dug to provide drainage and a series of 79 dark spots that contained wood remains in most instances were interpreted as former post-holes. The majority of these posts were inclined and set in the low bank and were considered to represent a succession of three lightweight timber-built huts possibly covered with hides or thatch. No hearth was found but some sherds of pottery and hundreds of flint and chert implements were recovered and included an exceptionally large number of concave scrapers. The second, about 70m to the west, was similar, and burnt limestone slabs in the centre were believed to represent a hearth; it too produced a large quantity of concave scrapers, mostly of chert, some showing signs of considerable use. The concave scrapers represented 39.5% and 25.8% of the total number of artefacts at these respective sites and clearly denote some particular form of work, though exactly what is unknown. Similar results came from two more hut sites on the southern side excavated in 1999. Along the walls, as in the hut sites, there is evidence of a very intensive lithic industry based on the locally available chert. The principal artefact is the concave scraper, while arrowheads, convex scrapers, decorated pottery and cattle bones have also been recorded. The banks have been radiocarbon-dated to a very short interval around 3350 BC. The large passage tomb most likely dates from the end of the fourth millennium BC as well, and the banks are presumably contemporary with some of the ritual activity on the flat summit. They served to emphasise the significance of the eastern side of Knocknarea, and when viewed from a cemetery of passage tombs in Carrowmore on the lands below they transformed the whole mountain into a monument. As Stefan Bergh (2000; 2002) has pointed out, 'the ritual space of the mountain was defined on the ground'.

The importance of the mountain has been further enhanced by Stefan Bergh's discovery of a large-scale prehistoric chert quarry on its northern slopes. The quarry activity covers an area *c.* 1km in length and *c.* 300m in width along the steep northern slopes. Finds consist of all aspects of the procurement sequence, from large chunks, bipolar and platform cores, flakes, flake fragments and splinters. Very few formal tools, such as concave scrapers, convex scrapers and arrowheads, have been found, however.

More intriguing upland settlement of Neolithic date has been recognised at Mullaghfarna, Co. Sligo, where over 150 enclosures of various sizes have been identified on a limestone plateau at an elevation of over 220m above OD. Most of these enclosures have an average diameter of about 10m and some limited excavation has produced some flint, chert and pottery similar to that found on Knocknarea. Some connection with the adjacent passage tomb cemetery of Carrowkeel seems likely (Bergh 2006).

These upland sites, like the coastal middens, emphasise how meagre our knowledge is about the diversity of settlement types and about the wider range of subsistence strategies in the fourth and third millennia. The recognition of a persistent pattern of sedentary settlement does not imply immobility. A family or kin group might occupy a site for a generation or more, or might move from time to time, occupying a series of favoured locations in an area. There may have been a greater degree of seasonal mobility than is generally believed. The relative importance of such activity in the economy as a whole is impossible to assess at present, but it does seem likely that some members of some settled communities exploited a range of resources and occupied seasonal camps, both coastal and inland, for purposes as varied as the procuring of the raw materials for the manufacture of stone axes and flint implements, pottery vessels, wooden artefacts and basketry work on the one hand and for activities that included food-gathering, fishing, hunting and even tomb-building and associated rituals on the other.

POTTERY

Because of its durability, pottery is one of the commonest artefacts to survive on a settlement site or in a tomb. It is assumed to be a characteristic feature of early farming communities but, of course, its manufacture does not prove the existence of a farming economy. Nonetheless, in Ireland, as in much of Europe, its first appearance is indeed associated with early agriculturalists. Several different types of hand-made pottery have been recognised in fourth-millennium Ireland and several general classifications have been proposed. The fragmentary nature of the evidence is, of course, a problem and considerable variety in form and decoration makes concise description difficult, but following the work of Humphrey Case (1961), Alison Sheridan (1995) and Alex Gibson (2002a) it is possible, with some modification of their preferred terminologies, to outline the principal types (Fig. 2.12).

The Carinated Bowl style is the earliest pottery found in Ireland and has close parallels with pottery found in eastern and northern England, Scotland and Wales. This is a well-made, hard, thin, often leathery-looking ware with smoothed or burnished surfaces, usually reddish brown to dark brown in colour but sometimes virtually black. Pots are round-bottomed with distinctive shoulders or

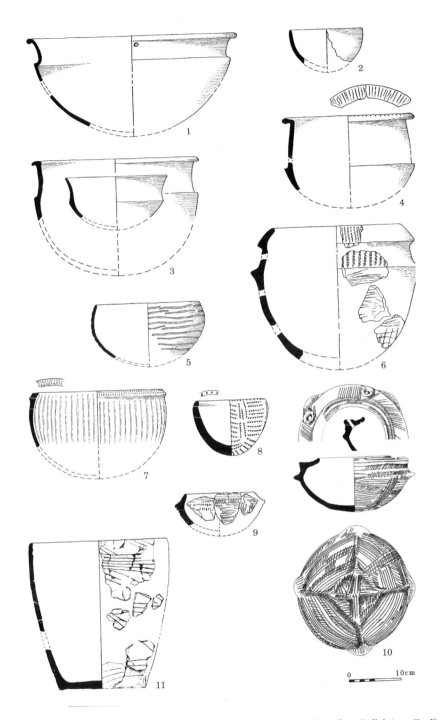

Fig. 2.12—Pottery. (1–2) Carinated Bowl style: bowl from Cohaw, Co. Cavan, and cup from Ballybriest, Co. Derry. (3) Lyles Hill-style bowls from Lyles Hill, Co. Antrim. (4) Limerick-style bowl with incised decoration on the rim from Lough Gur, Co. Limerick. (5–8) Decorated Bowl style. (5) Goodland bowl with impressed whipped cord decoration from Lyles Hill, Co. Antrim. (6) Bowl with collared rim from Island MacHugh, Co. Tyrone, with impressed twisted cord and incised ornament. (7) Newferry, Co. Antrim, with incised decoration. (8) Carrowkeel bowl with stabbed decoration from Lislea, Co. Monaghan. (9–10) Bipartite Bowl style. (9) Ballynamona, Co. Waterford. (10) Drimnagh, Co. Dublin. (11) Grooved Ware from Knowth, Co. Meath.

carinations, concave necks and simple pointed or slightly rounded rims. Almost all are open bowls with a mouth diameter as great or greater than the shoulder diameter. Some simple hemispherical bowls or cups also occur. Apart from some fingertip rippling or fluting executed in the wet clay before firing, decoration is usually absent and wall thickness may be no more than 5–6mm. Perforations, probably for the attachment of cords for suspension, occur on occasion but protruding lugs are rare. This style has a wide Irish distribution and has been found in reasonably securely dated contexts at sites such as Ballynagilly, Co. Tyrone, Ballygalley, Co. Antrim, Newtown, Co. Meath, Tankardstown, Co. Limerick, Corbally, Co. Kildare, and Pepperhill, Co. Cork. On present evidence (and discounting the earlier dates from Ballynagilly) this style appears about 4000 BC and is a feature of the first half of the fourth millennium, after which modified regional or local pottery styles appear. These developed styles include Lyles Hill style, Limerick style and Decorated Bowl style, which emerge in the middle of the fourth millennium. There is evidence that both they and the Carinated Bowl style (including its simple hemispherical bowl or cup component) were in contemporaneous use for a number of centuries thereafter.

Lyles Hill-style pottery, a term coined over 40 years ago and once synonymous with the generic 'Western Neolithic' pottery of some writers which included the fine carinated pottery just mentioned, is now applied to a developed pottery style with a markedly angular shoulder and a straight or almost straight neck; rims may still be simple but more often than not are flat, angular or even T-shaped, and wall thicknesses are greater, often 6–10mm or more. Open bowls are common; closed forms in which the mouth is notably narrower than the shoulder diameter are rarer. Decoration is virtually absent: fingertip rippling sometimes occurs on neck and rim, and some sherds from Lyles Hill itself and a few other sites have simple decoration usually in the form of one or more rows of impressions on or inside the rim. Suspension holes occur. Limerick-style pottery is a related regional pottery style, known from various sites in and around the Lough Gur area; this is the Class I pottery of Ó Ríordáin, the Limerick style of Case, and is noteworthy for the occasional occurrence of simple incised decoration mainly on out-turned rims and sometimes near the shoulder. Rim forms are usually simple or flat and out-turned. Mouth diameters are often much the same as that of the shoulder, which is often angular.

The Decorated Bowl style is a term used here to embrace a range of decorated round-bottomed bowls of various forms and fabrics given different names by different writers; some are of simple semi-globular form with rare shoulders which, when they occur, are usually poorly defined. This semi-globular form includes pots with rounded or bevelled rims that are often simple but may also be accentuated in several ways—including out-turned, in-turned, T-shaped, and thickened or collared examples. Decoration is frequent; short incised lines or jabs often ornament the rims, and the upper part of the vessel or the whole of the exterior may bear incised or cord ornament, often made by a twisted cord impressed in the wet clay before firing; simple patterns of parallel horizontal or vertical lines are common, and filled triangles and rectangular panels occur. This category includes a group called Goodland bowls, named after that site in County Antrim, which have an in-turned profile, simple rims and cord-impressed decoration; examples with characteristic basalt grit are more or less confined to east Ulster. Other prominent bowl types include examples with thickened, heavy, collared or flat rims, occasional lugs and cord-impressed, grooved or incised ornament, well known on northern sandhills and other sites. These latter types need further study but have been variously called 'Sandhills Western pottery', 'Dundrum bowls', 'Murlough bowls', 'Broad-rimmed vessels', etc.

The Decorated Bowl style also includes Carrowkeel ware, a distinctive, profusely decorated, round-bottomed bowl with simple rim. The fabric is usually hard and invariably relatively thick and coarse with large grits of crushed pebble or shell. The all-over decoration is impressed or incised or both; impressions are executed with a sharp or blunted implement—perhaps a piece of wood or bone, or even occasionally a bird bone or a shell edge. A characteristic decorative technique, unhappily termed 'stab-and-drag' ornament, consists of a line made by a pointed implement applied with intermittent pressure, producing an indented groove. Impressions are sometimes haphazard, linear ornament (including indented grooves) sometimes occurs in irregular zones or panels, and occasionally parallel lines form shallow arcs; one or two horizontal lines just below the rim is a frequent feature.

The Bipartite Bowl style consists of a series of finely made and finely decorated bowls with a sharp shoulder and in-turned upper body, producing pots with an acute bipartite profile and mouths noticeably narrower than the greatest diameter. Some have been called Ballyalton bowls and are well-made, shouldered, narrow-mouthed, round-bottomed bowls with distinctive decoration. The diameter of the rim is invariably less than that of the shoulder, sometimes very markedly so. The in-bent neck of these vessels may vary from slightly concave, as in the Carinated Bowl style and some Lyles Hill pottery, to straight with a quite acute shoulder angle; a variety of rims, including rounded, out-turned and in-turned examples, occur. Decoration both above and below the shoulder seems to be the norm: parallel grooved lines are common, and impressed lines executed with lengths of twisted cord or whipped cord (that is, thin cord or sinew wrapped around a stamp or another piece of cord) are also fairly frequent. Lugs and raised ribs are found on a few vessels, and the criss-crossing ribs on the bowl from Drimnagh, Co. Dublin, are a reminder that while some vessels were used as cooking pots others may have been suspended in rope containers and perhaps used for storage purposes. This County Dublin example and a significant number of others have been found in burials (Linkardstown Graves, Chapter 3), and some of these very finely decorated Bipartite Bowls may have had special symbolic significance (Cooney 2000). Some Bipartite Bowls have parallels in Scotland and the type may have been inspired by Scottish ceramic fashions. The suggestion that Ballyalton bowls and their Scottish counterparts were inspired by some early (late fifth-millennium) decorated carinated pottery in north-western France (Sheridan 2003a) has yet to be supported by firm radiocarbon-dating evidence. Decorated Bowl and Bipartite Bowl pottery was used throughout the later fourth and earlier third millennium BC, eventually being replaced by new ceramic fashions such as Grooved Ware, as well as fine and coarse Beaker pottery, which will be considered in Chapter 4.

The appearance of Grooved Ware, possibly early in the third millennium BC, demonstrates that flat-bottomed tub-shaped pots, some with decoration formed by parallel grooved lines, were also part of the ceramic repertoire at this time. A pottery tradition well known in Britain, sherds have been found in Ireland at sites such as Donegore, Ballynahatty, Knowth and Newgrange, and at Lough Gur (Brindley 1999; Sheridan 2004).

STONE IMPLEMENTS

The stone axe is an object that may have been used for at least five millennia. Though flint and polished stone axes were part of the tool kit of early hunters and foragers, the stone axe may have continued in use into the third millennium and possibly even much later. Nonetheless, the polished stone axe is still considered a particularly characteristic implement of the early farming communities, in which it was, no doubt, an important instrument in forest clearance. It could have been used for either ring-barking or felling; experiments have shown that substantial trees, particularly soft woods, can be relatively quickly felled by one person. It has been determined that a young birch tree 15cm in diameter can be felled in as little as fifteen minutes; larger trees were probably felled for planking, which was presumably radially cleft from split trunks with the aid of wooden wedges. Stone axes were effectively used in the construction of wooden trackways in Corlea and Cloonbony, Co. Longford, in the fourth and third millennia BC. Polishing the edge of an axe can improve its cutting capability, but the laborious polishing of the entire surface must also indicate a growing concern with the decorative elaboration of such artefacts.

A small number of stone axes from Britain and Ireland have been found with their perforated wooden hafts, and a variety of woods were used (Coles *et al.* 1978). In Ireland, the remains of a haft of alder still retaining its stone axe (Fig. 2.13) were found at a depth of some 2.4m in a bog south of Roosky, in Edercloon townland, Co. Longford. Another fragment of a perforated alder haft and an axe came from the lower levels of a bog at Carrowntreila, south of Ballina, Co. Mayo; a haft of pine was found in County Monaghan, and an example of apple wood comes from Maguire's Bridge, Co. Fermanagh. Other hafts are reported from Lissard, Co. Longford, and Carrickfergus, Co.

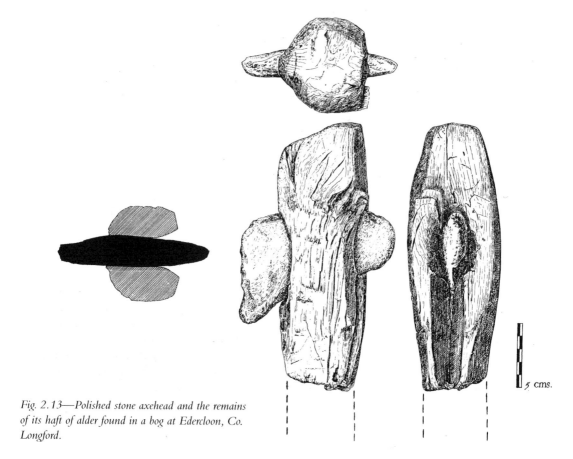

Fig. 2.13—Polished stone axehead and the remains of its haft of alder found in a bog at Edercloon, Co. Longford.

5 cms.

Antrim. The axes were inserted into perforated pieces of wood and it is possible that bindings of leather thongs or resin were used to secure them, though ethnographic evidence and experimental work suggest that these are not essential. It seems likely that axes 8–20cm in length were used for woodworking, the larger for tree-felling, the smaller for lighter work such as coppicing or for more specialised carpentry tasks. Not all axes were necessarily woodworking implements; some examples were probably used as weapons and others—including some very small and some very large ones—may have had a ceremonial and symbolic role.

A major research undertaking, the Irish Stone Axe Project, has demonstrated that these objects were particularly common in Ireland (Cooney and Mandal 1998). Over 20,000 have been recorded, a number that may be compared with an estimated 4,000 in Scotland. Different forms of stone axes have been recognised. The principal shapes, based on the plan or 'face shape' of the axe, comprise symmetrical oval axes, asymmetrical axes with one convex side, splaying straight-sided axes, parallel-sided axes, axes with diagonal butts, and a large miscellaneous category of other shapes. The latter and the asymmetrical axes are the commonest categories (Fig. 2.14).

Axes have a wide distribution, with a major concentration in the north-east of the country and a remarkable number in County Antrim. Other areas of relatively high density include the Lough Gur region, part of the area around inner Galway Bay, and the Shannon at Killaloe. Some regional concentrations probably reflect the energies of local collectors to a certain extent. The great majority of these axes are stray finds, casual discoveries with no apparent archaeological context, but, as already mentioned, examples have been found on various settlement sites, such as Ballynagilly, Ballygalley and Lough Gur, while significant numbers have been found in bogs and large numbers have been

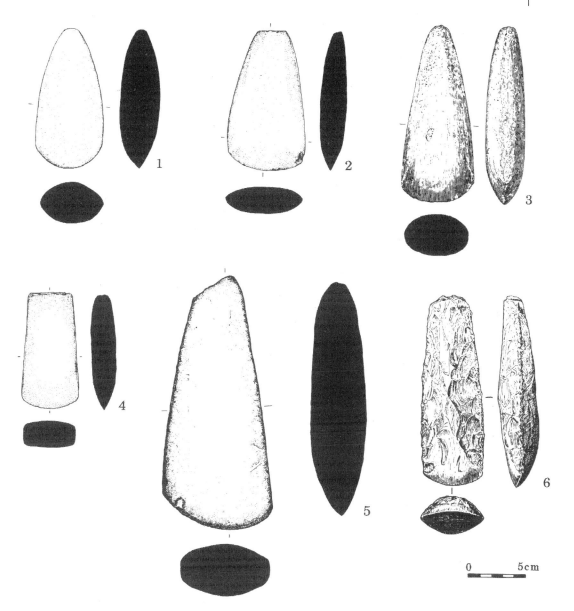

Fig. 2.14—Stone axes. (1) Symmetrical oval axehead from County Limerick. (2) Asymmetrical axehead with one convex side from Loughantarve, Co. Louth. (3) Straight-sided axehead from Mullacrew, Co. Louth. (4) Parallel-sided axehead from Dunbin, Co. Louth. (5) Axehead with diagonal butt from Ballynakill, Co. Meath. (6) Flint axehead with polished cutting edge from Killarida, Co. Kerry.

recovered from rivers, notably from the Bann, the Shannon, the Erne and the Barrow. Over 300 have been found in the River Bann, particularly at Portglenone and Toome Bridge, and over 700 are recorded from the River Shannon at Killaloe. While some of these were probably accidentally lost and some river finds may derive from riverside settlements, others may represent deliberate ritual

offerings, a practice which becomes particularly noteworthy in later prehistory with the formal deposition of metalwork in watery contexts. That deliberate stone axe deposition was an occasional practice is demonstrated by a number of possible hoards. The most notable of these is a group of about eighteen fine porcellanite axes found in glacial sand at Danesfort, on the Malone Road,

Belfast. The discovery was made about 1872 near a trackway that had been constructed on the side of a hill and the objects were found within a small area, 'each standing on its end in the sand with its edge turned upwards'. Some are exceptionally large and highly polished examples and they show no signs of use; they ranged from about 22cm to about 33cm in length. A number have that diagonal butt already mentioned which may be a mark of a prestigious item, and the manner of their deposition, with cutting edge upwards, suggests ritual activity. Three highly polished and unused stone axes, 20–26cm in length, found together in a bog in Canrawer townland, near Oughterard, Co. Galway, and a collection of two flint axes, 39 flint flakes, a nodule and two other flint implements discovered at the base of one of the stones of a megalithic tomb at Ballyalton, Co. Down, may be similar deposits. A number of complete or fragmentary stone axes have been associated with tombs and other sites (Sheridan *et al.* 1992). Whether a cache of a dozen stone axes found in the nineteenth century in a small copper mine on Ballyrisode Hill, near Goleen, Co. Cork, should be considered ritual or not is uncertain; it may be an abandoned tool kit (W. O'Brien 2003).

Petrological analysis, which attempts to identify the rock types used and the sources of this raw material, can in some cases provide important information about the distribution of specific axe types and about the extent of early prehistoric contacts. A systematic programme of such analyses has shown that a wide variety of rock types were used and, not surprisingly, locally available materials were often exploited. A hard, blue-grey porcellanite, which outcrops on the slopes of Tievebulliagh, near Cushendall, Co. Antrim, and at Brockley at the western end of Rathlin Island, was particularly popular. This rock type has long been known as a major source of material for axe manufacture, and it is now evident that these Antrim sources accounted for 53.8% of Irish stone axe production. Trace element geochemical analysis has demonstrated that it is possible to distinguish between Tievebulliagh and Brockley porcellanite, which otherwise appear identical, and the latter island has been just as important a source of this stone as the better-known Tievebulliagh (Mandal 1997; Mandal *et al.* 1997).

Porcellanite axes are widely distributed throughout the country but are particularly common in the north (Fig. 2.15). Fine-grained sedimentary rocks such as mudstone and shale are the next most common rocks used (9.6% and 13.6% respectively) but, in contrast to porcellanite, could have many possible sources, including glacial tills and alluvial and beach deposits. They commonly occur in the west, midlands and south. Among the other rock types exploited were sandstone (3.7%), schist (3.4%) and various coarse igneous types. A few other extraction sites have been identified. Naturally formed flat shale pebbles at Fisherstreet, near Doolin, Co. Clare, would have required very little modification to make them into axes with a sharp cutting edge. Coarse-grained igneous rocks such as porphyry and dolerite are commonest on the east coast, and a dark green porphyry was quarried on Lambay Island, Co. Dublin, for some limited axe production. Flint axes were also used but are rare (Woodman 1992); both unpolished or partly polished axes of flint are known, mainly from the flint-bearing north-east, and some may have had specialised uses as adzes or chisels (Fig. 2.14).

Antrim porcellanite was extensively worked at Tievebulliagh and Brockley and these extraction sites have been termed 'axe factories' because numerous waste flakes and axe rough-outs have been found there, the latter roughly shaped lumps of stone being normally transported elsewhere for polishing and sharpening. Because both the scale and the duration of the quarrying and chipping work are difficult to quantify, however, the term extraction site is preferable because centralised and large-scale specialised 'factory' production may not have been the case; rather the process may have been episodic and on a modest scale but over a long period of time. To complicate the picture, some porcellanite was probably derived from glacial erratics. A number of flaked axe rough-outs have been found in County Antrim in particular, including many from the valleys near Tievebulliagh. Sandstone polishers were used to smooth the rough-outs, sandstone with coarse quartz grains being particularly effective. At Loughaveema, just over 9km from Tievebulliagh, a site has been discovered where considerable trimming and polishing of porcellanite rough-outs seems to have been undertaken: a rough-out and fragments of polished axes were found. Although porcellanite axes did not occur on the Ballynagilly settlement,

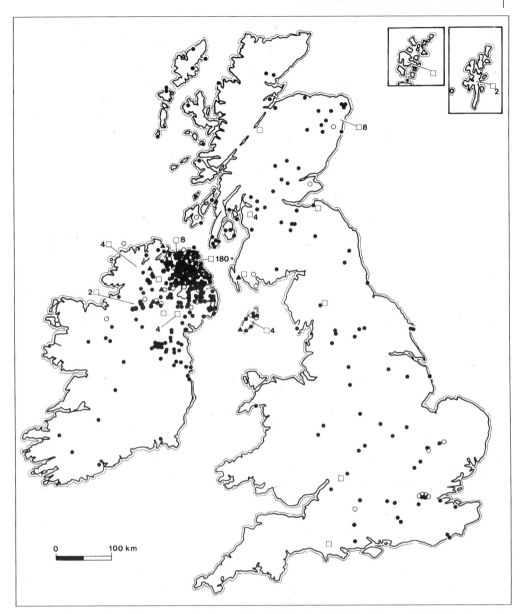

Fig. 2.15—Distribution of porcellanite axes and other artefacts in Ireland and Britain. Open symbols indicate imprecise or uncertain provenance and numbers denote multiple examples.

where the axes were made from the local igneous rock, evidence from Ballygalley and other sites indicates that this rock type was exploited from the earlier fourth millennium. It continued to be widely used throughout the third millennium, and a number of porcellanite implements come from early second-millennium BC contexts as well. The island location of the axe production sites at Brockley and Lambay may be noteworthy. Islands, like mountaintops such as Tievebulliagh, may have

been seen as liminal places situated between two worlds, places that in time gave added and magical value to the material extracted. On Lambay, excavation has revealed complex pit deposits containing potsherds (of vessels such as Goodland and Carrowkeel bowls), porphyry waste and other material (Cooney 2000; 2003). Far from being rubbish pits or casually discarded items, these may well represent the ceremonial returning to the earth of material full of social meaning, perhaps commemorating past activities and even negotiating the future.

Petrological analysis indicates that axes of Antrim porcellanite had a wide distribution (Fig. 2.15). While the majority occur in north-eastern Ireland, as already mentioned, axes of this rock type have also been found in various other parts of Ireland and as far away as the south of England and in Scotland, with distinct concentrations in the Clyde region and in the north-east in Aberdeenshire. Island finds include examples from the Isle of Man and from various islands off the west coast of Scotland, including the Hebrides as well as Orkney and Shetland. The apparent scarcity or absence of these axes in some localities, such as Wales, might be explained by the abundance of locally available axes in these areas. While finished axes were normally exported, a small number of rough-outs have been found in south-west Scotland.

How axes were traded or exchanged has been considered by various writers, including Alison Sheridan, who notes that part of the area of densest distribution in Antrim and Derry (and adjacent coastal regions in Scotland and elsewhere) might have constituted a supply zone in which people may have gone straight to the sources and extracted the raw material themselves. Beyond this there may also have been a contact zone in which finished objects or rough-outs were obtained directly from communities in the supply zone. In this contact zone and further afield, various forms of exchange seem the most likely distribution mechanism, in which communities passed on various supplies, including stone artefacts, to each other through a network of contacts. Exceptionally well-made axes, many with distinctive coloration and highly polished, may have had a powerful symbolic value and this is probably why they were sometimes carefully deposited in various ways. They were probably prestigious elements in ceremonial exchanges as well. Indeed, 'the gift of stones' may have been a complex process, perhaps undertaken as part of marriage or initiation rites, and the manipulation of such exchanges may have been the prerogative of community leaders, or even a factor in their emergence and in the development of greater social ranking. It is also possible that the axes involved may have circulated over a prolonged period of time (Edmonds 1995).

A striking example of an exotic ceremonial axehead type is a series of jadeite axes from Britain and Ireland; over 100 have been found in Britain and a number in Ireland. Jadeite is an extremely hard greenish rock. Its source is Continental, from an Alpine locality (Pétrequin et al. 1997). The Irish examples, like their British counterparts, were probably highly prized possessions, perhaps received as special gifts, never used for woodworking and maybe never even hafted. A significant number of axeheads that were imports from Britain have also been identified and include axes of a volcanic tuff from the Great Langdale region, Cumbria (one being found at Ballygalley), and examples of Cornish gabbro (Mandal 1997). It is possible that some stone axes considered to be the products of trade or exchange might be locally produced artefacts formed from rocks and pebbles transported there in glacial deposits (Briggs 2001; 2009).

Flint and chert were widely used to manufacture a range of implements. The extent to which raw flint or flint implements themselves were traded in prehistoric Ireland is not clear but may have been considerable. A major source of material was the good-quality flint that occurs in the basalt-covered chalk in north-eastern Ireland. The flint-bearing chalk is exposed on many parts of the Antrim coast and at several inland outcrops. Opencast mining has been identified at Black Mountain, near Belfast, and on the southern side of Ballygalley Hill, near Larne, Co. Antrim (Collins 1978), where a series of bands of flint nodules in the chalk were mined by flint-workers and numerous waste flakes and cores indicate that knapping took place nearby. Sherds of undecorated pottery and flint implements, found a short distance away on the summit, are from an occupation site possibly contemporary with the industrial activity. Flint found in deposits of glacial drift, river gravels and on beaches elsewhere in the country was another significant source of raw material.

A variety of arrowheads, scrapers and knives of flint and chert were in common use, and pressure retouch is a recurrent feature (Woodman et al. 2006). Small and approximately leaf-shaped or lozenge-shaped arrowheads are particularly characteristic of the fourth and third millennia: manufactured from thin flakes, they are usually carefully pressure-flaked on both faces and worked to a sharp point. They were presumably glued with

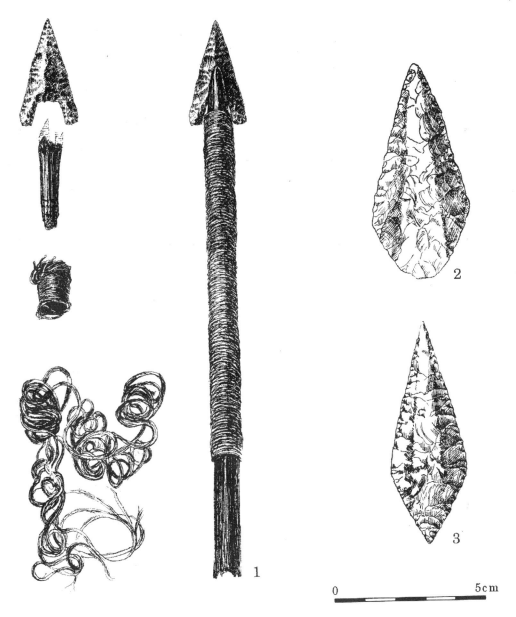

Fig. 2.16—Flint arrowheads. (1) Concave-based flint arrowhead found in Kanestown Bog, Co. Antrim, still attached to its wooden shaft with some sort of adhesive and with a binding of animal sinew. (2) Leaf-shaped flint arrowhead found in a bog near Glarryford, Co. Antrim. (3) Lozenge-shaped flint arrowhead found in a bog at Teeshan, near Ballymena, Co. Antrim.

some resinous substance into wooden shafts, and in a few cases differential staining on the surface indicates the former presence of the shaft (Fig. 2.16). A leaf-shaped flint arrowhead was found at a depth of about 3m in a bog south of Port Laoise, at Clonaddadoran, Co. Laois, with part of a birch shaft attached. Such arrowheads are not an uncommon find in megalithic tombs, particularly court tombs,

and on habitation sites, and their relative number is presumably a reflection of the importance of archery in both hunting and fighting. A fragment of a bow of yew wood was found in the last century at a depth of about 6m in a bog at Drumwhinny, Kesh, Co. Fermanagh, and has been radiocarbon-dated to 1680–1326 BC (Hedges *et al.* 1991). Yew was probably favoured for bow

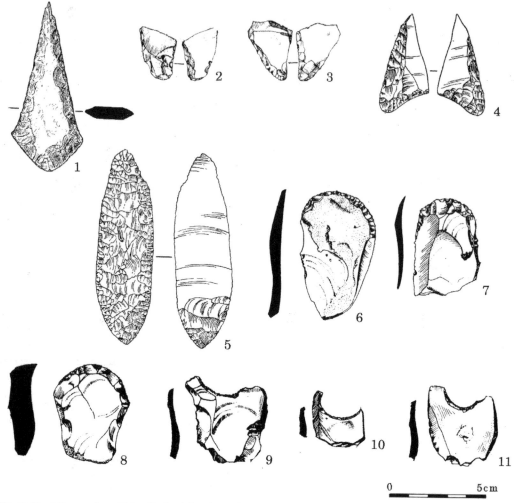

Fig. 2.17—Flint artefacts. (1) Javelin-head found in a bog at Killeelaun, near Tuam, Co. Galway. (2–3) Transverse arrowheads from Townleyhall II, Co. Louth. (4) Petit tranchet derivative from Lough Eskragh, Co. Tyrone. (5) Plano-convex knife from Barnes Lower, Co. Tyrone. (6–11) Convex (6–8) and hollow (9–11) scrapers from Townleyhall II, Co. Louth.

manufacture because it is a dense but pliable wood. Other arrowhead types, such as the concave-based or hollow-based arrowhead, were used particularly in the third millennium and later. One undated concave-based arrowhead recovered from Kanestown Bog, south of Glenarm, Co. Antrim, was found still attached to its wooden shaft with some sort of adhesive; the upper part of the shaft, probably ash, was bound with animal sinew to prevent it from splitting (Fig. 2.16).

A large leaf- or lozenge-shaped flint point was perhaps used as a projectile head and is commonly called a javelin-head; a polished lozenge-shaped variety is a peculiarly Irish type (Fig. 2.17). They are occasionally very finely made and may exceed 15cm in length. Regular pressure flaking may completely cover one or both faces and often part of the faces is carefully polished, sometimes before flaking, sometimes afterwards. While many are merely stray finds, several examples have been found in court tombs and passage tombs and some, like the finer axes, may not have been utilitarian objects but may have had prestigious connotations. That tip of a small arrowhead found embedded in a male hip bone at Poulnabrone, Co. Clare, and a stone axehead found with a male burial (with several old skull fractures) at Linkardstown, Co. Carlow, may be painful reminders, however, that some axes and arrowheads were male possessions sometimes used to lethal effect.

A series of flint implements of uncertain purpose occasionally found in third-millennium contexts have been called 'petit tranchet derivative arrowheads' because, in Britain, they were thought to derive from a symmetrical trapezoidal form of transverse arrowhead with a sharp primary edge at right angles to the long axis of the flake (that is, to the pressure rings on the bulbar surface); they may also have steep retouching on both sides (Fig. 2.17). Irish transverse examples with chisel-like cutting edges are not particularly common: they have been found, for example, on the Townleyhall II settlement and in the Dundrum sandhills. So-called derivative forms of this 'chisel-ended' arrowhead vary in shape and in extent of retouching. A pointed asymmetrical form is better known, with a sharp primary flake edge at an angle to a retouched edge, and it is thought by some that the sharp edge could have been mounted obliquely in an arrow-shaft, the longer retouched edge being set into the wood. It is a measure of how little is known about the use of these implements that they have also been considered to be knives rather than arrowheads. Examples have been found at Newgrange and in the Grange stone circle at Lough Gur, Co. Limerick (Woodman *et al.* 2006).

While a variety of worked and unworked flints and pieces of chert probably served as knives, a series of plano-convex flint implements are readily recognisable as such (Fig. 2.17). They are double-edged implements with the non-bulbar, convex surface wholly or partially pressure-flaked. Several examples have been found in court tombs and on other contemporary sites, but finds of similar knives in second-millennium graves indicate that the type was a long-lived one. Various flint shapes served as scrapers. Convex scrapers and concave scrapers are particularly common types. Convex scrapers are blades or flakes with a retouched convex scraping end and could have been used in many ways, including the preparation of animal hides. Concave scrapers have a concave working edge. Some are made from irregularly shaped flakes or blades; others are broad, thin trapezoidal flakes with a concave or 'hollow' worked edge, usually at the distal end of the flake. Woodman *et al.* (2006) would distinguish between these two forms. The latter are the classic 'hollow' scrapers of the Irish

Neolithic, occasionally found in the Isle of Man and in Scotland. It has been suggested that these seemingly quite specialised tools were used to prepare wooden rods for such purposes as arrow-shafts or to manufacture bone pins. Some microwear analysis suggests that the hollow was used primarily to scrape or whittle wood or sometimes bone, and that polish on the points on either side of the hollow perhaps indicates the occasional cutting of hide (Bamforth 2006). A hoard of over twenty flint implements, mainly hollow scrapers and convex scrapers, found in the valley of the River Braid, at Kilnacolpagh, Co. Antrim, has been interpreted as a workman's tool kit (Flanagan 1966). Another hoard, probably from the mid-Antrim area, comprised several flint flakes, a polished mudstone axehead, half a dozen convex scrapers and over 60 unfinished hollow scrapers; this may have been a manufacturer's or trader's hoard (Woodman 1967). As already mentioned, the discovery of numbers of hollow scrapers at upland sites such as Knocknarea, Co. Sligo, and Windy Ridge, Co. Antrim, also suggests some specialised purpose.

ORGANIC MATERIALS

Very little is known about the bone, leather, wood, basketry and textile work of this period. A variety of bone pins and beads were made; wooden pins, ladles and bowls were also probably widely used, and it is likely that leather and wooden containers were even commoner than pottery vessels. A finely made round-bottomed bowl carved from a single piece of oak and found at a depth of 3m in a bog at Timoney, near Roscrea, Co. Tipperary (Fig. 2.18), is believed to be of early date; it was found with the remnants of several basketry bags and the find illustrates just some of the range of organic materials which were probably very widely used (Earwood 1993). Fragments of a finely woven reed basket were found in peat exposed on the foreshore at Carrigdirty Rock, in the Shannon Estuary, Co. Limerick, and have been dated to *c.* 3600 BC (O'Sullivan 1997). A discovery in Twyford townland, north-east of Athlone, Co. Westmeath, shows what these basketry bags looked like. This was a small, handled bag about 40cm in diameter, found at a depth of over 3m in a bog; each side was made by coiling thin wooden rods into a flat spiral and binding them together with strips of some woody plant. The Twyford bag is undated but the depth at which it was discovered suggests the possibility of an early prehistoric date. Another bag from Aghintemple, near Ardagh, Co. Longford, seems to have been similarly made, and this example may well be of fourth- or third-millennium date for it was found at a depth of almost 4m and contained a miniature axehead of polished limestone only 8.6cm in length. Baskets and other containers of organic materials were probably much commoner than ceramic vessels.

Leather clothing and textiles of vegetal matter such as flax were probably worn, but Irish evidence is all but absent. The earliest Irish evidence for flax occurs in a pollen diagram from Essexford Lough, Co. Louth, shortly before 2000 BC (Weir 1995), and early sheep, being hairy rather than woolly, were probably raised for food rather than fleece at least until the second millennium BC. A weighted stick is all that is required to spin flax or wool fibre into thread, however, and such sticks or spindles are commonly weighted with a perforated circular spindle-whorl of stone or baked clay. But perforated stones may have various uses, and one possible spindle-whorl from an Irish fourth-millennium context—a flat, circular stone 37mm in diameter with a central perforation, from a court tomb at Ballyalton, Co. Down (Herity 1987)—could possibly be a large stone bead. Primitive looms consisting basically of two timber crossbeams and pegs would leave no archaeological trace in normal circumstances.

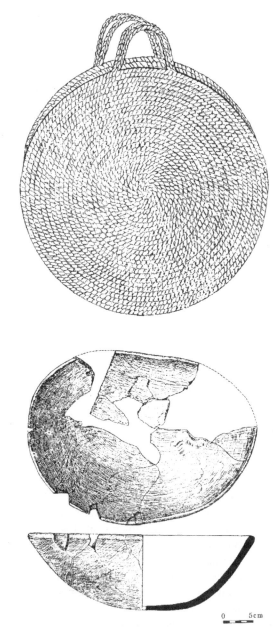

Fig. 2.18—Above: reconstruction of a basketry bag from a bog at Twyford, Co. Westmeath. Below: wooden bowl found in a bog at Timoney, Co. Tipperary.

3

THE CULT OF THE DEAD

The most prominent remains of the early prehistoric period are the megalithic tombs (from the Greek *megas* 'great', *lithos* 'stone'), the majority of which were constructed in the fourth and third millennia BC (4000–2000 BC). These are the 'cromlech' and 'dolmen' of earlier writers, and the 'giant's grave' and 'druid's altar' of popular folklore. Most of these monuments are now assigned to four major classes, each named after an important distinguishing feature: passage tombs, court tombs, portal tombs and wedge tombs.

Minor categories such as Linkardstown graves and boulder monuments also exist, as do a number of simple chambered tombs identified in Connemara and elsewhere that cannot be readily assigned to the traditional categories. Systematic field survey has now recorded some 1,600 megalithic tombs and the approximate numbers for each category are as follows: passage tombs, an estimated 236; court tombs, 412; portal tombs, 180; and wedge tombs, about 543. Unclassified tombs form the remainder and number about 215 (Shee Twohig 2004). A goodly number of excavations has meant that these monuments are comparatively well documented, but many tombs have suffered considerable damage over the millennia; often the covering mound or cairn of stones has been removed, and perhaps only a few of the stones of the tomb may survive. Such destruction naturally makes classification a difficult task. These classifications are modern constructs, of course, and archaeologists understand that prehistoric peoples may have interpreted and experienced the complex architecture of these monuments in a very different way (Jones 2007).

PASSAGE TOMBS

Some of the finest and most spectacular of the surviving Irish megalithic tombs are assigned to the passage tomb class, and the largest of these monuments, in the Boyne Valley, Co. Meath, have been described as the greatest architectural achievements of megalith builders in western Europe. Many small tombs occur among the 236 or so probable examples, however, and there is considerable variation not merely in size but also in tomb plan.

A typical Irish passage tomb consists of a chamber approached by a passage, both covered by a characteristic circular mound. The mounds may be built of earth or stones or a mixture of both, and they usually have a kerb or retaining wall of large, contiguous stones around their base (Fig. 3.1). The diameter of the mound may vary from just over 10m (the 'Druid Stone', Ballintoy, Co. Antrim) or even less to as much as 85m (as at Newgrange, Co. Meath: Fig. 3.3), but a majority of mounds range in diameter from about 10m to 25m. Mounds usually, but by no means invariably, contain just one chamber, which is centrally placed. Carved ornament on the stones of some tombs is a noteworthy feature.

The distribution and situation of these tombs are remarkable in several respects (Fig. 3.1). Unlike many other megalithic tombs, they are sometimes prominently sited on high ground, on occasion occupying commanding hilltop positions. Though the latter tombs are often the most spectacular, a majority (about 58%) are situated below 150m and

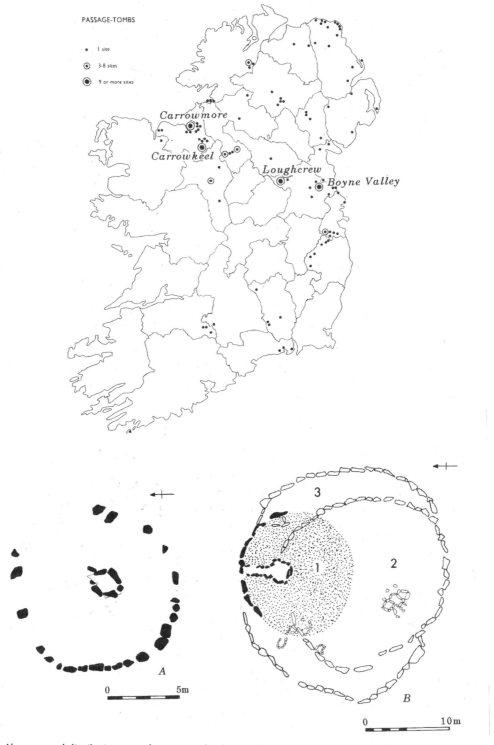

Fig. 3.1—Above: general distribution map of passage tombs, showing the major cemeteries. Below: (A) Small, simple polygonal passage tomb, the 'Druid Stone', Ballintoy, Co. Antrim. (B) Simple polygonal passage tomb in primary cairn (1) with later additions (2–3) at Baltinglass Hill, Co. Wicklow.

at no great distance from areas of potential settlement. They may occur in groups or cemeteries, with one large focal monument often surrounded by a number of smaller satellite tombs. Most passage tombs are to be found in the northern and eastern parts of the country; isolated examples occur in counties Limerick and Waterford and as far south as Kerry, and a possible site is recorded on Cape Clear Island, Co. Cork. There are four major cemeteries, variously containing from about twelve to about 60 tombs: the Boyne Valley and Loughcrew (Slieve na Caillighe) in County Meath, and Carrowmore and Carrowkeel in County Sligo. A few smaller groups of from two to five tombs are found, for example, in counties Armagh, Donegal, Dublin, Leitrim and Roscommon. Four small mounds beside a larger mound containing a passage tomb on the Bremore promontory in north County Dublin probably represent an example of a small cemetery (Cooney 2007). None are known for certain in Galway, Mayo or Clare, though various hilltop cairns in these and other counties may well cover such tombs.

Passage tombs are usually constructed of large quarried slabs or boulders, and the boulders are sometimes split. Passages are narrow and built of upright slabs (orthostats) and roofed in whole or in part with flat slabs (lintels); on occasion passages are divided into segments by one or more low transverse slabs set on edge in the floor (sill stones). Passage lengths vary from as little as 1m to over 40m at Knowth. Chambers are often simple: circular or polygonal, subrectangular or trapezoidal. These simple forms are commonest but more complex plans—with one or more additional cells—are well known. Internally, chamber diameters may vary from about 1.2m to 6.4m, as at Fourknocks I, Co. Meath (Fig. 3.7). They may be roofed with one or more flat slabs or boulders (capstones) or corbel-roofed with horizontally laid courses of slabs, each successive course oversailing the one below until it is possible to close the vault with a capstone.

The tomb known as the 'Druid Stone', near Ballintoy, Co. Antrim, has a simple polygonal chamber of five stones covered with a large capstone, and the short 'passage' seemingly consisted of only two stones (Fig. 3.1). Tomb no. 7 in the Carrowmore, Co. Sligo, cemetery is of similar plan (Fig. 3.11). One of three tombs in a cairn on Baltinglass Hill, Co. Wicklow, also had a polygonal

chamber, approached in this instance by a 4m-long passage (Fig. 3.1). Some tombs with chambers of subrectangular or trapezoidal plan are monuments in which it is difficult to distinguish between chamber and passage. Sometimes the chamber is slightly higher or of more massive construction than the rest of the tomb, and sometimes a sill stone demarcates the chamber area. Excavated examples of these 'undifferentiated' passage tombs include a number at Knowth and others at Townleyhall, Co. Louth, Carriglong, Co. Waterford, and Harristown, Co. Waterford (Ó Nualláin 1989 and references).

A tomb with three cells (a terminal cell and two lateral cells) is a well-known type. Such cruciform tomb plans are well represented among the Boyne Valley monuments. One of the tombs in the great mound at Dowth, Co. Meath, is circular with a single lateral cell, and complex plans with several additional cells are known. A tomb in the Loughcrew cemetery (cairn I) has a large chamber divided into seven cells (Fig. 3.10). There is considerable variation in tomb orientation: some face east and, like Newgrange, may be aligned on the midwinter solstice. Other solar or lunar alignments are claimed as well, and some tombs seem to be aligned on other hilltop cairns (Prendergast 2008). Occasional patterns are clearly discernible: at Knowth the entrances of many of the undifferentiated tombs face the great mound, and at Carrowmore there was a measure of internal focus as well, with a number of tombs orientated towards the centre of the cemetery. The range of tomb types and orientation and the popularity of the cruciform plan are apparent in the major cemeteries.

THE BOYNE VALLEY

The celebrated cemetery in the Boyne Valley is situated in a loop of that river in County Meath between Slane and Drogheda (Fig. 3.2). The term *Brú na Bóinne* ('the Otherworld dwelling place of the Boyne'), now applied to this landscape and to Newgrange in particular, is not used here because it is a fatuous attempt to aggrandise a Neolithic monument with later Celtic mythology (Ronayne 2001). The great mounds at Newgrange and Knowth, each with nearby smaller satellite tombs, are, along with the mound at Dowth, the largest passage tomb mounds in Ireland. Although not

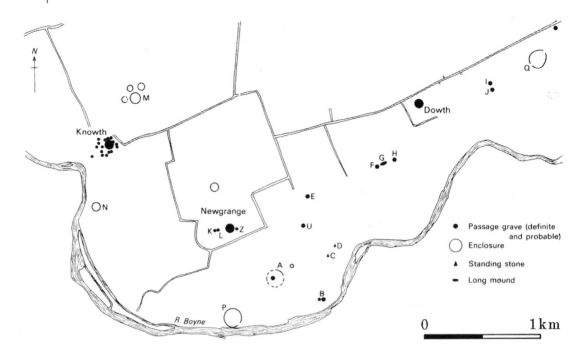

Fig. 3.2—Map of the Boyne cemetery, showing the location of the passage tombs at Newgrange, Dowth and Knowth. The embanked enclosure at Dowth (Q) is shown to the east.

situated on a hilltop like some other tombs of this class, these three exceptional monuments nonetheless occupy commanding positions in a landscape that had seen settlement since at least the early fourth millennium BC (Stout 2002).

Newgrange

The Newgrange mound was built on the highest point of a low ridge, some 61m above sea level, facing the Boyne (O'Kelly 1982; Stout and Stout 2008). This approximately circular mound (Fig. 3.3) measures 85m in maximum diameter and about 11m in height; it covers almost 0.4ha (one acre) and is composed mainly of water-rolled stones. The mound is surrounded by a continuous line of 97 kerbstones, many of which bear decoration. The entrance to the passage is on the south-east behind a richly decorated kerbstone (Fig. 3.4) and this entrance was originally closed by a large rectangular slab. A short vertical line in the middle of the decorative composition of the kerbstone is aligned on the entrance. The orthostatic passage is roofed with large slabs; near the entrance these slabs rest directly on the orthostats but elsewhere they rest on corbels (courses of slabs, the upper oversailing the

one below). The upper surfaces of some of these roof slabs have grooves or channels picked in them (with a hammer and flint point) to carry off rainwater percolating through the cairn. In addition, the roof joints were caulked with sea sand and burnt soil. The height of the passage roof increases towards the chamber, and the combined length of passage and chamber is just over 24m. Many of the orthostats and some roof stones are decorated, and this decoration is particularly frequent in the inner parts of the passage and in the chamber.

The chamber, with its two lateral cells and one terminal cell, is of the common cruciform plan. It would seem that the eastern cell was the more important; it is larger than the others and contains the most decoration. The cruciform chamber is roofed with a very fine 6m-high corbelled vault. Four large and slightly hollowed 'basin stones' occur in the chamber; such stones occur in other passage tombs and they may once have contained the burnt or unburnt bones of the dead.

Excavation revealed that a considerable amount of material had collapsed from the mound; a layer of cairn stones 8–10m wide lay outside the

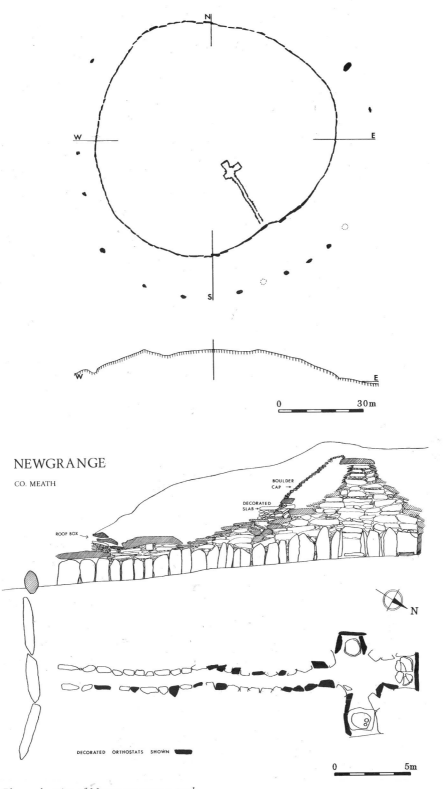

NEWGRANGE

CO. MEATH

BOULDER CAP →

DECORATED SLAB →

ROOF BOX →

N

0   30m

0   5m

DECORATED   ORTHOSTATS   SHOWN

Fig. 3.3—Plan and section of Newgrange passage tomb.

Fig. 3.4—The decorated entrance stone at Newgrange.

kerb, leading M. J. O'Kelly to suggest that a sloping wall of stones, almost 3m high, had rested on top of the kerbstones and that the original mound may have been steep-sided and flat-topped. On the south-east, a lot of angular pieces of quartz were found at the base of the collapse, and O'Kelly argued that the mound, in the area of the entrance at least, was faced with sparkling white quartz and oval-shaped granite stones. The monument that the visitor sees today is based on this assessment. This drum-shaped reconstruction with a quartz façade is controversial, not least because it imposes a particular interpretation on the visitor (Scarre 2006). It has been suggested, for instance, that a tall, near-vertical revetment would have been unable to withstand the outward pressure exerted by the mound for any length of time, but it has also been argued that cairns of stones, even steep-sided ones, may have been quite stable structures (Eriksen 2006). Cooney (2006) has proposed that the quartz and granite may have been laid down as a platform in front of the tomb. While O'Kelly believed Newgrange to be a single-period monument (even if its construction took several decades), turf lines recorded by him in the cairn material may in fact represent layers of vegetation that denote a complicated and protracted multi-period process of enlargement, perhaps spanning a thousand years (Eriksen 2008).

The discovery of what has been called the 'roof-box' above the entrance to the passage indicates that the face of the mound probably turned inwards at the entrance to permit access to this box. This stone-built feature was constructed beneath a decorated lintel and over a gap between the first two roof slabs of the passage. At dawn on the midwinter solstice, the shortest day of the year, the rays of the rising sun shine through the roof-box and briefly illuminate the chamber. The spectacle occurs for about a week before and after the solstice and lasts for a little over a quarter of an hour, but only on the solstice itself does the beam extend to the end cell; indeed, it has been calculated that at the time the tomb was built 5,000 years ago the beam of sunlight would have bisected the chamber and illuminated a triple spiral carved on the rear orthostat of the end recess (Ruggles 1999). Clearly the orientation of the tomb was of great importance to its builders, and solar phenomena had a very important place in their magico-religious beliefs and practices. Ritual chanting may have been a part of the rituals in the tomb; experimentation with the acoustic properties of chambers such as Newgrange has shown that the proportions were well suited for male chanting, 'deep-chanting women' or musical instruments (Devereux and Jahn 1996; Watson and Keating 1999).

Because the tomb has been open since at least the late seventeenth century, little has survived of the original contents. Excavation in the chamber recovered some cremated bone (of four or five people) and the position of these bone fragments suggested that the burial deposits might have been placed in the basin stones in the end and side cells. Objects found with the bones, presumably grave-goods placed with the remains, are typical of Irish passage tombs and include stone beads and pendants, fragments of bone pins and some small balls of polished stone (including a conjoined pair).

The decoration on the stones of Newgrange was generally picked out, probably with a hammer and a flint point; motifs usually consist of closely set small pock-marks executed in this fashion, and chevrons, zigzags, lozenges, triangles, spirals and circles are common. The decoration varies from the haphazard to the formal, from apparently casually and poorly carved designs to the superbly executed and aesthetically pleasing composition of spirals, arcs and lozenges on the celebrated entrance stone (Fig. 3.4). It is obvious that the designs on the entrance stone and on stones such as the tomb orthostats were meant to be clearly seen, but many, particularly the more casually picked ones, occur on the backs of stones and were lost to sight when these stones were put in place. Presumably the designs had some significance for their carvers, and the hidden motifs suggest, in some instances at least, that the very act of carving a particular design may have been more important than its display. Certainly, a lot of this imagery was not intended for public show and seems to be intimately connected with a cult of the dead. Christopher Tilley (2007) suggests that the continuous and unbroken kerb establishes a fundamental distinction between the interior and exterior and that both the architecture and spiral art of tombs like Newgrange were about symbolically containing the spirits of the dead and preventing their escape.

Only a fraction of the huge mound has been excavated and it is possible that it may, like Knowth or Dowth, cover a second tomb. While layers of turves occur now and then in the Newgrange cairn, limited excavation on the northern side of the mound revealed that the kerbstones there had not been set into or upon the old ground surface but were placed in sockets cut into a layer of turves which increased in thickness the further it extended inward under the cairn. This turf mound may cover some pre-cairn structure and it may be significant that the great mound bulges outwards at this point.

Palynological analysis of some turves revealed that they contained wheat pollen and they had evidently been stripped from fields in which cereals had grown. Open pasture was also indicated, and turves containing pollen of wet-loving plants probably came from the river valley. The stripping of this topsoil alone must have been a large undertaking, but the cairn, it has been estimated, contains about 200,000 tons of material, much of it transported from the bed of the River Boyne about 1km away. Some of the rounded stones, such as examples of granite, may have been deliberately selected many kilometres to the north, perhaps from the northern shores of Dundalk Bay, and transported south, while some of the quartz may have come from the Wicklow Mountains (Meighan *et al.* 2002; 2003). When it is remembered that the monument also contains at least 450 large slabs, some over five tons in weight, it would seem likely that it was the work of a substantial and wealthy population with considerable social organisation and engineering skill.

Indeed, the scale of monuments like Newgrange raises important questions about size and density of population, craft specialisation and social structure. The tomb in Newgrange was built towards the end of the fourth millennium BC. The burnt soil used to caulk the roof joints of the tomb contained charcoal fragments that provided radiocarbon date ranges of 3316–2922 BC and 3304–2922 BC which probably date the construction of the monument to sometime shortly before 3000 BC, after which, as already mentioned, the great mound visible today (and partly obscured by the modern quartz façade) may have been periodically enlarged over a long period of time.

Twelve large standing stones survive of what is sometimes assumed to have been a complete stone circle surrounding but not concentric with the mound. The original plan of this feature is not known with certainty, however; if ever complete it may have comprised 35–38 stones. While excavations have revealed the sockets of several missing stones on the south of the mound, results elsewhere have been inconclusive. It is possible that the circle was never completed. O'Kelly claimed that cairn material had apparently collected around some of the stones, thus indicating that these were in position when the mound commenced to decay, but subsequent excavations suggested that they post-date a circle of pits dug in the later third millennium BC (Sweetman 1985). It is possible, however, that the standing stones formed a great arc in front of the mound (Bradley 1998b).

There are three small, ruined satellite tombs in the immediate vicinity of the great mound, sites K and L to the west and Z to the south-east. Site K is a small, undifferentiated tomb: the chamber area is slightly wider than the passage and the two are separated by a sill stone 60cm in maximum height. Excavation revealed at least two phases of activity: the primary monument comprised the chamber with short passage covered with an earthen mound retained by a kerb of boulders. A penannular ditch (with its entrance aligned on the tomb entrance) surrounded the mound. Some time later the passage was lengthened, the mound enlarged and a new kerb 20m in diameter built; this kerb turned inwards towards the tomb entrance. While the primary tomb was disturbed, it had contained cremated human bone. The extension to the passage contained a homogeneous deposit of brown soil and cremated human bone, fragments of bone pins, small chalk balls and a pendant possibly of pottery. This mixture of soil and bone was apparently placed in the tomb as one deposit. Site L was a cruciform tomb, and traces of an earlier habitation site, a few pits, areas of burning, some pottery and flint were found beneath the mound. Site Z had been thoroughly destroyed: only the stump of one of the structural stones of the tomb survived, but the sockets of the others were located and it was thus possible to reconstruct the plan. Like site K, this was an undifferentiated tomb with a sill stone demarcating the chamber area, in which there was an irregularly shaped basin stone bearing some decoration. An unusual feature was a small cell opening off the inner end of the eastern side of the passage just before it joined the chamber. Fragments of both burnt and unburnt human bone were recovered. Decorated stones were found in each of these three satellite tombs (O'Kelly et al. 1978).

Knowth

Excavations at the great mound at Knowth, about 1km north-west of Newgrange, have revealed eighteen satellite tombs around a huge mound (Fig. 3.5) which itself contains two fine passage tombs (Eogan 1986). The large mound was modified in

early medieval times and souterrains and other features indicate extensive habitation on the site. The mound is approximately circular and comparable to Newgrange, being about 85m in average diameter, about 9.9m in height and surrounded by a contiguous series of 127 kerbstones. Unlike the Newgrange mound, it was constructed of alternate layers of earth and stones. The tombs are placed almost back to back, the entrance of one facing west, the other east. The first few metres of each passage were destroyed when a large ditch was dug around the mound in the earlier first millennium AD, and later still the outer parts of the passages were modified for use as souterrains, used for storage or refuge, and the interior of each tomb was apparently disturbed. Circular stone settings and spreads of quartz, granite and other stones were found in front of the entrances. The rituals associated with these features probably had some connection with the art carved on the adjacent kerbstones.

The kerb curves in slightly at the entrance to the western tomb, which lies behind a remarkable decorated kerbstone on which a design of concentric subrectangles is bisected by a vertical line more or less aligned on the centre of the passage entrance. The tomb was originally about 34m in length and has an almost square chamber divided in two by a low sill stone and separated from the passage by a higher one. Both the chamber and the passage are constructed of orthostats and roofed with capstones that rested on the side stones. The height and width of the passage increase near the chamber, and there is a marked curve to the south in the line of the passage about 6m from the chamber. Just before this bend there is a displaced basin stone, and just beyond it a sill stone. Like many of the kerbstones, several orthostats and capstones are decorated, notably in the area of the chamber.

The eastern tomb is slightly longer (over 40m) and has a more or less straight passage. The kerbstone at its entrance also bears a rectilinear design bisected by a vertical line. It has a fine corbel-vaulted cruciform chamber 5.9m high. As in Newgrange, the right-hand (northern) cell of the chamber is the largest of the three and has a pair of portal stones at its entrance. Within is a richly decorated basin stone that must have been put in place before the portal stones and the passage were built and therefore must be of very special

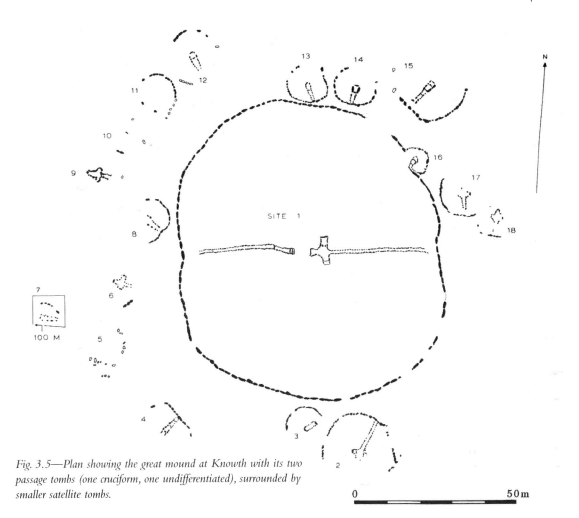

Fig. 3.5—Plan showing the great mound at Knowth with its two passage tombs (one cruciform, one undifferentiated), surrounded by smaller satellite tombs.

0   50 m

significance. The burial deposits had suffered some disturbance. For the most part they were confined to the cells and consisted mainly of burnt bone. A few unburnt bones were noted. Several deposits of cremated bone were recorded in the left-hand (southern) cell and a stone basin had been disturbed and upturned on top of them. The northern cell also contained a number of cremations around (but not in) the decorated basin stone. Finds included stone beads and pendants, antler pins and a remarkable decorated flint macehead (Fig. 3.6), found in the right-hand cell. Again, the majority of decorated stones occur in or near the chamber.

If the equinoxes had any importance for the builders of these monuments (and this is not certain), the eastern tomb may have been orientated towards the rising sun of the spring and autumn equinoxes (21 March and 21 September), and the

setting sun could also have shone into the western tomb at the same times. Like the midwinter solstice so important at Newgrange, the spring and autumn equinoxes, when day and night have equal lengths, could have been significant points in the calendar of a farming community. It is possible that burial or other rituals may have been timed to coincide with these events. It is also possible, of course, that our modern emphasis on astronomical precision is misplaced—the observation and experience of sunlight entering the darkness of a monument may have been an important ritual event in itself (Hensey 2008). The great mound at Knowth may have been completed, like Newgrange, towards the end of the fourth millennium BC. Charcoal believed to be contemporary with the commencement of construction has provided dates of 3358–2932 BC and 3292–2922 BC (Eogan

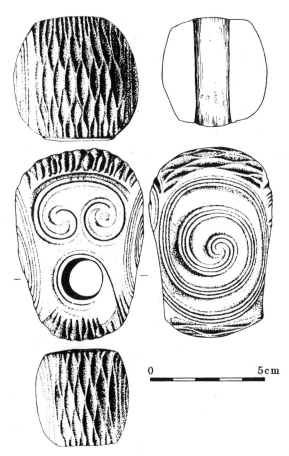

Fig. 3.6—Carved flint macehead from Knowth.

1991). A number of decorated orthostats in both the eastern and western tombs appear to have been reused and may have come from an earlier tomb (Eogan 1998a).

Excavation has revealed the remains of at least eighteen satellite tombs of considerably smaller size in the immediate vicinity of the large mound: most of these sites are situated close by, though one (site 7) is 145m away. All had suffered damage, in some cases so extensive that only a few stones or sockets of stones survived. In most instances it was still possible to recover the tomb plan; at least ten were small, undifferentiated tombs and five had cruciform chambers. The small mounds varied from just under 10m to about 20m in diameter. The passage entrances of the undifferentiated tombs were usually orientated towards the large mound. In contrast, all but two of the cruciform examples

faced east and the entrances of all five appeared to focus on an area to the south-east of the large mound. Excavation here produced no explanation for this, however.

Decoration occurs on some stones of kerb or tomb, or both, in the majority of these satellite sites. Several tombs had traces of cremated burials and a little unburnt human bone was found. For example, in addition to some cremated human bone (of several individuals) and some burnt animal bone, site 6, a cruciform tomb, produced a fragment of a small pottery bead and a bone pendant. Site 3 consisted of a rectangular chamber 3.5m in length set within the remains of a mound with kerb, presumably originally circular. Because of disturbance, a doubt remains as to whether or not this chamber ever had a passage. If not, this monument would bear some resemblance to a monument with passage tomb affinities at Millin Bay, Co. Down (Collins and Waterman 1955), where an oval mound was found to contain a long, narrow chamber, and is a reminder that passage tomb-builders may have constructed other types of monument as well. A little cremated bone was found in the site 3 tomb, along with a large pin or rod of antler or bone decorated with grooving; a sherd of Carrowkeel ware was found near the chamber. Site 4 had suffered considerable damage but was clearly an undifferentiated passage tomb; it is of particular interest because of a series of arcs of small stones found on either side of the passage, placed on the old ground surface and covered by the mound. The purpose of these stone settings is unknown, but a complex of arcs and radial lines of stones was associated with an undifferentiated passage tomb at Townleyhall, Co. Louth, not far away. A small circular area roughly paved with quartz pebbles occurred just outside the entrance to the site 4 tomb; it presumably served some ritual purpose (similar features have been found near the entrances of the two tombs in the large mound and near the entrance of the main Newgrange tomb). Site 2, a disturbed cruciform tomb, contained a stone basin in its surviving western recess, and a fragment of Carrowkeel ware was also found. A charcoal spread in the mound of this monument produced a radiocarbon date of 3090–2400 BC. Site 16, an undifferentiated tomb, yielded a date of 3334–2910 BC from a similar context. Both determinations may approximate to the construction dates of the two sites. A cremation in site 9 was dated to 3316–2920 BC.

While site 2 and other satellite tombs post-date the completion of the large mound, the relationship of all the various monuments to one another is still not clear. The small tombs at site 13 and site 16 are probably of earlier date; parts of the kerbs of both were removed to allow the completion of the large mound. It is possible that the large mound was built in several stages. The range of the available radiocarbon dates indicates tomb construction in the period 3300–2900 BC.

Dowth

The large mound at Dowth is the third of the great passage tombs in the Boyne cemetery (O'Kelly and O'Kelly 1983). It is comparable in size to those of Newgrange and Knowth and was considerably damaged in the course of nineteenth-century excavations. These revealed two tombs, both opening onto the western side of the mound. The more northerly of the two is a small cruciform tomb with its passage interrupted by three sill stones, and it has a small L-shaped annexe extending from the right-hand recess of the chamber. A souterrain has been added to the passage of this tomb. The southern tomb has a circular chamber with one lateral cell and its passage appears to be aligned on sunset (rather than sunrise) around the winter solstice (Moroney 1999). Of two small ruined mounds some distance to the east of Dowth, one, at least, contains a passage tomb.

Though often described as a cemetery, the Boyne Valley is more than a collection of individual tombs. While natural places—like the bend in a great salmon-rich river—may have their own significance, the building of monuments establishes or enhances the importance of particular locations and creates a new sense of order in the landscape (Bradley 1993). Cooney (2000) has suggested four phases in the development of the complex. A cluster of small tombs at Knowth and site K at the western end of the Newgrange ridge may mark an initial period of small-scale monument construction in sympathy with the terrain, with a general west to east spread across the valley. A later phase witnessed the emergence of the huge and complex tombs at Newgrange, Knowth and Dowth, with a greater interest in display and visibility in both art and architecture. The great tombs now dominated the area and became the focal monuments for other small tombs and for ritual activities that ordered space, time and mind. As Stefan Bergh (1997) has indicated, such large monuments are characterised by constructional complexity and a high investment in labour; they reflect a competitive socio-religious milieu, where certain knowledge was probably the preserve of a minority who, in their ability to predict certain celestial events, appeared to control time—the ultimate expression of power. Indeed, in these large complex monuments ritual practices may have been based on mystery. Large circular enclosures like a great earthwork just east of Dowth (site Q) and various monuments in the vicinity of Newgrange demonstrate the continued importance of this sacred landscape for ceremonial activity to the end of the third millennium BC (Chapter 4).

FOURKNOCKS I, CO. MEATH

The Fourknocks tomb (Fourknocks I) near Naul, Co. Meath, is some 15km south of the Boyne cemetery. Excavation revealed a cruciform monument covered by a circular mound of turves delimited by a very low drystone kerb, too slight to be a retaining wall and of a ritual rather than a functional nature. On the north-north-east the kerb curved in towards but did not connect with an orthostatic and unroofed passage that gave access to the chamber. The approximately oval chamber was unusually large, measuring 6.4m by 5.5m (Fig. 3.7). Its roof was partly corbelled but the quantity of collapsed stone found in the chamber was not sufficient to provide a complete roof. In the excavator's opinion the roof was originally completed in timber, and the discovery of a large post-hole in the centre of the chamber indicated that a timber post may have supported such a structure. A low sill stone separated each of the three slab-roofed cells from the chamber. There were no burials in the chamber; they were confined to the cells and the passage. The primary burial deposits in the cells comprised a homogeneous mass, 15–25cm thick, of burnt bone (with some fragments of unburnt bone) covered and sealed by a thin paving of stone flags (Hartnett 1957; Jones 2007).

Grave-goods were few and included stone and bone pendants and beads and bone pins, some of

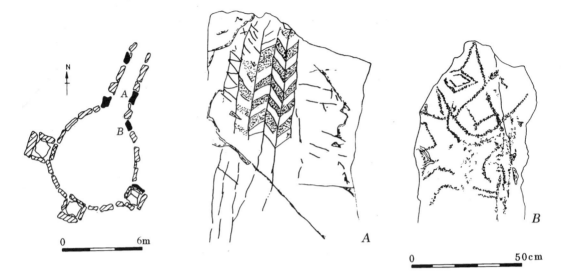

Fig. 3.7—Fourknocks I, Co. Meath: plan of tomb and two of the decorated orthostats.

which showed clear traces of burning. These were mixed through the mass of human remains. Several small chalk balls, also burnt, were found. One 19cm-long antler object, burnt and in fragments, was decorated with incised chevron ornament (Fig. 3.12, 1); it came from the terminal cell. No pottery was found in the tomb, though two sherds of Carrowkeel ware came from the mound.

Burials were found in the passage, mainly nearer the entrance; these consisted of a mixture of cremated and unburnt bone, the latter mostly in the upper levels of the layer of clay and stones which contained the human remains and which was sealed with stones and some clay right to the tops of the passage orthostats. The occurrence of a chalk ball and two bone pins with these burials, and a belief that the passage never had a roof, convinced the excavator that the passage deposits were primary and contemporary with the burials in the cells. A single collective burial, in which human remains were accumulated elsewhere over a period and then all deposited at the one time, is by no means a certainty, however. It may be that the cremations were the primary deposit and the unburnt remains in the passage were later insertions. Apart from some bones incorporated in the cairn, the bones from the tomb represented the remains of a minimum of 52 individuals (both adults and children). It was not possible to determine accurately the number of individuals represented: a

minimum of 24 persons (adults and children) were recognised among the bones from the chamber cells and a minimum of 28 from the passage. The unburnt bones comprised mainly skulls and disarticulated long bones.

Fourknocks I is one of a small number of burial monuments that display interesting evidence of ritual patterning in the funerary deposits. There appears to be a distinction between the way the remains of adults and children were treated, and some parts of the body seem to have been accorded special treatment. Cremated adults were normally assigned to the cells, while the unburnt bones of children formed a high proportion of the mix of burnt and unburnt bones in the passage. In the passage too there was the occasional deliberate deposition of unburnt adult skulls and long bones. The terminal cell was the most important location: it contained the most bones and the decorated antler rod and was roofed with a finely decorated lintel. Cooney (2000) has drawn attention to the ritual complexities here, including a pattern of activity in which children, peripheral location and unburnt burial may be compared with adults, cremation, central position (in the formal burial areas of the tomb) and the provision of accompanying artefacts. Very few of the children were cremated and most were under five years of age. The placing of a significant number of their unburnt bones in the passage must have had a

Fig. 3.8—Two decorated stones from Fourknocks I, Co. Meath.

special meaning in the complex closing rituals that evidently included the deposition of defleshed bones. Cut-marks on a jawbone from Millin Bay, which contained a large quantity of disarticulated bone, indicate that some defleshing was done with stone implements (Murphy 2003).

Some animal bones were found, a few mixed through the human bones in the cells and the passage, and some on the floor of the chamber; they were mainly unburnt but a few showed signs of scorching. They included cattle, sheep and pig and were considered evidence of funeral feasting. Even though many questions remain about the Fourknocks burial ritual, it was clearly an intricate process.

Ritual found further expression in the art that occurs on a total of eleven stones of the tomb. Picked zigzag, triangle and lozenge motifs are commonest and they are often arranged to form coherent geometric designs on either the whole surface or on part of the stone (Fig. 3.8). In this the art is comparable to the formal art at Newgrange. Fourknocks is one of the very few sites where motifs have been claimed to be anthropomorphic; a composition on one of the orthostats of the chamber bears a crescent-shaped motif, believed to be a mouth, with lozenges above suggestive of a nose and one eye (Fig. 3.7B), but caution is necessary and such assertions should be accepted as no more and no less than subjective guesswork.

A nearby mound (Fourknocks II), surrounded by a penannular ditch, was found to cover a small round cairn as well as a trench and passage thought by the excavator to be a crematorium. The latter feature consisted of a short megalithic passage placed within the gap in the ditch; the passage was roofed and contained burials. It terminated in a deep transverse trench, the bottom and sides of which showed considerable evidence of intense heat and which contained charcoal and several

Fig. 3.9—Passage tomb in the Mound of the Hostages, Tara, plan and section. One orthostat bears elaborate decoration.

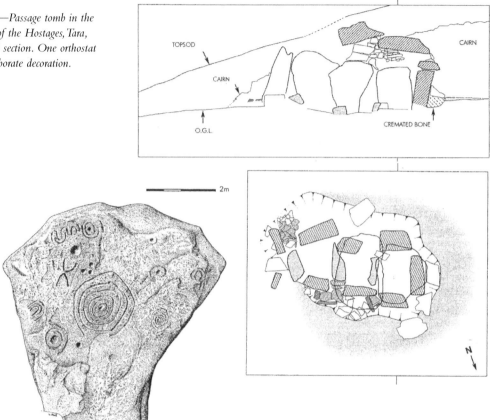

deposits of cremated bone. While some burning took place in the trench, it was not certainly a crematorium, but the finding of bone or antler pins with the burials and some Carrowkeel ware from the mound indicate that this puzzling monument was the work of passage tomb-builders. Here too differences in burial ritual have been detected: cremation was mainly an adult rite and adults were found in both the trench and passage, while children were mainly unburnt and disarticulated and deposited in the megalithic passage. Again the remains of the dead were used to seal the monument (Hartnett 1971; Cooney 2000).

Both of these mounds at Fourknocks were reused as burial places towards the end of the third millennium and in the second millennium BC, as was the Mound of the Hostages at Tara, Co. Meath (O'Sullivan 2005). The latter site, one of the earliest monuments in that celebrated complex, proved, on excavation in the 1950s, to be a passage tomb covered by a cairn and a mantle of clay that

contained a large number of early Bronze Age burials. The tomb was a small, undifferentiated monument, about 3m in length internally, with an entrance on the east (Fig. 3.9). A series of radiocarbon dates from bone and charcoal indicate that it was built around 3000 BC. A pair of portal stones flanked the entrance, which was also demarcated by a low slab set on edge (a sill stone). Two other sill stones divided the tomb into three. One orthostat had typical passage tomb art with concentric circles, U-shaped motifs and cup-marks. Cremated human bones were found both inside and outside the tomb and included a series of token deposits placed at the edge of the mound and three slab-protected concentrations of burnt bone placed outside but against the orthostats of the structure. Altogether parts of over 180 adults were identified, with a number of children and infants represented by unburnt limb bones. The extensive deposits in the tomb were greatly disturbed both by burrowing foxes and by the later insertion of a number of early

Bronze Age burials. Objects found with the human remains included Carrowkeel bowls, stone beads, bone pendants and pins, and stone balls.

THE LOUGHCREW (SLIEVE NA CAILLIGHE) CEMETERY

Loughcrew (Slieve na Caillighe), Co. Meath, is a name applied to a series of hills that, over an area of some 3km, are crowned by an extensive cemetery of at least 25 passage tombs (McMann 1994). The majority of these tombs are grouped into three clusters (Fig. 3.10). The most westerly group is on the hill called Carnbane West, where the huge and disturbed cairn D is partly surrounded by the remains of some eight sites (A1–3, B, C, E, F and G), of which F is a small cruciform tomb with a

number of decorated stones. About 150m north-east of D, a second large cairn (L) is partly surrounded by four smaller cairns (H, I, J and K). Cairn H is a small cruciform tomb and cairn L has a chamber divided into one terminal and seven lateral cells; both of these monuments and cairns I, J and K contain decorated stones. Cairn I, with its chamber with terminal cell and six lateral cells, is similar in some respects to L; the U-motifs, serpentiform motifs, radial motifs, dot and circle and concentric circle motifs are particularly common at Loughcrew. Most of these monuments were excavated in the nineteenth century after the fashion of the time, and several yielded fragmentary human bones and the occasional bone pin, bead or pendant and fragment of pottery. Although extensive digging took place in cairn D in 1865 and 1868, no tomb was found. Cairn H, also

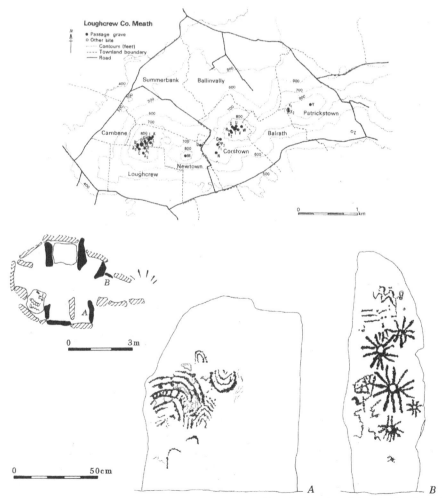

Fig. 3.10—Map of passage tomb cemetery at Loughcrew, Co. Meath, with plan of tomb in cairn I and two decorated stones.

investigated in these years, was re-examined in 1943 and both typical passage tomb material and a considerable quantity of later prehistoric material was recovered.

The second major group of tombs is situated on Carnbane East, where cairn T on the summit is partly surrounded by half a dozen smaller tombs (R, R1, S, U, V, W). Cairn T is a cruciform tomb with a cairn 35m in diameter; its entrance faces east and at the equinoxes the rising sun illuminates some of the decorated stones in the interior. Cairn S has a polygonal chamber with a single cell, U is a tomb that appears to be a variation of the cruciform type, and V and W are of uncertain plan. Investigation of these monuments also produced burnt bone, Carrowkeel ware and other finds. Many of the stones, particularly in cairn T, bear decoration. Four other tombs occur on Patrickstown, the next hill to the east. As in the Boyne Valley, this was a monumental complex where ritual was intimately connected with both tomb and landscape. In addition to being places of burial, some small earlier monuments may have had loosely defined spaces among them where communal ritual activities could have taken place. While their modest size and rounded form made them seem like natural extensions of the landscape, the later larger tombs themselves became landmarks that restricted the public space and, as Fraser (1998) has argued, the reduced communal participation may denote greater élite control and more prescribed formulaic ritual.

THE CARROWKEEL CEMETERY

One of the two major passage tomb cemeteries in County Sligo is to be found on the Bricklieve Mountains overlooking Lough Arrow. This cemetery, Carrowkeel, is named after one of a number of townlands in which several high limestone ridges bear some twenty round cairns, some of which are known to contain passage tombs (Bergh 1995). Fourteen cairns were partly and unscientifically investigated in 1911. Several were found to contain cruciform or related passage tombs, which produced mainly cremated bone and typical finds such as fragments of Carrowkeel pottery, bone pins, beads and pendants and stone balls. All but one of the cairns were circular. Cairn

E is a long, trapezoidal cairn with traces of a straight kerb; what seems to be an unusual orthostatic court occurs at the broader end but has no adjacent chamber, and a cruciform tomb occurs at the narrower end. Some fragments of bone, two bone pins and a boar's tusk were found. The numerous enclosures of various sizes identified by Stefan Bergh on the nearby limestone plateau at Mullaghfarna probably represent settlement that had some connection with the cemetery.

THE CARROWMORE CEMETERY

The cemetery of tombs at Carrowmore, Co. Sligo, is dominated by the great cairn, traditionally known as Miosgán Meabha ('Maeve's heap'), on the summit of Knocknarea near Sligo town (Fig. 3.11). This huge, unopened cairn probably contains a passage tomb and in its vicinity are the remains of five satellite monuments, one of which is a cruciform tomb. In a pioneering study of the Neolithic monuments and landscape of the Cúil Irra peninsula in north-west Sligo, Stefan Bergh (1995; 2002) has shown that this conspicuous cairn is deliberately located on Knocknarea to achieve the best visual impact when viewed from the east, from Carrowmore, and it is this eastern face that is distinguished by the presence of a series of linear banks that separate the summit from the land below and possibly controlled and directed the approach to the summit. This transformation of the mountain into a monument is a good example of the interrelationship between architecture and natural form that lies at the heart of the passage tomb tradition. In his study of Cúil Irra, Bergh (1995) has noted three clusters of monuments, Knocknarea in the west, Carrowmore in the centre and a pair of cairns on Carns Hill in the east, an intriguing tripartite manipulation of the landscape replicated at Loughcrew (with its three hilltop clusters) and in the Boyne Valley (with Knowth, Newgrange and Dowth).

The Carrowmore cemetery proper lies below and to the east of Knocknarea, and the surviving monuments are only a fraction of the original number. Some 60 monuments once existed, but only about 30 survive in various stages of dilapidation today. Most lie within an area measuring about 1,000m by 500m and are situated

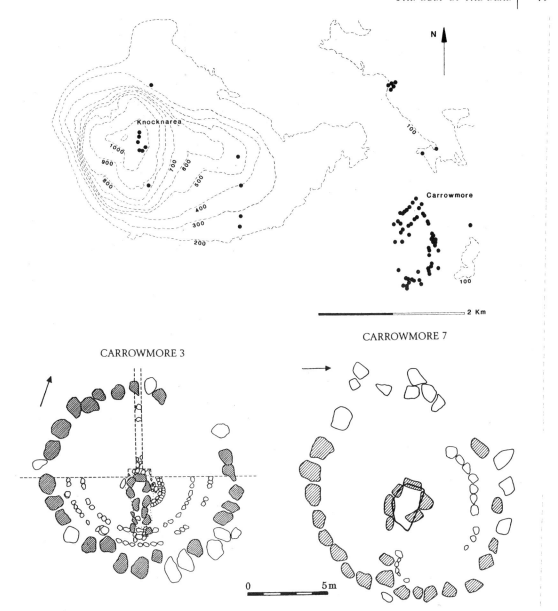

Fig. 3.11—Map of the Carrowmore and Knocknarea passage tomb cemeteries in County Sligo and plans of tombs Carrowmore 3 and 7.

on a series of low morainic hills; few are conspicuously sited. The majority are boulder circles, consisting of circles or parts of circles of stones that probably once contained centrally placed stone structures of some description; of the 25 remaining monuments, 24 have or had a central feature. For the most part, diameters range from 10m to 17m. Megalithic tombs survive within the circles in seventeen instances and most are monuments with polygonal chambers, some with short passages; they are built of boulders and the capstones are split boulders with a characteristic almost conical shape. There is also one cruciform tomb (Carrowmore 27) and several rectangular or subrectangular monuments. Many of the Carrowmore tombs were investigated in the nineteenth century and some produced typical finds such as Carrowkeel ware and bone or antler pins. Excavation has been undertaken here in the 1970s and 1990s by Göran Burenhult.

The largest tomb is Carrowmore 51 ('Listoghil'), more or less in the centre of the cemetery, a cairn about 35m in diameter with the remains of a boulder kerb and containing a subrectangular orthostatic chamber roofed with a single large capstone. Excavation has produced unburnt human bone and radiocarbon dates that suggest construction of the chamber around 3600 BC. Several large boulders found beneath the cairn and unconnected with the chamber may be the remnants of an earlier monument (Burenhult 2000). A series of picked arcs and a pair of concentric circles with a central dot have been identified on the edge of the limestone roof stone of the chamber (Curran-Mulligan 1994).

Carrowmore no. 7 is a small tomb set within a circle of boulders 12.5m in diameter; the boulders were supported by an internal packing of small stones (Fig. 3.11). Like so many of the other sites in the cemetery, it had been examined in the nineteenth century. The chamber was of polygonal plan, constructed of five stones and roofed with a large capstone. Excavation revealed traces of a very short passage but no evidence of a covering cairn. Despite the former disturbance, several intact deposits of cremated bone, burnt sea shells and charcoal were recovered; in one deposit fragments of an antler pin were found, but no pottery. The burnt sea shells, which included unopened mussels and oysters, were interpreted as funerary offerings. Several pits or post-holes may pre-date the tomb, and a mixed sample of charcoal from several contexts (including one of these pits or post-holes) provided an early radiocarbon date of 4226–3987 BC, giving a *terminus post quem* for the chamber (Bergh 1995). This was just one of four or five post-holes dug into the natural surface below the monument, however, and thus the date probably relates to some structure somewhat older than the tomb.

Carrowmore no. 26 is a boulder circle with a diameter of 17m and it lies in the eastern part of the cemetery. The boulders were supported by an internal stone packing and the circle had a paved entrance on the south-east. Cremated bone and a fragment of a mushroom-headed antler pin were found at the centre. The circle was reused in the first millennium BC as a ritual site, but the nature of the construction of the stone circle and the antler pin and cremation relate these particular features to the passage tomb monuments of the cemetery; there

may once have been a central chamber.

Carrowmore no. 27 is a relatively large monument: a boulder circle with a maximum overall diameter of 23m and a centrally placed cruciform tomb. Excavation showed that the large boulders were partly surrounded by stone packing, which also occurred within the line of the circle; the tomb too was surrounded by stone packing, delimited by an inner boulder circle 13.7m in diameter. There was no true passage but two stones flanked the entrance to the chamber, which was also marked by a sill stone. All parts of the chamber had been extensively disturbed and much cremated bone found outside had clearly been dug out in the past; antler pins, chalk balls and three sherds of Carrowkeel ware were recovered. The stone packing around the chamber was up to 40cm thick and served as a support for the stones of the tomb. No trace of a more substantial cairn was found and, in the excavator's opinion, the tomb was never covered in this fashion. Charcoal from beneath and between the stones of the lowest level of the stone packing has provided a series of early fourth-millennium radiocarbon dates (3958–3646 BC).

The small monument, Carrowmore no. 3 (numeration following Bergh; Burenhult's no. 4), consisted of a circle of boulders with a diameter of 13m. Like nos 7, 26 and 27, the inner edge of the circle was supported by a packing of small stones. At the centre was a small, more or less polygonal stone chamber measuring only 80cm by 100cm internally and roofed with a small boulder (Fig. 3.11). Four limestone slabs and several small boulders formed a narrow passage too small to permit access to the chamber; no roof stones were found. Both chamber and passage were constructed in a shallow pit about 30cm deep and surrounded by a packing of stones delimited by a circle of small stones. A second circle of small stones and two small cist graves were located between this circle and the circle of boulders at the edge of the monument. The central chamber and the passage had been greatly disturbed, but a considerable quantity of burnt human and animal bone was recovered along with fragments of antler pins. Both the small cists contained cremated human bone; one also contained a stone ball, the other a stone bead and fragments of antler pins. Charcoal from the base of one of the stones of the chamber produced a radiocarbon date centred on *c.* 4600 BC, but a charcoal sample associated with an arc of small stones east of the chamber, apparently part of the stone packing, has given a date of *c.* 3000–2900 BC. According to Burenhult, these dates indicate at least two distinct phases in the history of the tomb, the former representing the construction of the chamber, the latter the much later addition of a half-circle of stones east of the chamber. But in a careful assessment of the stratigraphical evidence, Bergh (1995) suggests that the charcoal that produced the exceptionally early date may be redeposited and brought in from elsewhere.

For the excavator, the radiocarbon evidence from the Carrowmore excavations implied that small and relatively simple passage tombs were being built as early as the fifth millennium BC. These supposedly early tombs may not have been completely covered by cairns and had rudimentary passages that did not run all the way from chamber to kerb. Because of the early radiocarbon dates, the quantity of sea shells recovered and the scarcity of pottery, Burenhult (1980; 1984) has speculated that the Carrowmore megaliths were initiated by a community with an essentially hunting and foraging economy. He suggested that the cemetery was the focus of a hunter-gatherer group with a subsistence pattern that included the seasonal exploitation of coastal shellfish and the fauna of the adjacent countryside. Excavations by Stefan Bergh on the summit of Croaghaun Mountain, south of Ballysadare Bay, Co. Sligo, revealed that a small oval cairn (which had suffered some disturbance) contained a small subrectangular megalithic tomb; a number of small deposits of cremated bone (one with an antler pin fragment) and some sherds of coarse pottery were found. Charcoal from this deposit produced a radiocarbon date of 5640–5490 BC, and a date of 4675–4460 BC was obtained from another similar sample (Bergh 1995). For Burenhult, these early dates offer support for his claim that hunters and foragers constructed simple megalithic monuments, but the samples may have been contaminated. The absence of diagnostic artefacts of these pre-farming folk is telling, however, and it is more sensible to see the Sligo tombs in general as a phenomenon of the fourth millennium, as most of the radiocarbon dates would suggest (Sheridan 2003b), their builders combining an agricultural economy with coastal fishing and shellfish-gathering.

BURIAL RITUAL AND GRAVE-GOODS

Many aspects of the burial ritual of the passage tomb-builders are not understood, but it is clear that these tombs usually contain remains representing several individuals, frequently cremated but sometimes unburnt. Because cremation was so frequent and because so many of the excavated tombs have been disturbed in the past, reliable details of the numbers buried are often unavailable. But in spite of damage and disturbance, it seems fair to say that cremation was the predominant rite. This was the case at Carrowmore and Knowth, for example, but unburnt bones are frequently reported. Animal bones may be evidence of funeral feasts, and the discovery of shells at some sites has prompted the suggestion that shellfish may have been consumed too. In some tombs it seems that human remains were deposited in a number of collective ceremonies: since the burials in the terminal and lateral cells at Fourknocks I, Co. Meath, formed a fairly compact homogeneous deposit, the excavator was of the opinion that each cell contained a single collective deposit that represented the cremation of a number of corpses accumulated over a period of time. The presence of some unburnt bones could be said to support this theory, for these were clearly fleshless and disarticulated when placed in the tomb and suggested that some corpses at least had been stored for a time elsewhere until they were defleshed. Some selection process clearly took place and, as we have seen, distinctions were made between adults and children and various bone deposits were deliberately placed in certain areas. All the evidence indicates a complex ritual both outside and inside the tomb.

Discrete burial deposits were found in several locations in the Knowth cemetery: all were cremations. In site 15, for instance, an undifferentiated tomb with three sill stones, one segment contained some burnt bones of a child covered by four flat stones. A second larger deposit representing at least one child and two adults lay on top of the slabs, but the length of time, if any, between the two deposits could not be ascertained. In site 16, a similar undifferentiated tomb, five separate cremation deposits of at least sixteen individuals were identified in both chamber area and passage. Three stratified deposits occurred in the chamber and two in the inner passage, each separated by one or more slabs. Here, as elsewhere, the interval between these burials is unknown but there is no evidence for large-scale and prolonged use.

It is not clear what role stone basins may have played in the burial ritual. Some may have once contained deposits of cremated bone, but most of those recorded to date come from disturbed monuments. Several Boyne tombs and a number at Loughcrew have produced these enigmatic objects and examples have occasionally been found elsewhere, at Baltinglass, Co. Wicklow, and Slieve Gullion, Co. Armagh (Collins and Wilson 1963), for instance.

A limited range of other artefacts occurs fairly consistently with passage tomb burials but their restricted character presents an intriguingly specialised and perplexing assemblage. Beads and pendants, bone and antler pins, stone balls and fragments of Carrowkeel pottery are characteristic finds (Fig. 3.12; Fig. 2.12, 8). The small, perforated pendants, made of stones such as steatite, limestone or occasionally semi-precious stones such as carnelian and jasper, are often of miniature pestle or hammer shape. Many bear traces of burning, cracking and heat-crazing, indicating some time in the funeral pyre. A few bone or antler examples have been found too. Simple cylindrical and flat circular beads of similar types of stone (and the occasional bone or baked clay example) are known. It is possible that some of the pendants are miniature versions of stone

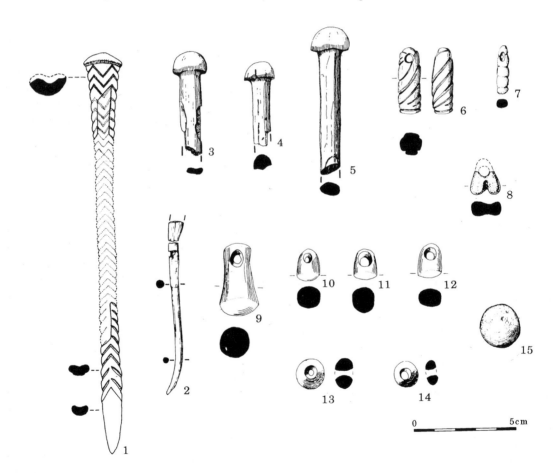

Fig. 3.12—Finds from passage tombs. (1–2) Decorated antler rod or pin and bone pin from Fourknocks I, Co. Meath. (3–5) Fragments of mushroom-headed pins from Loughcrew, Co. Meath. (6–8) Pendants from the Mound of the Hostages, Tara, Co. Meath. (9–12) Pendants from Carrowkeel, Co. Sligo. (13–14) Beads from the Mound of the Hostages, Tara, Co. Meath. (15) Stone ball from Fourknocks I, Co. Meath.

maceheads. Two of these maceheads or hammers have been found at Knowth: half of a perforated macehead of finely polished stone comes from the western undifferentiated tomb in the great mound there, and a complete decorated example was found in the cruciform eastern tomb. The latter is an extraordinary object (Fig. 3.6). Made of pale grey flint and 7.9cm long, it is cylindrically perforated and polished and decorated on all six faces. The principal decorative motifs are extremely finely carved spirals composed of three parallel lines in relief and hollowed lozenges that decorate either end. The polishing, perforating and decorating of this hard flint was a work of exceptional craftsmanship (Fenwick 1995) and the object may well have been a prestigious symbol of religious or political authority. Both maceheads are types well known in northern Scotland, particularly in Orkney.

The commonest type of bone or antler pin has a rounded mushroom-shaped head. Simpler skewer pins also occur. Many are fragmentary but were probably 10–20cm long and most show traces of burning. Their significance is unknown, but a calcined decorated antler example found in the Fourknocks I tomb was considered to be a cult object (Fig. 3.12, 1). It was decorated with incised chevrons and had, it seems, a shallow groove running for most of its length on one side. A somewhat similar antler or bone object was found in one of the Knowth satellite tombs (site 3), and a slender, 25cm-long grooved and conical sandstone object was found near the entrance to the western tomb. This object indicates that at least some of the decorated bone and antler rods were more than mere pins and had some symbolic significance.

Equally enigmatic is a series of carefully made balls of stone and other materials from passage tombs. Eleven of these so-called 'marbles' were found in Fourknocks I, for example; two were made from calcite pebbles, the others were of a chalky material identified as calcium carbonate. They ranged in size from 11mm to 25mm in diameter and some showed traces of burning. Small chalk balls from the main tomb at Newgrange may have been made of material from Antrim, and two examples possibly of serpentinite were also discovered there. Larger, highly polished balls 7–8cm in diameter are also known: examples in marble and ironstone are known from Loughcrew.

A large limestone ball comes from Fourknocks I. It has been pointed out that some balls fit neatly into some circular pits or cup-marks on the stones at Loughcrew and may have been used in ritual performances of some sort (McMann 1994). Pairs of small conjoined balls have been found at Newgrange and Tara. Needless to say, the significance of these latter objects is unknown but, not surprisingly, there have been suggestions that both they and the antler pins are expressions of some fertility belief. A strange collection of fossils was placed in a passage tomb at Ballycarty, near Tralee, Co. Kerry (Connolly 1999).

Stone implements, such as flint scrapers, are rarely found in the burial deposits. A flint convex scraper from site K at Newgrange is one of the few identifiably primary finds from such contexts: most of the flints from passage tombs come from the mound or its vicinity or represent some activity on the site prior to or during the construction of the tomb. Fragments of pottery are fairly consistently associated with burials, and invariably these are of Carrowkeel ware with characteristic profuse, impressed and incised decoration, hemispherical form and coarse friable fabric. The frequent occurrence of sherds of just parts of pots rather than fragments of complete vessels would seem to suggest that funerary custom often demanded no more than token deposits of pottery perhaps ritually broken elsewhere. Indeed, it is possible that some of these pots were specifically made for the burial ceremony. Complete Carrowkeel pots from tombs are rare. Two were found in the Mound of the Hostages at Tara and one is preserved from Donegore, Co. Antrim; it was found in a possible tomb, a 'subterraneous cavern'.

PASSAGE TOMB ART

Carved decoration on the stones of some tombs is a remarkable feature of this category of megalithic monument and, in Ireland, decoration of this sort is virtually confined to passage tombs. Not all of these tombs contain decorated stones, however; the decorated monuments, about 50 in number, are found in the north and east of the country, and the greatest concentration occurs in County Meath in the great cemeteries at Loughcrew and in the Boyne Valley. Decorated tombs, or decorated stones probably from tombs, are also known from counties Antrim, Armagh, Fermanagh, Sligo, Tyrone, Kilkenny, Louth, Wicklow and Cork (Shee Twohig 1981; 1996; Eogan 1986).

Ornament has been found on kerbstones, roof stones and orthostats; in some instances it is clear that it was carved after the stones had been put in place, while in other cases carved designs were hidden or inaccessible and must have been done prior to placing the stone in position. The designs were executed in two main ways: lightly incised and deeply incised lines are occasionally used, but most of the decoration was done by picking with a sharply pointed implement. A flint point or chisel was probably hammered with a wooden mallet to produce a line formed of a series of closely set 'pick marks'. Sometimes lines such as this were deepened by rubbing with a pebble to produce an even groove. Some stones bear designs in which broadly picked lines form a pattern that emphasises the unpicked or reserved areas. Area picking also occurs, particularly in the Boyne Valley: in such designs the picking extends over the whole surface of a motif, a triangle or lozenge, for example; in some cases it may cover large parts of the surface of a stone. No evidence of painting has ever been found in an Irish tomb (though this technique is known in megalithic tombs in the Iberian peninsula). The art varies from the seemingly haphazard to the remarkably formal. Although some of the more haphazard designs cannot be readily classified, it is still possible to group most of the motifs employed into some eleven general categories (Fig. 3.13). A full assessment of the components of this art style must await the study of the large amount of material revealed in the Knowth excavations, where over 300 decorated stones have been found in the great mound alone.

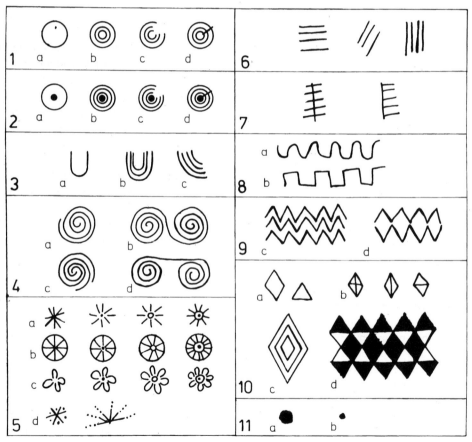

Fig. 3.13—Passage tomb art motifs. (1) Circles: single, concentric, penannular and with radial line. (2) Circle with central dot. (3) U-motif and boxed U-motif (b), arcs (c). (4) Spiral motifs. (5) Radial motifs. (6) Parallel lines. (7) Offset motifs. (8) Serpentiform motifs. (9) Zigzag. (10) Lozenge. (11) Cup-mark and dot.

Single and concentric circles are the commonest motif; they are sometimes penannular, as on the kerbstones of the great mound at Knowth. Similar circles with central dots also occur and are particularly frequent at Loughcrew. U-shaped motifs and 'boxed U's' (U-motifs set within other U-motifs) are also common and are noteworthy in the latter cemetery, where in fact they are the commonest motif. They are one of several superbly executed motifs decorating the entrance kerbstone at the main tomb at Newgrange. This stone also illustrates the fact that some of the finest art in this tomb incorporates the spiral motif. Simple clockwise or anticlockwise spirals, double spirals of two parallel lines and linked spirals occur, and many have a central circle or dot. They are a notable feature of the repertoire of the Boyne Valley carvers.

Radial motifs, in contrast, are common at Loughcrew but are rarely found elsewhere, though good examples do occur at Knowth. The name serpentiform is used to describe an undulating linear motif, though there is no suggestion that the motif represents a serpent. It is widely used and, when rather angular, is sometimes difficult to differentiate from a zigzag (or chevron) motif. The latter motif is sometimes used to form a panel of ornament, as are lozenges and triangles. Other simple motifs include parallel lines and offset motifs in which a series of lines usually project at right angles to a base line, the whole motif being sometimes enclosed in an oval or D-shaped frame. Dots and so-called cup-marks occur frequently; it is not always possible to differentiate between them but cup-marks are usually considered to be more than 2cm in diameter, though it is sometimes difficult to distinguish between natural hollows and picked cup-marks.

The listing of individual motifs is a convenient way of summarising the different elements in this megalithic art but, of course, overlooks the significance of compositional groups and of their location inside and outside the monuments. The decorative motifs are used in varying combinations and individual tombs seem to have their own distinct style. At Newgrange, and on some stones at Knowth, motifs are integrated to form a coherent overall design, but sometimes there appears to be no attempt to achieve an overall composition and many stones have just one or two motifs apparently placed at random. Concentric circles, dot and circle motifs, U-motifs and serpentiforms are common. The visitor to Newgrange might well assume that spirals, zigzags and lozenges are the principal motifs, but in fact circles and serpentiforms are well represented. They occur mainly on the upper surfaces of the roof stones of the tomb and on the backs of some of the kerbstones. Some of this hidden ornament may be no more than casual doodling or experimentation by some of the carvers of the water-grooves, for example, but the use of different motifs to those of the formal art is difficult to explain. Since such hidden art was not meant for display, as already mentioned, the act of inscribing it may have been its most important aspect. The very megalithic stones employed may have had magical significance, and their size, shape, colour and texture may have been important. In choosing to use large and often unmodified blocks (rather than smaller dry masonry) the builders of such monuments may have been expressing a belief that great stones had a meaning in their own right (Scarre 2004).

Muiris O'Sullivan (1986; 1993) has identified a depictive or standard style and a plastic style. The former consists of combinations of basic individual motifs such as spirals, circles, chevrons or lozenges; these usually appear haphazard without any obvious attempt to create a coherent pattern, though neat two-dimensional compositions may occur occasionally. This style includes the hidden art. In contrast, the plastic art is never hidden. It retains elements of the standard art, using motifs such as spirals, circles, lozenges, etc., but these are now boldly displayed in visually impressive patterns that take the general shape of the stone into account. There may be a shift in emphasis from individual decorative elements to the structural stone itself. This art seems rarely to extend to the bottom 30cm of a stone, implying that it was often executed when kerbstone or orthostat had been placed in position. The famous entrance stone at Newgrange is a classic example (Fig. 3.4). The plastic style may occur on the same surface as the standard style but when this happens it is usually superimposed, cutting through or even partly obliterating the latter. A complex sequence of five overlaid compositions has been proposed for one orthostat at Knowth (Eogan 1999a).

Various explanations have been offered for individual motifs in this geometric art style. Solar and anthropomorphic explanations have been popular: radial motifs, for instance, have been seen as sun symbols, and pairs of spirals have been considered to be stylised human eyes or faces ultimately inspired by vaguely anthropomorphic Iberian plaques and idols. Several Irish carvings have been declared to be stylised representations of human figures, among them the design on one of the Fourknocks orthostats where lozenges and arcs form what the excavator thought to be the head and upper part of a body (Fig. 3.7B). A face-like design has been seen in a combination of spirals and lozenge on one of the Newgrange orthostats, for example, and on the decorated macehead from Knowth (Fig. 3.6). It was once thought that this might be evidence that an anthropomorphic goddess was worshipped by passage tomb-builders, but this is a belief that rests on a subjective interpretation of evidence at best described as ambiguous. Since anthropomorphic designs and human faces are recorded in passage tomb contexts on the Continent, both in Brittany and, as already mentioned, in Iberia, stylised representations of this sort are not an impossibility, but clearly interpretation is difficult (Shee Twohig 1998; M. O'Sullivan 1996).

The study of compositional groups and of the locational patterns of these compositions may advance our understanding of this enigmatic phenomenon. It is clear that some stones and their art mark significant areas where specific rituals may have taken place: the decorated stone above the Newgrange roof-box is an obvious example, as are the highly decorated kerbstones at tomb entrances. The decorated kerbstones around the great mound at Knowth, like some adjacent settings of stones revealed by excavation, may denote important points on a processional circuit around the site. Here some groups of adjacent kerbstones appear to share similar overall designs; for instance, the entrance stone with that vertical line in a rectilinear design outside the entrance to the eastern tomb is flanked on either side by a kerbstone bearing another rectilinear design (Eogan 1996). The carvings in the passage at Newgrange are generally small-scale and the majority of spirals, circles and zigzags are not visible but are a part of the hidden art; in contrast, in the chamber these motifs are very visible elements (Shee Twohig 2000).

It has been claimed that the origin of some

motifs may be entoptic (from the Greek *entos* 'within', *optikos* 'vision'), sensory visual images produced in states of altered consciousness induced by hallucinatory drugs, by sensory deprivation or by some other means. Ethnographic evidence and laboratory experimentation suggest that abstract motifs such as U-shapes, arcs, spirals, zigzags and serpentiform motifs, and compositions of triangles or lozenges could have been inspired in this way (Dronfield 1995a; 1995b; 1996; Lewis-Williams and Pearce 2005). That hallucinatory images might reflect the experience of shamans in a trance-like state has also been proposed for similar symbols in Palaeolithic art, and while this may explain the ultimate origins of some such motifs, their meaning still eludes us. It may well be that individual motifs and combinations of motifs had multiple meanings, and meanings may have changed over time. Differences between tombs and between regions may be expressions of different group identities, while shared motifs may have facilitated communication. To recover some of the meaning encoded in passage tomb art is one of the great challenges in Irish archaeology.

Megalithic tombs were built in various parts of western Europe from as early as the fifth millennium BC. Passage tombs or related monuments are a widespread phenomenon found mainly in southern Scandinavia, western France, Iberia, Ireland and Britain. In Ireland the majority of examples date from the second half of the fourth to the first half of the third millennium BC. The nature of their relationship to the Continental tombs has been the subject of some debate and inconclusive discussion. Various writers have assumed a Breton origin, and it has been argued that the first Irish passage tombs were built by a group of people who sailed from the Gulf of Morbihan in southern Brittany to the mouth of the Boyne and then spread westward to Loughcrew and Sligo. Thus the simple monuments in the Carrowmore cemetery would be the ultimate derivatives of the great eastern tombs (Herity 1974). Sheridan (1986) has proposed a developmental sequence of five stages, beginning with simple tombs like the 'Druid Stone', Ballintoy, Co. Antrim, and culminating with the large monuments of the Boyne Valley. The idea that there was a general typological progression from simple to complex plans seems plausible, but obviously not all simple monuments are necessarily early. There is such evidence from Knowth, where small tombs pre-dated the great mound, and there are indications that other monuments may be of multi-period construction, the final form of such monuments perhaps differing greatly from the primary structure: this seems to have been the case at the passage tomb on Baltinglass, Co. Wicklow (where the small primary tomb was modified at least twice), and at cairn H in the Carrowkeel cemetery. This tomb seems to have had its passage lengthened at some time, and the same may have occurred in the western tomb in the great mound at Knowth. Sheridan (2003b) has also argued that the early simple monuments may be the result of maritime contacts with Brittany. There are intriguing parallels with aspects of the passage tomb phenomenon in the Iberian peninsula as well (Eogan 1990), and it is evident that the picture was a complex one. M. J. O'Kelly (1982) saw the passage tombs (and the other megalithic tombs of western Europe) as various regional manifestations of a cult of the dead that spread among early agricultural communities, no large-scale movements of peoples being involved. The practice of building sizeable stone monuments does broadly coincide with the development of agriculture, and the Irish tombs are a part of a western European megalithic phenomenon in which a network of contacts along the coasts and estuaries of the Atlantic façade played a major role (Cunliffe 2001).

COURT TOMBS

As the name court tomb suggests, a forecourt of some description is one of the characteristic features of these megalithic monuments. In contrast to passage tombs with their circular mounds, court tombs have long cairns. Essentially a court tomb consists of a long cairn of approximately rectangular or trapezoidal shape with an orthostatically defined, unroofed court giving access to a longitudinally placed gallery of one or more chambers. Cairn lengths vary, but dimensions of between 25m and 35m seem to be common and rare examples from about 40m to 60m in length are known. The maximum width is usually about half the length. Over 400 examples have been recorded and they display considerable variation in shape of court,

tomb plan, etc. (de Valera 1960; 1965; Ó Nualláin 1976; 1977; 1989 and references; Cody 2002). The distribution of these tombs is mainly a northern one, north of the central plain (Fig. 3.14). Very few examples occur south of a line from Galway to Dundalk: a few examples are recorded in County Clare, and one each in counties Kilkenny, Limerick, Tipperary and Waterford, for instance. A significant concentration (about 34% of the total) is to be found in the Mayo–Sligo area. Regional preferences for different types of court tomb are evident: simple tombs with open, crescent-shaped courts are found mainly in the north-east, while elaborate monuments with more complex courts occur mainly in the north-west. Many of these tombs have suffered considerable disturbance, and shape of court, number of chambers and other features are sometimes not discernible without excavation.

Several varieties of court tomb have been identified, including open court tombs, full court tombs, dual court tombs and transeptal court tombs. In some of these varieties the number of chambers in the burial gallery may vary but two-chambered galleries are most common. Approximately 70% of tombs with a known number of chambers have just two. Those monuments with a two-chambered gallery and with an open court appear to be the basic court tomb type, most of the other varieties being more complicated variations on this plan. A court tomb at Tully, near Derrygonnelly, Co. Fermanagh, is a good illustration of this two-chambered form with open court and an indication of how excavation can sometimes recover the original plan of even a badly damaged monument. Many of its structural stones had been removed but their sockets or bedding trenches survived. The original trapezoidal shape of the cairn, which would have covered the two-chambered gallery, was also apparent (Fig. 3.14).

The cairns of court tombs are generally retained by an orthostatic revetment (for example Ballyglass, Co. Mayo, and Annaghmare, Co. Armagh: Fig. 3.15); retaining walls of dry masonry also occur now and then, as at Tully, where the surviving eastern side of the long cairn had a functional revetment of large stones (with a second non-functional revetment set 45–90cm in front of it). Evidence of the original heights of cairns is scanty: at Carrowreagh, Co. Sligo, a long cairn almost entirely covered by peat is 3–4m high at the

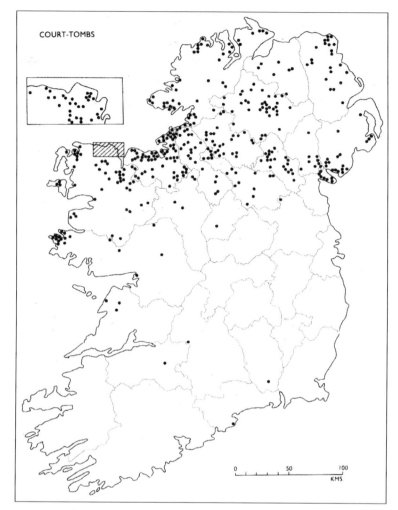

COURT-TOMBS

Fig. 3.14—Above: general distribution of court tombs. Below: court tomb with open court and two-chambered gallery at Tully, Co. Fermanagh.

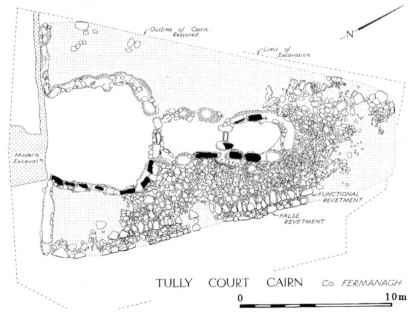

TULLY COURT CAIRN Co. FERMANAGH

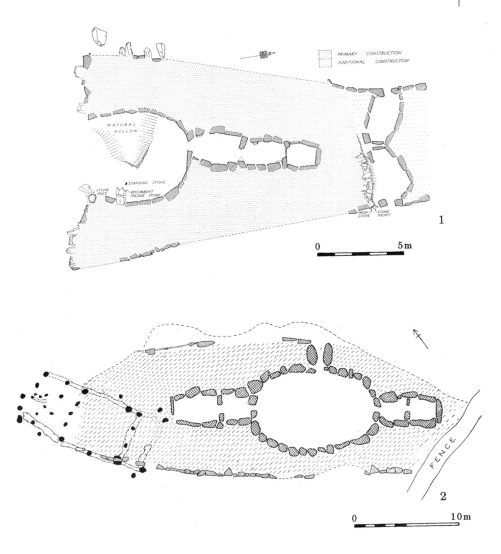

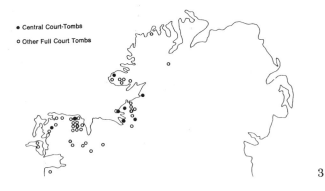

Fig. 3.15—(1) Court tomb with open court and three-chambered gallery at Annaghmare, Co. Armagh, with segmentation both by a pair of jamb stones and by jamb stones and sill stone. (2) Central court tomb at Ballyglass, Co. Mayo, with the pre-tomb structure visible on the west. (3) Distribution of central and full court tombs.

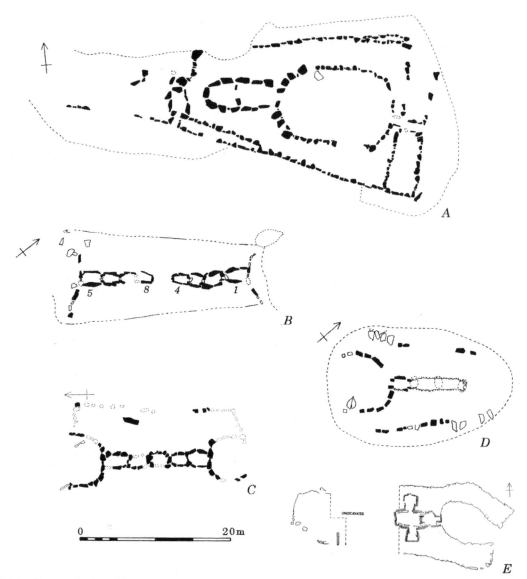

Fig. 3.16—Court tomb plans. (A) Full court tomb at Creevykeel, Co. Sligo. (B) Dual court tomb (with two four-chambered galleries) at Audleystown, Co. Down: the chambers in the north-eastern gallery are numbered 1–4, those in the south-western gallery 5–8. (C) Dual court tomb at Cohaw, Co. Cavan: post-holes in courts not shown. (D) Open court tomb with a single chamber at Ballymacaldrack, Co. Antrim, and pits of mortuary structure north-east of the chamber. (E) Transeptal court tomb at Behy, Co. Mayo.

chamber and slopes to a height of about 1m towards the rear of the monument. Several cairns show such a decrease in height from front of chamber to rear of monument.

Courts are usually defined by orthostats, and occasionally dry walling fills gaps between these stones. Courts of dry walling alone are rare. As the name suggests, open courts are concave: often one-half or perhaps two-thirds of a circle, sometimes slightly U-shaped as at Tully. The court gives access to the burial gallery, the entrance to which is sometimes flanked by two of the tallest stones of the façade of the court, usually a matching pair, which narrow the entry and form a sort of portal suitable for a lintel stone.

As already mentioned, galleries often comprise

two chambers but three- and four-chambered examples are known. Chambers are rectangular, occasionally subrectangular, perhaps with slightly concave sides (as at Annaghmare). Galleries are segmented or divided into chambers by pairs of jamb stones or a combination or jamb stones and sill stone. Jamb stones are upright stones, usually a matched pair, and they may be set against or inset into the side walls. Sill stones, those low transverse slabs set on edge in the floor (as seen in the Mound of the Hostages passage tomb), are sometimes placed between the jamb stones. Evidence for corbel roofing of the chambers is fairly common— several oversailing corbels survived at Ballyglass, Co. Mayo, and at Audleystown, Co. Down, for example. Back stones of galleries are occasionally pointed to a gable shape quite suitable for supporting corbelling. Use of corbels in this fashion would probably have demanded a substantial covering cairn to hold them and the roof stones in place.

A number of open and full court tombs have subsidiary chambers at right angles to the long axis of the cairn and opening onto the sides of the monument (such as Annaghmare—Fig. 3.15). They are normally of simple rectilinear plan, sometimes narrowing towards the rear; a pair of jamb stones (sometimes with long axes parallel to the long axis of the chamber) form a portal at the entrance, and in some examples a sill stone is placed between the jambs. Little evidence for the form of roofing of these subsidiary chambers has survived, but at Annaghmare one was corbel-roofed and several courses of corbelling were noted.

Single court tombs, whether with full or open courts, show a definite preference in orientation. In a clear majority of cases the broader court end faces in a general eastward direction, mostly between north-north-east and south-east. This possibly represents an alignment on the rising sun, which in these latitudes would give a splay of some 80° between summer and winter positions.

Elaboration of the basic open court plan may have produced the full court tomb in which the court is of more or less oval plan with a narrow entry terminally placed opposite the entrance to the gallery. At Creevykeel, near Cliffony, Co. Sligo (Fig. 3.16A), a narrow orthostatic passage 4.5m long connects the large court (14m by 9m) with the frontal façade, and it is possible that this passage may once have been roofed. Here too a difference in the

size of the orthostats of the court clearly differentiates the concave section at the tomb entrance from the rest. A few tombs of this type have a frontal concave forecourt as well.

A rare variant, the central court tomb, combines at least two tombs with a full centrally placed court with lateral entry. Ballyglass, Co. Mayo (Fig. 3.15), is a well-known example with a large pair of out-turned stones forming an entrance to the court, which is just over 11m long and has a two-chambered gallery at both its western and eastern ends. A drystone revetment delimited the long cairn that enclosed the court and probably once covered the tombs.

Dual court tombs appear to be another elaboration of the basic tomb plan (the two-chambered monument with open court) in which two galleries are placed back to back. Two-chambered galleries are normal but a few dual court tombs with pairs of three- or four-chambered galleries are known. Cohaw, near Cootehill, Co. Cavan (Fig. 3.16C), consists of a pair of two-chambered galleries (each segmented by jambs and sills) and separated one from the other by a closed chamber. Sometimes the galleries share a common back stone and sometimes they are simply separated by a large or small gap. Audleystown, Co. Down (Fig. 3.16B), unusual in having a pair of four-chambered galleries, has an intervening gap of just over 2m.

Regional preferences are discernible for different features of the court tomb series: the elaborate full court tombs and the central court variant (both consistently having two-chambered galleries) are to be found in the north-west, mostly in Mayo, Sligo and Donegal (Fig. 3.15). Open courts predominate elsewhere. Dual court tombs are mainly found in central and southern Ulster: a few examples are recorded in the Mayo–Sligo area and in eastern Ulster, but the majority occur in a broad region embracing the counties of Leitrim, Cavan, Monaghan, Fermanagh and Tyrone. A small number of court tombs in the Mayo–Sligo area have the unusual feature of one or two side chambers opening like transepts from the main gallery. These transeptal court tombs mainly have full courts of orthostatic construction. One tomb, at least, has an unusual drystone court. At Behy, Co. Mayo (Fig. 3.16E), excavation has revealed a long subrectangular cairn with an oval full court of dry walling leading through a lintelled entrance into a gallery divided into two by a pair of jambs and a high sill stone. An opposed pair of transeptal chambers open off the inner part of the gallery. Some regional bias in orientation is also apparent: the eastern rule for single court tombs is fairly constant in the west of the court tomb province but adherence to this custom is less marked in the east, notably in County Armagh.

In spite of damage and disturbance to many tombs, excavation has produced some interesting and puzzling evidence for burial and other ritual practices. A number of sites bear witness to collective burial but some have yielded little or no burial evidence. Browndod, Co. Antrim (Evans and Davies 1935), Goward, Co. Down (Davies and Evans 1933), Kilnagarns Lower, Co. Leitrim (Corcoran 1964), and Bavan, Co. Donegal (Flanagan and Flanagan 1966), for example, have yielded no trace of bone—but with the possible exception of Goward, all were extensively disturbed. In contrast, the much-damaged tomb at Tully, Co. Fermanagh, still contained the sparse remains of four individuals, all cremated, in the two-chambered gallery (Waterman 1978). It is possible, if burials were not destroyed by disturbance, that unburnt bones might have simply decayed without trace in certain circumstances. In the relatively well-preserved open court tomb at Ballymacdermot, Co. Armagh, for instance, the innermost two of the three chambers of the gallery were used for burial but only a few very small fragments of burnt bone survived, and here the acid soil conditions of the area would have been inimical to the preservation of unburnt bone. Phosphate analysis within and outside the gallery demonstrated a significantly high concentration in the inner chamber and, while this could be due to the deposition of material from a phosphate-rich context such as a settlement area, enrichment could be caused by the decay of skeletal material, a conclusion favoured by the excavators. Charcoal samples from the burial gallery produced radiocarbon determinations suggesting a date towards the middle of the fourth millennium BC (Collins and Wilson 1964; Jones 2007). The two chambers in Creevykeel, Co. Sligo (Hencken 1939; Jones 2007), each contained small deposits of cremated bone, but no human remains were found in the subsidiary chambers towards the rear of the tomb (Fig. 3.16).

Unburnt bones have been found on a few occasions: for instance, at Ballyalton, Co. Down, the very fragmentary bones of at least six individuals were recovered (Evans and Davies 1934), numerous unburnt bones were found at Audleystown, Co. Down (below), and some teeth and a fragmentary skull of one or two individuals came from Cohaw, Co. Cavan (Kilbride-Jones 1951). Cremated remains were also found at the latter two sites. Cremation is recorded from a majority of the excavated court tombs to yield human bone. Five or six individuals were represented at Ballymacaldrack, Co. Antrim (Evans 1938), and a minimum of two at Clady Halliday, Co. Tyrone (Davies and Radford 1936); at Cohaw, aside from the unburnt bone just mentioned, the burnt bones of a child were found, and possibly two or more individuals at Barnes Lower, Co. Tyrone (Collins 1966). As mentioned, there were four at Tully, Co. Fermanagh, and a few fragments of the bones of two children were all that was recovered from the large dual court tomb at Aghanaglack, Co. Fermanagh (Davies 1939a; Jones 2007). Creggandevesky, Co. Tyrone, produced cremated bone representing 21 individuals, and the bone was so fragmentary it may have been deliberately crushed after burning; here again acid soil may have destroyed unburnt bones (Foley 1988). Given the fragmentary nature of most of this evidence and the difficulties involved in the ageing and sexing of cremated bone, most if not all of these figures for court tombs are possibly minimal ones.

Particularly interesting funerary and ritual information comes from a small number of excavations. Carleton Jones's meticulous examination of a court tomb at Parknabinnia in the Burren, Co. Clare, with very detailed recording of each and every bone fragment recovered, allowed the use of GIS (Geographical Information Systems) to precisely map and analyse their distribution and with the application of re-fitting studies to track bone movement in the tomb. It appears that people moved disarticulated bone around in episodes of tomb-cleaning and further deposition: larger bones were moved more and smaller bones tended to stay closer to where they were first placed. A small number showed signs of cremation, and some material from funeral pyres was probably placed in the tomb as well. Use seems to have spanned the period from 3600 BC to 2800 BC. Some nineteen individuals were represented and included males, females and children. It seems that where unburnt burial was the norm in megalithic tombs like this, a protracted pattern of continuous disturbance and destruction of earlier burials coupled with the normal process of decay might result in misleadingly low numbers of surviving body parts (Beckett 2005; Beckett and Robb 2006).

The dual court tomb at Audleystown on the shore of Strangford Lough, Co. Down, had a trapezoidal cairn (Fig. 3.16B) retained by a drystone revetment (Collins 1954; 1959b; Jones 2007). Shallow courts and four-chambered galleries faced north-east and south-west respectively. Traces of at least partial corbel roofing of the galleries were found: it was not possible to ascertain whether corbelling alone completed the roof or whether a combination of corbelling and lintelling was employed. Each gallery was about 10m in length, 1.2m in width and, when empty, about 1.2–1.5m in height; the space between jamb stones varied from 30cm to 60cm. The two inner chambers, nos 3 and 4, of the north-eastern gallery were empty, except for the remains of a fire in no. 3. Burial deposits were found in the other six chambers, though in nos 5 and 7 in the south-western gallery they had suffered some disturbance. Only cremated bone had survived in no. 5, but in the other chambers there was a 15–30cm-thick and compact deposit of earth, or earth and stones, and cremated and unburnt human bone. Numerous fragments of pottery and some flint implements were mixed through these deposits, which were packed down and sealed with stones. A few animal bones—including cattle, horse, sheep or goat and pig—were also found.

The human remains from the tomb were unburnt, partially burnt and fully cremated and represented approximately 34 individuals. A majority of these (21 or 22) were represented by unburnt bones that had been placed in a defleshed condition, sometimes in small, neatly arranged groups, at all levels in the burial deposits (which contained burnt bone throughout). The remains were those of adults, both male and female, and children. The pottery found was all fragmentary and comprised plain and decorated round-bottomed pots of both Lyles Hill style and Decorated Bowl style (including Goodland bowl and Carrowkeel ware). Flint implements included scrapers, leaf- and lozenge-shaped arrowheads, plano-convex knives and a lozenge-shaped javelin-head. While the

number of persons in Audleystown was large enough to suggest successive burials in the tomb over a period of time, details such as the disarticulated nature of the bones, implying storage elsewhere, and the difficulties involved in re-entering the galleries led the excavator, A. E. P. Collins, to conclude that a single collective burial was the more likely possibility. A complex sequence of events of unknown duration is certainly indicated: there was possible evidence for the burning of the site before the tomb was built, burning within some of the chambers, deposition of the burial deposits, and then placing of packing stones on top of this. There seems to have been a tendency for a greater number of children and adult females to be deposited in an unburnt condition, but among the identifiable adult bones men were more than twice as common as women (Cooney 1992a).

Annaghmare, near Crossmaglen, Co. Armagh (Fig. 3.15), is a single court tomb with open court and three-chambered gallery. It also had a pair of subsidiary chambers placed back to back near the rear of a trapezoidal cairn, which was just 20m in length, 11.5m wide at the southern end and 6.5m wide at the northern rear end (Waterman 1965; Jones 2007). The 5.5m-deep forecourt was well preserved and was constructed of orthostats with dry stonework between them, in the so-called post-and-panel technique of building. A matching pair of 1.28m-tall orthostats flanked the entrance to the gallery, which, as excavation revealed, had been deliberately blocked with horizontally laid flagstones; these filled much of the court, sloping away from the portal. The blocking extended into the gallery for at least 1m or so; its full extent was not ascertainable because the outer chamber had been disturbed and a potsherd, a flint scraper and a few scraps of burnt bone were all that remained of its original contents.

In the inner chamber (approximately 1.65m by 1.28m) the burial deposit consisted of a 38cm-thick homogeneous filling of stones, soil, fragments of burnt human bone, a few scraps of animal bone, sherds of three decorated round-bottomed pots, six flint concave scrapers and charcoal. In the middle chamber (measuring approximately 2.4m by 1.2m) the filling consisted almost entirely of stones with just a little dark soil. Small fragments of burnt bone were mixed through this filling and a few further sherds of two of the pots discovered in the inner chamber were also found, along with a flint javelin-head, several concave scrapers and a convex scraper. On this stone filling lay a few unburnt bones of a child and a femur of an adult; these were the only unburnt remains found in the gallery. The burnt bone may represent one child and at least one adult but certainty was not possible. Examination of the subsidiary chambers at the northern end revealed that the eastern one had been dug out in recent times and all but one of the stones on one side removed. The western chamber, with orthostatic concave sides and portal stones narrowing the entrance, had been corbel-roofed. No traces of burials were found and phosphate values were normal.

In attempting to discover the sockets of the missing side stones of the eastern subsidiary chamber, the excavation exposed a drystone revetment surviving to a maximum height of 90cm. This wall seems to have been the back of the cairn as first planned and built, and the monument was evidently extended at some later time to accommodate the additional subsidiary chambers. This evidence for multi-period construction at Annaghmare is interesting and suggests continuing interest in and activity at the tomb over a period of time. One radiocarbon date of 3308–2914 BC obtained from charcoal behind the court blocking gives no hint, of course, of the possible duration of this activity. Both the position of several stones in the court blocking and the size of the gallery suggested to the excavator that re-entry was theoretically possible even with the burial deposits in place. Thus intermittent accumulation of these deposits over a period of time could have occurred, and the presence of sherds of the same pot in different chambers could be explained by the disturbance and relocation of the tomb contents. Since, however, the sherds of one pot in the inner chamber were found from top to bottom of the filling, the excavator, Dudley Waterman, concluded that the deposit was introduced in a single act, remaining undisturbed and unaugmented; in other words, the mixture of stone, earth, burnt bone, potsherds and charcoal were collected elsewhere and placed in the tomb as a unitary deposit.

Aside from the question of a single or collective deposit, the very nature of the Annaghmare deposit is intriguing. In an analysis of some fifteen court tomb fillings which were seemingly undisturbed, including Annaghmare, Humphrey Case (1973) noted the consistent occurrence of earth often containing bone, charcoal, stones and fragments of incomplete pots. Pottery was evidently deliberately deposited as sherds, and the absence of complete burials, either unburnt skeletons or entire cremations, raises the possibility that these monuments were not merely—or even primarily—sepulchral, and they may have been exercises in sympathetic magic. He suggested that the earth and pottery fragments might represent settlement debris buried as part of some magic rites for the needs of the living and possibly connected with fertility. He was struck by the resemblances between the contents of some court tombs and the contents of pits at a ritual site at Goodland, Co. Antrim (Chapter 4). Rather than deriving from a settlement, it is even possible that this material may be sacred soil from some other ritual site.

It is not difficult to see court tombs as both tombs and shrines of some description. As tombs, the cult of the dead may have never involved the full and formal burial of all members of the community. As cult places, various rituals may have taken place not just within but also outside the monument. It is generally assumed, for instance, that the unroofed courts had some ceremonial purpose, perhaps serving as a space between the world of the living and the domain of the ancestors. Traces of fires, fragments of pottery and evidence of blocking from some sites have all been generally considered indications of ritual practice. A few pits of uncertain purpose have been found. A small standing stone in the forecourt at Ballymarlagh, Co. Antrim (Davies 1949), a larger one in the court of Browndod, Co. Antrim, and another small example set in the blocking material at Annaghmare may have some ritual significance. At Creggandevesky, Co. Tyrone, cremated human bone was found in front of the tomb's entrance, and what was thought to be the remains of a fire had been placed in the middle of the forecourt. A fallen pair of tall, slender stones were thought to have once stood in the northern court at Cohaw, Co. Cavan, where excavation also revealed a series of post-holes, mostly just over 30cm in depth, placed at intervals across the fronts of both courts; their purpose may well have been to screen or close the courts and exclude some people.

A tomb with quite a narrow paved court at Shanballyedmond, Co. Tipperary, had its cairn delimited by a series of 34 spaced timber posts, which for the most part had diameters of 25–30cm (O'Kelly 1958a). These posts had, it seems, no functional purpose and a ritual explanation is likely—totem poles of some description is not an impossibility. A fire had been burnt for some hours in the outermost of the two chambers of the gallery; in the inner chamber a large pit in the floor also had a fire burnt in it, the ashes removed and some cremated bone of a young male then placed therein.

The creation of the full court at Creevykeel and the extension of the Annaghmare cairn to incorporate subsidiary chambers presumably reflect different secondary ritual requirements. Possible multi-period construction was also inferred in the much-disturbed court tomb at Barnes Lower, near Plumbridge, Co. Tyrone, where a two-chambered gallery (with traces of a slightly convex façade) may have been extended to form a four-chambered gallery with a flat façade. The trapezoidal cairn contained four, perhaps five, subsidiary chambers. Unusual ritual evidence comes from excavations in 1935 and 1975 at Ballymacaldrack, near Dunloy, Co. Antrim (Evans 1938; Collins 1976; Jones 2007). This tomb had a semicircular court and a single-chambered gallery (Fig. 3.16D). Occasional fragments of pottery were found scattered throughout a blocking of stones in the forecourt. Two polished stone axes were also found in this sealing material. The chamber contained a 90cm-deep deposit of earth and stones, and finds included potsherds, two lozenge-shaped flint arrowheads and a bead of serpentine. A few fragmentary animal teeth were found but no human remains. A paved and stone-lined trench was found behind the chamber, aligned on the same axis; this trench measured 6.5m in length, some 90cm in depth and 1–1.3m in width. Three roughly oval pits occurred in the floor of the trench: one in the middle and one at either end. These pits may have contained timber posts but possible traces of one or two posts were detected only in the westernmost pit, though all three contained stones that could have served as packing stones. The trench contained a large amount of charcoal, fire-cracked stones, pottery fragments, a calcined leaf-shaped flint arrowhead, and cremated human bone representing five or six adult individuals. Charcoal from the trench has given radiocarbon dates of 3930–3640 BC and 4226–3708 BC.

Axial pits containing traces of large timber posts have been found in some contemporary British burial mounds, and these and other features are considered to be the remains of mortuary structures of wood and other materials, built as a temporary protection for the human remains. In Scotland and in northern England these were sometimes burnt and, while the Ballymacaldrack evidence admits of no clear explanation, some sort of structure or structures may have been burnt and human remains may have been cremated in place. This does illustrate the point that there were some non-megalithic funerary practices perhaps eclipsed by the more visible megalithic tradition (Sheridan 2006), and it has been suggested that a wooden structure found in a bog near Inver, Co. Donegal, in the nineteenth century could have been a Neolithic mortuary house like Ballymacaldrack (Coles and Coles 1989). Gabriel Cooney (2000) has proposed a complex four-phase sequence at Ballymacaldrack: a wooden mortuary structure, possibly burnt as part of a cremation ritual (phase 1), was followed by the construction of a paved rectangular structure above the pits that was surrounded by some cairn material (phase 2). The court tomb was then built (phase 3) and used for the deposition of culturally significant material, and was then formally sealed (phase 4). A further puzzling feature at Ballymacaldrack is the collapse of at least one of the court orthostats early in the history of the tomb and prior to the deposition of the blocking. This and other evidence of early collapse at Ballymacdermot and Audleystown seem to suggest some lack of interest in cairn maintenance on the part of these tomb-builders. In some cases the more important act may just have been the construction of the monument.

In contrast to passage tombs, art is very rarely found in court tombs: a lozenge was carved on a loose stone found on the surface of the cairn at Goward, Co. Down, and two orthostats of a fine court tomb at Malin More, Co. Donegal, are also decorated with motifs including arcs, a lozenge and curving lines (Shee Twohig 1981).

A range of pottery and flint types occurs. Some or all may have been intended as funerary offerings but, in the light of the suggestion that some tombs may have settlement or other debris incorporated in their contents, it is worth bearing in mind that the term 'grave-goods' may not be the most appropriate. The pottery comprises both plain and decorated wares, invariably represented by sherds of incomplete vessels; the Carinated Bowl, Decorated Bowl and Bipartite Bowl styles are all represented, and a majority of the excavated examples have yielded sherds of decorated pottery. The range of pottery types found has led to suggestions that these tombs were in use over a period of several centuries but, as we have seen, the contents of their chambers often present interpretative problems and stratigraphical evidence, when present, is rarely conclusive. Various flint types occur and they occasionally show signs of burning; flint arrowheads, scrapers and knives are the commonest items found. The arrowheads are of the characteristic lozenge or leaf-shaped forms. Larger javelin-heads are known from over a dozen sites and for the most part these are of lozenge shape. Several are leaf-shaped, however, and one of these finely worked flints from Creevykeel, Co. Sligo, is an oval specimen 13cm in length. Broad oval examples such as this one could have served as projectile heads, but use as a knife is a possibility. Double-edged flint knives, sometimes of fine workmanship, have been found in a number of court tombs: two complete, finely made plano-convex flint knives (and the fire-damaged tips of two others) were found in Barnes Lower, Co. Tyrone (Fig. 2.15), and one comes from Ballybriest, Co. Derry. Less well-finished knives have also been found, as at Audleystown, Co. Down.

Quite a number of the excavated tombs have produced flint scrapers of both the concave scraper and convex scraper varieties. No less than fourteen concave scrapers (four of them burnt) were found in Annaghmare, Co. Armagh, all but one from the burial gallery. This tomb also produced one convex scraper. A few monuments have yielded stone axes: two small and rather poorly chipped axes of flint, found with a hoard of other flints, come from Ballyalton, Co. Down, and among the several examples of polished stone are two of Antrim porcellanite from Ballymarlagh, Co. Antrim, and two from Ballymacaldrack, Co. Antrim. The latter were found in the blocking material at the entrance and were possibly ceremonial offerings: the excavator suggested that they were 'the magic guardians of the tomb'. An axe of polished diorite

was also found in the forecourt at Creevykeel, Co. Sligo. Among the other artefacts occasionally found are various form of beads: usually of simple disc shape, as from Ballymacaldrack and Creevykeel. Two almost spherical beads of polished schist and a larger almost lozenge-shaped bead of similar material were found in the chamber at Bavan, Co. Donegal. The lozenge-shaped stone bead, with a length of 5.8cm, has a 5mm-wide longitudinal perforation. Another similarly perforated schist bead from Tully, Co. Fermanagh, has a length of 8cm, and Waterman suggested that the narrow cylindrical perforation was probably pierced through a larger mass of rock, which was then reduced to the requisite size and shape. The drilling demanded considerable stone-working ability. Similar beads were found in a portal tomb at Ballyrenan, Co. Tyrone (Davies 1937). A necklace of 112 stone beads is reported from Creggandevesky, Co. Tyrone.

Radiocarbon dates from a small number of court tombs suggest that these monuments, like some passage tombs, are essentially a feature of the fourth millennium BC (Sheridan 2003c). Few of these dates come from samples that are certainly coeval with the period of construction and primary use, but it is clear that the two tomb types were at least partly contemporary. The burning of the mortuary structure at Ballymacaldrack could have occurred around 4000 BC, and the blocking material of the megalithic tomb was possibly placed in position (or at least interfered with) some centuries later. The late fourth-millennium BC date for the blocking at Annaghmare, Co. Armagh, provides a terminal date for the tomb, and a series of dates for the house that pre-dated Ballyglass, Co. Mayo, may indicate a date in the early third millennium BC for that monument. Dates from pre-cairn samples from the dual court tomb of Ballybriest, Co. Derry, imply a construction date sometime in the fourth millennium BC for at least the eastern part of this monument. The radiocarbon evidence indicates that Ballymacdermot, Co. Armagh, was in use towards the middle of the fourth millennium BC. Dates from the chamber and forecourt at Tully, Co. Fermanagh, and from Shanballyedmond, Co. Tipperary, imply the same.

A relationship between court tombs and similar megalithic tombs in England and Wales (Cotswold–Severn tombs) and in Scotland (Clyde tombs) has been recognised for many years, and the derivation of the Irish tombs from the latter south-western Scottish monuments was generally assumed. Given that the knowledge of animal husbandry and cereal cultivation did spread westwards across Europe, the concomitant diffusion of certain tomb types, built by these early farmers, was a reasonable belief. Terms such as the Clyde–Carlingford culture or group emphasised the relationship of the Scottish and Irish monuments, but with the realisation that the bulk of the Irish examples were to be found not in the north-east but in the north-west, Ruaidhrí de Valera proposed a controversial alternative theory (1960; 1965). The density of the north-western distribution and the occurrence there of complex full and central court tombs were some of the factors that led him to suggest that these tombs were introduced along with the landfall of early farming communities on the shores of Mayo and Sligo. From this supposed primary focus court tomb-builders were thought to have spread eastwards, and the transeptal tombs suggested that their origins should be sought in north-western France, where a small number of transeptal passage tombs are to be found. Variations in tomb morphology were considered to represent a typological devolution from complex tombs in the west to simpler monuments in the east, reflecting a corresponding movement of early farming groups. The presence of fragments of plain, shouldered round-bottomed pottery in many tombs seemed to support the notion that these megaliths were built by pioneering farming colonists. This suggestion, though widely promulgated, never found general acceptance. The absence of suitable prototypes in north-western France for Irish forecourts, for example, as well as differences in pottery styles and flintwork, and the implausibility of seaborne landings in a very restricted area of the Atlantic coast of western Ireland were just some of the reasons for its rejection (Waddell 1978). General similarities in tomb plan, pottery and flintwork point—as has long been recognised—to a complex pattern of relationships with Scotland and England.

With the knowledge in recent years that early farming communities were widely scattered throughout the country some time before court tombs were constructed, the diffusion or adoption of these tombs need no longer be associated with the arrival or spread of pioneering agriculturalists.

Their origins may be more complex and various suggestions have been offered. They may, for instance, be elaborate translations into stone of the idea of a timber mortuary structure (ApSimon 1997), and thus, it has been argued, early megalithic tombs in Scotland may have been relatively simple quadrangular structures, with forecourts, long cairns and further chambers being later and more elaborate additions. The provision of a pair of prominent portal stones at one end of such a simple megalith would produce a monument akin to a portal tomb (below) and, indeed, it is suggested that in Ireland such a monument may have evolved into the court tomb. Indications of separate constructional phases in the history of particular monuments (as at Annaghmare, Ballymacaldrack and Barnes Lower) indicate just how varied and complicated the story of any one court tomb's development may be. It has been suggested that tomb design may be a reflection of the social organisation of a community. A. B. Powell (2005) has proposed that the linear segmented gallery may have housed elements of a descent group or lineage (descended from a common ancestor), and that complex arrangements like dual court tombs might represent a combination of lineages. The various features of long mound and tomb that together characterise these megaliths are found singly or in differing combinations in a variety of funerary monuments from southern England to northern Scotland. Behind the parallels and distinctions that can be recognised there must lie complicated tales of kinship and regional contacts, as well as of parallel evolution and divergence in both islands.

PORTAL TOMBS

Although the portal tomb is invariably a structure of simple plan, some of these monuments are remarkable examples of megalithic engineering. A majority have a single subrectangular chamber with an entrance flanked by a pair of tall portal stones (Fig. 3.17). The tomb is usually covered by a single capstone, sometimes of massive proportions, and, as far as can be judged from rather limited evidence, cairns are of elongated, perhaps subrectangular form, but short oval and round cairns also exist (Ó Nualláin 1983; Cody 2002; Kytmannow 2008).

Only a very few of the 180 or so Irish portal

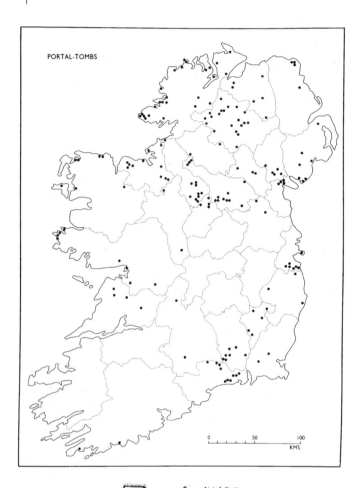

PORTAL-TOMBS

0   50   100
KMS.

Fig. 3.17—Above: general distribution of portal tombs. Below: plan and section of a portal tomb at Drumanone, Co. Roscommon, with the front of the large capstone resting on the portal stones.

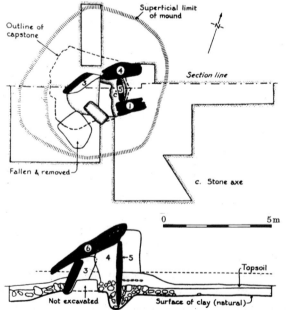

Superficial limit of mound

Outline of capstone

Section line

-N-

c. Stone axe

Fallen & removed

0   5 m

Topsoil

Not excavated   Surface of clay (natural)

tombs have been scientifically excavated and, because so many tombs of this class have been denuded of cairn material, the original form of the great majority of cairns is unknown. Indeed, even in the few excavated examples either partial excavation or poor preservation has meant that the original cairn shape could not be accurately ascertained, but long mounds, longer than necessary just to cover the tomb, are reliably attested at about one-sixth of the sites. Ballykeel, Co. Armagh, for example, had the remains of a long, subrectangular cairn, some 28m in length, with the tomb situated at the southern end (Collins 1965; Jones 2007). Normally just one tomb is terminally placed in this fashion but in a few cases there is more than one. Two portal tombs, both facing in the same direction, occurred one behind the other in a 13.7m-long cairn at Ballyrenan, Co. Tyrone (Davies 1937). Subsidiary chambers have been noted in some cairns. Excavations at a destroyed tomb at Melkagh, Co. Longford, revealed that the cairn may have been retained by a low drystone wall (Cooney 1997).

Chambers are usually subrectangular in plan, narrowing towards the rear, but a few tombs broaden towards the rear. Both sides and ends are often formed of single orthostats, and end stones are occasionally gabled as in court tombs. At the entrance a pair of massive portal stones are set inside the line of the side stones; these portal stones are usually the tallest and most imposing orthostats in the structure. In some tombs the space between the portals is closed with a large slab (as with stone 5 at Drumanone, near Boyle, Co. Roscommon: Fig. 3.17); occasionally a sill stone about half the height of the portals is present, and lower sills also occur. In many cases no evidence of closure, either partial or full, survives.

A large single capstone is often used to roof the tomb, resting on portals and end stone. When one end of the capstone is larger than the other, the more massive end is usually poised on the portals, no doubt to give further emphasis to the front of the tomb. Capstones of extraordinary size and weighing many tons were sometimes used. The largest is said to be that at Kernanstown, Brownshill, Co. Carlow, estimated to weigh over 100 tons (Fig. 3.18). Some denuded tombs, such as Proleek, Co. Louth, where all that survives is a huge capstone of 30–40 tons perched on two portals and a back stone, are imposing reminders of their builders' skill. It is not known how such impressive stones were transported and raised, but it is assumed that they were pulled by men and perhaps oxen, with the use

Fig. 3.18—A nineteenth-century depiction of the portal tomb with gigantic capstone at Kernanstown, Brownshill, Co. Carlow.

of ropes and timber sleds or rollers. While ropes and levers may all have been used to raise large orthostats like some of the portal stones, the larger capstones must have presented considerable engineering problems. These large stones may have been hauled up ramps of earth or stone (and some long cairns may have been thus employed), or they may have been lifted in stages by means of levers and timber platforms or cribs raised gradually to the required height.

The side stones of the chamber do not normally reach the capstone, and it has been suggested that these spaces may have been filled by corbelling. As already mentioned, one capstone is the norm, but occasionally a small second capstone occurs below the larger one and in a few instances two-chambered tombs have been recorded, as in one of the tombs at Ballyrenan, Co. Tyrone, which is divided in two by a large slab. Another very rare feature, perhaps reminiscent of the courts of court tombs, is the presence of some stones flanking the portals. The orientation of portal tombs seems to be fairly variable, though a number face in a general eastern direction, sometimes uphill. Some are located in valleys, often near streams as at Ballykeel. The siting of some tombs in sheltered valleys has provoked the suggestion that certain tomb-builders were exploiting some more heavily wooded lowland sites. A majority of portal tombs are found in the northern half of the country: a thin scatter of examples lies in the north-west, an area also favoured by court tomb-builders. A significant number of portal tombs occur in Donegal, Tyrone and Derry, and the type is represented in Cavan and Monaghan and eastwards to Down and Louth. A few are known in Mayo, Galway and Clare, where many are quite close to the coast, and a major group occurs well outside the court tomb province in Leinster and Waterford. Portal tombs are also known in Wales and Cornwall.

Finds are recorded from a small number of these monuments but few have been scientifically excavated in recent years. The examination of Ballykeel, near Camlough, Co. Armagh, yielded some interesting results. Here a long cairn measuring about 28m long and 9m in average width contained a tomb at its southern end. The cairn had been damaged in places but survived to a height of some 75cm. Several cuttings revealed that it was more than an amorphous dump of stones:

leaning pairs of stones propped together formed a sort of spine along the central long axis, and parallel to this were two symmetrical pairs of lines of stones which in places formed a flimsy wall three courses high. The inner stone rows were clearly buried features, their purpose unknown, but the outer two, in the excavator's opinion, originally may have delimited the cairn. The tomb survived as a large capstone resting on twin portals (averaging 2m in height) and on a back stone that had collapsed inwards. A large slab in front of the portals had once closed the entrance. There were no side stones and excavation revealed no suggestion that there ever were any. (If, however, like the back stone, they had been placed in a shallow bedding of stones indistinguishable from the cairn material itself, their former presence would have been virtually undetectable.) It is also possible that some light timberwork might have served as side walling, for the distribution of finds within the chamber area did suggest some sort of containment. Hundreds of sherds of pottery were recovered as well as three flints, but no bone, either burnt or unburnt. Acidic soil conditions may well have destroyed unburnt bones. Phosphate analysis did reveal extremely high concentrations in the chamber area compared to nearby fields, but the likelihood of localised rabbit activity contributing to the inflated phosphate values was recognised.

A small amount of plain shouldered, round-bottomed pottery was found inside and outside the chamber; it may be a relic of pre-tomb activity on the site but it is also conceivable that an attempt to clear out the contents of the tomb was made on some occasion. The fragmentary pottery consisted mainly of sherds of four finely decorated Bipartite Bowls and numerous sherds of plain, coarse, flat-bottomed pots. Sherds of coarse ware, all possibly from the one pot, came from the body of the cairn on its long axis, along with some charcoal. Charcoal also from the body of the cairn provided a radiocarbon date of 1742–1526 BC and might indicate a second-millennium BC date for the plain pottery. The remains of a cist, a small, slab-built, subrectangular structure measuring about 1m in internal length, were found near the northern end of the cairn. No capstone survived and the cist had been rifled in the past: no trace of any burial was found, but it did contain a few sherds of a Goodland bowl, a flint flake and a flint javelin-head.

Exceptional information has been recovered from the portal tomb at Poulnabrone in the Burren, Co. Clare. Excavation by Ann Lynch in 1986 and 1988 (Lynch 1988; Lynch and Ó Donnabháin 1994; Jones 2007) revealed that the side stones of the rectangular chamber simply rested on bedrock and were kept in place by the weight of the large capstone. A broken sill stone between the portals had been set in a gryke or crevice; its original height is unknown but it could have been large enough to close the entrance. Three slabs had been set on edge just outside this entrance and formed a small antechamber that had been filled with earth and stones and marked the limit of the edge of the cairn; its purpose is not clear. The surrounding cairn was approximately oval in plan and consisted mainly of large limestone slabs extending about 3m from the tomb and laid against the sides of the chamber. No trace of a kerb was found and it seems that the cairn may never have been more than about 55cm in height. It would have mainly served to support the chamber orthostats, and the tomb with its soaring capstone would always have been visible. The soil in the chamber was about 25cm in depth and this deposit and the grykes beneath contained numerous unburnt human bones and some animal bones; the latter included bones of cattle, pig, sheep or goat, dog, hare, stoat, pine marten, woodmouse and bird. The human remains represented at least 22 individuals, sixteen adults and six children. The bones, many of which had been jammed into the grykes, were disarticulated and had obviously been deposited in a defleshed condition. Since no cut-marks were noted, deliberate defleshing seems unlikely and, since even smaller bones were represented, exposure (allowing the bones to be dispersed by scavenging animals and birds) may not have been practised either. The remains could have been stored elsewhere and periodically transferred with some care to the tomb. Less than 50% of all skeletal elements were present, and the over-representation of small bones and corresponding under-representation of crania and long bones might indicate that the latter were deliberately removed or retained for curation or use elsewhere (Beckett and Robb 2006).

Ten radiocarbon dates obtained from samples of human bone have provided interesting information about the extent and duration of burial practice. Excluding the complete skeleton of one newborn child buried in a gryke beneath the antechamber that proved to be a later, second-millennium insertion, the dates suggest that burials were deposited at regular intervals over a period of 600 years between about 3800 and 3200 BC, though it could be that they were all kept elsewhere and transferred to this location as one major deposit around 3200 BC (Cooney 2000). The fragmentary state of the bones made it difficult to age and sex them accurately. Males and females were equally represented among the eight adults whose sex could be determined. Most of the adults were quite young, dying before the age of 30; only one was more than 40 years old. Apart from a couple of infants, most of the children were aged between five and fifteen. The numbers and the age and sex profile suggest that the remains are those of a select sample of a community chosen at various times over some six centuries for the special privilege of being reburied in this tomb. Some of the bones were scorched and the burning pattern shows that this was done when the bone was dry; they may have been purified by fire as part of the reburial process.

Why just some adults and children were selected is not obvious. Evidence of arthritic conditions indicates that the adults led physically active lives, carrying heavy loads, and though they merited special treatment after death, they were not spared the normal stresses and strains of everyday existence. One adult male had the tip of a flint or chert projectile embedded in a hip bone; there was no trace of infection or healing, so the wound occurred at the time of death. Two healed fractures, one on a skull, the other on a rib, were the sort of injuries usually produced by aggressive blows rather than by accidents. Dental wear suggested a diet that included stone-ground cereals. Artefacts placed with the burials included a triangular bone pendant, part of a mushroom-headed bone pin, a polished stone axe, two stone beads, several flint and chert implements and over 60 sherds of plain coarse pottery.

Traces of burials have been found in several other portal tombs—usually small quantities of cremated human bone. Burnt bone was recovered from the disturbed chamber at Drumanone, Co. Roscommon, but it was too fragmentary to permit any estimate of the number of individuals represented (Topp 1962). The only other significant find in the chamber was a small polished stone axe of Antrim porcellanite, which was found close to the inner face of the large closing slab. Cremated human bone was also found in excavations at Aghnaskeagh, Co. Louth (Evans 1935; Jones 2007), and Ballyrenan, Co. Tyrone, for example. Finds of pottery of Lyles Hill style and of Bipartite Bowl style from these tombs are similar in quite a few respects to those from court tombs (Herity 1982).

Stone implements have also been found, of course, but again not in great numbers. The polished stone axes from Drumanone and Poulnabrone have been mentioned, and flints include a small number of leaf-shaped arrowheads, convex scrapers and concave scrapers from several tombs. A chert concave-based arrowhead comes from a tomb at Kiltiernan, Co. Dublin. A few stone beads are known: simple disc-shaped beads were found in Poulnabrone, in Clonlum, Co. Armagh, and Ballyrenan, Co. Tyrone. The latter tomb also produced two longitudinally perforated ovoid beads of polished schist similar to those from the court tombs at Bavan, Co. Donegal, and Tully, Co. Fermanagh.

Some relationship between court tomb and portal tomb has long been recognised and various writers have thought that the latter evolved from the former. In 1960, de Valera suggested that the origins of the portal tomb lay in the subsidiary chambers found in the cairns of some court tombs. Both have a similar relatively simple plan: both are single-chambered, of subrectangular form, and both are entered through a pair of portal stones with a sill stone or closing stone between. The fact that both subsidiary chambers and most portal tombs lack forecourts was considered significant, as was the mutual usage of long cairns. While some portal tombs are of massive construction, others are quite small, and in general the internal dimensions of the type are said to be closely comparable to those of the subsidiary chambers of court tombs. The fact that they are essentially simple tombs was one reason for a belief that they could belong to an early date and it has been proposed that a simple structure like a portal tomb could be the primary stage in the development of the court tomb: the placing of a second chamber in front of the hypothetical primary structure would result in a two-chambered burial gallery, requiring only a long cairn and concave façade to give the basic court tomb form.

While a relationship to court tombs is not disputed, older arguments that portal tombs developed from court tombs or vice versa remain unresolved and are probably too simplistic. Portal tombs have a wider distribution as well, being also found in Wales and south-western England. Some Welsh examples have dramatically large capstones like a number of the Irish tombs, and this has prompted the interesting suggestion that these extraordinary feats of engineering may have been a deliberate and extravagant expression of a people's labour. The ability to mobilise such a workforce and the process of construction may have been the main social factors that inspired them. As at some tombs at Carrowmore, such capstones may never have been covered by cairn material but may have remained exposed as a permanent manifestation of a memorable event to be recalled by future generations (Richards 2004).

WEDGE TOMBS

With over 540 examples recorded, the wedge tomb is the most numerous megalithic tomb in Ireland, representing almost one third of the total. It is so called because many, though not all, examples have a chamber of a relatively narrow wedge shape or trapezoidal plan that decreases both in height and in width from front to rear (Cody 2002). This main chamber is constructed of orthostats and roofed with one or more capstones, which in most cases rest directly on the side stones (Figs 3.19–3.20). Some tombs have a short orthostatic portico or antechamber at the front and some have a small closed chamber at the rear. The division between antechamber and chamber is usually by a slab inset at the sides and of roof height. Occasionally a pair of jambs or, more rarely, a sill stone occur instead of this closing slab. The chamber is frequently flanked by one or more lines of outer orthostatic walling that taper in plan to form a straight or U-shaped rear end. A straight orthostatic façade is found at the front of the tomb, which consistently faces west. Cairns may be approximately round, oval or D-shaped, sometimes with a kerb.

These tombs vary considerably in size: the chamber at Labbacallee, near Glanworth, Co. Cork (Fig. 3.19A), measures some 9m in overall length, while some particularly small tombs in County

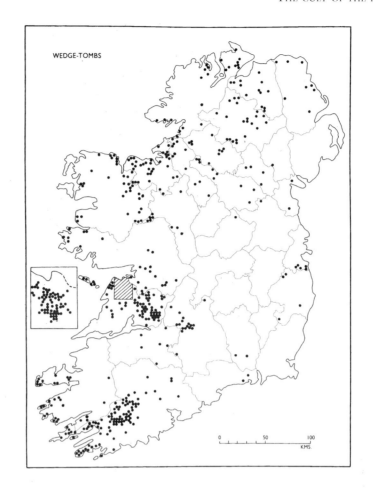

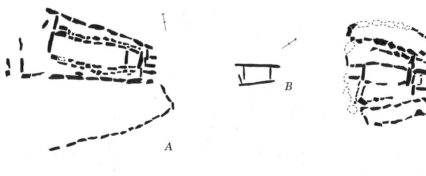

Fig. 3.19—Above: general distribution of wedge tombs. Below: plans of wedge tombs. (A) Labbacallee, Co. Cork. (B) Parknabinnia, Co. Clare. (C) Ballyedmonduff, Co. Dublin. (D) Kilhoyle, Co. Derry. (E) Loughash (Giant's Grave), Co. Tyrone.

Clare have chambers of 2m or less in length. The well-known Labbacallee tomb is a large, well-preserved example which was excavated in 1934 (Leask and Price 1936; Jones 2007). Some ancient disturbance at the western, front end of the tomb has meant that the original form of this part of the monument is uncertain: two straight lines of orthostats may have formed a double façade in front of the chamber. The long narrow chamber decreases in both height and width towards the eastern rear end. It is 1.8m high at the western end and is constructed of double rows of orthostats with a further row of outer walling 0.5–1.2m from either side, the intervening space being filled with cairn stones. An orthostat 1.45m high separates a small end chamber from the rest of the gallery. This slab effectively sealed the small chamber except at one of its upper corners, which may have been knocked away to provide some limited access; as the excavators discovered, however, the single three-ton capstone that neatly covered this chamber was capable of being moved aside with relative ease and thus access to both chambers was possible. One very large and one smaller capstone roofed the rest of the tomb. The rear of the tomb was supported by three buttress stones.

The contents of the main chamber had suffered some human and animal disturbance but they included a 60cm-deep fill of earth and stones with numerous animal bones, fragments of the unburnt bones of a young male adult and a child, as well as the skull of a female; fragments of one well-made pottery vessel with incised decoration (of uncertain type) and of some coarser flat-bottomed pottery were also recovered. Fragments of coarse pottery and a perforated piece of animal bone were found along with cremated human bone in the earth and stones that filled the small end chamber, and below these, on the floor, lay the unburnt remains of a headless skeleton. These unburnt bones were those of an adult female and, since they were partially in articulation, it seemed that the body had been partly decomposed when buried. A skewer-like bone pin was found with the bones and it was suggested that the skull from the large chamber belonged to this skeleton.

Over 50 years after the excavation, radiocarbon dating of samples of unburnt bone has shed further light on the Labbacallee burials (Brindley *et al.* 1988; Brindley and Lanting 1992b).

A long bone from the headless skeleton in the end chamber provided a date of 2456–2138 BC, while the two skeletons in the main chamber were dated to 2458–2038 BC and 2202–1776 BC respectively. A date in the second half of the third millennium BC for these primary burials is indicated, the three being placed in the tomb at intervals over several hundred years. The cremated bone was a secondary deposit and it has been suggested that the animal bone and the coarse pottery also represent secondary use of the chamber.

The wedge tomb at Kilhoyle, near Drumsurn, Co. Derry (Fig. 3.19D), examined in 1937, is a much smaller example, about 4.6m in length (Herring and May 1937). Excavation did not ascertain the original shape of the cairn, which, like the burial chamber, had suffered considerable disturbance. The tomb consisted of a main chamber with outer walling surviving on one side and a small antechamber separated from the larger chamber by a large slab of almost roof height. It faced approximately west and decreased in height from about 1.6m (excluding missing capstones) at the front to 0.6m at the rear. Both chambers had been extensively disturbed. The antechamber produced fragments of cremated human bone, sherds of Beaker pottery and a bowl, a flint concave scraper and a barbed and tanged arrowhead. The main chamber also yielded cremated bone, fragments of Beaker and of flat-bottomed, coarse, straight-walled ware. Possible cup-marks occurred on one orthostat. The outer walling at Kilhoyle may once have formed a rounded, U-shaped rear end, a feature of a number of wedge tombs such as Loughash (Giant's Grave), Co. Tyrone (Fig. 3.19E), Ballyedmonduff, Co. Dublin (Fig. 3.19C), and Island, Co. Cork (Fig. 3.20). At Loughash entrance to the antechamber was impeded by a centrally placed orthostat (bearing a dozen cup-marks) with a low sill stone on either side of it, and a pair of jamb stones separated the antechamber from the main chamber. Jamb segmentation has been noted in a number of tombs in the northern half of the country and in a few in the south-west. Here an orthostat of almost roof height (sometimes called a septal stone—a term used of slabs which, unlike sill stones, are high enough to prevent normal passage from one area to another) is more usual. Cup-marked stones are known from a number of other sites, including Ballyedmonduff and

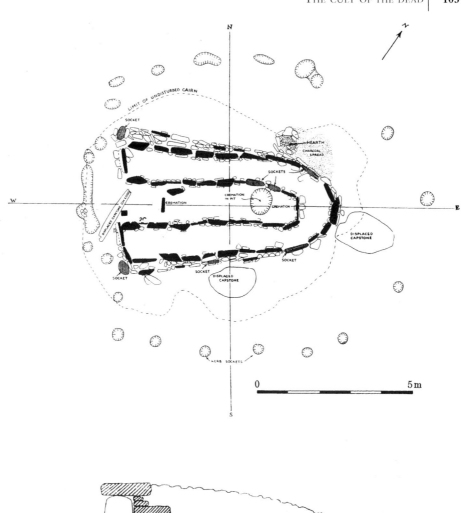

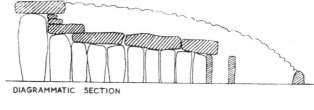

Fig. 3.20—Plan, section and reconstruction of a wedge tomb at Island, Co. Cork; the cairn as shown probably represents a later extension of the original monument and the reconstruction is not precisely to scale.

Baurnadomeeny, Co. Tipperary.

At Island, south of Mallow, Co. Cork, the antechamber was separated from the main chamber by a single small pillar stone and a 7cm-high sill stone (Fig. 3.20). Excavation has shown that the denuded cairn of this tomb had been approximately D-shaped with a maximum length of about 11.5m (O'Kelly 1958b; Jones 2007). A series of small sockets of varying depths spaced around the cairn were interpreted as sockets for kerbstones. The entrance to the tomb, on the south-west, was marked by a pair of tall portal stones, 1.65m in average height, and its length (including antechamber) was 5.74m. Its height decreased considerably from antechamber to main chamber. The small pillar stone, 0.68m high, stood just inside the entrance: its purpose is unknown though during the excavation it became known as the 'sentinel stone'. A socket for a similarly placed and, presumably, ritual stone was found in the antechamber at Ballyedmonduff. A stone standing in the centre of the tomb entrance is a feature of several sites in Ulster (including Loughash, mentioned above) and elsewhere. At Island the characteristic outer walling of the tomb formed a rounded rear end and at the front was joined to the portals of the antechamber by a straight orthostatic façade. The 2m of cairn on either side of this façade gave a slight concavity to the front of the monument. The upper fill of the tomb consisted of a 35cm-thick deposit of loose soil and stones cleared and thrown in from the surrounding field since the original cairn cover was removed. Below was a firmly packed layer of soil and small boulders that had been laid on the old ground surface, where the original turf line was readily recognisable. Beneath this layer a circular pit was found near the eastern end of the chamber; it contained charcoal, some finely fragmented cremated human bone and part of a burnt flint implement, perhaps a knife.

A little burnt human bone and two flint scrapers were found on the tomb floor, and a shallow pit just inside the sill stone contained the cremated bones of an adult female of 60–70 years of age. Some charcoal collected from a hearth site on the old ground surface outside the kerbstones provided a radiocarbon date of 1730–1000 BC, which was generally thought to be both unreliable and too young for the construction of the monument. But a duplicate sample from the same location and another of charcoal from the socket of one of the kerbstones have been dated in recent years, the respective dates of 1412–1226 BC and 1430–1274 BC confirming the original late date. According to Anna Brindley and Jan Lanting, these dates may be related to a later enlargement of the monument; it may be that the tomb proper dated from the early second millennium but that a secondary phase of activity in or about the fourteenth century BC, indicated by the radiocarbon dates, consisted of the addition of the D-shaped kerb.

Single-chambered wedge tombs, lacking an antechamber (or the rarer end chamber), are also recorded and are well known in County Clare (Fig. 3.19B), where their apparent simplicity is accentuated by the local availability of large tabular pieces of limestone that facilitated the construction of rather box-like monuments with perhaps just one or two slabs for side stones and capstones. In the absence of excavation certainty about details of tomb plan is often impossible, but only a few of these megaliths have traces of likely antechambers or end chambers and the majority appear to have been single-chambered. Many display a decrease in height and width from front to rear, and the broader, front end consistently faces approximately west. Outer walling is visible in quite a number of cases, and closure of the western end is sometimes by one large slab and sometimes by two overlapping slabs, one wider than the other. The use of such multiple closing stones may indicate that repeated access was intended. In a few instances one upper corner of the closing stone at the eastern end has been knocked or chipped away. A few of these openings may be fortuitous but others may be an original feature and some tombs may have been entered from the eastern end (Walsh 1995).

Whether there is any significant difference in purpose and function between such small, simple chambers and longer, more monumental galleries like Labbacallee is not clear. The orientation of wedge tombs in general is remarkably consistent: they almost invariably face somewhere between west-north-west and south, a majority being aligned to the south-west and west, towards the general position of the setting sun. Their distribution too has a western bias (Fig. 3.19): over 75% of them occur in the west and south-west of the country, with significant concentrations in

Sligo, in Clare and Tipperary, and in Cork and Kerry. The latter south-western group includes clusters of over 30 tombs on the major peninsulas of the indented coast from Mizen Head to Dingle. In the north these tombs are to be found in some numbers in Donegal, Derry, Antrim and Tyrone, as well as Cavan, Fermanagh, Leitrim and Monaghan. A few scattered examples occur in Leinster.

The relatively small number of wedge tombs excavated to date cannot be said to provide a clear picture of the funerary ritual and grave-goods of the class as a whole. Just over twenty examples have been investigated, and some have produced evidence of burials and a variety of artefacts, notably fragments of pottery. Cremation seems to have been the dominant burial rite, though unburnt bones have been found in several instances and a number of tombs have yielded no trace of burials at all. Very small quantities of cremated bone have been found at sites such as Ballyedmonduff, Co. Dublin (Ó Ríordáin and de Valera 1952), while Clogherny, Co. Tyrone, produced 'many fragments' of cremated human bone. They were mixed with charcoal through a layer of yellowish clay 30cm in average thickness, and the excavator surmised that the cremation pyre had been shovelled into the chamber along with some of the soil beneath it (Davies 1939b). Fragments of burnt bone were recovered from both antechamber and chamber at Kilhoyle, Co. Derry, and at least three persons were represented. At Largantea, Co. Derry, the cremated bones of at least six adults (male and female being represented), a twelve-year-old child and an infant were found (Herring 1938); the cremated bones of at least four persons came from the main chamber at Loughash (Cashelbane), Co. Tyrone (Davies and Mullin 1940), while some more burnt bone was recovered from two small chambers behind the main chamber; and at Loughash (Giant's Grave), Co. Tyrone, the antechamber contained some burnt bones of an adult male, while the burnt bones of two persons were found in a pit at the rear of the main chamber (Davies 1939c). A layer of clay up to 14cm thick in the chamber of a wedge tomb at Ballybriest, Co. Derry, was found to contain a large quantity of charcoal and burnt bone (Hurl 2001). The bones represented at least seven individuals, including an adult male, an adult female and a child, and sherds of several Beaker vessels were mixed with them. A sample of the cremated bone produced a radiocarbon date of 2139–1830 BC. The nature of the burial deposits in these tombs raises many problems: for example, the range of pottery styles represented (see below) suggests the likelihood that they were reused over a period of time. It is probable, however, that the cremation in a pit at Loughash (Giant's Grave) was primary; this was true of the similar pit containing unidentifiable cremated human bone at Island, already mentioned.

A complex sequence of deposition of cremated bones was observed in and around the wedge tomb at Baurnadomeeny, near Rear Cross, Co. Tipperary (O'Kelly 1960; Cooney 1992b). This monument comprised a chamber and broad antechamber set in a round cairn with kerb. A septal slab separated the chambers and the main eastern chamber had been completely dug out in modern times; nothing survived of the original deposit except a few minute scraps of cremated bone. The antechamber did contain burials, two of which were apparently primary: a rectangular slab-built structure constructed against the southern side contained fragments of cremated bone (possibly of an adult female) and 33 potsherds, and another deposit of cremated bone was found at old ground level, covered by two thin slabs. Three other deposits of cremated bone were found on a packing of boulders around the slab-built structure and are thus later, though perhaps not much later, than the primary deposits. Outside the tomb some fourteen other deposits of bone were found, all on the southern side of the monument. All were cremated and five were in diminutive rectangular or polygonal slab-built cists set in pits in the old ground surface. A sixth small cist was empty; this possible grave and three of the cremations were found under the cairn. Six other cremations were possibly primary and four were secondary; one of the latter had been inserted into the cairn and the rest were outside the kerb. Thus at least part of the funerary ritual at Baurnadomeeny seems to have involved, as far as can be judged, the deposition of the burnt bones of separate individuals within and outside the tomb over a period of time, and the deposits outside the tomb were seemingly token deposits, some deliberately mixed with soil and charcoal. Because acid soil had damaged the bones, little information was gleaned from their study: adult males and females as well as adolescents were represented.

Unburnt burials have been recorded in a few cases. Labbacallee, Co. Cork, has already been mentioned, unburnt bones being found in both the main chamber and the end chamber, although the cremated bone from the fill of the end chamber may be secondary. A wedge tomb at Lough Gur, Co. Limerick, produced a considerable quantity of pottery, a few fragments of cremated bone from antechamber and main chamber and numerous unburnt human and animal bones (Ó Ríordáin and Ó h-Iceadha 1955; Jones 2007). The contents of the tomb had been greatly disturbed and the unburnt remains were in a very fragmentary condition. The human bones from the main chamber represented at least eight adults (a figure based on the number of second cervical vertebrae found). Bones of children were also found both inside and outside the chamber, and some adult remains occurred outside the tomb too. The animal bones were mainly those of cattle and pig. A burial of the skeleton of a young ox was found to the south of the tomb and was considered contemporary. A series of radiocarbon dates from unburnt bone suggest a series of burials over a period of several centuries from about 2500 to 2000 BC. Nineteenth-century investigations of a wedge tomb at Moytirra, Co. Sligo, are said to have yielded the unburnt bones of at least six individuals, including one child, a 'long thin piece of bronze' and fragments of Beaker pottery (Madden 1969).

A remarkable sequence of ritual activity that sheds considerable light on the later use of wedge tombs has been identified by William O'Brien (1999) in two tombs at Toormore Bay, near Schull in west Cork. One megalith in Altar townland was a simple trapezoidal orthostatic gallery, 3.42m long, wider at the front (western) end. The monument seemed to have been aligned on Mizen Peak 13km to the south-west, and it has been suggested that this was an orientation towards the setting sun at Samhain in early November. Excavation produced a little cremated bone (just 15g) of a human adult found near the entrance, a single unburnt tooth, some charcoal from two pits near the rear of the chamber and some deposits of shellfish such as periwinkles and limpets. No artefacts were recovered. At first glance these results might be considered unpromising but a programme of radiocarbon dating of a number of samples from a variety of carefully selected contexts revealed a remarkable pattern of prehistoric depositional events.

Phase 1: the unburnt tooth associated with some cremated bone found inside the tomb entrance dated initial activity to 2316–1784 BC; this deposit may be broadly contemporary with the construction of the monument.

Phase 2: charcoal from a small pit near the centre of the chamber was dated to 1250–832 BC and might indicate some sort of depositional activity, which could have included offerings of food or some other perishables. Some charcoal found near the rear of the chamber provided slightly later dates of 998–560 BC and 766–404 BC.

Phase 3A: charcoal from a small pit on the south side of the chamber dates from the period 356 BC–AD 68.

Phase 3B: a deposit of periwinkle and limpet shells inside the entrance is of later date (2 BC–AD 230).

Phase 3C: a pit in the centre of the chamber contained various deposits of shells (periwinkle and limpet) and fish bones (wrasse and eel); three dates for the upper fill place some of this activity in the second century AD.

The ritual sequence at Altar initially seems to have involved just the token deposition of human remains, but the placing of food offerings, including fish and shellfish, may have figured prominently, particularly in later prehistoric times. It would appear that the depositional emphasis may have shifted from human remains to other votive offerings in the course of the second millennium BC. Obviously, late prehistoric communities (who otherwise remain archaeologically invisible in the region) also regarded the monument as a sacred place.

The second tomb, in nearby Toormore townland, had suffered considerable damage in the past but also revealed early and late prehistoric activity. A small deposit comprising a decorated bronze axe and two pieces of copper had been placed as an offering at the tomb entrance; it and some radiocarbon-dated charcoal indicate ritual practice in the general period 1800–1600 BC. Further charcoal from the tomb was dated to 1368–1002 BC and 818–412 BC.

Fragmentary pottery is the commonest artefact in wedge tombs generally and about half of the excavated examples have produced sherds of one sort or another. A puzzling variety of pottery types occurs, and at some sites at least this indicates the use of the tomb for some length of time. Beaker pottery and coarse ware are the two pottery classes most frequently represented, each being recorded from some eight or nine tombs. The coarse ware includes flat-bottomed plain pots, as from Kilhoyle, Co. Derry, from the two tombs at Loughash, Co. Tyrone, and from Largantea, Co. Derry, as well as other coarse wares from Ballyedmonduff, Co. Dublin, Lough Gur, Co. Limerick, and Baurnadomeeny, Co. Tipperary. Apart from the last mentioned, these tombs have also yielded sherds of Beaker pottery of various types, as have Moytirra, Co. Sligo, and Ballybriest, Co. Derry. A number of radiocarbon dates and some Beaker pottery seem to firmly date the beginnings of the wedge tomb type to the later third millennium. A few instances of Neolithic pottery, such as some decorated pottery from Lough Gur and sherds of a Goodland bowl reported from Boviel, Co. Derry (Herring and May 1940), may be redeposited material. Much of the artefactual and radiocarbon evidence now indicates a complex pattern of use throughout the later third and second millennia, and even later.

The origins of the commonest Irish megalithic tomb type remain a perplexing puzzle. Over the years various writers have seen parallels between Irish wedge tombs and certain megalithic tombs in western France, and at one time the builders of these tombs were thought to have arrived from the Continent to a point of entry in the south-west. Beaker, barbed and tanged arrowheads and coarse flat-bottomed pottery were seen as the characteristic finds, and the narrow, rectangular megalithic tombs of the *allée couverte* type in Brittany (with the occasional antechamber and outer walling) were thought to be excellent prototypes. It is also true that Beaker pottery in some parts of Europe seems to be contemporary with the acquisition of the knowledge of metal-working and some of the wedge tombs in west Cork and Kerry are situated not too far from copper deposits. This, coupled with the supposed Breton connection, led to the theory that these tomb-builders were copper-workers and a major element in the introduction of this new technology to Ireland. This hypothesis has its deficiencies, not least the absence of supportive evidence from the excavated south-western wedge tombs. The Toormore deposit does establish a connection between tomb-builders and metal-users but at a stage when the tradition of wedge tomb-building was well established.

The Beaker pottery comes only from a minority of tombs, mainly in the northern half of the country. Furthermore, this pottery is of types that, if not peculiarly Irish, are best paralleled in Britain. The Breton tombs themselves differ in important respects from the Irish examples: many are not wedge-shaped but rectangular, and many face east rather than west. It is true that there are parallels: antechambers and outer walling occur sporadically in Brittany and some tombs may face west. It is, in the absence of other evidence for contact, a question of attempting to gauge the relative significance of the morphological differences and resemblances. The parallels, if not coincidental, may indeed be an indication of Irish contact with Brittany, but it does not follow that the origins of the largest class of Irish megalithic tomb can be attributed to the same source. Features such as jamb stones in some wedge tombs raise the question of some relationship with court tombs and the possibility of indigenous development. As O'Brien (1999) has said, it is understandable that, at a time when the culture-historical model was dominant, external contact should have been emphasised above all else, but now a greater role must be allowed for the internal dynamics of past societies.

RITUAL IMPERATIVES

The four major classes of Irish megalithic tombs are remarkable expressions of prehistoric social organisation, engineering ability and ritual obligation. They were certainly the most permanent and probably the most conspicuous objects in the contemporary landscape. They were something more (or perhaps on occasion something other) than just burial places, for there are obviously more economic and no less effective ways of disposing of the dead. Since in some cases at least these monuments were situated on or near the farming land of the people who built them, they may have had a social and ceremonial role as significant as any funerary one. They may have been special repositories for sacred ancestral bones. It has been suggested, for example, that they were territorial markers, an expression of the community's claim to their land and possibly serving as ceremonial centres. It is interesting to speculate that, aside from the disposal of the dead, some megalithic tombs may have been locations for such activities as ceremonial gift exchanges, fertility rituals, ancestor worship and the observation of celestial events. There is now a large body of literature on their possible meaning (Bradley 1993; 1998a; Thomas 1999). The anthropological study of modern and recent primitive societies has always proved to be a particularly fruitful source of inspiration for possible explanations of archaeological phenomena and in recent years it has provided a number of social and economic models with interesting archaeological applications, some in the realm of megalithic tomb studies. As Alistair Whittle (2003) has pointed out, ethnographic analogy does serve a purpose. It may be used to widen the imagination and to open up possibilities of interpretation; it also challenges our modern western ways of thinking and may remind us of neglected aspects of human behaviour. It has been one of the factors that have encouraged the study of the use of colour and texture, for instance, in megalithic construction.

It is generally believed that some megalithic tombs may have served as the symbolic and functional centre of a community; in any event, they may have been expressions of communal solidarity. It has been argued that the tendency of court tombs generally to occur in isolated and scattered locations reflects the dispersed distribution of the social units of a segmentary society. Such societies are small, acephalous communities, lacking the centralised hierarchical structure of the chiefdom or state; the communities (or segments) are politically and economically autonomous rather than subordinate parts of a larger political and economic entity. Anthropological studies indicate that populations usually range from about 50 to 500 persons living in a village or in a small number of dispersed houses. The variety in plan of broadly contemporary court tombs could be a mark of a segmentary society in which a broad hierarchical control of tomb design would of course be absent. As already noted, details of tomb plan might reflect complex kinship relationships. In contrast, passage tombs, it has been suggested, may be the products of

a different sort of society. The use of cemeteries in particular has been considered significant, possibly implying denser population concentrations and a form of social organisation other than a segmentary one. A hierarchical society has been postulated, even one in which a group rather than an individual exercised control. This centralised control could explain the relatively limited variation in passage tomb plans and may be expressed too in the substantially greater input of labour represented by the largest monuments, such as those in the Boyne Valley and at Loughcrew. But there are other possible explanations. As we have seen, Alison Sheridan has argued that the construction of ever-larger passage tombs reflects the ambitions of various communities to enhance their power and status (and she draws an analogy with the ostentatious funerary practices of Victorian Britain). Different groups attempted to outdo each other in their treatment of the dead by building bigger and better monuments and by devising more elaborate rituals, which included the introduction of novel and exotic elements into the ceremonial repertoire. These elements could include architectural features or artefacts borrowed from abroad, and here we may have an explanation for architectural parallels with, for instance, passage tombs in Wales and the Orkneys and for the presence of objects such as the stone maceheads at Knowth. In both court tombs and passage tombs, however, there is an evident preoccupation with the ordering and control of access to parts of the tomb interior.

The distributions of various types of tomb overlap and there is also evidence that different types were in contemporaneous use, with no neat chronological succession of tomb types. Thus the development of complex forms of court tombs in the north-west, for instance, could be seen as a regional development similar to the passage tomb aggrandisement in the Boyne Valley but one for which another design option was chosen. Different tomb types may not represent different cultural groups but different responses, some regional, to various social and ritual imperatives. It is possible that communities may have had allegiances to more than one tomb type, and in this respect the existence of small groups of tombs of different categories may be significant: for example, two court tombs, a portal tomb and a wedge tomb at Wardhouse, Co. Leitrim (between Bundoran and

Cliffony), form a small cemetery; a group at Fenagh, also in County Leitrim, comprises two passage tombs, a court tomb and a portal tomb, and there is a concentration of wedge tombs as well as other monuments in Parknabinnia and adjacent townlands near Kilnaboy in the Burren, Co. Clare (Cooney 2000).

LINKARDSTOWN GRAVES AND OTHER BURIALS

In the 1940s a megalithic grave was discovered in the course of ploughing in the townland of Linkardstown, south-south-east of Carlow town, and this name is now applied to a small group of fourth-millennium burials (Ryan 1981; Brindley *et al.* 1983). At Linkardstown, a low circular mound some 75cm high and 25m in diameter had a kerb of low stones and covered a large, centrally placed grave. This megalithic cist was polygonal, formed of large, inward-sloping granite blocks, roofed with two capstones and built on the old ground surface, which formed the floor of the grave. The disarticulated unburnt bones of an adult male were found, and mixed with them were sherds of five incomplete bowls. The skull displayed several ancient fractures. A polished stone axe was also found. The most complete pot was a large round-bottomed bowl with grooved or channelled ornament and a heavy rim; the remaining sherds represented parts of one plain vessel and of three highly decorated pots, including two Bipartite Bowls.

Some half a dozen other graves are assignable to the Linkardstown type: each consists of a round mound covering a large cist containing one or two burials and few grave-goods apart from highly decorated round-bottomed pottery vessels. The cists, built on the old ground surface and covered by circular mounds, often have inclined walling and contain unburnt burials, but cremation is also recorded. The burials seem to be usually those of males.

At Ballintruer More, near Baltinglass, Co. Wicklow (Fig. 3.21), the destruction by bulldozer of a circular mound with kerb revealed a polygonal cist with a floor of fine sand and containing some disarticulated and apparently broken bones representing part of the skeleton of an adult male. An empty pottery vessel had been placed in the centre of the grave immediately to the west of the bones. This pot, like a number of vessels from other burials of this type, is a fine Bipartite Bowl. A large polygonal cist in a round cairn at Ardcrony, near Nenagh, Co. Tipperary, contained the unburnt skeletons of two men, one aged about seventeen, the other aged about 40. The bones were disarticulated and the individuals were placed in separate deposits on a paved floor on either side of a similar pottery vessel, found empty and mouth upwards in the centre of the grave. The cairn, which measured 33m in diameter, was not excavated and a report that it was once surrounded by a bank and ditch was not confirmed. At Jerpoint West, Co. Kilkenny, a circular mound, about 24m in diameter, covered a centrally placed polygonal cist that contained some cremated bone, the unburnt bones of a young adult male, some sherds of plain pottery and fragments of a highly decorated bowl, part of a leaf-shaped flint arrowhead and part of a bone object, possibly a pin. The contents of the cist had suffered some disturbance, possibly by rabbit activity, but it was clear that the adult male had lain in an extended position with head to the north. It was thought too that this burial and the cremation were contemporary.

A polygonal cist beneath a damaged circular mound at Baunogenasraid, Co. Carlow, contained some disarticulated unburnt bones of an adult male of large stature with a decorated bowl nearby; a worked, pointed piece of animal bone and a small perforated object (a toggle?) of lignite were the only other finds in the grave. The cist was built of five granite blocks that sloped inwards and a sixth stone, of limestone, which had no part in supporting the capstone. This stone, the smallest of the six, seems to have been selected for ease of movement to seal the 30cm gap between the two adjacent granite blocks. The cist was almost completely surrounded by a near-circular platform of stones 30cm high at its edge and rising to 1.2m at the centre, where it did not cover the tomb. This arrangement recalls the stone packing that Burenhult found at Carrowmore, for example, and which he thought to have comprised the entire cairn at these sites. At Baunogenasraid the rudimentary cairn was covered by a mound of turves with a maximum height of some 2m above ground level. Several penannular stone settings seem to have had some role in retaining parts of the stone platform and

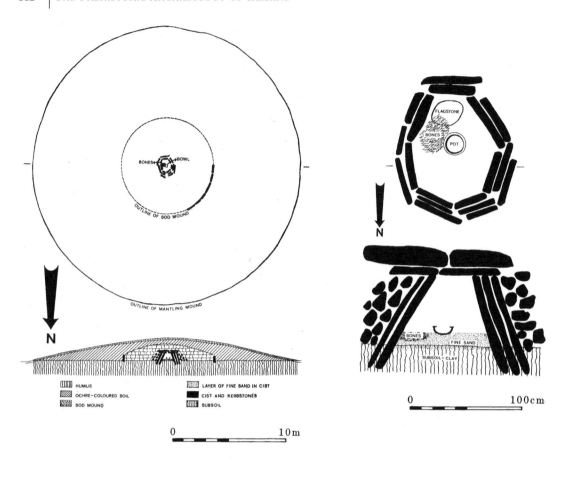

Fig. 3.21—Linkardstown-type grave from Ballintruer More, Co. Wicklow, and Bipartite Bowl with grooved decoration on rim, body and base.

mound. At some later date, in the early second millennium, the mound was enlarged to incorporate at least eleven simple burials. A mound at Drimnagh, Co. Dublin, had an even more complicated history, but the large primary mound, some 22m in diameter, covered an arc of stones, a cup-marked stone and a polygonal cist containing the unburnt skeletal remains of a male adult (possibly flexed) and a highly ornamented Bipartite Bowl (Fig. 2.12, 10). Very little is known about a mound at Norrismount, Co. Wexford, which was almost completely destroyed. It covered a rectangular cist with inclined side stones that contained the unburnt skeletal remains of a male adult (possibly flexed) and another highly ornamented Bipartite Bowl.

At Ashleypark, Co. Tipperary, just south-east of Ardcrony, a large mound was partly excavated and found to consist of a cairn with a mantle of clay surrounded by a pair of concentric banks, each with an internal ditch, with an overall diameter of about 90m (Manning 1985). The cairn covered a rectangular, open-ended stone structure with inclined side stones which incorporated part of a natural rock outcrop and contained a deposit of clay about 60cm deep through which were mixed unburnt human and animal bones and some sherds of pottery. The human bones were disarticulated and represented an elderly adult male and a child, the animal bones were those of cattle, sheep and pig, and the pottery fragments were from a Carinated Bowl-style vessel, a Decorated Bowl and a pot with grooved decoration, possibly a Bipartite Bowl. More animal bones were found in the cairn and the context of these bones is particularly interesting. Such bones from megalithic tombs are sometimes assumed to be the remains of offerings or of funeral feasts (as in the passage tomb at Fourknocks I, for instance), but direct association between the monument and food consumption is often difficult to prove. At Ashleypark the mantle of clay that covered the cairn was obtained from the surrounding ditches and sealed the animal bones found among the cairn stones. These bones represented three fully grown cattle, a small number of other cattle bones and a single pig femur, and in many cases were split or broken for marrow extraction and sometimes displayed butchering marks, indicating that they were discarded food remains. Thus the consumption of food seems to

have been part of the rituals enacted here, and a radiocarbon date for a cattle bone indicates that this activity may well have been contemporary with the deposition of the human remains and pottery fragments in the grave shortly after 3500 BC. The bones with the burials—a single pig bone, a sheep or goat bone and a few cattle bones—did not represent joints of meat and could have been token offerings perhaps representing the three most important domestic animals of the community.

The occurrence of the remains of individual unburnt male burials accompanied by complete or fragmentary pottery vessels in these Linkardstown Graves, the use of a large round mound, polygonal cist and other details of monument construction all indicate a distinctive burial ritual in Leinster and Munster for a number of centuries in the fourth millennium. Radiocarbon dates from the human bones from sites such as Ardcrony, Ashleypark, Ballintruer More, Baunogenasraid and others suggest a timespan of about 3600–3300 BC and demonstrate their contemporaneity with megalithic tombs such as court tombs and passage tombs (Brindley and Lanting 1990a). These graves also demonstrate a preference for a form of individual expression by some persons or groups at a time when some others, for whatever reason, practised a collective rite. The consistent inclusion of finely decorated pottery vessels suggests that these pots had some particular significance; they may have denoted special status and, like some stone axes, may have been the insignia of male community leaders. It is worth noting that the in-turned necks of these pots render them unsuitable for the consumption of food and drink, and they may have been suspended containers for some other purpose.

A variety of other burials are known, some related to the Linkardstown type. The primary burial in a cairn at Poulawack, in the Burren, Co. Clare, was a polygonal cist containing the disarticulated bones of an adult male and female, a child and an infant; a concave scraper, a boar's tusk and two sherds of unclassifiable pottery were also found. Radiocarbon dating indicates contemporaneity with Linkardstown Graves. At Martinstown, Co. Meath, fragments of a highly decorated Bipartite Bowl were found along with the unburnt bones of an adult male in a sand and gravel ridge. Unfortunately no details of the burial were recorded, though it seems to have been in a simple pit. A pit at Clane, Co. Kildare, contained the unburnt bones of two adolescents, a Decorated Bowl and a piece of polished lignite. Pottery and unburnt human remains have been found in a cave at Annagh, Co. Limerick, and human bones of Neolithic date have been identified from a number of other caves as well (Dowd 2008).

4

SACRED CIRCLES AND NEW TECHNOLOGY

Various megalithic tombs continued to be the focus of ritual activity in the third and in succeeding millennia. Other forms of ritual expression emerge, however, and, in time, a new metal technology had a profound effect not just on economy and society but in the ritual sphere as well. Although the circular kerbs of some passage tombs and the banks and internal ditches at Ashleypark, Co. Tipperary, for instance, are indications of the importance of large stone and earthen circles in funerary ceremonial in the fourth millennium, circular enclosures seem to assume new significance in the following millennium. A penannular ditch, about 1.1m wide and deep, enclosed a circular area with an internal diameter of some 12m at Scotch Street, Armagh (Fig. 4.1). Nothing survived within the circle, but the ditch contained silt, redeposited soil, charcoal, flints, animal teeth and many hundreds of pottery sherds, including fragments of Decorated Bowls (and a little Carrowkeel ware). Radiocarbon dating suggests that the ditch was dug around 2800 BC and some later wooden stakes were inserted in its fill (Lynn 1988). Some larger and more elaborate open circular areas offer greater space for more complex depositional and other practices.

In particular, a number of earthworks in the Boyne Valley, which were possibly built by the tomb-builders or their successors but which, in the absence of excavation, are of unknown date and purpose, may well have had a ritual function. These include several more or less circular enclosures. A large and impressive oval enclosure near Dowth is well known: located about 1.5km north-east of the passage tomb (Fig. 3.2), it has a maximum overall diameter of about 180m and consists of an oval area some 165m in greatest diameter, surrounded by an earthen bank 3–5m high in places and with an average width of 20m. Today there are two gaps in the bank, but only one, that on the south-west, seems likely to be original. Apart from a hollow outside the bank on the northern side, there is no trace of a surrounding ditch either outside or inside the bank, and it would seem that the material for the bank was scooped up from the interior. This was the case at an embanked enclosure, some 3km north of Newgrange, in Monknewtown townland (Sweetman 1976). Only a segment of the earthen bank of this circular enclosure survived, but originally the monument was about 107m in overall diameter. The bank, about 1.5m in height and about 11m wide at its base, was constructed by scarping between 1m and 1.5m of material from the interior. Excavation of part of the interior on the north revealed a dozen pits within some 15m of the bank. Some of these pits contained stones but no finds of any description, but small deposits of burnt bone were found in or near eight of them; in one shallow pit a small amount of cremated bone (of a child) had been placed in a Carrowkeel bowl, while in another pit a plain bucket-shaped pot contained some cremated bone. In the south-western quadrant of the enclosure, the remains of a flat-bottomed pot and some burnt bone were found in a pit at the centre of a small annular ring-ditch. Traces of a hut site associated with Beaker pottery were found 3m to the south-east. Charcoal from around a hearth in this hut produced a radiocarbon date of 2456–2138 BC. Samples of charcoal said to

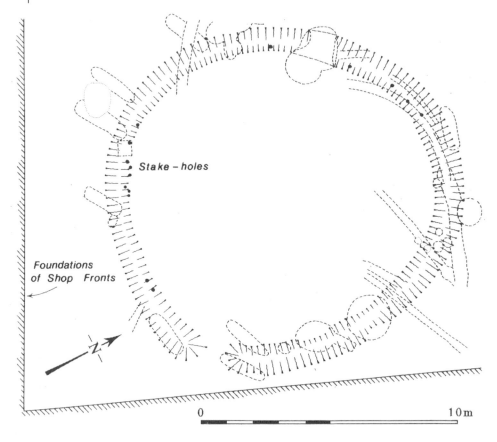

Fig. 4.1—Plan of penannular ring-ditch (disturbed by later features) at Scotch Street, Armagh.

be from the remains of hearths in the area of the pits and burials produced a series of dates that ranged over several thousand years, however, and contamination of some of the samples is a possibility. It is also possible that the site had a long and complicated ritual history. The occurrence of Carrowkeel pottery would seem to indicate that passage tomb-builders were associated with it, and there is a small passage tomb just 150m to the south-east. This may be true, too, of the Dowth earthwork and other circular enclosures, such as one at Micknanstown located 0.6km from the passage tomb at Fourknocks, Co. Meath.

Embanked enclosures such as Dowth, Monknewtown and Micknanstown belong to a well-defined group of earthworks characterised by their large size, with maximum external diameters exceeding 100m. These and ten others in the Boyne region have been surveyed by Geraldine Stout (1991), who notes their oval or circular plan, a slightly raised centre or hollowed interior (owing to the scarping of material to build the bank), and a flat-topped earthen bank generally with a single entrance. They are located on good agricultural land in river valleys and sometimes occur in groups of two or three. Small to medium-sized examples with diameters of 106–160m tend to have circular plans, while the four largest sites, with maximum diameters of 180–275m (like Dowth and Rath Maeve, at Belpere, near Tara), tend to an oval plan. Internal features have been noted in some examples: a burial mound is located in one near Newgrange, circular features have been recorded in several, including Rath Maeve, and limited geophysical analysis has revealed an arc of a possible trench or ditch 3–4m wide inside the bank at Micknanstown and at another 160m-wide enclosure at Balrath, Co. Meath.

The great earthwork known as the Giant's Ring at Ballynahatty, Co. Down, just south of

Belfast, is an exceptionally large example of an embanked enclosure (Hartwell 1998; 2002). With an approximately circular plan, it has an overall diameter of about 225m and an earthen bank about 4m high and of an average width of 19m, which was built of material scarped from a broad (20m wide), shallow quarry ditch on the interior (Fig. 4.2). A small polygonal passage tomb lies just east of the centre. Various prehistoric burials were found in the general area in the nineteenth century, mainly to the north-west of the enclosure, and aerial photography and excavation have shown that the Giant's Ring is just the largest of a complex of prehistoric ring-ditches and other monuments in an area of at least 33ha.

A large oval enclosure has been identified about 100m to the north-west of the Giant's Ring, and partial excavation suggests that it is just one of a number of timber circles in this ritual complex; this oval enclosure (Ballynahatty 5) was formed of a double ring of timber posts with a maximum diameter of about 100m. The paired timbers were each about 30cm in diameter and set in pits with an average depth of 1.8m; each pit had a substantial ramp to allow the timbers to be slipped into the holes and raised to a vertical position, and they could have been as much as 6m high. A small rectangular setting of timbers, 2m by 3m, was found just inside the line of these double posts. Another smaller timber circle (Ballynahatty 6) was found within the large enclosure and it too consisted of a double ring of timbers (Fig. 4.2). This structure had several constructional stages, and the cremation of an adult female in a shallow pit was associated with its primary phase. When completed, it consisted of a central square timber feature, perhaps a platform, with four large timber posts set in 2m-deep pits a short distance from either corner; the surrounding double ring of timbers, set in deep post-holes, had timber planking infill between the posts near the entrance. This timber circle, about 16m in diameter, may have been the focus for ceremonial activity over a period of time but was eventually burnt to the ground. Judging from the way in which the stumps of some timbers were dug out and the holes deliberately filled with charcoal-rich soil, flints and other material, the structure was destroyed on purpose. What form the rituals took is uncertain; some Grooved Ware, animal bones (notably pig), flint scrapers and stone balls were found. It is

possible, as Hartwell has suggested, that the central timber structure may have served as an exposure platform where corpses were defleshed by the elements or by carrion birds.

A smaller timber post structure, of slightly oval plan and about 8m across, has been found at Knowth, about 10m from the entrance to the eastern tomb; sherds of Grooved Ware, broken fragments of flint flakes and an unusual number of convex scrapers were deliberately deposited in some of the post-holes. It has been firmly radiocarbon-dated to the middle of the third millennium BC (Eogan and Roche 1997). Another, some 8m in diameter, is reported near Cloonbaul, between Balla and Claremorris in County Mayo; it surrounded a rectangular arrangement of four posts. Grooved Ware was recovered and radiocarbon dates span the period 3010–2470 BC (Cotter 2008). An even smaller timber circle with an internal diameter of 5.5m and several internal posts associated with Grooved Ware was found at Whitewell, Co. Westmeath, and radiocarbon-dated to *c.* 2500 BC (Grogan *et al.* 2007).

Limited excavation to the south-south-east of the large passage tomb at Newgrange has uncovered a series of concentric arcs of pits and some post-holes, which may have formed a large oval enclosure with an overall diameter of about 100m and which would have encompassed the destroyed satellite passage tomb, site Z. An outer arc of holes seems to have been dug to hold large, spaced timber posts; this was traced for just over 9m of its circumference but only occasional post-holes were identified elsewhere. Concentric rows of pits have, however, been traced for a circumferential distance of over 130m; some large pits were deliberately lined with clay and contained charcoal, burnt clay and redeposited boulder clay, while other rows of pits contained token deposits of burnt animal bone, sometimes on or under layers of small rounded stones. Charcoal spreads, paving, post- and stake-holes, Beaker pottery and Grooved Ware were found within the lines of pits, and a series of radiocarbon dates suggest that this activity and the pits date from the later third millennium. Further limited excavation 50m to the west of the large passage tomb has revealed a double arc of post-holes. Two main phases of activity were identified, the first consisting of a series of small and large pits, some of which displayed traces of extensive burning

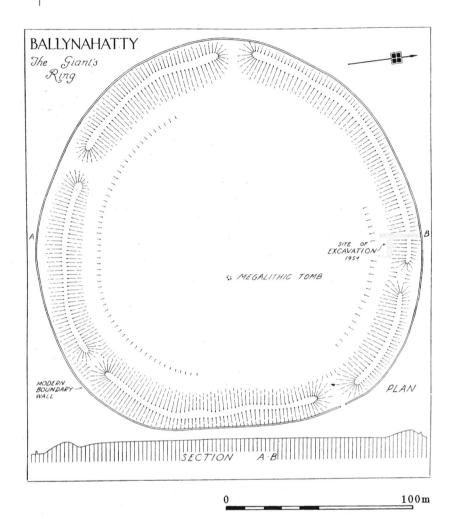

BALLYNAHATTY

The Giant's Ring

A — B

SITE OF EXCAVATION 1954

∴ MEGALITHIC TOMB

MODERN BOUNDARY WALL

PLAN

SECTION A·B

0   100m

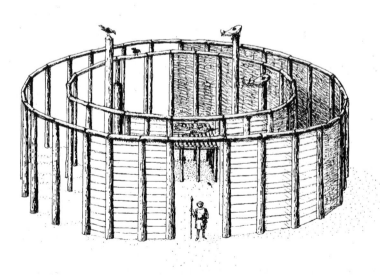

Fig. 4.2—Above: large embanked enclosure known as the Giant's Ring, Ballynahatty, Co. Down. Below: a reconstruction of a double timber circle (found within a larger timber circle) excavated to the north-west of the embanked enclosure at Ballynahatty (not to scale).

and produced Beaker pottery. In a second phase some pits were used as post-holes and other post-holes were dug to form what seemed to be a double timber circle with an outer diameter of about 20m (Sweetman 1985; 1987).

Geophysical survey on the Hill of Tara has revealed the existence of a huge oval enclosure measuring 210m north–south and 175m east–west (Fig. 4.3). A strong, curving magnetic signature about 5m wide represents a large ditch probably containing significant quantities of burnt material, while a series of regularly spaced circular anomalies 1.5–2m wide denote the presence of pits on either side of the ditch (Fenwick and Newman 2002). The pits form pairs placed about 8m from each other across the ditch and set some 4m apart centre to centre. If, as seems possible, they once contained large timbers, then the Tara enclosure was a truly monumental construction, comparable in scale to some very large later Neolithic palisaded enclosures in Britain (Gibson 2002b). A huge number of oak trees may have been felled to construct an edifice that was several times larger than Stonehenge. Situated as it was towards the eastern side of the hill, it was meant to be seen from the east, emphasising the importance of the Gabhra valley between Tara and Skreen at this early date.

A well-known monument at Grange, near Lough Gur, Co. Limerick, was excavated in 1939 and consists of a large circle of 113 contiguous stones set immediately within a penannular earthen bank with an internal diameter of about 46m (Ó Ríordáin 1951). Abundant finds included flint arrowheads and convex scrapers, a number of petit tranchet derivative implements, a polished stone axe and fragments of two others, and thousands of sherds of pottery both from under the earthen bank and from the interior. The pottery comprised coarse ware, Beaker and later Bowl Tradition wares and on this basis the Grange circle has usually been dated to the late Neolithic, but a re-evaluation of the pottery by Helen Roche (2004) has prompted the suggestion that it is a late Bronze Age monument built on a site with a protracted history of earlier activity. If so, it may be related to some smaller stone circles in the south-west enclosed by a bank with internal ditch (Chapter 5).

The large circles of the third millennium, whether of timber, earth, stone or delimited by pits, are linked by a number of features, of which the delineation of a circular space is only the most obvious. Limited excavation does suggest a ritual purpose, but the extent to which the rituals may have replaced the functions of megalithic tombs and represent, for instance, a shift from the worship of ancestral remains to some other form of religious expression is not clear; human bones are occasionally reported, but the occurrence of pottery sherds and animal bones may indicate the consumption of food and drink in non-funerary ceremonies. Some new pottery types, such as Grooved Ware and Beaker pottery, may have had specific roles in such activities. There is also a pattern of deliberate deposition in pits of certain materials such as charcoal and soil, and burnt animal bones as at Ballynahatty and Newgrange. But it would be unwise to assume that all these different circles had similar functions and there may be important regional differences.

Smaller circles were also constructed. At Millin Bay on the Ards peninsula, Co. Down, an oval setting of large standing stones surrounded an oval mound that covered a long stone-built grave containing the disarticulated bones of fifteen individuals (Collins and Waterman 1955). Some Carrowkeel pottery and some art carved on a number of stones indicated a relationship with passage tombs. Partial excavation of a stone circle at Ballynoe, near Downpatrick, in the same county revealed a complex multi-period monument comprising a large circle of closely set orthostats that enclosed a long, low, oval cairn containing two chambers, and an oval arrangement of stones partly surrounding the cairn (Groenman-van Waateringe and Butler 1976). The cairn and its associated stones were eccentrically placed within the larger stone circle and the relationship of the two is uncertain. Ballynoe is similar in some respects to Millin Bay and like the latter site it also produced a little Carrowkeel ware. Excavation of the remains of a possible stone circle at Kiltierney, Co. Fermanagh, revealed no less than seven cremated burials on its perimeter and within the interior (Daniells and Williams 1977). Near the centre a spread of cremated bone contained several pendants (two of baked clay and one of stone) and a few sherds of Carrowkeel ware. Below this deposit a pit contained another cremation, along with two stone and four amber beads. Only two of the remaining burials had any associated artefacts: a sherd of Grooved Ware was found with one and a small

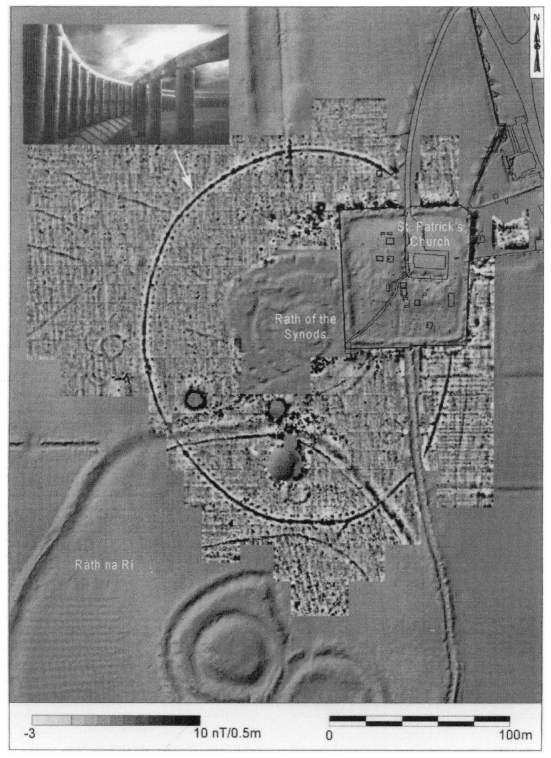

Fig. 4.3—*Magnetic gradiometry image of the great ditch and pit circle on the Hill of Tara. Inset: conjectural reconstruction showing the pits containing timber posts. The area of the huge structure was disturbed by later monuments on the hill such as the great enclosure called Ráth na Rí, the Rath of the Synods and St Patrick's Church.*

quantity of burnt bone near the perimeter was covered by an inverted cordoned urn of the early second millennium BC. A number of regional groups of small stone circles of second-millennium date will be considered in Chapter 5, and it seems that stone circles of different types were constructed over a long period of Irish prehistory.

INNOVATION AND CHANGE

The chronological period conventionally named the 'Neolithic' lasted in calendar years from at least 4000 to about 2500 BC, a period of at least fifteen centuries. Within this long time-span tomb-building fashions and pottery styles, for instance, clearly changed, and no doubt some of these changes reflect social and demographic developments. Population may well have increased, and some change may have occurred in social structures too. Major technological change and significant changes in pottery and burial fashions occur towards the end of the third millennium BC, and these and other developments mark the commencement of the period that has traditionally been called the 'Bronze Age'.

The period of the later third and much of the following millennium coincides with the latter half of the Sub-Boreal vegetation zone, in which temperatures continued to be slightly higher on average than those of today. There may have been some increase in rainfall, because there are indications in the pollen record, as at the Céide Fields, for example, of a growth of blanket bog from the early third millennium BC. High rainfall may leach a soil of nutrients like iron and may produce an acid podsol with a basal layer of impervious iron pan, causing waterlogging and peat formation. Farming activity such as overgrazing can also cause nutrient loss and soil degradation, with similar results. Thus peat formation may not be an indication of higher rainfall, and the contribution of human activity to the formation of upland peat may have been significant (O'Connell 1990). Along with the development of blanket bog, the process of deforestation and regeneration initiated some 2,000 years before continued, of course, though much of Ireland remained heavily forested. Elm never achieved its former status, and pine, in particular, shows a decline in the second millennium.

BEAKER POTTERY

The appearance of Beaker pottery in the latter part of the third millennium, about 2500 BC, is one ceramic innovation that is still imperfectly understood. Several types of Beaker pottery have a fairly widespread if irregular distribution in western and central Europe, and more localised types are also recognised in various regions from Hungary to Ireland. On the Continent and in Britain, these pots are often found in graves, usually accompanying the unburnt skeletal remains of one individual lying in a crouched position. Sometimes these graves also contain other distinctive items, notably copper knives, barbed and tanged flint arrowheads, stone wrist-guards or bracers (supposedly to protect an archer's wrist from the recoil of the bowstring), and buttons with a distinctive V-shaped perforation. For over a century the concept of a 'Beaker Folk' was generally accepted in European prehistoric studies, and some believed that this pottery and other artefacts, and the rite of single burial, represented the movement of early metalworkers from a homeland in Iberia or central Europe to other parts of the Continent as well as to Britain and Ireland (Harrison 1980). In recent years, as we shall see, the theory of a distinct Beaker culture or folk has come under increasingly critical scrutiny, and alternative explanations have been offered for the widespread if somewhat discontinuous European distribution of interrelated types of Beaker pottery.

Various Beaker pottery types have been recognised both in Britain and in Ireland and several classifications have been proposed. The Beaker pottery tradition comprises a range of forms, fabrics and sizes, and vessels were evidently used in everyday life and for special occasions. There is a wide range of sizes in both fine and coarse wares, and the fact that so many survive with capacities ranging from about 0.5 to 2 litres is probably because this was the preferred size for deposition with burials; some of these may have served as drinking vessels, while coarse Beakers may have been used as storage and cooking pots as well (Gibson 2002a).

Fine Beaker pottery is well made and is profusely and sometimes attractively decorated. Pots usually have a sort of S-shaped profile and for this reason are sometimes described as 'bell-shaped'. A common and distinctive type of decoration is 'comb' ornament, produced by impressing a toothed implement (probably of bone) into the wet clay before firing, but other decorative techniques are used too and include grooved or incised lines and impressions of twisted cord; many Beakers bear characteristic geometric ornament in horizontal zones. A range of fine and coarse wares come from very different contexts, including burials and settlements, but a considerable amount of this pottery from Ireland is not readily classifiable and to a great extent this is because of the fragmentary nature of much of the material, coming as it does from settlement or other non-funerary contexts.

The various typological groupings proposed for insular Beakers, for example by Clarke (1970), Case (1993; 1995a; 1995b; 2001) and Needham (2005), all illustrate in different ways the complexity of the regional patterns and chronological differences reflected in variations in shape and decoration in this ceramic style. In Ireland, the chronology of the different types of Beaker vessel that can be identified is quite uncertain (Brindley 2004). Some clearly have affinities with Beakers in Britain and some display a distinctively Irish character.

Among the types that can be recognised is the so-called all-over-cord (AOC) style, which may have persisted throughout the Beaker period. These vessels are usually decorated from rim to base with fairly closely set horizontal lines of twisted cord impressions and they are related to another style of Beaker with all-over ornament (AOO), which may take various forms, including horizontal grooving and comb-impressed lines (Fig. 4.4). Fragments of all-over-ornamented Beaker have been found in settlements of Beaker-using people at Newgrange, Knowth, Dalkey Island and Lough Gur. Sherds of all-over-cord Beaker fragments come from Newgrange and Dalkey Island, and have also been reported from later settlement at Ballynagilly, Co. Tyrone, and from sandhills at Whitepark Bay, Co. Antrim. A few such sherds occurred in the Beaker material in the wedge tomb at Loughash (Cashelbane), Co. Tyrone. The relatively small quantity of all-over-cord Beaker from Ireland represents the westernmost distribution of a widespread bell-shaped Beaker type, one also found in Scotland, England, Brittany, the Netherlands and in Germany in the middle Rhineland. In Britain and the Rhineland these Beakers are fairly

frequently found complete and accompanying crouched unburnt burials in flat graves or beneath burial mounds; in Brittany they have been found in megalithic tombs. Other bell-shaped vessels, often red in fabric and decorated with comb-impressed or incised ornament, have been called European (E) Beakers. Decoration is sometimes distinctive: multiple horizontal zones are usually alternately plain and decorated. The decorative motifs employed are invariably simple: horizontal, vertical or oblique lines (the latter sometimes forming a herringbone design); lattice and zigzag (chevron) motifs are also found. Horizontal lines of cord impressions may occasionally occur. Sherds have been reported from settlements such as Newgrange and Dalkey Island, in the Loughash (Cashelbane) wedge tomb and in other similar tombs at Moytirra, Co. Sligo (Fig. 4.4), and Lough Gur. Again the quantity is small and fragmentary—and, as with all-over-cord Beakers, there are interesting contrasts with the British and Continental evidence. The consistent association of these Beakers with crouched unburnt burials in single graves in Britain, for instance, is a striking difference in funerary context. It is true that the unburnt bones of two adults and a child were found along with some of the decorated Moytirra sherds, but the nineteenth-century account of this discovery is brief and direct association less than certain. In any event, it was not a classic Beaker burial, and the same can be said of the few other Beaker burials now known from Ireland (below). Other Beaker forms (such as examples from the Largantea, Co. Derry, wedge tomb and the Grange stone circle: Fig. 4.4) are related to rather loosely defined regional groups in Britain with either relatively tall curving or angular profiles, sometimes with prominent everted necks, variously called long-necked or short-necked Beakers. Simple decorative motifs such as herringbone and lattice continue to be used but broader zones of ornament are common and there is a wide range of motifs, including filled triangles and chevrons. Reserved decoration is sometimes prominent (decorative motifs juxtaposed with plain or reserved designs, notably triangles and chevrons). Incision, grooving and comb impression occur, and plain vessels are also known.

Coarse pottery of various sorts presumably served as domestic wares. Carbonaceous matter

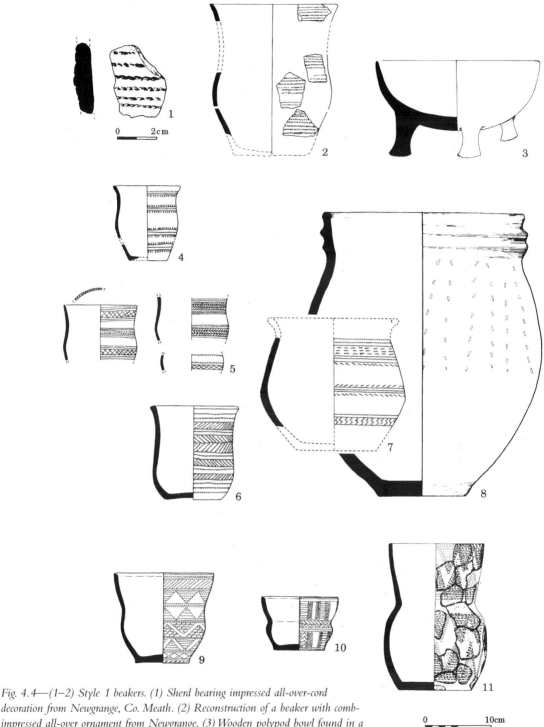

Fig. 4.4—(1–2) Style 1 beakers. (1) Sherd bearing impressed all-over-cord decoration from Newgrange, Co. Meath. (2) Reconstruction of a beaker with comb-impressed all-over ornament from Newgrange. (3) Wooden polypod bowl found in a bog at Tirkernaghan, Co. Tyrone. (4–8) Style 2 beakers. (4 and 6) Newgrange. (5) Three beakers from Moytirra wedge tomb, Co. Sligo. (7) Knowth, Co. Meath. (8) Cluntyganny, Co. Tyrone. (9–11) Style 3 beakers. (9–10) Largantea wedge tomb, Co. Derry. (11) Grange stone circle, Lough Gur, Co. Limerick.

adhering to the surface of some pottery at Newgrange suggests that they functioned as cooking pots. Decoration may consist of impressed lines or fingernail impressions, and one or more cordons, or raised ribs, may occur just below the rim. A very large and complete pot of this sort (with a height of over 41cm) was found in Cluntyganny, near Cookstown, Co. Tyrone (Brennan *et al.* 1978; Fig. 4.4), and sherds also come from sites such as Monknewtown, Co. Meath, Lough Gur and Dalkey Island, and the Kilhoyle, Co. Derry, wedge tomb. Bowls also occur and Newgrange produced fragments of polypod bowls, a rare type also known from Britain, the Rhineland and further east and which may be a pottery rendering of a wooden form with several legs. Several wooden examples have been discovered in Ireland: a circular five-legged wooden bowl found at a depth of 4.5m in a Monaghan bog at Lacklevera, north-east of Killeevan, is probably of prehistoric date, and another found in a bog at Tirkernaghan, just south of Dunnamanagh, Co. Tyrone (Fig. 4.4), with two small wooden round-bottomed cups has been radiocarbon-dated to the third millennium (Earwood 1992).

SETTLEMENT AND ECONOMY

Mention has been made of sherds of Beaker pottery from a number of settlements: aside from the several sandhill sites, these settlements include Dalkey Island, Co. Dublin, Lough Gur, Co. Limerick, Knowth, Co. Meath, Monknewtown, Co. Meath, Newgrange, Co. Meath, and Ballynagilly, Co. Tyrone. At Dalkey Island excavation revealed traces of intermittent activity from about 4000 BC to the early medieval period. The scattered Beaker ware—with no trace of any houses—suggested temporary occupation; some coarse ware was associated with a small shell midden. The absence of structural evidence, however, has prompted the suggestion that much, if not all, of this material may have a ritual explanation (Leon 2005). The Beaker finds at Knowth consisted of five separate pottery concentrations; in one or two instances these were associated with hearths or pits but no evidence of structures was uncovered. Scraps of flint indicated flint-knapping on site, however, and a layer of dark soil was probably the result of accumulated

habitation refuse. Beaker pottery, including a polypod bowl, pits, hearths, post- and stake-holes are reported from Newtownbalregan, Co. Meath (Bayley 2006), but no structures were identifiable. A large quantity of Beaker pottery was found in two pits at Rathmullan, Co. Meath, and included fragments of a handled vessel and polypod bowls. Again, apart from the truncated remains of two slot-trenches nearby, no clear structural remains were evident (Bolger 2003). Pits, stake-holes, Beaker pottery and charred seeds found at Curraheen, near Ballincollig, Co. Cork, may denote settlement activity there (Danaher 2004). A similar puzzling picture of pits and stake-holes but no clear trace of houses was excavated at Ballynagilly. This scarcity of 'Beaker structures' is a well-known phenomenon and is not confined to Ireland; it is just as true of Britain and elsewhere, and it seems likely that many of the huts and houses were lightly built. Structures of roughly oval or circular form have been recognised at a few sites. A structure composed of three concentric C-shaped arcs of stake-holes that perhaps supported a wattle hut or shelter about 7.6m across was associated with Beaker pottery at Graigueshoneen, near Kilmacthomas, Co. Waterford (Tierney *et al.* 2008).

At Monknewtown, Co. Meath, extensive traces of habitation were found in the south-western sector of that embanked enclosure which had also been used for burial and ritual purposes. A roughly oval area about 7m by 4.5m had been dug out to the underlying gravel, leaving a broad shallow pit containing some 50cm of occupation debris: dark soil heavily impregnated throughout with charcoal and potsherds. The pottery from the upper levels was similar to that from the lower levels. An approximately circular hearth, about 1m in diameter and partly stone-lined, lay on the underlying gravel near the centre of the pit, which also contained an irregular series of possible post-holes. The excavator, David Sweetman (1976), suggested that these had held timbers supporting a conical house of more or less oval plan. Pottery fragments included fine Beaker (mainly with incised decoration) and coarse pottery, some decorated. Very little flint and stonework was found: a few flint blades and convex scrapers, and three concave scrapers. The absence of animal bone may have been due to acid soil conditions.

Excavation to the south of the major passage

tomb at Newgrange revealed later activity beyond the limits and on top of the material that had slipped from that mound. There was evidence of considerable occupation: hearths, numerous pits, post-holes and stake-holes, short stretches of foundation trenches, concentrations of Beaker sherds, flints and animal bones were found (O'Kelly *et al.* 1983). The post-holes and trenches, however, did not provide any clearly identifiable house plans, though the existence of circular houses with central hearths has been postulated (Chapter 2). Three oval pits contained charcoal and two contained Beaker ware. One produced fragments of all-over-ornamented Beaker, charred grains of barley and emmer, and charcoal that was radiocarbon-dated to 2488–2284 BC. Another contained fragments of plain bowls and charcoal which yielded a comparable date. A few metres to the north-east of the hearth lay two boulders, one so picked and abraded that the excavator thought that it must have served as a metalworker's anvil. The discovery of a bronze axe and a number of stone tools, a perforated granite hammer, a quartzite hammer and a rubbing stone showing traces of use as a polisher, raised the possibility that at least some metal-hammering and finishing had also taken place on site (O'Kelly and Shell 1979). Elsewhere the occupation evidence included an L-shaped foundation trench thought to be part of a rectangular structure (though no other traces of this rectangle were detected). Here, in and near this trench, the pottery comprised some sherds of Grooved Ware and Beaker ware, including polypod bowl fragments. Besides pottery, pits in this area also contained much flint waste, flint artefacts and animal bones. The flint material indicated that knapping had taken place on the site and the raw material was probably small nodules collected from the glacial drift in the locality. In relation to waste flakes and cores, the percentage of finished implements was 8.6%. Scrapers of various sorts were the commonest implement type, convex scrapers being particularly frequent, but side scrapers, concave scrapers and other forms were represented too. Also found were petit tranchet derivative implements (or knives), as well as a few barbed and tanged and other arrowheads.

The animal remains were preponderantly those of domesticated cattle and pig (Van Wijngaarden-Bakker 1986). Most cattle were killed when they were between three and four years old, suggesting that they were reared primarily for meat and secondarily for milk. The absence of older cows suggests that milk and dairy products were not a significant dietary component. Bull calves may have been castrated and, though direct evidence was lacking, a small proportion of the docile results of this procedure may have been used for traction. Pig bones came from a large breed and with a few exceptions they were killed at two to two and a half years; they too were clearly an important food source, as noted in Chapter 2. The minimum number of individual animals represented suggests that pig may have been the dominant species (53% as opposed to 27% cattle) and this conforms to a pattern identified elsewhere, where pig becomes increasingly important towards the end of the Neolithic (McCormick and Murray 2007). Only about 3% of the identifiable bones were of sheep or goat and some dog bones were identified. Also found were some bones of horse (about 1% of the total). It is difficult to distinguish between the bones of wild and domestic horse. Wild horse is recorded from a considerable number of early sites in Britain but, in contrast, there is no certain evidence for native postglacial wild horse in Ireland. Thus the Newgrange horse bones are tentatively considered to represent a domesticated stock imported in the later third millennium, one of the several innovations that seem to coincide with the appearance of Beaker pottery. A small quantity of wild animal bones (1%) was also found and included wild cat, brown bear, wild boar and red deer. This activity may be a part of the ritual practices indicated by the pit and timber circles there, and the animal bones recovered may be the remains of ceremonial feasts (Mount 1994).

Exceptionally interesting traces of Beaker settlement have been found on Roughan Hill in the south-east of the Burren, Co. Clare (Jones 1998; 2004). An irregularly shaped stone enclosure wall contained the remains of several ruined stone structures, including a house (Fig. 4.5). Attached to this inner enclosure on the south and east was an outer enclosure wall, and radiating off both enclosures were mound walls that ran across the hill and demarcated the boundaries of contemporary fields. The mound walls are low grass-covered features, usually no more than 80cm high and 80cm to 1.5m wide, and they delineate ancient fields in

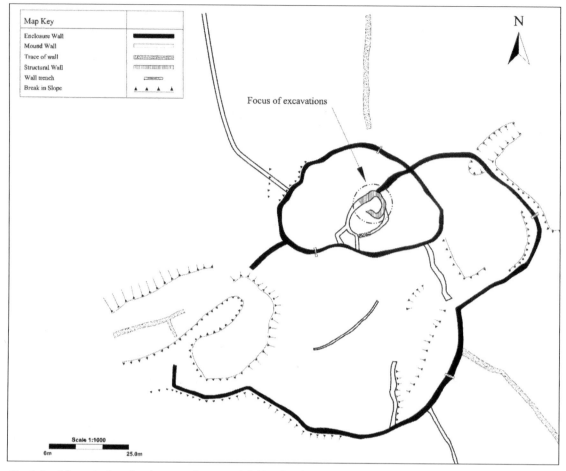

Fig. 4.5—Schematic plan of settlement enclosures and field walls of the Beaker period on Roughan Hill, Co. Clare; the house structure is arrowed.

various parts of the Burren. The fields on Roughan Hill are often small and irregular and some are broadly contemporary with the roughly circular structure at the centre of the site. This on excavation turned out to be the stone foundations of a prehistoric house 6–7m in internal diameter. Animal bones indicated that cattle, sheep or goat and pig were raised, and numerous quern fragments showed that plant foods were also being used. Finds included stone implements such as chert arrowheads and scrapers, and hundreds of Beaker sherds that date the farmstead and its associated field walls to *c.* 2000 BC. It seems likely that the settlement was contemporary with a number of wedge tombs in the immediate locality.

BEAKER BURIALS AND THE BEAKER ASSEMBLAGE

Allusion has already been made to the intriguing differences in Beaker funerary practice between Britain and Ireland. In England, Scotland and Wales, Beakers are consistently associated with crouched skeletons in graves. In Ireland the situation is very different. Fragments of Beaker pottery have been found in a number of excavated wedge tombs, which more often than not have also produced some cremated bone, though tombs such as Lough Gur and Moytirra, for instance, did yield unburnt human bones. Other Beaker burials are rare. The cremated bones of an adult and a child were placed in the passage of one of the satellite tombs at Knowth and sherds of a Beaker were found in and

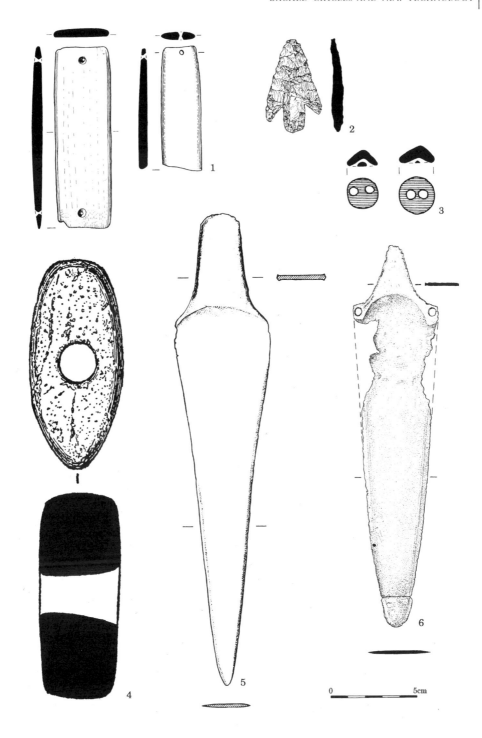

Fig. 4.6—(1) A pair of stone wrist-guards found at Corran, Co. Armagh. (2) Barbed and tanged flint arrowhead from a hoard of flints at Ballyclare, Co. Antrim. (3) Two V-perforated buttons of jet found in the Mound of the Hostages, Tara, Co. Meath. (4) Stone battleaxe from Drumeague, Co. Cavan. (5) Tanged copper knife from Blacklands, Co. Tyrone. (6) Tanged copper knife with rivet holes in the shoulders from Derrynamanagh, Co. Galway.

close to the burial; the pot is a well-made bell-shaped vessel without decoration. Three small sherds with incised zonal ornament found with a cremation in the stone circle at Kiltierney, Co. Fermanagh, have been compared to Beaker. The varied nature of these burials and the uncertainties about some of them only emphasise all the more that difference in funerary custom. In Ireland, it is some makers of pottery of the Bowl Tradition of the late third millennium who adopt the practice of crouched unburnt burial with accompanying pot in classic Beaker fashion. The widespread European distribution of some Beaker pottery, the occurrence in many areas of a consistent burial rite and the recurrence in these graves of a variety of artefacts such as copper knives, archer's bracers, buttons and arrowheads have all helped to give credence to the concept of a culturally distinct 'Beaker Folk'. True, this Beaker assemblage came mainly from graves, but when, as in Britain for instance, the broad-skulled or brachycephalic skeletons from those graves appeared to differ from the narrow-skulled or dolicocephalic remains from earlier contexts, then arguments for a new intrusive population group seemed persuasive. Such differences in cranial morphology remain unexplained, but they could have been caused by a range of environmental factors and head shape can change in populations over time (Brodie 1994).

In addition to pottery, other elements of what has been called the Beaker assemblage are found in Ireland, though not, of course, in direct association in single graves. Over 100 bracers (or wrist-guards) are known, most of them unfortunately stray finds without any documentation as to their archaeological context and many without even their provenance recorded (Harbison 1976). The great majority of the Irish examples (95%) are of slender rectangular or subrectangular shape, of more or less flat or of plano-convex cross-section with two holes, one at either end (Fig. 4.6, 1). This type is a western European fashion, found in the Iberian Peninsula and France and well represented in Britain. A very small number are of broader rectangular shape, of flat or concave–convex cross-section, and have four perforations, two at either end. Bracers of this sort are frequent in central Europe but examples have been found in Britain and the Netherlands too. Irish specimens are made from quite a variety of polished stone, including red

jasper, siltstone, porcellanite, sandstone, porphyrite and slate, and there seems to have been some preference for stones of a reddish colour. Of the provenanced examples a remarkable number, no less than two-thirds, come from County Antrim, with the remainder scattered as far west as County Galway and as far south as County Limerick. This Antrim concentration is extraordinary but it may in part be due to the activities of a number of antiquarian collectors in that part of the country. As mentioned, the find circumstances of most of these objects were not recorded. One was found in a burial at Longstone, Co. Kildare, where a large stone-lined grave at the foot of a standing stone contained fragments of a two-holed bracer, a few coarse potsherds, a flint, a stone bead and cremated bones. A number have been found in bogs, and two grey siltstone bracers from a bog at Corran, about 10km south of Armagh, were found in 1833 'in a box bound with a gold band, together with some gold circular plates, and several jet beads of various shapes' (Case 1977). Unfortunately no more precise details are recorded and only the bracers appear to have survived, though it has been suggested that an unprovenanced gold disc may be one of the lost circular pieces (Fig. 4.12, 6). It is generally accepted that most of these objects were either intended to protect the archer's wrist from the recoil of the bowstring or were decorative versions of such a protective device. Since the modern archer's wrist-guard is a piece of leather that protects the inner arm and has thongs or clasps on the outer arm, some bracers may have been the equivalent of the clasp or have served to provide tension to the thonging and been worn on the outer arm (King 1999). The Corran find indicates that some were highly prized; certainly many were carefully made and polished, and the finest examples may have been emblematic rather than functional items. Some very finely made specimens in Britain, including several with gold-capped rivets in the perforations, suggest that these were highly valued objects, perhaps symbolically representing the status of the archer (Woodward *et al.* 2006; Fokkens *et al.* 2008).

Buttons of various types are known in Beaker contexts in Europe and in Britain, where the commonest form is conical with a basal V-shaped perforation and where examples of jet and amber have been found singly or in pairs mainly in later

Beaker graves. A small number of these V-perforated buttons from Ireland may be of Beaker period or later date. Of jet, shale, steatite and bone, most are stray finds but a small number come from burials. Three (one of shale and two of jet) were found in the passage tomb in the Mound of the Hostages at Tara, Co. Meath (Fig. 4.6, 3), for example, where the two jet examples were associated with unburnt burials and Bowl Tradition pots. They may have served as dress-fasteners or as pouch-fasteners (Shepherd 2009).

Another innovation attributed to Beaker-using people is the barbed and tanged arrowhead (Green 1980). In Britain, flint arrowheads of this variety occur in Beaker contexts and, like buttons, continue in use in post-Beaker times. A number have been recovered from Irish wedge tombs and Beaker settlements such as Ballynagilly and Newgrange. Among the numerous stray finds, several have been found with part of their wooden shafts still attached: one from a bog at Tankardsgarden, near Newbridge, Co. Kildare, had an incomplete hazel shaft, 42cm in length, split for the insertion of the point and bound with animal sinew or gut; a second, from Gortrea, near Killimor, Co. Galway, is said to have had an alder shaft, and a third such find comes from Ballykilleen bog, near Edenderry, Co. Offaly. Different types of barbed and tanged arrowheads have been identified, including large and small forms, and one large type, named after a find from Ballyclare, Co. Antrim (Fig. 4.6, 2), seems to be a favoured Irish type. The Ballyclare discovery consisted of a hoard of 22 finished arrowheads and seventeen roughly oval flint flakes which have been interpreted as blanks or rough-outs from which other arrowheads could be made; the finished examples have an average length of 6.5cm (Flanagan 1970). A perforated stone axe, a so-called 'battleaxe' (Simpson 1990), is another item occasionally associated with Beaker pottery in Britain, and some Irish examples may be of this period too (Fig. 4.6, 4).

An important and novel artefact occasionally found with Beaker pottery abroad is a tanged copper knife, one of a series of metal objects and trinkets recorded in such contexts from Britain to central Europe. It was associations such as these which inspired the belief that the 'Beaker Folk' were the first metalworkers in certain parts of western Europe, including Ireland and Britain, and

it was once widely believed that wholesale migrations of these people were responsible for innovations like copper-working, new funerary customs like single burial, and even the introduction of domesticated horses. Tanged copper knives are amongst the earliest metal objects known in Ireland but, like wrist-guards and V-perforated buttons, they have not been found in direct association with Beaker pottery. Most of these knives, and they are few in number, are stray finds, often from bogs. They are simple flat implements of copper with a rather rounded point and sometimes with bevelled cutting edges; the sides of the tang are occasionally serrated to give better purchase to a hilt of some organic material (Fig. 4.6, 5–6). A few related knives have one or two holes for rivets to improve the stability of the hilt. Two tanged knives come from important hoards containing other metal types, which of course provide a possible indication of some of the range of implements in contemporary use. At Knocknagur, near Tuam, Co. Galway, a nineteenth-century bog find has provided a name for the first metalworking phase in Irish prehistory. This hoard comprised one tanged copper knife, three flat copper axes and three copper awls (Fig. 4.9, 1). At Whitespots, just north of Newtownards, Co. Down, a very corroded tanged knife was discovered in a rock crevice along with an axe and a riveted copper blade variously considered to be a dagger or a halberd. The Corran find mentioned above is just one piece of evidence that suggests that some sheet goldwork was manufactured at this time as well, and it is contended that some gold discs, lunulae and earrings could be 'Beaker work'.

It was not until the early 1930s that excavations in a number of wedge tombs in the north of Ireland revealed the existence of Beaker pottery in any quantity in Ireland. Thereafter it was generally assumed that 'the Beaker Folk' must have been a significant element of the population, and some believed that these people introduced the knowledge of metalworking and in effect initiated a copper or bronze age. The traditional concept of 'a Beaker Folk' has received considerable scrutiny in recent years and various attempts have been made to reassess the significance of the widespread geographical distribution of 'the Beaker assemblage'. It has become increasingly clear that there are significant differences between regional

Beaker-using groups and this is particularly evident in the settlement material. To a lesser extent these regional differences are also apparent in funerary contexts (the differences here between Britain and Ireland being a good example). One common link is the bell-shaped Beaker vessel itself but, as already noted, the material from single graves also includes some other widely distributed objects, such as bracers, tanged copper daggers and buttons, which are rare in settlement contexts. The wide-ranging objects, however, are not subsistence-producing tools; the Beaker pot is sometimes—though not always—finely made and decorated, and items such as the polished stone wrist-guards were probably highly prized pieces more for display than protection. If this limited series of artefacts was an indication of the social status of the deceased in life, then their function was primarily a social one.

As emblems of status, items such as copper knives could have been exchanged, traded and copied over wide areas by late third-millennium societies in which individual ranking and social differences were becoming more marked. If the attractive Beaker were also associated with the ceremonial drinking of some alcoholic brew such as beer or mead, its importance would only be enhanced. Indeed, the residue in one Beaker from a Scottish grave, at Ashgrove, Fife, has been identified as mead made from fermented honey flavoured with meadowsweet (Dickson 1978). Since pollen indicated that this honey was derived from lime trees, which then, as now, only grow further to the south, it may have been an imported and presumably costly funerary offering. Some association with alcohol and possibly with ceremonial drinking or even with the consumption of plant-derived hallucinogens would offer a plausible explanation for their initial widespread distribution. That said, the shape and size of some Beakers indicates that they were not likely to be used as drinking vessels, and elsewhere they evidently served a variety of purposes (Guerra-Doce 2006). The regular occurrence of this pottery in settlement contexts also suggests mundane usage; it will be recalled that Roughan Hill was a very simple farmstead whose inhabitants nonetheless shared in a widespread ceramic fashion that probably had a variety of social roles.

The hypothesis of a distinct population group, 'the Beaker Folk' of older archaeological literature, has therefore been replaced by a functional model in which various artefacts, including Beakers, are considered as expressions of individual status. While this model does not preclude the possibility that some users of Beaker pottery travelled from place to place, it does obviate the need to presuppose complex population movements to account for the European spread of 'the Beaker assemblage'. Small-scale events, such as the movement of marriage partners, may have been a factor (Vander Linden 2007). As far as Ireland is concerned, the adoption of certain Beaker period fashions by some of the indigenous population seems to be a reasonable explanation. Like the Beaker pot and the stone bracer, it is possible that the knowledge of metalworking was introduced by a small number of metalworking specialists at this time, but the Irish evidence at present is rather equivocal. If the tanged copper knife was one of the high-status metal artefacts of the period, then the argument that it and the knowledge of copper-working and some forms of Beakers were all interrelated would have much to recommend it.

There may be important differences between the earliest Irish and British metal industries, however, and in Ireland the scarcity of Beaker pottery associations means that the importance of this pottery type as a status symbol is very difficult to estimate. Other objects, like the more numerous copper axes or some of the goldwork or some perforated stone battleaxes, for instance, may have played a more important role in this sphere. What evidence there is suggests that most Beaker pottery was locally made and not widely distributed. At Newgrange, scientific analysis of clay and grit tempering of the Beaker pottery indicated local production. Some petrological analysis of the grit tempering of the Knowth and Monknewtown Beaker ware as well as small samples from Dalkey Island and Lough Gur all point to local manufacture. An increased emphasis on status and display may be only part of the explanation. Domestic coarse Beaker wares may not have been particularly significant in this respect, and when fine and coarse Beaker pottery is considered together it is possible that a whole range of pottery types became familiar over large areas primarily through a constant pattern of seasonal movements and exchanges between small communities, a pattern of interaction as old as the fourth millennium. Metal artefacts and the knowledge of metallurgy were probably transmitted to Ireland through participation in such Beaker exchange networks. The discovery of early copper mines associated with Beaker pottery at Ross Island, near Killarney, Co. Kerry, is an important link.

Copper-mining was undertaken on Ross Island on the shores of Lough Leane in early prehistory, in early medieval times and from the eighteenth to the early twentieth century (Fig. 4.7). Because the rich copper ore was relatively close to the surface, this was an attractive location for early miners. Despite all the more recent activity that destroyed much of the earlier workings, it has been possible to identify very early mining activity dating from the period 2400–1900 BC (O'Brien 2004a). The remains included dozens of flooded vertical mine shafts and cave-like openings cut into exposed limestone rock faces. Excavation at two locations confirmed the exceptional early date of some of this mining work. Traces of fire-setting showed that, to extract the copper ore, the miners lit wood-fuelled

fires against the rock face and hammered and prised out the heat-fractured stone using stone, bone and wooden tools. This practice has been examined in greater detail at a slightly later mining location on Mount Gabriel in west Cork (below). The most impressive mine visible today at Ross Island is a cave-like opening in a 5–6m-high cliff face. This shaft measures over 10m wide, 2.7m in height and extends inwards at an incline for over 8m. Excavation was confined to the front area, where spoil from the mine contained numerous stone hammers or mauls, charcoal and animal bones, including cattle spatulae. These shoulder blades were probably used as crude shovels to move broken rock that was then transported in leather or wooden containers.

Extensive evidence for nearby occupation was discovered, indicating intermittent work-camp activity over the five centuries when the mines were worked. This consisted of lines and arcs of stake-holes and shallow foundation trenches, representing flimsy structures or shelters possibly

Fig. 4.7—Artist's reconstruction of the Beaker period copper-mining settlement at Ross Island, Killarney, Co. Kerry.

covered with cattle hides. Some of the stake-holes may have supported screens or racks that served as windbreaks or were connected with animal butchery. Finds included Beaker pottery, animal bones, stone hammers and some worked chert and flint. The latter included knapping debris, scrapers, a hollow-based arrowhead and a plano-convex flint knife. The pottery and animal bone deposits seem to be domestic refuse. Cattle (67%) and pig (25%) were the main animals exploited; some bones of sheep, dog, red deer and hare were also present. The Beaker pottery conforms to that recovered from domestic contexts elsewhere and some of it was quite well finished. It seems to be ordinary domestic ware brought to the mining settlement as drinking vessels and water-containers.

The mineralised rock extracted from the nearby mines was sorted and crushed at the work camp, and all this was probably done on a seasonal or part-time basis. Many thousands of hammer fragments were recovered. Rounded cobbles from nearby riverbeds were used, and some had pecked grooves to secure rope or wooden handles. Evidence from Mount Gabriel shows that twisted hazel or willow rods or withies were sometimes used as hafts. Boulders of sandstone or larger limestone blocks were used as anvils. Numerous pits were found and in some cases, judging from fire-reddened walls and the presence of charcoal and copper ore, were used as furnace pits associated with the processing of copper ore. The ore concentrate was roasted and smelted in these furnace pits to produce droplets of copper. No artefacts were manufactured here; this was presumably done at a nearby parent settlement. The extensive mining of arsenical copper by users of Beaker pottery at Ross Island suggests that Killarney was the principal source of the first copper metal made in Ireland.

NEW TECHNOLOGIES: COPPER, BRONZE AND GOLD

With significant copper and gold resources, Ireland was one of the important metal-producing areas in early prehistoric Europe. The large number of copper and bronze axes and gold objects that have been found is testimony of this. The morphological developments of various metal types have been studied, and these changes in form, when coupled with evidence for relative contemporaneity provided by hoard deposits and grave groups, permit the construction of a sequence of overlapping metalworking traditions (below). The most primitive copper axe is a typologically simple, flat, almost straight-sided implement: the sides are straight for most of its length but curve very slightly outward near a slightly convex cutting edge; the butt is flat and thick. The shape is almost trapezoidal. Peter Harbison (1969b) in a study of flat copper and bronze axes includes these trapezoidal examples along with axes with more curving sides (like those from Knocknagur: Fig. 4.9, 1) in the one category named after a find at Lough Ravel, Co. Antrim (below), but Colin Burgess (1980) has argued that the simple straight-sided trapezoidal axes in this Lough Ravel category represent a copper-working tradition which pre-dates the curving-sided flat axe and tanged knife tradition as found at Knocknagur. A study of over 200 flat, thick-butted axes noted a very small number (about 4%) of straight-sided specimens that compared closely in their proportions to early Continental trapezoidal copper axes, some from Beaker or possibly pre-Beaker contexts. Axes with more or less straight sides (showing only a slight curvature) and still displaying some resemblance to Continental trapeze-shaped axes comprised about 30% of the total sample. These axes have been found mainly in Ulster, Leinster and Munster, the latter province producing almost as many as the other two combined. Given their rarity in Britain, they may represent an early Munster copper industry that Burgess has named the Castletownroche stage after a possible hoard of four axes found near Mallow, Co. Cork. The principal problem as far as this Irish material is concerned is that it is poorly dated. The one hoard containing trapeze-shaped axes is not particularly helpful. Only two of the Castletownroche axes survive: one is trapezoidal but the other has slightly curving sides (Fig. 4.9, 2), departing from the primitive Continental straight-sided form and foreshadowing the preferred shape of Irish and British axe-makers. The significance of these trapeze-shaped copper axes remains a puzzle.

Inspiration from Atlantic Europe is a possibility, conceivably from Brittany with later Continental influence coming via Britain. There is now a measure of agreement that this innovation is

Phases Ireland	Harbison 1973	Burgess 1974	Needham (Britain) 1996	Approximate dates partly following Brindley 2007
Knocknagur	Knocknagur Phase	Stage I Castletownroche	Metalwork Assemblage I and II	2500-2000 BC
		Stage 2 Lough Ravel		
	Frankford-Killaha-Ballyvally Phase	Stage 3 Frankford		
Killaha		Stage 4 Killaha	Metalwork Assemblage III	2000-1900 BC
Ballyvally		Stage 5 Ballyvally	Metalwork Assemblage IV	1900-1700 BC
		stage 6 Scrabo Hill	Metalwork Assemblage V	
Derryniggin	Derryniggin	Stage 7 Derryniggin	Metalwork Assemblage VI	1700-1600 BC

Fig. 4.8—Metalwork phases of the earlier Bronze Age.

contemporary with the spread of Beaker pottery and related fashions from about 2500 BC and, given the complexity of the technological process involved, a small group of specialist metalworkers was probably involved. Two sources are possible, one from the Iberian Peninsula perhaps via Atlantic France, the other from the Rhineland to Britain and Ireland. Trapeze-shaped copper axes do occur in Iberia and France but the rarity of other artefacts of likely Iberian extraction in Ireland may be important negative evidence. The very occasional parallel may indicate sporadic southern contact through the medium of an overlapping network of coastal traffic along the Atlantic façade. The bulk of the evidence, however, seems to point to Britain and ultimately the Rhineland and, given the evidence from Ross Island in particular, the claim that the makers of Beaker pottery had some role to play in the transmission of the new technology seems to be the likeliest explanation. Copper objects, notably tanged knives, and sheet-gold artefacts do have parallels in Beaker burials in Britain, but it is fair to say that the appearance of selected metal items in a funerary context there

may not reflect the full range of metalwork in circulation. The large number of Irish copper axes and halberds (below) raises many questions, not least because these artefacts are relatively scarce in Britain. This contrast between the Irish and British copper industries is one reason why some writers have been reluctant to see both as having a similar Continental source.

Several writers have attempted to divide the metalwork of the late third millennium and the earlier second millennium into a series of chronological and metalworking stages. In these schemes the typological development of axes and daggers in particular is the basis of a sequence that in very general terms is supported by associated finds in a small number of significant hoards and by a number of radiocarbon dates. These hoards provide the names for the different phases, and various schemes have been proposed and correlated with similar sequences in Britain. The general chronological framework of successive metalwork phases spanning some nine centuries below incorporates very general absolute dates partly following Lanting in Brindley (2007), who modifies some earlier schemes (Fig. 4.8).

While the broader sequence of metalworking development is clear, the postulated stages or phases of development are imprecisely dated and a degree of overlap is likely. As already mentioned, Burgess has suggested an early copper industry producing trapeze-shaped axes, his Castletownroche phase, but Harbison has placed both trapeze-shaped and curving-sided copper axes in the one typological category and in the one Knocknagur phase. This name is retained here for the earliest stage of Irish metalworking, including the production of the primitive Castletownroche axes.

METALWORK OF THE KNOCKNAGUR PHASE

The copper axe is the principal metal artefact of the Knocknagur phase, named after that hoard found in a bog near Tuam, Co. Galway, with a tanged copper knife and three awls (Fig. 4.9, 1). The typological evolution of Irish copper and bronze axes broadly conforms to the classic developmental sequence first recognised in the nineteenth century. This progressive sequence, from broad flat copper axe to narrower forms of flanged bronze axe, is generally believed to reflect a desire for improved efficiency, both technological and functional. In a general way this sequence has also some chronological significance, albeit a quite imprecise one, as we shall see. Over 2,000 early copper and bronze axes have been recorded by Harbison; unfortunately over 56% of them are unprovenanced, with no record of where and in what context they were discovered. Of those with some information about these circumstances, almost 95% are isolated finds. Four types of copper axe have been identified (Schmidt and Burgess 1981):

—Type Castletownroche: the straight-sided form of copper axe with a broad, straight, thick butt (Fig. 4.9, 2 left).

—Type Growtown: another straight-sided axe named after a find of two copper axes (found with two rounded stones and a boar's tusk) near Dunshaughlin, Co. Meath; it differs from Castletownroche-type axes in having a thin butt and some examples are broader and shorter (Fig. 4.9, 3).

—Type Lough Ravel: named after a group of five axes (considered a possible hoard because of their similar coloration or patina) from a bog midway between Toome and Randalstown, Co. Antrim. These are flat copper axes with broad thick butts and slightly curving sides (Fig. 4.9, 4). There are two important associated finds with tanged copper knives: the axe in the Whitespots hoard and two of the three axes in the Knocknagur hoard are of this type.

—Type Ballybeg: a similar flat copper axe with slightly curving sides but having a thin butt is a type named after a County Cork hoard (Fig. 4.9, 5). A mixture of thick- and thin-butted axes was found in a hoard from Carrickshedoge, Co. Wexford, and in the Knocknagur find one of the three axes has a butt which, as Harbison puts it, 'could almost be described as thin'; clearly the identification of a thin butt sometimes presents difficulties and may sometimes be a subjective assessment. The association of thick- and thin-butted forms indicates, however, that some measure of contemporaneity is likely. Some are also contemporary with a typologically more developed form of dagger: several Ballybeg-type axes and a Lough Ravel type were found with a small riveted dagger and a halberd in a hoard found together in 1892 at a depth of 10m in a bog at Frankford, near Birr, Co. Offaly.

The large number of Castletownroche, Growtown, Lough Ravel and Ballybeg copper axes (over 400 are known) is generally considered to demonstrate Ireland's importance as a centre of early copper-working, particularly when compared with Britain, where some 40 examples are recorded in northern England and Scotland. Indeed, the latter mostly have the distinctive Irish copper composition and may even be the product of some early metal exchanges across the Irish Sea.

All the Irish axes are usually quite small, 10–15cm in length, and they were possibly mounted in club-shaped wooden hafts (Fig. 4.9, 7). They could have been cast in simple open stone moulds (Fig. 4.9, 6), and some axe-shaped objects called 'ingots' with a plano-convex cross-section may be unfinished axes.

Metallurgical analyses (including lead isotope analysis) have indicated that while a few axes were

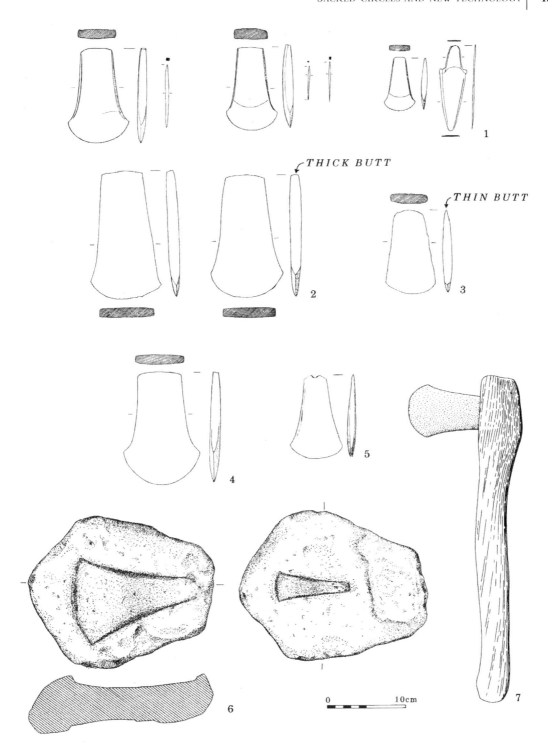

Fig. 4.9—Copper axes. (1) Hoard of copper axes with thick butts, awls and a tanged knife from Knocknagur, Co. Galway. (2) Two axes from Castletownroche, Co. Cork (the example on the left is a straight-sided trapezoidal specimen and both have thick butts). (3) Straight-sided axe with thin butt from Growtown, Co. Meath. (4) One of the thick-butted axes from the Lough Ravel hoard, Co. Antrim. (5) The one surviving thin-butted axe from the Ballybeg, Co. Cork, hoard. (6) Stone mould for two flat axes from Lyre, Co. Cork. (7) Axe mounted in a club-shaped wooden haft.

made of unalloyed copper (a relatively soft metal), a greater number were made of copper with significant traces of arsenic and trace elements of antimony and silver. It was these ores with their distinctive arsenic–antimony–silver composition that were exploited at Ross Island, Co. Kerry. Indeed, Ross Island itself may have been the main source of early Irish arsenical copper, and the importance of this region is demonstrated by the fact that 34% of all provenanced copper axes (and a number of important hoards) come from this part of Ireland. The new and effective copper axe may have been rapidly and widely adopted; timbers used in bog trackways at Corlea and Annaghbeg, Co. Longford, dating from shortly before 2000 BC, were cut with copper or bronze blades (A. O'Sullivan 1996).

Apart from the copper awls in the Knocknagur hoard, the only other copper artefact assigned with certainty to this early metalworking phase is the tanged copper knife. A small number are known and, apart from the Knocknagur and Whitespots examples, all are isolated finds. Like Knocknagur, some have come from watery contexts and may have been votive depositions. One from Blacklands, near Fivemiletown, Co. Tyrone, was found at a depth of 1.2m in a bog (Fig. 4.6, 5). They were probably cast in simple open stone moulds; one such mould, possibly from Ireland, is preserved. Developed variants include examples with one or more rivet holes in the tang or with a rivet hole in each shoulder. A bog find from Derrynamanagh, near New Inn, Co. Galway, is a fine example of the latter (Fig. 4.6, 6); in addition to the two rivet holes it displays differential corrosion indicating the former presence of an organic haft, and the tang bears characteristic hammered indentations to give it greater purchase in the hilt. A dagger with a single rivet hole and a total of five rivet notches in the sides of the tang was recovered from the Sillees River, near Enniskillen, Co. Fermanagh, and like most of these tanged daggers has the typical arsenic–antimony–silver impurity pattern of Ross Island copper. The Killaha dagger (below) is one exception: with a pair of rivet holes in the shoulder as on the Derrynamanagh variant, it has grooves on its blade that recall the grooving found on some British tanged daggers and it is interesting to note that its composition, with high arsenic, some nickel and almost no other impurities, also finds parallels

in Britain (Sheridan and Northover 1993; Needham 2000a).

METALWORK OF THE KILLAHA PHASE

The Killaha phase marks the commencement of the widespread adoption of bronze *c.* 2000 BC. It is named after a hoard from Killaha East, near Kenmare, Co. Kerry, found in 1939 under a limestone slab below a sandstone outcrop, which comprised the tanged copper dagger just mentioned, a halberd, four axes, one or two unfinished axes and a fragment of another. Like the Frankford hoard, this find suggests that axes, daggers and halberds continued to be the principal metal products. The four bronze axes are examples of type Killaha, and it seems that most axes of this type may well be made from an alloy of tin and copper. They are of broad and approximately triangular shape with a shallow crescent-shaped cutting edge, which is occasionally clearly bevelled (Fig. 4.10, 1). Most are flat, but slight hammered-up flanges are found on a few examples; butts are thin and rounded. These large, broad-bladed axes with evenly curved sides have a length to maximum width ratio of 1.5 or less to 1, and the largest example, found in the ruins of Kilcrea Castle, near Ovens, Co. Cork, measures 31cm in length, 22cm in width and is 9mm thick. As was the case with some polished stone axes, large bronze examples like this may have had a ritual purpose.

A hoard of ten or eleven axes found at Carhan, Cahersiveen, Co. Kerry, was probably a votive deposit. The find was made when an attempt was made to remove a large stone in the middle of a small channel of a river; this stone (which served as a stepping stone between an area of marshy ground and dry land) contained a slab-covered hollow in which the axes were arranged in a circle, cutting edge outwards, around a deposit of wood ashes and small fragments of deer bones. Only four of these axes are preserved: two are of type Ballybeg and two of type Killaha, suggesting a measure of contemporaneity between the two types. A ritual use for some bronze axes should not obscure the fact that experiment has shown that these bronze implements are about twice as efficient as stone axes and the appearance of such superior tools must have contributed to major developments in woodworking.

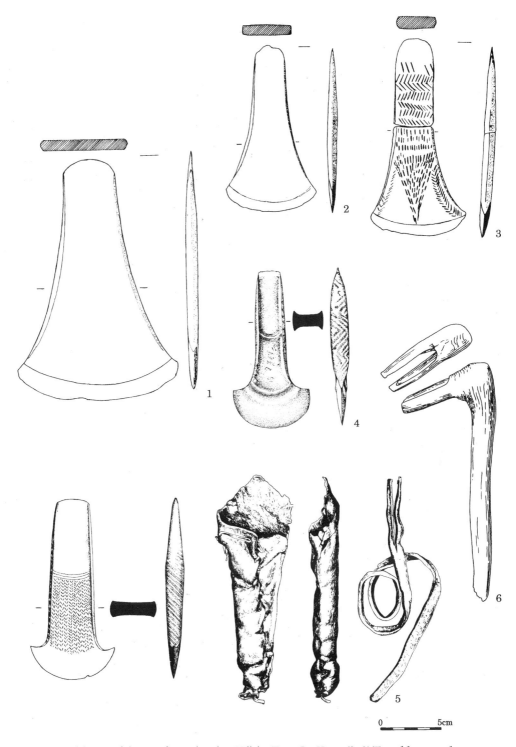

Fig. 4.10—Bronze axes. (1) One of the axes from a hoard at Killaha East, Co. Kerry. (2–3) Two of four axes from a possible hoard at Ballyvally, Co. Down. (4) A Derryniggin-type axe with flanges and stop-ridge from Clondalkin, Co. Dublin. (5) A decorated Derryniggin-type axe from Brockagh, Co. Kildare, found in a leather sheath. (6) A split knee-shaped wooden haft for flanged axes (not to scale).

A few type Killaha axes bear decoration that usually consists of longitudinal grooving, possibly produced by grinding and polishing. Their general distribution provides no clue as to the whereabouts of any manufacturing focus, if such there was, and unfortunately just over 70% have no recorded provenance. Analyses demonstrate that the tin content in these bronzes varies somewhat (from about 7% to 15%) but a majority contain in the region of 10%. The origins of the new alloying technique are uncertain. Continental inspiration for bronze-working has been assumed, given the scarcity of tin in these islands, and a central European stimulus for this new process of alloying copper with tin is generally accepted. There may have been wide-ranging trade and exchange in tin and copper, and the rich tin resources in south-western England, in Devon and Cornwall, were probably utilised. Alluvial tin, mainly in the form of pebbles of cassiterite, was presumably the first source to be exploited, but tin ores near the surface were possibly mined as well. Early smiths could well have fortuitously discovered the benefits of including pebbles or grains of cassiterite when smelting copper, or could even have perceived the improved casting properties of the rarer mineral stannite, an ore containing both copper and tin. Unfortunately, evidence for early tin-mining is all but absent, much of it conceivably destroyed by later working (Barber 2003). It seems as if south-western England may have been the source of tin for the Irish bronze industry (Budd *et al.* 1997), and while it is possible that alluvial cassiterite from the Gold Mines River in County Wicklow and other rivers in the area was exploited (Jackson 1979), evidence is lacking.

AXES OF THE BALLYVALLY AND DERRYNIGGIN PHASES

Developed flat axes are the principal artefacts of the Ballyvally and Derryniggin metalworking phases and are the result of a developmental trend from broad, simple and more or less triangular axes to narrower forms with straighter parallel sides. This trend is discernible in axes of type Ballyvally, named after a find of four axes on Ballyvally Mountain, east of Newry, Co. Down, in 1843. Nothing more is recorded about the discovery but it may have been

a hoard. Axes of this type (and various subdivisions of this category; see Schmidt and Burgess 1981) are flat or slightly flanged with thin, rounded butts; sides are more or less parallel for about half the length and they then diverge gently towards the cutting edge. They are usually 15–20cm in length with a maximum width to length ratio of 1 to more than 1.5. About 50% are decorated, usually with fairly simple hammered or engraved geometric motifs, herringbone and stroke ornament being particularly common (Fig. 4.10, 2–3). The presence of slight hammered flanges or a median thickening or both on some examples is an indication of a change or improvement in hafting methods: it is believed that these axes were intended to fit into the split or forked end of a knee-shaped or angled wooden haft (Fig. 4.10, 6). The narrow flanged portion would fit firmly into the split end and a median thickening would help to prevent the axe being driven further into the haft. The differential colouring of the patina of the Newgrange axe retained traces of this sort of haft. The Ballyvally type of axe is the commonest Irish form: over 800 are recorded. Most occur in the east and north-east of the country. The small number of hoards is widely distributed: the only concentration is to be found in the north-east and there is a possibility that this region was a centre for their manufacture. Ritual deposition is attested at the Toormore wedge tomb, Co. Cork, for instance, where a developed flat axe with faint traces of decoration on faces and sides and two pieces of raw copper were placed as an offering near the tomb entrance.

Harbison included a range of developed axes in his type Derryniggin. This County Leitrim hoard was found in a bog near Newtown Gore in the course of turf-cutting and comprised two fragmentary axes and two plano-convex flint knives. The deposition of parts of broken axes is unusual and—if not scrap bronze—may recall the ceremonial destruction of some daggers placed in burials. The Derryniggin axe is fairly small, under 13cm in length, with straight and more or less parallel sides that curve out abruptly to an expanded crescentic cutting edge. Butts are usually flat and low hammered flanges are present in many cases, though a few axes are flat; a median thickening or ridge often occurs. A number of axes have flanges several millimetres high (possibly cast) and a few have a true stop-ridge (Fig. 4.10, 4). Decoration occurs on a majority of examples. The presence of high flanges on both faces is a significant development for it may imply the use of a bivalve or two-piece mould. No stone moulds for these axes are known at present and baked clay moulds may have been used, but it is also possible that high flanges could have been produced by laborious forging and grinding. Many of these bronze axes were presumably used for woodworking and tree-felling, or even as weapons, but again not all may have been functional. A decorated Derryniggin-type axe in mint condition from Brockagh, near Robertstown, Co. Kildare (Fig. 4.10, 5), was found in a leather sheath at a depth of 4m in a bog; the sheath was slit for attachment to a strap or belt, and it seems that the axe was not hafted but carried around in this fashion, perhaps as a ceremonial object or a status symbol. The overall decoration on some other examples may imply that they too were meant to be seen in an unhafted state on certain occasions.

HOARDS

Axes occur in about 90% of early metal hoards, and over 40 hoards containing at least one axe have been recorded (O'Flaherty 1995). Almost 60% of these are hoards of axes only, the largest being a group of 25 found in a bog at Clashbredane, near Ballineen, Co. Cork; all but two are lost and the survivors belong to type Lough Ravel. Deposits containing other objects are not common, although a few axes were accompanied by copper cakes or pieces of copper, as at Toormore. Other implements are rare and the small number of hoards, such as Knocknagur, Killaha, Frankford and Derryniggin, containing a range of items such as knives, daggers, halberds and awls are the exception. The frequent occurrence of axes in hoards is also in marked contrast with their rarity in graves. Clearly axes had some particular significance at this time. As with some stone axes, copper and bronze examples may have been an important element in a system of competitive gift exchange in which social prestige was enhanced by the acquisition of highly prized objects in a display of wealth and munificence. If this was so, the deliberate deposition of hoards containing axes may have been votive offerings for communal gain; of course they could also have

served to increase individual status if publicly perceived as an act of conspicuous generosity, a pattern of activity prominent in later prehistory.

While a majority of hoards have been found in dry-land contexts, often on or protected by stones, almost half have been found in wet conditions, usually in bogs. Indeed, individual axes may have been deposited in this fashion as well; of those whose context has been recorded no less than half come from wet contexts such as rivers, lakes or bogs and, as the Carhan find demonstrates, such contexts were evidently deliberately chosen on some occasions. Various trends are detectable in the practice of hoard deposition: the smaller numbers of typologically later axes (and the fewer axes in these later hoards in whatever context) may denote a decline in the custom of including axes. There is also a suggestion that a greater number of typologically later axes may come from wetland contexts, a preference for watery offering that also becomes particularly marked in later prehistoric times.

HALBERDS

The halberd—a pointed, dagger-like metal blade mounted at approximately right angles to a haft—is an intriguing object (Fig. 4.11, 1–5). It was fashionable in various parts of Europe in the third and second millennia BC, in areas as widely different as Ireland, Iberia and central Europe. A relatively large number have been found in Ireland: over 170 have been recorded, of which, unfortunately, over half are unprovenanced (Harbison 1969a; O'Flaherty 1998; 2007). In some cases it is difficult to distinguish halberds from daggers but most halberds are heavy, broad, slightly asymmetrical blades, usually of copper rather than bronze, with low rounded midribs to strengthen the blade and holes for stout rivets. Where differential patination reveals traces of a haft, this invariably forms a straight line across the butt in contrast to the more or less concave hafting mark sometimes found on daggers.

A majority of halberds belong to two closely related types: type Carn and type Cotton. A bog in Carn townland near Ballina, Co. Mayo, yielded an example with at least part of its wooden haft still attached. As found, the oak haft was about 1m in

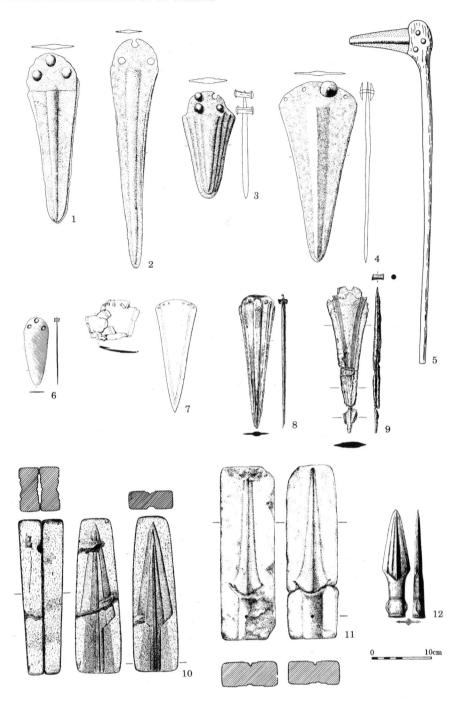

Fig. 4.11—*Halberds, daggers and spearheads. Halberds: (1) Carn, Co. Mayo; (2) one from a hoard at Cotton, Co. Down; (3) Clonard, Co. Meath; (4) Breaghwy, Co. Mayo; (5) the Carn halberd mounted on a copy of its original wooden haft (not to scale). Daggers: (6) River Blackwater at Shanmullagh or Ballycullen, Co. Armagh; (7) Grange, Co. Roscommon (with reconstruction); (8) Gortaclare, Co. Clare; (9) Kiltale, Co. Meath. Spearheads: (10) stone two-piece mould for casting a tanged spearhead from Omagh, Co. Tyrone; (11) stone two-piece mould from Omagh, Co. Tyrone, for an early socketed spearhead; (12) end-looped spearhead found near Ballymena, Co. Antrim.*

length and riveted at right angles to the blade by means of three large cylindrical, round-headed rivets. The blade, 24.6cm long and 8cm in maximum width, has a straight, rounded midrib on both faces and is slightly asymmetrical, one edge being very slightly concave (Fig. 4.11, 1 and 5). This sort of asymmetrical blade (possibly grooved) with straight midrib and the rounded butt with a triangular arrangement of three rivet holes are the distinguishing features of type Carn halberds. Type Cotton, named after three examples found in a bog south-east of Bangor, Co. Down, is similar but has a curved midrib corresponding to the curvature of one side of the blade (Fig. 4.11, 2). About a dozen examples are assigned to a type Clonard, named after a single County Meath find, which has a squared or shouldered butt with four large rivet holes arranged more or less in a rectangle (Fig. 4.11, 3). A halberd found in a bog near Ballina, Co. Mayo, has given its name to a type Breaghwy: a small group characterised by a fairly straight blade and a rounded butt with three or more narrow rivet holes arranged in a shallow arc (Fig. 4.11, 4). One of this type of halberd was also reportedly found with its wooden haft still attached but this was not preserved. Another was found in a cist grave at Moylough, Co. Sligo, with a cremation; the capstone was decorated with a series of arcs, and a radiocarbon date from the cremated bone suggests a date *c.* 1950 BC (Brindley 2001). In contrast to the other types, most type Breaghwy halberds are of bronze, and the one rivet surviving on the eponymous example suggests that the narrow rivets may have been three-piece objects with conical caps on a slender stem—a rivet type common on the Continent. One type Cotton halberd bears similar but stouter three-piece rivets.

It is not certain whether the various halberd types form a chronological sequence. A few typological straws have been grasped by several writers: the use of bronze as well as multiple narrow rivets (as found on developed bronze daggers) have prompted the suggestion that type Breaghwy is late in a developmental series. Harbison has claimed that some evidence of re-hafting indicates that narrow rivets were a later fashion than large rivets. Since the halberd with a straight midrib is the Continental norm, the earliest Irish type (assuming Continental inspiration) may have been type Carn. The closely related type Cotton was presumably partly

contemporary. The inadequacy of this sort of evidence is widely recognised and needs no further comment here. Unfortunately the few associated finds are not very enlightening. Halberd hoards are not common: a hoard of seven (two of type Carn, the rest of type Cotton) was found in 1850 at Hillswood, near Kilconnell, Co. Galway; they were discovered stuck point downwards in a bunch in the ground beneath some bog and may well have been a ritual deposit. In two instances other objects have been associated with halberds: in the Frankford hoard one copper halberd (type Cotton) was found with five axes (of types Lough Ravel and Ballybeg) and a flat riveted dagger. The Killaha hoard included four bronze axes, a bronze halberd of type Breaghwy and that tanged and riveted grooved dagger. Harbison has tentatively suggested a halberd sequence commencing with type Carn, followed in turn by types Cotton and Clonard and culminating with type Breaghwy. While Ireland, Iberia, Italy and central Europe have all been suggested as the original centre where these objects were invented, he finds a German origin most likely.

The substantial midribs of Irish halberds imply that they were cast in bivalve moulds of stone or clay (none of which survive). Because of their large and unwieldy blades, it has been thought that they would have made clumsy weapons and were more likely to have had some ceremonial or emblematic function, perhaps belonging to the parade weapon tradition like the polished stone macehead or battleaxe. A number show impact damage, however, and experimentation with a copper replica (type Cotton) and a number of (dead) sheep's heads has shown that a short chopping blow, in poleaxe fashion, was sufficient to pierce the skull. Some halberds may have been effective weapons (O'Flaherty 2007; O'Flaherty *et al.* 2008). Whether they were used as weapons remains uncertain, however, but they may have been effective implements for slaughter or sacrifice (Skak-Nielsen 2009).

DAGGERS

Although flat axes and halberds together represent the bulk of the material of the early Irish copper and bronze industry, the repertoire of early metalworkers also included a series of knives or daggers, ranging from the early tanged copper knives to typologically advanced bronze examples with riveted hafts, midribs and grooved blades. Quite a variety of forms were manufactured and Peter Harbison (1969a) has attempted a classification, identifying nine separate types and several miscellaneous categories. Because of the paucity of associated finds these are, in the main, imprecisely dated, but a very general typological sequence is apparent. To simplify matters, a fourfold classification is summarised here. The earliest form, the tanged copper knife (Harbison's type Knocknagur) has been briefly described (Fig. 4.6, 5–6). Flat riveted daggers (type Corkey) are a more developed type. Most if not all of these simple flat daggers are of bronze; they vary in shape from short triangular specimens to longer, rather tongue-shaped blades and may have a U- or V-shaped hafting mark. Butts are rounded and contained two to six rivets to affix an antler or bone haft (Fig. 4.11, 6). The Corkey example was found in a cist grave near Loughguile, Co. Antrim, and, along with a bowl, accompanied an unburnt burial (Fig. 4.15, 2), and an example found in a cist near Derry with the crouched skeleton of an adult male and the pelvis of a piglet had a bark and leather sheath decorated with embossed ornament (McConway and Donnelly 2006). Simple riveted daggers with a midrib also occur; one was found in a cremated burial in the Mound of the Hostages and had apparently been burnt on the cremation pyre.

A series of grooved daggers are not easily classifiable but two major groups are identifiable, with some intermediate forms and variants. Grooved triangular daggers (such as Harbison's type Topped Mountain) comprise a small number of daggers, with a gently rounded butt and straight cutting edges giving a triangular form. Blades may be almost flat, have a central thickening (giving a biconvex cross-section) or even a distinct midrib. Two or more grooves run parallel to the edges and four or six slender rivets are placed in a very shallow arc in the butt. A dagger from Gortaclare, Burren, Co. Clare (Fig. 4.11, 8), probably had six rivets and a prominent midrib and has parallels in southern England and Brittany. A find from a grave at Grange, near Tulsk, Co. Roscommon (Fig. 4.11, 7), has a flat grooved blade and six rivets, and the Topped Mountain dagger with its similar blade and four rivets is a smaller version, found in a grave in

County Fermanagh along with a fragment of sheet gold. The piece of gold is generally believed to have once decorated the organic hilt or its pommel and is one of the very rare instances of gold in a burial context.

Grooved ogival daggers (various types in Harbison) are slender blades usually expanding in a gentle curve from point to butt. Sometimes the curve is pronounced but occasionally so slight as to give an almost triangular shape; usually three or more grooves run parallel to the cutting edges and reflect their curvature. Cross-sections of the blade are occasionally biconvex but frequently display a fairly distinct midrib. Butts are often trapezoidal, usually with two rivet holes; a few have three or more rivet holes, and an indentation in the heel of some, as on an example from Kiltale, Co. Meath, may have been for a notch for a third rivet (Fig. 4.11, 9). Some are decorated with engraved triangles or lozenges on the upper blade. Miscellaneous daggers include small nondescript blades, some flat, some with midribs, of various shapes and sizes, and include several with triple midribs.

Except for the riveted flat daggers of type Corkey, a simple type that may have been in use for much of the earlier second millennium, there is some evidence to suggest a typological sequence obviously commencing with the tanged copper dagger but followed in turn by grooved triangular daggers and then grooved ogival daggers. It is this sort of typological succession for axe, dagger or halberd, when combined with the slender evidence of associated finds—be they from Irish hoards or British graves—and supplemented by a small but important number of radiocarbon dates, that provides the basis for the various overlapping typo-chronological phases from Knocknagur to Derryniggin. The goldwork, pottery and burials as well as some of the later bronze types (such as the earliest bronze spearheads) can be loosely correlated with this sequence.

EARLY SPEARHEADS

The bronze spearhead was an important development in the Derryniggin phase, but the lack of associated finds makes it difficult to relate it to other bronze types and to chart its development accurately. The typologically earliest form of spearhead was a tanged blade, a development of grooved ogival daggers in southern England (Needham 1979a). A few examples have been found in Ireland and their manufacture is indicated by the survival of a bivalve or two-piece stone mould from near Omagh, Co. Tyrone (Fig. 4.11, 10), with matrices for a dagger as well as a tanged spearhead. This is one of a group of stone moulds found about 1880. A second mould demonstrates the contemporary manufacture of a typologically more advanced form of spearhead with a hollow socket (Fig. 4.11, 11). It is believed that the spearhead was initially created by inserting a tanged dagger into the end of a wooden shaft in spear-like fashion, and to prevent the shaft from splitting it would have been necessary to bind it with leather at this vulnerable point or to provide it with a bone or metal collar. A third mould from Omagh is for the production of a detached metal collar (with side loops) that would have served as this sort of strengthening device on the top of the shaft. An obvious typological improvement was the casting of collar and spear-blade in one piece to produce a socketed weapon. The casting of a collar or socket would have entailed the use of a core, perhaps of charcoal, in a complex two-piece mould and represents the earliest attempts at hollow casting. The socketed bronze spearhead quickly became a relatively popular weapon and different forms were fashionable at different stages throughout much of later prehistory. The first socketed spearheads in this long typological sequence display features recalling the dagger blades and the separate collars that inspired their development. These include ogival blades and rare features such as oval-sectioned sockets and small bosses or dummy rivet heads on the socket, emulating the rivets that once attached the separate collars to the wooden haft. They invariably have a pair of cast loops near the mouth of the socket, a consistent feature of the standard type (Burgess and Cowen 1972).

The standard type is a small weapon with a solid-cast, channelled or broadly grooved blade, a short circular socket (terminating at or near the base of the blade) and loops near the socket mouth (Fig. 4.11, 12); this has been named the end-looped spearhead and was popular not just in Ireland but also in Scotland and Wales in particular. A stone mould for one of these end-looped spearheads (and

a small lugged chisel) was found at Inch Island, Co. Donegal, and another mould for several examples comes from Lough Gur, Co. Limerick. Derryniggin-type axes and end-looped spearheads are the two principal products of the Irish metalworking industry at this time and the manufacture of both may well have continued into the succeeding metalworking phase, which is distinguished by further developments in axe, dagger and spear, and loops of one sort or another remain a distinctive feature of insular spearheads for many centuries. The numerous minor variations in spearhead form (like dummy rivets and tiny loops) are, as Barber (2003) points out, a reminder that materials may be physically and culturally manipulated in many different ways, and innovations might mark differences in the user's physical, economic or social rank.

GOLD

In early times, as today, gold was doubtless a highly prized and prestigious metal. Yet despite its ancient and modern value a remarkable number of Irish gold objects of early prehistoric date have survived, and the preference, as we shall see, was for the manufacture of objects of sheet gold, in the main earrings, decorative discs and collars or lunulae (Eogan 1994). Unfortunately, most are isolated finds with unrecorded or uninformative archaeological contexts: the gold strip found with the Topped Mountain dagger, the gold discs discovered with the Corran wrist-guards and a gold button cover associated with the cremation of a child at Screggan, near Tullamore, Co. Offaly (Lalonde 2008), are rare exceptions.

Two Irish earrings are of the basket earring type but now consist of a slender flattened plaque of sheet gold with a narrow tang for attachment to the ear. Both are plain and may have formed a pair but their find-spot is unknown (Fig. 4.12, 1). Half a dozen pairs are known from Beaker graves in Britain and, while it has been suggested that they may have been hair ornaments worn as plait-rings (Sherratt 1986; 1987), it does seem certain that they were worn on either side of the head and the earring explanation may be the more plausible. A third sheet-gold ornament is a roughly oval disc of thin sheet gold with a tang found at Benraw near

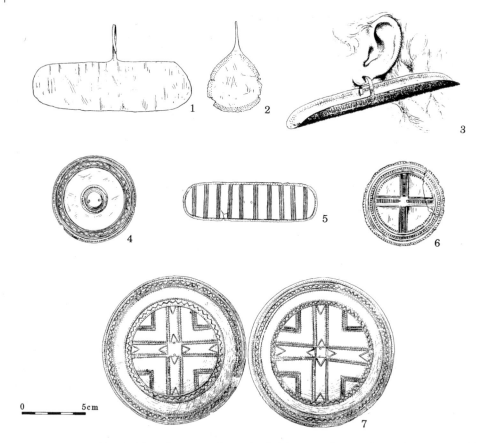

Fig. 4.12—Beaker period goldwork. (1) Basket earring from Ireland. (2) Earring from Deehommed, Co. Down. (3) Wearing a basket earring. (4) Gold plaque from Bellville, Co. Cavan. (5) One of a pair of gold discs from Cloyne, Co. Cork. (6) A gold disc with no recorded provenance but possibly one of the discs from Corran, Co. Armagh. (7) Pair of gold discs from Tedavnet, Co. Monaghan.

Deehommed, Co. Down (Fig. 4.12, 2). It has been considered a basket earring, and more oval, less elongated, forms are known from Britain, but its simple repoussé dotted ornament around the edge finds a close parallel on a pair of tanged gold ornaments from late Beaker contexts in Portugal (O'Connor 2004).

Some twenty decorated discs of sheet gold are also thought to date from the Beaker period but are invariably poorly documented finds. In about half a dozen cases they form matching pairs and they vary in diameter from about 4cm to about 11cm. All are of thin sheet gold and bear repoussé decoration (Fig. 4.12): on several this consists of a few concentric circles, including on occasion circles of zigzags or dots or short lines, pressed up with a pointed implement from behind. A majority also bear a cruciform design, usually a simple double

cross with a ladder pattern set within a circle. A well-known pair from Tedavnet, Co. Monaghan, found between the roots of an old oak tree, and the surviving specimen of a pair from Ballyshannon, Co. Donegal, have somewhat more complex cruciform decoration with triangles in the quarters of the circle. On some of the more elaborate discs decoration is raised on both faces: on the Tedavnet pieces, for instance, the repoussé linear decoration is carefully raised from the back and emphasised by dots punched from the front. Centrally placed pairs of perforations were presumably for attaching these discs to something, and some minute holes or nicks near a part of the circumference of discs from Kilmuckridge, Co. Wexford (said to have been found near a great stone), and Castle Treasure, Co. Cork, have been thought to imply some additional stitching to give extra security. Pairs of these discs may have been permanently attached to some perishable substance such as cloth or leather. It has also been suggested that the cross and circle motif was inspired by Continental decorative pin fashions: a series of bronze disc-headed pins in central Europe have a cruciform pattern very similar to that on the Kilmuckridge disc and on a pair from Ballina, Co. Mayo. The symbolism of this motif is unknown but the use of pairs of these discs from time to time may indicate that they were for personal adornment. Four narrow gold plaques may have had a similar purpose. At least three of them were found in a stream at Bellville, near Crossdoney, Co. Cavan, and all have centrally placed pairs of perforations and simple linear repoussé ornament; they too may once have been attached to something. Eogan (1994) has described these decorative objects as 'Primary bell beaker goldwork'.

LUNULAE

The numerous gold lunulae represent the greatest volume of insular gold of this period. The name, a diminutive of the Latin *luna*, 'moon', was first given to these crescent-shaped objects in the middle of the eighteenth century. Just over 85 examples have been found in Ireland, and of these about 50 have their provenance recorded. About a dozen have been found in Britain, notably in Cornwall and Scotland, and about eighteen have been found on the Continent, mainly in north-western France. None of the Irish finds comes from an archaeological context. Some were found on dry land, a few in bogs and some were seemingly associated with prominent landmarks such as large stones. One, from Newtown, Crossdoney, Co. Cavan, was found at a depth of about 2m in a bog and was contained in a two-piece oak box. A number of lunula hoards are known: four from Dunfierth, north-east of Carbury, Co. Kildare, were said to have been found together 'with several bones' in hard gravel thought to be the remains of an ancient bog trackway, three were found in a bog at Banemore, south of Listowel, Co. Kerry, and two were found at a depth of 60cm in a field at Rathroeen, near Ballina, Co. Mayo. None have come from certain burials.

A typical lunula is a decorated, crescent-shaped object of burnished, thin, sheet gold with impressed or incised geometric ornament on one face only, where it is invariably confined to the horns of the crescent and the edges of the widest part (Fig. 4.13). The horns end in flat, expanded, oval or subrectangular terminals usually turned at right angles to the plane of the lunula. Internal diameters are generally about 14–16cm. Joan Taylor's detailed study of shape and decoration has revealed three lunula styles: Classical, Unaccomplished and Provincial. Analysis of the thickness and width of the sheet gold at the widest part of the crescent has shown that Classical lunulae have the thinnest and widest collars, the Unaccomplished are of broadly similar thinness but noticeably narrower, and the Provincial examples are of thicker sheet gold and overlap both the others in width (Taylor 1970; 1980).

The thinner and wider Classical lunulae are superb examples of sheet-gold craftsmanship. They were skilfully beaten from a single rod, then polished and decorated with precision. Most were worked to give a thicker inner edge to provide greater strength. On lunulae generally the decoration was applied with a fine pointed implement and impressed or incised, with the sheet gold being firmly held in a bed of resin or pitch or some such, for in a few cases it has come through on the other face. On Classical examples the commonest motifs are triangles, lozenges, zigzags and lattice patterns, all carefully executed. The latter two motifs often occur on the edges of the broadest part of the lunula, which is otherwise plain. All four motifs and others are found in complex zonal patterns on the crescent tips; on some the whole tip is filled with zonal ornament, on others three major decorated panels are separated by undecorated zones. This juxtaposition of plain and decorated areas is also frequently found in the patterned zones, where reserved triangles, lozenges and chevrons are prominent. The overall effect of balance and contrast thus produced is elegant and restrained. Taylor has demonstrated that symmetry was an important decorative consideration: the decorative scheme on one horn of the crescent is more or else the mirror image of that on the opposing horn. On some examples one half of a horn's decoration is a mirror image of the other half—divided on a central longitudinal line.

The Unaccomplished lunulae are inferior but

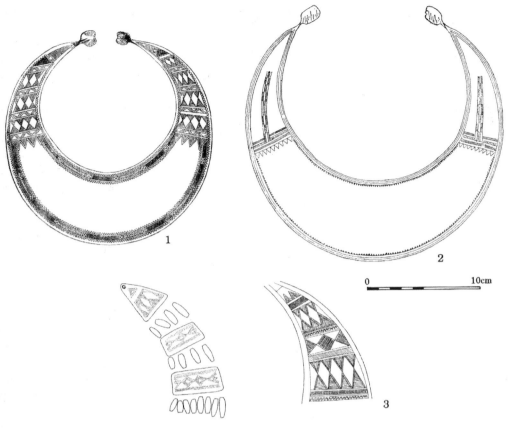

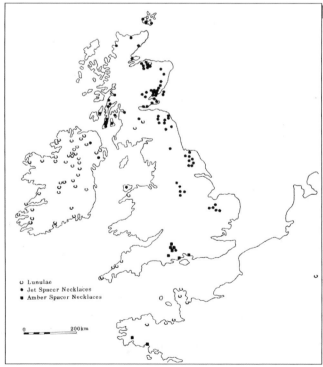

Fig. 4.13—Gold lunulae. (1) Classical lunula from Killarney, Co. Kerry. (2) One of four Unaccomplished lunulae found at Dunfierth, Co. Kildare. (3) Comparison of part of a jet necklace with spacer beads from Mount Stuart, Bute, Scotland (left), with a lunula from Blessington, Co. Wicklow (right). (4) General distribution of gold lunulae and necklaces of jet and amber.

close relatives of the Classical type; they are narrower and more crudely decorated. Symmetry was still sought but only roughly achieved, as over-run lines, truncated designs and misapportioned spaces show. A broadly similar range of motifs is used and sometimes placed in the familiar zones or panels; sometimes the decoration is placed in a novel fashion longitudinally along the centre of the horn of the crescent. A small number bear no decoration.

While there is a scatter of these lunulae in the south-west, the majority of both types have been found in the northern half of the country. If this distribution pattern of provenanced examples (about 60% of the total) is any guide, then northern gold resources were exploited and the western Mourne Mountains in Co. Down have been suggested (Warner *et al.* 2009). No Unaccomplished lunula has been found outside Ireland, but three Classical examples have been found in Cornwall, one possibly found with a Provincial example near Harlyn Bay. Classical lunulae are generally believed to have been manufactured in Ireland and exported.

With the single exception of a lunula found in a bog at Cooltrain, near Enniskillen, Co. Fermanagh, all Provincial lunulae have been found outside Ireland—hence their name. They are characterised by their thickness and scanty decoration; they also often have distinctive deep crescentic terminals. Ornament may be linear: several incised lines parallel to the edge, perhaps with a simple zigzag. When uncomplicated panelled ornament occurs it is usually executed in the dot-line technique (an incised line embellished with punched dots). Like some Classical lunulae, these Provincial pieces were also traded or exchanged: the Provincial specimen from Harlyn Bay is identical to one from a hoard of three lunulae from Kerivoa in northern Brittany, and all of these may have been manufactured by the one craftsman whose patron or patrons constituted one link in a chain of contacts which evidently extended from Ireland to southern England to north-western France.

Though some antiquarian commentators believed that lunulae might have served as diadems, their shape and size have long convinced many writers that they must have been decorative collars. Obvious signs of prehistoric use have been detected on only two, however, and Taylor suggests that they may not have been used as personal ornaments very often, if at all, and that they may even have decorated inanimate objects like wooden idols. Since they do not occur in burials as personal grave-goods, she suggests that they may have been the property of the community, serving as the insignia of a chieftain or a priest.

The absence of associated finds makes the dating of lunulae particularly difficult, but the fact that Beaker pottery decoration, in Britain in particular, offers a parallel for every motif found on Classical lunulae prompted Taylor to suggest a Beaker date for this goldwork. Motifs such as hatched triangles, lozenges, lattice patterns, and zigzags or chevrons are shared, as is the preference for reserved designs and for symmetrical presentation. Analysis of trace elements in a number of Irish basket earrings, discs and lunulae using a pulsed laser beam (Laser Ablation Inductively Coupled Plasma-Mass Spectrometry or LA-ICP-MS) appears to confirm their Beaker period context (Taylor 1999). Lunulae also show a close resemblance to a somewhat later series of necklaces of jet and amber well known in Britain in the early second millennium. The decorated subrectangular spacer beads of the jet necklaces in particular recall the panelled decoration of the goldwork, but stylistic parallels are uncertain dating evidence and some of these necklaces may have been old heirlooms when buried. Such necklaces are rare in Ireland but the general distribution pattern does suggest that lunulae may be an Irish version in gold of a widespread fashion for crescent-shaped neck ornaments which finds a commoner expression in either jet or amber in Britain (Fig. 4.13, 4). These were probably the personal possessions of a minority, but all were probably prestigious and symbolic objects. The amber and jet necklaces from graves in Britain are seen as expressions of high status, a further indication of the increasing significance of certain materials in the definition of social relations (Harding 1993). The greater use of gold in Ireland may be another expression of this phenomenon, and the wide distribution of the lunula fashion, whatever its precise date, may denote, like the distant contacts suggested by other metalwork, a continuing interest by social élites in the acquisition of prestigious objects and a wider network of reciprocal contacts to further this objective.

EXCHANGE AND PRODUCTION

Three Classical lunulae from Cornwall, including the one from Harlyn Bay, and the parallel, already mentioned, between the Provincial lunula from that site and the example from Kerivoa in Brittany are just some of the indications of far-reaching trade and exchange in the early second millennium. Cornish tin, Irish copper and gold, as well as some finished objects, may have travelled considerable geographical distances. Like the polished stone axes of Antrim porcellanite of earlier centuries, metal axes and other items may have been exchanged in various social circumstances. A number of halberds of Irish type have been found on the Continent. An Irish axe found at Dieskau, Germany, may have passed through many hands before being finally deposited in an enormous hoard of bronzes there, and several axes from Denmark and southern Sweden have been claimed to be of Irish origin. Reciprocal contacts no doubt allowed Continental fashions to reach these shores. It is possible that finished products were not the only objects exchanged. The so-called ingots, if that is what they were, may have been a means of transporting raw metal, and the presence of broken items or scrap metal in a small number of hoards may reflect some collection and recycling of metal at this early date. Few certain tools for metalworking have been recognised. The copper and bronze as well as the sheet goldwork demonstrate that highly skilled hammering was a very common and important technique, as indeed was the subsequent grinding and polishing. Stone or metal hammers were probably used. It has been claimed that some perforated stone implements of subrectangular or oval shape were metalworkers' hammers, and it will be remembered that part of a perforated, oval granite hammer was found at Newgrange along with a bronze axe, a quartzite hammer and a rubbing or polishing stone, and these were considered to be the equipment of a metalworker. Two rounded subrectangular polished pieces of stone from the north of Ireland have been compared to similar objects from Beaker contexts on the Continent, where cushion stones, as they are called, seem to have served as hammers or polishing stones (Lynch 2001).

Evidence of early casting methods is provided by a number of stone moulds (Eogan 1993a).

Mostly of medium-grained sandstone or similar stone, many are for the production of flat axes. One such mould from Lyre, near Carricknavar, Co. Cork, has two matrices or cavities, for a large and a small axe (Fig. 4.9, 6). The irregularity of the surfaces around each matrix on this and other similar moulds shows that they are single-piece open moulds, for no cover or lid could have effectively converted them into closed moulds. The objects cast can only have been rough-outs requiring further working: according to M. J. O'Kelly (1970), 'a thick rough-out would be drawn out to a larger size than a thin one in the hammer finishing, as one may legitimately assume that the smith did not waste scarce and valuable metal by unnecessary grinding away. In fact, different sizes and shapes of axe can be produced from the same matrix by pouring in more or less metal and by drawing out to a greater or lesser extent in the hammer finishing'. The Newgrange axe, for instance, was shaped by extensive hammering. This is just one of the difficulties facing any attempt to identify the products of a particular matrix in the surviving axe population. Since crucibles of fired clay were presumably a necessary part of the casting process, clay moulds may have been used at this early date too, but none have yet been found. It is also conceivable that moulds of some substance like sand mixed with animal dung were used, and these, not surprisingly, would rarely if ever survive. The cast flanges on some Derryniggin axes and the high midribs on both faces of some halberds all imply the use of two-piece moulds at an early date; the development of the early spearheads with tubular metal collars or short sockets indicates more complex hollow casting.

While the arsenic-rich ores at Ross Island were an important source of raw material for the copper and bronze artefacts of the Knocknagur and Killaha phases, the use of these ores began to decline c. 1900 BC and the attention of early copper-miners shifted to other sources on the Beara and Mizen peninsulas of west Cork. The best known is Mount Gabriel, near Schull, where there is important evidence of prehistoric mining activity in the period 1700–1500 BC (O'Brien 1994). In contrast to the long-term working of a single rich ore deposit at Ross Island, a whole series of low-grade and essentially arsenic-free copper ores are now exploited in relatively short-lived episodes

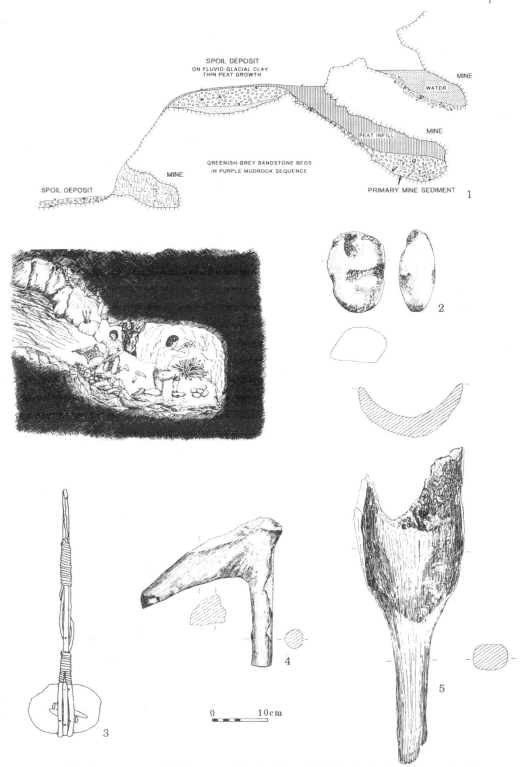

Fig. 4.14—Mount Gabriel copper mines. (1) Schematic profile of a Mount Gabriel mine based on mines 1–4 and a reconstruction of underground mining with hand-held stone hammers and pine lighting chips (no scale). (2) Stone hammer with modification for hafting. (3) Reconstruction of the hafting mechanism with a flexible withy. (4) Hazel pick. (5) Alder shovel.

across a wider landscape. The Mount Gabriel mining complex has provided a wealth of information about this form of copper extraction. Some 32 mines have been identified, mostly on the eastern slopes of the hill just below the summit, where beds of copper ore are exposed in the near-vertical rock outcrops. These workings consist of short inclined openings or tunnels that followed the ore-bearing green sandstones in the hard siliceous rock (Fig. 4.14). The poorer-quality copper necessitated the extraction of large quantities of rock, and sizeable spoil heaps outside the bigger mines are characteristic. Mines are up to 10m in length, depending on the amount of copper present and on problems posed by water seepage. Workings are small, able to accommodate only a few workers at a time. The smooth concave profiles of the mine walls are one of the telling signs of the use of fire-setting. As at Ross Island, wood fires were lit against the rock face to cause heat fracturing that might be aided by sudden water quenching. Rock was then removed by pounding with stone hammers or mauls. These are mostly rounded sandstone cobbles, about 10cm by 15cm and generally weighing 1,000–2,000g, very likely collected on the coast at Schull some 4km to the south. Tens of thousands were probably used; easily broken, large quantities of fragments of these hammers were recovered. They were hand-held or hafted and some show light pecking or abrading around part of the circumference to give purchase to a wooden haft; the remains of a flexible twisted withy, possibly of hazel, was found in one mine. Pointed hazel sticks were used to help prize out the heat-shattered rock, which was then removed with the aid of wooden shovels and containers of some kind. Pine splints were used as torches at Mount Gabriel and, though none were found, ropes and ladders were probably used as well.

The mineralised rock extracted from the mines was crushed nearby and the ore removed elsewhere for smelting. The location of smelting sites associated with the Mount Gabriel mines remains unknown; they may have been on the mountain or near the coast. Certainly the ten or so wedge tombs on the Mizen peninsula, including those at Altar and Toormore, indicate extensive second-millennium settlement there. The size of the mine workings and the mounds of spoil provide a general indication of the amount of rock extracted, but it is difficult to estimate annual ore production. Over a 200-year period the mines as a whole may have yielded anything from 1.5 to 26.5 tonnes of copper, but in any one year the production was more likely to have been in kilograms rather than in tonnes. O'Brien suggests that Mount Gabriel may have produced as little as 15–20kg per year, enough to make 40 to 50 bronze axes and requiring a kilogram or less of tin. Tin, a vital raw material in bronze production, must have been obtained through some exchange mechanism, possibly from County Wicklow, where cassiterite occurs, as already mentioned. Cornish sources are another possibility. Though the Cork–Kerry region may not have been the only source of copper at this time, the distribution of contemporary metal products such as the developed axes of types Ballyvally and Derryniggin, which are mainly concentrated in the midlands and the north-east of the country, suggest that ore from Mount Gabriel could have had a wide circulation. The concentration of type Ballyvally axes along with stone moulds for their manufacture in Antrim and Down suggests important metal workshops in this region, and they may very well have been supplied by a long-distance metal trade. It is possible that various local communities had access to the Mount Gabriel ores but, given the more complex technology and the fact that axes generally display considerable uniformity, it is more likely that both access and production were controlled and organised. Communities in the locality may have mined the ore and smelted it into either ingot form or finished products or both, which were then transported by land into the Cork hinterland or by boat along the coast. The social differentiation implied by finely crafted objects such as lunulae and reflected in the burial record (below) serves as a reminder that élite individuals or groups may have had a controlling role in these metal exchanges.

INNOVATIONS IN THE FUNERARY RECORD

While the wedge tombs of the west and north demonstrate the continuing importance of megalithic tombs in ritual and funerary practice towards the end of the third millennium and early in the second millennium BC, this period also saw the development of novel burial customs and

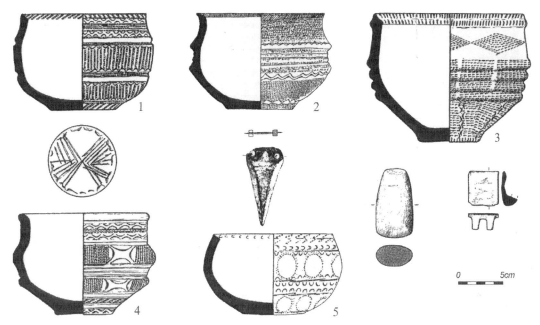

Fig. 4.15—Pottery of the Bowl Tradition. (1) Stage 1 bowl from Crumlin, Co. Dublin. (2) Bowl and bronze dagger from Corkey, Co. Antrim. (3) Bowl from Killycarney, Co. Cavan, found with a miniature stone axe and a bone belt-hook. (4) Stage 2 bowl from Rush, Co. Dublin. (5) Stage 3 bowl from Rubane, Co. Down.

ceramic types. Some of the significant innovations in pottery and in funerary practice were inspired by Beaker fashion, while others correspond to contemporary developments in Britain. The burial evidence is varied and complex; some of this diversity in grave form or content reflects changing fashions over a period of time, some variations are regional and others may denote differences in social status. Pottery vessels of different types are the commonest artefacts found with these burials and provide one way of summarising this diverse body of evidence.

These different pottery types and burial customs overlap with one another and are partly contemporary with metalworking phases Knocknagur to Derryniggin, but because metal artefacts were rarely placed in graves it is still difficult to correlate the major categories of metal objects with the various pottery types from funerary contexts. Our understanding of burial ritual is hampered too by the unfortunate fact that many graves have been casual discoveries in the course of agricultural activities or gravel-digging and have often been less than adequately recorded. The relative scarcity of contemporary settlement evidence is also a problem. Notwithstanding these

difficulties, material from these graves reveals new ceramic fashions and social customs. Thanks to the fact that bone and charcoal are susceptible to radiocarbon dating and, most significantly, since it is now possible to date cremated bone (Lanting and Brindley 1998; Lanting *et al.* 2001), a relatively secure chronology is possible. Four major pottery and burial traditions are evident: almost a thousand pottery vessels may be assigned to either a Bowl Tradition, a Vase Tradition, a Collared Urn Tradition or a Cordoned Urn Tradition, a ceramic and funerary patterning which implies the existence of ordered social groups. The pottery in each of these traditions has been analysed by Anna Brindley (2007) and, with the aid of radiocarbon dating, she has identified three broadly successive stages in their development over several centuries.

The Bowl Tradition

The pottery of the Bowl Tradition, the so-called 'bowl food-vessels' of some writers, consists mainly of several forms of highly decorated, hand-made bowls, usually 8–15cm in height (Ó Ríordáin and Waddell 1993). The exterior is almost always covered with impressed or incised designs, and bases and rims are sometimes decorated too (Fig. 4.15).

Impressed ornament is particularly characteristic and the use of comb-impressed lines (as on Beaker pottery) is noteworthy, as is the technique of false relief in which a line of impressions executed with a triangular-pointed or spatulate implement gives a raised zigzag or chevron or other pattern. Other decorative techniques include the use of twisted and whipped cord impressions and broad grooving. The principal forms comprise simple and bipartite bowls, necked bipartite bowls, tripartite bowls and ribbed bowls, but these and other differences in shape appear to have little or no chronological significance. Brindley's analysis suggests that decoration is the most important variable and she has identified three stages spanning the period *c.* 2160–1920 BC. Stage 1 bowls are decorated with simple zonal ornament, usually comb-impressed, while in stage 2 the decorative range is extended to include larger triangular and lozenge motifs filled with lines or placed against a filled background, with comb impression and incision commonly employed. In stage 3 broad bands of ornament with a more open character are popular and ribbed vessels are frequent, but other forms are made as well. Incised lines and broad grooves are preferred but cord and comb impressions still occur. In part, these stages may reflect changing decorative fashions, but it is very likely that the motifs employed sometimes carried a symbolic charge. Some features seem to echo organic containers: small lugs sometimes occur and a few are perforated. They would seem to be decorative renditions of one-time functional elements. It is possible that they and false-relief ornament are elements borrowed from the woodworker's craft.

Bowls have been mainly found in the north and east of the country: notably in counties Antrim, Derry, Down and Tyrone, and in Meath, Westmeath, Dublin, Kildare and Wicklow (Fig. 4.16). Sherds have also been found on a few habitation and ritual sites, but the majority are known from funerary contexts. A small number have been found in megalithic tombs: one in the Audleystown, Co. Down, court tomb and several in various passage tombs. These were secondary depositions either in the tomb or inserted into its mound or cairn. Two bowls were found in the Loughash (Cashelbane), Co. Tyrone, wedge tomb; in Kilhoyle, Co. Derry, sherds of the one bowl came from various levels both inside and outside the tomb. Fragments of

bowl, possibly associated with late Beaker pottery, came from the wedge tombs at Largantea, Co. Derry, and Lough Gur, Co. Limerick. Two bowls were found with unburnt burials in the passage tomb in the Mound of the Hostages, Tara.

By far the greater number of bowls have been found in cists or pits, and graves such as these, when they contain a crouched unburnt skeleton accompanied by a pot, are the classic Irish representatives of the single-burial tradition so popular, for instance, among Beaker communities in Britain. The Bowl Tradition burial rite is more varied, however: about 43% of these bowls have been found with unburnt burials and about 57% with cremations. The unburnt corpse was almost always placed on its side in the grave in a crouched position, with the bowl usually in front of or behind the skull. Bowls have been found with the remains of adult males and females, as well as with children. Unburnt burial was popular in the midlands and the south-east; it was occasionally practised in the north but here cremation was commoner. Again these pottery vessels were usually placed beside the pile of burnt bone, but on occasion they contained some of the bone as well. In a few rare instances bowls have been found placed mouth downwards with cremated burials. The relatively few cases in which the cremations have been scientifically examined and successfully aged and sexed demonstrate that both adults and children were cremated, and now and then the remains of several individuals have been noted in the one grave. Details of burial ritual such as this will be considered further when the interesting and varied funerary ritual of the cemeteries of this period is examined. Since bowls of all types have been found with both unburnt and burnt human remains, it would appear that both burial rites were in contemporaneous use and each must have had important and different meaning.

Grave types differed too. Approximately 78% were stone-built cists and 22% simple pit graves. Cists were usually short, rectangular slab-built boxes, at most large enough to contain an adult corpse in a crouched position: usually with a capstone, they sometimes had paved floors as well (Fig. 4.16). Some cists were flat graves placed in the earth below ground level with no surviving superimposed monument; others were above ground level but covered by a mound of earth or

Fig. 4.16—(1) Large rectangular cist grave in a cemetery at Keenoge, Co. Meath, containing the crouched skeleton of an adult female with a bowl placed in front of the face. (2) General distribution of pottery of the Bowl Tradition.

stones. Why some individuals were accorded very different rites remains an intriguing puzzle: there is some evidence that unburnt burial of both adult males and females in well-made cist graves was a mark of special status (Mount 1995; 1997b). Such graves seem to be in a minority and, from time to time, occupy focal positions in cemeteries (Waddell 1990).

Some graves may have been isolated single burials; others have been found in cemeteries. At Carrickinab, Co. Down, for instance, a cist was discovered when a plough struck its capstone; it was a small slab-built box, some 70cm in length and 35cm in width internally, and it had a paved floor. It contained a bowl, the cremated bones of an adult (possibly male), a copper or bronze awl, a small flat bronze knife in a fragmentary condition, and two flint scrapers. In contrast, a cist at Keenoge, Co. Meath (Fig. 4.16), contained the crouched skeleton of an adult female and a bowl and was one of fourteen graves in a flat cemetery in which the majority of graves were pit graves (below). A mixture of burial rites and pottery types is a fairly

common and puzzling feature of such cemeteries, but now and then just the one pottery tradition is represented. A cemetery mound at Corrower, south-east of Ballina, Co. Mayo, consisted of a low circular mound some 13m in diameter without any encircling ditch. It was found to contain nine graves. Eight burials survived and all of these were cremated; five were accompanied by one or more bowls. The majority were unprotected, perhaps placed in small pits; four, however, were in cists. One cist, slightly off-centre, seems to have been the principal grave; this was a small polygonal structure with capstone and paved floor. Three bowls stood mouth upwards on this floor and, in an unusual ritual, they and the cist were filled with fine sand through which were mixed the cremated bones of at least five persons.

There were three burials with bowls in a flat cemetery of some nineteen burials at Edmondstown, Co. Dublin (Fig. 4.21), that displays much of the funerary variety so frequently found. Two short rectangular cists each contained crouched skeletons with a bowl placed in front of the face, while a third contained a deposit of cremated bone also accompanied by a bowl. The other burials were all cremated and the majority lay south and south-west of the cists mentioned. Other pottery included encrusted urn and collared urn.

Artefacts of stone or bronze are now and then found with bowls: flint scrapers (as at Carrickinab) or flint knives (some of the plano-convex type) have been placed in the grave on a small number of occasions. Flint leaf-shaped arrowheads and small polished stone axes have been recorded too. Bronze is surprisingly rare: the small, flat, bronze riveted dagger from Corkey, Co. Antrim, was found in a cist with an unburnt skeleton and a bowl (Fig. 4.15, 2). The much-corroded flat bronze blade from Carrickinab is believed, judging from the one rivet recovered, to have been a riveted specimen as well. A small bronze knife, two bowls and several flints came from a pit grave in the cemetery at Keenoge, Co. Meath. A small hooked bone object, a bowl and a miniature stone axe came from a double grave at Killycarney, Co. Cavan (Fig. 4.15, 3); the bone artefact is thought to be a belt-hook and finds a counterpart in gold in a rich contemporary grave, Bush Barrow in Wiltshire.

It is possible that bowls contained a funerary offering of food or drink but evidence is lacking; the in-turned rims of simple and bipartite bowls would seem to render them unsuitable as drinking vessels. If they were ever meant to contain edible material, wooden or bone spoons were probably used—and a ceramic spoon has been found with a Cordoned Urn burial (below). The makers of bowls also manufactured a range of vessels, however: smaller miniature vessels and larger pots have been found. The miniature bowls occur only very occasionally in burials and, like other small cups or 'pygmy' cups, some specific ritual purpose seems quite likely. Larger vessels are also rare but this may be due to the scarcity of settlement evidence. Indeed, the evidence for domestic usage is so scarce that this pottery type may have emerged as a response to a new funeral rite, as Brindley (2007) suggests, and may have had a limited domestic role. Sandhills at Magheragallan, Co. Donegal, however, have produced sherds of some large vessels up to 25cm in height which, judging from the presence of false-relief ornament, may have affinities with bowls from funerary contexts. Sherds have been found on various sandhills sites in the north of

Ireland (ApSimon 1969b), including Ballintoy and Whitepark Bay, Co. Antrim, Castlerock and Portstewart, Co. Derry, Ballykinlar and Dundrum, Co. Down, and on Dalkey Island, at Lough Gur and Coney Island in south-western Lough Neagh. On Coney Island traces of prolonged prehistoric occupation were obscured by subsequent activity, notably of medieval and later periods. A few sherds of bowls were associated with what appeared to be rectangular structures, a number of pits and a hearth (Addyman 1965).

As already mentioned, the distribution of these bowls is essentially a northern and eastern one, and their scarcity or absence in the west and south is possibly because the use of megalithic wedge tombs was the dominant funerary ritual in these areas. A significant number occur in south-west Scotland and attest to the importance of cross-channel contacts. A series of radiocarbon dates indicates that the Bowl Tradition was contemporary with some Irish Beakers from wedge tombs and overlapped with the use of some vases but was a short-lived phenomenon perhaps spanning less than three centuries.

The Vase Tradition

There is no doubt that the makers of pottery of the Vase Tradition did manufacture a range of pottery sizes, for they had occasion to place both small pottery vessels, the so-called 'vase food vessels', and large vessels or 'cinerary urns' in graves. In contrast to the Bowl Tradition, where the one pot type was placed with either an unburnt or a cremated burial, in this tradition a small vase or a larger vase urn or encrusted urn are all usually found with cremated burials. Unburnt burial is rare, though it does occur with a relatively small number of vases.

Vases are small, hand-made, well-decorated pottery vessels, usually 11–16cm in height. There are two main forms (Fig. 4.17, 1–2). One is a bipartite vase with a slightly everted rim and a biconical profile, often with a rounded shoulder. The other is a tripartite vase with an angular profile, having an everted or even a vertical neck above a sloping shoulder. The distinct neck, shoulder and body give the characteristic tripartite shape. A small number bear imperforate or perforate lugs on the shoulder; these are found, for the most part, on bipartite vases. The great majority of all vases bear incised decoration on most of the exterior;

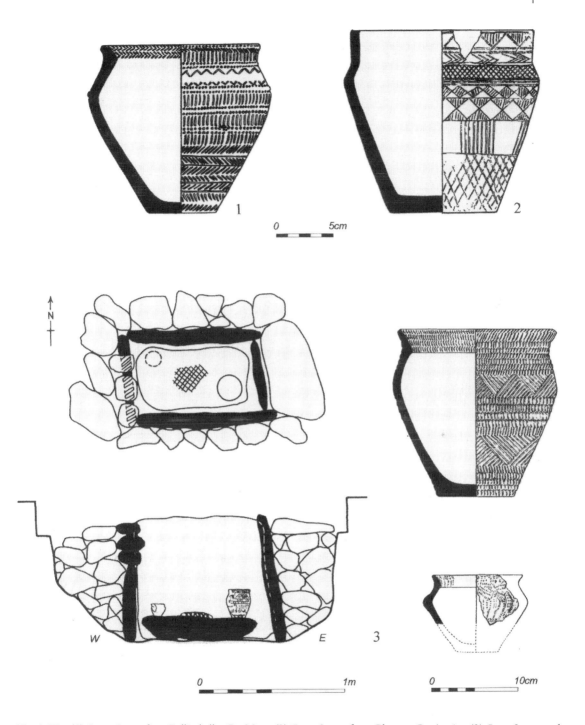

Fig. 4.17—(1) Stage 1 vase from Ballinchalla, Co. Mayo. (2) Stage 3 vase from Glenavy, Co. Antrim. (3) Stage 2 vase and miniature vase found accompanying cremated bone in a rectangular cist at Ballynahow, Co. Cork.

impressed decoration occurs occasionally (including comb and cord impressions). The principal motifs employed are simple herringbone patterns, zones of vertical or oblique short lines, and filled triangles. Brindley's study suggests that the form developed in three stages over a period of some three centuries c. 2000–1740 BC. Bipartite vessels with short everted rims and a preference for short line decoration are followed by an intermediate stage in which everted rims become larger and neck and shoulder become more pronounced; broad zonal ornament and filled triangles are common. A third stage is characterised by prominent everted or vertical necks and well-defined and often broad decorative bands including reserved ornament.

Like bowls, vases have been frequently found in the east and north but a significant concentration of bipartite vases is found in the west, in Galway and Mayo, and tripartite vases have a curious twofold distribution pattern, one major group scattered across the north of the country and the other in the east and south-east. Some fragments of vases come from likely habitation sites but most finds come from funerary contexts. A few have been associated with megalithic tombs: sherds of vases were found in court tombs at Ballymacaldrack, Co. Antrim, and Clontygora, Co. Armagh. Like bowls, of course, most have been found in cists or pits. While a small number accompanied unburnt burials (notably in counties Galway and Mayo), the majority were placed in the grave with cremated remains and here there is some variety in funerary practice. A majority of vases were placed in a short rectangular cist, mouth upwards beside a deposit of burnt bone. This was the case, for instance, in a cist discovered at Ballynahow, near Fermoy, Co. Cork (Fig. 4.17, 3). A slab-built cist (placed in a pit below ground level) was found in the course of ploughing; the contents were disturbed, but it seems that a miniature vase and a vase stood mouth upwards on either side of a small amount of cremated bone placed on a floor slab. The bones, unfortunately, were not preserved. In some graves, vases contained some cremated bone or were placed mouth downwards beside the bones (indicating that these pots probably held no offering of food or drink). Vases have been found with the bones of adults as well as children, and analysis of the burnt remains has sometimes revealed the presence of bones of more than one individual in the one grave. Vases have sometimes

been found as isolated burials but often in cemeteries. While most of these cemeteries have produced a range of pottery types, a small number, such as Cloghskelt, Co. Down, and Clonshannon, Co. Wicklow, may possibly be attributed to the Vase Tradition alone.

While objects of stone and metal are also occasionally placed along with vases as grave-offerings in burials, the commonest item is another pottery vessel, either a second vase, a larger vase urn or an encrusted urn. This triangular pattern of association contrasts with the relatively infrequent direct associations between other pottery types, and these funerary associations and the typological resemblances between vases, vase urns and encrusted urns are the two reasons for the identification of a distinct Vase Tradition. Just as the proponents of the Bowl Tradition had a varied burial ritual embracing both unburnt burial and cremation, so too did those of the Vase Tradition, who not only practised cremation and some unburnt burial but also favoured the use of urns. These larger bucket-sized vessels, of sufficient size to hold a deposit of burnt bone, were intended to be either containers for or perhaps, when inverted, protective coverings for cremated burials. In this the contrast with many vases is apparent, for vases more often than not were placed beside the human remains. This distinction between urns as containers for bones and both vases and bowls ('food-vessels') was once thought to be an important cultural difference and led to a long-held and erroneous belief in separate 'food-vessel' and 'urn' communities.

Other artefacts occasionally found with vases include plano-convex flint knives and, more rarely, bone pins. A faience bead was found with a tripartite vase and a cremation (mixed through a 15cm fill of clay) in a rectangular cist at Ballyduff, Co. Wexford. A small triangular dagger and an awl were found with a bipartite vase and a cremation in a similar cist at Annaghkeen, near Headford, Co. Galway, and the grooved dagger and the strip of gold from Topped Mountain, near Enniskillen, Co. Fermanagh, were found in a cist that also contained a vase. Some of these pottery vessels were seemingly used as domestic vessels; sherds of vase are reported from sandhills sites in the north, and possible vase also comes from sandhills at False Bay, near Ballyconneely, Co. Galway (McCormick et al. 1996).

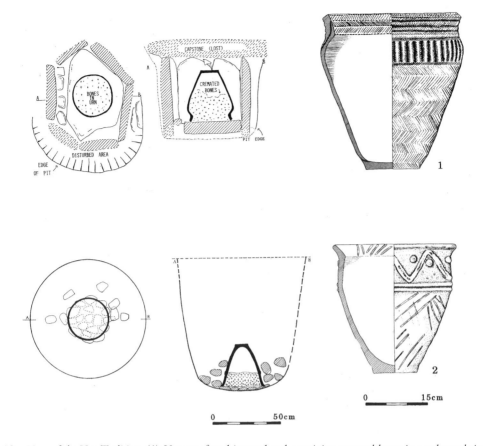

Fig. 4.18—Urns of the Vase Tradition. (1): Vase urn found inverted and containing cremated bones in a polygonal cist at Ballinvoher, Co. Cork. (2) Encrusted urn found inverted and containing cremated bones in a large pit at Coolnahane, near Kanturk, Co. Cork.

Vase urns, which have sometimes been called 'enlarged food vessels' or 'food-vessel urns', are large vessels, invariably over 20cm high and on average just under 30cm in height (Fig. 4.18, 1). Though obviously larger than vases and of thicker and coarser fabric, there is a clear typological relationship in both form and ornament between the two. Both the slack, curving profile of bipartite vases and the angular form of tripartite vases are found in the vase urn category. Some of these urns have the sharp shoulder and everted or near-vertical neck of the former and are usually decorated with incised lattice, filled triangle or herringbone motifs. Others have a round-shouldered form with a slightly everted rim, again with a predilection for incised decoration, notably herringbone designs. Again it is possible to identify early, intermediate and late stages in their development, with vessels with vertical necks and sparse ornament coming

late in the sequence. They appear to have been in use for some three centuries *c.* 2000–1750 BC. The distribution of vase urns (and encrusted urns) broadly coincides with the distribution of vases. Minor differences do exist, however; for example, the absence or rarity of these urns in parts of the west from Galway to Donegal, where there is a significant cluster of bipartite vases, is puzzling.

Most vase urns come from funerary contexts, both from simple pit graves and from cists. A few cists were short and rectangular but the majority were polygonal and just big enough to contain the urn. The vessel was usually inverted, as at Ballinvoher, near Castletownroche, Co. Cork (Fig. 4.18, 1), where a polygonal cist was discovered in the course of bulldozing work on a farm. A vase urn containing the burnt bones of at least one adult and one child had been deposited mouth downwards on the floor slab of the cist. Presumably a cloth covering or some such had been placed over the mouth of the urn to keep the bones within it. A partly stone-lined pit at Knockroe, near Sion Mills, Co. Tyrone, contained an inverted vase urn which in turn held the cremated remains of five individuals, an adult male, an adolescent female and three children; a fragment of a flint blade, part of a tubular bone object, some burnt animal bones and a plano-convex flint knife were also found in the vessel. Most of these plano-convex flint knives from burials have been found with pottery of the Vase Tradition. A secondary pit burial in a cemetery mound at Grange, near Tulsk, Co. Roscommon, contained an inverted vase urn which held the cremated bones of a young adult male; in the bone deposit lay the twisted remains of a bronze grooved dagger (Fig. 4.11, 7) and its bone pommel. The dagger had been deliberately twisted and ritually destroyed and burnt on the funeral pyre. Here, though the urn was a crudely made vessel, the dagger—related to a well-known type found in rich burials in southern England—suggests an individual of exceptional importance. Sherds of vase urn were found in a court tomb at Clontygora, Co. Armagh, and in the Kilhoyle and Largantea wedge tombs in County Derry: all were secondary deposits. A secondary cist in the cairn of the Kilmashogue wedge tomb, Co. Dublin, contained an urn of this type also.

Encrusted urns are so called because they bear distinctive encrusted, or applied, ornament (Kavanagh 1973). By and large they tend to be slightly taller and broader than vase urns (Fig. 4.18, 2): over two-thirds have heights and rim diameters in excess of 32.5cm (to a maximum of about 40cm). The larger examples also tend to be the most ornate as far as applied decoration is concerned. A typological relationship to vases and vase urns is evident: the majority have a curving profile with a short everted rim, while others have a more distinct neck and rim and a shouldered body. As with vase urns, the final stage of their development is represented by pots with vertical necks and sparse decoration. Encrusted ornament consists of applied strips or bosses of clay and ranges from simple zigzag or wavy motifs to complex net-like designs on a number of urns which recall vessels suspended in rope netting; applied strips with short incised lines on them may be echoes of strips stitched to leather containers. Incised ornament is common,

and simple impressed decoration occurs too. A few of these urns are of such coarse and friable fabric that it is a reasonable assumption that they were made specifically for burial purposes. They seem to have had a shorter lifespan than the vases or vase urns of this tradition, extending from c. 2000 to 1800 BC.

A small number of encrusted urns have been found as secondary burials in or near megalithic tombs of court, wedge and passage tomb type, but the great majority have been found inverted (with cremated bones) in pit or cist graves. As with vase urns, simple pits and polygonal cists are the preferred grave types; a small number have been found in rectangular cists. A number of urns have been found with the bones of adults, but cremations of children are also reported and occasionally more than one individual is represented. An example from Ballyveelish, near Clonmel, Co. Tipperary, was found inverted in a stone-lined pit along with two cups and the cremated bones of two adults and three children; the grave lay at the centre of a ring-ditch and was protected by a timber structure which has been interpreted as a mortuary house.

Urns have been recovered from possible habitation sites: fragments of vase urn and encrusted urn are recorded from various northern sandhills (ApSimon 1969b), from contexts that presumably can be described as non-funerary and possibly domestic. The presence of pottery vessels of both the Bowl Tradition and the Vase Tradition in western and south-western Scotland confirms, if such were necessary, the fact that the narrow stretch of water between north-eastern Ireland and the adjacent parts of Scotland inextricably linked the two areas together. Radiocarbon dating suggests that pottery styles like these were widely adopted fairly quickly. Two important British urn traditions, represented in Ireland, are probably good examples of this process and a further illustration of contemporary cross-channel links. One of these, the Collared Urn Tradition, is the major urn tradition in Britain, and the Cordoned Urn Tradition is prominent in Scotland.

The Collared Urn Tradition

Over 2,000 collared urns have been recorded in Britain by Ian Longworth (1984) and some 60 examples are known in Ireland, where they are dated to the period c. 1850–1650 BC (Kavanagh

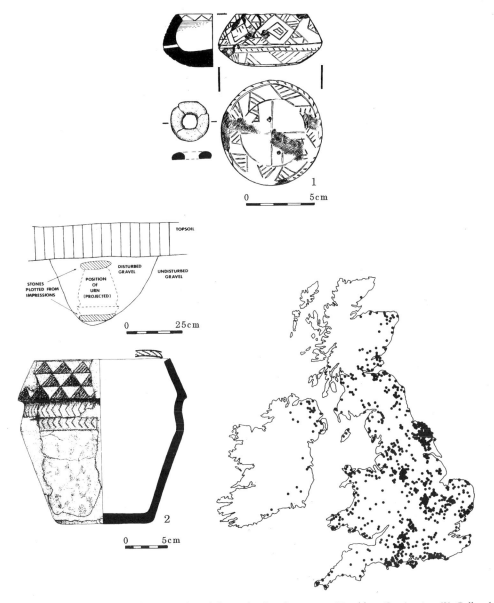

Fig. 4.19—(1) Biconical cup found with a quoit-shaped faience bead and an urn at Knockboy, Co. Antrim. (2) Collared urn found inverted in a pit at Killeenaghmountain, Co. Waterford, and general distribution.

1976; Brindley 2007). A distinguishing feature of these urns is a collared rim above a concave neck (Fig. 4.19, 2), which gives the vessel a distinctive, angular, tripartite profile. Rims are often broad and flat or bevelled, and are sometimes expanded internally and externally. Collars are often concave, sometimes straight, and the curvature of the neck may vary from pronounced to slight. The collars and necks are frequently decorated with cord-impressed or incised designs; both techniques are

more or less equally popular in Ireland. Lattice, filled triangle and herringbone are the commonest motifs. In a few cases the body below the shoulder is decorated, usually with a lattice design. Early stage urns usually have ornament on collar, neck and body; intermediate examples share some traits with the Vase Tradition and some decorative motifs and the use of cord ornament suggest interaction with the makers of Cordoned Urns. In a third stage of development, the tripartite shape of these urns is

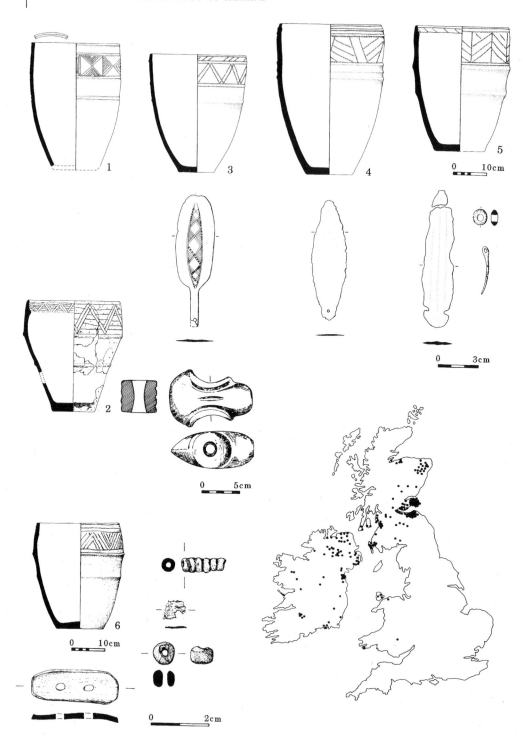

Fig. 4.20—The Cordoned Urn Tradition and distribution in Ireland and Britain. (1) Urbalreagh, Co. Antrim. (2) Laheen, Co. Donegal, and stone battleaxe. (3) Pollacorragune, Co. Galway, and tanged bronze razor. (4) Knockast, Co. Westmeath, and bronze knife or razor. (5) Harristown, Co. Waterford, and bronze knife, quoit-shaped faience bead and bone pin. (6) Kilcroagh, Co. Antrim, and segmented faience bead, stone bead, perforated bone object and fragment of a bronze knife or razor.

produced not so much by a division between neck, collar and body but by a pair of cordons or ribs, as on Cordoned Urns.

The majority of these urns (no less than 72%) have been found in the north and north-east, in counties Antrim, Derry, Down and Tyrone; the remainder have a scattered distribution in the east and south of the country. The general distribution pattern clearly shows how a British fashion impinged on the eastern half of the country. While sherds have been recovered in domestic as well as funerary contexts in Britain, in Ireland they have so far only been discovered in burials—sometimes singly, occasionally in cemeteries. By far the greater number occurred inverted in pit graves and containing cremated bones. Very few were in cists and few were placed mouth upwards. The urn from Killeenaghmountain, near Kilwatermoy, Co. Waterford, is fairly typical: found in the course of gravel-working, it had been placed on a flat stone in a pit and protected by another stone on the base. It contained a small quantity of burnt bone, possibly the remains of a child. Bones of adult males and females have been found in these urns too. At Ballymacaldrack, Co. Antrim, where an urn contained the cremated bones of a female and a burnt barbed and tanged arrowhead, it was suggested by the excavator (since an arrowhead seemed an inappropriate funerary offering for a woman) that the flint may have been the cause of her death. At Creggan, Co. Antrim, a plain urn reportedly held the burnt bones of three persons: an adult female, a child, and an infant.

Associated finds with collared urns are relatively few but some are of interest. Several contained small bronze daggers: a small dagger of type Corkey was found with another Creggan, Co. Antrim, urn, and two collared urns (stage 2 examples) in the cemetery in the Mound of the Hostages, Tara, contained daggers, burnt and broken or twisted out of shape. A superbly crafted stone battleaxe was found in one of these urns, which was accompanied by an inverted vase. Another bronze dagger was found in an inverted urn at Bay Farm, Carnlough, Co. Antrim, along with a shell button and a carved piece of chalk.

The Cordoned Urn Tradition

Cordoned Urns are so named because they usually have one or more horizontal cordons or raised ribs

encircling their exteriors, with a simple (almost straight-sided or slightly barrel-shaped) or a slightly bipartite profile, and a single horizontal zone of ornament on the uppermost part of the exterior (Fig. 4.20). The cordons are usually applied or pinched up and, since these vessels are coil-built, it has been suggested that cordons might have been made to mark coil junctions. While this may be true in some cases, the presence of narrow, closely set multiple cordons on some urns and the occasional presence of false cordons, produced by grooving or by impressing pairs of lines, indicates that some were intended to be decorative. This is evident on the superbly made urn found in a pit in the centre of a small penannular ring-ditch at Urbalreagh, Co. Antrim, where the decoration is produced by fine whipped cord impressions. It and the urn from a cemetery mound at Knockast, Co. Westmeath, are examples with simple, slightly curving profiles with simple rims (Fig. 4.20, 1 and 4). The Knockast urn has an internal cordon just below the rim, an occasional feature of the type. An urn from Laheen, north-east of Ballyshannon, Co. Donegal (Fig. 4.20, 2), is an example with a bipartite profile. Most cordoned urns are about 30cm or more in height, but a number of miniature examples 12–15cm high are known (Kavanagh 1976; Waddell 1995a).

As already mentioned, decoration is usually confined to one broad zone below the rim and cord-impressed designs are usual, occurring on about 75% of examples. Incised decoration is found on a minority of pots. Other techniques such as comb ornament are rare. Filled triangles, chevron and lattice patterns are favoured motifs, and it is worth noting that reserved designs, sometimes in elegant panels as on the Urbalreagh vessel, are a feature of over a third of these urns. A few are undecorated. According to Brindley (2007), early urns (stage 1), usually with a single zone of cord-impressed ornament, emerge *c.* 1730 BC and the type continues to *c.* 1500 BC; intermediate examples often have panelled ornament, while in the final stage (stage 3) urns tend to have simple open ornament without hatched motifs or triangles.

The great majority come from burials and the simple pit grave is the commonest type; few have been found in cists. Cremation is the invariable rite and most urns were inverted; a minority stood mouth upwards. Bones of adults, both male and female, as well as those of children have been identified. Some urns have been found in cemeteries and several interesting instances are known where cordoned urns have been found to be the principal and, sometimes, the only burial in burial mounds. The Pollacorragune urn was found in the centre of a small circular mound; the urn was inverted, half-full of cremated bone, and also contained a decorated, tanged bronze razor (Fig. 4.20, 3).

Sherds of cordoned urns have been recovered from a significant number of settlement contexts. At Downpatrick, Co. Down, traces of two roughly circular timber houses were uncovered (Pollock and Waterman 1964). The remains of an important and extensive habitation were revealed in the course of the construction of a housing estate during which most of the archaeological remains were destroyed. Only a narrow cutting, for the most part 2m wide and some 42m long, could be excavated, and this only with difficulty. The excavation revealed the greater part of two approximately circular timber houses set about 18m apart, and a few pits, a hearth and some isolated post-holes. A post-hole in one house contained part of an axe of Tievebulliagh porcellanite but acid soil conditions precluded the survival of any animal remains other than a few cattle teeth. Of particular interest was the fact that, though a greater variety of decorative techniques were used, the pottery in general did not differ in any significant way from the funerary series. Plain cordoned urn was associated with a post- and stake-built circular house with a central hearth set within a ditched enclosure at Knockhouse Lower, near Waterford; charred seeds demonstrated the cultivation of barley and some wheat, but again soil conditions were not suitable for the preservation of bone (Richardson and Johnston 2007). Sherds of cordoned urn have been found on destroyed habitation sites at Ballyrenan and Sheepland, Co. Down, and on a number of sandhill sites in counties Antrim, Derry and Down (ApSimon 1969b). Pottery of this type is also associated with a number of wetland settlements. Sherds come from a lakeside settlement at Moynagh Lough, Co. Meath, where two circular houses approximately 6m in diameter, stone scrapers and fragments of saddle querns have been uncovered (Bradley 1999). A brushwood platform retained by a timber palisade some 20m across has been partly excavated in Ballyarnet Lake,

north-west of Derry, and has produced numerous sherds, remains of a circular house 5m in diameter, a large hearth, a fragment of a quoit-shaped faience bead and stone implements (Ó Néill and Plunkett 2007; Ó Néill et al. 2007).

The Cordoned Urn is an Irish–Scottish type: in Ireland there is a distinct concentration in the north-east, in counties Antrim, Derry, Down, Tyrone and Louth. Scattered examples extend from Donegal to Inis Oírr, Aran, Co. Galway, to counties Limerick and Waterford. The number recorded in Scotland is about double the Irish figure and their general distribution is another indication of Irish–Scottish contact: a scatter of finds links a south-western group of urns in Ayrshire and Wigtownshire (including Arran and Kintyre) with major concentrations in the east and north-east. A few examples are known in northern England, the Isle of Man and Wales. As Brindley notes, the Cordoned Urn Tradition is a regional expression of a funerary phenomenon whereby a cord- or cordon-decorated pottery type is associated with cremated bones and occasionally beads or trinkets and small bronze blades that is also found in Cornwall (Trevisker Urns) and in the Netherlands and Belgium. The associated finds with cordoned urns are intriguing. The rarity of bronze artefacts in burials generally has been readily apparent, but the Cordoned Urn Tradition offers an unusual exception. A number of small bronze knives or razors have been found with as many of these urns, and they and a limited range of other artefacts are probably tokens of particular importance.

Prestigious tokens

The small knives or razors found with cordoned urns may have been male equipment; in the few cases where the cremated bones have been analysed it seems that they did accompany male burials (Kavanagh 1991). They do occur, albeit rarely, with other pottery types but seem to be a favoured artefact in this burial tradition, both in Ireland and in Scotland. A fine tanged and decorated razor (Fig. 4.20, 3) was found with the Pollacorragune urn, and a somewhat similar but plainer tanged example was associated with a vase and vase urn burial in a cemetery mound at Knockast, Co. Westmeath. The commonest type of blade is a simple, more or less oval, flat knife less than 9cm long, usually with one or two rivet holes in a rounded or broadly tanged butt for the attachment of a hilt (Fig. 4.20, 4). While the name 'razor' may be justly applied to tanged implements like that from Pollacorragune, the purpose of the miniature knives is less apparent. Some were burnt on the cremation pyre and some were not. Their use is uncertain; they may have been shaving implements or used for cosmetic mutilation, but they do seem to have had some symbolic significance. It is interesting to note that one cordoned urn in a small cemetery at Kilcroagh, Co. Antrim, contained the cremated bones of a male teenager and an adult female; a bronze knife or razor in the urn may have been a male offering, while a small faience bead may have accompanied the female. A second similar burial in the same cemetery also contained a fragment of a razor and a faience bead (Fig. 4.20, 6). In addition to knives or razors and those beads of a glassy substance called faience, a number of bone pins, a few plano-convex flint knives and other flints, and two stone battleaxes have also been found with these urns. An unusual ceramic spoon and two miniature cups (one with a human face modelled on it) were found with a cordoned urn in a pit at Mitchelstown, Co. Cork; the urn had been placed mouth upwards and there were no human remains (Kiely and Sutton 2007).

While the significance of small bronze blades or single beads may be difficult to determine, the finely made and often highly polished perforated battleaxes are evidence of a considerable investment in time and craftsmanship and presumably were items with exceptional prestige value. The cordoned urn found at Laheen, Co. Donegal, had been inverted in a pit and contained cremated bones; the stone axe had been placed beside the urn and showed some traces of use—its cutting edge was slightly blunted and its flat butt was slightly abraded (Fig. 4.20, 2). Another cordoned urn from Ballintubbrid, near Kilmuckridge, Co. Wexford, contained a burnt perforated axe of simpler form, and another battleaxe, also burnt in the pyre, was found in a collared urn burial in the Mound of the Hostages. Several types of perforated battleaxes are known in Ireland, though—compared to Britain—they are not particularly common (Simpson 1996a). The Laheen and Tara battleaxes belong to a distinctive Irish form, the Bann type, characterised by a widely splayed crescentic blade, a deeply cut waist and a truncated-conical butt; decoration, usually in the form of a carved moulding on the

sides, also occurs. A number of battleaxes from Scotland have affinities with this Bann type and experiments have shown that it takes several days of intensive pecking, drilling and polishing to produce one example. These axes, like the various flint knives, scrapers and other implements occasionally found with other burials, are a reminder that stonework still had significant uses in an age of metal. Indeed, for many stone may still have had a predominant role.

The faience beads found in the cordoned urn burials at Kilcroagh, Co. Antrim, are two of a small number of such finds; similar associations with cordoned urns are recorded at Carrig, Co. Wicklow, Longstone, Co. Tipperary, and Harristown, Co. Waterford. At the latter site one of three cordoned urns in a small cemetery contained a faience bead, a bronze knife and a bone pin. Other faience bead finds include Ballyduff, Co. Wexford, where one was found with a cremation and a vase, and at the Mound of the Hostages at Tara, where an unburnt burial was accompanied by a bronze knife and a necklace of faience, jet and amber beads and of beads of bronze tubing. A biconical cup, a faience bead, a cremation and a (lost) urn were found at Knockboy, near Ballymena, Co. Antrim (Fig. 4.19, 1). Most Irish beads are of a segmented tubular variety, as at Kilcroagh; those from Harristown and Knockboy are circular and flat, a form sometimes called quoit-shaped, and a few are star-shaped. In prehistoric archaeology the term 'faience' is given to a synthetic substance widely distributed in Europe and the Near East in the second millennium in particular. Beads made of powdered quartz or sand with a surface glaze coloured with copper salts to produce a blue-green glassy finish were evidently highly prized and, like amber, some may have been exchanged over considerable distances. Various analyses demonstrate regional groups and production, and X-ray fluorescence spectroscopy indicates that Irish beads, for the most part, have a similar tin content to British finds. Usually found singly or in small numbers in cremated burials, they may have served as amulets and appear to have a mainly female association. Faience may have been considered a mysterious and exotic substance because its manufacture involved the magical transformation of certain raw materials by a privileged few (Sheridan and Shortland 2004).

The Carrig, Co. Wicklow, association is

particularly interesting because the deposition of faience beads was part of a complex ritual sequence (Grogan 1990). A rectangular cist grave in a damaged cemetery mound south-east of Blessington was seemingly used on no less than six separate occasions and contained two vases accompanying cremated bones which were covered by a clay filling through which small pockets of burnt bone were mixed; these deposits were followed by three further cremations in inverted cordoned urns inserted into the fill and a final token deposit of a few cremated bones and some coarse potsherds (Fig. 4.21, 3). Two of the cordoned urns produced bronze knives or razors, and one also contained star-shaped and segmented faience beads.

Miniature pottery cups ('pygmy cups') are a rare find with urns of all types; like the limited range of metal and stone artefacts, no cup form is clearly restricted to any one of the major pottery traditions but several have been discovered with cordoned urns. While some of these puzzling cups are evidently miniature bowls or vases, the commonest form is a small biconical vessel no more than 6cm high. Incised geometric decoration is common but a number are plain. About half of these have a pair of small perforations in the shoulder, as in the Knockboy cup found with the faience bead. A few related cups have larger triangular perforations in their sides, giving them an openwork appearance; these and the perforated cups have inspired the suggestion that these small pots were meant to hold a pleasant-smelling substance (such as incense) and they have been variously called 'incense cups' as well as 'pygmy cups'. Their purpose is unknown and it has been suggested that they may have served as burners for narcotic substances, but residue analysis in Britain has—so far at least—produced negative results. Though the evidence is limited, they have frequently been found with the remains of adults, both male and female (Ó Donnabháin and Brindley 1990).

CEMETERIES

These burials with their occasional grave-goods were the interments of representatives of small agricultural communities whose settlements remain elusive but were presumably nearby. Most of the burials and pottery mentioned in the preceding pages were casual discoveries in the course of ploughing, gravel-digging and other such activities, and many, unfortunately, were disturbed and further damaged by the finders. This was particularly the case with flat graves—cists or pits *in* the ground with no surviving superimposed monument or marker—but mounds containing burials were frequently damaged too. Thus an enormous amount of information about details of burial ritual has been irretrievably lost. Some burials appear to have been isolated, solitary interments, a number occur in small groups of two or three, and others were grouped in small cemeteries. Whether those solitary burials were actually just one of a group destroyed in the past or one of a group just not detected is often an unanswerable question. The last-mentioned certainly has happened: at Cloghskelt, Co. Down, two urn burials were accidentally found many decades before an excavation in the area in 1973 undertaken after a further accidental discovery revealed that the old finds were but two graves in a flat cemetery of over twenty burials (Waddell 1990). Charles Mount (1997b) has shown how the circumstances of discovery have significantly influenced the present picture: it is clear that pit graves are under-represented because ploughing in particular has led to the discovery of more cists than pits. Thus small groups of cists are probably the remnants of larger cemeteries where pits were not recognised. Solitary burials do occur, however. Some burial mounds which have been carefully excavated have produced just one grave: Pollacorragune, Co. Galway, with its cordoned urn burial mentioned above, and a vase urn burial found at the centre of a very low mound with encircling ditch at Lissard, Co. Limerick, are just two examples; it is clear that some flat graves may indeed have been isolated ones. Such may have been the case at Ballyveelish, Co. Tipperary, where an encrusted urn was found with the cremated bones of five individuals and where the one grave was, in effect, a small collective burial.

Judging from the poorly documented evidence, sites with just two or three graves are surprisingly numerous (comprising about 58% of all multiple grave sites). Small cemeteries of four to ten graves represent about 32%, larger cemeteries of eleven to nineteen graves about 8%, and more extensive sites of more than twenty are rare: only

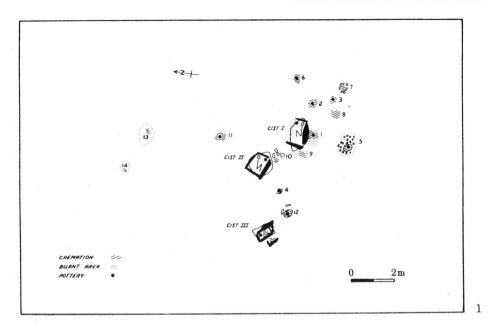

Fig. 4.21—(1) Simplified plan of a flat cemetery at Edmondstown, Co. Dublin. (2) Ring-ditch containing three urn burials at Urbalreagh, Co. Antrim. (3) Cist grave containing successive burials in a cemetery mound at Carrig, Co. Wicklow.

about 2%. Mount has shown that in the south-east of the country the average number of graves is four and three is the most common number, but many of these are sites with only cists recorded. In the mixed cemeteries (those with cists and pits) the average number is higher, about six. Thus the relatively large number of very small sites is due in part to inadequate or incomplete excavation and to

the failure to discover or recognise pits. It is still apparent, however, that in most instances only small numbers were given formal burial and not everyone was entitled to this privilege.

There are two contrasting forms of cemetery: flat cemeteries where the graves have no surviving superimposed monument, and cemetery mounds where a round mound or cairn may contain a number of graves. Since many burials were not accompanied by a pottery vessel, be it bowl, vase or urn, a summary of the pottery traditions is not a summary of burial fashions. The cemeteries of the time offer a clearer picture, and a number of well-excavated examples are excellent illustrations of the remarkable diversity of burial practice and provide important information about the social significance of some of the complex variations in the funerary record.

Flat cemeteries

Most flat cemeteries have been incompletely or inadequately recorded but Cloghskelt, Co. Down, is one of the few to have been excavated in recent years. In addition to an encrusted urn burial, and a vase urn 'in a small stone cist', found years before, the flat cemetery contained a further 23 graves within an area measuring about 13m by 5m. One grave was a small and approximately polygonal cist holding a vase urn and a vase; another, possibly the remains of a long cist, contained two vases. The other graves were pit graves, some protected by one or more stones. Nine contained no pottery and, apart from a few stray sherds of bowl found, all the pottery was of the Vase Tradition, mostly vases but a vase urn and several encrusted urns as well. Other grave-offerings were few: a plano-convex flint knife and a flint convex scraper, for instance. An interesting feature of the site was the apparent division of the cemetery into two areas: a southern concentration of burials consisted of urns and vases, while only vases were found in a northern group. Whether this reflects some social distinction or is of chronological significance is not clear. Excavation also revealed the possible cremation site; a thick black deposit containing minute fragments of burnt bone covered an area about 9m by 6m. Evidently at least some of the dead were buried near the remains of their funeral pyre.

While a very small number of cemeteries seem to contain just one pottery tradition, in most cases a mix of traditions is present. This was the case at the Edmondstown, Co. Dublin, flat cemetery (Mount and Hartnett 1993). Here it seems that four rectangular cists may have formed the nucleus of a cemetery of some nineteen burials (Fig. 4.21). Cist I contained the crouched skeleton of a young adult male lying on his right side with a bowl mouth upwards in front of the face while Cist II held the crouched skeleton of a teenager with a bowl standing in front of his or her face; the cist was almost filled with soil containing both burnt and unburnt bone. A mixture of clay fill and cremated bone (of a young adult male) was found in cist III, along with another bowl. Cist IV was a small addition to III and just contained the cremation of an adult male. Most of the other burials were situated south and south-east of the cists and were all cremations. Some of these were just scatters of bone but others were pit burials; the accompanying pottery included complete or partially complete vase urns, encrusted urns and collared urns. One of the pit burials with an inverted encrusted urn contained the bones of four individuals, and another burial was a collared urn containing the cremated bones of three persons. Several cremations had no accompanying pottery.

Apart from the two unburnt individuals in cists I and II, the cremated remains represented 27 individuals, including four adult males, one adult female and six adults of uncertain sex, four children, three to four infants and eight deposits of bone which were unidentifiable. All the burials in the cists were adults and all but the youth in cist II were positively identified as male. These were the only burials associated with bowls. This contrasts with the treatment of women and children, who were all cremated, though some adult males were cremated as well. A similar pattern occurs in the cemetery mound at Knockast (below). Another interesting feature at Edmondstown was the number of multiple burials in the one grave: three of the nineteen (16%) contained the remains of more than one person and these were mostly children and infants, with the occasional adult. This pattern of adult males predominating in single interments and women and children figuring more in multiple burials has also been noted by Mount in southern Leinster generally and by Martin Doody (1987) in Munster.

At Keenoge, near Duleek, Co. Meath, a flat cemetery of fourteen graves was gradually uncovered in a low esker from 1929 to 1936 in an area measuring about 14m by 10m (Mount 1997a). A mix of cist and pit burials was found and only a minority were cremated. Two small cists simply contained cremations, a third contained the unburnt remains of an infant, and several pit graves held crouched skeletons—none of these accompanied by any pottery. A polygonal cist contained a cremation and an encrusted urn and a vase urn. Bowls and crouched skeletons occurred in three pit graves and in two rectangular cists. One of these pit graves was distinguished by a paved floor and contained the crouched skeleton of an adult female, two bowls, a small bronze knife and several flints; a small deposit of cremated bone was found beneath and behind the head of the skeleton. One cist was built of massive stones (Fig. 4.16, 1); it contained the crouched skeleton of an adult female and, in addition to a bowl in front of the skull, had two more placed outside it, on either side. These two burials would seem to have been the most important in the cemetery, but a simple pit contained the crouched skeleton of a young adult female with a necklace of 40 jet beads around her neck, an unusual grave-offering and possibly another indication of status. Like at least two of the cremations and six other unburnt burials, this grave contained no pottery; and while it might be assumed that the crouched skeletons should be assigned to the Bowl Tradition, certainty is not possible. A minimum of 26 individuals were represented in the cemetery, with adult males predominating (64%) and children and infants clearly under-represented. Nevertheless, it is also evident that when some women were accorded formal burial they sometimes received exceptional treatment. The high proportion of multiple burials is also noteworthy, with five single and nine multiple interments (69%). Some of the graves may have been used for successive burials, as was so clearly demonstrated at Carrig, Co. Wicklow (Fig. 4.21, 3). Judging from a number of radiocarbon dates for human bone samples, the Keenoge cemetery was used for at least 500 years, and possibly for as long as 760 years, perhaps with just one or two burials taking place in each generation.

Given the limited extent of excavation at sites such as Keenoge, it is unclear whether cemeteries were normally enclosed or not. At Urbalreagh, south-east of Portrush, Co. Antrim, a penannular ring-ditch with a diameter of about 6m surrounded three burials (Fig. 4.21, 2). The central pit burial (no. 1) was a fine inverted cordoned urn (Fig. 4.20, 1) containing the burnt bones of a male and the remains of a possible razor or knife. A secondary urn (no. 2) and the burnt bones of a child were placed in the upper levels of this pit, and a third

cremation (no. 3), representing part of the remains of a juvenile, were placed in a pit just to the north. The positions of these burials may once have been marked by very low mounds. On the south-west, the ring-ditch had cut through an area of intense burning which produced some small pieces of cremated bone and may have been the site of a funeral pyre (Waterman 1968).

Cemetery mounds

A number of cemetery mounds have been scientifically excavated but many have been less than adequately recorded in the past. The term embraces earlier mounds reused for multiple burials in the later third and second millennia, as well as circular mounds specifically constructed to cover several burials, or perhaps built to cover just one or two graves, with secondary burials inserted at a later date. On present limited evidence there seems to be no great difference in the variation in numbers in cemetery mounds or flat cemeteries, though one cemetery mound, at Knockast, Co. Westmeath, is exceptional in having over 40 burials. Between 25 and 30 Bronze Age burials were found in the Mound of the Hostages, eight inserted in the passage tomb and the rest placed in the covering mound. Most of these were cremated. The one unburnt burial in the mound is of unusual interest: it was the unprotected skeleton of a youth, lying on its back with the legs flexed. There was no pottery, but a necklace of beads of jet, amber, faience and bronze tubing lay in the neck area and a small bronze knife and a pin or awl had been placed beside the corpse. Exotic materials from different sources made up the composite necklace (the amber may be of Baltic origin and the jet may have come from northern England, for instance) so there may have been complex meanings encoded in its diverse elements. The range of pottery, which included Bowls, Vases, Vase Urns, Encrusted Urns and Collared Urns, the V-perforated buttons, beads, bronze daggers and stone battleaxe all indicate the importance of this cemetery. At Tara, as occasionally elsewhere, an earlier monument was reused as a burial place, and this was a monument that was in active use at various times from 3000 BC to at least 1700 BC in a location whose significance spanned millennia.

The reuse or augmentation of older mounds is recorded elsewhere too: at Baunogenasraid, Co.

Carlow, a mound covering a Linkardstown-type grave was enlarged to contain at least ten burials, all in shallow pits protected, in a few cases, by some small stones. Both cremated and unburnt crouched burials occurred in the secondary mantling, and two of the latter (one with a bowl) were disturbed by subsequent cremations. The remains represented both adults and children (B. Raftery 1974). The well-known passage tomb at Fourknocks I, Co. Meath, was also used as a later cemetery. A secondary mantling of clay was spread only over part of the northern half of the original mound. This covered four of five cists that had been constructed in pits dug into the primary mound. No bones were found in one cist but four held the unburnt remains of children, one with a bowl. Three pit burials were also found: fragments of a bowl and some human teeth were all that survived of one, and the other two were cremations in inverted vase urns.

The radiocarbon dating of some material from a 1934 excavation of a cemetery mound at Poulawack, in the Burren, Co. Clare, suggests the possibility of remarkable ritual persistence in some cases (Fig. 4.22). The primary burial on the site was a polygonal cist related to the Linkardstown type of grave and dated to 3614–3373 BC (graves 8 and 8A), which was probably covered by a low cairn and encircled by a stone wall or kerb with a diameter of about 10m. A thousand years later, towards the end of the third millennium, a rectangular cist (grave 4) containing the unburnt remains of an adult and a child was inserted into the cairn at a point where some of the kerb may have been removed. Two other cists (graves 5 and 6) were inserted about this time as well, and these various acts could have taken place over several generations. Towards the middle of the second millennium BC the cairn was enlarged; it was heightened by about 1m and extended by about 2m around its circumference. Judging from the radiocarbon evidence, graves 1 and 3 were added or incorporated at this time, and graves 2 and 7 were then evidently inserted into the enlarged cairn. Far from being a simple and relatively short-lived cemetery containing the remains of some sixteen people, mostly unburnt, with no significant grave-goods, this complex monument had a protracted ritual significance for at least 1,800 years. The evidence suggests three periods of funerary activity in this long time-span,

but during this millennium and a half Poulawack, a prominent monument on a broad limestone plateau, may well have been a focus for other sorts of ritual observance which have left no archaeological trace (Brindley and Lanting 1992a; Jones 2007). A large circular mound at Grange, south of Tulsk, Co. Roscommon, contained the unburnt and cremated remains of some 25 people, several accompanied by finely made pottery vessels of the Bowl Tradition (Ó Ríordáin 1997). The great majority of burials occurred in its eastern half and, while both adults and children were represented, only one unburnt juvenile was buried alone. In all other cases the juvenile remains were cremated and were mixed with the bones of adults. Of the fourteen adults, the sex of only nine could be determined with some degree of certainty, and all of these were male or probably male. Here, as in some other cemeteries (Mount 1998), a study of skeletal pathology indicates a physically active lifestyle involving the manipulation of heavy loads or some other strenuous activity. One cremation in an urn of the Vase Tradition was the burial of a young adult male accompanied by the bronze dagger noted above, which was evidently a prestigious status symbol. It had been deliberately and ritually destroyed by folding it over several times and burning it on the cremation pyre. Judging from the half-dozen radiocarbon dates available (Brindley 2007), it is possible that the burial activity at Grange was also protracted and may have spanned a period of about 400 years.

A shorter span of activity of several centuries probably obtained at Moneen, just south of Glanworth, Co. Cork, where a circular cairn enclosed by a shallow annular ditch covered four cists. A primary, central cist was of massive megalithic construction and it contained the unburnt bones of a male and a possible female, placed on a paved floor. At some later date, these were displaced and the cremation of a youth spread on the floor. This cist was surrounded by a kerb of large stones, one in-turned slab on the north-east conceivably being the remains of an entrance. Three subsidiary cists lay to the west of the central grave: two on the pre-cairn surface, one partly on this surface and partly on the lowest layer of cairn material. The latter contained the disturbed unburnt bones of an adult male, a diminutive cist was empty, and a third (only about 90cm by 55cm internally)

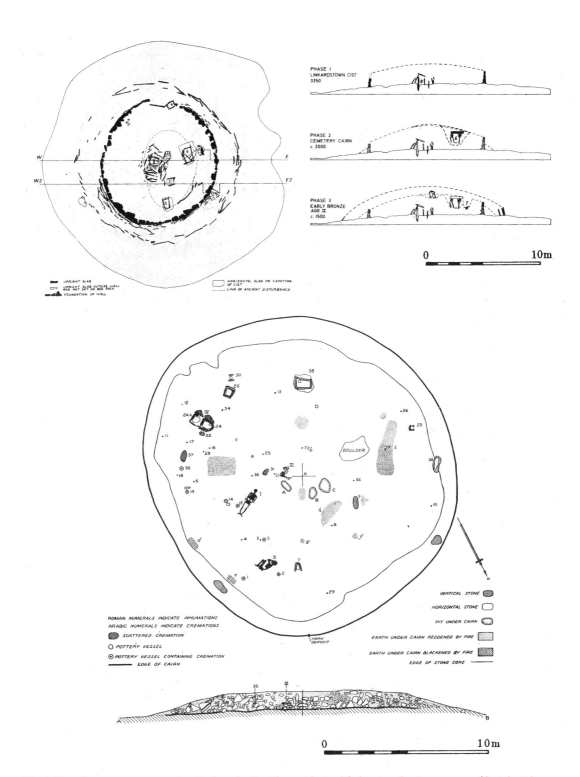

Fig. 4.22—Above: cemetery mound at Poulawack, Co. Clare, with simplified section showing sequence of burials. Below: cemetery mound at Knockast, Co. Westmeath.

held the disarticulated unburnt bones of a male, a female and a child, whose remains must have been stored for a period elsewhere, and defleshed, to allow them all to fit in this grave. Two further burials were found near the cairn on the south-west. One, an encrusted urn burial, had been placed within an arc added to the annular ring-ditch that encircled the cairn; the other, a cremation and bowl sherds, had been disturbed when this added arc was dug. Several pits, some spreads of charcoal, Beaker pottery, a few fragments of a human skull (some burnt), a few flints and a scatter of stake- or post-holes were found beneath the cairn and within the area of the ring-ditch. This activity could have been either temporary occupation or of some ritual significance, and radiocarbon dating now places it in the period 2854–2294 BC. The central grave is radiocarbon-dated to 2284–2046 BC (from human bone). The other cists are probably broadly contemporary, and the two other burials associated with the extension to the ring-ditch are somewhat later (Brindley *et al.* 1988).

The cemetery mound at Knockast, near Moate, Co. Westmeath (Fig. 4.22), was a broad, low, flat-topped, kerbless circular mound just over 18m in diameter and with a maximum height of 1.2m. It was situated on the summit of a low but conspicuous hill. Excavation in 1932 (Hencken and Movius 1934) revealed a core of clay and stones covered by dark soil. Burials were found both on the old ground surface and at different depths within the cairn. One unburnt, extended, adult male skeleton found about 50cm beneath the surface in the eastern half of mound disturbed two cremated burials; because it differed somewhat in physical type from the other unburnt burials, it was thought to be of different date. In fact its date is unknown and, while extended burial is unusual in early prehistory, it does occur. Burial 2 was the unburnt skeleton of a man in the more usual crouched position, which lay at the base of the cairn. This unfortunate individual suffered from chronic arthritis and as a youth had an abscess of the inner ear that had left his face badly distorted. The only find in the grave was a pig's tusk. Unburnt burials 3 and 4 were disturbed by subsequent cremations. In addition to these four unburnt burials, 39 cremations were found, the majority of all burials being in the eastern half of the mound. The cremations were placed in cists in a few

instances, in spaces between the stones of the cairn, on the earth at the base of the cairn, or in small pits made in the old ground surface. Ten cremations were accompanied by pottery, in some cases so decayed as to be unrecognisable but which included bowl (cremation no. 28), encrusted urn (no. 2), vase and possible vase urn (no. 14), vase urn (no. 15) and cordoned urn (Fig. 4.20, 4), found with cremation no. 36. The latter was the cremated burial of an adult male accompanied by a small bronze knife or razor. Other grave-goods included a small decorated bronze knife and a plano-convex flint knife with cremation 18 and small bone cylinders (no. 6). The excavator noted that the burials accompanied by non-pottery artefacts such as these were confined to a restricted area near the south-eastern edge of the cairn. Some two dozen cremations had no accompanying grave-goods of any description.

A study of the cremated bones revealed the remains of twenty males, eight females and twelve individuals whose sex characteristics were not clearly defined, probably because these bones were more fragile and had disintegrated more in the intense heat of the pyre. If these were the remains of females, the unusual preponderance of males over females would be reduced. Only two female burials (nos 2 and 30) were accompanied by pottery and all the bronze items were found with male burials. Of the 40 individuals identified in 39 burials (one was a double burial), only eleven could be identified as having reached middle or old age (that is, over 36 years of age). A high mortality rate up to and in early adulthood would be normal in early prehistoric societies. In studying the Knockast bones, Movius detected an interesting difference between the people who were buried unburnt, who were of larger and more rugged appearance, and those who were cremated, who were of a smaller and lighter-limbed physical type. He thought that this pointed to a racial difference between the two, but socio-economic circumstances, or better diet or different work patterns, could be a causal factor too. Beneath the Knockast mound there were three clearly defined pits containing earth, charcoal and bones of cattle, horse, and sheep or goat; there were also patches of well-burnt earth and charcoal, and some fragments of plain pottery of possible fourth-millennium date.

There was no obvious primary or focal burial

in the Knockast cemetery but, since a few graves disturbed others, there was clearly a sequence of burials there. Other cemetery mounds, such as Cornaclery, Co. Derry, with five graves (May 1942) and Corrower, Co. Mayo, with nine graves (Raftery 1960), had more or less centrally placed primary graves, with the majority of the other burials being placed on the eastern and southern sides of the mound respectively, a pattern noted in the Mound of the Hostages as well.

The variation in numbers of burials, in types of grave, in the rituals practised and in the range of grave-goods found is a remarkable feature of cemeteries, both flat cemeteries and cemetery mounds. They offer a conspectus of the variety of burial rite and funerary pottery of the period. Some, such as Knockast, could have been the communal burial place of a small community, the different pottery types perhaps reflecting changes in ceramic fashion through time, or different social caste or ancestry, or even family affiliation. A relatively small number of cemeteries have contained pottery of just one tradition, but more commonly two or more pottery traditions are represented. There is evidence that only a fraction of the members of a family or community were formally buried, others presumably being disposed of in other ways. The occasional mixture of pottery types, particularly in small burial groups, suggests that some mixed deposits may have had some magico-religious, social or political significance, rather than just a funerary one. These do not seem to have been cemeteries in the ordinary sense of the word, with a continuous sequence of individual burial from generation to generation; other social or ritual factors must have applied. While there is evidence that some individuals had special status, clear evidence of a social hierarchy is still lacking.

Social interpretation of burial data has a long history in archaeology, and grave-goods are often seen as the personal property of the dead, reflecting their role or status in life. But just as all members of the community were not formally buried, not all aspects of social organisation may be reflected in the funerary record, which may be distorted by individual action or by ideology. Artefacts may have a symbolic role, and their selection and deposition may echo the beliefs of those performing the burial ritual rather than the status of the deceased. As Heinrich Härke (1997) has remarked, burials are

not 'mirrors of life': if anything, they are a 'hall of mirrors of life', providing distorted reflections of the past.

Nonetheless, choices were made in these cemeteries in the placing of one burial in relation to another and, in the process, specific relationships with earlier generations were reaffirmed. Their periodic use denotes a particular concern with ancestry and lineage, signified both in the use and reuse of existing monuments and in the siting of burials. The distinct phases of burial activity sometimes detected may have occurred in times of social stress or instability, or at times deemed propitious for some other reason, when there was a special need to express a sense of history and social continuity. Thus the sheer variety of ritual, which is often one of their more striking features, might actually be a reflection of the infrequent use of these monuments, with ceremonial details being remembered imprecisely from one generation to the next. In these circumstances there would be many possibilities for the introduction of novel elements or the manipulation of existing practices, all with the intention of affirming the historical social order (Garwood 1991).

It is perhaps not surprising that pottery fashions and burial customs such as these should eventually cease. The four major pottery traditions altogether span some six centuries from shortly before 2100 BC to 1500 BC. What is intriguing is that they are apparently not immediately followed or replaced to any extent by new pottery or equally visible funerary customs. Once again the nature of the archaeological record, at least as we perceive it today, undergoes a significant change. The decline in formal burial practice was possibly a gradual one and may have varied from place to place. The significance of this change is uncertain. Cremations placed in plain, coarse bucket-shaped urns, as at Tankardstown, Co. Limerick (Gowen and Tarbett 1988), for instance, are often considered to denote the end of the urn burial tradition. There is no suggestion of social decay or economic disintegration. Other less visible or less easily detectable forms of disposal of the dead were presumably adopted. Simple cremations in pits or token burials of very small amounts of burnt bone seem to have become the norm. Such token deposits might mean that some of the remains were retained as ancestral relics by the living, perhaps distributed amongst the mourners. As Joanna Brück (2006) argues, this might also explain the presence of fragmentary pieces of unburnt human bone on settlement sites such as Chancellorsland, Co. Tipperary (Chapter 6). A series of discoveries during the construction of a major gas pipeline in 2002 are good examples of this tokenism: in County Limerick at Kiltenan South, near Adare, eleven simple pits contained a little cremated bone; a dozen similar burials, several with the remains of coarse pottery, were found at Rathcannon, west of Bruff; and of seventeen pits excavated at Williamstown, near Moate, Co. Westmeath, only a few contained small amounts of burnt bone (Grogan *et al.* 2007). The fairly widespread presence of charred cereal grains, notably barley, in some of these cremations suggests that such offerings may have been a part of the funerary ritual. Sometimes it seems as if the bones in these token burials were not just well cremated but processed further by crushing or pounding the remains—as in another pit burial at Rockfield between Castleisland and Tralee, Co. Kerry (Collins and Lynch 2001). At Darcystown, north Co. Dublin, eight plain domestic vessels containing token cremations were placed mouth upwards in pits and formed a small cemetery dating from about 1000 BC (Carroll *et al.* 2008). Another cemetery at Ballintaggart, Co. Down, comprised eight small annular ring-ditches that contained centrally placed cremations, some in plain urns, and judging from the radiocarbon dates the burials spanned 35 to 40 generations, assuming a generation to be 20–25 years. Whether these ditches once enclosed small, low burial mounds is uncertain (Chapple *et al.* 2009).

A U-shaped ring-ditch at Shanaclogh, near Croom, Co. Limerick (Gowen 1988), enclosed several pits, some of which contained minute quantities of burnt human bone. Some twenty low barrows or ring-ditches were investigated by Seán P.

Ó Ríordáin (1936) in the vicinity of Lissard, near Galbally, Co. Limerick, and only one produced a few fragments of cremated bone. A series of barrows at Mitchelstowndown West, Knocklong, Co. Limerick, also produced no evidence of burial and it has been suggested that a tradition of token burial had there progressed to the stage where barrows became cenotaphs without formal burials (Daly and Grogan 1993). There is some evidence, however, for the continuation of a tradition of barrow burial in the later Bronze Age. A complex ring-barrow at Mullaghmore, Co. Down, contained a central burial consisting of the cremated bones of four persons accompanied by sherds of a number of coarse bucket-shaped pots and a blue glass bead (above a large pit filled with loose stones); sherds of a coarse bucket-shaped urn accompanied another cremation outside the ring-barrow to the south-east (Mogey and Thompson 1956), and comparisons with the burials and pottery from Rathgall suggest a late Bronze Age date. Several small deposits of comminuted cremated bone (one with a black glass bead) in a burial mound at Kilmahuddrick, near Clondalkin, Co. Dublin, were radiocarbon-dated to this period, and the weathered fragments of a human skull also dated to 911–802 BC were found in the encircling ditch (Doyle 2005). The skull fragments may have been exposed for a time before deposition, and some small deposits of cremated bone from the upper fills of the ditch were dated to the Iron Age (Chapter 10).

From at least 1500 BC, contemporary in part with that period of funerary change, new developments in bronze types are characteristic of the metalwork of the Killymaddy phase (Chapter 6). More so than ever before, the archaeological evidence consists of a wide range of metal types and an increasing body of settlement evidence whose study offers interesting insights into society and technology and new interpretative challenges as well.

5

ENIGMATIC MONUMENTS

Embanked enclosures, timber circles, burials, burial mounds and artefact hoards are not the only evidence of ritual activity in the third and second millennia BC. A series of monuments including rock carvings, stone circles, standing stones and stone alignments testify to other ceremonial preoccupations, and a puzzling group of boulder monuments seem to combine some elements of the megalithic tradition with the custom of token burial. Burnt mounds and the hot stone technology they represent would seem to be a part of the settlement pattern of the period, but they too offer interpretative challenges.

ROCK ART

The carving of symbols on some exposed rock surfaces may have been a means of imbuing natural rock outcrops or certain parts of the landscape with special significance. Rock art, sometimes called rock carvings or petroglyphs, is found in several locations in Ireland and seems to be part of a wider western European or Atlantic fashion (Bradley 1997). Five stones at Reyfad, north-west of Boho, Co. Fermanagh, are fairly typical. They are low rock outcrops on high rising ground and there are wide and impressive views to the east. The largest rock measures over 3m in length and its surface is covered with a profusion of cup-and-ring motifs (Fig. 5.1). This combination of a hillslope siting and a viewpoint is a feature of some rock art sites. A major complex of over twenty stones occurs at Derrynablaha, Co. Kerry, about 12km north-east of

Sneem; it lies at the head of the Kealduff river valley and some of the stones, located at heights above sea level of over 200m, also command extensive views. Cup-marks and cup-and-ring motifs, some with radial lines, are common. This is one of over 120 rock art sites on the Iveragh peninsula, where most examples have been found in elevated positions around the 180m contour and towards the upper reaches of river valleys. Some groups of carvings occur in relatively inaccessible places but at viewing points that may overlook routeways; others are more accessible and may mark routeways (Purcell 2002b). Elsewhere a majority of sites are found below 133m. Other concentrations have been identified, for example in the Dingle peninsula, in Inishowen in north Donegal, in County Louth and in south Leinster (Johnston 1991).

This art is executed by picking with a stone or metal implement often on flat or gently sloping rock surfaces. Compositions may be widely or closely spaced; motifs may be linked or unconnected to one another. A quite limited range of basic abstract motifs occurs: particularly common are cup-marks, cup-marks with a tail or radial groove, cup-and-ring marks, sometimes with a radial groove and sometimes with multiple rings, and cup and penannular rings—again sometimes with a radial groove and with multiple rings. On sloping surfaces the radial grooves often run downwards and circular motifs are often conjoined. Less common are rectilinear motifs such as parallel lines sometimes in subrectangular fields, circles of cup-marks and cruciform designs. True spirals are rare, if not absent. This detail is not unimportant

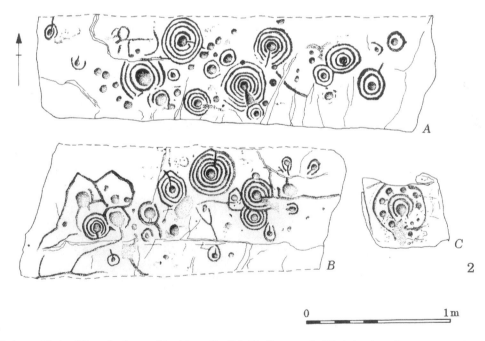

Fig. 5.1—Rock art. (1) A rubbing of a decorated boulder at Reyfad, Co. Fermanagh. (2) A drawing of art on two sections (A and B) of a boulder at Derrynablaha, Co. Kerry, and on a small detached boulder (C) nearby.

because the question of the relationship of rock art to the art on passage tombs is crucial in any consideration of the date of this phenomenon (Johnston 1993). There are some parallels between the two: cup-marks, dot and circles and concentric circles with a radial line do occur in the passage tomb repertoire but the sum of the differences is considerable. There are certainly significant differences in both context and distribution, and the variety of passage tomb motifs is not found in rock art. The relationship between the two styles remains uncertain, and the mutual occurrence of cup-marks may be of little significance in this respect. Various writers would distinguish between stones with rock art (including cup-marks) and stones with just cup-marks by themselves. Stones bearing cup-marks have a long history in western Europe, appearing as early as 4000 BC and continuing in fashion until about 1800 BC (Waddington 1998). As George Eogan (2008b) has pointed out, they have been ignored in some rock art and passage tomb art studies.

Some carved motifs on the capstones of several cists, including the rectangular cist at Moylough, Co. Sligo, which contained a cremation and a halberd, have suggested a second-millennium date for rock art, but the arcs, rough lozenges and concentric circles found on these cist stones have, if anything, closer parallels with passage tomb art and in some cases may even be reused stones. The precise date of rock art remains uncertain, though a third-millennium date is usually assumed.

There has been much theorising about the possible meaning of individual motifs. The cup-and-ring marks on the Reyfad stone were thought to be 'votive sun symbols', for instance, and fertility interpretations have been freely offered too, but no satisfactory explanation has emerged. The motifs undoubtedly had some special meaning and it may be that the circle and the cup-mark, if derived from passage tomb art, were selected because they were especially potent symbols in their own right and lost none of their significance when deployed in a very different context. The size, spacing and intricacy of the design elements may have conveyed complex information too. Recent studies have emphasised the role this art may have played in the ordering of the landscape. The location of some at viewing points or on possible routeways has been mentioned. Some are close to fresh water, usually a river or lake, and, while many are situated in rocky areas, they are, in some cases, on the margins of land that would probably have been suitable for agriculture and may have overlooked or have been adjacent to settlement sites. Excavation of rock art sites is rare, but investigation at Drumirril, Inishkeen, Co. Monaghan, did reveal traces of human activity nearby, including pits and evidence of burning (O'Connor 2003; 2006).

Irish rock art finds parallels in Scotland and northern England and some of its motifs, such as cup-and-ring marks, are also found in the rock art of Portugal and north-western Spain, in Galicia in particular, where strikingly similar compositions of concentric circles occur. Galician art, however, also contains figures of daggers, halberds and animals such as deer. To what extent the abstract motifs form an international Atlantic art style or to what extent they reflect a common ancestry in the symbolic art of megalithic passage tombs is not clear.

STONE CIRCLES, STONE ALIGNMENTS AND STANDING STONES

The term 'stone circle' is applied to ritual monuments consisting of a circular or almost circular area delimited by a number of stones, which are usually spaced but are occasionally contiguous. The area within the circle is usually open, as in the Kiltierney, Co. Fermanagh, stone circle briefly described in Chapter 4, but, as we have also seen, some circles may have surrounded cairns like Newgrange, and in some cases circles of contiguous stones may be the kerbs of denuded cairns.

Various types of stone circle are widely distributed in Ireland, and different forms include circles with widely spaced stones, examples with almost contiguous stones, and circles combined with an earthen bank. They are testimony to the enduring significance of a circular space as a location for ritual activity. Scattered examples occur in Connacht and Leinster and major concentrations are found in Ulster and Munster. Apart from a small group in County Limerick, the majority of Munster examples are situated in Cork and Kerry, where over 90 are recorded (Ó Nualláin 1984). Here recumbent stone circles are the typical form: these are circles of free-standing orthostats arranged

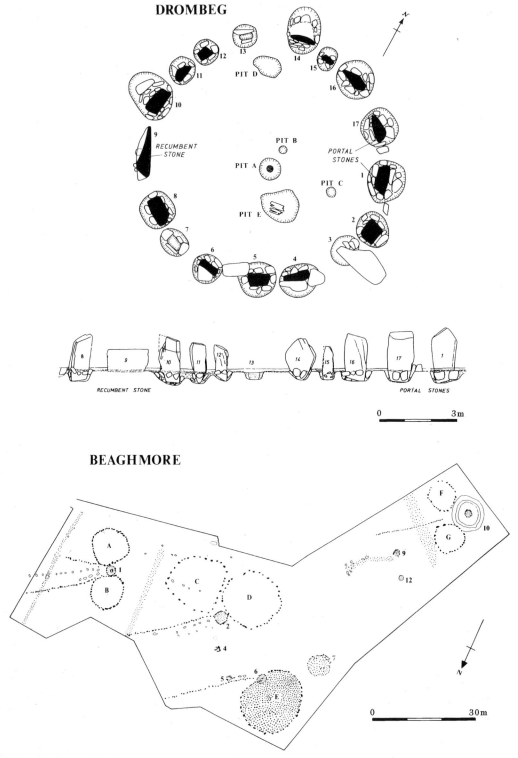

Fig. 5.2—Above: Drombeg, Co. Cork. Below: plan of part of the complex at Beaghmore, Co. Tyrone.

symmetrically and varying in number from five (five-stone circles) to a greater number (multiple-stone circles). The entrance to the circle is through a pair of matched portal stones, usually the tallest in the circle. Opposite the entrance is a stone called the 'recumbent' or 'axial' stone, normally the lowest in the monument. The recumbent stone is so called because in many cases it appears to be a long stone placed on its side rather than on end, often with a horizontal upper edge. The other stones decrease in height from portal to recumbent stone. The main axis of these circles is considered to extend from the middle of the gap between the entrance stones to the centre of the recumbent stone and divides the monument into more or less symmetrical parts. This axis consistently lies approximately south-west to north-east, with the recumbent stone on the south-western side and the portals on the north-east; this has prompted the belief in an alignment in the direction of the rising or setting sun. Detailed study, however, appears to indicate that as a group there is no consistent relationship with any specific astronomical body or event and no evidence for preferential orientation towards conspicuous hill summits (Ruggles 1999). About half of the Cork–Kerry recumbent stone circles are multiple-stone circles with seven or more stones. These have uneven numbers of stones—nine, eleven or thirteen for the most part—and internal diameters vary from almost 3m to 17m. The other half of the series comprises five-stone circles, which often have a rather irregularly circular or D-shaped plan (in which the recumbent stone forms the straight line of the D); their maximum dimensions on their main axis varies from 2.3m to about 4m. Half a dozen of the southern circles have been excavated: one five-stone circle at Kealkil, Co. Cork (Ó Ríordáin 1939), and one multiple-stone circle at Reanascreena South, Co. Cork (below), produced no artefacts at all. A small stone circle at Lissyviggeen, near Killarney, appears to lack a recumbent or axial stone but (like Reanascreena) is surrounded by a ditch and external bank; limited excavation did not produce conclusive dating evidence (O'Brien 2004a).

Drombeg stone circle, between Glandore and Ross Carbery, Co. Cork, is situated on a natural terrace overlooking a shallow valley, with the Atlantic visible to the south (Fahy 1960). Excavation showed that it had originally consisted of seventeen stones set in an almost perfect circle 9.3m in diameter (Fig. 5.2). A pair of portal stones on the north-east averaged 2m in height, and the recumbent stone on the south-west was an almost flat-topped slab 2.1m long and 90cm high. The upper surface of this stone bears a cup-mark, and a second cup-mark nearby is set within a carved oval shape that has been compared to a stone axe. The axis of the monument, from portal to centre of recumbent stone, seems to have been aligned on the midwinter sunset and on a conspicuous notch on the horizon. Ruggles points out that this alignment is not precise and is not repeated in other circles. A circle at Bohonagh, just over 6km to the east-north-east, is aligned on a low flat hill and more or less due west. Two of the Drombeg orthostats (nos 14 and 15) in the northern half of the circle differed noticeably from the others: one was a carefully erected, large, lozenge-shaped boulder, flat on its inner face; the other, beside it, was a small pillar stone standing just over 1m in height and the smallest stone in the monument. The excavator believed that these stones might have had some fertility significance, representing respectively the female and male sexes. A similar sort of juxtaposition has been noted in an avenue of paired stones at Avebury in Wiltshire. The interior of the circle was found to have been covered with a compact layer of pebbles and gravel. Five pits were discovered beneath this layer: three (C–E) contained mainly stones, one (B) contained a deposit of dark soil and a few flecks of charcoal, and a circular pit (A) in the centre, 82cm wide and 28cm deep, contained a cremated burial. The bones of an adolescent were very fragmentary and may have been broken up after burning; they had been placed, along with some sweepings from the funeral pyre, in a broken pottery vessel which, the excavator suggested, had been wrapped in some organic material before being placed in the pit. The pot, which lacked its base and most of its rim, was of plain, coarse ware. Charcoal scraped from the pot produced a radiocarbon date range of 1124–794 BC.

The stone circle at Bohonagh, not far from a boulder monument described below, was a multiple-stone circle of thirteen stones (Fahy 1961). In the centre a small, very low mound covered a cup-marked slab and a shallow pit containing soil, pebbles and flecks of burnt bone; the pit had been disturbed. The Reanascreena circle, about 6km to the north-west, also of thirteen stones, had a soil-filled pit at its centre, and a few metres to the north a second pit near the edge of the circle contained some minute fragments of cremated bone (Fahy 1962). The stone circle was surrounded by a ditch with external bank, and the monument had an overall diameter of 24m. Radiocarbon evidence suggests a date *c.* 1252–835 BC (O'Brien 2004a). At Cashelkeelty, near Lauragh, Co. Kerry, a circle of eleven or thirteen stones had been greatly disturbed; the only find was a flint convex scraper (Lynch 1981). A second circle at Cashelkeelty was a five-stone monument situated about 80m east of the multiple-stone example; a slab-covered pit in the centre contained the cremated bones of an adult of 25 to 30 years. A short alignment of four stones stood just south of this circle. Stone implements found in or near the circle and alignment included a leaf-shaped flint arrowhead, a barbed and tanged flint arrowhead, two scrapers and part of a sandstone point, but direct association with the monuments was impossible to prove. Two radiocarbon dates indicate the possibility of a date around 1000 BC for the circle, and a slightly earlier date may be indicated for the stone alignment on stratigraphical evidence.

Standing stones and stone alignments are associated with a small number of circles (Ó Nualláin 1994). At Kealkil, Co. Cork, a pair of standing stones had been erected just north-east of the circle; one was originally over 6m in height. Nearby a small cairn covered a ring of stones and sockets, some set radially. Most stone alignments are isolated monuments, however. A stone alignment is a row of three or more standing stones, intervisible and in a straight line. Three to six stones is the norm in stone alignments in west Cork and Kerry, and many have the stones graded in height, with the tallest stone at either the eastern or western end; in the Iveragh peninsula the tallest stone is often found at the western end. Their purpose is obscure, and excavation at both Cashelkeelty and at Maughanasilly, Co. Cork, revealed nothing about this aspect of these puzzling monuments. At the last mentioned site a row of five standing stones was excavated, and two charcoal samples believed to represent the burning and clearance of the area produced identical radiocarbon dates of 1678–1438 BC. At Dromatouk, Co. Kerry, charcoal that

provided a date range of 1740–1520 BC has been tentatively related to the construction of a three-stone alignment. Ann Lynch has suggested that a circle and alignment at Cashelkeelty, Co. Kerry, and an alignment at Maughanasilly, Co. Cork, were erected on marginal farmland whose soils were degenerating (as evidenced by developing podsolisation), and the settlements of their builders, which were not located in the immediate vicinity, may have been several kilometres away.

Two standing stones, of course, may form an alignment too, and over 100 stone pairs have been identified in counties Cork and Kerry. A pair of standing stones at Ballycommane, Co. Cork, set 3m apart and situated a few metres from a boulder monument, were aligned in a north-north-east to south-south-west direction; one stone had a very small stone-lined pit nearby which contained two thin deposits of fine clay containing flecks of charcoal separated by a thin lens of boulder clay and a small flat stone (O'Brien 1992). Another stone pair in the Barrees valley, near Eyeries in west Cork, was associated with two small deposits of burnt bone, some quartz offerings and episodes of burning (W. O'Brien 2009). An unusual double stone alignment with a similar orientation has been found at Askillaun, west of Louisburgh, Co. Mayo (Corlett 1997). A row of six quartz boulders at Gleninagh, Connemara, Co. Galway (Gosling 1993), is located on the crest of a low moraine, both to be visible and to offer a view of the surrounding valley; it points to a high pass between two mountain peaks to the south-south-west, and the midwinter sun sets in the gap between the mountains.

Alignments and circles appear to be related (particularly in the north of Ireland), and in the Cork–Kerry area evidence suggests a chronological range of about 1700 to about 800 BC. Both monument types may have had some related ceremonial and ritual purpose. The idea of a sacred ceremonial circle had a long life in various forms in different parts of prehistoric Britain and Ireland, and it is an intriguing fact that recumbent stone circles find their closest affinities in north-east Scotland. The belief that the occasional deposits of cremated bone in the stone circles are dedicatory seems reasonable, but whether there was a general preoccupation with the position of the rising or setting sun is uncertain. As already mentioned, while the axis of Drombeg when projected to the horizon coincides with the point of sunset at the winter solstice, others seem to have had no more precise astronomical focus. In contrast, the stone alignments in the south-west do tend to focus on certain prominent hilltops, which were also locations on the horizon where the moon (not the sun) rose or set (Ruggles 1999).

A group of some 50 or so monuments in the south-west, in counties Cork and Kerry, have been named 'boulder-burials' by Seán Ó Nualláin (1978) and evidently have some connection with the stone circles of the region. The name 'boulder monument' is preferred here; they consist of a large boulder or thick slab, usually 1–2m long, set above three or more very low flat-topped stones, which rarely form a recognisable chamber. A few of these low monuments have small stones inserted between the supporting stones and the capstone. Covering cairns or mounds are not recorded. In eight instances boulder monuments are placed within stone circles, two are present in one, while four are set within a large stone circle at Breeny More, near Kealkil, Co. Cork. At Bohonagh, the boulder monument is situated 18m to the east of the stone circle. The boulder, which rested on three low stones, measured 2.9m by 2.4m and 1.1m in thickness. Two of the supporting stones were of quartz; the other stones (including the capstone) were of sandstone. Beneath the boulder a shallow pit contained a few fragments of cremated bone. The underside of this stone bore at least seven cup-marks. Two boulder monuments at Cooradarrigan, near Schull, Co. Cork, each covered a pit, while a third, in Ballycommane, near Durrus, Co. Cork, covered a thin layer of what may have been burnt clay. Some charcoal from the pit beneath one of the Cooradarrigan monuments provided a radiocarbon date of 1426–1266 BC and, though no human bones were found, a funerary association is possible because it is conceivable that the burnt material was a token deposit from a funeral pyre (O'Brien 1992).

These south-western boulder monuments, stone rows and stone circles represent new ritual practices in the region in the period *c.* 1800 or 1500–800 BC. Wedge tombs ceased to be used for burial, though some, such as Toormore and Altar (Chapter 3), continued to be a focus for offerings of organic materials. These new monuments may be related to an expansion of settlement and an intensification of agriculture reflected in the pollen record and pre-bog field systems.

The second major concentration of stone circles (and alignments) in Ireland is to be found in mid-Ulster, in counties Tyrone, Derry and east Fermanagh. Many of these circles are very different from the south-western examples, being often of irregular plan and built of a greater number of quite small stones, rarely over 50cm in height. The alignments are different too, being constructed of closely set small stones as well. The circles often occur in groups, as at Beaghmore, Co. Tyrone.

A small number have been excavated. A circle at Castlemahon, Co. Down, consisted of half a dozen widely spaced orthostats enclosing an area about 20m in diameter (Collins 1956). A large circular pit near its centre had contained a hot fire of ash wood that had been quenched with a layer of clay. Nearby a burnt plano-convex flint knife and a few cremated bones of a child were found in a small cist; a pit on the perimeter contained oak charcoal, a few worked flints and some sherds of plain round-bottomed pottery. Two radiocarbon dates, however, suggest that the circle may be contemporary with either the Vase or the Collared Urn Tradition (Brindley 2007).

At Drumskinny, near Kesh, Co. Fermanagh, a circle with adjacent alignment and cairn which had been partly obscured by upland bog has been examined; the stone circle originally comprised 31 stones set in a fairly accurate circle with a diameter of just over 13m (Waterman 1964). The stones varied considerably in shape and size, were usually between 60cm and 1.2m in height, and were normally placed 30–60cm apart. There was no clearly defined formal entrance to the circle, though there were slightly larger than usual gaps between stones at three points in the perimeter; any one of these could have served the purpose. The only finds within the circle were a flint convex scraper, a flake and a burnt blade. These came from the natural clay surface, as did a minute fragment of pottery found near one of the stones. Immediately north-west of the circle, a small circular cairn with kerb had a diameter of just 4m. Nothing was found but a burnt flint flake and a crude concave scraper beneath a small spread of stones adjoining the cairn. The alignment of small stones ran north–south and at its nearest point this row of 24 uprights was only 1.2m from the circle; heights ranged mainly from about 30cm to 60cm. Some of the stones had been set in shallow sockets but others stood more or less on the natural surface. The few finds from Drumskinny give little or no indication of the date or purpose of the monuments.

A similar group of monuments has been partially examined at Castledamph, near Plumbridge, Co. Tyrone, on the southern slopes of the Sperrin Mountains; like some other northern circles, these were apparently first revealed when some 2m of peat were cut away in the late nineteenth century (Davies 1938). A circle of low stones measured about 19m in diameter; the stones were set almost contiguously and enclosed a semicircle of similar stones, within which was a low cairn. A small cist in this cairn had been disturbed: some cremated bone was recovered and represented one eighteen-year-old individual. A cup-marked slab was found near the grave. An alignment of relatively large stones, about 1m high, ran southwards from the circle. A nearby small cairn was trenched but produced no finds, and a second subsidiary alignment was observed to the west of the main stone row.

A complex of over nine circles, a standing stone, a cairn and an alignment has been recorded at Copney Hill, Co. Tyrone, and at least three of the circles enclosed a low cairn containing a robbed cist. Each circle also contained roughly concentric rings of hundreds of small stones (Foley 1998). Some 11km away is the well-known group of circles, alignments and cairns at Beaghmore, north-west of Cookstown (Fig. 5.2), first uncovered in the course of turf-cutting. It is located on the eastern slopes of the Sperrin Mountains about 195m above sea level, and the monuments so far exposed include seven stone circles, eight stone alignments (and the sockets of a ninth), and a dozen small cairns (May 1953; Pilcher 1969). Some have been excavated. At least two other circles and cairns have been recorded in the vicinity. Three pairs of stone circles (A–B, C–D, F–G) occur along with one isolated circle (E). Associated with each pair, and with circle E, are at least one stone alignment and one small cairn. Most of the stones of the circles and alignments are of quite small boulders or slabs. Several of the alignments run over lines of stony rubble—possibly the remains of collapsed field walls or the results of field clearance. The small cairn (no. 1) between circles A and B measured 3m in diameter and contained a small cist in which was found a porcellanite axe. Circles C and

D with average diameters of some 16m are quite irregular, and to some extent this irregularity seems to have been intentional. Circle C, for example, seems to extend eastwards to enclose a flat stone, and three stones that form part of a bulge on the south-west were, for some reason, set on a bank of small stones. Two pits within this circle contained charcoal, stones, sherds of Lyles Hill pottery and a few flints. The nearby small cairn (no. 2) was also excavated and found to contain a small cist but, apart from what may have been the very last vestiges of a pot sherd, the contents—if any—had been destroyed by peat water.

No bones were found in cairns 4 and 9, but a few decayed particles were found beneath no. 5, while nos 6 and 12 produced some cremated bone. An intriguing feature of cairn 4 was a small stone-lined pit containing a short section of an oak tree trunk. No. 10 proved to be the most elaborate cairn on the site: a small cairn with kerb was covered with a clay capping, and this was surrounded by a ditch and external bank with an average overall diameter of about 10m. The cairn contained a small cist, empty but for a few decayed fragments of bone. A second small and empty cist was found outside the kerb. The soil under the cairn contained enough charcoal to give a radiocarbon date of 1950–1684 BC, and organic material from a sample of the lowest layer of peat that had formed in the encircling ditch provided a date of 990–808 BC. The monument's construction lies between the two dates. A small hoard of pieces of flint, including several cores, was found near the stone alignment that ran north-eastwards from cairn 10, and charcoal from the soil in which they were embedded gave an early second-millennium radiocarbon date. This is a possible date for the flints and the nearby stone row but, of course, the dated sample was not directly associated with either. Charcoal from a hearth found near the alignment running from cairn 6, when radiocarbon-dated, suggested activity in the period 2900–2500 BC. The small hoard of flints recalls a larger cache of over 60 flints, including convex scrapers, knives and points, which was found at the base of one of the stones of another circle at Cuilbane, near Garvagh, Co. Derry (Yates 1985).

The cremation in cairn 6 was unusual: bones were deposited in two lots, one on a flattish stone just below the surface of the cairn, the other outside it on the floor of a small cist; it is possible that the former deposit represented just the skull of the individual in the cist. This cairn was incorporated in the puzzling monument called circle E, which is in fact an oval arrangement of over 880 closely set stones with a maximum diameter of 18m. Like the similar stone-filled circles at Copney, its purpose is unknown—and even the ritual epithet so often applied on the basis of negative evidence to ostensibly non-utilitarian sites seems not very illuminating here. Whatever rituals took place in and around the various sites at Beaghmore, astronomical practices do not seem to have been a part of them. The irregular shapes of the circles and the small size of the stones used would appear to support the suggestion that no significant celestial observations could have been made.

The date for the Beaghmore complex as a whole is uncertain; some monuments, such as cairn 10, were built between 1800 and 800 BC (a date range somewhat similar to those so far obtained for the circles in the south-west). The discovery of Lyles Hill pottery in circle C and the possible date of 2908–2504 BC for the hearth should not be forgotten and indicate earlier activity there, though not necessarily connected with the stone circle. Palynological work at Beaghmore has shown clearance of pine and elm and cereal cultivation there from about 3800 BC, a phase which lasted for several centuries (until approximately 3400 BC) and during which cereal cultivation was superseded by grazing.

A small group of four stone circles occurs just north-east of Cong, Co. Mayo, and is part of a scattered complex of monuments including a large circular enclosure and several cairns (Lohan 1999). The Grange embanked stone circle, near Lough Gur (Chapter 4), is also a part of a larger complex and it has been suggested that it is a late Bronze Age ceremonial monument. It is possible that it and an embanked circle at Lugg, Saggart, Co. Dublin, excavated in 1939, may be late Bronze Age ceremonial sites (Roche and Eogan 2007).

A number of standing stones, numerous cairns and small circles of stones are among a series of ritual monuments identified on the western side of the Monavullagh mountains, north of Dungarvan, Co. Waterford (Moore 1995). In the absence of excavation, it is difficult to assess the significance of complexes of prehistoric monuments like these, but

here, as at Beaghmore and at Ballynahatty, Co. Down, and Tara, Co. Meath, whole landscapes may have had a prolonged ritual significance. Rituals in these locations may have been enacted at particular times of the year, and monuments such as mounds, cairns, stone circles, alignments and standing stones provide a link between the megalithic tombs of earlier times and other special centres of ceremonial activity in later prehistory, such as hilltop enclosures. But man-made monuments were not the only special places and are not the only evidence of the persistent importance of ritual. The second millennium also sees natural features such as rivers, lakes and bogs becoming increasingly significant as special places for the ceremonial deposition of metalwork (Chapter 6). As later evidence demonstrates, even trees may mark special places (Manning 1988).

Numerous isolated standing stones were also markers of important locations but on a smaller scale. Though the particular significance of an individual stone is more difficult to assess, many are considered to date from the second millennium. It is probable, however, that this monument type spans a long period of time, from at least the third millennium to the later centuries BC, and had a variety of functions. Standing stones are widely distributed, with over 200 recorded on the Iveragh and Dingle peninsulas alone, where they range from 1m to 3m in height (O'Sullivan and Sheehan 1996; Cuppage 1986). A few bear cup-marks and some mark burials. A squat 1.37m-high stone in Drumnahare, near Loughbrickland, Co. Down, had a few fragments of cremated bone in the very shallow pit in which it stood (Mallory 1984), and a pit had been dug to contain a token deposit of cremated human bone beside a stone at Moneyreague, near Dunmanway, Co. Cork (McCarthy 2003). One of several stones at Kilmurry, near Slieverue, Co. Kilkenny, was surrounded by a circle of twelve timber posts (Carroll 2006). Some stones, such as one near Newgrange (Shee and Evans 1965), appear to have had no direct funerary purpose.

THE ENIGMA OF THE BURNT MOUNDS

Burnt mounds and spreads of burnt stones have been found in extraordinary numbers in various

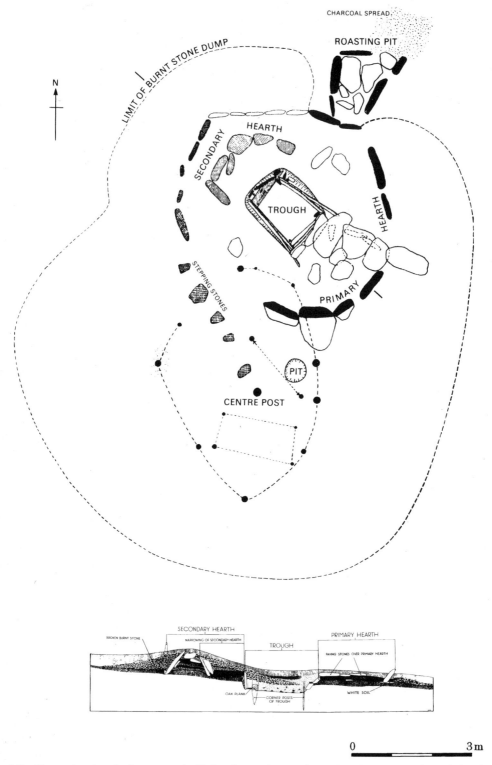

Fig. 5.3—Plan and section of a burnt mound with hearths, wooden trough, roasting pit or oven, and post-holes of structures at Ballyvourney, Co. Cork.

parts of the country. They are the most numerous prehistoric site: at least 7,000 have been recorded to date and many hundreds have been excavated (Grogan *et al.* 2007). They are the product of hot stone technology, in which stones were heated in a fire and then used to heat a liquid in a container of some description. The result is usually an accumulation of charcoal and heat-shattered stone, and this sort of evidence has been found on occupation sites of diverse periods from the Mesolithic (as at Mount Sandel and Ferriter's Cove) to the medieval era. It may have been an understanding of this technology that encouraged the seventeenth-century historian Geoffrey Keating to pen an account of a *fulacht fiadh* in which water was heated in pits for boiling meat and for washing. For him the resulting mounds of burnt stones were monuments that testified to the existence of the legendary Fionn Mac Cumhaill and the warrior-hunters of the Fianna, whereas the megalithic tombs that the general population called 'beds of the Fian' were really 'Druids' altars' for sacrificial rites (Waddell 2005b). Terms such as *fulacht* or *fulacht fian* are found in other early literary sources as well and from the mid-nineteenth century were applied to mounds of burnt stones believed to be the remains of these ancient cooking places, which were then, of course, assumed to date from late prehistoric and early medieval times. Despite the fact that the meaning of the term *fulacht fiadh* is debatable (Ó Néill 2004) and has as much relevance to an archaeological site as Keating's 'Druid's altar', writers still persist in using it if only to distinguish between burnt mounds with associated pits or troughs and more amorphous spreads of burnt stone.

A burnt mound is a relatively low grassy mound often of crescent, U-shaped, circular or oval plan; some may have a more irregular form. Often small and inconspicuous, most are 1–2m high and may range in greatest dimensions from a few metres to over 20m in a few instances. They are usually close to water, often near a stream or by a lake or river, or in marshy ground. They sometimes occur in groups, with clusters of two to six occasionally located within quite a small area.

Two burnt mounds at Ballyvourney, Co. Cork, were the first to be scientifically excavated. They were investigated in 1952 by M. J. O'Kelly, who in a classic piece of practical experimentation

also demonstrated how they could have served as cooking places as Keating imagined (O'Kelly 1954). One of these mounds, Ballyvourney I (Fig. 5.3), proved to be a roughly oval accumulation of burnt stone measuring just over 12m in maximum width and about 60cm in maximum height; this dump of burnt material partly surrounded a rectangular wooden trough, two hearths, a stone-lined pit and a series of post-holes. The mound consisted of some 27 cubic metres of burnt and broken sandstone with abundant charcoal and some ash. The subrectangular trough was 1.8m long and 40cm deep, constructed of branches of birch and oak, an oak plank and stones; it had been set into the peat that lay beneath the mound and it naturally filled with about 450 litres of water from the surrounding bog. A hearth was found beyond the south-eastern end of the trough and this area of burnt material was partly delimited by a line of slabs. A second, later hearth was found at the opposite end of the trough and it too was delimited in part by an arc of slabs. Each hearth showed several phases of use. A nearby stone-lined pit displayed traces of burning and seemed to have been an oven. A series of inclining post-holes to the south of the trough formed an approximate oval and were interpreted as the foundations of a timber hut which had a central post as well. A pit dug into the peat, four stake-holes forming a rectangle and a pair of post-holes were found inside the hut. Apart from five small stone discs and a stone pounder, there were no finds and no bones were discovered.

O'Kelly reconstructed the hut, the wooden trough and a hearth and determined, by experiment, that stones heated in the fire, removed with a long-handled wooden shovel and placed in the trough could bring the water to the boil in 30–35 minutes. Adding the occasional well-heated stone kept the water at boiling point, and a 4.5kg leg of mutton wrapped in straw was cooked to perfection in three hours and forty minutes. After this process, it was found that the trough was about two-thirds full of cracked and broken stones, amounting to about 0.5 cubic metres in volume. This material and ash and charcoal from the hearth were thrown to one side to eventually form the stone dump. Assuming that the stones were not used more than once, the size of the mound suggested some 54 cooking episodes. A further experiment demonstrated that the stone-lined pit could well have been an oven, for another similar piece of mutton was equally well cooked by placing hot stones around and over it for a similar length of time. The boiling experiment has now been repeated many times.

A burnt mound at Drombeg, Co. Cork, situated just over 40m from the stone circle, had a stone-lined trough and a stone-built hearth enclosed by a penannular bank that was built piecemeal during the period of use of the site; at one time associated features included a substantial circular hut (Fahy 1960). While the question of permanent or temporary occupation could not be resolved, the lack of occupation debris suggested a prolonged though periodic use of the site, and the excavator calculated that the volume of burnt stones indicated a minimum of 300 episodes of use.

A large number of burnt mounds and spreads have been excavated in the last decade but only a small proportion of these have been published, so it is not possible to offer a considered overview of this phenomenon. It is clear, however, that a mound of heat-fractured stones, a trough, a wetland location and traces of fires—sometimes a formal hearth—are consistent features of burnt mounds. Burnt spreads usually just contain heat-fractured stones and charcoal but lack evidence for troughs for boiling water. Two major studies—*The Lisheen Mine Archaeological Project*, undertaken in the late 1990s as part of the proposed development of a lead and zinc mine north-east of Thurles, Co. Tipperary (Gowen *et al.* 2005), and *The Bronze Age landscapes of the Pipeline to the West*, initiated in 2002 as a gas pipeline was constructed from north County Dublin across the midlands to County Limerick (Grogan *et al.* 2007)—each contain important studies of significant numbers of so-called *fulachta fiadh* (and summary accounts of the excavations). A total of 109 burnt mounds and burnt spreads were excavated as a part of the pipeline project, and of these 48 had the characteristic trough of the burnt mound. Some of the burnt spreads could, of course, be the spoil from unidentified burnt mounds or the remains of destroyed sites. In some burnt mounds multiple layers of heat-fractured stone and charcoal and changes in the position of troughs indicated prolonged use. A few examples appeared to have been used on just a few occasions. They were associated with a wide range of lined and unlined pits or troughs. While some evidently had their

lining removed, a number still contained a lining of timber planks or stone slabs. While timber-lined troughs tended to be rectangular, unlined examples might be rectangular, subrectangular, circular or oval. Depths varied from about 20cm to 50cm, though one exceptionally deep example (1.6m) had evidently been dug to this depth to reach the water-table to allow the trough to fill naturally in the usual manner. Sizes varied considerably, from a stone-lined example measuring 1.35m by 92cm to an unlined pit 4.5m by 2m, and obviously volumes differed greatly too. In one case a channel connected two troughs. In addition to troughs or pits and deposits of burnt stone, some sites had hearths and remains of stake-built structures, and one produced a well-made mallet of yew wood. While no charred cereal grains were found, animal bones were recovered from two sites, cattle from one and cattle and sheep or goat from another. Interestingly, analysis of beetle remains found above a trough at Cahericon, south of Killadysert, Co. Clare, revealed the remains of a weevil whose larvae live in oak-galls, and these growths on oak trees have had a long history in cloth-dyeing and in tanning.

Eighteen burnt mounds and ten burnt spreads were identified in the Lisheen Mine area. Again the shape and size of troughs varied, lengths ranging from 1.2m to 3.45m and volumes from 195 to 1,745 litres. Some had a thin clay lining, others had plank linings, one may have had a stone lining, one had a lining composed of wickerwork of coppiced hazel and moss or peat, and one had a trough (2.7m by 60cm) hollowed from an oak tree trunk. A saddle quern was found near one site and sheep bones were recovered on four. Analysis of the volume of one burnt mound (Killoran 240) produced interesting results; this also involved estimating the capacity of its trough and taking the fact that the limestone and sandstone used would have fared differently in repeated firings into account. The trough was a timber example that had been re-lined: the original one may have been used in 3,967 firing episodes, the re-lined one 3,167 times. A similar assessment of the amount of burnt debris at another site (Derryfadda 216) suggested 400–500 firing episodes.

The diverse nature of burnt mounds and the scarcity of animal bones indicate that the popular belief, encouraged by O'Kelly's pioneering experiment, that all were cooking places cannot be sustained. The occasional recovery of animal bones does suggest that this may have been the case in some instances. Faunal remains have been recovered from one mound at Fahee South, near Carron, in the Burren, Co. Clare, where a mound with a wooden trough produced five cattle teeth, one deer tooth, two deer antlers, one horse jawbone and other fragments. The horse bone had been chopped and two other bones showed breaks that might have been due to butchering (Ó Drisceoil 1988). In another important study of sixteen burnt mounds and spreads investigated during road development in Sligo, two burnt spreads (without evidence for troughs) in Caltragh townland were found to contain animal bone—some with butchery marks. One burnt mound at Caltragh had a puzzling drain-like feature running from the trough, and it has been suggested that this narrow gully might have been covered and used to hold split timbers, steam being employed to soften and manipulate slender timbers or rods (Danaher 2007). A number of sites in Carlow and Kildare have produced some animal bone—mainly cattle but also horse, deer, pig and sheep or goat—and, as the beetle evidence from Cahericon suggests, dyeing or tanning or the processing of horn or antler may be the purpose of some (Tourunen 2008). Others, such as a burnt mound at Ballymaley, near Ennis, Co. Clare, where post- and stake-holes could have supported a structure over the trough, may have been saunas or sweat-houses (Tierney 2002). A circular stake-built structure beside a burnt mound at Rathpatrick, Co. Kilkenny (north-east of Waterford), has been interpreted as a sweat-house and an adjacent subrectangular pit as a pool to plunge into (J. Eogan 2007). A similar sweat-house-type structure with adjacent trough or pool has been excavated at Ballykeoghan, in southern County Kilkenny

(Laidlaw 2008). Some troughs may have been used for boiling meat to extract fat, while in others the fatty flavoursome water could have been used to cook dough dumplings (Wood 2000).

Burnt mounds do seem to have been used to prepare large quantities of boiling water and some were repeatedly used over a period of time, with the resultant accumulation of quite large mounds of burnt stones. The diverse uses proposed for them are all possible, and even ritual activity cannot be ruled out. Two of the pipeline mounds produced fragments of human skulls that seem to have been deposits marking the decommissioning of the sites. These and the occasional unusual find of objects such a gold ring, a gold dress-fastener, an amber bead, a bronze axe and a musical instrument consisting of a set of graded pipes made of yew all hint at special activities, perhaps of a votive nature (Grogan *et al.* 2007). Several of the Caltragh sites were close to a small settlement of three contemporary circular houses dating from *c.* 1500 BC, and it seems highly likely that these enigmatic sites generally served a variety of functions as an integrated part of a wider pattern of settlement activity.

An extensive series of radiocarbon dates from the three studies mentioned and from other discoveries (Brindley *et al.* 1990) place the majority of burnt mounds firmly in the second millennium BC. Some, however, date from the late Neolithic and early Bronze Age as early as *c.* 2400, and their use extended to at least the eighth century BC. The range of dates spans a millennium and a half and demonstrates that these sites have no connection with the supposed cooking places of those warrior-hunters referred to in early Irish literature. The dates also indicate that the Irish monuments are broadly contemporary with similar sites in England, Wales and Scotland.

6

BRONZE AND GOLD AND POWER: 1600–1000 BC

The changing pattern of bronze types produced in later prehistory allows part of the broad time-span from about 1600 to 600 BC to be subdivided into a series of industrial and chronological phases. The absolute chronology of these phases is often somewhat uncertain and they are best considered as no more than loosely delineated stages in the general picture of metalworking development. Their use, no doubt, masks considerable variation in the duration of some types from region to region, as well as considerable chronological overlap and uneven development. Nonetheless, they do offer a convenient means of assessing the changing character and context of artefact types and their relationships (particularly in hoards), and of correlating these developments with those in various parts of Britain and even further afield. Some commentators have divided the Bronze Age into an Earlier Bronze Age to about 1400 BC followed by a Later Bronze Age. Others, following the common and understandable archaeological practice of dividing typological or chronological developments into threes (usually clearly defined early and late stages with a less well-defined intermediary stage), prefer to see an Early Bronze Age (2500–1600 BC) and a Middle Bronze Age (1600–1200 BC) followed by a Late Bronze Age (1200–700 BC). Again, in the later Bronze Age a series of chronological and metalworking stages have been identified by various writers such as George Eogan (1964) and named after a small number of significant hoards and supported by a small number of radiocarbon dates (Brindley 2001). These can be broadly correlated with developments

in Britain. All these attempts at periodisation are, of course, imprecise simplifications offering useful divisions for the purpose of study and analysis but undoubtedly concealing regional differences. There are, moreover, areas of disagreement between specialists as well. The general chronological framework of successive metalwork phases in Ireland summarised here is based in part on the work of Needham (1996) and Lanting in Brindley (2007), and though the term 'phase' is a convenient label they are best considered as broadly successive and sometimes overlapping metal assemblages:

Killymaddy phase	1600–1400 BC
Bishopsland phase	1400–1100 BC
Roscommon phase	1150–1000 BC
Dowris phase	1000–600 BC

A group of stone moulds found during ploughing near Killymaddy, south of Ballymoney, Co. Antrim (Eogan 1993a), includes moulds for socketed kite-shaped spearheads, dirks, sickles and tanged blades (Fig. 6.1) and has given its name to one metalworking phase characterised by the production of dirks and various flanged axes, palstaves and certain types of spearheads. It should be remembered that Derryniggin material continued in use, and end-looped spearheads, for instance, were probably partly contemporary with the new kite-shaped and side-looped types.

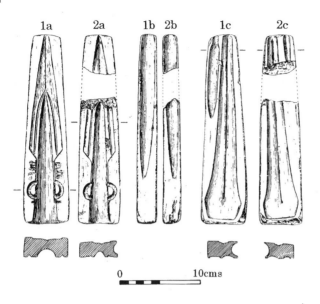

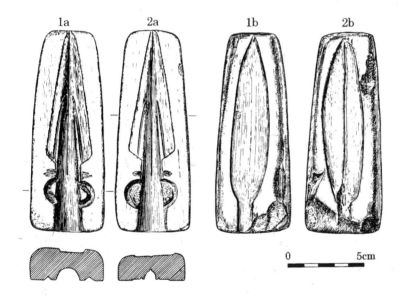

Fig. 6.1—Two of the stone moulds from Killymaddy, Co. Antrim, showing various faces with matrices for casting kite-shaped spearheads, tanged blades and a dirk.

METALWORK OF THE KILLYMADDY, BISHOPSLAND AND ROSCOMMON PHASES

Spearheads

Kite-shaped spearheads are characterised by a kite-shaped (approximately lozenge-shaped) blade, usually with distinctive ribs or grooves parallel to the edges and sometimes with a median rib on the socket as well (Ramsey 1995). A small hoard of three examples of this type was found in a bog at Tattenamona, south-west of Enniskillen, Co. Fermanagh (Eogan 1983), and demonstrates the range of sizes commonly found (Fig. 6.2). Another common feature is a pair of rather lozenge-shaped side loops placed more or less midway along the socket. No longer does the socket terminate at or near the base of the blade, as with end-looped spearheads: in a significant development the hollow socket extends into the blade, a technological improvement giving a stouter weapon with a longer socket. Several hundred examples of this type have

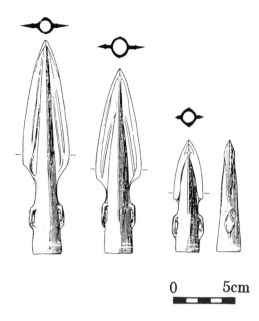

This is a figure illustration.

0   5cm

Fig. 6.2—A hoard of three kite-shaped spearheads with lozenge-shaped side loops from Tattenamona, Co. Fermanagh.

traditions. The nature of the relationship between them is a matter of debate. The leaf-shaped blade has been variously thought to be of Continental inspiration, or even derived from the Irish kite-bladed series. The limited hoard evidence from Scotland and southern Britain suggests a date more or less contemporary with the Bishopsland phase.

A reminder of the lethal purpose of these weapons comes from a remarkable discovery at Tormarton, Gloucestershire, where the skeletons of two young men aged about nineteen were found. One had a hole in its pelvis apparently made by a lozenge-sectioned spearhead; the other also had the pelvis pierced in this fashion, with part of a bronze spearhead still embedded in it, but in addition had part of a second spearhead embedded in the lumbar vertebrae. Evidently not all bronze spears were mere status symbols or used in the hunt. Extensive cut-marks produced by a spear and a sword have been identified on the bones of a crouched skeleton found in a cist at Sonnagh Demesne, near Mullingar, Co. Westmeath (Sikora and Buckley 2003).

The basal-looped spearhead, with loops at the base of the blade, is an interesting development (Fig. 6.3, 4–5). These loops may be incorporated into the lower part of the blade or be separate but joined to it. Blades with a slender leaf shape are common and usually have flattened loops that more or less complete the curve of the blade. On a few the loops are narrow rectangular appendages to the base of the blade, which is long, slender and approximately triangular in shape. Blades often have a groove on either side of the midrib. Occasionally, a rib occurs on the midrib itself. A small number have blades that seem to have been modelled on the shape of the rapier (below). It is possible that placing the loops close to the base of the blade gave them greater protection. The basal-looped spearhead is an Irish–British form with some significant Continental concentrations, notably in western France (Davis 2006). A majority of examples come from rivers. Associated Irish finds are very few and thus the chronology of these weapons is unclear. Three hoards, from Tempo, Co. Fermanagh, a possible one from Knockanbaun, Co. Sligo, and another from Kish, Co. Wicklow, show their continued use into the Dowris phase. But evidence from Britain and the Continent indicates that the type had appeared at least by the Bishopsland phase.

been found in Ireland, where it is widely distributed. It is only occasionally recorded in Britain and thus seems to be a product of the Irish bronze industry. It is very difficult to estimate its date with any accuracy because the type is rarely associated with other material; the Killymaddy moulds imply contemporary manufacture with early dirks and rapiers (below), yet two hoards hint at survival into the Dowris phase, perhaps into the ninth century BC.

Side-looped spearheads have a leaf-shaped blade which may be short and broad or long and slender, and the side loops usually placed midway on the socket may be leaf- or lozenge shaped or semicircular 'string loops'. Rare examples have been found in Ireland (Fig. 6.3, 1–2). One half of a stone mould for a leaf-shaped example (with the ribs on blade and socket reminiscent of those features on kite-shaped spearheads) comes from Ballyshannon, Co. Donegal. This leaf-shaped side-looped spearhead was the most popular form in Scotland, and in Britain generally. The preponderance of kite-shaped spears in Ireland and the preponderance of leaf-shaped examples in Britain suggest two broadly complementary and contemporary weapon

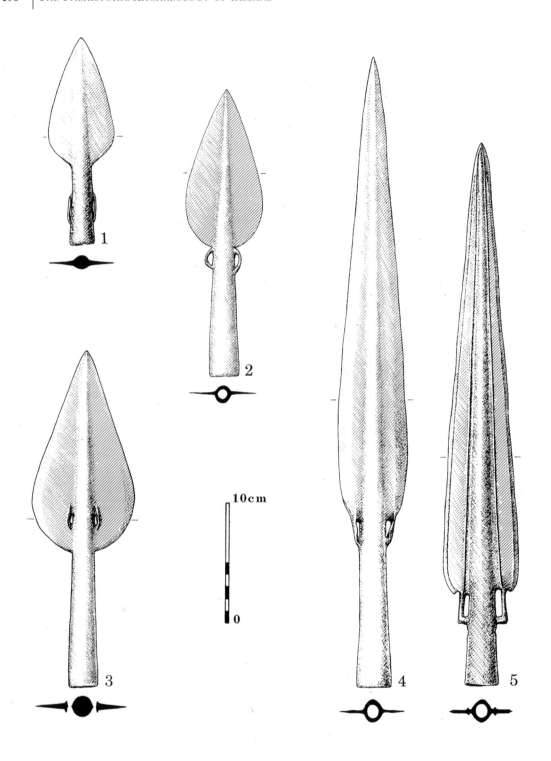

Fig. 6.3—(1) Side-looped spearhead with leaf-shaped blade from Edenvale, Co. Antrim. (2) Side-looped spearhead from Larkfield, Co. Leitrim. (3) Protected-looped spearhead from the River Bann, Co. Antrim. (4) Basal-looped spearhead from Toome, Co. Antrim. (5) Basal-looped spearhead with triangular blade (no provenance).

The origin of these basal-looped spearheads is uncertain. It has been suggested, for example, that they represent a hybridisation between British side-looped spears and the Continental leaf-shaped type, or that they are an Irish development from the kite-shaped (side-looped) spearhead. In the earlier phases of its development the basal-looped type seems not to have exceeded 25–30cm in length, but the late hoards such as Tempo or Knockanbaun (with its spearhead 46cm in length) demonstrate that some late examples are very long. The tendency to lengthen the blade may have commenced as early as the Bishopsland phase and presumably indicates some development in fighting practice. While the very longest examples may have been prestigious items primarily for parade and display, there is evidence that some were put to murderous use: the tip of a spearhead (with a groove on either side of the midrib) was found impaling the pelvis of a human skeleton at Dorchester, Oxfordshire, and is presumably part of a basal-looped weapon. A combination of long and short spear may have been used in combat: the short one used as a throwing spear, the long one as a thrusting weapon, as was the case in first-millennium BC Greece.

A series of bronze spearheads called protected-loop spearheads, with loops set well within the blade as perforations (Fig. 6.3, 3), may be an Irish form as they are infrequently encountered in Britain. A raised outer edge to the perforations has prompted the term 'protected-loop' and it is believed that they are a development of the side-looped and basal-looped types. The basal and protected loops can hardly have had a functional role, and the size of some of these spears (over 60cm in maximum length) and the narrowness of the sockets suggest that they were mainly for display.

Dirks and rapiers

The second popular weapon type of the Killymaddy phase (and the following Bishopsland phase) was a narrow, stabbing, elongated version of the grooved dagger, the so-called dirk or rapier (Fig. 6.4). They have been studied by Colin Burgess and Sabine Gerloff (1981) and Greer Ramsey (1995), and the name 'dirk' is conventionally and arbitrarily applied to blades less than 30cm in length that could have served as cutting knives or daggers as well as stabbing implements. The longer rapiers were probably specifically intended as thrusting

weapons. Almost 1,000 dirks and rapiers are recorded from Britain and Ireland and detailed study has shown that there is considerable variety. Indeed, Burgess and Gerloff's typology comprises four major groups, within which are some 60 types or variants plus quite a number of miscellaneous categories. It is debatable whether or not this sort of complicated typological scheme is really workable, particularly when some of the criteria such as butt shape and blade cross-section are occasionally subjective. Furthermore, because butts were often made of thin metal and rivets were often positioned very close to the butt edge, the hafting mechanism (usually a handle of animal horn) often failed and numerous torn rivet holes testify to this. Many so-called rivet notches are in fact torn rivet holes. Six Irish examples retain their horn hafts (as Fig. 6.4, 3), and two Irish finds, from Kanturk, Co. Cork, and Belleek, Co. Fermanagh, have hollow-cast metal hilts; the latter was separately cast and attached to the butt with rivets. One is known from southern England. Only two solid hafts (cast in one piece with the butt) are known, one supposedly from County Cork and one in a late hoard from Ambleside, Cumbria.

The four major groups (groups I–IV) are distinguished by blade cross-section and, in broad general terms, they represent a chronological evolution. It is also likely, however, that all of these groups overlap in time: evidence from several British hoards reveals that at least one example of each group has been found associated with an example of every other group, yet on typological grounds, or on the evidence of associations with other metal types, most group I blades are early and most group IV blades are late. The four blade forms are fairly readily recognisable (Fig. 6.4, top): I is characterised by a rounded midrib, which may be flanked by grooves, ribs and channels; II has a central ridge, giving a slender lozenge-shaped cross-section, and blade edges are sometimes distinctly bevelled; III has a triple-ribbed blade; and IV has a flattened or slightly rounded centre section.

In form and blade section, group I rapiers (and particularly dirks) are close to earlier daggers. So close is the resemblance between some of the dirks and grooved daggers that it is sometimes impossible to distinguish between them. It is this resemblance which suggests that many, if not all, group I weapons are early. Their lengths vary from 13cm to

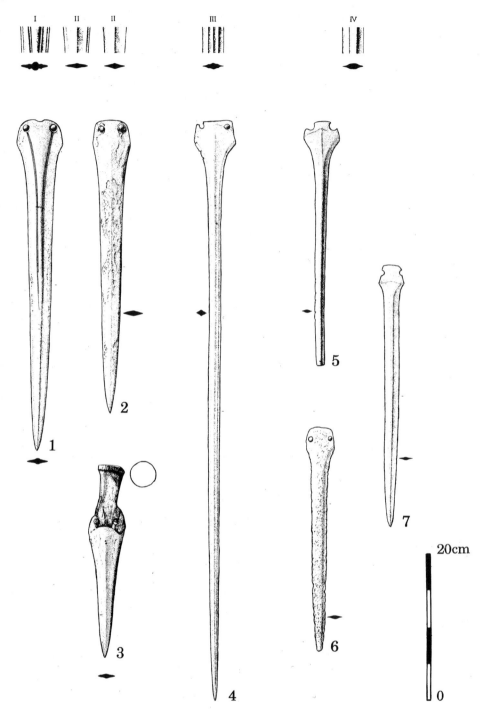

Fig. 6.4—Above: blade cross-sections of rapier groups I–IV: (I) rounded midrib usually with grooves and/or beading; (II) flattened lozenge section with or without bevelled edges; (III) triple-ribbed; (IV) flattened mid-section (after Burgess 1974). Below: (1) group I rapier from the River Barrow, Riverstown, Co. Kildare; (2) group 2 rapier from Keelogue, Co. Galway; (3) group 2 dirk with horn handle from a bog in Beenateevaun townland, Co. Kerry; (4) group 3 rapier from Lissan, Co. Derry; (5) group 4 rapier from Cloonta, Co. Mayo; (6) group 4 rapier from Carndonagh, Co. Donegal; (7) group 4 rapier from Killukin, Co. Roscommon.

58cm but are for the most part 20–30cm; butts are rounded to trapezoidal in shape, mostly with two rivet holes, though occasionally a central rivet notch or former rivet hole also occurs (Fig. 6.4, 1). A number bear engraved decoration. These weapons are known from Britain, notably from south of the Wash, and from Ireland, where they were even more popular. Grooved daggers were evidently a significant element in their development, but inspiration for the production of longer, slender, stabbing weaponry probably came ultimately from the Continent, where trapezoidal-hilted rapiers are common. The presence, notably in eastern and southern England, of some rapiers with Breton features presumably reflects this influence.

All the Irish examples are stray finds and unfortunately some 50% are unprovenanced. Of the provenanced pieces, a large number may have come from watery locations such as lakes, rivers or bogs (Cooney and Grogan 1999; Bourke 2001). The absence of associated finds makes dating difficult, but some British evidence suggests continued use into the equivalent of the Bishopsland phase there. It is possible that the group I examples in later hoards were heirlooms, but the bulk of Irish finds may conceivably date from the Derryniggin and Killymaddy phases. Two valves of a fine stone mould for casting one dirk and three rapiers of this group come from Inchnagree, Co. Cork. This mould also contains a matrix for a small, leaf-shaped tanged blade of the sort found on one of the Killymaddy moulds (Fig. 6.1). The important Killymaddy mould assemblage also contained matrices for casting group II rapiers.

Group II rapiers, with their distinctive lozenge-shaped cross-section, usually have more or less trapezoidal butts with two rivet holes. Occasionally there are four rivet holes as on Continental rapiers. Blade edges are sometimes distinctly bevelled. Most are 20–40cm in length, and a few are over 50cm. The longer blade on one of the Killymaddy moulds is almost 38cm long. Those blades over 30cm long are thought with some justification to have been specifically made as thrusting weapons. Burgess and Gerloff attempt to identify several types of group II rapiers, among them type Keelogue, named after two examples found in the River Shannon at Keelogue, near Portumna, Co. Galway. These are broad, heavy weapons with wide trapezoidal butts (about 6cm

across), usually 30–40cm long, and with two or perhaps three rivets (Fig. 6.4, 2). Almost two-thirds of them have been found in Ireland and, whenever find circumstances have been recorded, all have been found in watery contexts, in river, lake or bog. Group II rapiers are slightly more frequent in Ireland than in Britain (where there are two remarkable concentrations in the Thames area in and near London, and in the Fens of East Anglia). Apart from the Killymaddy mould there is a dearth of Irish dating evidence, but typological similarities to group I rapiers, as well as British and Continental associations, may imply development late in the Derryniggin period (alongside group I) and use in the Killymaddy and Bishopsland phases.

Weapons of group III are almost all 30cm or more in length with a distinctive triple-ribbed blade (which very occasionally is difficult to distinguish from the group II form with distinct blade edge bevelling). Butts are generally trapezoidal with two rivet holes near the corners. This group includes the longest and most elegant blades of the Irish–British rapier series, some being over 60cm in length. A well-known example from a bog at Lissan, near Churchtown, Co. Derry (Fig. 6.4, 4), is 79.7cm long; its length and extraordinary slenderness must imply that it was made more for display than for stabbing. It shows hardly any signs of use and, like many dirks and rapiers, may well have been purposefully deposited, perhaps as a votive offering. Almost three-quarters of group III rapiers have been found in England, where a few hoards provide the main dating evidence and indicate a date equivalent to the Bishopsland phase.

More than half of all Irish–British rapiers belong to group IV, with a flattened or slightly rounded centre section. On the basis of butt form they are divided into two general categories: (a) weapons with archaic trapezoidal butts with corner rivet holes as in groups II and III, and (b) what Burgess and Gerloff call weapons in the Appleby tradition, which mark a distinct change in the insular rapier tradition. One identifiable type in the first category is type Cloonta, named after a bog find in County Mayo; in addition to the characteristic rivet holes near the corners of a trapezoidal butt, it has a vertical rib on the butt that broadens out as it extends onto the blade (Fig. 6.4, 5). Lengths vary from 25cm to over 50cm.

Several rapiers in a hoard from Appleby,

Lincolnshire, display the characteristic features of the second category: smaller, less shapely trapezoidal butts now have rivet holes or notches (some of which are now genuine cast notches) in their sides, not their corners, and blade lengths are generally shorter, between 30cm and 40cm. They continue, of course, to have the more or less flattened centre section (Fig. 6.4, 6). Of a number of types identified, one, mainly Irish, is type Killukin (named after a Roscommon find), characterised by small butts with side notches for rivets (Fig. 6.4, 7), a feature found on several other types. This butt form finds its ultimate development in a series of rapiers with deeply indented or constricted butts in which the traditional trapezoidal outline is lost completely. Many of these rapiers come from Ireland, where a type Cutts (named after another find from the River Bann) has a constricted butt and a slightly leaf-shaped blade showing the influence of early leaf-shaped swords.

Group IV rapiers in the archaic tradition are found both in Britain and in Ireland; those in the Appleby tradition are relatively scarce in Ireland, where notched butt forms predominate and continued to be more popular. Indeed, it is suggested that rapier manufacture ceased in the south and east of England with the development of the insular leaf-shaped sword c. 1200 BC there, but elsewhere, in northern Britain and, possibly, in Ireland, the rapier continued perhaps for a number of centuries. The absence of Irish associated finds means that dating again depends on the evidence of a number of British hoards containing rapiers. Indeed, the scarcity of hoards of bronzes in (and just after) the Bishopsland phase generally means that chronological developments are uncertain. In any event, the dirk and rapier fashion was a long-lived one, conceivably spanning at least six centuries throughout which designs—notably in butt and blade shape—continually changed. Ireland shared in a vigorous way in a widespread weapon fashion for slender stabbing implements. The fact that both short dirks and longer rapiers were in contemporary use raises the possibility, as Burgess and Gerloff note, that two-handed combat was practised, with dirk in one hand and rapier in the other. The wetland context of so many finds is noteworthy, as is the likelihood that some of the more splendid pieces (like Lissan) were made for display rather than practical use.

Deposition or loss?

It has been estimated that 45.7% of Irish rapiers with details of discovery recorded have been found on wet sites, and the percentages from wetlands for Burgess and Gerloff's four main groups are 26%, 38%, 45% and 51% respectively. If these groups do represent a broad typological and chronological sequence, then these figures may indicate an increase in the practice of wetland deposition through time. Rivers seem to have been the most desirable location (68%), followed by bogs (22%) and lakes (10%). It may be that the formal disposal of prestige bronzes was now more or less confined to wetland contexts, particularly in the open water of rivers, and certain rivers like the Shannon (notably at Keelogue), the Bann and the Barrow seem to have been particularly favoured. These bronzes were valuable commodities, not lightly discarded, and this, therefore, may well have been an élite ritual activity.

It is a great pity that the find circumstances of most dirks and rapiers are poorly recorded, but given that so many of them have been recovered from such wetland contexts it does seem strange that only one scabbard has ever been recorded: traces of a wooden scabbard (made of flat laths of hazel bound with narrow bronze bands) were found with a Suffolk rapier from West Row, near Mildenhall. This scarcity of scabbards might support the belief that all or almost all of these finds are the results of ritual activity in which just the weapon figured. The high proportion of prehistoric weaponry from riverine contexts at certain times in prehistory is one of the principal arguments in favour of this thesis, and in the case of rapiers the numerical evidence is certainly compelling. That said, some finds may reflect the proximity of settlements and others may be the result of loss—for river systems were undoubtedly important routeways and may also have provided suitable locations for barter and exchange. Rapiers are the commonest bronze object found in the River Shannon at this time, and are replaced by spearheads in the following Dowris phase; it does seem likely that at least a proportion of this material was ritually deposited. In contrast, a concentration of bronzes of various dates from the River Blackwater comes from just downstream of a ford and these may have been casual losses. But it is also possible that some rivers served as boundaries between warring communities and became the focal points for confrontations. Indeed, the development of weaponry—such as spear, dirk and rapier—gives an increasingly warlike cast to the Bronze Age. The production of items, like the Lissan rapier, that might be described as 'parade weaponry' suggests that conspicuous display may have been a part of warrior activity.

Axes and palstaves

A series of axes and palstaves is the third major bronze product of this period. The Irish material has yet to be studied in detail. Derryniggin-type axes and related forms continued in use in the Killymaddy phase but were in time superseded by their typological successors, the short-flanged axes (Schmidt and Burgess 1981; Ramsey 1995). Included in this category are what some writers have called haft-flanged axes, with long low flanges rounded in side-view, and wing-flanged axes, with high flanges angular in side-view and sometimes bent inwards to grip the haft more firmly (Fig. 6.5).

Short-flanged axes are so called because prominent flanges were shortened (presumably to economise on metal) and confined more or less to the upper, hafted part of the axe, with little or no continuation down the sides of the blade. Viewed from the side they often have a convex appearance. In typologically early specimens, the axe splays in plan from butt to broad, crescent-shaped cutting edge. Later short-flanged axes have slender, parallel-sided hafts and splay is confined to the lower blade. Some short-flanged axes have a stop-ridge, but on some typologically later ones the thinning between the flanges is accentuated and ends in a ledge-like stop. Early and late short-flanged axes display considerable variety of form. This variety contrasts with the more standardised Continental products of the time and perhaps implies smaller and more individualistic workshops in Ireland as in Britain. A significant number of Irish finds are unprovenanced and the virtual absence of helpful hoard associations means that dating is difficult. An early short-flanged axe (of the haft-flanged variety) and a typologically later example (with wing flanges) were seemingly found together in a bog at Doagh Glebe, near Derrygonnelly, Co. Fermanagh (Fig. 6.5, 1–2), in the last century, and two wing-flanged specimens were found in similar circumstances at Kilnamanagh, near Collooney, Co. Sligo (Fig. 6.5, 3–4).

The palstave is an implement that represents a development of the flanged axe principle but one burdened with an antiquated and ill-suited name. This unfortunate term was borrowed from Danish archaeology in the nineteenth century and came originally from Icelandic *Paalstab*, a digging tool. Various definitions of a palstave have been offered. An important characteristic is a ledge stop or a bar-ledge stop, with the blade below the stop being

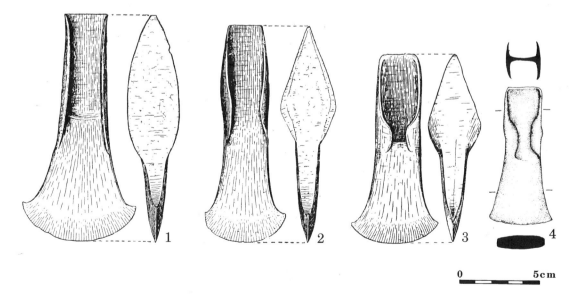

Fig. 6.5—Short-flanged axes. (1–2) Doagh Glebe, Co. Fermanagh. (3–4) Kilnamanagh, Co. Sligo.

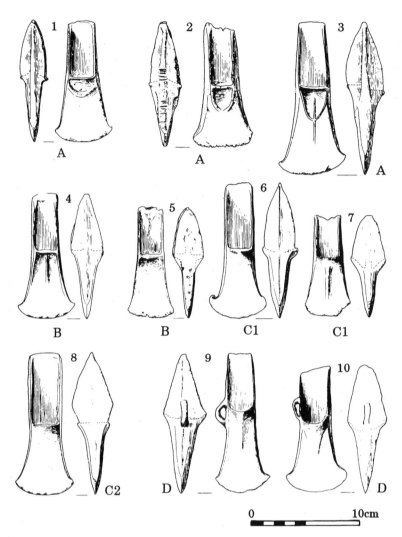

Fig. 6.6—The Irish palstave series. (1–3) Group A (shield pattern). (4–5) Group B (flanges extend below stop). (6–8) Group C (continuous flange-stop line): (6–7) C1, low-flanged; (8) C2, high-flanged. (9–10) Group D (looped, narrow blade). All 'Ireland': unprovenanced.

significantly thicker than the septum between the flanges; also important is the height of the stop, which should be more or less the height of the adjoining flanges, and all should usually form a continuous U-shaped feature (Fig. 6.6). This fusing of stop and flanges is a distinguishing feature of the palstave. Some examples of the so-called 'West European' palstave series occur in Ireland. This is a widespread form characterised by a broad blade and correspondingly narrow body, with a cast U-shaped (shield-shaped) or Y-shaped motif below the stop. This form was particularly popular (instead of the flanged axe) in southern Britain, including north

Wales. Similar palstaves in north-western France, the Netherlands and northern Germany are testimony to a vigorous pattern of contact. The cross-channel impact of the Irish bronze industry declined in the Killymaddy phase, however, and north Welsh metal sources seem to have supplied much of England, where the novelty of lead alloying makes its appearance for a relatively short period. The addition of small amounts of lead (2–7%) to bronze improves its casting capabilities and lowers its melting point.

A number of these Anglo-Welsh shield-pattern (also called group I) and midribbed (group

II) palstaves occur in Ireland, and a bronze mould for one of the former from 'Ireland' but with no precise provenance has been identified. A looped, low-flanged (group III) palstave with a trident pattern below the stop comes from the Annesborough hoard (Fig. 6.8), and another with a midrib from a lost find in County Westmeath.

Most Irish palstaves have a distinctively local character, tending to be short, squat pieces with deep stops and high flanges. An undercut stop that acts as a type of socket for the haft is a distinctively Irish feature. A number of stone moulds are preserved. The typological development of these Irish palstaves broadly follows that of the British series and they are provisionally divided into four basic groups. Group A comprises shorter and broader versions of British shield-pattern palstaves, with the characteristic U-shaped motif below the stop; occasionally a vertical rib forms a trident pattern. Ledge and bar-ledge stops occur and flanges may extend below them, curving inwards to form the shield. Many have the peculiarly Irish feature of prominent casting seams on the sides, and flanges may vary from low rounded to high angular forms when viewed from the side. Group B are broadly similar but instead of a shield pattern have a vertical midrib (like British group II palstaves) or are plain. Flanges extend below the stop and are usually rounded in side-view.

In group C, flanges are not extended but may, in side-view, form convex curves from stop to butt (low-flanged: C1) or have their highest point above the butt and be often angular in outline (high-flanged: C2). This differentiation on the basis of the treatment of the flanges recalls British group III palstaves but otherwise there are few similarities. Plain and midribbed specimens are known and blades may be splayed or narrow. Undercut stops occur and are presumably the culmination of attempts to strengthen and improve the split haft method.

In Britain, the name 'Transitional palstave' has been given to examples chronologically and typologically placed between broad-bladed palstaves and later examples with narrower blades. Blades are only slightly expanded and often have a midrib; flanges, in side-view, form a straight line from butt to stop. A loop (presumably to help secure the object to its haft) is a characteristic feature. Group D seems to be the Irish version of this Transitional type. They may have slightly expanded blades, usually with a midrib. A loop is a regular feature and flanges tend to have the straight line from butt to stop. One occurs in the Bishopsland hoard (Fig. 6.7), described below. Again, associated finds are rare in Ireland and, as with short-flanged axes, the pattern of development and the date of these objects are difficult to assess. There is no Irish version of the British late, narrow-bladed and looped variety.

The range and diversity of short-flanged axes and palstaves is remarkable and, at least in part, may be due to a continuing concern to improve hafting methods. They also show considerable variation in size (52–192mm) and weight (44–903g), however, and it is likely that they served a range of woodworking functions, though use as weapons is possible too. If they did have this multiplicity of purposes then a wider range of designs is likely and, moreover, they may not have been subject to the control of specialist weapon-smiths (if such existed). They may have been valuable objects nonetheless: the average weight of a flanged axe (370g) and palstave (313g) is significantly higher than that for spears or dirks and rapiers; in other words, they were not insignificant in terms of metal quantity.

The Bishopsland and Annesborough hoards

Two significant finds of bronzes are attributed to the Bishopsland phase (Eogan 1983). The hoard from Bishopsland, Co. Kildare (Fig. 6.7), was found in 1942 near Ballymore Eustace during work on the Poulaphuca hydroelectric scheme. Unfortunately it was dispersed after discovery and may originally have contained items other than those recorded. As it stands, it appears to be a remarkable hoard of the tools and other possessions of a smith. It includes such metalworking implements as bronze socketed hammers (nos 3–5), a possible vice (no. 12) and a miniature anvil with three work surfaces and a stem, presumably for insertion into a block of wood. A small anvil like this would obviously have been used for delicate work. Other implements include two chisels (nos 6 and 7) and a double-edged saw (no. 10). Three items of particular interest are a sickle blade (no. 9), a simple form of flesh-hook (no. 17: so called because such objects are thought to have been used for hooking meat from a boiling cauldron or cooking pit) and a square-mouthed socketed axe (no. 2).

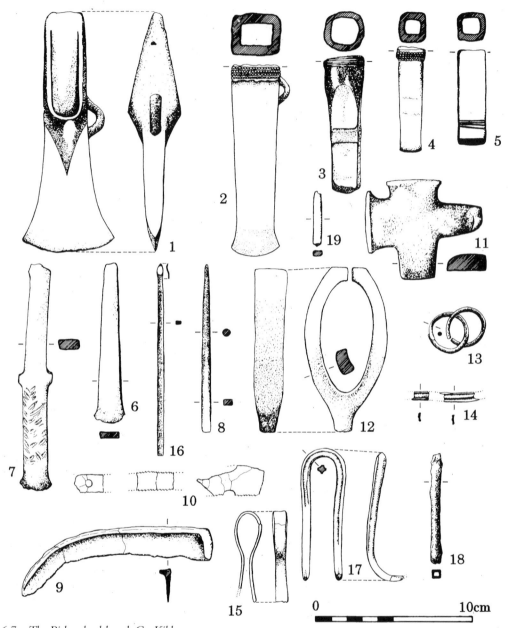

Fig. 6.7—The Bishopsland hoard, Co. Kildare.

Several of these types find parallels in southern British hoards. One such is the looped socketed axe, a small, narrow tool presumably used like a chisel for light wood or other work. This is the earliest socketed axe form and the multiple mouldings on the Bishopsland piece imply casting in a clay mould. Hollow-cast sockets, of course, were familiar to the makers of bronze spearheads. This axe, like the three socketed hammers from the same hoard,

should possibly be considered part of a general tradition of specialised craftsmen's tools. It has been suggested more than once that these tools were the equipment of a travelling smith, perhaps hidden for safekeeping, but little is known about the nature of the socio-economic role of the metal-worker at this time (below).

The Annesborough hoard, found near Lurgan, Co. Armagh, in 1913, raises other questions (Fig.

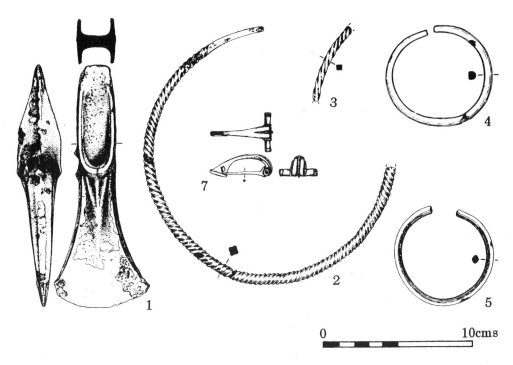

Fig. 6.8—The Annesborough hoard, Co. Armagh.

6.8). It was found at a depth of about 23cm when a tree root was being removed and consisted of a low-flanged palstave, a bronze spiral-twisted neck-ring or torc, a fragment of another, two penannular bracelets (one of D-shaped and the other of lozenge-shaped cross-section), and a fibula or brooch of provincial Roman type. Apart from the fibula, which dates from about the first century AD, all the objects find parallels in southern British hoards, where palstaves and bronze personal ornaments such as twisted torcs and bracelets, and plain bracelets often of lozenge-shaped cross-section, are among the characteristic finds. For this reason it is generally assumed that the fibula is simply a later intrusion, but it is also possible that a genuine ancient hoard, first discovered in the first century AD, was reburied with the addition of a fibula, perhaps to personalise a later votive offering to placate whatever spirits may have been disturbed (Waddell 2005b). It is worth remembering after all that a recurved terminal of a Bishopsland phase gold torc bearing a Roman inscription was found at Newgrange.

A third small hoard, found in 1959 at a depth of about 2m in a bog at Clooneenbaun, north-west of Roscommon town, Co. Roscommon, contained just two bronze objects: a bracelet of circular cross-section with tapered terminals and a small cast ribbed bracelet; they have Continental parallels and may even have been imports.

Goldwork

A series of novel gold types form an important and remarkable addition to the range of Bishopsland phase metalwork (Eogan 1994). Found singly and in a significant number of hoards, this goldwork is evidence of exceptional gold-working skill and further testimony to wide-ranging contacts with Britain and with north-western continental Europe. Various forms of what seem to be personal ornaments, torcs, bracelets, earrings and tress-rings, are commonest, and gold bar work now represents a noteworthy innovation.

Torcs

Torcs or neck-rings, usually made of twisted gold, include bar torcs, flange-twisted torcs and ribbon torcs. Various writers have suggested typological classifications based on the nature of the spiral-twisting and on terminal form, and some would

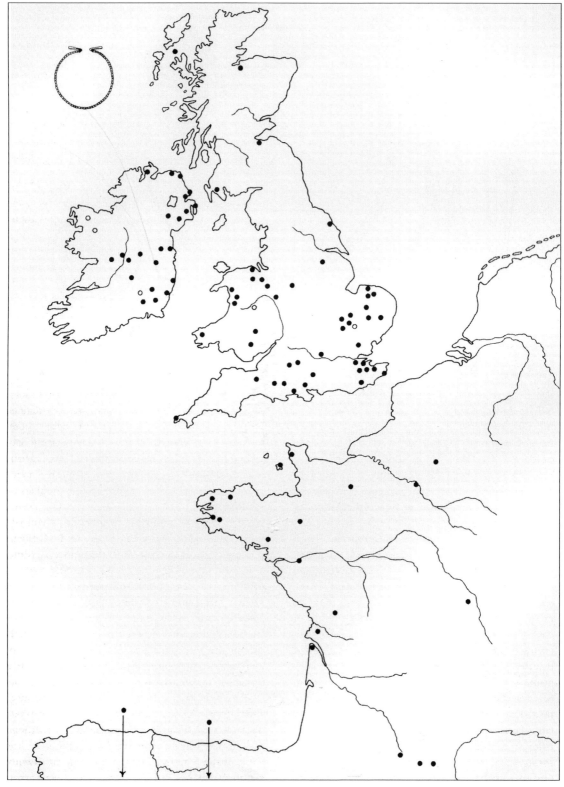

Fig. 6.9—General distribution of gold bar torcs.

distinguish between torcs made from a stout wire and those made from a more substantial bar or rod, but here the general term bar torc is used of both and also embraces both the bar-twisted and the flange-twisted varieties.

As their name implies, bar torcs are made from a thick wire (up to about 3mm in thickness) or a more substantial bar of gold (usually 4–9mm in thickness) that may be of square, triangular, circular or oval cross-section. Bars of square cross-section are commonest. The great majority are elegantly spiral-twisted, usually in a right-handed or clockwise manner, and, as already mentioned, the torsion or twisting may be described as either bar-twisted or flange-twisted. All are penannular, with terminals that are often hooked or recurved and tapering; some have described them as club-shaped.

Some 38 bar torcs are recorded from Ireland, mostly from the east and north-east, almost 50 from Britain and a scatter of about twenty examples from the Continent, mainly in north-western France but extending as far south as Spain (Fig. 6.9). In Ireland many are fragmentary and almost 40% are unprovenanced or with county only recorded. Precise details of circumstances of discovery have been very rarely recorded.

Bar-twisting consisted of spiral-twisting a bar of gold, possibly holding one end in a vice and the other in a pliers of some sort. The results presumably gave the object greater aesthetic appeal, allowing light to play in different ways on the surface, and both fine tight twisting and looser twisting occur. A large untwisted example of square section with a diameter of about 27cm found (with a smaller gold torc) near Enniscorthy, Co. Wexford, is believed to be an unfinished piece (Fig. 6.10, 1).

About a dozen bar-twisted examples are recorded from Ireland and a slightly greater number in Britain; Irish finds include a bog find from Carrowdore, Co. Down, one unprovenanced example and two nineteenth-century discoveries from near Athlone, Co. Roscommon, with diameters ranging from about 14cm to 20cm (Fig. 6.10, 3–5). All but one of these have simple hook-shaped terminals; one of the Athlone finds (like the large Enniscorthy example) has elongated recurved tapering terminals. It is generally believed that the bar-twisted gold torcs with simple hooked terminals in Ireland and in Britain are versions of the similarly twisted bronze form seen in the

Annesborough and Bishopsland hoards and more widely distributed in southern England.

Flange-twisted torcs are more intricate pieces of work: again an ingot of gold was forged to the appropriate length and diameter but then three or four deep longitudinal cuts were made in the bar, which was hammered to a threefold or cruciform section with three (or four) protruding flanges, and finally spiral-twisted (Fig. 6.11). This provided a deeper spiral and presumably accentuated the effect achieved by simple bar-twisting. Experimentation has shown that this sort of flange-cutting can be done with a small chisel, a punch and an anvil, and an even width may have been achieved by drawing the twisted torc through a die or by rolling it between two flat surfaces. It has also been suggested over the years by a number of writers that these torcs could have been made by soldering or fusing or hammer-welding strips of gold together, but this, if done at all, was rare; soldering on examples from Shropshire and Essex has been shown to be due to ancient repairs. A few Irish torcs of this type have hooked terminals, three flanges and are loosely twisted; these appear to be a specifically Irish form. Coolmanagh, Co. Carlow (Fig. 6.12, 1), though untwisted, is a good illustration of the three-flanged form. Most flanged torcs, however, have tighter spiral-twisting with four flanges and invariably have tapering terminals. These terminals are usually round-sectioned and some were clearly made before the rest of the body was flange-twisted (as on the Enniscorthy example). Joan Taylor (1980) differentiates between these integral terminals, which are an integral part of the torc and usually associated with broad flanges and wider twisting, and separate terminals that were evidently soldered or fused to the twisted body. The latter torcs have an abrupt termination of the fluting caused by the flanges, and usually have narrow, more tightly twisted flanges that have been hammered directly on the edge to produce a slight thickening or expansion of the edges themselves; she suggests that this form is a later development. A few terminals are faceted and one fine torc from County Mayo, with a diameter of about 27cm, has its faceted terminals decorated with engraved herringbone ornament. Two exceptionally large torcs were found at the Rath of the Synods at Tara in the early nineteenth century; one has broad flanges, the other narrow flanges—but both have separate terminals. One

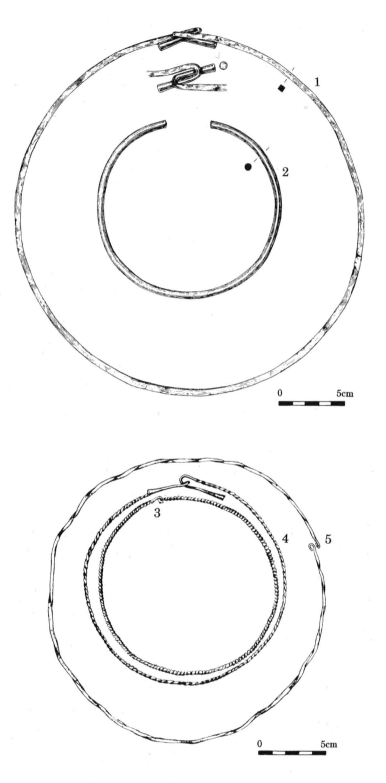

Fig. 6.10—(1–2) Gold bar torcs from Enniscorthy, Co. Wexford. (3–5) Bar-twisted torcs: (3) unprovenanced; (4–5) two bar-twisted torcs from Athlone, Co. Westmeath, one loosely twisted.

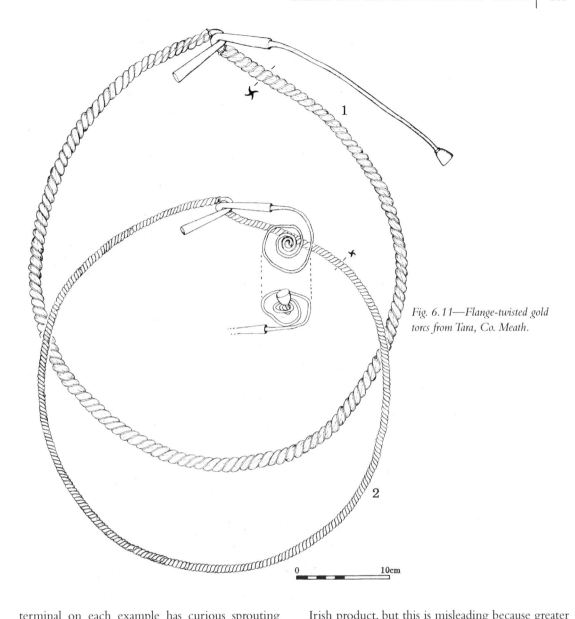

Fig. 6.11—Flange-twisted gold torcs from Tara, Co. Meath.

terminal on each example has curious sprouting extensions (Fig. 6.11). The largest of the Tara torcs has a diameter of some 42cm (and, if extended, a total length of about 167cm, including the extension). As their name suggests, it is generally assumed that these torcs were worn as neck ornaments, but the Tara pieces and some others are large enough to have been worn around the waist, if indeed they were ever worn at all, and some English and French examples (found wound into several coils) may well have served as armlets.

Flange-twisted torcs have, in the past, been labelled the 'Tara type', giving the impression of an Irish product, but this is misleading because greater numbers have been found in Britain, with significant concentrations in Wales and East Anglia in particular, where there may have been other important centres of production (Fig. 6.9). There is also a possible correlation between weight and distribution: large torcs have weights in the region of 750g and examples come from Tara, Wales and Jersey, but torcs in the weight range 316–567g are mainly found in Ireland and north-western France, while examples in the range 200–275g are largely found in Wales and the Marches. The weight range 160–186g also seems to have a regional distribution

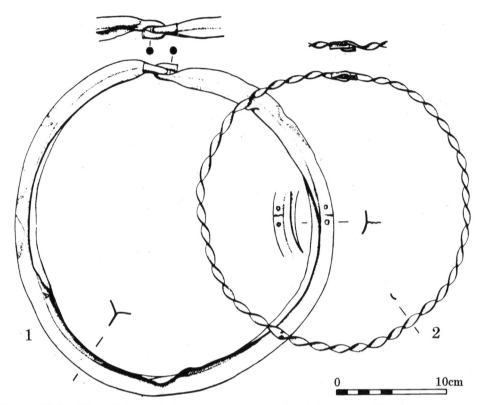

Fig. 6.12—Possible hoard from Coolmanagh, Co. Carlow. (1) Untwisted triple-flanged torc. (2) Ribbon torc.

but in southern and eastern England. The significance of these possible 'regional weight standards' is not clear; they may be a further indication of regional production centres or reflect regional fashions. The presence of the very large torcs in several of these regions may indicate a hierarchy of torcs, and possibly a hierarchy of owners as well. The resemblance between bar-twisted gold torcs and their bronze counterparts confirms a Bishopsland phase date, and flange-twisted examples with similar simple hooked terminals (like Coolmanagh) may be broadly contemporary. English associations suggest that at least the majority of four-flanged torcs with tapering terminals are somewhat later, belonging to the thirteenth–twelfth centuries BC. English and Continental four-flanged torcs also differ in their copper and tin content from their Irish counterparts (Warner 2004).

Ribbon torcs are relatively simple ornaments made from a band of gold loosely or moderately spiral-twisted. The unique Coolmanagh association of a flange-twisted torc and a ribbon torc (Fig. 6.12)

demonstrates that a small number of gold ribbon torcs with simple hooked terminals belong to the Bishopsland phase and are distinct from another large group of ribbon torcs, mostly with knobbed terminals, that are much later in date and belong to the Iron Age (Chapter 8). This distinction is confirmed by gold analyses, which display differences in copper and tin content in particular between the two groups. These two Coolmanagh objects were found together in 1978 in the course of disc-harrowing a field, but the finder reported finding 'similar pieces' six years before this and throwing them away.

Earrings
Various sorts of penannular gold earrings are another innovation of the Bishopsland phase and amongst these are bar-twisted and flange-twisted examples (Eogan 1994). There are some sixteen recorded from Ireland, a few in Britain and about twenty from France. Two bar-twisted examples, each slightly different, were acquired by the National Museum in 1927 and are said to have been

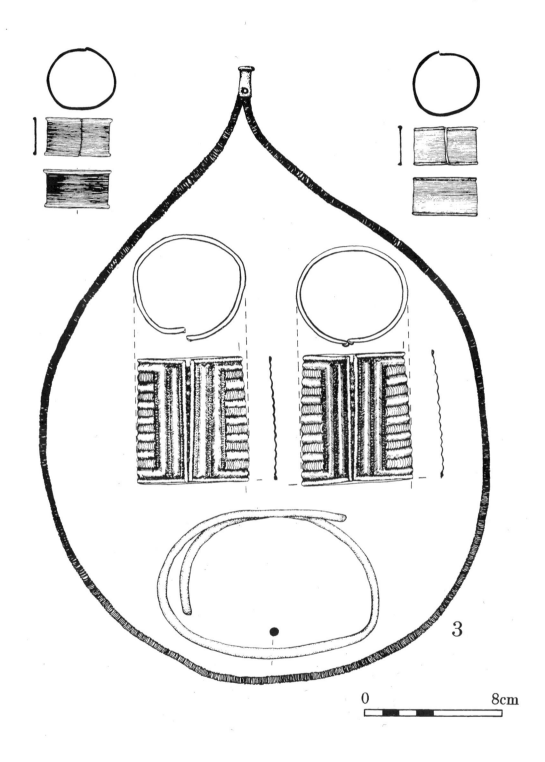

Fig. 6.13—(1) Pair of bar-twisted gold earrings from Tara, Co. Meath. (2) Pair of flange-twisted gold earrings said to have been found near Castlerea, Co. Roscommon. (3) The Derrinboy hoard, Co. Offaly.

found at Tara, Co. Meath, 'with some bronze objects, since lost' (Fig. 6.13, 1). Another bar-twisted example was found with a spiral finger-ring at Ardmayle, Co. Tipperary. These and the half a dozen other Irish bar-twisted examples have parallels in France, where acceptable associations are known. A flange-twisted pair are said to have been found near Castlerea, Co. Roscommon (Fig. 6.13, 2), probably in the eighteenth century but their find circumstances are not recorded. Another type of earring is a beaded form: one of the two recorded is unprovenanced, the other was found in a bog near Macroom, Co. Cork. Again flange-twisting seems to be an ingenious way of achieving a deeper spiral twist with a greater contrast of light and shade and, while bar-twisting in gold may indeed have been inspired by Continental fashions for spiral-twisted bronzework, the practice of decorating a leather piece with spiralled gold wire, as on the composite necklet in the Derrinboy hoard, may have been a contributing factor.

The Derrinboy hoard

A unique discovery was made in a County Offaly bog in 1959. Turf-cutting in Derrinboy, near Ballyboy, uncovered a hoard of objects at a depth of about 4m. It comprised two gold cuff-shaped bracelets, two tress- (or hair-) rings, also of gold, and a composite necklet (Fig. 6.13, 3). All the items were found within a circle about 13cm across formed by a piece of stout copper wire. The necklet consists of a leather core just over 90cm in length, a strip folded over and sewn with gut, covered with closely coiled gold wire. The core measures 4mm across and the gold wire, of D-shaped cross-section, is 1mm wide and 0.5mm thick. Unwound, the wire, apparently hammered in several pieces, has a total length of 15.25m. The other objects are made of sheet gold. Two small items, formed of a rectangular sheet of gold, are bent into a circular shape just 37mm in diameter and are assumed to be tress-rings; they are 27mm wide and the outer surfaces are decorated with fine horizontal grooves. Two larger pieces, also of sheet gold, are similarly formed cuff-shaped bracelets with average diameters of about 65mm; they bear ribbed repoussé decoration. Two similar bracelets are known: one found at the base of a stone along with a piece of pottery and a copper object at Dysart, Co. Westmeath, the other found at Skrene, Co. Sligo. They have parallels in

Britain (Needham 2000b). The Derrinboy hoard would appear to be a set of personal ornaments deliberately deposited in boggy ground, presumably as a votive offering of some sort. This ritual explanation may also apply to the other hoards of gold objects of the period and perhaps to many of the single finds as well.

Bracelets

Bracelets, whether of sheet gold as at Derrinboy or made from a bar of gold, are the commonest ornament. Those made from a penannular bar belong to a common form of bracelet in later prehistoric Ireland and Britain but one with many different types of terminal and forms of cross-section. Dating is often difficult, depending—particularly in the case of the simpler types—on typological details and a few associations. The earliest examples of this penannular form are found in the Bishopsland phase. They usually have simple unexpanded terminals and the body may vary in cross-section: simple circular cross-sections, lozenge-shaped cross-sections and square cross-sections with spiral-twisted body are all recorded. Some twenty examples of the type with circular cross-section with simple terminals (that is, plain or at most very slightly but evenly expanded) are known from half a dozen hoards, the majority coming from two found on Cathedral Hill, Downpatrick, Co. Down (Fig. 6.14).

The Downpatrick hoards are rare instances of well-documented discoveries. Hoard no. 1, found in the course of grave-digging in 1954, had been carefully deposited in a very small pit, 20cm in greatest diameter, covered by some stones; it consisted of eleven bracelets and part of a neck-ring which had been carefully stacked one upon the other, the smaller ones at the bottom, the three largest at the top and separated from the rest by an inch of clay filling. Five of the bracelets had lozenge-shaped cross-sections, and six had circular cross-sections. One of these (no. 11: several times heavier than the others) was represented by just one half, and a chisel mark clearly showed that it had been partly cut by such an implement. Another (no. 9), also more massive than the rest, had some decoration on the terminals: engraved concentric rings on the flat end and engraved triangles on the body. Only about half the neck ring (no. 12) had been deposited and it too had been partly cut with

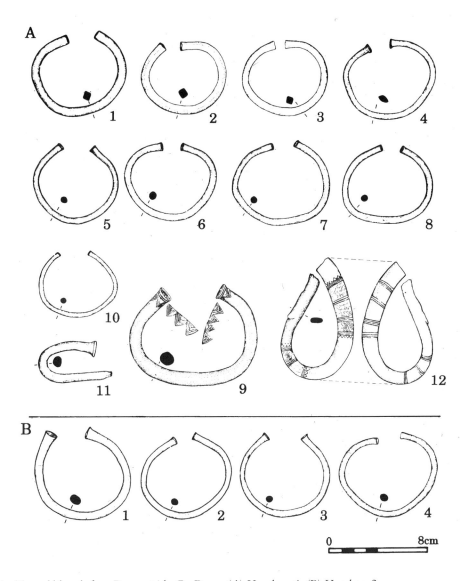

Fig. 6.14—Two gold hoards from Downpatrick, Co. Down. (A) Hoard no. 1. (B) Hoard no. 2.

a chisel and one terminal hammered back against the body. Whether this represented ritual destruction is not clear, but two of the three heaviest pieces in the hoard were singled out in this way. The neck-ring was decorated with panels of engraved herringbone ornament and it may be that it is related to Iberian decorated neck-rings of Berzocana type.

Hoard no. 2 was discovered in similar circumstances two years later some 20m from the site of the first. This time four bracelets had been stacked in a very small pit and three small stones had

been placed in the pit on top of them. All four are of more or less circular cross-section with slightly expanded terminals.

Both hoards were found within some 20m of the site of limited excavations undertaken on the south-western side of the hill in the 1950s. These excavations had revealed extensive traces of late prehistoric occupation, mainly in the form of coarse pottery, but whether hoards and settlement are contemporary is uncertain and the site was not a hillfort, as was once thought.

The association of the rare form of lozenge-sectioned bracelet with those of circular cross-section at Downpatrick implies the contemporaneity of the two types, and the chronology of the Bishopsland phase goldwork rests in great measure on the evidence of a limited number of hoards, as well as on typological parallels with material elsewhere. A poorly documented hoard found in 1858 at Saintjohns, near Castledermot, Co. Kildare, contained five gold ornaments: a circular-sectioned bracelet, two spirally twisted armlets and two tress-rings of grooved sheet gold. In this instance the so-called tress-rings were both large and heavy enough to be bracelets (Fig. 6.15). Like Downpatrick hoard no. 1, it provides a crucial, if tenuous, link between several different types of goldwork. Unfortunately, most of the dozen or so gold hoards attributable with some degree of plausibility to the Bishopsland phase are inadequately documented or questionable in some other way. Trustworthy associations between different types are surprisingly few and dating rests on this sort of slender evidence.

Gifts to the gods?

The practice of depositing hoards of metal objects in the ground is not a new departure. Axes and halberds were the favoured objects at an earlier date but hoard deposition was not common in the ensuing Killymaddy phase, though single finds of rapiers, for example, may in some cases represent another sort of depositional pattern in wet locations. What is new in the Bishopsland phase is the range of personal ornaments and the predilection for the use of gold. The belief that these are valuable possessions buried for safekeeping in a time of danger is an old one, but it should not be

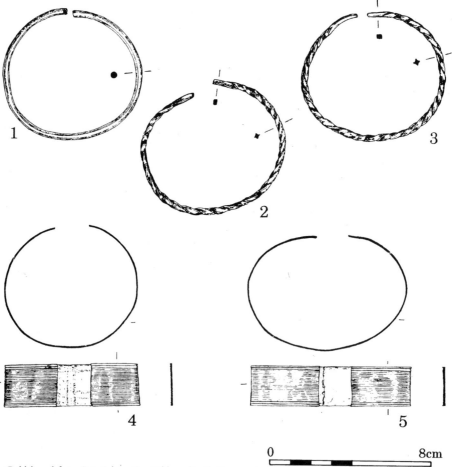

Fig. 6.15—Gold hoard from Saintjohns, Co. Kildare. (1–3) Penannular bracelets: two spirally twisted. (4–5) Two gold 'tress-rings' or bracelets.

dismissed entirely because it may yet be testable if, for instance, settlement excavation ever demonstrates a contemporary concern with fortification, in turn suggesting political instability. But at present it seems to be a less than adequate explanation. Why conceal just a selection of gold objects and not some prized bronzes as well? The restricted range of artefacts and the rarity of combined finds of gold and bronze artefacts indicate that other factors may apply.

It is possible that the decline in urn burial may have ushered in an alternative cult of the dead that demanded the burial of some of an individual's prized possessions instead of the corpse, which was presumably disposed of in some way that left no archaeological trace. This is a possibility, though it should be recalled that flamboyant grave-offerings were not a feature of earlier times and now the range of objects is so restricted that it is not even possible to know whether we are dealing with sets of male or female ornaments. A ritual explanation, though not necessarily one associated with death, seems plausible, and ritual activity might well increase in times of social or economic stress. Such a ritual purpose could explain the selectivity but there are other possibilities too. It is by no means certain that all the objects are simply personal ornaments; like earlier lunulae, they could have had other social roles, perhaps as emblems of caste or rank. The votive offering of special objects may have been one way for an individual or a group to distinguish themselves from others. Offering 'gifts to the gods' in this fashion could have had the coincidental effects of combining the symbolic and the practical by placating the otherworld and conferring status on the donor (Bradley 1990). While some of these deposits may have been intended to be permanent, it is possible too that these rituals allowed for the retrieval of some objects in certain propitious circumstances (Needham 2001).

The contemporary bronzework should not be forgotten. There is an intriguing contrast between the deposition of weapons such as rapiers in wet locations and the tendency to deposit many (though not all) gold ornaments on dry land. If casual loss is an inadequate explanation for river finds, then these contrasting contexts offer very different instances of processes of selective deposition that have yet to be analysed. Detailed study may yield surprising results: there is, for instance, too little information to gauge the significance of the total weights of gold hoards, but it has been suggested that there may have been precisely calculated units of weight. The weight of the combined pieces in the Downpatrick hoard no. 1 (1,037.98g) finds some comparisons in a number of other European hoards that are multiples or fractions of 1,037.25g (Spratling 1980).

The wide distribution of the finer types, such as flange-twisted torcs, does suggest an élite fashion in prestigious metalwork and demonstrates that the eastern half of Ireland had contacts with areas such as north Wales, southern England and East Anglia. Indeed, finds of Irish bronze metalwork in Hampshire and Dorset as well as in East Anglia may be significant too, though the nature of the patterns of exchange and circulation, like the patterns of deposition, is far from clear. In Britain, the thirteenth century BC witnessed important new developments. These included such significant types as the leaf-shaped sword (which probably inspired the earliest Irish swords of Ballintober type), the bronze shield and large vessels of sheet bronze, all of which are just part of a large body of evidence for frequent and diverse contacts with the Continent. The novel type of sword implies new forms of personal combat; the bronze slashing sword is a prominent weapon in succeeding centuries and will be examined when the metalwork of the Dowris phase is considered.

In 1880 a Cork antiquarian and collector, Robert Day, reported that in January 1870 he had inspected a collection of bronze objects acquired by a dealer in Mullingar. This consisted of 'a hoard of bronze fragments, about two hundred in number, and weighing over sixteen pounds, which had all been found together, somewhere in the county of Roscommon, by a labouring man'. Unfortunately, the exact location of this discovery was not recorded and, because the dealer demanded too high a price for the whole hoard, Day only purchased a selection. Fragments of eleven broken socketed axes, part of a sword blade, fragments of three long slender chapes (mounts for the tips of scabbards), three mould 'gates' (waste bronze pieces cast in the channel through which molten metal flows into a mould) and 21 pieces of bronze, some evidently waste, are preserved. Day also referred to 'numerous small portions of spear-heads and bronze

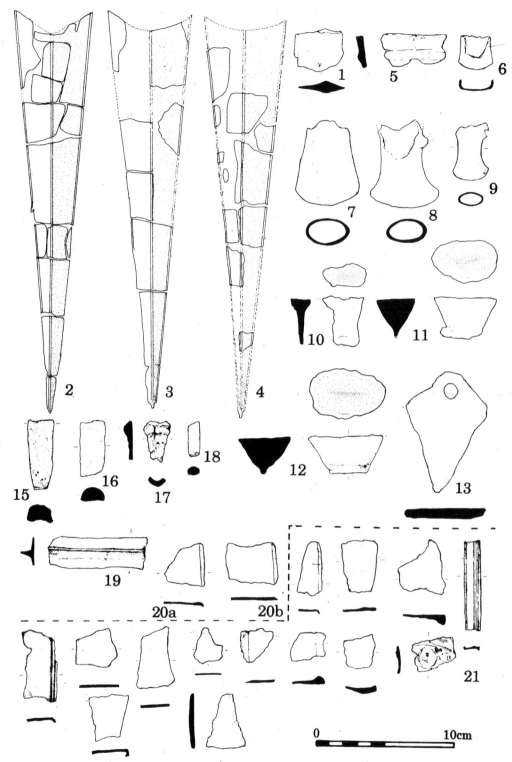

Fig. 6.16—The Roscommon hoard. (1) Fragment of a sword blade. (2–4) Fragments of tongue-shaped chapes. (5–9) Fragments of socketed axeheads. (10–12) Mould gates. (13 and 15–20) Bronze fragments. (21) Pieces of waste bronze.

vessels' or 'bowls', and he identified the hoard as the stock-in-trade of a 'bronze founder'.

This large hoard of scrap bronze, which has given its name to Eogan's Roscommon phase, is, if genuine, an exceptional find in an Irish context (Fig. 6.16) and, while Day undoubtedly acquired it in Mullingar, how and where the dealer got it is unknown. It may even have come from a settlement site. This sort of collection has numerous parallels abroad, notably in southern England and on the Continent. Called founder's hoards because they contain a significant quantity of broken objects and bronze fragments as well as casting residues, they are well known in England and appear to have had a role in the recycling of bronze metal. Such deposits of scrap metal have prompted discussion about the role of the bronzesmith and the nature of the metal industry at this time. But one hoard of scrap metal and one collection of craftsman's tools (Bishopsland) do not shed much light on bronze production in Ireland.

The elusive smith

While a votive explanation is possible for the Roscommon hoard, it and other founder's hoards may have been buried with the intention of recovery and may have been part of an efficient system of collection and recycling, a suggestion perhaps supported by the scarcity or absence of bronze on settlement sites like Lough Gur, Co. Limerick, Rathgall, Co. Wicklow, Dún Aonghasa, Co. Galway, or Lough Eskragh, Co. Tyrone, which have produced evidence for metalworking usually in the form of fragments of clay moulds. It has often been assumed that prehistoric bronze-workers were itinerant high-status specialists but this is by no means certain: metalworking may not have been a full-time occupation and could have been a local seasonal event, or even one regularly practised by particular kin groups. In England, it has been suggested that smiths—whether travelling or settled—produced material such as tools, small spears and ornaments on a local basis for communities within a radius of 15–20km, but in addition there were wider regional weapon industries producing rapiers, large spears and eventually swords.

There could even have been both itinerant full-time and settled part-time bronzesmiths in prehistoric Ireland and the situation may well have been a complex one. The belief that smiths were persons of high status in society is commonly held, but their position may have been ambiguous and surrounded by taboos. It is possible that the supply of raw materials to the smith was controlled, and the general scarcity of metalworkers' tools such as hammers, tongs and anvils and the puzzling absence of metal-working debris on sites where moulds have been found may point to some procedures of selection and exclusion.

Roscommon phase metalwork

The metalwork of the Roscommon phase has parallels with material in northern England, where Transitional palstaves and square-mouthed socketed axes with flat collars occur. As already mentioned, group IV notched-butt rapiers probably continued in use if not in production, and the same may be the case with various types of spearheads such as basal and protected-looped. Though their beginnings are unclear, spears with lunate (half-moon-shaped) openings in the blade, thought to be derived from the protected-looped type, probably appeared at this time and were a long-lived weapon type that continued into the Dowris phase. The flange-hilted sword may have first appeared at this time too, replacing the primitive Ballintober sword and also becoming a common weapon in the Dowris phase. The appearance of the first chapes is presumably another reflection of a growing interest in weaponry and related fitments: of thin cast bronze, they would have served as both protective and decorative extensions and guards for the tips of sword scabbards of wood or leather. The so-called tongue-shaped chapes of the Roscommon hoard (Fig. 6.16, 2–4) are long, slender objects (up to 28cm in length and 6cm in greatest width) of flat lozenge-shaped cross-section with curving mouths, midribs and a short projecting tip. Two or three related chapes of a shorter form have also been found in Ireland.

The Ballintober sword

The first sword in Irish prehistory designed as a slashing weapon is named after a find from a bog in Ballintober, Co. Mayo (Fig. 6.17). The type has a flat rectangular hilt or tang, usually with four rivet holes in two pairs; this tang broadens to pointed shoulders. Below these, on about half the examples, the blade edge is blunted to form a ricasso (a

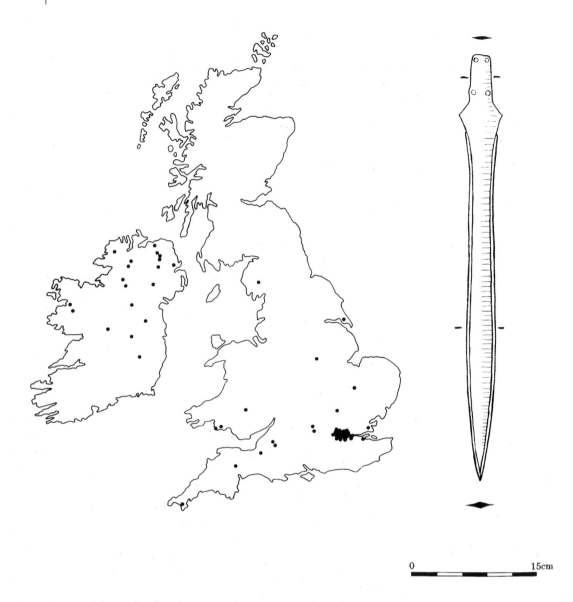

0   15cm

Fig. 6.17—Sword from Ballintober, Co. Mayo, and general distribution of the type.

blunted indentation replacing the sharp edge). Blades are slightly leaf-shaped, sometimes with bevelled edges, and usually have a ridged, narrow, lozenge-shaped cross-section. Lengths vary from about 43cm to 61cm. Compared to the rapier, the hilt or tang obviously provided an improved hafting mechanism. The leaf shape is also significant because, with the greater weight of the weapon in the lower part of the blade, it is clear that these weapons were designed more for slashing blows than for stabbing and thrusting in rapier fashion. It is assumed that this indicates an important change in fighting methods.

Some two dozen are recorded but only half have even brief details of find circumstances documented: almost all of these come from rivers or bogs. Distribution is mostly confined to the northern half of Ireland, but examples in Britain show a remarkable concentration in the Thames valley, which emerges as a major centre of bronze production and of Continental imports and influences from about 1200 BC. Sporadic finds occur elsewhere, including in the Penard hoard in Glamorgan with its early Rosnoën sword, narrow socketed axe and leaf-shaped spearhead. Contacts between Ireland and the Thames valley may have been via south Wales. British examples of the Ballintober type tend to have less prominent and less widely splayed shoulders (with a variant having a flat or rounded cross-section with bevelled edges), and using these criteria it is possible to identify Irish pieces in Britain and vice versa (Colquhoun and Burgess 1988). Ballintober swords have long been considered the result of a process of hybridisation between rapiers and early leaf-shaped swords, and their cross-sections do recall the lozenge and flattened lozenge cross-sections of group IV rapiers. The earliest swords in Britain, however, are the north-western French Rosnoën swords with subrectangular riveted hilts and more or less parallel-sided slender blades, and the slightly broader and ever so slightly leaf-shaped Ambleside swords, both responses to early central European sword fashions. One or both of these could have prompted the development of Ballintober swords, or at least their distinctive hilts. It may be that their leaf-shaped and lozenge-sectioned blade was inspired by early rod-tanged swords of the type recovered from the site of a possible shipwreck at Moor Sand, Salcombe, but the chronology of Ballintober swords is so uncertain that it is possible that the leaf shape may have been inspired by the earliest leaf-shaped (and flange-hilted) swords, which appear in the Thames valley in or about the thirteenth century BC and are derived from imported Continental leaf-shaped swords.

This preoccupation with swords is but one facet of a wider interest in weaponry and may well be an indication of an increase in martial activity. It is also necessary to remember that while some weapons were undoubtedly functional (and lethal), others were for show, as we have already seen with some spears and rapiers. This may imply the continued presence of a warrior aristocracy with an interest in diverse 'heroic' activities such as raiding and ostentatious exhibitionism. This evidence and the appearance of defended enclosures as well as a possible hierarchy of settlement types may point to significant social change towards the end of the second millennium BC.

SETTLEMENT, ECONOMY AND SOCIETY 1600–1000 BC

Evidence for settlement and economy in the period 1600–1000 BC has increased significantly in the last two decades, mainly owing to factors such as archaeological excavation in advance of major construction projects and archaeological survey and research projects such as the work of the Navan Research Group and the Discovery Programme. Excavation is beginning to illuminate a complex area crucial to a better understanding of a society that did not live by bronze and gold alone. The evidence is still very fragmentary, however, and the study of economy and of settlement patterns has barely begun. Thus the correlation of settlement with metalwork production and distribution remains an unresolved but important problem. Too little is still known about the agricultural base, the contemporary landscape and territorial organisation. As a part of the Discovery Programme's Ballyhoura Hills Project, Martin Doody (2008) has reviewed the growing body of settlement evidence for the later Bronze Age. Though some rectilinear and subcircular structures are known, wooden oval and circular houses predominate. Size and construction methods vary, but one or two circles of timber posts or circular foundation trenches—sometimes with internal timbers for roof support—are common. The majority have diameters of 5–9m but a small number of large examples with diameters in excess of 10m are known. Hilltop enclosures, lowland and wetland settlements and temporary occupation sites have all been identified and, as already mentioned, the range and size of settlement types hint at increasing social complexity. A village of 52 circular houses excavated at Corrstown, near Portrush, Co. Derry, is an exceptional illustration of this (Fig. 6.18). Most of the houses seem to have been occupied at the same time, and they were closely spaced and of fairly uniform construction and size. Possibly built of a turf superstructure on a drystone wall footing, their entrances, usually facing south-east, had porches and stone paving. Numerous trackways linked the houses and a metalled roadway ran across part of the site. A large quantity of coarse, flat-bottomed pottery and several stone moulds were found, and radiocarbon dates indicate occupation in the period 1500–1300 BC (Conway 2005).

It is difficult to be certain, given the restricted

Fig. 6.18—Simplified plan of a settlement of over 50 circular houses at Corrstoun, Co. Derry.

areas excavated elsewhere, but Corrstown may not be unique. Some houses, however, may be isolated single examples. There is a growing body of evidence to indicate the widespread presence of small clusters of two or more houses that are sometimes contemporary but sometimes successive buildings on the one site. Some may be unenclosed settlements but some are enclosed. Just one house was found on a south-facing slope at Knockdomny, near Moate, Co. Westmeath, during gas pipeline construction. A penannular foundation trench with an internal diameter of 8.5m may have contained a timber footing for upright posts, and some post-holes across the centre may have been roof supports; an arrangement of over 70 stake-holes formed some sort of internal division. There was an external hearth to the north-west and a number of pits contained heat-shattered stones. As is often the case, artefacts were few, just a few flint and chert scrapers and other pieces and a possible loom-weight. Some small amounts of wheat cereal were recovered and radiocarbon dates suggest occupation *c.* 1400 BC

(Hull 2006; Grogan *et al.* 2007). A single house was excavated within the narrow, 12m-wide corridor of another pipeline at Kilmurry North, near Kilmacanogue, Co. Wicklow. Of double-ringed form with a diameter of 11.5m and a south-eastern entrance, it had a central hearth. A few pieces of struck flint were found and some sherds of coarse pottery were recovered nearby (Ó Néill 2001; 2003). This double-ring house type has now been recognised at a number of locations, including Killoran on the edge of Derryville Bog during work on the Lisheen Mine Archaeological Project near Thurles, Co. Tipperary (Gowen *et al.* 2005). At Killoran the remains of at least three houses were found, and two of these consisted of a circular foundation trench with a concentric ring of timber posts within it (Fig. 6.19). Entrances were on the south-east and diameters were about 8m and 9m respectively. The outer wall (in the trench) would have been a non-load-bearing wattle-and-daub structure; the inner ring of posts would have supported the roof. Again finds were few but

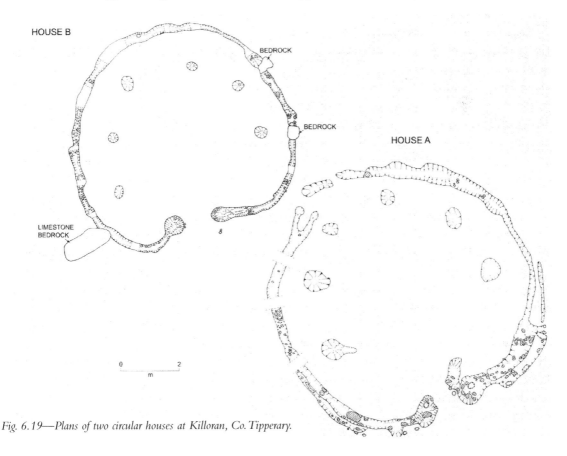

Fig. 6.19—Plans of two circular houses at Killoran, Co. Tipperary.

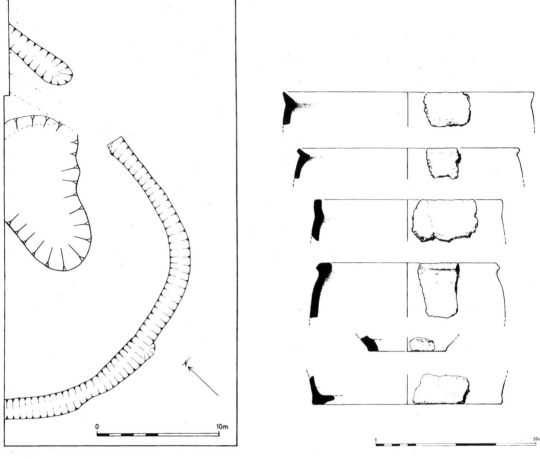

Fig. 6.20—Ballyveelish, Co. Tipperary. Left: plan of excavated part of subrectangular ditched enclosure; the central hollow was the site of a natural spring later filled with stones. Right: coarse flat-bottomed pottery.

included saddle quern fragments and some sherds of coarse pottery. A few sites such as Colp West, Co. Meath (O'Hara 2006), have produced burnt cereals and faunal remains, but subsistence evidence is often meagre or absent.

Enclosing features may of course have been no more than simple wicker fences: a series of stake-holes found to the north and south of a circular house at Tober, Co. Offaly, not far from Moate, may have been part of a wattle fence (Walsh 2007). More substantial ditched enclosures occur, and sometimes the ditches offer the prospect of well-preserved faunal and other remains. Excavations on the Cork to Dublin gas pipeline in 1981–2 at Ballyveelish, just north of Clonmel, Co. Tipperary, revealed part of a subrectangular enclosure that may have measured about 47m north–south by 25m

east–west (Doody 1987). Less than half of its southern area lay within the pipeline corridor and only this section was examined (Fig. 6.20). The site had also suffered considerable damage in more recent times (some of it associated with a nearby medieval moated site) and the surviving features were clearly truncated; if, for instance, an occupation horizon containing domestic refuse had existed within the enclosure, it had been stripped away. The enclosure consisted of a shallow, V-sectioned ditch about 1.8m wide at the top and 50cm wide at the base with a maximum depth of 1.2m: its upper layers had been removed too, so it may once have been somewhat more substantial. No evidence of an internal bank was found, and a gap in the ditch on the east may have been an entrance.

The recovery of a quantity of animal bones and sherds of coarse pottery from the fill of the ditch provided the main evidence for occupation. Indeed, the excavator had the impression that the ditch had been deliberately allowed to fill with silt and domestic refuse, and it was this refuse that offered the most useful information about the site's inhabitants. Two samples of wood charcoal from the ditch provided radiocarbon dates that suggest occupation around 1130–810 BC. The animal bones demonstrated that cattle were the most important livestock (about 42.9%). Next in significance came pig (about 35.7%) and caprovines (sheep or goat: about 16.7%). Since cattle provide more meat than pig it is possible that beef may have been by far the major component of the meat diet. Large numbers of broken bones were evidence of marrow extraction. Many of the cattle bones represented mature animals but the presence of numbers of immature specimens may be important; it has been argued that the presence of calf bones in quantity indicates that dairying was not important, an argument partly based on the premise that primitive cows needed their calves to maintain lactation. The Ballyveelish economy may well have been cattle-based and focused on beef production, but cows may still have been milked. Isotopic analysis of pottery residues has revealed milking in England since the early Neolithic (Copley *et al.* 2003), and this has been identified in similar residues at Chancellorsland, Co. Tipperary (below). Horse and dog bones were found in small numbers and, since they too were broken, these animals may have occasionally formed part of the diet. Hunting seems to have been of minimal importance, but red deer was occasionally hunted and eaten on site. Cereals were also cultivated: processing of a soil sample from the ditch by water flotation and sieving produced a number of grains of barley and one possible grain of wheat.

Over 200 sherds of coarse plain pottery were recovered, including some fragments of rims, shoulders and bases. These suggested flat-bottomed bowls and squat jars (Fig. 6.20). Only one sherd was decorated with a few incised lines. The pots were coil-built and some had sooty accretions, suggesting that some were cooking vessels. A detailed study of fabric demonstrated a range of possible uses: a majority of the sherds (95%) were 10–18mm thick and were tempered with varying amounts of calcite

grits. The amounts of temper may relate to function: the greater the degree of tempering (to produce a coarser-textured pot), the better the capability of the vessel to withstand the thermal shock of an open fire. Petrological analysis indicated local manufacture. A minority of sherds (5%) were about 22mm in thickness and were tempered with crushed pottery (variously termed grog or chamotte) to produce a vessel with a dense texture suitable as a dry-goods container. Some of the sparsely tempered calcite-gritted pots could have had a similar function. The thicker pottery was calcite-free and the clay used probably originated outside the Ballyveelish area; thus a little pottery—or perhaps just the clay—was imported. Other artefacts were few. Two small stone chisels or adzes, two stone spindle-whorls, a fragment of a lignite bracelet and three bone points were found. The evidence indicates a relatively simple and self-contained agricultural community, living in a small enclosed settlement, who were engaged in cattle-raising and cereal cultivation with some other activities such as spinning and pottery-making.

The gas pipeline work revealed another settlement at Curraghatoor, Co. Tipperary, south-west of Cahir, and again there were no surface traces of the archaeological remains. Excavation exposed a site with more than one phase of settlement activity (Doody 2007). The main phase comprised a small cluster of five houses, four circular and one subrectangular, dating from *c.* 1000 BC. They were of similar construction, with a foundation trench containing a number of posts and diameters varying from 3m to 5m. Finds were few and very little pottery was recovered. Some burnt cereals were found in two pits: barley predominated, with smaller quantities of wheat. A little burnt animal bone survived the acidic soil conditions but was insufficient to provide a reliable picture of the fauna exploited.

A larger oval enclosure at Chancellorsland, near Emly, Co. Tipperary (site A), measuring about 60m by 50m, has produced important settlement evidence. It and a nearby barrow cemetery (site C) were first identified in a series of aerial photographs and survived as low earthworks. The enclosure was surrounded by a ditch that had been recut three times, and in at least the last two phases there was an internal palisade as well, a wattle fence being replaced by a stouter timber post structure in the

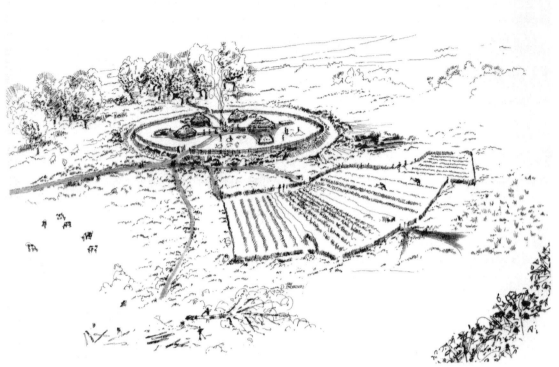

Fig. 6.21—Artist's reconstruction of an enclosure at Chancellorsland, near Emly, Co. Tipperary.

last phase. The second-phase ditch was waterlogged and produced significant occupation debris because it seems as if the ditches served as dumps for domestic refuse. Approximately 30% of the interior was excavated by Doody (2008) as part of that Discovery Programme study of prehistoric settlement in the Ballyhoura Hills region. Remains of at least eleven circular and rectangular structures and several lines of fences representing a number of phases of activity were uncovered. There was little direct evidence for the purpose of the various buildings but diverse domestic uses seem likely. Two rectilinear stake-built structures (structures 4 and 24) were interpreted as possible animal pens. Later disturbance destroyed a great part of the foundation trench of a rectangular building (structure 6) but there was no trace of a hearth and nothing to indicate its purpose. Two approximately circular houses of post-and-wattle construction with porch-like entrances (structures 12 and 15) did contain large internal hearths, each partly protected by a stake-built screen. There was evidently a long sequence of building, but it was not clear how many houses and other structures stood in the enclosure at any one time (Fig. 6.21). The various phases of settlement may have spanned the sixteenth century or even several centuries *c.* 1500 BC.

Apart from a large quantity of coarse pottery, artefacts were relatively few. There was little struck chert and flint and the only metal objects found were two bronze awls, but tool marks on some timbers from the ditch indicated the use of metal axes. Fragments of two crucibles were the only hint that metalworking may have taken place. Some points and awls of bone were a reminder that organic materials were probably widely used in many ways, and an amber bead and part of a small amber ring are two important finds. Amber probably originates in the Baltic region or on the eastern coasts of Scotland or England, and there is a discernible increase in the exchange of this prized material in the later Bronze Age. Several fragments of a human skull were found in the second-phase ditch, which also produced an important faunal assemblage. The deposition of skull fragments alone (and not any other part of the skeleton) may suggest that this was more than just a casual act of disposal. Unburnt plant remains from the ditch include grains of barley and wheat as well as seeds of elder, blackberry and hawthorn.

Cattle and pig were the main animals reared, but a significant quantity of sheep bones were present as well. The high proportion of young cattle bones suggests an emphasis on meat production, with only animals for breeding, traction or milk production being allowed to reach maturity. Residue analysis on a dozen pottery sherds indicated that these vessels were used for dairy products such as milk or butter. Butchery marks were identified on cattle and pig bones, and cut marks occurred on some sheep bones as well. The low incidence of mature sheep suggests that few were required for wool or fleeces; they may have been mainly reared for their meat. The large numbers of bones of young calves and lambs might indicate that calving and lambing took place in the enclosure. Chancellorsland was a substantial farmstead, and while its enclosing ditch and palisade were not defensive except in so far as they might offer some protection for livestock, they clearly demarcated the settlement and perhaps were an indication of the social standing of its inhabitants, who practised an extensive mixed farming economy.

The barrow cemetery (site C) and a circular enclosure lay about 55m north-east of site A. The circular enclosure appears to be an early medieval ringfort, and of the three burial mounds excavated (out of 42 in the general area) none were contemporary with site A. Nonetheless, it is quite likely that some of the unexcavated examples represent funerary monuments contemporary with the Bronze Age settlement.

Several timber structures and enclosed house sites on Knockadoon at Lough Gur, Co. Limerick, represent a sequence of occupation over a period of time from about 1200 to 800 BC, judging from a series of radiocarbon dates. As elsewhere, artefacts, apart from coarse pottery, were few; plain, coarse flat-bottomed bowls and squat jars were the principal forms. It is worth noting that the number of pig bones at Lough Gur, in contrast to other sites, implies that pig here may have been as numerous as cattle. Like the relatively high incidence of sheep at Chancellorsland (and at some other sites in the southern half of the country), these figures suggest that regional patterns of livestock exploitation may yet emerge. Some of the enclosed sites were once

thought to be of Neolithic date but may belong to the later Bronze Age. At site K an irregularly rectangular house was surrounded by a low enclosing wall. The enclosure had an average diameter of about 25m and consisted of a double ring of low boulders with a fill of earth and rubble between them; four post-holes at an entrance passage on the south-east suggested a double wooden gate. The remains of a similar enclosure at site L surrounded an irregular oval structure (Cleary 1995; 2003). Site K and a number of other sites at Lough Gur, and some other settlements like Chancellorsland, have produced human burials or human bones. These may denote complex rituals in which the living negotiated with the dead (Cleary 2005).

Circular enclosures would have provided some protection for the occupants and perhaps for some of their animals but are too slight to be truly defensive; they and the elaborate entrance at site K may, however, denote a house of some status. An enclosure with an average diameter of about 20m and possibly constructed of vertical timber planking surrounded an oval house at Ballybrowney, near Rathcormac, Co. Cork (Cotter 2005), a ditched enclosure 31m in average diameter enclosed house remains at Kilsharvan, near Drogheda, Co. Meath (Russell and Corcoran 2002), and a house in a similar enclosure with a diameter of about 36m at Knockhouse Lower, near Waterford, was associated with a late plain variant of Cordoned Urn (Chapter 4). An even larger enclosing ditch, 48m across, seems to have surrounded one or more houses at Lagavooreen, near Drogheda (Murphy and Clarke 2003). At Carrigillihy, near Union Hall, Co. Cork, a small oval enclosure measured 24m by 21m internally and consisted of a stony bank some 2.7m wide with an entrance, with post-holes for a gate, on the east facing the sea (Fig. 6.22). The excavator estimated that the bank might originally have been about 1.4m in height. Within was an oval house, 10m by 6.7m internally. It too was stone-built, with a 1.5m-thick wall faced with boulders and with a core of small boulders and earth. It survived to a maximum height of about 54cm and an asymmetrical arrangement of post-holes in the interior provided roof support. Before this house was completed, a level surface was made on the east by filling a natural hollow there with soil scooped from the immediate vicinity. No hearth was found,

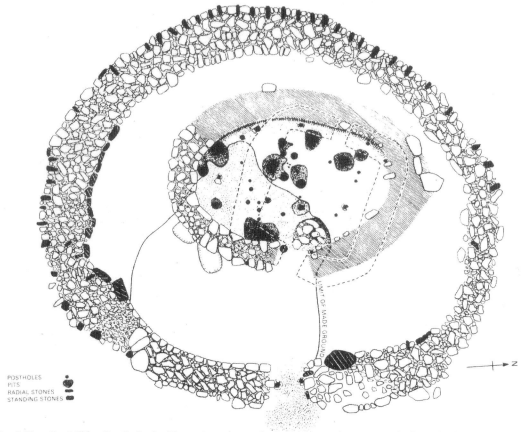

POSTHOLES
PITS
RADIAL STONES
STANDING STONES

Fig. 6.22—Carrigillihy, Co. Cork. Oval house in oval stone-built enclosure. A later rectangular house built on the site is dotted on the plan.

but the floor was covered with a layer 10–15cm thick of black habitation refuse, including charcoal and pottery. The occupation layer contained numerous fragments of pottery representing at least nine coarse flat-bottomed vessels. Many sherds were carbonised and were evidently cooking pots; their tempering was similar to the pottery from Lough Gur. Because of acid soil conditions no animal bones survived, but a small quantity of periwinkle shells showed that the resources of the nearby coast were exploited. Radiocarbon dating of charred twigs from a pit in the house and from the habitation layer produced dates with calibrated ranges of 1510–1220 and 1130–850 BC (O'Kelly 1951; 1989). Thus a fragment of a bronze socketed axe, a stray find in modern rubble covering the site, may have come originally from the later phase of prehistoric settlement. A later rectangular house (with opposed doors) was built on the site, probably in early medieval times, and used stone robbed from

the earlier house and the enclosing bank; it was separated from the earlier occupation by a thick layer of archaeologically sterile soil leached to a grey-white colour.

Clonfinlough, Co. Offaly

Another oval enclosure of a very different sort has been excavated at Clonfinlough, Co. Offaly (Moloney 1993). Here, investigations in a midland raised bog have added an important dimension to the varied settlement picture of the period. On the southern shore of Finlough, just over 2km southeast of the River Shannon and Clonmacnoise, a palisaded enclosure had been built on shallow peat on the lakeshore. It had been revealed at a depth of 2–3m in the bog in the course of mechanical peat extraction, which had unfortunately caused considerable damage and destroyed most of any occupation levels.

A stoutly built but irregularly oval palisade

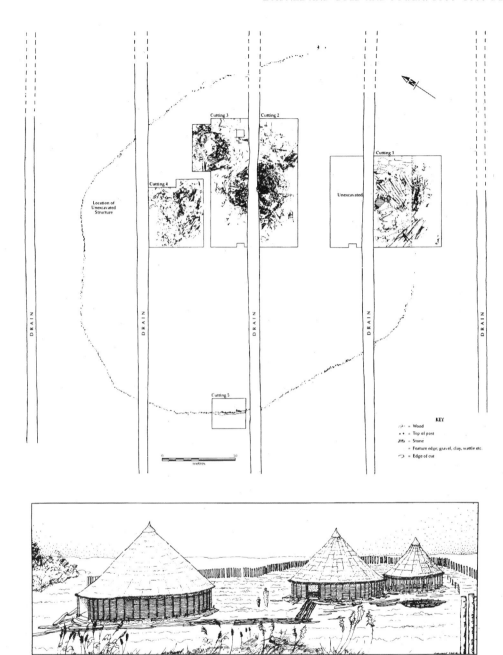

Fig. 6.23—Above: plan of palisaded enclosure at Clonfinlough, Co. Offaly, showing (from right to left) platform 1 in cutting 1, platform 2 in cuttings 2 and 3, structure 4 in the northern corner of cutting 3, and hut 3 in cutting 4. Below: reconstruction of Clonfinlough.

enclosed an area some 50m by 40m (Fig. 6.23). The ashwood posts were closely set and were 16–20cm or more in diameter; in places they were set in a trench but were sometimes driven up to 2.5m into the shallow peat and lake marl below. The pointed ends of the timbers showed cut-marks of bronze axes with blades 4–6cm across. It was thought that these posts could have formed a stockade 1–1.5m in height and probably open on the east at the lake edge. Within the enclosure four timber platforms, three of which probably supported circular houses, and the remains of several timber trackways were found. The platforms, up to 60cm or 70cm deep, were built to provide a dry surface above the damp ground.

Platform 1, to the south-east, was the best preserved. It measured 9.35m in diameter and was a carefully constructed complex structure of layers of wood including ash posts and split oak timbers, brushwood, stones and gravel. There was a roughly circular central hearth built of large stone slabs, and several layers of sand and clay along with ash and charcoal suggested a number of relining episodes. Pockets of occupation debris did survive and consisted of charcoal with burnt and unburnt animal bone. An amber bead and sherds of coarse pottery were also found.

The floor of this platform underwent one major reconstruction and layers of split oak planks were laid down, the uppermost around a square, slab-built hearth. The platform was surrounded by a double post-and-wattle wall, the tightly woven wattle walls being about 30cm apart on average. Whether this outer wall supported a roof is unclear but there could also have been internal roof supports simply resting on some of the stone slabs. There was a stepped entranceway on the north-east. Dendrochronological analysis of some oak timbers demonstrated that this platform had been constructed in the period 917–899 BC.

Platform 2, 10m to the south-west, was badly damaged but of broadly similar construction. It too was surrounded by a double post-and-wattle wall with an outer diameter of 7.2m. Part of a central slab-built hearth survived, as did some occupation debris including pottery and charcoal. There was also a stepped entrance on the east, with a brushwood path or trackway leading to it. Two broken wooden paddles (Fig. 6.24, 6–7) were found beneath this path, and a saddle quern was discovered near the entrance (Fig. 6.24, 8). Timber from the upper level of the entrance produced a felling date of 886 BC. A smaller structure (called hut 3) was uncovered 6m to the west. With a diameter of 5.2m, it consisted of a platform of several layers of timbers with a central slab-built hearth (rebuilt on a number of occasions) and surrounded by many posts. A small, perforated wooden disc (Fig. 6.24, 5) was found in the upper timbers here and bears some resemblance to the perforated lids of modern milk churns of the dash churn variety.

A fourth platform (structure 4), 4.4m in diameter, may have been a work area; there was no sign of a hearth, but organic material, charcoal, burnt and unburnt bones were found here. A second amber bead was found nearby.

A site like Clonfinlough would probably have been part of a network of settlements, and its inhabitants evidently had wider contacts and were able to acquire relatively exotic items. The two amber beads (Fig. 6.24, 1–2) are small but significant discoveries. It is highly likely that proximity to the Shannon was an important factor in whatever social communication there was, and the two paddles were probably used to row or scull some sort of wooden or hide-built craft on the waters of this major routeway. Log boats were probably a common feature on rivers and lakes. In addition, there may have been an important fording place near Clonmacnoise. It is also possible that Clonfinlough was part of a widespread network of timber trackways. The period of use of a trackway at Annaghcorrib, Co. Galway, 10km to the east across the Shannon, is partly contemporary, with a dendrochronological determination of 892 ± 9 BC (Raftery et al. 1995).

Besides the paddles and the perforated wooden disc, parts of possible wicker baskets were recovered and there was, of course, abundant evidence for woodworking. There was also evidence for woodland management. Ash was the dominant species exploited (75%) and was deliberately selected in two sizes: brushwood 3–6cm in diameter and roundwood 12–24cm across. The brushwood used showed particular uniformity and indicated the coppicing of ash rods of similar ages. It appeared that a stand of 1–2ha of ash was carefully grown and periodically cut to provide the necessary sort of wood over a period of time.

Other finds were mundane: stone objects were few and included a whetstone, an axe-like object of siltstone and the saddle quern mentioned above. The pottery was the familiar coarse, flat-bottomed ware, some with sooty accretions and used for cooking. At least two vessels were quite large, and one broad, basin-like pot (Fig. 6.24, 3) with a complete profile was found to have a capacity of 11.5 litres.

Much of the animal bone was burnt and

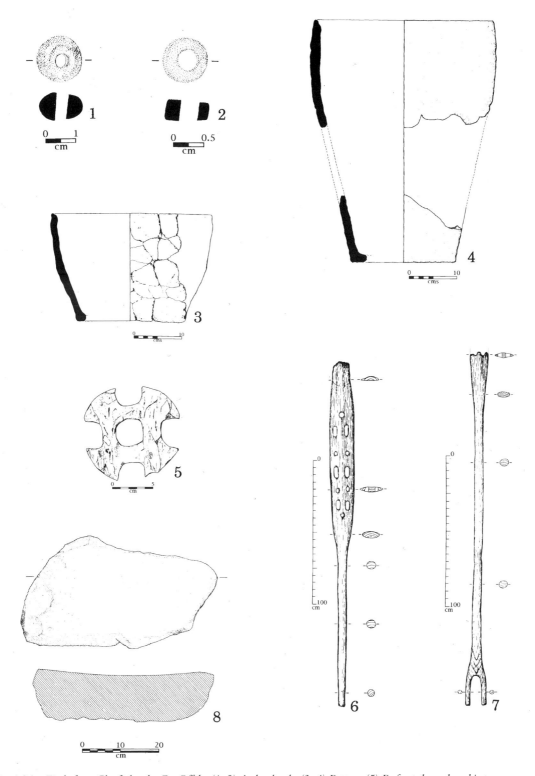

Fig. 6.24—Finds from Clonfinlough, Co. Offaly. (1–2) Amber beads. (3–4) Pottery. (5) Perforated wooden object. (6–7) Wooden paddles. (8) Saddle quern.

fragmented and identification was necessarily tentative. As at Ballyveelish and other sites, cattle were clearly dominant, with pig, sheep or goat and dog also represented.

The dendrochronological evidence suggested that the construction and occupation of the Clonfinlough settlement could have extended from 917 to 886 BC, perhaps representing one or two generations of an extended family. The substantial platforms and hearths do seem to imply permanent occupancy, but intensive seasonal occupation, and some specialised economic purpose, is also a possibility. Such a wetland location may have had a particular attraction as a permanent settlement, however, because of the security it offered. While the stockade could have served to keep animals in or out, like the stone wall at Carrigillihy, it was not a defensive measure. The Clonfinlough settlement was naturally protected, being situated in an area of bogland with a lake to the north and a large raised bog to the south. A strip of dry land to the east could have been reached by a path or trackway that would have allowed restricted access. If it can be established that there was a significant increase in the occupation of naturally defended wetland sites at this time, then the latter part of the second millennium BC may well have been a time of unrest and increasing social pressures. But for the inhabitants of Clonfinlough there may be simpler explanations: the proximity of the Shannon offered several advantages, the possibility of trading contacts being but one. There was no surviving evidence that the rich wildlife of the area was exploited but this may have been another factor; there certainly was vegetation suitable for cattle.

One similar though smaller site was excavated at Cullyhanna, Co. Armagh, in 1956. A lakeshore enclosure of irregular oval plan, about 20m in maximum dimensions, was formed by a line of oak stakes. Within was a circular hut about 6m across with a central hearth on a timber platform. Just south of this hut, an outdoor hearth protected by a screen or windbreak was found. The only artefacts recovered were a few flint scrapers and the excavator thought that the site was a hunting camp of the early medieval period. Timber samples taken from the site in 1969, however, provided both radiocarbon and dendrochronological dates; the latter demonstrated that the hut and palisade were contemporary, and with the completion of the

Belfast master tree-ring chronology Cullyhanna was eventually dated to 1526 BC. Though now securely dated, its purpose remains a puzzle and it may well have been a temporary and specialised site (Hodges 1958; Baillie 1982).

Considering the large amount of bronze in circulation, the scarcity of metalworking evidence is surprising. As we have seen, apart from occasional finds such as the moulds from Corrstown and the crucibles from Chancellorsland, evidence on or near settlement sites is rare. At Lough Gur, Co. Limerick, Seán P. Ó Ríordáin (1954) excavated a hut site, partly stone-built against a cliff face, on the southern side of Knockadoon. This hut (site D, house 1) was quite small, measuring about 5m by 3m, and of partly oval plan. There was no trace of a hearth inside or immediately outside. The discovery of part of a stone mould for a looped palstave inside and another fragment of the same mould outside on the north-east, and the further discovery of ten fragments of clay moulds for casting spearheads (one possibly basal-looped), led Ó Ríordáin to conclude that the occupants were engaged in bronze-working. If this was indeed the case, then bronze-casting here may have been an activity undertaken somewhere in the vicinity and some distance from any settlement, as was the case at Lough Eskragh, Co. Tyrone (Chapter 7). At site F at Lough Gur a rectangular structure was found to contain a hearth, and finds included fragments of clay moulds for casting spears and rapiers and waste pieces from bronze-casting. Some minute fragments of gold suggesting fine metalworking were recovered at Haughey's Fort, Co. Armagh, and clay moulds for casting various bronze objects have been found at the ritual site known as the King's Stables nearby and at Dún Aonghasa, Aran, Co. Galway.

Haughey's Fort

Haughey's Fort, named after a local landowner, is situated on a low but prominent hill just over 1,000m west of the celebrated Navan enclosure (commonly called Navan Fort) in County Armagh. Several seasons of excavation have revealed evidence for occupation in the general period 1300–900 BC (Mallory et al. 1996; Boreland 1996; Neill 1996; Murphy and McCormick 1996). The fort was trivallate, with an approximately oval outer ditch measuring some 340m by 310m in diameter (Fig. 6.25). The inner enclosure was first recorded in

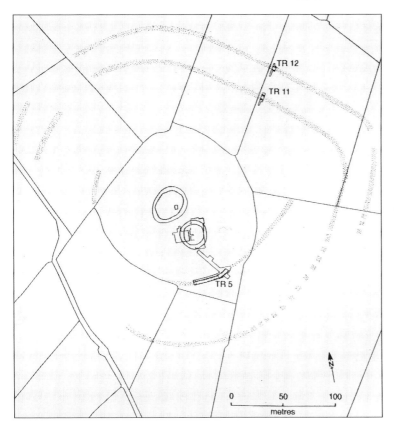

Fig. 6.25—Schematic plan of Haughey's Fort, Co. Armagh, showing position of trench 5, which sectioned the inner ditch, trench 11 at the middle ditch and trench 12 at the outer ditch. The approximate positions of the two circular structures in the inner enclosure are indicated.

the nineteenth century, when it may still have been visible on the ground, but today no superficial trace survives and the two outer ditches were only identified through aerial photography in 1989. The middle ditch is 25m from the outer one, with the inner ditch a further 55m upslope and enclosing an area measuring *c.* 150 by 140m in diameter.

No traces of an earthen bank survived near any of the ditches, but the excavated ditch sections revealed the slip of material from the interior, indicating the former existence of internal banks, and it seems that the site was a defensive one, a hillfort. The ditches were substantial, more or less V-shaped in section and 2.3–3.2m in depth. A small palisade trench was found near the lip of the inner ditch. This innermost ditch was waterlogged and yielded a considerable quantity of faunal and floral remains. Samples of short-lived organic remains (small branches, twigs, etc.) from the base of the ditch provided a number of high-precision radiocarbon dates. These demonstrated that the filling of this ditch began in the period 1160–1042 BC. A sample extracted from 1m above the base of the ditch produced a date of 1047–941 BC, and

another from 30cm above this yielded a date of 841–806 BC, which suggests that the defences may have been established about 1100 BC and that abandonment of the site may have occurred within a century or two, perhaps around 900 BC.

Limited excavation of the interior of the fort has revealed numerous small stake-holes presenting no clear structural pattern, as well as three lines of stake-holes and small post-holes running in an arc from north to south-east, perhaps part of a stockade. Radiocarbon dates from two of the posts indicated a date range of *c.* 1250–900 BC (although others produced a series of seemingly anomalous dates from 2450–1550 BC, and whether all are contemporary or not remains uncertain). Two possible lines of pits were also found: these measured about 1m or more in depth and at least 1m in diameter. There were no traces of posts in the pits, which produced quantities of coarse pottery, carbonised grain and fragments of gold and bronze, suggesting that they had been filled with occupation debris. The enhancement of a series of vertical aerial photographs indicates that the excavated pits actually form part of a double ring structure about 25m in diameter. The excavator suggests that the large pits may be the remains of a dismantled double-ringed timber structure, the timbers having been removed from their post-pits, with the subsequent accumulation of settlement debris therein. A radiocarbon date from one of the pits has a calibrated range of 1260–910 BC. Aerial photography also revealed a second and slightly larger double-ringed structure with a diameter of some 30m just to the north-west of the first.

A number of pits containing pottery, carbonised grain and hazelnut shells, burnt bone, fragments of quern stones and metal artefacts with radiocarbon dates ranging from 1250 to 900 BC indicate occupation broadly contemporary with that of the ditches and post-pits. Some later occupation on the site (possibly transitory) is also indicated by fragments of iron and later glass beads in a few of the pits. One pit, which contained a small iron object, possibly a strap handle, produced two charcoal samples that provided radiocarbon dates ranging from *c*. 400 to 200 BC and demonstrate that the latest evidence for activity at Haughey's Fort is more or less contemporary with the complex timber structures at the Navan enclosure (phase 3ii) to be described in Chapter 9.

Artefacts recovered included a considerable quantity of pottery, generally classic coarse ware. A number of pots could be reconstructed and were about 30–40cm in height with rim diameters of about 23–32cm. Analysis of organic deposits on the interior of some of the vessels suggested that carbonised residues were produced both by a cellulose material derived from plants and from the meat or skins of cattle. The fact that some large vessels, with capacities of as much as 16 litres, showed traces of plant remains suggested that they may have been part of some manufacturing process, perhaps the tanning of leather.

Metal finds included some minute fragments of gold leaf or wire recovered after flotation of material from the large post-pits. One complete object was a gold stud about 4.5mm in diameter from the post-pit radiocarbon-dated to 1260–910 BC. These might indicate fine metalworking on site. Bronze items included a sunflower pin, a fragment of a possible bracelet and three rings. A number of glass beads were found. The largest stone object recovered was a cup-and-ring-marked block of sandstone found in a shallow pit containing

charcoal radiocarbon-dated to *c*. 1250–900 BC. Carved with a double ring with a groove running from the centre to the outer edge of the stone, this sort of rock art is normally dated to the third millennium BC but, being portable, this stone could obviously have been brought to the site from elsewhere and need not be evidence of early prehistoric activity there. A few saddle quern stones and rubbing stones were also discovered. Evidence of woodworking included poles made of alder and hazel, split-wood oak used for structural purposes, two perforated handles of ash (possibly for socketed bronze axes which would have had wooden dowels in their sockets set into mortises in the hafts) and fragments of a round-bottomed bowl.

Faunal remains were mainly those of cattle (54.33%), with some pig (33.8%) and only few traces of sheep or goat (3.1%), horse and dog. A single red deer, a fox and a wild pig were the only evidence for hunted animals. The cattle are identified as short-horned, some with a shoulder height of 100–112cm (comparable to cattle from the early medieval period). A few larger animals, one with an estimated shoulder height of 129.5cm, may denote selective breeding. The pigs were large, with some up to 77.2cm at the shoulders. The horns of two goats measured 344mm and 348mm respectively, considerably larger than other recorded examples. The presence of unusually large animals is also evident in the dog remains, where several skulls represent the largest canine skulls known from prehistoric Ireland. Measurements suggest heights of *c*. 63cm and 65cm for some of these animals. It has been suggested that animals of large stature may be one of the criteria for the identification of a high-status site, since such élites might well be engaged in the selective breeding of larger animals or be the recipients of very large animals as prestigious gifts.

The interior ditch also yielded the remains of an insect assemblage: a preliminary report identified diverse species of beetle, some of which are generally associated with water or at least wetland areas, while a variety of dung beetles are associated with decaying animal and plant remains. This suggests that a certain amount of dung may have been deposited in the ditch from time to time; while much of this may have been from herbivores, it is also possible that the ditch could have been used as a latrine and was certainly used as a dump for rotting vegetable matter.

The environment of the Navan complex has been studied by David Weir (1994), mainly through pollen samples from nearby Loughnashade. This work has revealed a series of prehistoric clearance episodes culminating in the period *c.* 1400–1000 BC, when there was a significant reduction in elm, hazel, ash and oak. The increasingly open landscape appeared to be primarily for grassland. Arable agriculture was also important, as evidence for cereals, present since *c.* 1760 BC, rose to reach levels of *c.* 6%, which are among the highest known from Irish prehistoric contexts. The recovery of large quantities of carbonised barley from the pits at Haughey's Fort is further evidence of the importance of this cereal. Preliminary analysis indicates that these samples are free of contaminants and may indicate that the grain was processed elsewhere before being brought to the fort. The wood and seed remains, and an apple, from the lower levels of the interior ditch provide additional botanical evidence for the period *c.* 1100–900 BC. Pollen from both rye and flax was identified in the contemporary levels of the lake cores. The end of the major clearance phase occurs about 1000 BC and more or less coincides with the fort's abandonment. Hazel scrub was the first to recover, but by *c.* 850 BC ash and elm begin to expand again and grass values fall.

It was first thought that Haughey's Fort might have been the secular component of the Navan complex, with Navan Fort itself being the ritual centre of the area. This division between the sacred and the profane has not been supported by the radiocarbon dating, which shows that the main floruit of Haughey's Fort preceded most of the activity so far uncovered at Navan Fort. The possibility that the two large, double-ringed enclosures in Haughey's Fort could be ritual structures is a reminder that the fort may have been more than just a settlement. Indeed, the food remains could be interpreted as the debris from occasional ceremonial feasting, and the relatively pure barley might be the offerings of farmers who lived in the area but not in the enclosure. But settlement and ceremony are not incompatible activities on the one site. The faunal evidence, the size and hilltop location, the bronze artefacts and the limited evidence for fine metalworking, and even the possible indications of some ritual practice,

might all be considered as indicators of a high-status settlement. Ritual practices are certainly attested at the so-called King's Stables nearby, and possible entrances to Haughey's Fort are aligned on the latter monument (Conway 2006).

The importance of Haughey's Fort is confirmed by the discovery of the exceptional Tamlaght hoard about 700m to the south-west. Found in marshy ground, it consisted of a leaf-shaped sword and a small bronze bowl placed near its hilt; fragments of a complete decorated bronze cup and a small bronze ring had been placed in the bowl. The sword is of native manufacture but the bowl, cup and ring are imports from central Europe, where they date from approximately 1000 BC (Warner 2006; Macdonald and Ó Néill 2009). These are just the sort of prestigious drinking vessels that might have accompanied some of the earliest bronze buckets that are also of Continental origin and illustrate the complex networks of exchange that were the norm in Europe around the last millennium BC (Chapter 7, Fig. 7.4).

The King's Stables

The monument traditionally known as the King's Stables was once described as a sort of a 'ringfort with a sunken floor' and was popularly thought to be the site where the ancient kings of Ulster stabled and watered their horses (Lynn 1977). It lies just below and to the north-west of Haughey's Fort and is a flat-surfaced and approximately circular sunken hollow, about 2m below the surrounding ground surface and surrounded by a low, broad, penannular earthen bank, about 1m high and up to 10m wide, with a broad gap on its western side. The interior filled with water in wet weather but normally the surface appeared as a soft moss. A very small part of the site (about 5%) was excavated, with intriguing results. It proved to be an artificially constructed flat-bottomed basin with steeply sloping sides, a diameter of about 25m and a depth of 3.5–4m. The surrounding bank was formed by the upcast from the interior. Stratification in the basin basically consisted of a layer of fibrous peat on top of about 1m of mud on bedrock, and some 50cm of clear water above the peat had a layer of floating vegetation on top of it. The depth of the basin and the high level of the modern water-table suggest that it must originally have contained a considerable depth of standing water.

The limited excavation produced eighteen fragments of clay moulds, all for the manufacture of leaf-shaped bronze swords, two sherds of coarse pottery, a small plank of alder, two items of worked bone, some animal bones (mostly cattle, dog and pig) and a cut portion of the skull of a young adult human, probably male. Twigs from the basal silt and charcoal from beneath the earthen bank produced three radiocarbon dates that suggest contemporaneity with Haughey's Fort.

The King's Stables seems to have been an artificial pond deliberately constructed for cult purposes that included offerings of animal and human remains as well as material associated with bronze-working. What prompted this ritual development and the construction of the nearby hillfort is not clear. It has been tentatively suggested that both fort and pond were in some way a response to various economic and social pressures precipitated by climatic deterioration perhaps caused by the eruption of the Icelandic volcano Mount Hekla. This event (known as Hekla 3) and the ensuing dust-veil have been dated to about 1150 BC but, as already mentioned, the pollen record suggests a steady increase in land use at this time and Weir thought the hillfort a response to the social stresses caused by overpopulation. Some environmental change does seem to have occurred, however, as shown by narrow growth rings in oak trees at this time (Baillie and Brown 2002), but there may be no connection between this and the volcanic eruption (Plunkett 2006). The social and economic consequences of fluctuations in prehistoric climatic conditions are very difficult to assess. Short-term climatic problems might not be recognisable in coarse pollen records, yet a quick succession of poor harvests owing to bad weather might be disastrous for a community dependent on arable agriculture. But if there was significant and widespread climatic deterioration, societies with a predominantly pastoral economy may have been able to accommodate its consequences to a greater degree. English data may suggest that prehistoric farming communities were less vulnerable than we think and, while it should not be discounted, environmental catastrophism is a common explanation at present (Tipping 2002).

Dún Aonghasa

One of the surprises of the excavations initiated by the Discovery Programme at the great stone fort of Dún Aonghasa on the Aran Islands, Co. Galway, was the discovery of prehistoric settlement there long before the celebrated fort visible today was built (Cotter 1993; 1995; 1996). This well-known monument stands dramatically on the edge of a sheer sea cliff 87m high and dominates the lower lands of Kilmurvey to the north-east. It consists of an inner stone-built fort surrounded by two outer walls, a fragment of a third and a stone *chevaux-de-frise* (a term used to describe wooden stakes or upright pointed stones placed in the ground to hinder attackers and said to derive from spikes used by the Frisians to impede enemy cavalry in the seventeenth century). Its outer defences enclose a total area of 5.7ha (Fig. 6.26). The rampart of the inner fort survives to a height of 4.9m and has a slight external batter—that is, it slopes inwards from base to top to give greater stability—and has a maximum thickness of over 5m. The low, narrow, lintelled entrance is on the north-east. This inner fort is of irregular U-shaped plan, with an average internal diameter of about 47m and open to the Atlantic at the southern cliff edge. Presumably the enclosure was once an oval or at least D-shaped, with a wall or rampart on the seaward side.

Excavations conducted from 1992 to 1995 have revealed occupation broadly dating from the period 1300–800 BC within the inner enclosure of the fort and in the middle enclosure between the inner rampart (wall 1) and the next rampart (wall 2). The remains of a number of circular huts and other structures have been identified in the inner enclosure (Fig. 6.27). These include the remains of certain or possible hut foundations (nos 1, 2, 5 and 8), paved areas possibly the remains of dwellings (nos 4 and 6), paved areas possibly representing work areas (the 'North area' with a large hearth) and traces of walling (no. 3).

Hut 1 was about 4.8m in diameter and survived as several lines of low edging stones (all that remained of the foundation course), part of a paved floor and a stone-lined hearth; a horizontal slab marked the entrance on the east. An occupation layer of compact charcoal-flecked clay on the paving contained limpet shells, animal bones, sherds of coarse pottery, fragments of clay moulds (Fig. 6.27) and two crucibles. A sample of animal bone,

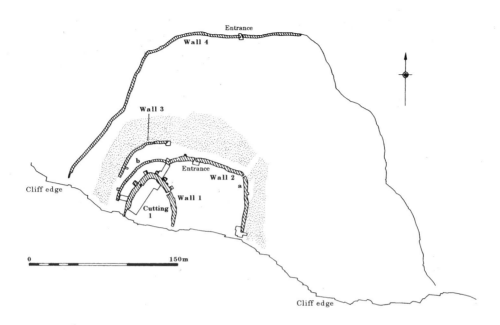

Fig. 6.26—General plan of Dún Aonghasa, Aran, Co. Galway.

when radiocarbon-dated, suggested occupation in the period 1063–924 BC, but traces of earlier occupation were found beneath the floor of hut 1 and extended beyond its limits.

Finds included more coarse pottery and clay mould fragments, bone pins, four small hollow bronze rings and a small bronze chisel. Again, animal bone indicated date ranges of 1379–1127 and 1266–1092 BC. This earlier occupation, *c.* 1300–1000 BC, was traced elsewhere under walls and paving, but further radiocarbon dates suggest that the other structures, like hut 1 itself, date from the period 1000–800 BC. Not all were in use at the same time; the foundations of hut 5 partly overlay hut 8, and there clearly was a sequence of occupation on the site. A stone-built trough found to the east of hut 1 had been constructed in pre-existing occupation debris. The large hearth uncovered in the 'North area' measured 3.6m by 1.8m by up to 17cm deep and produced coarse pottery and a number of bone points, as well as animal and fish bones.

Traces of similar occupation were also found outside the rampart in the middle enclosure to the north. The foundations of a stone wall were

uncovered here, running for a distance of 9m in a north-east to south-west direction. It was 2m in average width and survived to a maximum height of 50cm. Occupation material containing animal bone, limpet shells, pottery, part of a bronze ring, bone pins and some stone artefacts abutted the eastern face of this wall and continued southwards under the foundations of wall 1. Two radiocarbon dates from the upper level of this material provided a date range of 900–540 BC for this occupation and also provided a terminal date for the wall foundations and a terminal date after which wall 1 was built.

Determining the relationship of the occupation to the enclosing walls was not an easy task. In the middle enclosure, no trace of any habitation material was found to the west of the wall foundations uncovered north of wall 1 or outside wall 1 on the west between it and wall 2b. Occupation material (animal bone and coarse pottery) was found in a small cutting abutting wall 1 in the middle enclosure near the entrance to the inner fort, near the entrance through wall 2a and, to the east, in a cutting excavated near where wall 2a runs to the cliff edge. Here the material extended in

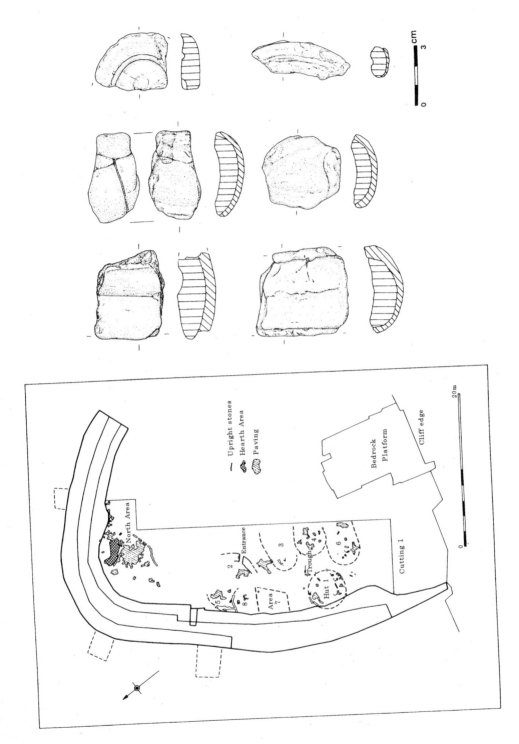

Fig. 6.27—Left: area excavated in inner enclosure at Dún Aonghasa. Right: fragments of clay moulds for casting a bronze sword, spearhead and bronze rings or bracelets.

under the inner face of the wall for a distance of 30–40cm. In effect, the late prehistoric occupation seems to have been confined to what is now the inner enclosure and to that part of the irregularly shaped middle enclosure east of the wall foundation found running from wall 1 to the junction of walls 2b and 2a.

The excavation in the inner enclosure demonstrated that the occupation material ran under the inner side of the rampart (wall 1). It seems as if this massive rampart had been built of a series of vertical walls of masonry, and its construction may have begun with a double-faced core wall (now contained within the thickness of the rampart) with additional skins of masonry added later to each face, the innermost skin resting on the interior occupation. The core wall would have been part of the original enclosing wall of the late second-millennium BC settlement. It is possible that this original enclosure consisted of a stone wall that ran, on the west, along the line of wall 1 to join with the foundation wall uncovered in the middle enclosure, and then joined an earlier element of wall 2a. The enclosing wall must also have extended along the Atlantic side of the settlement to provide essential protection from the elements.

It has been suggested that the outer wall (wall 4) may have been contemporary with this enclosure, but whether this was a multivallate monument remains uncertain. What does seem clear is that the great stone fort as it stands today represents a large-scale remodelling of the original enclosure, but when this took place is also uncertain. Quite limited material indicates activity on site in the last century or two BC and in the early medieval period, but there is no evidence of extensive occupation at these times.

The finds from the inner and middle enclosure excavations are particularly intriguing. Preliminary analysis of the animal bones has indicated a considerable emphasis on sheep-rearing (over 52%), with cattle and pig of lesser importance. About 34% of the sheep were killed at less than one year of age and only 20% were more than three and a half years at death, suggesting that this animal was reared primarily for its meat rather than for secondary products such as wool.

While the pottery conforms to the usual coarse, flat-bottomed fashion, the fragments of clay moulds demonstrate the casting of bronze swords, spearheads, rings or bracelets and pins on or near the site. At first glance, a cliff-top location on the edge of the Atlantic might seem to be an unlikely place for this sort of work. If the spectacular cliff setting is ignored, Dún Aonghasa is actually located in a commanding position—almost, but not quite, at the highest point of the southern end of a north–south ridge that dominates lower land to the north-east and east. This prominent location is only 15m or so higher above sea level than Haughey's Fort and was probably occupied for much the same reasons. Status, prominence and possibly defence were in all likelihood intertwining factors in the choice of location for both these monuments. Dún Aonghasa was, in effect, a coastal hillfort. A study of marine erosion processes on the Atlantic coast suggests that it was possibly situated about 1,000m inland from the shore in the Bronze Age (Williams 2004). It may have been strategically located to dominate seagoing traffic and defence may have been important. Most if not all of the resources needed for metal production would have been imported and, as Barry Cunliffe (2001) has demonstrated, Atlantic waters allowed the transmission of materials and technologies over great distances; similar evidence for metalworking has been found on the settlement at Jarlshof on the even more remote island of Shetland. It is also possible, of course, that Dún Aonghasa's liminal siting in a high place on the edge of the known world gave added magical value to swords and other objects made there.

A hierarchy of settlement

The exceptional bronze and gold objects of the Bishopsland phase have prompted the suggestion that they were the prized possessions of an élite element of society, and it is possible that social ranking is reflected in the broadly contemporary settlement evidence as well. If it is correct to consider Haughey's Fort and Dún Aonghasa as higher-status sites, possibly at the top of a hierarchy of settlement, then Clonfinlough, Ballyveelish, Chancellorsland and Carrigillihy may represent lesser orders of habitation site. The evidence is still limited but a range of distinguishing characteristics may be tentatively identified. For important sites, these include a prominent hilltop location, possibly chosen for defensive reasons but also chosen for visibility—as a proclamation of status and even as a focus for the organisation of the surrounding landscape. Scale may be important too: both the size of the enclosure and the presence of one or more ditches, banks, walls or palisades will indicate a greater measure of labour investment and, possibly, coercive control.

Given the importance of bronze and gold at this time, the possession of metal objects may be revealing. Since the evidence for metalworking seems particularly scarce, the presence of items like clay moulds is probably significant and, since weapons such as rapiers, swords and spears were sometimes of symbolic significance, evidence for weapon manufacture may denote special importance. More difficult to quantify is access to exotic materials. Prized materials, like the amber beads from Clonfinlough, may find their way into the archaeological record only in exceptional circumstances. The same is true of faunal assemblages, which are only preserved in special conditions. Cattle, in both size and quantity, may have been a major indicator of wealth and status.

Since cooking and storage were universal activities it is probably not surprising that so many settlements should share the same coarse cooking pottery. What is curious is that the supposedly more important sites should lack finer wares, especially since the clay moulds show that the capability to manufacture finer pottery did exist. Most of the coarse pottery was locally made, but a small amount at Ballyveelish and Lough Gur, for instance, was made of different clays and may have come from further afield. Organic containers of wood, basketry and leather must have been very common.

Finally, the evidence from Haughey's Fort and from the nearby King's Stables is a reminder that ritual activity in or near a settlement may be a mark of special status as well. Too few sites have been excavated and too little is known about economic and territorial organisation to clarify the picture. It is possible that we are seeing the emergence of powerful community leaders, even theocratic chiefdoms in which tribal leaders had both a political and a religious role. The control of long-distance exchange networks, which become even more marked in the succeeding Dowris phase, may have been an important factor in the development and maintenance of these social hierarchies. Élite power and control were possibly enhanced by complex depositional rituals which themselves may have been monopolised by a chiefly element. The appearance of the bronze sword, in particular, suggests that warfare, or at least aggressive and combative activities such as persistent raiding, may also have become a prominent part of a male-dominated system. Not all hillforts were settlements. Excavation at Cashel, Co. Cork, a large, bivallate hilltop enclosure north-east of Bandon, produced little or no evidence for occupation in the inner enclosure but did demonstrate the presence of significance defences (O'Brien 2008). A large timber palisade was constructed along the line of the inner enclosure and a fence of timber posts was also built on top of the outer rampart, which was found to have an external ditch. Radiocarbon dating indicates construction around 1200 BC and it seems that this monument was a defensive refuge for the Cashel community.

7

THE CONSOLIDATION OF WEALTH AND STATUS: 1000–600 BC

METALWORK OF THE DOWRIS PHASE

The first half of the last millennium BC saw the culmination of many of the developments in ornament and weaponry initiated in the preceding centuries. There seems to have been a significant increase in the amount of metal in circulation and a considerably greater variety of objects manufactured. Some writers have seen this as a time of conspicuous wealth expressed in a remarkable range of weaponry and gold ornaments. Certainly some of the most outstanding pieces of prehistoric gold and bronzework belong to this period. Technological skills developed as well, with the production of exceptional examples of hollow-cast and sheet metalwork. This was also a time that saw the consolidation of a warrior and aristocratic society, with an even greater emphasis on ostentatious display and on depositional cult practices. Indeed, almost 80% of the metal hoards of Irish prehistory, including some of the most remarkable, belong to the metalworking phase that George Eogan (1964) named the Dowris phase after a major find of bronze artefacts in the midlands.

THE DOWRIS HOARD: 'A HORSE-LOAD OF . . . BRONZE ANTIQUITIES'

What has become known as the Dowris hoard is the largest collection of bronze objects ever found in Ireland and originally it may have comprised over 200 objects. This extraordinary discovery of 'at least a horse-load of gold-coloured bronze antiquities', as one early report described it, was made in the 1820s by two men digging potato beds in reclaimed bogland in a small field just over 0.5km south of a lake called Lough Coura and about 7km north-east of the modern town of Birr. Named after the adjacent townland of Doorosheath, this great find has given its name to the major phase of the late Bronze Age in Ireland. Lough Coura no longer exists—the land has been drained and reclaimed—but in the early nineteenth century it formed an area of open water about 40ha in extent and some 56m deep. In late prehistoric times it was probably a much more extensive body of water located at the foot of several low glacial ridges encompassed by bog. It was certainly situated on the edge of a vast expanse of midland bog. This immense and inhospitable area stretched northwards and was broadly demarcated to the south and east by the higher, undulating good agricultural land that formed a broad arc at the foot of the Slieve Bloom Mountains. The lake's liminal location—on the interface between the wild and the tamed—may have invested it with special meaning, and the area of open water may have been perceived as an opening in the earth giving access to an other- or under-world. The bog would have been a place shaped by non-human forces, and both water and bog may have demanded a votive offering from time to time to placate the spirits or gods who lived there. The term hoard was applied to the Dowris find because it was assumed that it represented a collection of objects all buried in the ground at the one time, but the range of material

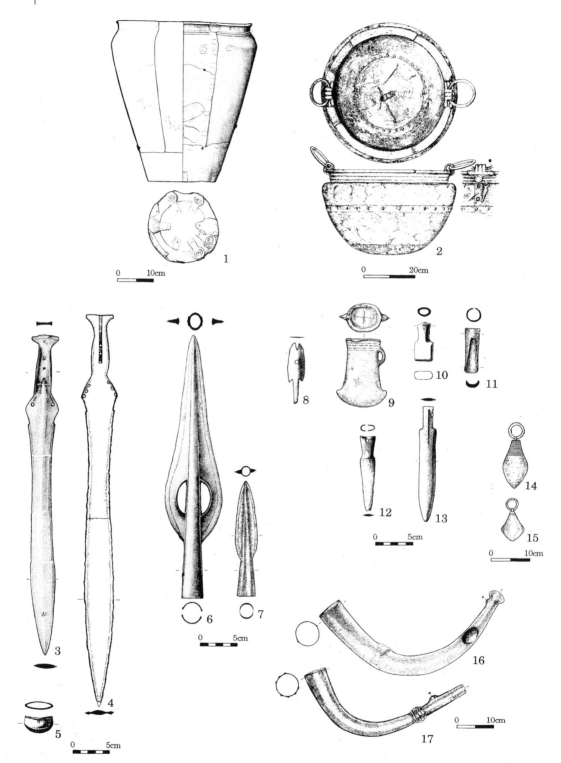

Fig. 7.1—The Dowris hoard, Co. Offaly, selected bronze objects. (1) Bucket. (2) Cauldron. (3–4) Swords. (5) Scabbard chape. (6–7) Spearheads. (8) Razor. (9) Socketed axehead. (10) Socketed hammer. (11) Socketed gouge. (12–13) Knives. (14–15) Pendants. (16–17) Horns.

and its watery context suggest that it may have been a diverse set of objects deposited over a period of time, perhaps several centuries. Indeed, some pieces may have been heirlooms when finally consigned to the depths of the greater Lough Coura. Extrapolating from dates assigned elsewhere to some of the bronze types, it seems probable that the watery rituals at Dowris began shortly before 1000 BC.

No precise details of the original contents of the find exist and some of the collection was dispersed. Today 110 bronze objects are preserved in the National Museum and a further 67 in the British Museum (of which most, though not all, probably came from the find); the latter collection also contains two pieces of waste bronze and six sandstone rubbing or polishing stones (Eogan 1983). Of the surviving items (Fig. 7.1) the most numerous are hollow-cast bronze pendants (48), spearheads (36), socketed axes (35), cast-bronze trumpets or horns (26), knives (7), swords (5), socketed gouges (5), buckets (3) and cauldrons (3) of sheet bronze, and razors (3). A socketed hammer and a scabbard chape are also preserved.

Many of the surviving objects are complete or in reasonably good condition. All of the swords are damaged or broken, but most of the axes, apart from half a dozen broken and incomplete examples, are, like the spearheads, well preserved. A majority of the horns are complete or nearly so, though six are represented only by parts or fragments. Two of the surviving buckets and two of the cauldrons are represented by parts or fragments as well. It is said that the complete cauldron had contained 'an assortment' of bronzes. The pendants are in good condition except for two which seem to be broken and flawed castings. The deposition of musical instruments, such as horns, is a new departure that may echo northern European customs. The bronze bucket is a remarkable object that had been repaired several times and was probably a number of centuries old when deposited. To dispose of a complete bronze bucket or cauldron, even one that had seen some use as the centrepiece of a long series of élite ceremonial feasts, must have been an act of particular significance. Its submergence in the lake may have been a part of a public ceremony conducted by someone of religious or political importance. Some of the trumpets found may have been sounded on such special occasions. The deposition of a broken spear or sword, on the other hand, might conceivably have been a more private commemorative event coinciding with the death of its warrior owner. A woodworker's axe or gouge may have been a craftsman's tribute, and scrap bronze or polishing stone the offering of a metalworker. Some poorly made or poorly finished axeheads may even have been specially made or selected for ceremonial discarding. In short, the diverse range of objects may denote a hierarchy of participants as well as a protracted series of different sorts of performance, some communal in the hope of benefiting a social group, some perhaps of a more individual nature. A number of objects in the collection, such as the cauldron, horns and pendants, are good illustrations of some of the significant metal types in use in the Dowris phase.

The Dowris bucket

The intact bucket from Dowris is one of two that stand at the head of an accomplished sheet-bronze industry in late prehistoric Britain and Ireland (Gerloff 2004). It and a bucket from Nannau, Merioneth, south Wales, are generally considered early imports from central Europe, perhaps in the thirteenth century BC, which inspired insular craftsmen to produce local forms of flat-bottomed buckets and round-bottomed cauldrons of similar riveted multi-sheet construction (Fig. 7.2).

Made from very thin sheet bronze (0.8mm thick), the Dowris vessel is over 40cm high and in good condition, apart from missing handles and a number of riveted repairs and patching (Fig. 7.1, 1). It is constructed of three pieces of sheet bronze. The lower part is a single sheet beaten into a tub shape with a slightly dished base surrounded by a foot ring. The upper body consists of two overlapping sheets of bronze of equal size riveted together along two vertical seams and riveted to the basal portion. The edge of the everted rim was bent around a bronze wire to strengthen it and there are two low corrugations on the neck. Two opposed handles (which would have held solid-cast bronze rings) were originally riveted to the vessel at the top of the vertical seams and the basal foot ring was originally protected externally by six equally spaced base plates consisting of a small decorated disc with a tab or strap-like extension. Two other unprovenanced Irish buckets are of Continental form but have had their original riveted strap handles replaced by cast-

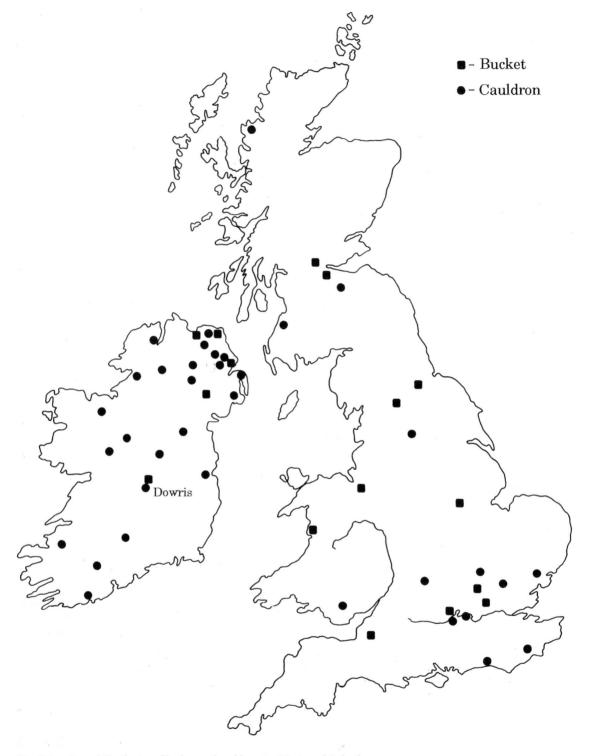

Fig. 7.2—General distribution of buckets and cauldrons in Britain and Ireland.

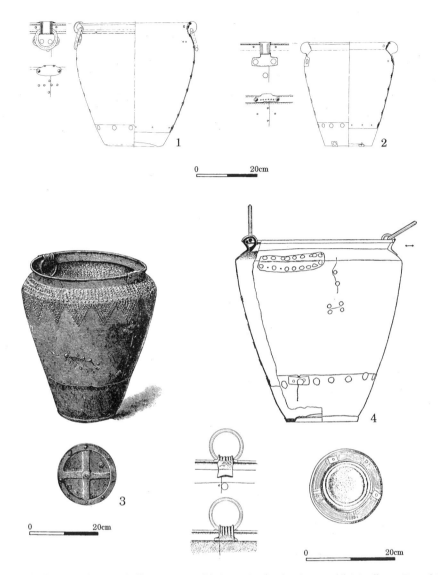

Fig. 7.3—Bronze buckets. (1–2) Hosszúpályi, Hungary. (3) Cape Castle, Co. Antrim. (4) Magilligan, Downhill, Co. Derry.

on handles, a distinguishing feature of the locally produced examples.

Parallels between the Dowris- and Nannau-type buckets and buckets of Hosszúpályi type in Hungary and Romania are intriguing: the latter are of similar size, manufactured of three riveted sheets of bronze, with deep tub-shaped lower portions, riveted strap handles and, on rare occasions, what may be similar protective base plates. These Hosszúpályi vessels (Fig. 7.3, 1–2) are a variant of the smaller Kurd buckets (named after another Hungarian find) that occur further west. They were probably important status symbols: one Kurd bucket

was found in a chieftain's cremation grave of about 1100 BC at Hart, in Bavaria, associated with a bronze cup and a strainer, and bronze fitments from a four-wheeled wagon. It has been suggested that such buckets, cups and strainers may have been special drinking sets, even connected with wine-drinking, and it is possible that the insular buckets may also have served as containers for some alcoholic drink, perhaps of a ceremonial nature. The small bronze bowl and the decorated bronze cup of central European type found in the Tamlaght hoard near Haughey's Fort (Warner 2006) were probably part of just such a drinking set and are testimony to

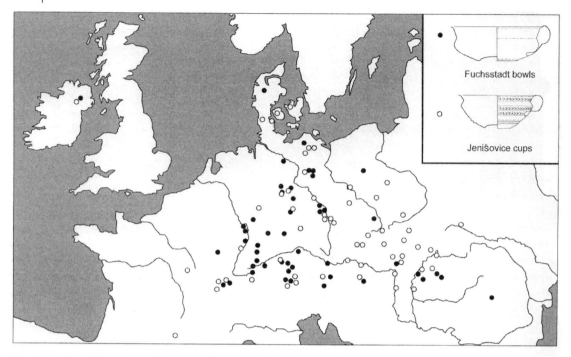

Fig. 7.4—General distribution of the types of bronze bowl and bronze cup found in the Tamlaght hoard, Co. Armagh.

the great distances covered by some fashionable bronze objects (Fig. 7.4). Whether buckets such as these are actual imports or close copies of a Continental fashion, they demonstrate the long-distance transmission of material fashion and ideas and are just one element in a much larger body of evidence, which includes bronze swords and shields and other objects, for interaction between élite societies in Ireland, Britain and continental Europe at this time. More mundane wooden cauldrons were being manufactured at this time: an unprovenanced round-bottomed wooden cauldron, probably from the north of Ireland, has been radiocarbon-dated to 1055–795 BC (Earwood 1993).

A fine bronze bucket from a bog at Cape Castle, Co. Antrim, now in the Hunt Museum, Limerick, is a local product judging from its shape, wheel-shaped base plate and cast-on handles. The wheel-shaped base plate replaced a series of separate angular base plates and seems therefore to be a later development. There is repoussé geometric decoration on the shoulder of this bucket (Fig. 7.3, 3) that recalls central European fashions and prompted the suggestion that its Irish maker must have been acquainted at first hand with the modes

and methods of Continental schools of workmanship. Other Irish–British buckets are for the most part of evident local manufacture and include the tub-shaped lower part of one and two angular base plates of another in the Dowris hoard.

The principal distinguishing features of locally manufactured buckets are the presence of cast-on rather than riveted handles and developed base plates. A complete example found at Magilligan, Downhill, Co. Derry, is made of the usual three sheets of bronze, each about 1mm thick (Fig. 7.3, 4). The skill required to hammer each of these from a heavy piece of cast metal was considerable; the basal part of the bucket is estimated to weigh a little under 1.2kg and was beaten into shape on a matrix using a metal hammer at least in the final stages. The rivets used have flat heads beaten tightly against the body. Several riveted patches are later repairs. The two handles (or staples as they are sometimes called) are cast onto the rim and neck and each projects inwards, forming a semicircular loop, to hold a free-riding bronze ring. These cast staples and rings are typical of insular bronze cauldrons and it is far from clear why this sort of complicated attachment was preferred on both buckets and cauldrons to a simpler riveted one. The casting-on must have been a difficult process, perhaps undertaken in more than one stage; great care was needed to see that the molten metal did not burn through the thin sheet bronze, and the bronze ring (cast separately) had to be carefully held in place. This sort of complex metalworking probably denotes the existence of specialised craftsmen who may have worked for aristocratic patrons. The Magilligan bucket has its base reinforced by a circular, ribbed, cast-bronze fitment that fits over and is riveted to the foot ring. This type of protective base ring or plate may be a development of the wheel-shaped base plate found on the Cape Castle and other insular buckets.

Cauldrons

The complete cauldron from Dowris (Fig. 7.1, 2) belongs to a well-known series of round-bottomed sheet-bronze vessels found in Ireland, Britain and in western continental Europe in Denmark, France and the Iberian Peninsula that have been called 'Atlantic cauldrons' to differentiate them from various bronze vessels found elsewhere in Europe. They have been divided into two classes, an earlier class A and a later class B, with various subdivisions, and the earlier examples have been studied by Sabine Gerloff (1986). The Dowris cauldron is a class A example characterised by a spheroid or slightly conoid body, usually with a corrugated neck and a rim that is turned sharply inwards to give a flat top. Two staples consisting of semicircular ribbed tubes are cast onto the rim and hold ring handles that are usually (but not always) of circular cross-section. The body is always made of three bronze sheets riveted together: two upper sheets with vertical seams set inside and riveted to a bowl-shaped bottom part (Fig. 7.5, 1). Other sheets invariably represent later additions and repairs. The Dowris cauldron has suffered some damage but was originally made in this way and the lowest basal part is a later and rougher addition. It is just over 50cm in external diameter with a characteristic corrugated neck and in-turned flat rim rolled around a bronze wire. Both corrugations and wire served to strengthen the sheet bronze. The staples are cast triple-ribbed tubes and hold cast rings.

Gerloff has assigned class A cauldrons in Ireland and Britain to four types, the earliest of which are represented by finds from England, one example coming from Colchester, Essex, and another from Shipton-on-Cherwell, Oxfordshire.

The Dowris cauldron belongs to her Tulnacross type, named after a bog find in County Tyrone about 5km south-east of the Beaghmore stone circles. The Tulnacross example itself (Fig. 7.5, 2) is a much-repaired piece with a conoid body and a maximum height of about 47cm. The lip of the in-turned flat rim is rolled around a bronze wire in the usual fashion, and the several later repairs to the body may reflect distinct phases of work. What was thought to be a strengthening iron band inside the rim has proven, on analysis, to be an organic deposit. Found mainly in Ireland, this Tulnacross type usually has a rather conoid body with heights of 33–40cm and a capacity of 35–45 litres; there are three corrugations on the neck and characteristic cast-on staples in the shape of a half-tube with three ribs, a staple form which 'in its entirety represents a triple-ribbed arch on two T-shaped supports'. Staples of this sort have been found in a huge founder's hoard from Isleham, Cambridgeshire, and this association and several other strands of evidence have convinced Gerloff that the manufacture of Tulnacross cauldrons began before 1000 BC. The distinctive triple-ribbed staples may be a development of the staples found on the earlier English cauldrons of Colchester and Shipton types, which are not ribbed tubes but formed of two or three closely set but separate three-quarter rings. One Irish cauldron from a bog at Derreen, near Bellanagare, Co. Roscommon (with ring handles of lozenge-shaped section), seems to have staples that consist of three separate rings simply fused together and thus, typologically at least, may represent an intermediate stage between the primitive Shipton and later Tulnacross forms. The Tulnacross type and later cauldrons are remarkable products of the bronzesmith's craft, displaying familiarity with sophisticated casting techniques, seemingly using lead-alloyed bronze for handle fitments and unleaded bronze for the carefully beaten sheet work and rivets.

The Portglenone type is named after two finds from a bog at Portglenone, Co. Derry (Fig. 7.5, 3). The triple-ribbed staples now have a flange at either end and a basal element usually formed by two transverse bars across the rim with a small space between them (this bracing presumably strengthened the attachment and protected the flat rim from contact with the free-riding ring handle). One of the cauldron fragments from the Dowris

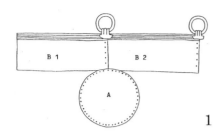

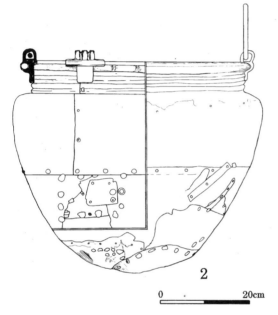

hoard is a staple of this type. The neck of these cauldrons has two rather than three corrugations and, judging from the complete examples, it seems as if the type is generally smaller: 29–35cm in height, with a capacity of 20–38 litres.

A significant number of complete cauldrons have been found in bogs but details of their discovery are all too rarely recorded. One, revealed at a depth of about 1m in the course of turf-cutting in Barnacurragh townland, near Tuam, Co. Galway, had the lip of its rim rolled around a wooden rod rather than a bronze wire. This cauldron had been deposited in an inverted position, but nothing else was found and nothing was noted in the vicinity when more of the bog was cut away.

According to Gerloff, a number of associated finds indicate that cauldrons of the Portglenone type date from the Dowris phase. Since all the complete cauldrons have been found in Ireland (and the one complete Scottish example—of Tulnacross type—from Hattenknowe, Peebleshire, may be an Irish export) and since the British finds and one from a large western French hoard at Vénat, near Angoulème in the Charente, are represented by fragments, Gerloff also suggests that cauldron production may have been confined to Ireland at this time, the fragments reflecting a trade in scrap metal.

Class B cauldrons are bronze round-bottomed vessels of multi-sheet construction but without a

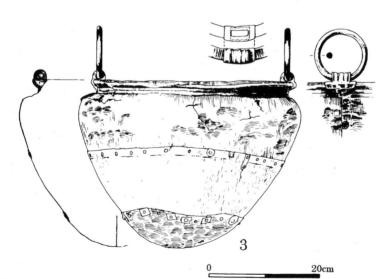

Fig. 7.5—(1) Method of construction of early cauldrons. (2) Tulnacross, Co. Tyrone. (3) Portglenone, Co. Derry.

corrugated neck. Now the rim is everted with rolled lip (sometimes rolled around a bronze rod or tube) and the staples are cast onto the inner part of the slanting rim. The staples are the familiar ribbed tubes with pronounced flanges at either end, but the T-shaped element is now usually confined to the exterior and various sorts of external or internal riveted struts or stays may be added. The rim may be decorated with corrugations and repoussé dots. The fragment of the third cauldron from the Dowris hoard is a part of a rim with repoussé ornament. Conical-headed rivets sometimes occur and are occasionally purely decorative; these are believed to have been inspired by north German and south Scandinavian fashion and are also found on some of the bronze horns of the period. There is some greater elaboration of handle rings, which may be fluted or ribbed. A small number of vessels have staples (of half-tube form with a base and with quite pronounced flanges) that were cast separately and then affixed to the neck by various means, including riveting. A cauldron found at a depth of some 3m in a bog at Lisdrumturk, Co. Monaghan, has a body basically made from three large sheets of bronze, a lower saucer-shaped piece with two broad sheets above, but the upper body and rim is formed of two further pieces and also bears several triangular attachments (Fig. 7.6, 1). All are riveted together with flat-headed and conical-headed rivets. Most of the vertical seams of rivets are decorative. The ribbed and flanged staples with faceted ring handles are cast on, and a number of patches on the interior are ancient repairs. An intriguing feature of this cauldron is the presence of what seem to be iron rivets. A dozen or so have been noted on different parts of the vessel. As we shall see, there is some evidence for the use of iron in Ireland in the seventh century BC. Some of the iron rivets may be repairs or replacements but some may be original and may imply that the cauldron was made around this time. A second good example of a class B cauldron was found in a bog at Castlederg, Co. Tyrone, and is also made of multiple bronze sheets and bears conical rivets, a large number of which form purely decorative seams, some with a reinforcing bronze strip on the interior. The handle rings are of octagonal cross-section (Fig. 7.6, 2).

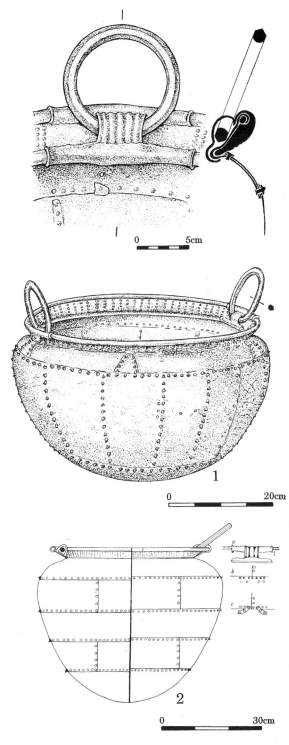

Fig. 7.6—Class B cauldrons. (1) Lisdrumturk, Co. Monaghan, with detail of cast-on staple and ring handle. (2) Castlederg, Co. Tyrone.

Cauldrons of plenty?

A number of writers have speculated on the purpose of these large bronze vessels and have been particularly struck by references to the special significance of cauldrons and their role in feasting in medieval Irish and Welsh literature (Green 1998). It has been claimed that there is some evidence that they may have been used as media for commercial barter in ancient times, and legend has it that some cauldrons were magical vessels providing the right amount of food for an assembled company and sometimes miraculously large enough to hold the carcasses of several sheep or hogs. Medieval legend may be an unreliable guide to late prehistoric practice, but David Coombs (1975) noted the magical properties and aristocratic associations of cauldrons in other contexts: 'It is possible to see the cauldron as epitomising the chief and his power. "The main symbol of being powerful is to be wealthy and of wealth is to be generous" sums up the redistributional chiefdoms known from anthropological studies. The giving away of selected portions of food out of the cauldron during certain ceremonies could have symbolized the whole process of the power of the chief to redistribute wealth.'

Bronze cauldrons were valuable objects, as demonstrated by the technical skills required in their manufacture, which demanded a knowledge of complex casting processes as well as beating and riveting. The care with which they were repaired from time to time is a further indication of just how prized they were. It is reasonable to see them as aristocratic possessions that were put to periodic use, and the fact that so many of them seem to have been single deposits in bogs may denote a special ritual significance. Their considerable capacity suggests the boiling of meat and, if primarily cooking vessels, this may have been for ceremonial purposes only. An early cauldron (of Colchester type) found during ploughing of a field at Feltwell Fen, Norfolk, contained a bronze flesh-hook. This is a socketed single hook, a more developed version of the simple double-pronged hook found in the Bishopsland hoard (Fig. 6.7) and at the settlement at Ballinderry, Co. Offaly (below). A famous example found in a bog at Dunaverney, near Ballymoney, Co. Antrim (Fig. 7.7), is decorated with small model swans and ravens and must have been a very prestigious piece indeed (Bowman and Needham

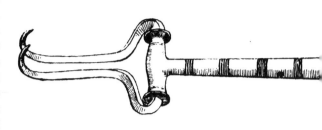

2007). These different types of bronze hooks, as the name 'flesh-hook' implies, are believed to have been used to pick pieces of boiled meat out of a vessel or a cooking pit and were an important part of feasting paraphernalia. Whether these cauldrons were set in the ground and their contents heated with hot stones like the contents of a trough at a burnt mound, as has been suggested, remains uncertain. The attention given to neck and handles may imply that suspension was the norm, and of course they could have been used to hold liquids too.

If bronze cauldrons were used to prepare special ceremonial food or drink, they may have been the centre-pieces at ritual meals or at elaborate feasts that were occasions for conspicuous hospitality and social competition conducted by a wealthy élite. The eventual votive deposition of a cauldron in a bog or some other place could have been the ultimate way of breaking an economically exhausting cycle of competitive feasting. What rituals may have accompanied such an event are unknown, but more than metalwork may have been involved on some ceremonial occasions at some bog sites. Ritual locations—like Dowris—may have been demarcated in some way by timber structures or trackways. A crudely carved wooden idol found in a bog at Ralaghan, near Shercock, Co. Cavan, has been radiocarbon-dated to 1096–906 BC (Coles 1998). Carved from yew, this primitive and sexually ambiguous figure (Fig. 7.8) stands just over 1m in height and when discovered it had a basal tenon that was inserted into a square block of wood, which was not preserved. It is conceivable that it had once formed part of some larger structure,

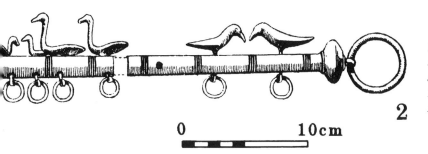

Fig. 7.7—Bronze flesh-hook decorated with small model swans and ravens found in a bog at Dunaverney, near Ballymoney, Co. Antrim.

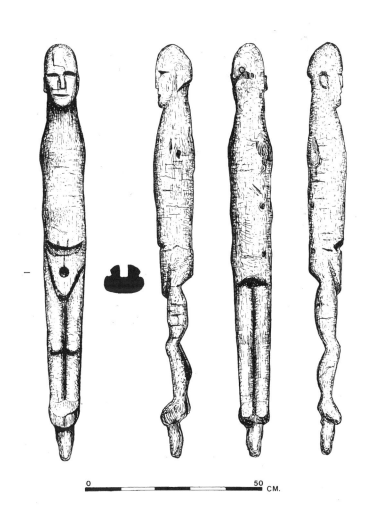

Fig. 7.8—Wooden idol from a bog at Ralaghan, Co. Cavan.

perhaps a shrine. The Bog of Cullen, Co. Tipperary (below), which produced an enormous quantity of gold and bronze objects over a number of years in the eighteenth century, also yielded—at the same time as a bronze sword was found—a 'fragment which was said to be part of an image . . . of black wood entirely covered and plated with thin gold'. Also found was 'another fragment of the same kind of wood', which contained some golden studs or rivets (which could have been bronze) and which was described as 'of an human form . . . of sufficient size to make a gate-post, to which use it was applied'. Unfortunately, it did not survive this treatment (Waddell 2005b). The Ralaghan figure is just one of two obviously anthropomorphic wooden figures recovered to date; another, radiocarbon-dated to about 2000 BC, comes from a medieval crannog at Lagore, Co. Meath, and, if not made of old wood, may be genuine. A small group of roughly carved wooden pieces with knobbed terminals and of various dates are much less explicitly representational (Stanley 2007).

Horns

It is probably not surprising that fine metalwork, like sheet-bronze vessels, should be associated with status and ceremony, and the same appears to be true of a remarkable series of cast-bronze horns or trumpets which were a particularly Irish development (Coles 1963; 1967). The Dowris hoard contained at least 26 examples, a few represented by parts of fragments; it is the largest assemblage of these objects found and it contained examples of the two principal forms, those blown through an aperture on one side and those blown through a mouthpiece at one end (Fig. 7.1, 16–17). Over 120 horns have been recorded and over 90 of these are extant.

These objects were recognised as wind instruments in the nineteenth century, a development which may have produced Ireland's first (and only) martyr to archaeology. An antiquarian, Dr Robert Ball of Dublin, demonstrated that these could be blown as musical instruments and he produced 'a deep bass note, resembling the bellowing of a bull'. Sadly, 'it is a melancholy fact, that the loss of this gentleman's life was occasioned by a subsequent experiment of the same kind. In the act of attempting to produce a distinct sound on a large trumpet . . . he burst a

blood-vessel, and died . . .'. The most detailed study of these horns is that by John Coles, who happily survived to produce a comprehensive report.

The horns were cast in two-piece moulds formed of two outer clay halves and a clay core: the technology was complex and inventive. Presumably wooden models or actual cow horns were used to form the moulds because some pairs of horns exist and suggest the production of identical castings. No clay mould fragments have yet been found.

A summary of Coles's classification is a convenient way of describing the basic features of these instruments; he divided the horns into two classes, each class containing end-blow and side-blow examples (Fig. 7.9). Class I end-blow horns are slender curving horns with both the bell (or wider) end and body either plain or simply decorated with ribs, grooves, bosses, or small spikes like conical rivets. The characteristic feature is a tubular piece at the narrow end, designed to fit inside a short tube that usually formed the mouthpiece. Most of these short tubes are removable but a few are cast on. The latter horns, those with the cast-on mouth-tube, are the longest examples known, measuring almost 1m in length. Side-blow horns in this class may also be plain or decorated in a similar simple fashion. Their closed end is either flat or knobbed and most have one or two loops. All class I horns have at least one loop and are generally smaller than class II.

Class II end-blow horns are characteristically decorated with large cast conical spikes at the bell end and often have perforations as well; they have a narrow tubular end, often with four holes, enclosing (rather than fitting inside) the tubular straight piece, which has a narrow inserting collar at either end each with four holes. These perforations may have served to lock the horn and tube, and sometimes a mouthpiece (none of which survive), together. The tube is decorated with ribs and conical spikes and has a loop and ring. The perforations at the bell end may have been used to fasten an extension. The same is true of the side-blow horns; they too have plain bodies and the mouth usually has conical spikes and, sometimes, four perforations. The closed end is shaped like a stepped cone with a loop and ring. Another ring occurs on the body between the end and the mouth-hole.

This classification confirmed an interesting twofold fashion in horn design and an equally

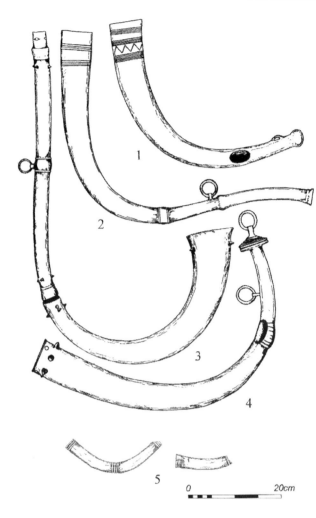

Fig. 7.9—Bronze horns. (1) Class I, side-blow: no provenance. (2) Class I, end-blow: Drumbest, Co. Antrim. (3) Class II, end-blow: Clogherclemin, Co. Kerry. (4) Class II, side-blow: Derrynane, Co. Kerry. (5) Two tubular pieces from one or more Irish trumpets found in the River Loire, near Orléans, in the nineteenth century.

distinctively Irish type: only two finds are recorded in Britain, a class I end-blow from Battle in Sussex in south-eastern England and a fragment of a side-blow horn from Innermessan, Wigtownshire. In France, two tubular pieces (Fig. 7.9, 5) were recovered from the River Loire, near Orléans, in the 1870s; destroyed in a fire in a museum in Orléans in 1940, casts are preserved (Clodoré and LeClerc 2002).

They are rarely associated with other types of bronze objects. Apart from the Dowris hoard, the only other associated find of this kind is a small hoard of bronzes from a bog at Boolybrien, south-west of Ennis, Co. Clare, which contained a class I end-blow horn, a hilt fragment of a sword, two socketed axeheads, a sunflower pin, a chain and several rings. But in about eleven instances horns have been simply deposited with other horns. This is a curious exclusivity, even more so when it is remembered that there is a noteworthy number of finds of large numbers of horns. Unfortunately details are scanty, but these finds include, for example, four horns found in a bog at Drumbest, Co. Antrim, in 1840; six found near Chute Hall, near Tralee, Co. Kerry, thought, when discovered in the course of turf-cutting, to be parts of 'an ancient

divergent distribution (Fig. 7.10) that later proved to be part of two major regional schools of both bronze- and gold-working in the Dowris phase. Class I end- and side-blow horns have a northern distribution, while class II examples are a distinctly south-western phenomenon. The Dowris hoard is one instance where the two classes overlap. Indeed, over half of the number of known class I horns are from Dowris. The only other northern horn found in the midlands was found at Griffinrath, near Maynooth, Co. Kildare, in 1725. These horns are a

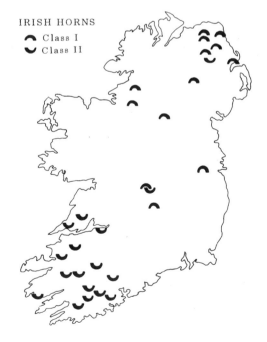

IRISH HORNS
Class I
Class II

Fig. 7.10—General distribution of bronze horns in Ireland.

distilling apparatus'; eight ('four of one make, four of another') from near Dungannon, Co. Tyrone; and thirteen or fourteen found in a bog between Cork and Mallow around 1750. There are several pairs of more or less identical horns: the two side-blow and two end-blow horns from Drumbest may be the best examples. Coles has also suggested that the two side-blow horns from this hoard and two other finds may be, in either case, products of the same moulds. Finds of two horns, from a bog at Drunkendult, north of Ballymoney, Co. Antrim, and from Macroom, Co. Cork, where each find contained one end-blow and one side-blow, might indicate that on some occasions these two forms may have been played together.

Nineteenth-century writers sometimes referred to these horns as war trumpets and believed that they could have been cast away in the haste of retreat by war parties. Today the contexts in which they have been found and the nature of the horns themselves, including their musical capabilities and the occasional pairing, suggest to most writers that they were ceremonial pieces.

In 1963 John Coles thought that side-blow horns were effectively one-note instruments and that the end-blow examples—judging from the two examples with cast-on mouth-tubes which can be considered proper mouthpieces—were capable of producing four or five notes at most, and possibly yielded only two notes with any clarity. Experimentation has since shown, however, that trying to blow these like modern instruments, and attempting the impossible in trying to achieve melodic higher notes, may not be the best way to proceed. Different blowing techniques may have been used. If played like the Australian didjeridoo, with lips given greater freedom of movement, considerable variation is possible in both pitch and tone-colour and much greater harmonic and rhythmic variety is possible. Modern replicas of both a Drumbest end-blow and side-blow horn together, and original horns from Drunkendult, Chute Hall and elsewhere, have produced impressive rhythmic effects (O'Dwyer 2004).

The horns were an indigenous development and were essentially translations into bronze of the simple curving cattle horn. Some very different bronze horns in northern Europe are unconnected: the production of metal versions of animal horns presumably occurred in those areas where casting techniques were sufficiently advanced.

Bulls and rattles?

The Dowris hoard included a collection of bronze pendants (Fig. 7.1, 14–15), and it has been argued that these objects and the horns were part of a wider European bull cult in the last millennium BC (Coles 1965). This suggestion was prompted in part by the fact that horned helmets or other horned head-dresses are recorded from Iberia to northern Europe (though not in Ireland) in bronze or in rock art and by the belief, at the time, that Irish horns produced a very limited range of bull-like sounds and could, of course, be representations in bronze of a bull's horn.

A further element in this argument was the pendant. These hollow-cast bronze objects are unusual and puzzling artefacts. They have been called crotals, an antiquarian term adapted from the Latin *crotalum* (rattle), are somewhat pear-shaped and often contain a loose piece of bronze or perhaps stone. The largest number (48) come from the Dowris hoard itself and, surprisingly, only two seem to have been found elsewhere. One was reportedly found in the ditch of a fort at Calheme, east of Ballymoney, Co. Antrim, and the other has no recorded provenance. They vary slightly in shape and size, and are usually about 12cm long with twelve or fourteen grooves on the upper part, with a suspension loop and ring above. Since they were meant to be suspended, one commentator thought that they might have formed a sort of musical glockenspiel struck in scalar sequence with a hammer. According to Coles they are heavy objects, weighing about 270g, and are thus unlikely to have been attached to clothing. He was struck by a resemblance between these supposed rattles and the scrotum of a bull, and it was this that inspired his suggestion of a cult with bull-horn and rattle, the latter being the 'outward sign of the virility of the beast'. He does note that the rattling sound produced is very faint, and indeed it has been claimed that this is accidental, being caused by nothing more than bits of loose metal. It does seem likely that the horns were used for musical rituals, and indeed a combination of end-blow and side-blow may have been employed, but any association with 'rattles' rests solely on the Dowris evidence and remains uncertain. The purpose of the so-called rattles is equally unclear and for that reason the term pendant is employed here. The suggestion that they bedecked the necks of prize cattle in parade has as much, if not more, to recommend it at present. Judgement both on a bull cult and on rattles is best suspended.

WEAPONRY

The Bishopsland phase saw the development of the earliest Irish swords of Ballintober type by about the thirteenth century BC, and ensuing developments in sword production and in other forms of weaponry give a distinctly warlike cast to a large section of the corpus of metalwork of later prehistory, particularly in the Dowris phase.

Swords and chapes
The flange-hilted leaf-shaped sword has generally been considered an important improvement in sword-making: the manufacturing of a broad hilt with flanges (to take a riveted haft of bone or some other organic material) cast in one piece with the blade was a major step. This combination of improved hafting mechanism and blade form produced a much more effective slashing and cutting bronze weapon which remained in use, with relatively minor changes, for over half a millennium.

The earliest flange-hilted leaf-shaped swords in Britain are concentrated in south-eastern England, notably in the Thames valley, where, after the introduction of different types from the Continent, native forms emerged. These early swords include imported or local copies of swords of Hemigkofen type, with short, wide leaf-shaped blades and high-flanged terminals with short projecting wings and poorly formed rivet holes. Erbenheim-type swords are similar but the flanged hilt has curving sides (and a distinctive small projection to support a pommel) and blades are of long, slender leaf shape. A well-formed ricasso is

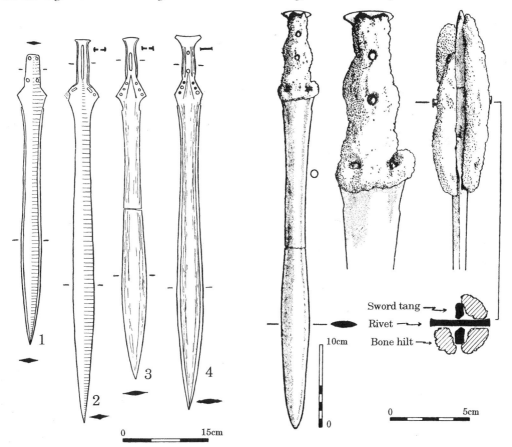

Fig. 7.11—Bronze swords of classes 1–4 and (on right) a class 4 sword with antler hilt plate from Mullyleggan, Co. Armagh.

absent in both types. Local versions with minor variations exist. Swords with convex (or U-shaped) shoulders—instead of the usual Erbenheim straight shoulder—represent a later British development, as do short heavy swords with straight (V-shaped) shoulders, considered to have developed from Hemigkofen swords. Some other early British flange-hilted swords have a curved ricasso and hilt slots.

The only detailed account of Irish bronze swords is Eogan's 1965 classification (Fig. 7.11), which requires revision. His class 1 is the Ballintober sword type already described (Chapter 6). His class 2 contains versions of the British Erbenheim-derived swords, and his class 3 swords are versions of Hemigkofen-derived forms. Eogan's class 4 contains over 400 flange-hilted leaf-shaped swords that evidently demand further study. These are the Irish counterparts of the equally numerous British Ewart Park type (named after a Northumberland find) and, though a significant number of Irish examples are fairly short weapons, they share a series of basic features, including hilts that are generally slightly convex-sided (sometimes lacking flanges) with expanded straight or flat terminals and steep straight shoulders usually with a straight (or sometimes slightly concave) ricasso. Slots are rare, a variable rivet pattern being preferred; blades usually have a gently rounded mid-section flanked by a slight concavity and then slightly bevelled cutting edges. One example, just over 50cm long, found at Mullyleggan, near Loughgall, Co. Armagh, has part of its deer antler hilt plate still attached (Fig. 7.11). No scabbards have been found, but bronze chapes of slender elongated form and lozenge-shaped section and small purse-shaped chapes are known. One of the latter type was found in the Dowris hoard (Fig. 7.1, 5). Swords of Eogan's classes 5 and 6 are described in Chapter 8.

The relatively short size of some Irish swords is surprising; given the technological skills of the bronzesmiths, longer weapons could surely have been made if required. Judging by the measurements given in Eogan's corpus, they range in overall length from just over 40cm to a little over 60cm, the average being 52.7cm. Only some 22% are 60cm or more in length. The smallest comes from Knocknalappa, Co. Clare, with a length of 40.5cm, while the longest, at 66.5cm, is said to have

been found with four other swords in County Tyrone. While the leaf-shaped sword may denote a change in fighting methods, from stabbing and thrusting in rapier-like fashion to cutting and slashing, the depositional pattern of the swords remains the same, the greater number coming from rivers, lakes and bogs. A significant number of hoards of the Dowris phase also come from bogs and, in contrast to the Bishopsland phase, 26% of them contain weapons (Cooney and Grogan 1999).

A small number of weapon hoards are known, mostly containing just two or three objects. Eogan has noted fourteen finds: seven of swords alone, four of swords and spears, one of a sword, spear and axehead, and two containing sword fragments and other items including spears, axeheads and several tools. The association of sword and spear reflects the popularity of these weapon types at the time (Fig. 7.12) and is a common enough association in Britain. One might speculate that a small hoard of such weapons could be the grateful votive offering of a happy warrior, but this was not always, if ever, the case. One hoard, from Ballycroghan, near Bangor, Co. Down, may have been deposited near the site of a former wetland settlement by a bronzesmith: it consisted of three swords cast in moulds from the same model and in various stages of completion, one a raw casting straight from the mould with unperforated dimples instead of rivet holes.

The association of a weapon such as a sword or spear and a socketed axehead, as at Blackhills, Co. Laois, is rare but does raise the question of whether some socketed axes were used as weapons too. The sword, however, was evidently a weapon related to high status across a wide area of Europe. As Anthony Harding (2000) indicates, its role was partly symbolic as an expression of warrior prowess, but it had a real role in combat too. A number of Irish swords show evidence of use; over 90% of a sample of swords examined displayed edge damage, assumed to be the result of direct impact in combat (Bridgford 1997). Interestingly enough, a high proportion of swords found in rivers had little or no damage, implying a selection process for this form of ritual deposition.

Spears

Different types of spear were fashionable; the Tempo discovery and the find from Kish, near Arklow, Co.

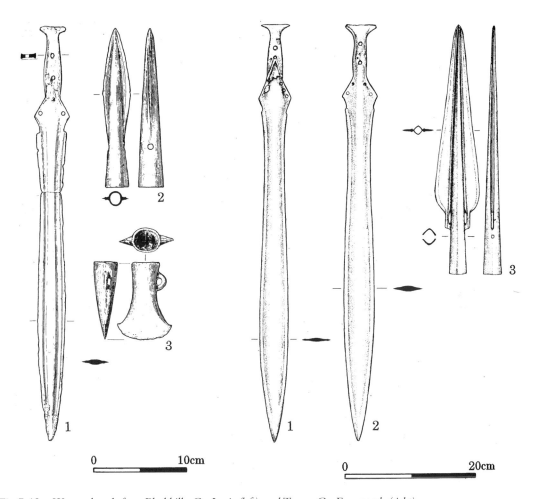

Fig. 7.12—Weapon hoards from Blackhills, Co. Laois (left), and Tempo, Co. Fermanagh (right).

Wicklow, and the possible association at Knockanbaun, south of Easky, Co. Sligo, demonstrate that the basal-looped type continued in use in the Dowris phase. The Knockanbaun find, with a length of 46cm, was probably a parade weapon. Also current were spears with lunate openings in the blade—undoubtedly related to the protected-loop form (Fig. 6.3, 3); a good example occurs in the Dowris hoard (Fig. 7.1, 6). Found in both Ireland and Britain (Ehrenberg 1977), this is a distinctively Irish and British type. Some are elegantly ribbed and some are exceptionally long; that from Dowris is almost 35cm in length. There are others that exceed this figure, such as an unprovenanced example from Ireland with gold band decoration on its socket (Fig. 7.13, 5); it would have been an unwieldy thrusting weapon and was obviously intended more for display than for combat. One example, a casual find in a gravel pit near Ballinasloe, Co. Galway, has an additional detail in the form of small decorative perforations above and below the lunate openings, perhaps an attempt to individualise the object (Fig. 7.13, 1). This is a very rare feature and bears a remarkable resemblance to a spear found in the great tenth-century ritual deposit of bronzes at Huelva in south-western Spain (Fig. 7.13, 2; Ruiz-Gálvez Priego 1995). A related spear with five small perforations around the pair of lunate openings was found with a bronze sword at Denhead near St Andrews in eastern Scotland. All three are a good demonstration of how idiosyncratic weapon fashions were transmitted and copied over large distances.

Many spearheads of the simple leaf-shaped type, whether long or short, were probably more

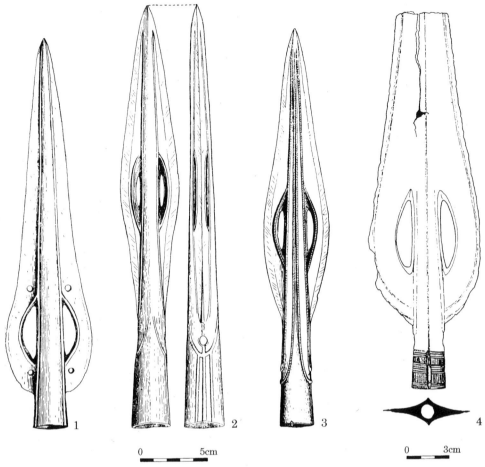

Fig. 7.13—Spearheads with lunate openings in the blade. (1) Near Ballinasloe, Co. Galway. (2) Example from the Huelva deposit in south-western Spain. (3) Unprovenanced from Ireland. (4) River Shannon. (5) Unprovenanced from Ireland with gold band decoration on the socket.

functional weapons. This type, also with peg or rivet holes in the socket to attach it to a wooden haft, is a very widespread form and may have been introduced into Britain from the Continent in the thirteenth century BC. It is well represented in the Dowris hoard, which contained 35 examples (Fig. 7.1, 7), and there is one in the Blackhills hoard as well (Fig. 7.12). Some very small examples are known: one 4cm in length was found at Navan, Co. Armagh, but many are 15–25cm in length and longer ones, though rare, are recorded. One splendid example found near Belturbet, Co. Cavan, is 53.6cm long. This, like a leaf-shaped spearhead with gold band ornament on its socket from Lough Gur, Co. Limerick, which is 41.7cm long, was probably intended primarily for display (Coles 1971).

Shields

A small number of circular shields of various materials have been found (Raftery 1982). The development of a defensive device like a shield is probably one telling indication that many of the swords and spears we have been considering were sometimes put to effective use, and the basic equipment of a warrior may have consisted of sword, spear and shield. Ireland has provided some remarkable evidence for the use of leather shields, and these are reminders that leather helmets and body armour may have been worn as well and that, across continental Europe, the bronze helmets, shields and breastplates (Fig. 7.18, 3) found there were exceptional and had more functional leather counterparts. Evidence for organic shields includes decorative metal fitments for a leather cuirasse from a warrior burial at Hagenau, Kr Regensburg (Demakopoulou *et al.* 1999) and from a rich grave at Milavče, Bohemia (Kytlicová 1991). It is surprising that so little prehistoric leather has survived even in anaerobic wetland conditions, but this may be because hides and skins were smoke-dried with a fatty agent applied to keep the skin soft and pliable; since this process was not irreversible, hides treated in this fashion would not be preserved in waterlogged conditions (Groenman-van Waateringe *et al.* 1999).

A unique leather shield was found during turf-cutting in 1908 at Cloonbrin, near Abbeyshrule, Co. Longford. It is made of a piece of leather about 50cm in original diameter and 5–6mm thick. It has a hollow, oval central boss capped externally with another sewn-on leather piece and inside the boss is a leather handle. Decoration consists of a raised penannular rib around the boss and two other concentric ribs, each with a V-shaped indentation or notch (on the same axis as the handle); between the ribs are four sets of three bosses (Fig. 7.14, 1). When found it was assumed to be a quite ineffective object, but John Coles (1962) has shown, by experiment, that soaking a suitable piece of leather in cold water, repeatedly hammering it with wooden punches, pressing it with weights on a mould over a period of several days, and finally impregnating it with wax produces a very hard and inflexible shield which is both capable of withstanding heavy blows with a sword and is impervious to water.

Two wooden moulds for the production of leather shields are known, both apparently made from circular slabs of wood cut from the trunk of a tree but now badly shrunk. One comes from Churchfield, Co. Mayo (Fig. 7.14, 2), the other from Kilmahamogue, near Ballycastle, Co. Antrim. Both have central depressions (to produce a central boss) surrounded by deeply grooved circles with V-shaped notches. The Kilmahamogue mould has produced the surprisingly early—but not impossible—radiocarbon date of 1950–1540 BC (Hedges *et al.* 1991). Protective leather goods may have had very early beginnings.

It is an intriguing fact that shields with V-shaped notches have only been recorded in Ireland (in organic form) and in western Iberia (in stone), where a series of engravings on stone slabs depict,

in a schematic fashion, a range of objects including shields, swords, spears and the occasional human figure, representing a warrior and his equipment. The decorated slab from Brozas, Cáceres, in western Spain (Fig. 7.14, 4) bears a shield (with handle on the same axis as the notches) that is very similar to the Cloonbrin shield. Here and on other carved slabs the trappings of a warrior may include sword, spear, shield, helmet, chariot, mirror and large ear ornaments, and the absence of the bow and arrow reinforces an impression of an ethos of close-quarter combat (Harrison 2004). As Marion Uckelmann (2008) has pointed out, the dates for these Iberian stelae might indicate a date as early as the twelfth or thirteenth century BC for Cloonbrin; even more significantly, she has identified the widespread employment of a readily identifiable decorative motif. The presence of three ribs, a penannular motif set within two concentric circles each with a V-shaped (or U-shaped) notch, is found not just in Ireland and Iberia but also repeated on bronze shields in central and northern Europe and would appear to be a potent symbol with warrior associations.

Two curious wooden shields carved from slabs cut from tree trunks are also preserved. One find from Annadale, south-east of Drumshanbo, Co. Leitrim, was found 3m deep in a bog; it shrank as it dried and now measures 66cm by 52cm but originally may have been nearly circular and about 10cm thick. A handle has been cut out of the alder wood behind a raised central boss. Decoration on the front consists of seven very narrow concentric ribs, which are purely ornamental; six have shallow U-shaped notches. A second, also of alder, from Cloonlara, near Swinford, Co. Mayo, is slightly smaller but has quite a high central boss with cut-out handle behind (Fig. 7.14, 3). Four narrow ribs each have shallow U-shaped notches, and on both shields the handle axis is at a right angle to the notches. The Cloonlara object has been radiocarbon-dated to about 1200 BC (Hedges *et al.* 1993). These wooden shields could have been functional, they could even have been leather-covered, but equally they may have been votive models made for ritual deposition. Bronze ribbed shields with that puzzling warrior symbol (but with U-shaped notches) are known in central and northern Europe, where they are named after a find from Herzprung in northern Germany.

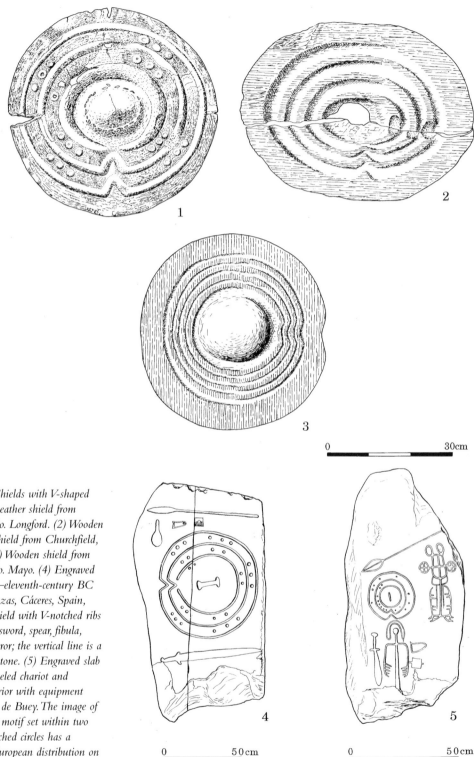

Fig. 7.14—Shields with V-shaped notches. (1) Leather shield from Cloonbrin, Co. Longford. (2) Wooden mould for a shield from Churchfield, Co. Mayo. (3) Wooden shield from Cloonlara, Co. Mayo. (4) Engraved slab of twelfth–eleventh-century BC date from Brozas, Cáceres, Spain, depicting a shield with V-notched ribs and bosses, a sword, spear, fibula, comb and mirror; the vertical line is a break in the stone. (5) Engraved slab with two-wheeled chariot and helmeted warrior with equipment from Cabeza de Buey. The image of a penannular motif set within two concentric notched circles has a widespread European distribution on bronze shields and was a potent symbol with warrior associations.

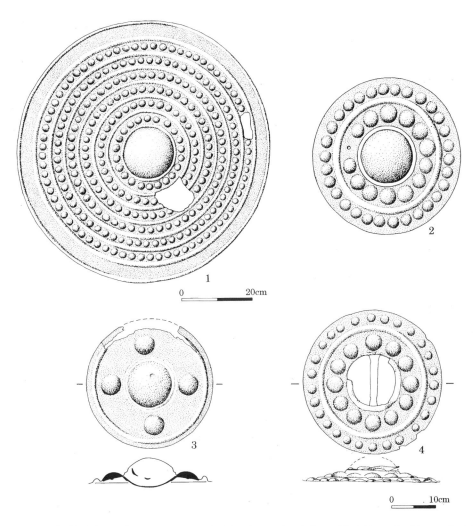

Fig. 7.15—Bronze shields. (1) Lough Gur, Co. Limerick. (2) Athenry, Co. Galway. (3) Athlone, Co. Westmeath. (4) Lough Gara, Co. Sligo.

The surviving bronze shields from Ireland find their closest analogies in Britain. One type of bronze shield, the Yetholm type, named after a Scottish find, is well represented in Britain. Generally of large size (averaging 60cm in diameter), they are characteristically decorated with concentric ribs and rows of small bosses, as on a well-known example from Lough Gur, Co. Limerick. This superb sheet-bronze object was found in a bog near Lough Gur and may have been wrapped in a textile when deposited (Fig. 7.15, 1). It has a diameter of 71.3cm and bears multiple repoussé ribs and bosses; on the back there is a riveted handle and a pair of perforated bronze tabs for a suspension strap, presumably to allow the shield to be slung from the shoulder. A second bronze shield, said to have been found in County Antrim, is similar, with a diameter of 66cm. A third, also decorated with ribs and bosses, was found in the River Shannon near Athlone in 1987 (Demakopoulou *et al.* 1999).

Three other circular bronze shields (Fig. 7.15, 2–4) are of very different form. They are quite small, from 27cm to 35.5cm in diameter, and have only one or two raised ribs and one or two sets of large bosses around a prominent central boss. One, with two rings of bosses, was found near Athenry, Co. Galway, with a large spearhead (now lost), and another similar shield was found on the shores of Lough Gara, Co. Sligo. The third, recovered from generally considered to be prestigious items for ceremonial purposes. Experimentation has confirmed their non-utilitarian nature: using a modern copper replica of comparable thickness and hardness revealed that the point of a leaf-shaped bronze sword could easily penetrate the metal and that a slashing blow could cut completely through the shield. The bronze shields, along with some other exceptional bronze weapons, may indicate the existence not just of a hierarchical society whose élite had sufficient wealth and patronage to commission the finest craftsmanship and follow the latest fashion but also of one dominated by a warrior aristocracy preoccupied as much with flamboyant display as with warlike activity.

GOLD

The finest goldwork of the Dowris phase is a good illustration of a propensity for spectacular exhibitionism, and three objects in particular are excellent examples of this: a group of sheet-gold objects called gorgets, generally believed to be neck ornaments or pectorals (Fig. 7.18), lock-rings and dress-fasteners (Eogan 1994). The greatest number of prehistoric gold objects date from this period, and a number of types, particularly made of sheet gold, are uniquely Irish.

The gorgets are impressive ornaments, and six more or less complete examples and one fragmentary find are preserved and provenanced; five others are recorded and have uncertain provenances, and as many as four may have been present in the large assemblage of objects found at Cullen, Co. Tipperary. They basically consist of a broad crescentic collar of beaten sheet gold with elaborate decoration (Fig. 7.16). A series of concentric semicircular ribs in high relief usually have narrow rows of rope moulding between them, produced by a combination of repoussé and chasing techniques. The edges of some collars are reinforced by wrapping them around gold wire. The circular terminals are double discs attached to one another by lapping the edges of the larger back disc around the edge of the front disc; these terminals are usually stitched to the collar with gold wire, and the uppermost discs are decorated with finely stamped concentric circles, round or conical bosses and raised herringbone or rope patterns. There is some

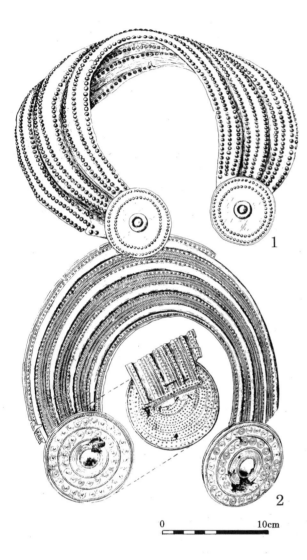

Fig. 7.16—Gold gorgets. (1) County Clare. (2) Borrisnoe, Co. Tipperary.

the River Shannon at Athlone in 1981, has a stepped central boss encircled by four bosses and one rib; the bosses are, in fact, large domed rivet heads. The four rivets secure a handle and two suspension tabs on the back. Features such as size, stepped boss and domed rivets indicate some relationship to Continental Nipperwiese shields, which also inspired a small number of British bronze shields (Needham 1979b).

Bronze shields, whether small or large, are

evidence that gorgets may have been worn: a small perforation on either side of the inside upper edge probably held a cord or light chain for suspension. One from a bog at Borrisnoe, Co. Tipperary, has one link of a gold chain in one of these holes. Details of discovery are usually scanty; examples from Ardcrony, near Nenagh, Co. Tipperary, and from Shannongrove, near Pallaskenry, Co. Limerick, were each found in a bog.

A well-preserved example was found in 1932 in a rock fissure at Gleninsheen, in the Burren, Co. Clare; it measures 31.4cm across and is decorated with characteristic ribbing, which includes seven plain ribs with intervening rows of triple rope mouldings produced by working the gold from the front. The terminals bear a large central conical boss

within concentric circles surrounded by a pattern of similar boss and circle ornament. It has been described as one of the finest achievements of the goldsmiths of the period.

The only associations occur in a hoard of gold ornaments found at Gorteenreagh, Co. Clare. This hoard was found beneath a large slab just below the surface in a field south-west of Feakle and comprised six gold objects, a gorget, two lock-rings, two bracelets and a plain dress-fastener. The gorget is an unusual piece (Fig. 7.17) in so far as the collar is composed of three broad ribs with lines of punched dots between them. Though of stout sheet gold, its edges are also strengthened by wrapping them around a gold wire. The terminals bear the familiar conical boss and concentric circle

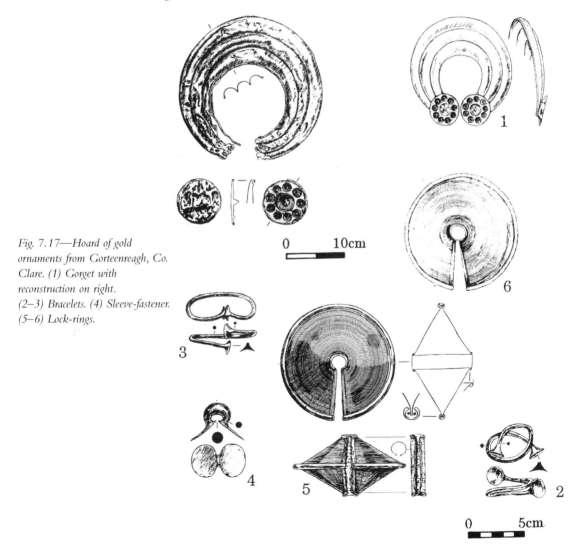

Fig. 7.17—Hoard of gold ornaments from Gorteenreagh, Co. Clare. (1) Gorget with reconstruction on right. (2–3) Bracelets. (4) Sleeve-fastener. (5–6) Lock-rings.

0   10cm

0   5cm

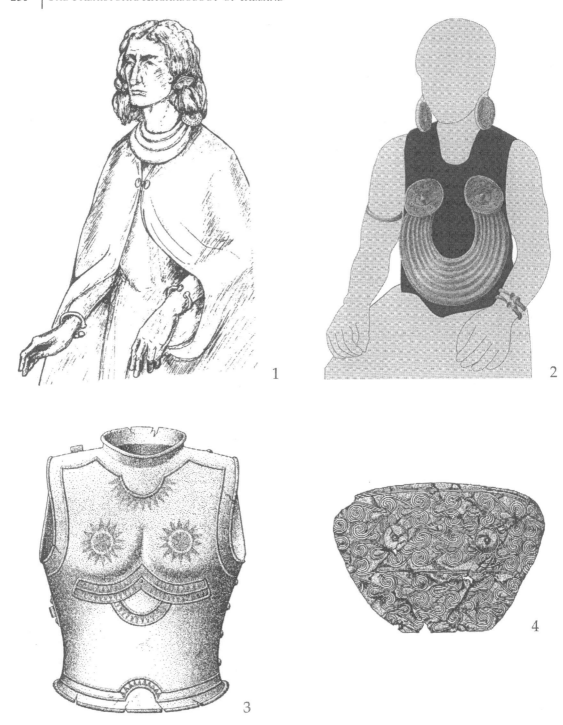

Fig. 7.18—(1) Suggested manner of use of the Gorteenreagh gold ornaments with the gorget worn as a collar; the gender of the figure, who is also wearing bracelets, a dress-fastener and lock-rings, is suitably ambiguous. (2) Alternative representation of gorget use, with the object displayed as suspended low on the chest as a pectoral ornament; the wearer is also sporting ear-spools, an armlet and bracelets. (3) Bronze cuirasse from Saint-Germain-du-Plain (Saône-et-Loire). (4) Gold breastplate from grave circle A at Mycenae. The emphasis given to the male breast is noteworthy.

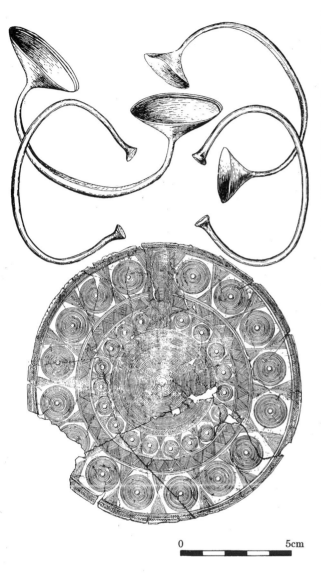

of personal ornaments. The gorget may have been ritually mutilated before being placed in the ground, but it has also been suggested that this damage might hint at violence and plunder.

The distribution of gorgets is quite confined: they have been found mainly in counties Clare, Limerick and Tipperary and form one element in a remarkable regional industry which includes other gold objects such as lock-rings, bowls and other collars and some of the largest gold hoards ever found (Fig. 7.21). Sheet gold seems to have been particularly popular here.

Gorget origins are disputed. General shape and the concentric circle decoration in particular have suggested north European inspiration, and George Eogan sees other objects, such as certain types of pin (including sunflower pins), U-notched shields and amber, as further evidence of Nordic influence. For Joan Taylor (1980), however, this influence is a myth. Mary Cahill (2005) has suggested that the gorget could be an item of warrior adornment and has drawn attention to the remarkable parallels between the arrangement of their discs and ribbed collars and the representation of male breasts and ribs on some Continental bronze cuirasses and on a celebrated gold breastplate from a grave at Mycenae. Thus they may have been worn not on the neck but lower down on the chest as decorative pectorals (Fig. 7.18). Since there were probably many less prestigious pieces of body armour made from studded leather, as that Bohemian leather cuirasse reminds us, parallels between the broad ribs of a gorget found somewhere in County Clare (Fig. 7.16) that resemble the stiff folds of a leather collar (like a horse collar) may be relevant too.

Dress-fasteners and lock-rings

The term 'dress-fastener' has been used to describe a series of puzzling penannular gold objects with large terminals of various sorts that are assumed, on no certain evidence, to have served as garment-fasteners. They appear to be exaggerated versions of simpler gold bracelets with expanded terminals (Fig. 7.19). Small examples, like that from the Gorteenreagh hoard (depicted as a cloak-fastener: Fig. 7.18), have been called sleeve-fasteners or cuff-fasteners and have been studied by Eogan (1972), who does allude to the fact that the discovery of just one in such a hoard does not help in determining

Fig. 7.19—Armstrong's (1933) illustration of a gold hoard of two dress-fasteners, two bracelets and a disc from Lattoon, Co. Cavan.

decoration and were apparently deliberately torn from the collar before deposition. The bracelets are penannular with expanded cup-shaped terminals; one is of circular and the other of lozenge-shaped cross-section. The dress-fastener and the two lock-rings are gold types that will be considered below. With the possible exception of the bracelets, the way in which all the objects were actually worn is uncertain; nonetheless, the hoard seems to be a set

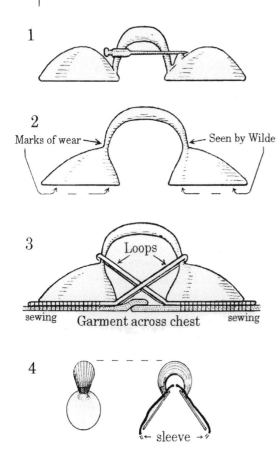

Fig. 7.20—An illustration depicting the possible method of attachment of a gold dress-fastener (2 and 3) and the prototypical Nordic bronze fibula (1). The method of attachment of a sleeve-fastener (4) is also shown.

function. These are small, hoop-shaped objects, some of which may be hollow, others cast. They invariably have elegantly grooved bows and a narrow zone of engraved lattice ornament between the bow and the terminals, which are expanded and often disc-shaped. The terminals may be cast in one piece with the bow and then expanded by hammering, or they may be soldered on; decoration on the terminals is rare, occurring on only a few examples. A number of examples without terminals exist and these have been called 'striated rings'.

Various writers have accepted that sleeve-fasteners could indeed have served as a garment-fastener, in cuff-link style, the discs being slipped through eyelets in the clothing (Fig. 7.20), but the space between the terminals of some is so narrow that only the thinnest clothing could pass through

it. It is possible that they could have been worn in some other way, perhaps as ornamental ear weights (Cahill 2004b). Over 80 of them are known and the type seems to be an Irish fashion (Fig. 7.22), being a smaller version of the large dress-fastener, which has a wider distribution.

The larger penannular dress-fasteners, or cup-ended ornaments as they have also been called, are no less puzzling (Cahill 1995; 1998b). A broad hoop of gold, which may be either solid or hollow, ends in prominent concave or cup-shaped terminals (which lie almost horizontally more or less on the same plane—as in Fig. 7.20, 2–3). Decoration occurs on a small number. As already mentioned, there is a general relationship between the simpler examples and penannular bracelets with expanded terminals and both are represented in a small hoard of objects found at a depth of over 3m in a bog at Lattoon, north-east of Ballyjamesduff, Co. Cavan (Fig. 7.19). The dress-fasteners vary in size and Mary Cahill has studied twenty extraordinary examples that are distinguished by their large size and weight (from 311g to 1,353g). Weights obviously depend on whether bows are hollow or solid, and three specimens of solid gold, all weighing over 1,000g, could never have been worn. Presumably of symbolic significance, at the very least they must have represented considerable wealth: the heaviest known is an example found near Dunboyne, Co. Meath, which weighed about 1,353g (over 43oz.) and contained enough gold to make 20–40 lunulae. A well-known example from Clones, Co. Monaghan, which is unusual in that it also has very fine decoration including dot and concentric circle motifs, weighs 1,031.5g.

Some 80 gold examples of dress-fasteners of all sizes (and two bronze specimens) have been recorded from Ireland, and eighteen gold and one bronze from Britain (Fig. 7.22). It is generally claimed that dress-fasteners are an adaptation of a Nordic fashion, being inspired by north European bronze fibulae (formed of separate pin and bow) which have convex disc-shaped terminals (Fig. 7.20, 1), but it has also been argued that the large gold dress-fasteners and the bronze fibulae are each the exaggerated culmination of two independently evolving and unrelated ornament fashions.

As the name and a reconstruction of how the Gorteenreagh ornaments may have been worn suggests (Fig. 7.18), gold lock-rings are believed to

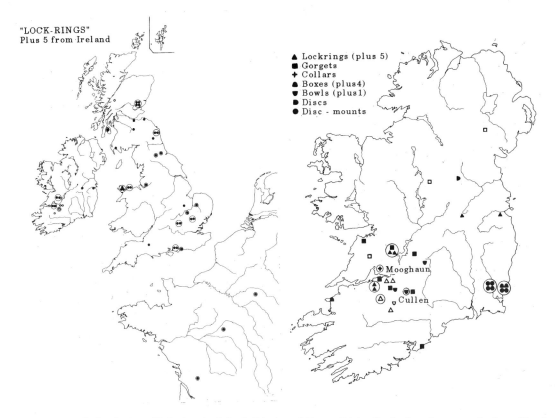

Fig. 7.21—Left: distribution of lock-rings in Ireland, Britain and France. Right: distribution of gorgets and other goldwork.

have been hair ornaments. They have been studied by Eogan (1969), who does note that it has not been established that they were used in this fashion. The only merit of the name 'lock-ring' is that it is a little more convenient than the descriptive 'penannular hollow ornaments of triangular section' used by other writers. Whatever their purpose, they are complicated objects. Two penannular conical plates are held together by a narrow C-shaped binding strip to form a large biconical bead-like piece; a penannular tube, usually of sheet gold, fits in the centre, but triangular side plates (in the gap or slot) rarely survive and may not always have been used. In a small number of cases, including the Gorteenreagh specimens, repoussé bosses occur in the central tube, and it is suggested that these might have helped to hold locks of hair in place. The method of manufacture of the conical plates is their most remarkable feature: in one Irish case these are of sheet gold decorated with light

repoussé ribbing, but in most instances each plate has been constructed of concentric rings of gold wires joined together with an average of about three to the millimetre. This work of extraordinary delicacy is unparalleled and it is a good illustration of specialised craftsmanship in which patronage and wealth are expressed in the creation of exclusive and exceptional objects.

These lock-rings were clearly an Irish–British fashion and the region of the lower Shannon may have been the main centre of production in Ireland (Fig. 7.21), but they are also well represented in north Wales, northern England, Scotland and south-eastern England, with a few known in northern France. Outside of Ireland, conical plates of sheet gold, plain or with engraved ornament, are commoner in Britain, and sheet-gold-covered bronze is found in France. The type does seem to be an insular innovation; prototypes elsewhere are unknown. Eogan would see them as an Irish

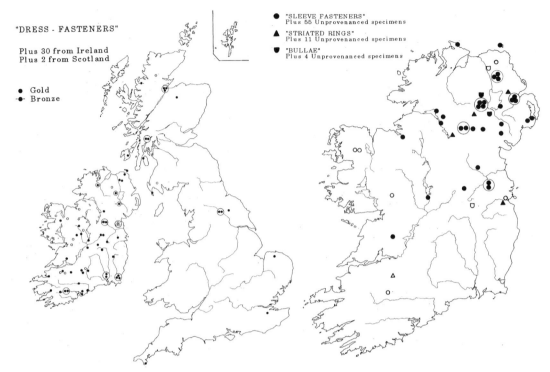

Fig. 7.22—Left: distribution of dress-fasteners. Right: distribution of sleeve-fasteners, bullae, etc.

development but he suggests the possibility of some Mediterranean inspiration—from a part of the world where hair ornaments such as small penannular round-sectioned hair-rings are found.

Hair-rings, ring-money and bullae

Dress-fasteners and lock-rings are not the only puzzling artefacts in the repertoire of the Dowris phase goldsmiths. Even more enigmatic are the unfortunately named ring-money and bullae. For many years the name 'ring-money' has been given to a series of small, thick, penannular gold or gilded rings because it was thought that a series of standard weights could be identified among them. Standard weights have yet to be satisfactorily demonstrated, however. These rings have also been compared to Egyptian hair-rings and there is a striking resemblance, but connections are difficult, if not impossible, to prove. For want of a better name the term 'hair-ring' is now employed (Eogan 1994; 1997), but they could have decorated other parts of the human body or have served as amulets. These little hair-rings are of circular cross-section, about 2.5cm in diameter, and may be of solid gold or may

be composite pieces with cores of copper, tin or lead covered with gold (Fig. 7.23). Some striped examples are solid pieces that have been inlaid with gold with a high silver content and cast using the lost-wax method (Meeks *et al.* 2008). Over 170 have been recorded, the great majority, over 125, from Ireland but some also from Britain, France, Belgium and the Netherlands. This remarkably widespread distribution and their complex and varied manufacturing methods indicate, notwithstanding their small size, that these were very highly prized and sought-after objects. One was found in a pit near the centre of a circular house at Rathgall, Co. Wicklow: it and a small token deposit of burnt human bone had been placed in a layer of carbonised organic material and may have been a foundation deposit.

A small group of larger decorated penannular rings of rounded or oval section appear to be related but are confined to Ireland (Eogan 2008a). They consist of a lead core (or in a few cases cores of clay) encased in thin sheet gold decorated with geometric motifs, including filled triangles and lattice patterns (Fig. 7.23). Examples of these thick

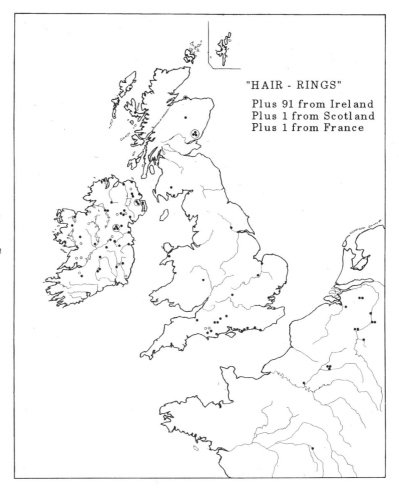

"HAIR - RINGS"

Plus 91 from Ireland
Plus 1 from Scotland
Plus 1 from France

Fig. 7.23—Above: Distribution of hair-rings or ring-money. Below: (1–2) hair-rings with no recorded provenance as illustrated by Wilde in 1862; (3–4) larger penannular rings or crescent-shaped bullae with no provenance.

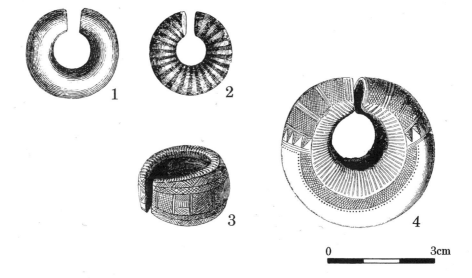

0   3cm

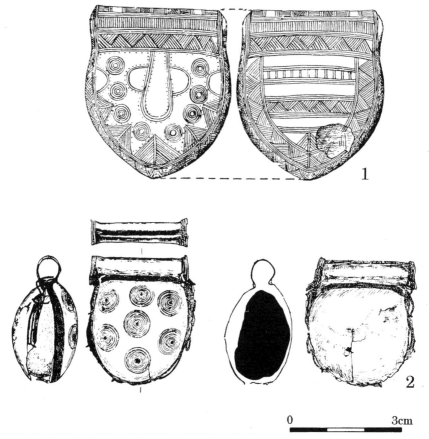

Fig. 7.24—Gold bullae. (1) Bog of Allen, Co. Kildare. (2) Arboe, Co. Tyrone, front and back.

penannular rings have been found in hoards at Tooradoo, near Athea, Co. Limerick, which also contained bronze rings and amber beads, and at Rathtinaun, Lough Gara, Co. Sligo, with bronze rings, amber beads, boars' tusks and other items. These large penannular rings have also been called crescent-shaped bullae and their decoration may indeed suggest some relationship with bullae of pendant form.

Named after a type of Roman pendant or amulet, bullae are heart-shaped objects consisting of a lead or clay core covered with decorated thin sheet gold with a transverse perforation for suspension (Eogan 1998b). Decoration may include filled triangles and concentric circles. A U-shaped motif on one face of a find from the Bog of Allen, Co. Kildare (Fig. 7.24), has been variously described as phallic and anthropomorphic. Five examples are recorded, all from Ireland. One found on the edge of the River Bann was said, after a nineteenth-

century chemical analysis, to have contained traces of blood. Another may have been associated with a number of sleeve-fasteners and gold discs near Arboe, Co. Tyrone (below). Needless to say, the purpose of these mysterious objects is unknown but they are further testimony of the capabilities of those innovative goldsmiths, and the suggestion that they and some of the other puzzling artefacts, like hair-rings, might be magical charms has as much to recommend it as any other. Though obviously difficult to quantify, much of the goldwork under consideration probably had a symbolic role.

Bracelets

The great diversity of personal ornaments is one of the noteworthy features of the later Bronze Age in general and the Dowris phase in particular. Most numerous of all is a series of gold penannular bracelets. Three principal types have been identified and over 300 examples recorded. The first

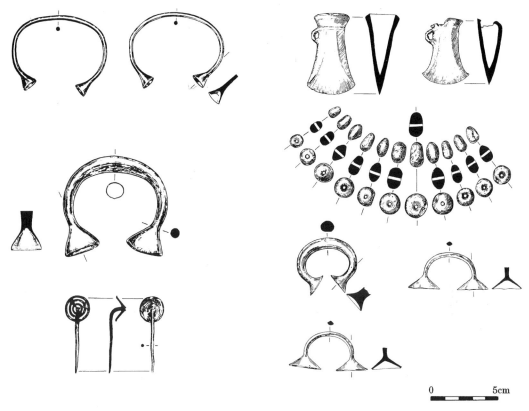

Fig. 7.25—Left: hoard from Drissoge, Co. Meath, containing two gold penannular bracelets, a larger gold bracelet with a hollow body and inclined terminals, and a small gold sunflower pin. Right: hoard from Mount Rivers, Co. Cork, containing two bronze socketed axes, amber beads, a large bronze penannular bracelet and two gold dress-fasteners.

comprises examples formed of a thin rounded or oval bar of gold with evenly expanded solid terminals, like those found in the Lattoon hoard (Fig. 7.19); over 150 may have formed part of 'the great Clare find' at Mooghaun (below). A second type is similar but has hollowed terminals, as in the Gorteenreagh hoard (Fig. 7.17, 3) and in another small hoard of personal ornaments found at Drissoge, near Athboy, Co. Meath (Fig. 7.25). The third type, also represented in the Drissoge hoard, is a larger bracelet with a thick body of rounded or oval cross-section, which may be solid or hollow, with hollow terminals set at a marked inclination to one another. Rare bronze examples of all three types have been found and a bronze version of the last-mentioned was found in a hoard at Mount Rivers, near Fermoy, Co. Cork, which, along with other items, also contained two gold dress-fasteners, neatly illustrating the difference between these and the bracelets (Fig. 7.25). Hoards like this containing

a mix of bronze and gold are fairly rare. A number of these penannular bracelets have been found in Britain (Fig. 7.26), mainly in Scotland and in north Wales. One large gold example has been found in a pottery vessel at Gahlstorf, near Bremen in northern Germany, and has often been cited as a further indication of Nordic contacts. In a small number of puzzling instances in Ireland, Wales and western England, a bracelet or fragments of bracelets have been found placed inside a socketed bronze axe. A study of several of these finds has shown that the bracelet fragments were cut into broadly similar lengths and weights, and among complete bracelets there appears to be a series of weight ranges at 5.5–7g or multiples thereof. In addition to being high-status objects, these bracelets may have been a form of portable wealth (Gwilt *et al.* 2005).

Ribbon-like bracelets of British type are rare in Ireland, where round- or oval-sectioned solid or

10 ● plus 43 from Ireland
11 ■ plus 18 from Ireland
12 ▲ plus 15
〇 either British or Irish

*Fig. 7.26—General
distribution of penannular
bracelets of Irish type.*

hollow forms are the norm. Of the various sorts of gold and bronze penannular bracelet found in Britain, only three have been recorded in Ireland, two with a flat ribbon-like body with expanded terminals, and a third of similar form but with coiled ends. A small hoard of ribbon-shaped gold bracelets with simple terminals found in a bog at Vesnoy in Strokestown demesne, Co. Roscommon, in 1849 may be related.

REGIONAL TRADITIONS

Another noteworthy feature of the Dowris phase is the identification of what appear to be regional metalworking traditions. Local fashions probably existed at an earlier date and may yet be revealed by detailed analysis. But the study of distributional

densities of widespread artefact types is a crude analytical method and naturally hampered by a range of circumstances, not least patterns of retrieval and collection. For example, the concentrations of rapiers, swords and spearheads in the Irish midlands and in central Ulster have been compared to weapon concentrations in the Thames valley and contrasted with areas of northern Britain and Wales where weapons are less common (Ehrenberg 1989b) but they cannot be said to form a well-defined Irish weapon zone. Nonetheless, typological differences may offer useful evidence of broad regional patterning, particularly if chronological questions can be resolved. Two broad regional concentrations of bronze horns have already been noted (Fig. 7.10), and Eogan has demonstrated that not only class I horns but also buckets, cauldrons of class A and sleeve-fasteners

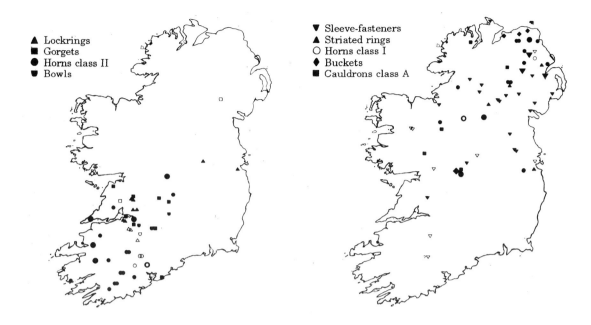

Fig. 7.27—Two regional groups of Dowris phase metalwork as depicted in 1974.

had a primarily northern distribution, while class II horns, lock-rings, gorgets and a series of gold bowl-shaped objects had a mainly south-western focus (Fig. 7.27). More tentative, perhaps, is his identification (1993b; 1994) of a midland province, mainly reflected in the distribution of penannular bracelets (Fig. 7.26). Such localised patterns may well hint at distinct production centres or even reflect regional identities but, in the absence of contemporary settlements and workshops, it must be remembered that these distribution maps, since they are often a record of gold finds in bogs, may be essentially maps of varied depositional or recovery practices.

There is no doubt about the significant concentration of fine goldwork in the north Munster region, and it may be argued that the lock-rings and gorgets alone would suggest that the lands about the Shannon estuary were an important and wealthy gold-working centre in the Dowris phase. The presence of a number of exceptional hoards would seem to support this.

'The great Clare find', as it has been called, was made in 1854 by labourers working on the Limerick to Ennis railway in the townland of Mooghaun North, near Newmarket-on-Fergus, Co. Clare. Sadly, details about the discovery and the original contents

are scanty. It may have been buried in a burnt mound near Mooghaun Lough. The hoard was dispersed, a considerable portion was melted down and its full extent will never be known. It is known that at least 146 gold objects were displayed at a meeting of the Royal Irish Academy a few months after the discovery but today the whereabouts of only 30 gold objects are known, though casts of the rest of the items displayed survive (Cahill 1998a). The original pieces include two penannular neck-rings and six collars (Fig. 7.28); the neck-rings of circular section with expanded terminals and the collars of C-shaped cross-section are of types otherwise unknown, though a somewhat similar neck-ring of bronze was found in a hoard from Ballykeaghra, south of Tuam, Co. Galway. Twenty-two penannular gold bracelets, casts of 137 more and casts of two gold ingots are also preserved. This is all that survives of what has been described as 'by far the largest associated find of gold objects found in Ireland and also in Bronze Age Europe outside the Aegean'. Yet another large collection of both gold and bronze objects came from 'the golden Bog of Cullen', north-west of Tipperary town, in the eighteenth and nineteenth centuries and possibly included gorgets, a gold bowl and a gold disc, as well as a bronze cauldron, swords and spearheads.

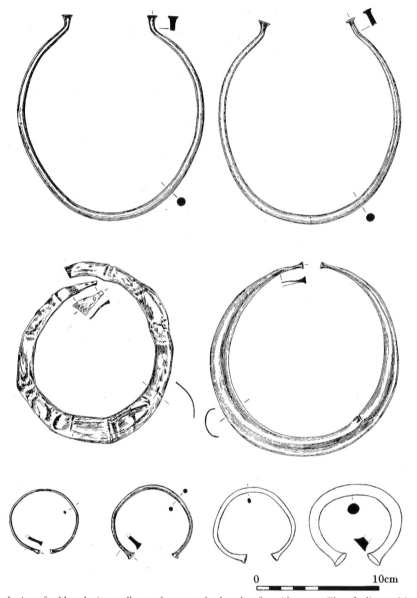

Fig. 7.28—A selection of gold neck-rings, collars and penannular bracelets from 'the great Clare find' near Mooghaun.

'Boxes', ear-spools and hats

A number of other puzzling objects also demonstrate the exceptional nature of the gold-working tradition of north Munster and show that innovative goldwork is found further afield in the south of the country (Fig. 7.29). Seven gold box-like and two gold bowl-shaped objects are known from Ireland. Except for two recent discoveries, they are all old finds and poorly documented. Of the seven small box-like objects of sheet gold, the circumstances of discovery of only three are

recorded. One was found in boggy land at Ballinclemesig, near Ballyheige, Kerry. It is a small cylindrical object, only 6.5cm in diameter and 1.8cm in maximum height; both top and base are separate pieces but attached by overlapping the edges of the sides and are decorated with repoussé boss and concentric circle ornament. Four other boxes, all fairly similar, are unprovenanced and appear to be two pairs. A pair was found in a dump of topsoil at Ballinesker, near Curracloe, Co.

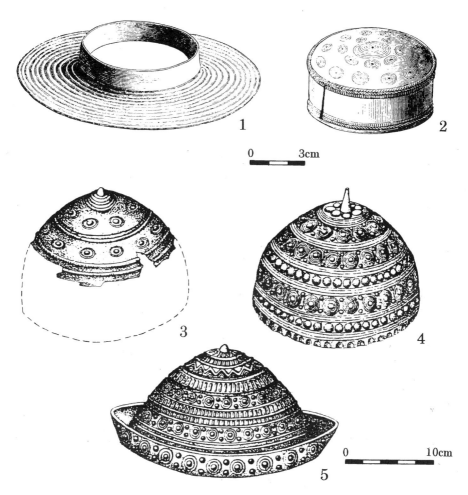

Fig. 7.29—Gold objects. (1) A 'hat-shaped gold plate', now recognised as one half of an enigmatic gold reel-like object, possibly a decorative ear-spool, possibly found near Enniscorthy, Co. Wexford. (2) Unprovenanced gold box-like object (as illustrated by Wilde), also possibly worn as an ear-spool. (3) Unprovenanced sheet-gold bowl-shaped object from Ireland. (4) Sheet-gold hat or crown from Rianxo, Corunna, Spain. (5) Gold hat or crown from near Devilsbit Mountain, Co. Tipperary.

Wexford, along with two gold 'reels', two dress–fasteners and a bracelet. It seems that these boxes were meant to be sealed and removal of any one of the closing discs would damage them. The Ballinesker pair each contained two small beads of solid gold. Their purpose is a mystery and the term 'box' seems a less than adequate term. Mary Cahill (2001) has made the very interesting suggestion that they and the gold spools or reels may have been ear ornaments. The gold spools or reels from Ballinesker have the appearance of two discs joined together by a very short cylinder and each face consists of two discs (joined in the same way as gorget terminals). The Ballinesker discovery led to

the recognition of other examples: an unprovenanced piece of sheet gold that had been simply called a 'hat-shaped gold plate' (Fig. 7.29, 1) and may be one of four discs found near Enniscorthy, Co. Wexford, in the eighteenth century (two of which do survive), and an example found near Cashel, Co. Tipperary, which also contained a solid gold bead. Both the decoration and method of manufacture of these curious reel-shaped pieces indicate some relationship to gorgets. They and the box-like objects with diameters ranging from about 5.5cm to 7cm could have been inserted as ornaments in greatly enlarged and distended ear lobes (Fig. 7.18, 2).

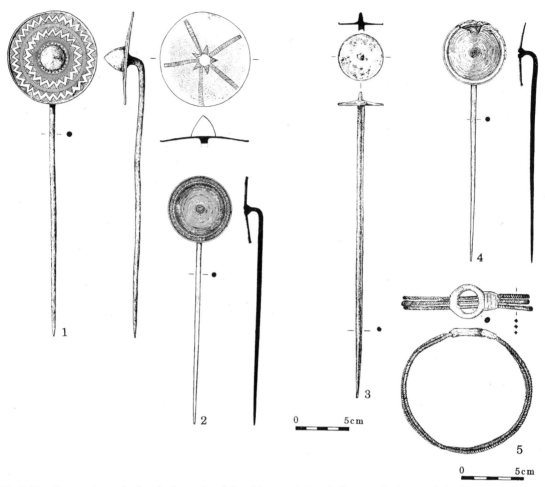

Fig. 7.30—Bronze pins and a bracelet from a hoard found in a sandpit at Ballytegan, Co. Laois, which also contained two bronze socketed axeheads and numerous bronze rings of various sorts. (1) Disc-headed pin with horizontal head. (2 and 4) Sunflower pins with gold foil decoration. (3) Sunflower pin. (5) Triple bracelet.

A series of bowl-shaped objects may be gold vessels but only one of these supposed bowls survives; it is a shallow, circular, dish-shaped fragment of sheet gold, now 11.3cm in diameter and obviously once somewhat larger (Eogan 1981). Repoussé decoration consists of a small central boss surrounded by concentric circles (Fig. 7.29, 3). It bears some similarity to a gold object found in the seventeenth century in a bog near Devilsbit Mountain, north-west of Templemore, Co. Tipperary, and depicted in an eighteenth-century engraving (Fig. 7.29, 5). The four others are known only from vague references to 'crowns' in the literature and include 'a golden crown weighing 6 ounces' found in that golden bog at Cullen. It has

been suggested that the two Irish pieces could have been headgear. Sheet-gold objects that may have been crowns or hats of both hemispherical or skullcap and conical shape are known elsewhere in Europe. Similar hemispherical hats have been found in north-western Spain and may reflect an Atlantic fashion in ceremonial headgear (Gerloff 1995).

Pins

A wide range of other ornaments and implements were produced by the bronzesmiths of the time. Chief among the bronze personal ornaments are different pin types, and for the first time the bronze pin becomes a relatively common feature of the Irish archaeological record (Eogan 1974). Whether this is just another ornamental expression of a widespread predilection for display or some indication of a change in dress fashion is not known. In short, since none have been found with unburnt burials, for example, questions such as how these pins may have been worn and whether a long-established practice of using buttons or toggles, if such existed, became unfashionable cannot be answered.

The majority of pins are divided into two major classes: disc-headed and cup-headed. The disc-headed variety includes both pins with straight stems and a horizontal circular head and those pins with a bent stem and circular heads placed at right angles to the length of the stem—the so-called sunflower pins. Both are represented in a hoard from Ballytegan, near Portlaoise, Co. Laois (Fig. 7.30). Disc-headed pins with straight stems have discs with a central conical boss and are otherwise plain or simply decorated with concentric circles,

other motifs being rare. Pins of this general type are scarce in Britain but well known in northern Europe, particularly in Denmark and northern Germany, and Irish examples with small heads, small hemispherical central bosses and concentric circle ornament are, in Eogan's opinion, closest to the Nordic forms and some may even be imports. Sunflower pins are generally more elaborate objects: the head, at right angles to the stem, provides a field for more complex ornament, which in addition to a central boss and concentric circles may include filled triangles, lattice and chevron patterns. Simply decorated examples occur, and one small plain pin, lacking even a boss on its disc, from Knocknalappa, Co. Clare, is a very down-market piece. A unique gold sunflower pin with an abnormal conical head from Drissoge, Co. Meath (Fig. 7.25), is even smaller, however. In contrast, two of the three Ballytegan examples are particularly ornate; the patterns on the large heads (one with a prominent

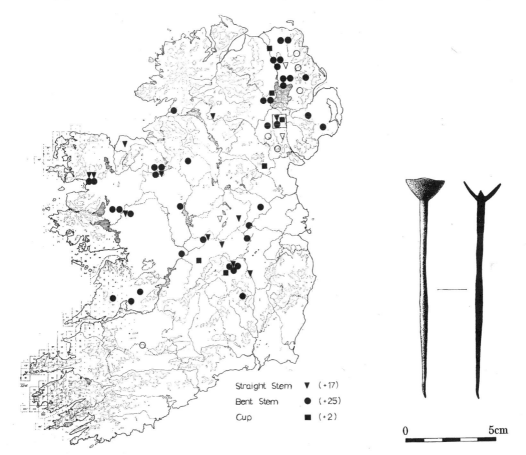

Fig. 7.31—General distribution of disc- and cup-headed pins and (right) a cup-headed pin from Arboe, Co. Tyrone.

conical boss) may have been engraved in the bronze rather than cast, and this was then reproduced on a thin covering of gold foil fitted to the head and pressed into the underlying decoration. Other gold foil decoration of this sort has been noted in a hoard from Arboe, Co. Tyrone. Again pins with small hemispherical bosses and concentric circle ornament are held to be earlier than those with large conical bosses, and these have been called primary and secondary series pins respectively. Sunflower pins are found in Scotland, where they differ in having a recurved neck. They also occur in Denmark and northern Germany, and those of the primary series are deemed to be closest to the supposed Nordic prototype.

The second major class of pin is the cup-headed variety, which is not particularly common and mainly recorded from the northern half of the country. These are invariably undecorated, though one from Arboe, Co. Tyrone, has a small conical boss in the centre of the cup (Fig. 7.31). This is an interesting minor detail; a few pins with somewhat cup-shaped heads are known from Britain, and one from a hoard at the Point of Sleat on the Isle of Skye has a similar pointed cup, a detail that has been noted on the Sintra gold collar from Portugal and on other Iberian ornaments. Cup-shaped decoration, derived from Iberian floral-cup ornament, has been claimed to be just one indication of venturers, perhaps even goldsmiths and their gold, along the Atlantic seaways (Hawkes 1971).

THE ATLANTIC SEAWAYS

The words of R. A. S. Macalister, who once declared that Britain was essentially an island of the North Sea and Ireland an island of the Atlantic Ocean, have been sometimes quoted when the thorny question of the role of the Atlantic seaways in Irish prehistory is discussed. There has been a long-held belief that this island on the Atlantic border of Europe had important contacts by coastal sea routes with France, Spain and the western Mediterranean on the one hand, and with Scotland and Scandinavia on the other. This belief has found some support in the archaeological evidence, which is sporadically intriguing, if not exotic. It has also found occasional support in quainter and less

reliable sources such as early origin-legends: Goidelic Celts, for instance, were said to have come from Scythia via Spain, being preceded by various other invaders, including the Fir Bolg from Greece. A belief in direct and influential contacts with France and Iberia must have appealed to some nationalist minds in the nineteenth and twentieth centuries. For them a non-British source for the main cultural influences to impinge on these shores had obvious attractions (Waddell 2005a). Egyptians, Phoenicians, megalithic tomb-builders and missionaries, prospectors, early metal-workers and stone fort-builders (with or without *chevaux-de-frise*) have all been credited with use of the Atlantic seaways at one time or another. Parallels have been drawn between Irish passage tombs and their Iberian counterparts, Iberian elements have been claimed in some early pottery types, careful consideration has been given to the possibility that early copper metallurgy may have been inspired by Atlantic contacts, some early metal objects and Irish and Galician rock art have been studied, and some of the claims for contact with the Mediterranean world in the last two millennia BC have been reviewed.

The decorated gold neck-ring from Downpatrick, Co. Down, may be related to Iberian decorated neck-rings of Berzocana type and may indicate connections with western France before 1000 BC. The Dunaverney flesh-hook too is part of an Atlantic phenomenon in which ritual feasting was an element of élite social practice. The gold headgear studied by Gerloff may be another indication of this élite interaction. Other contacts may be demonstrated by a range of interesting parallels, many of which demand careful assessment and include such disparate stylistic details as V-shaped notches on shields and Hawkes's floral-cup ornament. A bronze penannular bracelet with evenly expanded hollow terminals from an unrecorded location in northern Portugal is considered an Irish type by Eogan (1994), who also notes the resemblances between golden bowl-shaped objects in Ireland and northern Iberia. He suggests connections with north Munster, the gold-working traditions in this region possibly containing elements of both north European and southern fashion. Terence Powell (1974) provided a measured assessment of the conflicting stylistic parallels offered by the gold gorgets of the Shannon area, where the decorated circular terminals with their northern-inspired ornament find no parallels on bronze neck ornaments in northern Europe. He tentatively suggested that in shape and position they could be more splendid versions of the smaller floral-cups of Iberia.

The importance of the Atlantic seaways as a means of long-distance communication in Irish prehistory may have been exaggerated in the past but there is no denying the probability of contacts along shorter stretches of the Atlantic coasts in prehistoric times. While some exotic objects may hint at long-distance exchange, more restricted contacts over shorter distances were probably the norm. Short coastal journeys between communities must have been common and could well have formed an interconnecting chain of contacts extending considerable distances along the Atlantic coasts of Europe (Cunliffe 2001; Henderson 2007). This is neatly illustrated by that version of an Irish–British spearhead with lunate openings in the blade found in the Huelva hoard in south-western Spain. As we have seen, this example is remarkably similar to one found near Ballinasloe, Co. Galway (Fig. 7.13, 1), and, like the bronze trumpet pieces found in the Loire (Fig. 7.9), is a reminder that Ireland, southern Britain, western France and south-western Spain could have been linked together by a network of coastal connections. Such a process of exchange from coastal community to community was possibly the means by which objects and ideas were transmitted along the Atlantic façade, and this may also have been the way some exotic fashions in goldwork found their way to the south of Ireland and a bewildered North African ape came to Navan, Co. Armagh, some centuries later (Chapter 9).

AMBER AND THE NORDIC QUESTION

The wealth of gold in the Bishopsland and Dowris phases has tended to eclipse the less spectacular amber bead, but amber seems to have been particularly popular in Ireland in the latter phase especially (Eogan 1999c). Over 30 finds have been recorded, and beads of spherical, oval and disc shapes are common. A series of hoards that contained numbers of amber beads have already been mentioned: Mount Rivers, Co. Cork (Fig.

7.25: thirteen beads), Tooradoo, Co. Limerick (105 beads), and Rathtinaun, Co. Sligo (31 beads). In addition to these, 109 beads were found with a cup-headed pin and a number of bronze rings near Portlaoise, Co. Laois, and several finds totalling over 200 amber beads (one at least with a bronze spearhead) were made in Ballycurrin Demesne on the shores of Lough Corrib, north-west of Headford, Co. Galway. A gold dress-fastener, a bronze penannular bracelet and two bronze rings were found with a necklace of 128 beads near a large rock at Meenwaun, near Banagher, Co. Offaly. Even larger collections of beads have been found: at Derrybrien, east of Gort, Co. Galway, over 500 beads and a small fragment of sheet gold were found scattered over an area about a metre square at the bottom of an upland bog; the beads vary from 3cm to 6mm in diameter and the presence of a number of doubly perforated spacer beads suggests a complex multi-strand graduated necklace. Another large necklace of over 400 beads was found in a bog at Kurin, just south of Garvagh, Co. Derry. Smaller finds occur, of course, such as the ten beads from Ballylin, near Ferbane, Co. Offaly.

The relatively large quantity of Dowris phase amber recovered in Ireland is interesting because this material seems to have been less common in Britain at this time. The amber found in British and Irish contexts is 'Baltic amber'—that is, amber derived from natural deposits extending from eastern Scotland and England to Holland, Scandinavia, northern Germany and the eastern Baltic. This general north European source has been confirmed by infrared spectroscopy but more precise origins cannot be identified. It is impossible to distinguish between a British and a Scandinavian origin, for example, but since it is probable that fairly small amounts of amber were available in eastern Britain, importation from the Continent was more likely than not. To date, the evidence would appear to discount claims that Irish sources may have been used. The exchange of Baltic amber extended over wide areas of Europe in the second millennium BC in particular and it was clearly a highly prized material, occurring in rich graves in the south of England, in central Germany and Poland and in Mycenean Greece. Aside from any possible magical properties, its value in these locations may have been amplified by its far-distant source, a cosmic charge enhanced by geographical distance. For these reasons it may have been an item strictly controlled by élite societies. Its association with gold finery in several Irish hoards and its occasional votive deposition as a single item indicate that it had a special significance in the Dowris phase in Ireland, and Mary Cahill (2004a) has shown that a series of large gold beads from Tumna, Co. Roscommon, were probably gold copies of large amber beads. But why amber should seem to be less important in Britain is not easy to explain. Because it was readily available, and control was therefore difficult, amber was less of a status symbol in the Baltic region than elsewhere; it was valuable, however, because it could be exchanged for coveted metal. A similar situation may have obtained in eastern Britain at this time, and those penannular bracelets may have been one sought-after Irish item exchanged for exotic amber.

A whole series of objects and decorative motifs, and of course amber itself, have long prompted the widespread belief that there were pronounced and sometimes direct contacts with northern Europe. A few writers have alluded to the possibility of contact in early prehistoric times, and some comparisons between megalithic tombs in Ireland and Scandinavia and some later ceramic parallels have been claimed and questioned. It is not until the last millennium BC that significant contacts are thought to have developed: as Eogan (1964) put it, 'during the initial stages of the Dowris Phase, Ireland came into direct contact with the Nordic world, particularly Denmark and the north German plain'.

Some of the evidence has already been mentioned, and amber, of course, may have been one of the links in a chain of Nordic contacts. A range of decorative features such as U-shaped notches on shields, concentric circle ornament and conical bosses or rivets have been traced to Scandinavia. The well-known gold disc from Lattoon, Co. Cavan (Fig. 7.19), with its central boss surrounded by concentric circle decoration has been compared to the famous Trundholm gold disc from Denmark mounted on a vertical bronze disc on a six-wheeled model bronze wagon and generally accepted as a solar symbol. An unprovenanced small bronze disc from Ireland, with ornament similar to Lattoon, has prompted a similar comparison. Concentric circle ornament also occurs on gorget terminals whose collar shape has

been ascribed to Nordic prototypes. Dress-fasteners too are seen to have been inspired by northern fibulae, and the gold-plated sunflower pins in the Ballytegan hoard have been considered imports from northern Europe—though this has been disputed. Two small bronze bar toggles, one from Rathgall, Co. Wicklow, the other from Navan, Co. Armagh, are thought to be imports also (Raftery 1975).

Others have considered northern influence to be superficial, if not quite exaggerated and very debatable. It is claimed that the parallels so often cited are generalised and unconvincing, and it is worth noting that there are chronological discrepancies as well. The absence in Ireland of the spiral ornament that is such a striking feature of some Scandinavian metalwork (including the Trundholm disc) is one noteworthy difference. It has been argued that northern Europe had no great impact on British–Irish material culture, particularly goldwork, and that what contacts there may have been were casual and over a long period of time (Taylor 1980; Thrane 1995). It may be that we are witnessing parallel analogous developments.

It is not easy to resolve the conflicting opinions on the Nordic question but two important factors are worth considering. On present evidence much of the amber in Ireland may be of Baltic origin. It could conceivably have arrived in this island via a network of coastal traders and communities around the coast of Scotland, and the presence of a Scandinavian-type socketed axehead in both south-western Scotland and County Antrim is a reminder that this is a possibility (Schmidt and Burgess 1981). Even though the abundant evidence in bronze and gold for Irish–British contacts across the Irish Sea and across the North Channel makes a route across northern Britain seem more plausible, it should not be presumed that prehistoric trade or exchange would take the shortest route, and the discovery of a number of amber beads at a strategically located settlement at Runnymede on the Thames, Berkshire, and at a number of other locations in southern England and north Wales is a reminder that amber might have come via southern England too. Clearly those involved in Britain seem to have had little use for amber themselves, but if amber travelled so could other objects and stylistic inspiration. The transmission of stylistic elements is

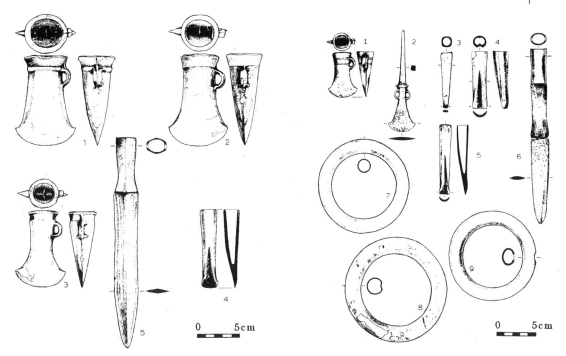

Fig. 7.32—Hoards of tools (including socketed gouges and a tanged and looped chisel or leather knife) and other bronzes from Crossna, near Boyle, Co. Roscommon, and Ballinderry, Co. Westmeath.

an elusive phenomenon but it was probably a constant fact of prehistoric communication. From time to time it may have become an especially important fact, particularly when stylistic features, with a symbolic significance we may never recapture, could serve the eclectic needs of craftsmen and their patrons. It is surely significant that the evidence for supposed long-distance contacts, whether with Iberia or northern Europe, survives in what must be the material culture of a wealthy élite ever anxious to express their exclusive status in novel ways.

There were contacts that extended to central Europe too, as the Dowris and Nannau buckets and their Hosszúpályi counterparts in the Carpathian Basin indicate. Buckets of this Hosszúpályi type are extremely rare (Patay 1990) and, as already mentioned, are a part of a tradition of sheet-bronze manufacture in south-eastern Europe which includes the smaller so-called Kurd buckets (15–20cm high). In this part of the world, the large vessels may have been ceremonial containers for a special alcoholic drink and the smaller ones may have been serving or drinking vessels in a society where drinking sessions may have been a part of

martial élite behavior. The scattered distribution of Hosszúpályi-type buckets across Europe, from Hungary to Switzerland to south Wales, gives only a faint indication of how this fashion may have been transported across the Continent to Britain and Ireland. The distribution of such prestigious items is now seen as the material expression of interaction between the aristocratic elements of various communities. This is a well-documented phenomenon in continental Europe: Mycenaean swords have been found in Albania and Bulgaria, for instance, and bronze vessels from the Carpathian Basin were imported into Scandinavia (Harding 2000). Swords, shields, personal ornaments and a whole range of other metal artefacts are only the most visible expression of interrelationships that must also have included the movement of less durable items such as slaves, amber, animal hides, furs, leatherwork, prized cattle and exotic animals.

BRONZE TOOLS AND IMPLEMENTS

A series of bronze tools and implements had more mundane roles in society, though their occasional presence in hoards suggests that they may sometimes have been symbols of social position and may even have had a ceremonial use. Double-edged knives (including socketed and tanged examples), socketed sickles, gouges, punches or hammers, chisels (both socketed and tanged), razors and tweezers have been recorded (Eogan 1964; O'Connor 1980). The commonest implement is the socketed axe.

A small number of hoards containing two or three bronze items such as socketed axes, gouges and knives, in varying combinations, and sometimes a few other bronzes, suggest that some groups of objects had some special significance, perhaps as a mark of caste or trade. Examples include a hoard from Enagh East, near Mooghaun, Co. Clare, comprising three axes, a gouge, a knife and several rings; a small hoard found in a bog at Crossna, near Boyle, Co. Roscommon, containing three axeheads, a knife and a gouge; and another bog find at Ballinderry, Co. Westmeath, containing an axehead, a tanged and a socketed chisel, two gouges, a knife and three rings (Fig. 7.32). A hoard containing a socketed axe, a socketed gouge, a razor and a pin found in a bog at Cromaghs, near Armoy, Co. Antrim, had apparently been wrapped in a textile and the razor was contained in a leather pouch. The textile remains are unique in the Dowris phase and comprise a large piece of plain woven woollen fabric, possibly a bag, and several pieces of a woven horsehair belt. Two socketed axeheads, a gold bracelet and a gold dress-fastener were found under the corner of a large stone at Kilbride, near Newport, Co. Mayo, and both bronze and gold may have been equally prized.

While some axes and knives may have been put to offensive use on occasion, and a socketed knife was reportedly found driven into a human skull discovered near Drumman More Lake, north-east of Armagh, it is probably safe to assume that most of them, like gouges and chisels, were used for more conventional tasks. Gouges were woodworking implements and are widely distributed. Socketed chisels were undoubtedly woodworking tools as well. Some tanged examples with curved blades (as from Ballinderry) may have been for leather-working or woodworking (Eogan 2007); they too are found in Britain and France. A number of different types of knives, both socketed and tanged, have been identified (Fig. 7.33), and a few curious examples with curved blades may have had some specialised purpose. These socketed knives are widely distributed in Ireland and Britain, with a number in western France. They, like the tanged type, appear to be an Irish–British form. The great majority of small tanged razors in Ireland are like the example in the well-known Dowris hoard (Fig. 7.1, 8). Bronze anvils are rare but include the example in the Bishopsland hoard (Fig. 6.7, 11). Their small size suggests that they were used for delicate work.

Irish bronze sickles are a varied lot and have a relatively long history. Over 30 examples of what presumably was an important agricultural implement are recorded. Some early stone mould fragments for casting sickles are known from Killymaddy, Co. Antrim, and the Bishopsland hoard contained a bronze sickle with a knobbed haft. This primitive form may have been replaced around 1200 BC by a ring- or cylinder-socketed type in which the blade is more or less at right angles to the socket (Fig. 7.33, 1). A tanged form (with a perforation in the tang) found with a leaf-shaped spearhead and some bronze rings in a hoard from Ballygowan, Co. Kilkenny (Fig. 7.33, 5), may be related to British and Continental examples. Socketed sickles are an insular fashion, and two basic forms have been recognised in Britain and Ireland; in one the blade springs almost vertically from the socket, while in the other the blade is set at right angles, as already mentioned. A small number of the latter, in which the outer edge of the implement continues across the top of the socket to produce a projecting heel, are particularly interesting because this type was copied in iron in a hoard from Llyn Fawr, Glamorgan, and may represent the final form of the bronze sickle. While ceremonial usage for some small slender examples cannot be excluded, experimentation has shown that these implements could cut cereals with reasonable success but were noticeably less effective than iron examples.

Socketed axes

Over 2,000 socketed axeheads have been found and there is considerable variety in shape and size (Eogan 1999b). Classification is complex and only a summary of the principal types is presented here. Early examples include a narrow socketed type as in the Bishopsland hoard with a characteristic

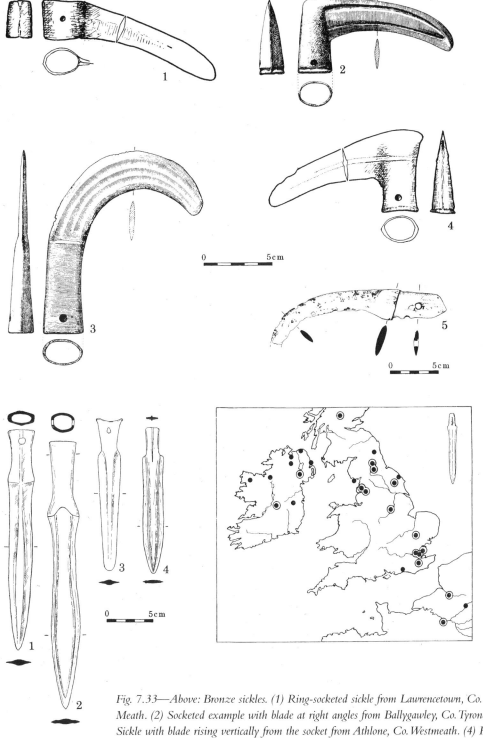

Fig. 7.33—Above: Bronze sickles. (1) Ring-socketed sickle from Lawrencetown, Co. Meath. (2) Socketed example with blade at right angles from Ballygawley, Co. Tyrone. (3) Sickle with blade rising vertically from the socket from Athlone, Co. Westmeath. (4) Heeled example, unprovenanced. (5) Sickle with perforated tang from Ballygowan, Co. Kilkenny. Below: Socketed bronze knives. (1) Ireland. (2) Kilmore, Co. Galway. (3) County Antrim. (4) Tanged knife from the Dowris hoard with the distribution of this type.

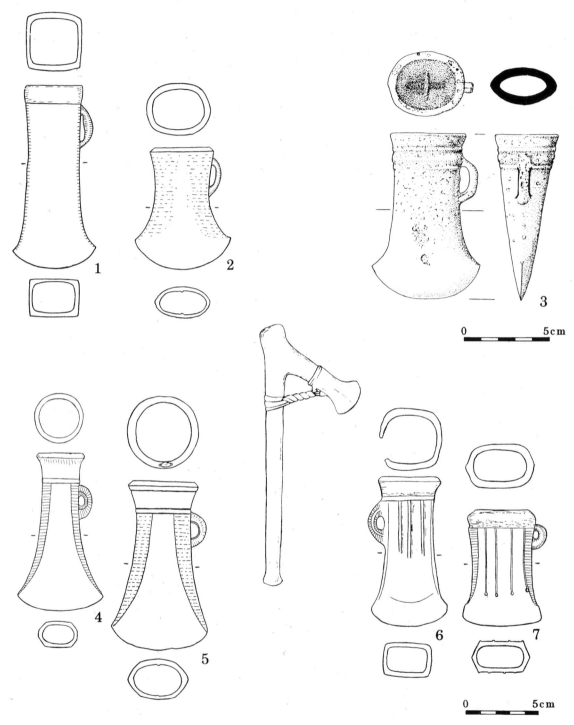

Fig. 7.34—Bronze socketed axeheads. (1) Early narrow socketed type from Rossconor, Co. Down. (2–3) Bag-shaped type from Glenstal, Co. Limerick, and from near Armagh. (4–5) Faceted axeheads: Kish, Co. Wicklow, and Mount Rivers, Co. Cork. (6) Ribbed axehead: Crevilly, Co. Antrim. (7) A nineteenth-century drawing of a socketed axehead mounted in a knee-shaped wooden haft from the River Boyne near Edenderry, Co. Offaly. (8) Some socketed axeheads may have been mounted on pegs set in mortised wooden handles.

rectangular cross-section and parallel sides with a slightly expanded cutting edge (Fig. 6.7, 2; Fig. 7.34, 1). Other specimens have a circular or oval mouth and a faceted body cross-section (Fig. 7.34, 4–5). This is a widespread form, found in Britain and in western continental Europe. The Irish socketed axe series, however, is dominated by small and large 'bag-shaped' axeheads with an oval, subrectangular or circular mouth, a body of oval cross-section and a widely splayed cutting edge. Loops are positioned at varying distances below the mouth, which may be plain or surrounded by one or more mouldings or a collar (Fig. 7.34, 2–3). Over 1,300 examples are recorded and they are well represented in the Dowris hoard (Fig. 7.1). Similar axeheads occur in northern England and Scotland. A small number of ribbed axes also have parallels in Britain (Fig. 7.34, 6).

These axeheads have generally been considered to have been used for carpentry and tree-felling and in many instances this seems a reasonable supposition. The great diversity in size and shape suggests a variety of functions, however. Some were mounted in a bent knee-shaped wooden haft but others were mounted on a stout wooden peg inserted into a socketed haft, and both were presumably lashed with leather thongs (Fig. 7.34, 7–8). An example of the former was found in the River Boyne near Edenderry, Co. Offaly, and two mortised wooden handles—possibly for socketed axes—were found at Haughey's Fort. Some socketed axes may have been used in adze-like fashion for some specific purposes, and a number of miniature examples, only a few centimetres in length, can hardly have been functional pieces. The most notorious non-functional socketed axeheads are the Breton *haches armoricaines*, known in their tens of thousands in that part of France. Of slender trapezoidal shape and rectangular cross-section, with a prominent biconical collar, these small axes are made of such thin metal with a high lead content that it is doubtful whether they ever had any practical use, but they were manufactured in such quantity that it is assumed that they were made specifically for trade or barter. Their association with iron in Brittany indicates survival into the seventh century BC. Some 30 examples have been found in Ireland (almost all unprovenanced), and the British distribution, not surprisingly, is concentrated in southern England.

SETTLEMENT AND SOCIETY 1000–600 BC

A relatively small number of settlements are assigned to the Dowris phase, but the same variety of sites found in the later second millennium BC continues to be represented and ranges from large hilltop enclosures to small wetland sites.

Lough Eskragh, Co. Tyrone

A wetland site at Lough Eskragh, near Dungannon, Co. Tyrone, was investigated in 1953 and in 1973 (Williams 1978). Three areas of timber posts were found projecting from the lake mud on its eastern shore (site A), and two smaller areas of timber piles (B and C) were discovered further to the north. A linear concentration of timber posts (D) was noted near the western shore. Site A consisted of two separate concentrations of timber piles, mostly birchwood with some ash and about 12cm in diameter (Fig. 7.35). One of these concentrations, to the north-west, was approximately circular with a diameter of 10.5m and constructed of brushwood, horizontal timbers and vertical piles to consolidate the brushwood. The discovery of two complete coarse pottery vessels, a cylindrical two-piece wooden vessel, a number of sandstone saddle querns, a polished stone axehead and part of a jet bracelet indicated occupation. This would seem to have been a small settlement accessed by boat, and two flat-bottomed dugout log boats of oak (one containing fragments of another tub-shaped wooden vessel) were found close by. The two tub-shaped wooden vessels, both of alder, from Lough Eskragh are further reminders that two-piece containers of wood were in common use. Another two-piece cylindrical vessel with at least three perforated lugs for suspension, also of alder, was found in a bog at Altanagh, near Carrickmore, Co. Tyrone. These are early examples of wooden vessels with the circular base held in a groove cut near the lower edge of the inner wall. The Altanagh vessel has been radiocarbon-dated to 838–408 BC (Earwood 1993). An elongated 35m-long concentration of almost 600 birch and ash piles, situated some 15m to the south-east of the Lough Eskragh site A settlement and between it and the lakeshore, produced the surprisingly large number of sixteen sandstone saddle querns and one large

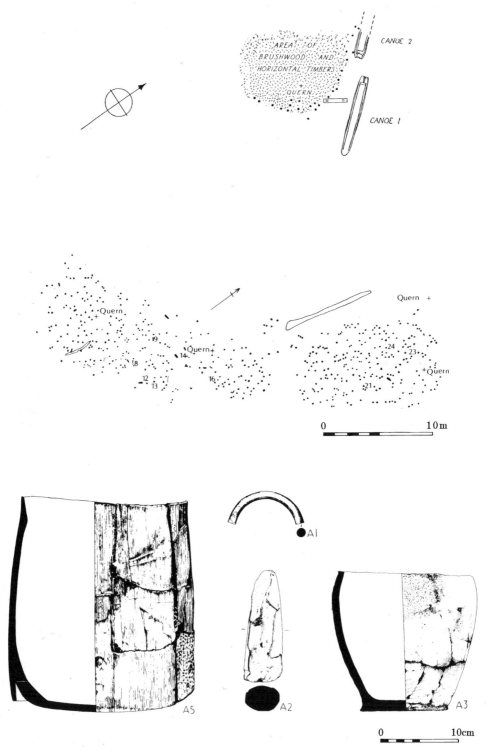

Fig. 7.35—Lough Eskragh, Co. Tyrone. Above: plan of site A, showing on north-west a small crannog with dugout canoes and to south-east a pile structure with tree trunk. Below: cylindrical wooden vessel, part of a lignite bracelet, polished stone axehead and pottery vessel.

granite example but no other domestic artefacts. This puzzling pile structure may have been used for some specialised activity but the suggestion that the querns could have been used to grind ore for metal production has yet to be proven.

Site B was located just over 108m to the north-east of site A. This was an approximately circular structure, 9m in diameter, built of brushwood with horizontal timbers on top and vertical piles defining its perimeter. It seems to have been a lakeside platform with a clay floor surrounded by a wattle fence which seems to have eventually been destroyed by fire. This too was a site for specialised activity: fragments of clay moulds for casting bronze swords, a single-edged tool (perhaps a sickle) and a socketed axe were found, as well as some baked clay fragments, possibly part of a pouring gate for a mould, and pieces of crucibles. Fragments of several saddle querns were also discovered and their presence here might support the ore-grinding hypothesis. A flat-topped boulder showed traces of hammering and may have served as an anvil. No furnace was found but only a limited area was excavated. A small bronze finger-ring was the only metal object recovered, though a socketed axe found on the lakeshore may have been made on the site.

Sites C and D were not investigated in any detail. An oak plank from the settlement at site A was radiocarbon-dated to 960–800 BC and confirmed by a tree-ring date of about the tenth century BC. The elongated pile structure to the south was radiocarbon-dated to 790–400 BC and a timber from site B provided a radiocarbon date of 1520–1150 BC which may be anomalous, being somewhat too early for the swords and axes manufactured there. If sites A and B are contemporary, then the deliberate distancing of dangerous metalworking area from settlement is interesting. This may have a purely practical explanation, of course, but the transformative magic of metalworking may have demanded this sort of isolation.

Ballinderry, Co. Offaly

Excavations in 1933 by Hugh Hencken of the Harvard Archaeological Expedition in Ireland revealed that a crannog of the early medieval period had been preceded many centuries before by a lakeside settlement of the Dowris phase, which survived as a thin black layer about 10cm in

thickness (Hencken 1942). This was in turn sealed by a layer of mud deposited by rising lake waters which extended over an irregular area about 45m by 25m. The main late prehistoric features comprised two rectangular timber structures (Fig. 7.36). One on the north-west was a very large and approximately rectangular timber platform situated on slightly higher ground. It measured 11.5m in length and consisted of eight rows of flat oak planks of varying lengths and measuring 5–10cm in thickness and 20–60cm in width. These were embedded in the black layer and lay about 1.5m apart. Each plank had a row of squarish holes set at intervals of about 40cm and containing the remains of narrow posts 6–7cm across. There was no trace of any wickerwork but a thin layer of brushwood and a thin layer of gravel covered different parts of this structure, which was partly surrounded by a number of lines of light wooden posts. Its purpose is far from clear but it was possibly meant to be a foundation platform for a house. According to Conor Newman (1997a), in a revealing re-evaluation of the excavation evidence, a series of timber posts to the east may represent a second rectilinear wooden structure of broadly similar dimensions and there may have been a pathway between the two. Artefacts recovered included sherds of coarse pottery, a bronze socketed knife, two flesh-hooks, the stem of a sunflower pin, two awls and two rings. Two amber beads, fragments of lignite bracelets, bone and stone spindle-whorls, a bone toggle, a saddle quern, rubbing stones, part of a wooden bowl, other unidentifiable wooden pieces and some fragments of leather were also found. Animal bones from this level were predominantly those of cattle (around 80%), with a little pig, less sheep or goat and some horse. A few bones of wild animals such as red deer and some wild fowl were also recovered. While the finds suggest that this may have been a domestic settlement of some significance, ritual activity was attested by the presence of two human skulls and a portion of a third found at the base of the occupation layer. These were considered to be foundation deposits. All were of adults, two probably male and one probably female. One of the male skulls and the female skull had part of the facial bone deliberately removed after death, and the other was just represented by a cut rectangular fragment. These and other finds of fragmentary skulls, like those

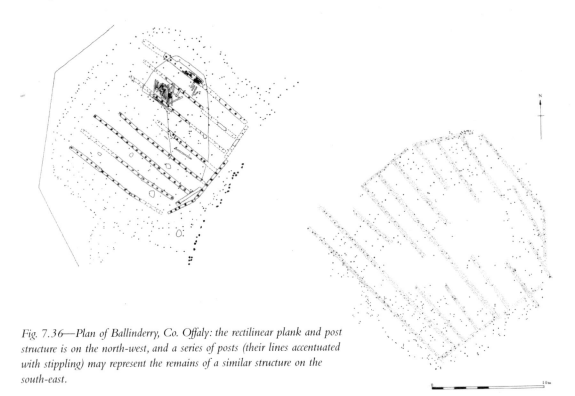

Fig. 7.36—Plan of Ballinderry, Co. Offaly: the rectilinear plank and post structure is on the north-west, and a series of posts (their lines accentuated with stippling) may represent the remains of a similar structure on the south-east.

noted from Chancellorsland and from the King's Stables, are further reminders of the special significance attached to the human skull in later prehistory. The quantity of bronze recovered is unusual (and in fact a large number of other finds of metalwork come from the general area) and it is possible that there was a ritual dimension to the activities at Ballinderry.

Knocknalappa, Co. Clare

In another reappraisal of an old excavation, settlement evidence dating from 1033–848 BC has been identified at Knocknalappa, on Rosroe Lake near Newmarket-on-Fergus, Co. Clare, which was excavated with inconclusive results in 1937 (Grogan *et al.* 1999). After an early second-millennium BC occupation phase, successive layers of stone and timber were laid on peat; associated finds included coarse pottery, amber beads, a polishing or rubbing stone, a polished stone axehead, a lignite bracelet, a bone spindle-whorl, bone toggles, two saddle querns, a very small bronze sword, a gouge, a small sunflower pin and a bronze ring. Animal remains recovered included bones of cattle, pig and a large dog, scanty remains of sheep and some red deer

antler. No structures or hearths were found. The amber beads, the metal finds including the sunflower pin and the bronze sword, small though it is, have prompted the suggestion that this was a settlement of some importance.

Other important wetland sites are known (O'Sullivan 1998) and include Moynagh Lough, Co. Meath, which probably dates from about the ninth century BC, where excavation revealed post-holes, hearths and stone spreads (many showing signs of heat fracturing). Among the artefacts were bronze pins, a hair-ring, two leaf-shaped bronze spearheads, parts of lignite and shale bracelets, lignite and amber beads, sherds of coarse pottery and an antler toggle or cheek-piece (Bradley 2004). A settlement on the shores of Lough Gara, west of Boyle, at Rathtinaun, Co. Sligo, was excavated between 1952 and 1955 and produced evidence of activity at various times from the Dowris phase to the early medieval period. Little survived of the earlier phase, but parts of wooden vessels, sherds of coarse pottery and bronze objects including tweezers, several rings, a razor and disc-headed pins were recovered. Some clay mould fragments, a penannular gold hair-ring and a hoard of bronze objects in a wooden box (comprising rings, tweezers and a pin, as well as several hair-rings, amber beads and boars' tusks) were also found. Island MacHugh, near Baronscourt, Co. Tyrone, has produced a bronze sword, and radiocarbon dating of timber piles indicates some construction there just before, or early in, the Dowris phase. Christina Fredengren (2002) has remarked that archaeologists tend to overdo their search for houses and that there may be explanations other than a domestic one for the presence of fires and animal bones. Noting that some bronze finds (as at Rathtinaun) occur at the edge of sites and that the finds sometimes recall the contents of votive hoards, she suggests that these wetland sites had a role to play in the depositional rituals that were such a feature of later prehistory. It may be an oversimplification to see them just as high-status settlements because of the wealth of material they produce.

Aughinish, Co. Limerick

Small enclosures, similar to Carrigillihy, Co. Cork, were also occupied. Two on Aughinish Island, near Foynes in the Shannon estuary, were excavated in 1974 (Kelly 1974). Both enclosures were about 35m in overall diameter, with a bank faced internally and externally with limestone slabs and with a rubble core. Site 1 was built on bedrock and no post-holes were found, but the ground had been levelled, presumably for a house. Traces of occupation included shell-filled pits, coarse pottery, two saddle querns, a bronze tanged chisel, a bronze knob-headed pin and the remains of an iron object, possibly a bridle-bit. The iron object was a significant find but was heavily corroded; it had one surviving circular ring and one link with the openings at either end set at right angles to each other but it is not clear whether it was originally a two- or three-link bit. Site 2, about 200m to the south-east, also contained pits filled with shells and produced coarse pottery; the plan of a circular house 8m in diameter was recovered.

A small part of the stone wall (possibly timber-laced) of an oval enclosure has been excavated at Clogher, Co. Tyrone, and dated to the Dowris phase. Some pottery sherds have been tentatively considered to represent vessels that were ceramic copies of bronze cauldrons (Warner 2009). Limited excavation at Carrownaglogh, west of Ballina, Co. Mayo, revealed part of a farmstead dated to around

the ninth century BC. Now covered by blanket bog, a combination of probing and excavation suggested the existence of an irregular stone-walled enclosure about 2.2ha in maximum extent. Traces of a robbed stone wall in the south-western part indicated that it had been enlarged at some time, and a small hut some 7m across with a central hearth was reportedly found in the northern half. Much of the enclosure was occupied by well-marked spade cultivation ridges averaging 1.5m in width. Further cultivation ridges were found outside the enclosure on both north and south. Pollen analysis supported by radiocarbon dates demonstrated an intensive phase of both arable (wheat and barley) and pastoral agriculture that probably lasted for about 250 years (O'Connell 1986). Pre-bog field systems at Derryinver, Renvyle, Connemara, are somewhat later: radiocarbon-dated pollen analyses indicate a sixth-century BC date (Molloy and O'Connell 1993).

Mooghaun, Co. Clare

The hillfort at Mooghaun, near Newmarket-on-Fergus, Co. Clare, is the most prominent monument in that part of south-east Clare and, though situated on a low hill about 80m above sea level, it commands wide views of the Shannon estuary (Grogan 2005). It is a large enclosure with three stone ramparts encompassing a total area of 11ha (Fig. 7.37). All three ramparts were of broadly similar construction and, though more or less concentric, built of fairly straight stretches of varying length, suggesting individual work-groups operating to an overall plan. Excavation in the inner enclosure demonstrated that the rampart here was of more or less dump construction with a low inner facing of a few courses and several lines of low internal revetments. In size it measured 6–9m in width and 1.5m in average height above the interior, but it was built to take advantage of the natural slope and on the north-eastern half of the site in particular there was a steep drop outside the rampart. It had a narrow angled entrance passage on the south-east. The middle rampart was 8–11m wide and over 2m high in places. For most of its circumference the outer rampart was composed of a large bank of stone with an average width of 5m, and it had a low outer facing of six courses of stones. It had a wide ditch and low outer bank, though on part of the south-west the inner bank

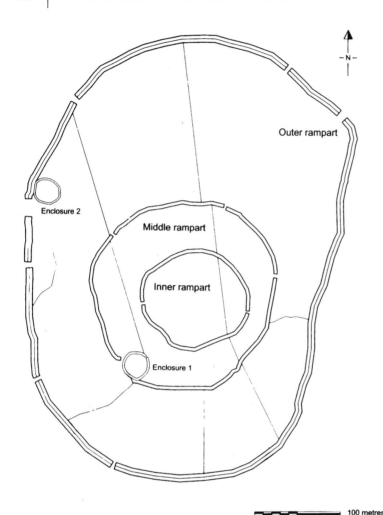

Fig. 7.37—Schematic plan of Mooghaun hillfort, Co. Clare: the small circular enclosures are later features.

alone was set on the edge of a steep slope; the ditch was over 5m wide in places and rock-cut to a depth of 1.74m. Lacking any semblance of vertical walling (as at Dún Aonghasa, for instance), the ramparts were not defensive in any military sense. Nonetheless, they were very substantial structures and each may have been slightly stepped in profile originally so would certainly have impeded access or egress. Their construction and the digging of the ditch involved the movement of an estimated 192,000 tons of stone. As Grogan points out, when viewed from a distance the light grey limestone ramparts carefully spaced on this rounded hill would have given the appearance of a great single wall.

Only meagre evidence for settlement was discovered, and some excavated areas produced no evidence of occupation. Stake- or post-holes representing the foundations of just two or perhaps four small circular houses were found inside the middle rampart. Some sherds of coarse pottery and animal bone (mainly cattle, pig and sheep or goat) were recovered. A series of radiocarbon dates from cattle bones from various contexts suggest that the ramparts were built as a single enterprise shortly before 900 BC. Presumably they were built by elements of the surrounding agricultural population. Pollen analysis has shown extensive forest clearance in the region and sustained cereal growth from 1450 BC, with the major reduction in tree cover occurring around 1100 BC. In the period 1100–650 BC woodland appears to have been replaced by pasture, and cereal-growing, mainly wheat, was also an important part of the economy.

The purpose of the Mooghaun enclosure is difficult to determine. The absence of significant evidence for occupation is intriguing and this recalls the situation at the somewhat earlier Cashel, Co. Cork (Chapter 6). Mooghaun's construction clearly demanded a considerable expenditure of human resources, but it cannot be described as a high-status settlement site and the term hillfort may be inappropriate as well. Apart from recognising the enormous amount of labour involved, there is little excavated evidence to demonstrate how society may have been structured. The monument may have been a great communal undertaking to provide a ritual focus or assembly place for the community, or it may be the expression of the power and organisational capability of an élite, perhaps a chiefdom. Even though it may be an oversimplification, a chiefdom model seems a good way of describing a hierarchical socio-political system. At present, as in Bronze Age Europe generally, material culture probably offers the best insights, since there is evidence of ranking in the contemporary bronze and goldwork (Harding 2000).

Mooghaun was clearly built as a prominent and focal monument in the landscape and presumably had some role in the social and economic organisation of the surrounding territory. It appears to dominate a lakeland zone to the north and east of Newmarket-on-Fergus and a natural routeway extending from the Fergus and Shannon estuaries to Broadford, north of Limerick, where the Broadford river valley runs westward to Formoyle Hill, crowned by another trivallate hillfort, 10km south-west of Killaloe. Grogan has identified a Mooghaun territory defined on the west by the Fergus estuary, by the Shannon to the south and by the Cratloe hills to the east. There is an important concentration of late prehistoric material in this area, the 'great Clare find' being the most noteworthy. The deposition of this great collection of gold near Mooghaun Lough some 750m to the north-east has prompted comparisons with both Haughey's Fort and Navan, Co. Armagh, both of whom also have lakes or ponds with associated ritual depositions on the north-east. It may be that large and important sites like Haughey's Fort and Navan had associated pools for 'the insertion of special items into the natural order', but whether the deposition near Mooghaun is

comparable is uncertain (Cooney and Grogan 1999). The lakeshore site at Knocknalappa is located about 4km to the south-east, and there are over 70 burnt mounds or burnt spreads in the region as well. Though not of the same scale as Mooghaun itself, a number of small defended enclosures, 0.2–1ha in area, are situated on hills or ridges, and some smaller habitation enclosures 15–36m in diameter occur also. If contemporary with Mooghaun, they may suggest a hierarchy of settlement and a series of territorial subdivisions.

The wetlands of the Shannon and Fergus estuaries were probably significant elements in flexible farming economies that also utilised the diverse resources offered by riverbank and estuarine marsh at various dates, including the Dowris phase. An intertidal wooden structure on the west bank of the Fergus estuary adjacent to the townland of Islandmagrath, Co. Clare, was built of two parallel rows of closely spaced stout roundwood posts. It was over 35m in length and at least 2m in width, with interwoven wattle between the posts. Horizontal panels of hurdlework were laid down between the two lines of posts and pinned to the underlying clays with sharpened pegs. A sample of hazel rod provided a radiocarbon date of 797–551 BC. This structure may have been a hard for beaching boats, or a jetty or causeway giving access to the lower part of the shore (O'Sullivan 2001). Riverine and coastal environments were exploited elsewhere as well (Woodman 2004b). The radiocarbon dating of a hearth in a shell midden to 770–600 BC at Culleenamore, near Sligo (Burenhult 1984), and the discovery of fragments of clay moulds for casting bronze swords in the sandhills at White Park Bay, Co. Antrim (Collins 1970), are just two examples.

There is a possibility that some coastal promontory sites may have been occupied too: the early medieval defences at the promontory fort of Dunbeg, Co. Kerry, were preceded by a ditch that cut off part of the promontory, and charcoal from this feature produced a radiocarbon date in the earlier half of the last millennium BC (Barry 1981). Hilltop enclosures of various forms other than Mooghaun also occur and, while the evidence is still limited, it is likely they had different purposes. A small enclosure at Freestone Hill, Co. Kilkenny, with a single stony bank and external ditch, enclosing an area of about 2ha with an average

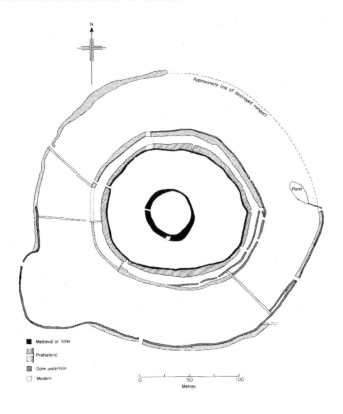

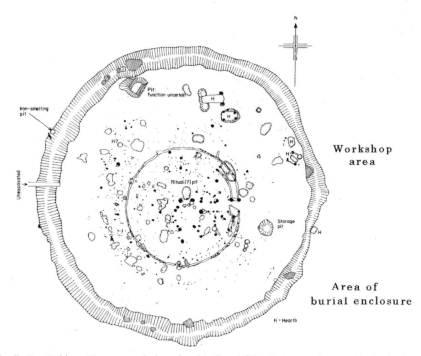

Fig. 7.38—Rathgall, Co. Wicklow. Above: general plan of multivallate hillfort. Below: enclosure with circular house, pits and hearths. The workshop and burial areas are indicated.

diameter of 140m, was excavated in the late 1940s. Some glass beads and coarse pottery were found, and parallels between the pottery from here and from Rathgall, Co. Wicklow, have prompted the suggestion that there may have been Dowris phase occupation on Freestone Hill as well. The recognition that some of the glass beads could be early and the dating of an old sample of charcoal from the site to 810–550 BC confirm this. The site also produced some provincial Roman bronzes and a coin of Constantine II of the fourth century AD and may have been a cult centre in the late Iron Age (Ó Floinn 2000). Another small hilltop enclosure at Knockacarrigeen, near Tuam, Co. Galway, measured about 160m across, and limited excavation demonstrated that it was simply enclosed by a low rampart of dump construction bearing some similarity to those at Mooghaun. No dating evidence was found, however (Carey 2002). A large multivallate hilltop enclosure at Rahally, near New Inn, Co. Galway, comprised a double outer ditch and two concentric widely spaced inner ditches with simple entrances on east and west. It had an overall diameter of 450m. No structural remains were found but the ditches contained butchered animal bone and some sherds of coarse pottery; charcoal from the base of the inner one provided a radiocarbon date of 994–827 BC (O'Sullivan 2007).

Rathgall, Co. Wicklow

The multivallate hillfort of Rathgall is situated on the western end of a low but prominent ridge some 137m above sea level in south-west County Wicklow (near Tullow, Co. Carlow) and is a site of major importance (Raftery 1976a; 2004). Four more or less concentric ramparts enclose an area of some 7.3ha (Fig. 7.38, upper). The inner enclosure is surrounded by a polygonal stone rampart 45m in average diameter; 27–53m outside this are two further ramparts set 10–12m apart. The irregular outer rampart is much denuded but had a diameter of about 310m. Excavations in the central enclosure, and on the southern slope of the hill beyond the outer rampart, have shown that the story of Rathgall was quite a complex one. The various ramparts have not been securely dated and the inner stone enclosure may be of medieval or more recent date, but it is possible that the three other ramparts are contemporary with late

prehistoric occupation on the hilltop that lay in part beneath the late stone enclosure.

Excavation within the late stone monument revealed an annular ditched enclosure surrounding another circular enclosure (possibly a large house) that produced evidence for occupation and bronze-working. The annular ditch was circular with an internal diameter of 35m but somewhat irregularly dug, with depths varying from 50cm to 1.5m. There was no entrance causeway so it may have been crossed by a timber bridge, possibly facing the eastern entrance to the house. The inner enclosure was 15m in diameter and formed of timber posts set in a bedding trench 15–25cm deep. Two large posts flanked an entrance on the east, and the walls turned inwards to form a small porch with a second inner doorway. Many post-holes were found in the interior and presumably served as roof supports but no coherent plan was discernible, though there did appear to be a parallel row of posts leading from the doorway towards the centre of the structure.

A large oval pit (pit 119), which measured 1.75m by 1.25m and 40cm in depth, was located just north of the centre of the house; its base and sides had been lined with some organic material and it contained a large boulder, which had been carefully sealed in the pit with sandy soil. A very small scatter of burnt human bone and a gold hair-ring were found beneath the boulder in the basal carbonised matter. The organic lining was radiocarbon-dated to 1290–1040 BC. Several other irregularly dug pits were discovered and, except for a small fire-reddened area in the north-eastern part, no clear traces of a hearth were found. Numerous other pits and post-holes were found outside the structure and within the annular enclosure. One pit just to the south-east of the house entrance contained traces of a wicker basket that had been renewed once, if not twice, and was evidently a storage pit. A series of hearths were found mainly on the north-east, and several of these had associated post-holes suggesting shelters of some description. The bedding trench of the house cut into one of these, so some of them at least may belong to an earlier phase of activity. For others, however, a Dowris phase date is confirmed by a series of radiocarbon dates; potsherds and bones found in several hearths suggested domestic use, but clay mould fragments were found in one.

Large quantities of coarse pottery were

discovered, a little of it decorated in simple fashion. Other artefacts included saddle querns and stone rubbers, a bronze bar toggle of north European type (Fig. 7.39, 1), bracelet fragments, and a bronze conical rivet of the type found on some cauldrons. A large number of glass beads were an exceptional discovery (Henderson 1988). Most are simple annular beads of blue or greenish-blue colour but some are decorated with circle or concentric circle designs. Chemical analysis has shown that most of these beads are of a low-magnesium, high-potassium type found in continental Europe, but whether these are exotic imports or of local manufacture is still uncertain.

Some of this material came from the enclosure ditch on the east and was derived from a workshop area found just outside it, where there were deposits of organic material up to 35cm deep. Numerous post-holes may be the remains of a number of timber structures reflecting a series of phases of activity. There were hundreds of fragments of clay moulds for weapons, including swords and spearheads, and for probable socketed axes and gouges or chisels. There was also a mould fragment for a flanged implement. Some lumps of waste bronze were found here, and artefacts such as a small socketed gouge, a tanged punch and other bronze objects. Bracelets of jet or lignite, numerous glass beads, some small pieces of amber, saddle querns and whetstones were also recovered. Gold objects included a biconical gold bead, another hair-ring—a penannular bronze ring covered with gold foil—and a finely made cylindrical bead or pendant consisting of a dark green glass bead with a gold inset. This was evidently a major workshop that produced weapons on a significant scale and probably manufactured finer prestigious items as well.

The presence of several cremated burials proved to be another exceptional feature. To the south of the workshop area, a circular ditch 19m in diameter enclosed a series of features including a central pit containing the cremated bones of a young adult (Fig. 7.39). This pit had been dug into an area of reddened burnt soil enclosed by a dense U-shaped arrangement of some 1,500 closely set stake-holes. Fragments of human bone in this burnt earth suggest that the cremation had taken place on site. Elsewhere in the enclosure, the cremated bones of a child were found in a small pit at the end of one

of the arms of the U-shaped setting, a coarse bucket-shaped pot placed mouth upwards in a second pit contained the cremated bones of an adult and child, and a third contained a hoard of bronzes comprising a small chisel, parts of a spearhead and a sword blade. Later activity is attested by a small bowl-shaped furnace for iron-working dated to the period AD180–540.

Further evidence of settlement was found on the southern slope of the hill outside the outer rampart. This included the foundations of a small D-shaped hut and another larger circular structure with associated coarse pottery. Nearby pits contained more pottery, parts of saddle querns and fragments of clay moulds, and the remains of hearths were also discovered. A small annular ditch enclosed a few post-holes, one associated with some fragments of burnt human bone, and a pit, and may be a ritual site. The sheer quantity of metalworking evidence, the weapon-manufacturing, the gold, the glass beads, the amber fragments, the cremated burials and associated ritual, and the hoard of bronzes all combine to set Rathgall apart from other settlements of the time. These factors, the unusual ritual evidence and its prominent hilltop location clearly imply a site of considerable status.

Aristocrats, warriors and craftsmen?

It is generally believed that significant social changes occurred in prehistoric Europe in the third millennium BC. The importance of ancestry, so significant in the Neolithic, may have diminished, and social relationships may have been increasingly defined not just by kinship and lineage but in terms of alliances and competition in which material goods played an important role. Prestigious artefacts were key factors in defining social relationships, and since in some areas such artefacts could only be obtained through contacts with other societies with similar preoccupations a pattern of reciprocal demand developed. In Ireland this process may have been a long and uneven one. The appearance of symbolic objects like stone battleaxes, halberds and gold lunulae, and of individual burials in pits and cists with distinctive pottery and the occasional flint knife, bronze razor or faience bead, suggests that it could have commenced by about 2500 BC.

Metalwork and metalworking may have given greater impetus to the development of social hierarchies, and the scarcity of evidence for

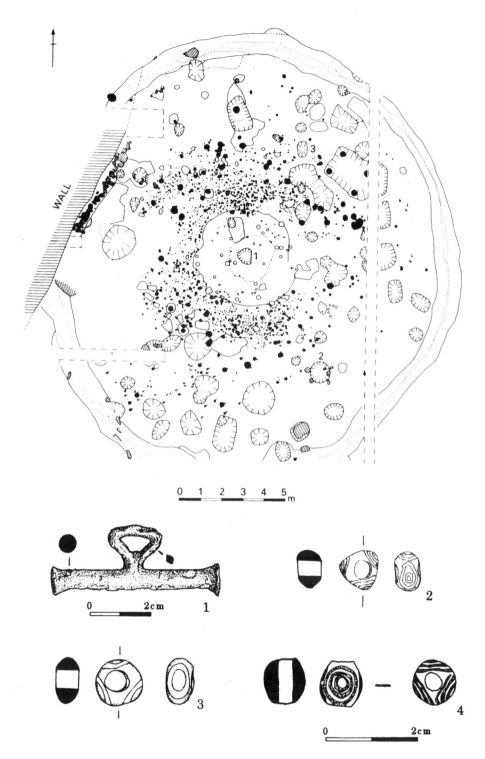

Fig. 7.39—Rathgall, Co. Wicklow. Above: plan of burial enclosure, showing central cremation pit (1) with U-shaped setting of stake-holes. Below: exotic material from Rathgall. (1) Bronze bar toggle. (2–4) Glass beads with inlaid concentric circle or circle ornament.

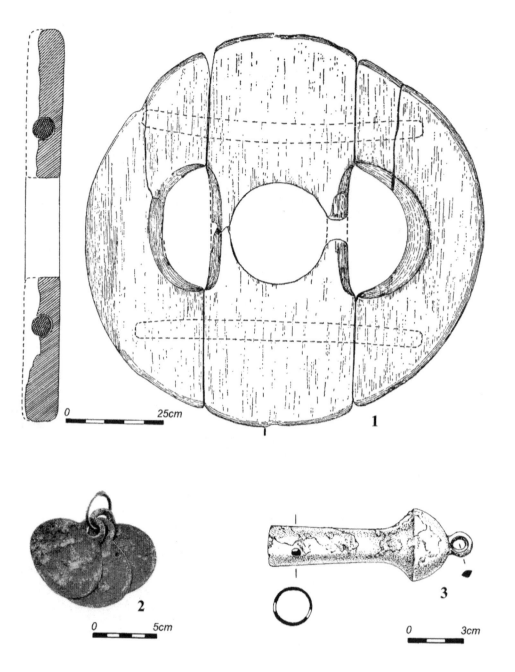

Fig. 7.40—(1) One of a pair of block wheels found in a bog at Doogarymore, Co. Roscommon. Three large pieces of alder are held together by two large dowels of yew; the wheel was originally circular with a diameter of about 1m. (2) Rattle-pendants from Lissanode, Co. Westmeath. (3) Bronze ferrule, possibly for a goad, from Moynalty Lough, Co. Monaghan.

metalworking on settlement sites may be an indication of its exclusive character. From about 1400 BC objects such as exceptionally long bronze rapiers and spearheads and finely executed goldwork represent greater technical specialism. Whether in lock-ring, hair-ring or cauldron, craftsmen display an extraordinary interest in technical virtuosity and this, presumably, was to indulge the aesthetic tastes of their patrons. An increasing appreciation of the visual and artistic qualities of fine metalwork and a concern with ostentatious display became the mark of an élite minority. As already mentioned, with evidence of ranking in the contemporary bronze and goldwork, a chiefdom model seems a good way of describing a hierarchical socio-political system. The appearance of prestige weaponry is revealing, and when the martial repertoire consists of sword, spear and bronze shield, some evidently symbolic, then it may be that this reflects an élite warrior aristocracy who may have distinguished themselves by drinking rituals, equestrian feats, ritualised combat, modes of dress, personal weaponry and bodily ornament (Treherne 1995). They could well have sported some of the contemporary gold ornaments.

Since the control of rituals such as hoard deposition and ceremonial feasting is also an important mechanism for the maintenance of power, these activities may have been the preserve of the élite as well. The presence of tools such as gouges and chisels in a small number of hoards indicates that certain craftsmen had high status and were also entitled to representation in the ceremonial sphere.

It is tempting to speculate that the two-wheeled cart or chariot may have been another status item, but Irish evidence is lacking. It is a possibility since there is abundant evidence elsewhere, including carved representations of two-wheeled vehicles in such diverse locations as Iberia (Fig. 7.14) and Scandinavia. The use of wooden ceremonial carts with block wheels and drawn by either horses or oxen is conceivable. The remains of a pair of massive wooden block wheels found in a bog at Doogarymore, near Kilteevan, Co. Roscommon (Fig. 7.40, 1), are radiocarbon-dated to 760–260 BC; a 1m-long piece of perforated

timber found 3m away may have formed part of the vehicle (Lucas 1972). An unprovenanced wooden ox-yoke has been dated to 920–780 BC (Hedges *et al.* 1991).

There is very little evidence for horse trappings: cheek-pieces such as the antler example from Moynagh Lough are rare, and metal fitments, like the possible handle for a goad from Moynalty Lough, Co. Monaghan (Fig. 7.40, 3), are often of uncertain purpose. A bronze phalera, a small circular bronze mount thought to be for horse harness, possibly of seventh-century BC date, was found on Inis Cealtra, near Mountshannon, Co. Clare. A second is reported from Rathtinaun, Co. Sligo, and a third from Mullagh, near Bantry, Cork (Cahill 2006). A series of bronze discs considered to be rattle-pendants may be horse-gear too: several unprovenanced examples are recorded, and a set of three suspended from a bronze ring were found at Lissanode, south-west of Ballymore, Co. Westmeath, along with bronze objects which may have been cheek-pieces (Fig. 7.40, 2). Both phalera and pendants have parallels in Britain and on the Continent. Bronze rings of various types are sometimes considered to be harness-strap holders but obviously, like mounts and rattles, all were not necessarily placed on horses. Some, like a collar of bronze rings forming two broad chains, found in a former bog near the town of Roscommon, may have been personal ornaments or insignia of rank (Eogan 2001).

Whatever about the uncertainties of horse harness and the limited nature of the evidence for a hierarchical society, it may be tentatively suggested that prehistoric Ireland from the later second millennium BC was populated by numerous small chiefdoms linked with one another (and with similar communities in western Britain) by an extensive system of alliances. It is not an unreasonable speculation that an élite stratum preoccupied with status, display and ritual was ensconced at the summit of a social hierarchy that also included warriors and craftsmen. This élite element is difficult to identify in the burial record, however, and the funerary evidence is relatively sparse.

8

FROM BRONZE TO IRON

The date of 600 BC proposed for the end of the Dowris phase and the commencement of the following iron-using period is only an approximation. The later first millennium BC and the early centuries AD are amongst the most obscure periods in Irish prehistoric archaeology. The decline of the bronze weapon industry and its replacement by iron sometime in the last millennium BC, and the disappearance of characteristic artefacts such as bronze swords and socketed axeheads, events which should theoretically mark the end of the Dowris phase, are imperfectly understood developments to say the least. There is general agreement that the development of an iron technology was a significant factor in the eventual demise of bronze-working on a large scale, but how, why and when this came about in Ireland is far from clear.

The use of iron on a modest scale is sporadically recorded in various parts of Europe from the second millennium BC onwards, and iron implements were used with increasing frequency in central Europe from about 1000 BC. Iron was in widespread use on the Continent by the late eighth century BC. In Britain there are sporadic traces of iron-working as early as the tenth century (Collard 2005), but the earliest evidence for iron-working in any significant way dates from about the middle of the seventh century: that iron copy of a bronze sickle in the Llyn Fawr, Glamorgan, hoard, just one of a number of early instances. How long it took for the new technology to supplant bronze to any significant degree is uncertain and it is possible that the process may have taken several centuries. It is

also possible, of course, that the appearance of iron had a more immediate effect on the value of bronze, which in turn resulted in a rapid reduction and eventually a cessation in its widespread use and in extensive hoard deposition.

THE GÜNDLINGEN SWORD

A series of bronze swords display some features that sharply distinguish them from the common class 4 sword of the Dowris phase. These are class 5 swords in George Eogan's classification, the insular Gündlingen swords of J. D. Cowen (1967). The Gündlingen sword, named after a possible grave-find in south-western Germany, is one of the classic Continental bronze sword types of the eighth century BC and was in contemporaneous use with iron swords. This sword has a number of quite distinctive features, including a convex-sided hilt, usually flangeless, with a prominent perforated rectangular pommel-piece (an extension to take a large decorative pommel of bone or antler), narrow pin-like rivets (occasionally with a punched head with a central nipple), wide-angled shoulders and a long, slender, leaf-shaped blade of thick oval central cross-section with a beaded edge. While a few have subrectangular perforated pommel-pieces, versions of the bronze Gündlingen sword in Ireland and Britain are characterised by a distinctive pommel-piece with a notch in its upper edge or an even more exaggerated winged form in which the notch is widened and the ears extended outwards and downwards to form hooks (Fig. 8.1, 1). The hilt is

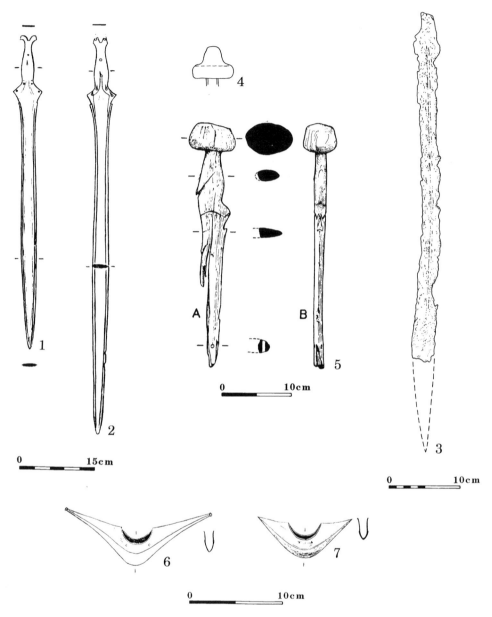

Fig. 8.1—(1) Gündlingen sword from Ireland with no precise provenance. (2) Another example from near Athlone. (3) Iron sword from the River Shannon, near Athlone (the slight bend is not ancient). (4) Possible pommel shape based on contemporary Continental forms (no scale). (5) Wooden model of a sword from Cappagh, Co. Kerry. (6) Winged chape from Ireland with no precise provenance. (7) Boat-shaped chape from Keelogue, Co. Galway.

usually flangeless and convex-sided with wide-angled shoulders below. The long slender blade may have the characteristic rounded central cross-section with a ridged or beaded bevelled edge, but more often than not Irish examples have a simpler blade cross-section with a rounded or flattened centre with very wide, hollowed bevelled edges. Rivets are characteristically pin-like, some with the distinctive ring-punched head with central cone or nipple; the rivet pattern is apparently variable.

The origins of this sword type have been the subject of much debate, a complex tale summarised by Gerloff (2004). Once thought to be a Continental form originating in southern Germany

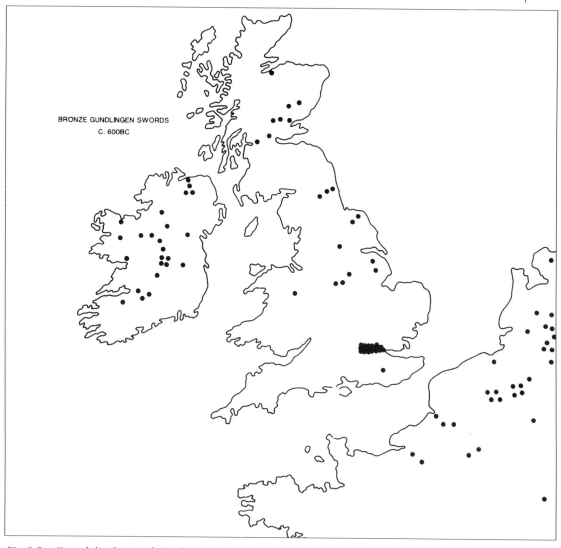

BRONZE GUNDLINGEN SWORDS
C. 600BC

Fig. 8.2—General distribution of Gündlingen swords.

and Bohemia and introduced to Britain and Ireland by early Iron Age 'sword-bearers', a British origin has been argued in recent years mainly because convincing prototypes are absent on the Continent and because this type shares some features with indigenous Ewart Park swords. Gerloff favours an origin in south-eastern England in the late ninth century. The distribution of the various forms of the Gündlingen sword (Fig. 8.2) clearly depicts a widespread weapon type with an Irish, British and Continental dimension, but typological differences indicate regional forms. The type as a whole is part of a tradition of bronze sword-making over five centuries old. Over this time-span there was a

continuous process of change in the forms of the weapons actually used, and here we have the final regional expression of a long-lasting fashion for bronze sword usage. The distribution is a reflection of a shared fashion and the contact this implies.

In Ireland these swords are, on average, longer than class 4: they vary from about 58cm to about 84cm in length, the average length being 67.3cm, with 89% measuring 60cm or more. The longest known, with an original length of about 84cm, was dredged from the River Moy in Coolcronaun townland, north of Foxford, Co. Mayo. Surprisingly, associations of complete swords in hoards seem to be unknown: four swords are said to have been found with a few others 'upon an ancient battlefield near Athlone' and a number were recovered from the celebrated Bog of Cullen, Co. Tipperary, but neither can be described as an associated find. A number of hybrid swords are known in Ireland, as in Britain, and they are possibly an indication of the willingness of swordsmiths to experiment with various permutations of old and new features. A few have T-shaped terminals to the hilt, or combine features of classes 4 and 5. Though no scabbards have been found, a number of bronze chapes are known (Fig. 8.1, 6–7). Boat-shaped and winged types have been recognised and are of Irish–British forms inspired by Continental fashions (Eogan 1965). All are stray isolated finds, but a boat-shaped example was found in the Bog of Cullen (which also yielded a number of swords).

It has been suggested that swords of the Gündlingen family were dual-purpose weapons, intended for use on foot or on horseback, and the contemporary appearance on the Continent of horse equipment such as iron bridle-bits might add some weight to this hypothesis. Nevertheless, the belief that winged chapes were functional and capable of being hooked beneath the foot of a horse-riding warrior to facilitate the drawing of the sword seems implausible. The small size of the rivet holes for attachment to the scabbard tip suggests that these objects could not have withstood robust treatment and were probably primarily decorative. Though no pommels have been found, some contemporary Continental swords had large decorated 'hat-shaped' pommels, and this may have been the fashion in Ireland too: a small wooden sword found in boggy ground at Cappagh, Co. Kerry, has been claimed to be a model of a class 5 example and it certainly has a quite prominent pommel (Fig. 8.1, 5). One of the Bog of Cullen swords, found in 1748, is said to have had rivets about 2cm long still in place, with 'a thin piece of gold' attached to one. Cowen accepts the description as that of a Gündlingen sword and it is possible, therefore, that some of these pommels were richly ornamented.

A number of other bronze artefacts are thought to reflect further shared fashions with Britain or the Continent, but compared to the preceding Dowris phase there is a disconcertingly small amount of metal in the archaeological record. In part, at least, this might be explicable by a shift in depositional practices, fewer hoards meaning fewer objects. Significant single finds of objects assignable to the last few centuries of the millennium are scarce too. These include a heavy knobbed bronze ring of Italian type said to have come 'from Co. Derry' which, like a number of other stray discoveries of exotic objects, could well be an antiquarian acquisition of recent centuries rather than an ancient import. A small bronze figurine of an Etruscan warrior 'found in a bog in Ireland' and another Italic bronze statuette 'from Sligo' could conceivably be early imports, but obviously, given the lack of information about the circumstances of their discovery, certainty is impossible (Jope 1958). A small number of Italic safety-pin brooches or fibulae have been found, again as stray finds (Fig. 8.3). One is said to have been found in County Dublin and the others are unprovenanced, but since a considerable number are known from Britain the Irish finds could be genuine (Jope 1962).

One find is relatively well documented. This is a small hoard of bronze artefacts from Kilmurry, near Castleisland, Co. Kerry, found in 1944 during quarrying operations (Fig. 8.3). It consisted of a small leaf-shaped spearhead, a bag-shaped socketed axehead, two simple penannular bracelets and a small knobbed bracelet with its outer body decorated with transverse grooves (Eogan 1983). Bracelets of this sort are known in the seventh and sixth centuries BC in various parts of France. The association suggests that Dowris phase bronzes may still have been in use around 600 BC or even 500 BC. The evidence for any later survival of Dowris phase metalwork is very slight, however; the claim that a class 4 sword bears traces of a scabbard form of the third or second century BC (Harbison 1970) and is thus an indication of the very late survival of Dowris metalworking traditions should be treated with due caution. While the very late survival of Dowris phase bronze-working in some parts of Ireland cannot be ruled out, the limited evidence suggests that the late seventh century and the sixth century BC probably saw the displacement of bronze by iron. Axe signatures on dated worked timbers from Derryville Bog, near Thurles, Co. Tipperary, suggest the use of iron axes from about 630 BC (Ó Néill 2005). Iron-working waste and some coarse pottery from a pit near Kinnegad, Co. Westmeath, have been radiocarbon-dated to 810–420 BC; the date, from oak charcoal, may be

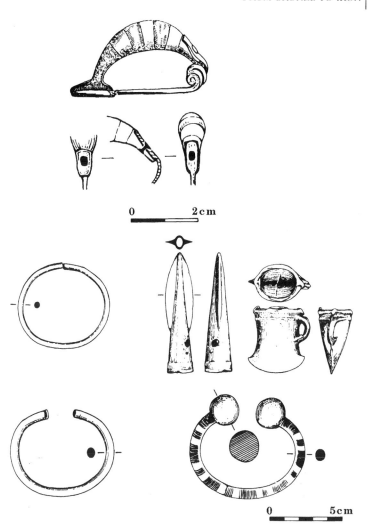

0   2 cm

Fig. 8.3—Above: Italic leech-shaped safety-pin brooch or fibula from Ireland, repaired with the addition of a riveted spring or pin. Below: hoard with bronze spearhead, socketed axehead, two simple bracelets and an imported knobbed bracelet, from Kilmurry, Co. Kerry.

0   5 cm

from old wood, but the presence of pottery might imply an early date nonetheless. Iron slag from another pit near Kinnegad, at Rossan, has been radiocarbon-dated to 820–780 BC, but again the date comes from oak charcoal; this large pit may have been used for the production of charcoal (Carlin *et al.* 2008). The use of iron was a technological development that may well have initiated some significant social and economic changes.

THE EARLIEST IRON-WORKING

A small number of iron objects have been considered to be early examples of the new technology and some are believed to be versions of well-known bronze types (Scott 1990). Two looped and socketed axeheads are probably iron copies of the familiar bronze form but are from undated contexts. One, said to come from 'one of the Lough Mourne crannogs' in County Antrim (Fig. 8.4), has been made from a single piece of iron, forged flat and folded into a cylinder, one end of which was then beaten flat. The loop was formed by pinching out a lobe of metal on one side of the completed socket and then punching a hole through it with a rectangular punch. It seems as if the smith went to considerable trouble to copy a bronze model, even though a loopless, rectangular-mouthed socketed form would have been simpler to make and equally effective, as an iron axe from Feerwore, Co. Galway, demonstrates.

The second example is from Toome, Co.

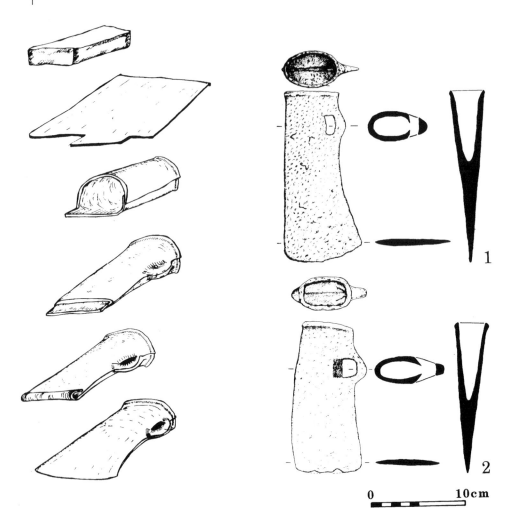

Fig. 8.4—Left: method of manufacture of an iron socketed axe from Lough Mourne. Right: (1) axe from Lough Mourne, Co. Antrim; (2) axe from Toome, Co. Antrim.

Antrim (Fig. 8.4, 2), and was made in much the same way, though the blade was formed not by folding over a tongue of metal but by welding the two faces together. Interestingly, even though older models were being copied, these two axes display a fairly sophisticated knowledge of the potential of iron to achieve a high degree of hardness when alloyed with carbon. The cutting edges of both have had carbon deliberately added, this carburisation producing a superior metal approaching the quality of steel. Care was taken to position the carburised surfaces so that the steeled cutting edges were protected by more flexible metal with a lower carbon content.

Chemical analysis has shown that the Lough Mourne specimen was possibly made from Antrim ores and is unlikely to have been an import. Similar looped and socketed iron axeheads have been found in Britain, where the same process of copying bronze prototypes occurred and where the earliest iron-working is just as hard to find and equally difficult to date. The iron rivets identified on the Lisdrumturk, Co. Monaghan, bronze cauldron (Fig. 7.6) are obviously an instance of early iron-working, though difficult to date precisely and possibly later repairs. It has been claimed that a riveted sheet-iron cauldron from Drumlane, Co. Cavan, may be early too, though the use of multi-sheet construction and round-headed rivets is rather slender dating evidence.

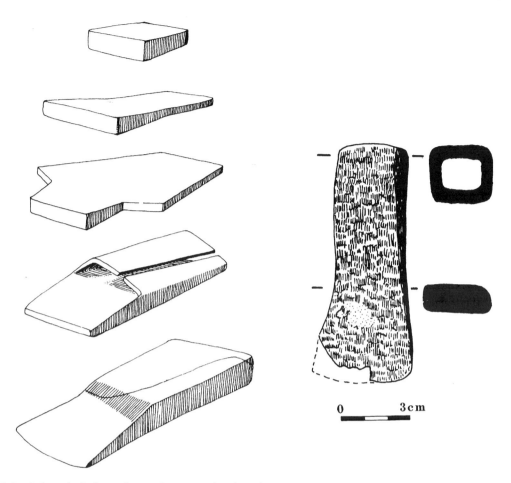

Fig. 8.5—Left: method of manufacture of an iron socketed axe from Feerwore, Co. Galway. Right: the Feerwore axe.

An axehead from Feerwore, near Loughrea, Co. Galway, is of a simple socketed type (Fig. 8.5). Made from a single piece of iron, one end was forged into a blade while the rest was hammered out and folded over to form a rectangular socket, and here the smith had evidently mastered the technique of expertly forging a right angle. It was found beneath the bank of a small ringfort and is not securely dated. Axes of this sort had a wide currency on the Continent from about the third century BC, and Barry Raftery suggests that the Feerwore example might date from the late second or early first century BC. Another example found beneath the bank at Ráth na Rí on Tara is imprecisely dated to the last three centuries or so BC (Roche 2002).

The date of a number of iron artefacts from Rathtinaun, Co. Sligo, is uncertain, but a shaft-hole axehead from there could possibly be of much the same date. It was rather crudely made but is nonetheless of complicated manufacture: a piece of iron was folded over and welded on to itself to make a socket, the welded area was covered by a flat plate hammered over both sides of the blade, and the blade was then drawn down and folded back on itself and welded to the plate. As on the looped socketed axes, the blade edge was carburised.

Three other shaft-hole axes from Kilbeg, Co. Westmeath (Fig. 8.6), were of simpler manufacture, being made of two pieces of iron, one folded over to form the socket with its two ends welded to the faces of a second, which formed the blade. These were found with a pair of horse-pendants (one of bronze, one of iron), a type not easily datable but which may belong to the first century AD or thereabouts. These shaft-hole axes are a reminder

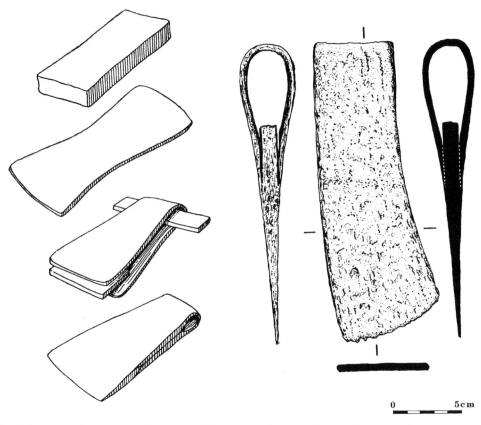

Fig. 8.6—Left: method of manufacture of an iron shaft-hole axe. Right: one of three shaft-hole axes from Kilbeg, Co. Westmeath.

that simple axe designs of a basic sort had a long lifespan and illustrate one of the consequences of the new technology. Percussive shaping reflecting the skills of individual smiths may now produce significant differences in shape in the one artefact type. Furthermore, the medium also imposed new and simpler lines on many artefacts, producing basic forms of axe, chisel, knife and other implements that were to remain essentially unchanged for many centuries. A further complication, of course, is the susceptibility of iron to corrosion and decay, which must explain to a great extent the scarcity of surviving material. The problems of poor preservation are clearly demonstrated by the relatively small number of iron swords and spears that survive in comparison to the many hundreds of bronze examples. Indeed, experimentation has shown that in certain bog conditions the complete dissolution of an iron object could take place within a century (Kelly 1995).

An iron sword found in 1847 in the course of drainage in the River Shannon at Athlone, Co. Westmeath, has been claimed to be a seventh-century BC Continental type (Fig. 8.1, 3) because, in particular, its haft was flat and its blade expanded towards the point and may have been leaf-shaped. But its triangular cross-section with slight midrib does not resemble the normal ribbed section of these iron swords, as seen, for instance, on the only example known from Britain from the Llyn Fawr, Glamorgan, hoard. It is possible that the Athlone sword is an iron copy of an indigenous bronze Gündlingen sword, and if its original length was about 60–65cm this would place it within the appropriate size range. Analysis also suggests that it could be an early piece; though low in carbon and therefore never a particularly effective weapon, its edges were cold-hammered to increase hardness, a technique that would have been familiar to a bronzesmith.

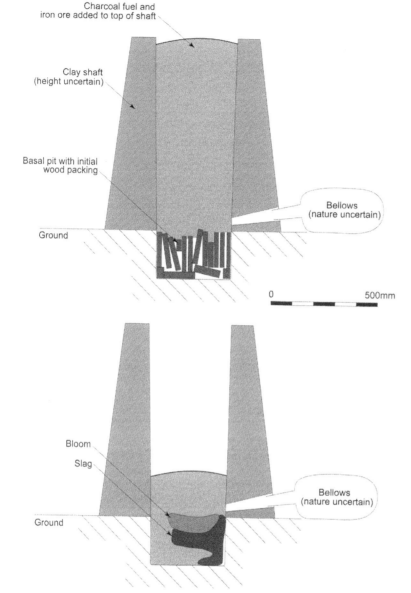

Charcoal fuel and
iron ore added to top of shaft

Clay shaft
(height uncertain)

Basal pit with initial
wood packing

Bellows
(nature uncertain)

Ground

0   500mm

Bloom

Slag

Bellows
(nature uncertain)

Ground

Fig. 8.7—Artist's reconstruction of an early iron-smelting furnace.

The production of iron was a skilled process but required relatively simple equipment. Iron was extracted through heating the ore by burning charcoal in a small furnace with a shallow bowl-shaped base and a low cylindrical shaft about 70cm high (Crew and Rehren 2002). The required temperatures of 1,100–1,250°C would be achieved comparatively easily with a bellows. This smelting process would produce a deposit of slag, which would accumulate at the base of the furnace below a bloom (Fig. 8.7). The bloom, a spongy mass of metallic iron, had to be reheated and carefully hammered to weld the iron particles together and to remove extraneous matter such as slag. Once this was done, the smith had a piece of iron from which artefacts could be made. Traces of iron-working have been found at Ráth na Rí on Tara and at several locations near Kinnegad, Co. Westmeath, and Enfield, Co. Meath. As already mentioned, a large pit at Rossan, near Kinnegad, may have been used to produce charcoal essential for the smelting process; charcoal was made by carbonising wood under oxygen-limited conditions so the wood was roasted but not burnt (Carlin *et al.* 2008). That the smelting process may have had a ritual dimension is suggested by the discovery of traces of a brief spell of iron-working in a circular timber structure set within a discontinuous circular ditch at Knockcommane, south-east Co. Limerick, and radiocarbon-dated to 357–47 BC (McQuade *et al.* 2009).

If the Athlone sword dates from around 600 BC, and allowing for the poor survival rate of iron, it is still surprising that the next recognised group of iron swords should number only about 30 and should seem to date from a period spanning the last two or three centuries BC and the first century AD. An even smaller number of iron spearheads is preserved and, while many are virtually impossible to date with any degree of accuracy, a number probably belong to this general period as well. The nature of the bronze industry changes too: in the main, bronze is no longer used for weapons but is used instead for a range of personal ornaments, horse harness, ferrules and other decorative attachments.

The remarkable scarcity of archaeological material datable to the period 600–300 BC is not solely an Irish problem; there is some decrease in the number of metalwork finds in Britain and in parts of the Continent as well. In Ireland this scarcity seems more acute, but this may be due to several factors, including not just the virtual cessation of metalwork deposition but also the absence of a burial tradition that included the practice of placing grave-goods such as weaponry with the remains of the dead and the failure to identify and excavate settlement sites in any number. The latter deficiency will, no doubt, be remedied in time, but the present lack of settlement evidence means that the archaeology of Iron Age Ireland does seem to be 'an archaeology of the non-routine of ceremonial centres, routeways and boundaries, and rich metalwork offered up in bogs, rivers and pools' (Armit 2007). This rich metalwork and other material will be considered below; most of it has been the subject of detailed study by Barry Raftery in a series of major publications (1983; 1984; 1994a).

DISCONTINUITY AND CHANGE OR CONTINUITY AND INNOVATION?

The apparent demise of a large-scale bronze industry at this time would seem to be a dramatic transformation reflecting at least some equally

significant social and economic developments. This may well be what is implied by the disappearance of a whole range of gold and bronze types from the archaeological record. If, as seems likely, these metals had an important role in the maintenance of status relationships, then the adoption of iron-working may indeed have disrupted this structure, reduced the value of gold and bronze in this sphere and precipitated a decline in associated customs like hoard deposition. Why a new and potentially disruptive technology should be adopted is a difficult question. There are several possibilities and many years ago the answer seemed a deceptively simple one, as, for example, when R. A. S. Macalister (1928) asserted that this change was brought about by the immigration of Celtic peoples about 400 BC, the invading Celts subduing the aboriginal inhabitants with superior iron weapons. But there is no good archaeological evidence to support the theory of an influx of new peoples on any scale. Another possibility is that a shortage of bronze might have prompted the search for some other metal, but it seems that local copper resources may have been sufficient for Irish requirements. Of course, if early iron objects had a prestigious value, then their acquisition along with the new technology would be just another step in a familiar acquisitive process by élite elements of society. But such prestigious early iron items are conspicuous by their absence, and numerous bronze objects, notably the local versions of the Gündlingen sword, demonstrate both the continuing value of bronze and likely contacts with iron-using communities elsewhere. As already mentioned, these contacts, part of a long-established network of communications between Ireland and Britain, are the probable mechanism by which knowledge of the new technology was eventually transmitted. There is the intriguing possibility that the impetus for the widespread substitution of one locally available metal for another came not from the élites but from other, lower levels in the social hierarchy. Small though the sample is, it may be significant that socketed and shaft-hole axes should figure so prominently, and it is possible that hewers of wood rather than wielders of swords were the principal beneficiaries of the new iron technology, and possibly its main proponents too. The potential of iron to supply a range of basic tools must have been quickly realised. If there were any disadvantageous

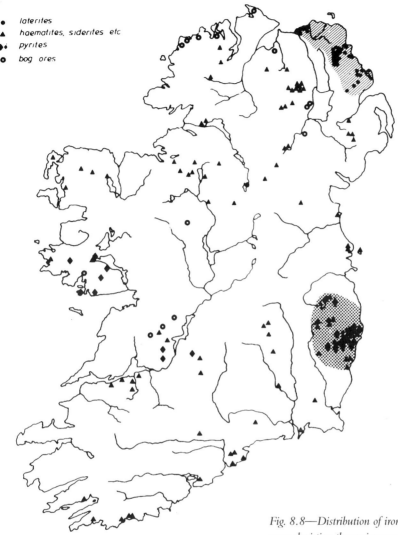

Fig. 8.8—Distribution of iron ores in Ireland, with hatched areas depicting the major sources in Antrim and Wicklow.

differences in the relative hardness of bronze and iron edged tools, and this may not have been as significant as has been claimed, then these were offset by the ready availability of iron ore. It is also possible, of course, that iron production remained, like earlier bronze-working, a craft associated with élite patronage. It undoubtedly had magical associations (Giles 2007), and this may explain why traces have occasionally been found in megalithic tombs (Scott 1990) and on sites such as the Bronze Age cemetery mound at Grange, Co. Roscommon (Chapter 4).

Iron ores are widespread in Ireland (Fig. 8.8)

and sources include lateritic ores in Antrim basalts, pyrites in County Wicklow and siderite around Lough Allen in County Leitrim and at the aptly named Slieve Anierin or 'Iron Mountain' near Drumshanbo. Bog ores may also have been a plentiful source, and theoretically ore can form in any peat deposit where conditions are suitable. Substantial quantities have been identified in recent times in counties Donegal, Tyrone and Roscommon. To what extent these different sources were exploited in ancient times is not known, but the general availability of iron must have offered many small communities the possibility of manufacturing their own tools and weapons free of the constraints imposed by the limited and controlled supplies of copper and tin. This development would no doubt have caused some considerable discomfiture to those individuals or communities who controlled the raw materials of the bronze industry. If rank and power depended on this control, then there could have been a collapse in the various exchange systems and political alliances that linked communities, even leading to a more fragmented social landscape by the end of the sixth century BC, as has been surmised elsewhere in Atlantic Europe. At present the Irish evidence provides few clues, but it is possible that rank and power did not depend solely on access to supplies of a particular metal and, dramatic though the disappearance of so many bronze artefact types appears to be, it does not necessarily follow that there was a wider socio-economic collapse, since bronze was probably just one element, though admittedly a prestigious one, in a wider spectrum of activity. There may have been some dislocation, but if, for instance, wealth and status also depended to a significant degree on cattle or sheep, then another order may quickly have asserted itself.

There was some dislocation in the votive sphere, as the apparent halt in the deposition of fine metalwork suggests. It is possible that other materials may have replaced the gold and bronze, or different rituals entirely may have developed. In any event, offerings of fine metalwork reappear in the archaeological record after 300 BC but on a somewhat reduced scale. This seeming hiatus between the two episodes of metalwork deposition is one of the puzzles of Irish archaeology.

THE PROBLEM OF THE CELTS

As already noted, the arrival of Celtic-speaking peoples was once a popular explanation for the beginnings of iron-working and for the social and economic changes that followed. It was also a convenient explanation for the historical fact that by Roman times Ireland, like Britain and much of western Europe, spoke a Celtic language or languages. Since terms like 'Celtic Ireland' and the 'Celtic Iron Age' are popularly used to describe the Ireland of the last few centuries BC and the early pre-Christian centuries AD, and since the study of

Celtic literature and our knowledge of the Celtic-speaking peoples of other parts of Europe have deeply coloured our interpretation of the archaeology of later prehistoric Ireland, the problem of the Celts must be briefly addressed.

It has long been believed that the Celtic languages, represented today by modern Irish, Welsh, Scots Gaelic and Breton, are descended from an ancestral language-family that developed in a central or western European homeland, whence its speakers spread to various parts of the Celtic world as well as to Britain and from there to Ireland. This is an enduring belief and it is still claimed in some quarters that the first speakers of a Celtic tongue arrived in Ireland as late as about 200 BC. Indeed, some of a more nationalist frame of mind have argued that these Celtic immigrants included some who came directly from continental Europe and were uncontaminated by any British influences (Waddell 2005a). The problem with such assertions is that Irish prehistoric archaeology reveals no trace whatever of any significant incursion of new peoples from either quarter in later prehistoric times. Rather it demonstrates a considerable degree of cultural continuity and invariably offers other, more plausible explanations for the discontinuities that do exist in the archaeological record. There is simply no archaeological trace of the large-scale immigration necessary not just to implant a new language but also to eradicate virtually all traces of the pre-existing language as well.

The genetic, family-tree model of linguistic reconstruction, which implies fission and divergence from a common ancestor as the significant factor in language change, has supported and has been supported by migrationary archaeological theories. The inevitable equation of ancient Celtic languages such as Goidelic or Brittonic with a people such as 'Q-Celts' and 'P-Celts' or with aspects of material culture has had a long history. In Ireland, various writers have, in the past, equated 'the coming of the Celts' with the introduction of such diverse archaeological phenomena as the 'Beaker Folk', the appearance of bronze swords, the knowledge of iron or a Celtic La Tène art style. The debate has been a prolonged and convoluted one and is further complicated by the claims made by a number of English writers in recent years that the ancient Celts were never a cultural entity but are a construct of modern times.

There seems to be general agreement among linguistic scholars that the Celtic family of languages emerged sometime in the last millennium BC, though ironically it is archaeological evidence that is often presented in support of this general date. With rare exceptions, however, there has been a great reluctance among Celtic linguists to consider alternative models of language diffusion, and migrating Celts remain the favoured explanation. Prehistoric archaeology, by its very definition, cannot reveal what languages were spoken at any time before written records appear; bronze swords are just as mute as stones. Archaeology can offer models of linguistic change that are at least in keeping with archaeological evidence and interpretation. A non-genetic model of the prehistory of European languages, in which the rate of the creation and demise of languages will change through time owing to a variety of social processes, would envisage the existence of large language areas in early prehistoric times, but with increasing sedentism and population growth and the formation of small, self-sufficient territorial groups there would have been a considerable increase in the number of languages spoken in Europe from about 5000 BC. Language proliferation would have halted and then declined in the third and second millennia BC, with the gradual formation of fewer, larger language groups (Robb 1993).

The emergence of the Celtic languages in later prehistory would be due to an intensification of a complex series of processes operating across parts of Europe since the third millennium BC: these would have included economic intensification, increasing polity size, developing gender and social stratification, and increasingly active trade along coasts and rivers. Indeed, Colin Renfrew (1987) has suggested that the European 'homeland' of the Celts might be constituted by the full extent of the area where Celtic languages came to be spoken, parallel linguistic development being precipitated by the interaction of the élite elements of ranked societies.

While Ireland had its own regional idiosyncrasies, there is good evidence that it participated at an élite level in wider European fashions in later prehistory and that the Irish Sea and the Atlantic façade of Europe, far from being a barrier to communication, may have been a focal area for interaction and exchange, displaying evidence for recurring cycles of contact over long periods of time (Cunliffe 1997; 2001; 2009; Koch 1991; 2007; Waddell 1992; 1995b; Waddell and Conroy 1999). The prehistoric reality may have been a constant pattern of communication that must have had interminable consequences in many spheres, not least in terms of linguistic developments. The emergence of a Celtic language in Ireland was arguably not the result of mass immigration but the culmination of a long process of social and economic interaction between Ireland and Britain, and between these islands and adjacent parts of Atlantic continental Europe, a picture now gaining support from genetic evidence, including the study of mitochondrial DNA, that suggests a lengthy history of shared Atlantic ancestry (McEvoy *et al.* 2004). In short, the Celticisation of Ireland was not an event but a process, and a Bronze Age process at that. The Atlantic façade was not the only axis of communication, of course; there was an east–west axis as well, in which such great river systems as the Rhine, the Seine, the Loire and the Garonne had a role to play. This interactive scenario does not exclude the possibility of movements of people; these may be difficult or impossible to detect in the archaeological record, but if such movements did occur in later prehistoric times then they only gave added impetus to diachronic linguistic developments long under way. Other possibilities have been suggested, of course; the role of the Atlantic seaways has been questioned and, as far as Ireland is concerned, it has been argued that changes were more abrupt and that influential immigrants did initiate significant language change in, for example, those enigmatic centuries between 600 and 300 BC (Mallory 1992b).

Whatever the outcome of this debate, many archaeologists would consider it quite appropriate to speak of 'Celtic Ireland' after 300 BC, and if by these words is meant a 'Celtic-speaking Ireland' there would then be no further disagreement. But the distinction between these two phrases encapsulates yet another debate about another stimulating Celtic problem. The claim that the ancient Celts were never a cultural entity but are a construct of modern times is encapsulated in the title of Simon James's (1999) book *The Atlantic Celts: ancient people or modern invention?* This work and others, such as Malcolm Chapman's *The Celts:*

the construction of a myth (1992) and *The Celts: origins, myths and inventions* by John Collis (2003), give particular emphasis to the archaeological diversity that is such a striking feature of the world of those Celtic-speaking peoples of the last millennium BC. Equal emphasis is not given to the significance of the emergence of a common language family.

Celtic-speaking peoples occupied large areas of Europe in the last few centuries BC and there is no dispute that Ireland was a Celtic-speaking land at this time as well. To the Greeks, these *keltoi* were one of four great barbarian peoples of the ancient world, and they believed that the entire known northern world was occupied by just Celts and Scythians. Even though they were linguistically related, it is disputable whether the peoples whom the Greeks called Celts ever considered themselves to belong to an ethnically identifiable group, yet linguistic compatibility must have facilitated communication and relationships and provided a measure of group identity. That said, the modern ethnic definition of the ancient Celts is indeed a recent construct. The nineteenth century saw the development of both the genetic family-tree model of linguistic development and the idea of distinct, biologically defined racial groups. The Celts were given an archaeological identity with the discovery of characteristic artefacts in a great cemetery at Hallstatt, near Salzburg in Austria, and at La Tène, on Lake Neuchâtel in Switzerland. These artefacts were part of the body of evidence that enabled the construction of the first detailed chronology of the 'Iron Age', which was divided into the two major phases named after these two sites. Finds of La Tène swords or brooches or art were then considered to represent the material remains of the Celtic peoples known to Greek and Roman writers. Whether in central Europe or in Ireland, La Tène material was simple confirmation of the presence of Celts and an illustration of how these people shared not just a material cultural assemblage but religious beliefs and social structures as well. This cultural-historical approach appeared to demonstrate the spread of Celtic peoples across a wide area of Europe, and a Celtic 'homeland' was usually placed in the region of the upper Rhine and Danube, where the La Tène art style developed. The concept of a 'Celtic World' extending from Ireland to central Europe and beyond is therefore of recent vintage, and the extent to which, in this world, there were common factors

in material culture, in rural economy and in social institutions is now the subject of some healthy scrutiny thanks to the 'Celtoscepticism' of some writers (to use the term coined by Sims-Williams 1998). Despite their common linguistic stock, there are great variations in subsistence and economy and in social structures discernible across the 'Celtic World'. The supposed homogeneity often implied by the adjective 'Celtic' is now being questioned by archaeologists conscious of these contrasts and concerned that its too-ready acceptance has diverted attention from the difficult questions posed by difference and diversity.

Some elements of the fragmentary ethnographic accounts of Greek and Roman writers appear to be corroborated in evidence from early Irish and Welsh literature almost a thousand years later, and these parallels may have given the 'Celtic World' a misleadingly cohesive and timeless image. The Classical references need to be assessed with caution; it is possible, for instance, that some references in Greek sources such as Poseidonius and some similar features in early Irish literature may have been quite separately inspired by heroic episodes in Homeric tradition. Other elements of the later Irish tales are probably imaginative fiction; they may be depictions of an ideal world, for it seems as if the learned classes of medieval Ireland thought it quite a proper thing to offer their perceptions of what the prehistoric past should have been like, or even to rewrite the past to make a moral point or to support a political cause. Their accounts may often be an unreliable guide to late prehistoric Ireland. But not all elements in early Irish literature are necessarily learned fiction, as we shall see, given the growing evidence for some continuity of tradition from pagan to Christian times.

In the last few centuries BC a Celtic-speaking Ireland was demonstrably in contact with a Celtic-speaking Britain, and possibly with the Continent as well, and the patterns of contact were probably broadly similar to the patterns that had obtained since the later second millennium BC at least. The significance of these later prehistoric contacts needs to be critically assessed, and doubtless, as in earlier times, there were similar or shared social and religious customs. It is reasonable to suggest that these are best identified or confirmed without the imposition of preconceptions about such things as a specifically Celtic society or a Celtic religion with a pan-European dimension. Yet it is not unreasonable to speak of Celtic art and, as Barry Cunliffe (2003) has remarked, to some degree archaeological evidence supports the idea of a broad cultural similarity between some Celtic groups.

The period from about 300 BC to an ill-defined point in the early centuries AD has been variously called the Irish La Tène horizon and the Celtic Iron Age. It is a time when novel metal types, some—but by no means all—with British or Continental affinities, are once again prominent in the archaeological record. Equally remarkable, however, is the reappearance of a limited range of quite exceptional metalwork and, albeit on a reduced scale, the reappearance of depositional customs of the sort last encountered in the Dowris phase. A small number of hoards, probably spanning a number of centuries, may faintly echo the extravagant practices of half a millennium or more before.

THE KNOCK HOARD

Two gold objects were found in 1861 in the course of turf-cutting in Ardnaglug bog in Knock townland, Co. Roscommon, about 7km north-east of Ballinasloe. They were found in a wooden box that was not preserved and for many years were believed to have been found near Clonmacnoise (Ireland 1992). The objects are torcs of quite different types: one is a buffer torc, the other a ribbon torc. The buffer torc is a celebrated and much-discussed piece (Fig. 8.9) belonging to a well-known British and Continental type of penannular neck-ring with broad, flat, expanded, circular terminals or 'buffers'. The Knock example is a version in which the terminals have been joined together to form a single element. It basically consists of two semicircular hollow tubes of sheet gold that fit into hollow decorative expansions at front and back. At the front (and worn beneath the chin) a biconical element, the conjoined buffers, is flanked by bosses, one of which is perforated to take a pin that secured one detachable tubular section of the torc. At the back a rectangular element is decorated with pronounced convex mouldings that form in part a pair of interlocking oval loops ornamented with a sinuous pattern of applied gold

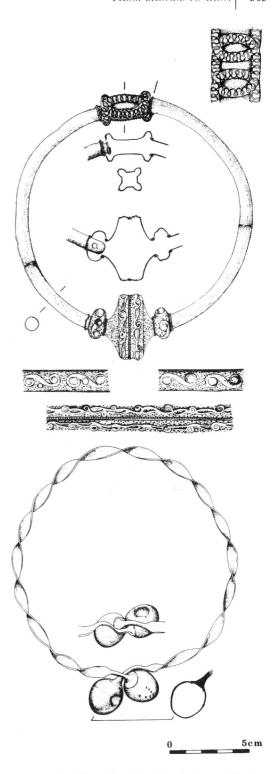

Fig. 8.9—Gold hoard found in Ardnaglug bog in Knock townland, Co. Roscommon. Above: gold buffer torc. Below: gold ribbon torc.

wire. The decoration on the flanking bosses of the biconical element at the front consists of pairs of repoussé S-scrolls, while that on the central part of the biconical piece consists of two narrow panels of irregular, asymmetrical, sinuous tendrils with spiral bosses. The background is finely stippled.

This type of torc and the repoussé ornament, in particular the asymmetrical tendril motif, find general parallels on the Continent in the early La Tène period and, if not an import as sometimes suggested (Jope 2000), it was made by someone familiar with torcs and other fine metalwork in the Rhineland around or shortly after 300 BC. It thus represents the earliest evidence for contact with or emulation of exponents of La Tène or 'Celtic' art. This remarkable art style developed in eastern France and western Germany, in the region of the Marne and the Rhine, in the fifth century BC and is found mainly on fine metalwork in rich aristocratic burials. Many of the motifs, like the tendril, are derived from Classical plant motifs, sometimes transformed almost beyond recognition. Some motifs are deliberately ambiguous and difficult to classify, and some may have had magical significance. The gold ribbon torc is loosely twisted and has unusual hollow pear-shaped terminals.

THE SOMERSET HOARD

A second gold torc of the ribbon variety comes from a hoard of bronze and iron objects found in a field in the townland of Somerset, south of Ballinasloe, Co. Galway (Fig. 8.10). Unfortunately the hoard was dispersed after discovery and the iron objects were not preserved, but several bronzes dating from the last century BC or the first century AD were recovered. These include five circular mounts, a fibula, part of a horse-pendant and the handle of a bronze cup or bowl. The torc had been coiled and placed inside a sort of box formed by two of the mounts. It is fairly tightly spiral-twisted and has unusual straight terminals of rectangular cross-section.

The unique Coolmanagh association of a flange-twisted torc and a ribbon torc (Fig. 6.12) was considered in Chapter 6. Apart from a few examples with similar gold to the Coolmanagh pair that may be assigned to the Bishopsland phase, analyses have shown that a majority of ribbon torcs, usually with

knobbed terminals, generally contain traces of platinum, which, when combined with the values for copper and tin, demonstrates that the gold used is quite different from that of the Bishopsland phase and is of Iron Age date (Warner 2004). Poorly documented hoards, each containing a number of ribbon torcs, are recorded from Largatreany, Co. Donegal, Derryvony, Co. Cavan, and Ballylumford, Co. Antrim, two of them at least being dry-land finds. A probable hoard of three examples was found along with seven amber beads, two bronze bracelets and fragments of a third on an eroding part of the seashore at Dooyork, near Gweesalia, Co. Mayo (Cahill 2002). Of the many single finds of ribbon torcs, several have been found in bogs but the majority have no details of discovery recorded. It would be unwise to simply assume a votive purpose but this does remain a possibility. Gabriel Cooney and Eoin Grogan (1999) have demonstrated how the contexts of other objects, such as horse-bits and pendants and iron swords, follow Dowris phase patterns, with rivers, lakes and bogs continuing to serve as a focus for ritual offerings of metalwork. Evidently ribbon torcs formed a major component in the depositional rituals of a period in which gold objects and gold hoards are otherwise relatively uncommon. While no ribbon torcs have been recorded from counties Cork and Waterford, Mary Cahill (2006) has drawn attention to several old finds of gold from these southern counties that are of probable Iron Age date and include two unusual penannular neck ornaments with Iberian parallels. They, like the extraordinary find of the skull of a Barbary ape from Navan, Co. Armagh (Chapter 9), are an indication that the Atlantic seaways may still have had a role to play in the dissemination of prestige items.

THE BROIGHTER HOARD

The most exceptional hoard of the period is undoubtedly that found at Broighter, near Limavady, Co. Derry, in 1896. Seven gold objects were discovered during ploughing near the shore of Lough Foyle, and it is possible that they had been intentionally deposited at a spot on a raised beach which was originally just below the old shoreline of the lough. The hoard comprised a fine buffer torc, a simpler twisted torc and a fragment of another, two

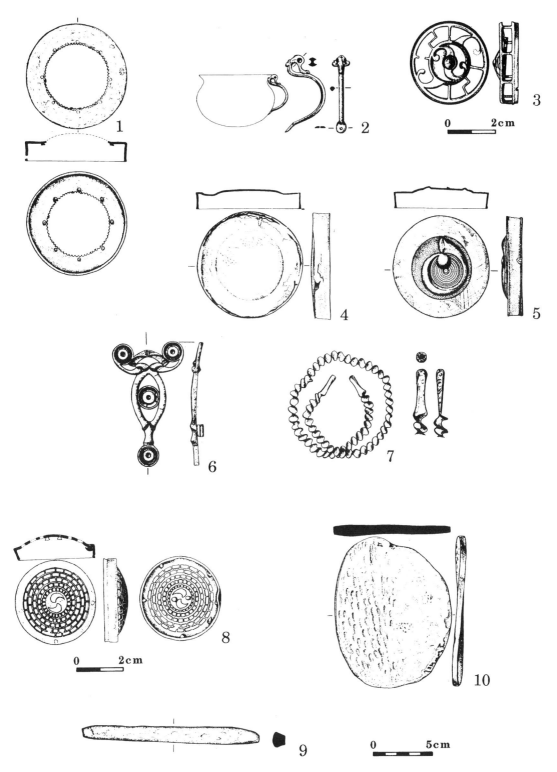

Fig. 8.10—Some of the objects found in the Somerset, Co. Galway, hoard. (1, 3–5, 8) Bronze mounts. (2) Cup handle. (6) Fibula of Navan type. (7) Gold ribbon torc. (9–10) Bronze ingot and cake.

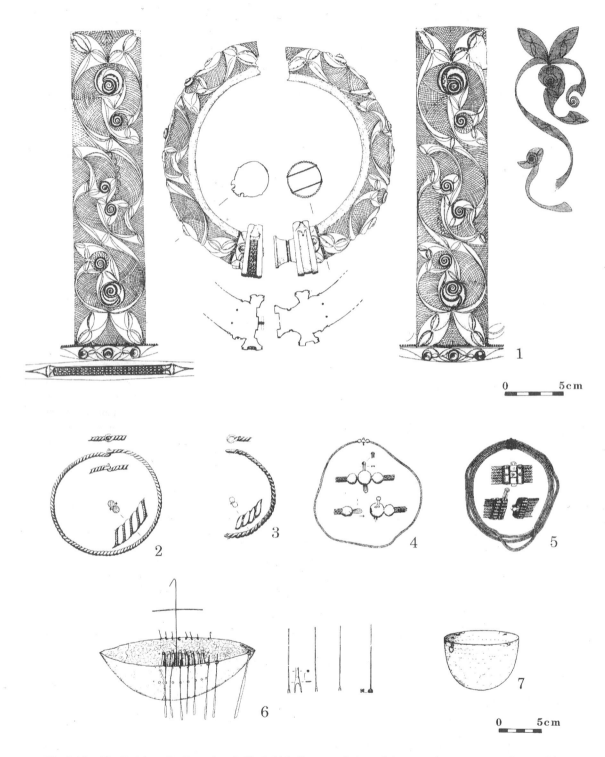

Fig. 8.11—The Broighter, Co. Derry, hoard. (1) Gold buffer torc with (on right) suggested interpretation of some of the curvilinear motifs. (2–3) Gold twisted torcs. (4–5) Gold wire necklaces. (6) Gold model boat with oars and (on right) three barge poles and a grappling iron or anchor. (7) Gold vessel or model cauldron.

gold wire necklaces, a small bowl of sheet gold and a model boat also of sheet gold (Fig. 8.11).

The miniature gold boat, just under 20cm in length, originally had nine benches for rowers and eighteen oars with rowlocks, most of which survive, along with one steering oar at the stern, three forked bargepoles, a grappling iron or anchor and a mast with yard-arm. It gives us a very general idea of what one type of sailing vessel of the first century BC may have been like, propelled by sail or oarsmen, or punted in shallow waters. It is usually assumed to be a model of a hide-built boat but, if it is to scale, the length of the original may have been about 15m and could therefore have been plank-built. The small bowl-shaped vessel is more or less hemispherical and has four rings for suspension; it may be a model of a cauldron. The wire necklaces are imports from the Roman world, ultimately from the Mediterranean region, and may date from the period between the first century BC and the third century AD. One is a triple-strand necklace formed of single-looped gold chain work, and the other is a single-strand piece made of a chain of multiple loops.

The twisted torc and the fragmentary example are each made of a twisted gold rod of circular cross-section, which was spiral-twisted with a narrow gold wire. The terminals are of a hook and eye type. This form of torc may be an Irish version of a type of neck ornament, made by spiral-twisting two rods of gold together, found in Britain in the first century BC.

The buffer torc from the Broighter hoard is a magnificent object and one of the masterpieces of artwork in the La Tène style. It is a hollow tubular neck-ring of hammered sheet gold, now in two halves, with separate buffer terminals held in place by gold pins. The ends of the terminals could be locked together by rotating them and locking a T-shaped tenon on one into a corresponding slot on the other. A small number of tubular torcs of this general sort are known from Britain, Belgium, France and Switzerland, and are well dated to the first century BC. The tubular portion of the torc is richly decorated with engraved and repoussé ornament (Jope 2000; Avery 1997). The superb relief design consists of a series of slender trumpet motifs, lentoid (pointed oval) bosses and spiral roundels. The overall pattern, mainly formed by the attenuated trumpets that distantly echo earlier vegetal tendrils, basically consists of two overlapping S-scrolls on each half of the torc. Though essentially a symmetrical composition, the effect of sinuous movement is accentuated by a static background of engraved compass-drawn cross-hatching. The curvilinear decoration on the torc is undoubtedly insular and implies a skilled workshop somewhere in the north of Ireland shortly before or after the turn of the millennium, with craftsmen who must have been in contact with others in Britain and even further afield.

Elusive or ambiguous imagery is a frequent component of La Tène art, and though Michael Avery saw the designs on the torc as visually pleasing, elegant abstract decoration, Richard Warner (1982) has argued that some of the trumpet curves and spirals combine to represent stylised sea horses (Fig. 8.11). He has also speculated that the hoard was a votive offering to an undersea god, the possible hippomorphic element having some connection with the sea god Manannán mac Lir, who in various legends is associated with a horse capable of journeying over land and sea, with Lough Foyle, sea travel and a large cauldron. It is quite possible that the various elements of the Broighter hoard had some individual and collective symbolism. The exceptional decorated torc may have been more than just a finely crafted status piece; it could have been a magical talisman, even a symbol of divinity. It has been suggested more than once that some special torcs may have been placed on the necks of idols rather than on human necks.

HORSE HARNESS

It would be unwise to assume that most archaeological deposits of metal objects necessarily have a ritual explanation, but when it comes to deciphering consistent patterns of deposition it is difficult to ignore this possibility. We tend to forget that in the prehistoric past, as in more recent medieval times, the world and everything in it was richly invested with magical and superstitious meaning. After 300 BC a different spectrum of fine metalwork has a role in the votive sphere, and items of horse harness, apparently highly prized objects, now seem to play a significant part in the resumption of depositional practices. A proportion of this metalwork was seemingly deliberately placed

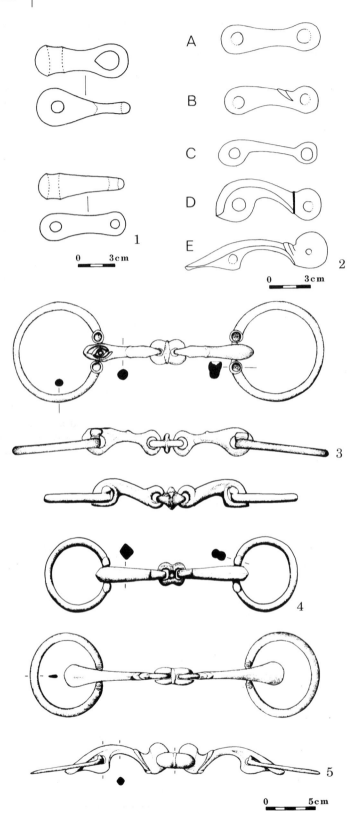

Fig. 8.12—Bronze horse-bits. (1) Side links, showing British form above with perforations at right angles and Irish form below with perforations in the same plane. (2) Typology (A–E) of side links. (3) Type B bit with asymmetrical ornament from Lough Beg, Co. Antrim. (4) Type D bit from Loughran's Island, River Bann, Co. Derry. (5) Type E bit from Tulsk, Co. Roscommon.

in river, lake and bog, and harness hoards are now the commonest type of collective deposit (Cooney and Grogan 1999): of 22 hoards, no less than thirteen are hoards containing either bridle-bits or pendants or both. Unfortunately approximately 68% of this material is unprovenanced and without details of discovery. Of the 27 horse-bits with recorded provenance, three came from rivers, four from lakes and seven from bogs, in all about 52% from watery contexts. Of pendants with recorded contexts, the figure is about 75%.

Bridle-bits

The great majority of horse-bits are of bronze and, surprisingly, they are the commonest surviving metal artefact from the period. Two bronze examples have iron rings and two iron bits are known, an unprovenanced fragmentary find and that possible example from Aughinish. The typical bronze bit has a mouth piece made of three links with two side rings for the attachment of the reins; the three-link section is formed of a small centre link of approximately figure-of-eight shape with two longer side links. Three-link bits of bronze or iron are also found in Britain but are rare on the Continent, apart from a number in north-eastern France. In contrast to most British bits, the holes in the side links of Irish examples are in the same plane (Fig. 8.12, 1).

While there are differences in the shape of both centre links and rein rings, variations in the shape of the side links have formed the basis for the most recent classification, but the degree to which these typological differences are of chronological significance is uncertain. The simplest and presumed

early side links are few in number; they are hollow-cast, sometimes retaining their clay casting cores, lacking any decoration and are horizontally symmetrical (type A). An example found in a well-known votive deposit of metalwork in a bog at Llyn Cerrig Bach, Anglesea, Wales, may date from the second or first century BC, but the material from this find spans a number of centuries and obviously it provides no precise indication of date.

A common form of side link is slightly bowed and has a cast decorative V-shaped feature or moulding above the inner perforation that attaches to the centre link (type B). This is the most numerous type (about 42% of the total), and there is considerable variety in detail; some side links are hollow-cast but others are of solid bronze. Decoration on the outer ends is rare, and while some V-mouldings are quite simple, others are more elaborate and occasionally seem to resemble ducks' heads. That this ambiguous ornithomorphism was sometimes deliberate is demonstrated by an unprovenanced fragment (Fig. 8.13) that has what seems to be a bird's head at the inner end of the side links and an extraordinary stylised human mask at the other end of the one complete side link. Both motifs are ambiguous, however, and also resemble stylised plant forms found in earlier La Tène art. The bit shows evident signs of use and wear and the bird's-head motifs would be invisible when the object was in use—and indeed any decoration on the outer ends would be obscured too. Why a bird's-head design should be placed in a horse's mouth is mystifying but may imply that some of these designs were more than just ornamental and had some magical charge. Strange human or animal masks

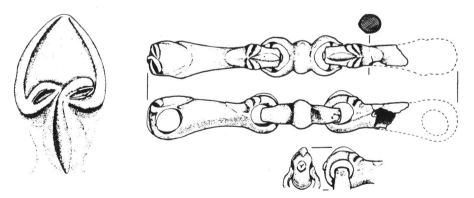

Fig. 8.13—Fragmentary bronze bit with stylised birds' heads at inner ends of side links and stylised human mask at the one surviving outer end.

0   5 cm

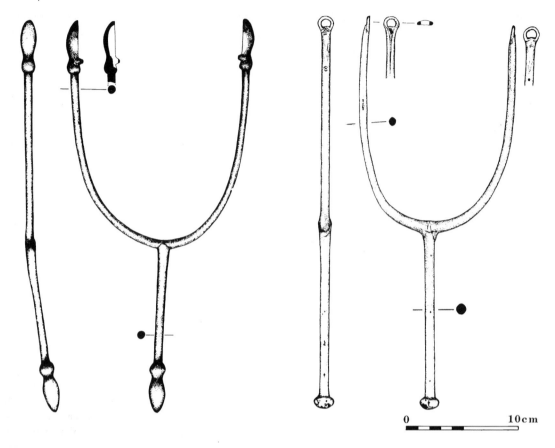

Fig. 8.14—Bronze pendants. Left: type 1, from the River Boyne, Moyfin, Co. Meath. Right: type 2, found in a ploughed field with a horse-bit at Clongill, Co. Meath.

occur on the link ends of another unprovenanced bit.

A few simple, solid-cast, very slender side links (type C) are without decoration and if they have V-mouldings these are rudimentary. Links of type D (representing about 21% of the total) are sharply bowed and are frequently decorated on their outer ends. This decoration may be either cast or incised but one unprovenanced link has its decoration created by cutting away a number of fields for *champlevé* enamel. The most developed side links (also about 21%) are markedly curved (type E) with a pronounced central spine and they expand in width towards their outer ends. V-mouldings are prominent but only a few have cast decoration on their outer ends. Examples such as those from Attymon, Co. Galway (Fig. 8.15), probably date from the early centuries AD.

Most of these horse-bits show signs of extensive wear, and much skill and ingenuity were sometimes displayed in undertaking repairs. A pair of bits from Streamstown, Co. Westmeath, between them were repaired no less than twelve separate times. Their manufacture was a skilled process involving the casting and linking together of five separate elements. They were evidently highly valued and this may be one reason why they were eventually selected as votive offerings even in a fragmentary condition. Presumably their iron counterparts were commoner but were not favoured in this way. Of course, leather and wooden harness and items like antler cheek-pieces could well have been widely used as well and may have had a long history. Thus the appearance of bronze bits in such numbers does not necessarily mean that horse-riding suddenly became a popular pastime, though they may indicate a greater concern with expert horse management. Compared with two-link bits, the three-link type is considered to have a milder action, less severe on the horse's mouth, and may imply the use of a finer breed, more sensitive to skilled control. The centre link and the curved side links of types D and E may have been designed to give greater adjustability; depending on how they were worn, they offer a variable mouth-piece width of between 13cm and 16cm. While such general mouth-piece dimensions may indicate a relatively small horse of pony size, it is possible that mouth width may have no correlation with withers height and that 'broad-faced' and 'narrow-faced' breeds may have coexisted (Palk 1984; Piggott 1983).

Pendants

A series of Y-shaped pendants are a peculiarly Irish type of harness piece, unknown elsewhere, and almost all are of bronze (Fig. 8.14). Various sorts of pendant pieces of horse harness are known on the Continent but nothing exactly like the Irish objects. These Y-shaped objects are puzzling artefacts, basically consisting of a finely cast stem and a pair of prongs; the overall length is usually 28–32cm and the distance between the prongs between 12cm and 16cm, although it may be as narrow as 7.8cm. Two basic types have been recognised. Type 1 are rarely decorated and have separate terminals cast onto the prongs; these terminals are usually hollow but of the same general design as the stem terminal and have inward-projecting loops. Type 2 pendants have perforated prong terminals and decoration may occur on these and on the stem terminal, which is often knobbed. Regional fashions are faintly discernible (Warner 2002a). These objects were clearly meant to be attached to something, and some apparently show signs of wear. Since they have been found with bridle-bits there is little doubt that they were some part of horse harness, but their precise function remains uncertain. They have been thought to be head-pieces, curbs, leading pieces and even spurs but, as Barry Raftery has pointed out, the least unlikely explanation is that they were pendants, suspended beneath the horse's mouth and used as leading pieces on ceremonial occasions.

Not all bits and pendants were used in horse-riding. Three matching pairs of bits and two pairs of pendants show that some at least may have been used for paired draught, worn by a yoked pair of horses presumably pulling a cart or chariot.

Asymmetric decoration on a few bits (as on Lough Beg, Co. Antrim: Fig. 8.12, 3) and on a pendant may indicate that these pieces were parts of sets of two as well. A good illustration of this pairing is a hoard of two bits and two pendants found at a depth of over 7m near the bottom of a bog near Attymon, Co. Galway (Fig. 8.15). Both bits have identical cast curvilinear decoration and show signs of wear. Curvilinear decoration also occurs on the flattened perforated terminals and the knobbed stem terminal of the pendants. It is most unlikely that this discrete assemblage of just horse-bits and pendants could be anything other than a deliberate votive offering placed in a watery or boggy context. The general date of these bits and pendants is not easily determined. Bits may have been used from the second century BC to the early centuries AD, and the pendants were probably fashionable in the early centuries AD and possibly earlier. Decorative details, like the curvilinear designs on the Attymon bronzes, are obviously meagre dating evidence, though the pattern on the side links finds parallels on Romano-British metalwork of the second or third centuries AD. Fragments of several bits of this type were found in the promontory fort at Drumanagh, Co. Dublin, which also produced Roman material, and the discovery of a copy of an Irish three-link type E bit in far-off Romania may reflect contact with Roman Britain and Roman military contact with that part of the Continent in the early centuries AD (Raftery 2000).

Cart or chariot fitments

The pairs of bits and pendants just mentioned imply the use of pairs of horses for traction, but fitments for the vehicles in question are remarkably scarce. Two-wheeled chariots are known from Britain and the Continent and were probably used in Ireland too, but evidence is still lacking. Of course a scarcity of metal fitments does not mean a scarcity of wheeled vehicles, and metal wagon fitments are not all that common in Britain or on the Continent either. Two bronze objects said to have been found on an island in Lough Gur, Co. Limerick (Fig. 8.16), are probably yoke mounts. Of cast bronze, they are similar but not identical pieces, each with cast S-shaped scrolls decorating their tips. Once thought to be horn caps or hand-grips at the rear of chariots, it is now believed that objects like these decorated the upturned ends of some yokes and

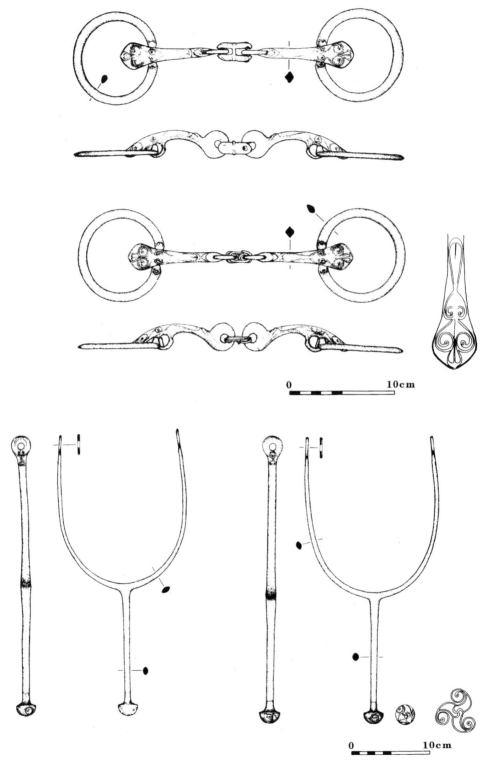

Fig. 8.15—Hoard of two bronze horse-bits and two bronze pendants found near Attymon, Co. Galway. The illustrated details of the decoration on the ends of the side links and the stem terminals of the pendants are not to scale.

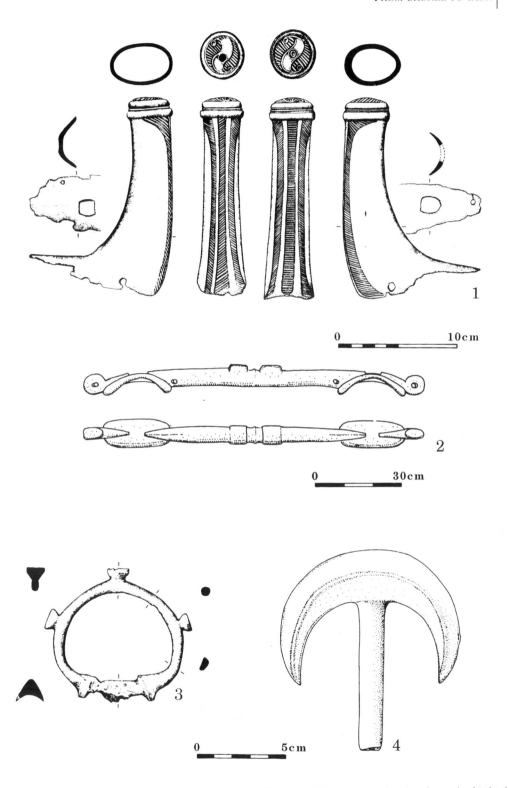

Fig. 8.16—(1) Two bronze yoke mounts from Lough Gur, Co. Limerick. (2) Wooden yoke found in the north of Ireland. (3) Bronze terret from County Antrim. (4) Bronze linchpin found near Dunmore, Co. Galway.

were similar to the wooden knobs found on some examples. Several wooden yokes have been radiocarbon-dated to the late Bronze Age–Iron Age (Stanley *et al.* 2003). One bronze terret, a guide for reins mounted on some types of yoke, was found somewhere in County Antrim and has close analogies in southern Scotland. The large rectangular perforations on the Lough Gur objects might have held attachments for terrets like this. A bronze linchpin for securing a wheel hub to an axle comes from Dunmore, Co. Galway.

WEAPONRY

A limited number of swords and spears are known, a striking contrast with the large quantities recorded in the Dowris phase (Rynne 1982; 1983). Some 30 iron swords form a varied and rather imprecisely dated assemblage. The inevitable problems posed by corroded iron mean that blade shapes are often difficult to determine, and the identification of swords of late prehistoric date often rests on very basic distinguishing features such as short size and parallel-sided blades. The presence of distinctive arched mounts or hilt-guards, a feature of Continental and British La Tène period swords, is an important characteristic detail, however (Fig. 8.17). Blades are parallel-sided, tapering gently to a point, with cross-sections of varied form that may be lozenge-shaped, a flat pointed oval or, in a few cases, with midrib and flanking grooves, as on a fine example found in Ballinderry bog, Co. Westmeath (Fig. 8.17, 3).

The hilt-guards are usually curving pieces of hammered or cast bronze, often with a campanulate or bell-shaped profile (which may be steeply arched or a shallow curve); a few are decorated, and the Ballinderry example bears raised trumpet motifs on both faces. The hilt-guard on a sword from Knockaulin, Co. Kildare, is heavily corroded and may be of iron. A small group of swords have organic hilt-guards of materials such as antler and may represent a distinct type (Fig. 8.17, 1). One of these thicker organic hilt-guards is depicted on a small wooden model of a sword found in a bog at Ballykilmurry, Co. Wicklow, which also has a prominent subtriangular pommel. Made of yew (with an unexplained projection on its blade), this may be a toy sword but is important because it

appears to have a skeumorphic representation of an arched metal hilt-guard of La Tène type below the organic hilt-guard, implying that those swords with the latter feature may be of this date too (Fig. 8.17, 4). A few other strands of evidence point to a possible late La Tène date for large oval antler pommels like that on a fragmentary sword found somewhere in the area of Edenderry, Co. Offaly, which has an organic hilt-guard as well as a tubular grip of bone (Fig. 8.17, 5). A couple of pommels of this sort have been found in Scotland, and it seems probable that both these prominent pommels and organic hilt-guards are features of a late Irish–Scottish sword series perhaps dating from the early centuries AD.

A unique Irish find is a bronze sword hilt dredged up in a fishing net from the seabed in Ballyshannon Bay, Co. Donegal, about 1916. When found it still had its blade attached and this was completely encrusted with a marine deposit of sand and shells. The hollow-cast bronze hilt is of stylised human form (Fig. 8.17, 6). Such swords with anthropoid hilts are known in Britain and on the Continent, and the Ballyshannon find has been considered an import representing direct contact between the west of Ireland and France. This is by no means certain and it could even have been acquired in Britain or be a local copy. It certainly implies coastal traffic of some description in or around the first century BC.

The Irish swords are remarkable in one particular respect: where blade lengths can be established, they vary from about 46cm, as on the Ballinderry specimen, to as little as 29cm, as on a sword from near Edenderry, Co. Offaly. In overall length, which varies from about 57.9cm to 41.8cm, they are notably shorter than the earlier bronze Gündlingen swords, but all of them do fall comfortably within the lower range of the Dowris phase (class 4) sword series. Their small size is in marked contrast, however, to contemporary iron swords in Britain and, in particular, to those on the Continent, which are effective weapons with an average overall length of 72cm and with later examples exceeding 1m in length. The Irish swords may have been intended for stabbing and hacking in close hand-to-hand combat, but most of them are more appropriately described as elongated daggers than as slashing swords. Their size has also prompted the comment that warfare in Ireland at this time

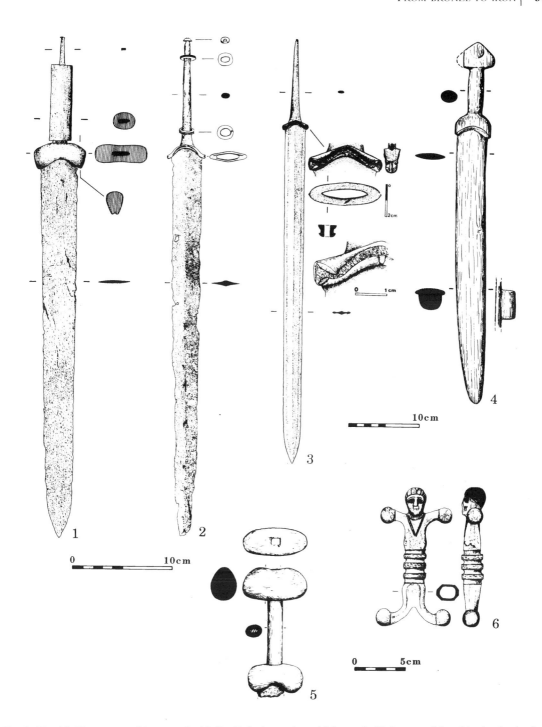

Fig. 8.17—(1) Unprovenanced iron sword with flat blade, bone grip and hilt-guard. (2) Iron sword found in the thatch of a derelict cottage at Cashel, Co. Sligo, with lozenge-sectioned blade and bronze hilt-guard of shallow bell shape. (3) Iron sword from Ballinderry, Co. Westmeath, with grooved and ribbed blade and decorated bronze hilt-guard. (4) Wooden model of a sword from Ballykilmurry, Co. Wicklow. (5) Hilt portion of an iron sword found near Edenderry, Co. Offaly, with bone grip and prominent deer-horn pommel and hilt-guard. (6) Bronze anthropoid hilt from Ballyshannon Bay, Co. Donegal.

may have been something of a ritual farce. Since it was technologically feasible to produce longer iron swords, sword size was probably dictated by fashion. If display was a paramount consideration, it is possible that decorated scabbards and hilts were more important than blade lengths. Indeed, serious fighting may have been done with the spear.

It was a comparison of these short swords with those described in the epic *Táin Bó Cúailnge* or the 'Cattle Raid of Cooley' that first demonstrated that heroic tales like this were not an accurate depiction of the material culture of a late prehistoric society, and were probably not 'a window on the Iron Age', to use K. H. Jackson's expressive phrase. The swords described in the *Táin* are akin to longer early medieval swords and would be the weapons familiar to storytellers of the seventh century AD onwards, when such tales were written down (Mallory 1982). The degree, if any, to which medieval Irish literature and tales such as the *Táin* reflect the world of the prehistoric Iron Age has been the subject of much debate.

A window on the Iron Age?

K. H. Jackson (1964) had argued that some Irish medieval literature, and in particular the tales of the Ulster Cycle, depicted a pre-Christian Iron Age world. For instance, for him the great epic the *Táin Bó Cúailnge* with its heroic warriors, endemic warfare and archaic material civilisation—as he put it—did reflect a genuine Iron Age. He did not, of course, suggest that the main protagonists in this tale, Queen Maeve of Connacht and the Ulster hero Cú Chulainn, were historical figures. Since elements of Irish La Tène art survive or reappear in the early medieval period, he thought it reasonable that the memory of other pre-Christian traditions might have survived too. But his thesis has not fared well. Further study confirmed this picture of an early medieval date for the material culture of the *Táin*, 'demonstrably or probably later than the 4th century AD' (Mallory 1992c). In a nuanced conclusion, however, Mallory has also pointed out that the learned class who contributed to the formation of the epic were producing a historical fiction but were also attempting to portray a past world. This was a complex world that may have included some memory of what constituted antiquity. In contrast, Aitchison (1987) in a lengthy critique of Jackson's approach argued that early

Irish epic literature does not constitute a legitimate source for the study of pagan Celtic society either in Ireland or in Celtic Europe. For him the Ulster Cycle was an early medieval literary composition. John Koch (1994) reviewed the near-total deconstruction of Jackson's case and had to conclude that the only really salvageable part of Jackson's work was the memorable subtitle. It did seem likely, however, that some features of these tales (such as head-hunting, chariotry, feasting and the champion's portion) might well have been a part of a pre-Christian world.

The essence of the question has been whether such elements represent a measure of survival and continuity or were, in John Barrett's expressive phrase, like Homeric Greece, 'pasts dreamt of, artefacts for past glories' (1981). Not surprisingly, there have been few attempts to prise open Jackson's window since. One exception has been the use of early Irish literature and other ethnographic analogies to examine the ritual aspects of warfare in the Iron Age and to suggest that while the sword was an élite weapon, the sling did not have a similar high status (Finney 2006). Parkes (2004) has undertaken a wide-ranging study of fosterage, where the ambiguities of foster-kinship are illustrated in the *Táin* when Cú Chulainn has to fight some of his foster-brothers, and Karl (2003) has compared Iron Age chariots to those in the *Táin* and other tales. There is, of course, much more to early Irish literature than epic stories of kings, queens and warriors. Besides the tales of the Ulster Cycle, place-lore and legal tracts also raise questions of survival and continuity. Early Irish law, elements of which are clearly pre-Christian, depict an early medieval world that, in a famous phrase, was 'tribal, rural, hierarchical, and familiar—in the sense that the family not the individual was the unit' (Kelly 1988). It was this hierarchical society, composed of king (*rí*), a noble class of warriors and skilled men, and a class of freemen, that Barry Cunliffe has tentatively applied to the social organisation of the southern English Iron Age and the hillfort of Danebury (1984; 2005). He recognised that Celtic social structure may have differed considerably from place to place and time to time but—reasonably enough—thought that this historical model might be marginally more relevant than African or Asian analogies. In rejecting this use of the picture we have of the hierarchical nature of Irish early medieval society to explain Iron Age social structure, various writers have emphasised the thousand-year gap between the two worlds, stating, for instance, that 'continuity and straightforward evolution cannot be assumed; they must be proven' (Hill 1995). The question of continuity of tradition is therefore a crucial one. It has to be acknowledged that tradition may not be a constant; it is not immutable; it may be modified, recast and reinvented, and the means of transmission may be difficult to determine. Various social practices described in early Irish narratives could well have roots in the Iron Age; the challenge is to show that this is possible. A number of studies have addressed the question of the survival of Irish La Tène art into the early medieval period, as Jackson noted. This is the Ultimate La Tène style found in manuscript decoration, on zoomorphic brooches and on other metalwork (Megaw and Megaw 2001; Warner 1987). Continuity has been detected in dress-pin fashion (Newman 1995), and it has been suggested that the deposition of early medieval brooches in wetland contexts (and at Knowth, Newgrange and Tara) could be a continuation of Iron Age votive practice (Ó Floinn 2001). There is a growing body of evidence demonstrating continuity in the burial record from Iron Age to early medieval times but nowhere, however, are the deeply rooted links with a pre-Christian past more in evidence than in recent work in several of the celebrated royal and assembly sites: Teltown, Tara and Rathcroghan (Chapter 9).

The Irish scabbard style

A series of finely decorated bronze scabbards are amongst the finest examples of Irish La Tène art and provide clear evidence that some of these iron swords were the possessions of a warrior aristocracy who were preoccupied with decorative display and who were also the patrons of skilled iron-workers, bronzesmiths and artists (Raftery 1994b; Jope 2000; Harding 2007). Presumably scabbards of organic materials were used as well but none have survived. Altogether eight bronze scabbards or parts of scabbards are preserved; two are plain and six have engraved decoration. One of the plain examples is of interest because it is the only substantially complete find; the others are represented by one scabbard plate only. The complete scabbard is one of four found at Lisnacrogher, Co. Antrim (below).

This piece (Lisnacrogher 4) consists of two sheets of hammered bronze held together by folding the edges of the front plate, which has a hammered midrib, over the edges of the back plate. There is a corroded iron blade within the scabbard and the scabbard tongue is protected by a cast-bronze openwork chape. Two small perforations near the centre on both plates were probably for a suspension loop attached at different times to one or other of the scabbard faces (Fig. 8.18, 1). The second plain scabbard is represented by a single bronze plate from Toome, on the River Bann. Of the six decorated specimens, two are of less refined workmanship than the rest. One from the River Bann, near Coleraine (Fig. 8.18, 2), is decorated with an engraved curvilinear pattern which has been described as a design based on a running wave; this motif is a continuous and sinuous wave-like line with spiral offshoots and is ultimately of Classical origin. Here the offshoots form pelta shapes with tightly coiled spiral ends. In the occasionally weird and often imprecise world of La Tène art terminology, the term 'pelta' or 'pelta-shape' is sometimes used to describe a crescent shape with a point or stem emanating from the centre of its concave underside (see Fig. 9.32, 1E). Minor motifs include hatched triangles, leaf shapes, a crude step pattern along one edge and, in the spaces between the major curvilinear motifs, triangular arrangements of three dots, a tiny but symbolically charged motif found on pottery and metalwork in Britain and on the Continent. The second, from the River Bann at Toome (Fig. 8.18, 3), bears a basic design of alternately disposed C-shaped motifs that are probably ineptly executed loose spirals. Minor motifs include leaf shapes, curves and circles that fail to form true spirals, and parallel hatching. This decoration was not to someone's liking because the scabbard plate was cut down, reused with the decorated face turned inwards and some punched ornament added to the edges. The remaining four are finely crafted pieces. Three come from Lisnacrogher and one from Toome on the River Bann. Lisnacrogher 1 (Fig. 8.19, 1) has no midrib and the overall pattern is basically a sequence of four S-scrolls with spiral-filled comma-leaf motifs filling the intervening spaces and touching the returned ends of the scrolls. The term 'comma leaf' is sometimes used of a leaf-shaped motif (often plastic, i.e. three-dimensional)

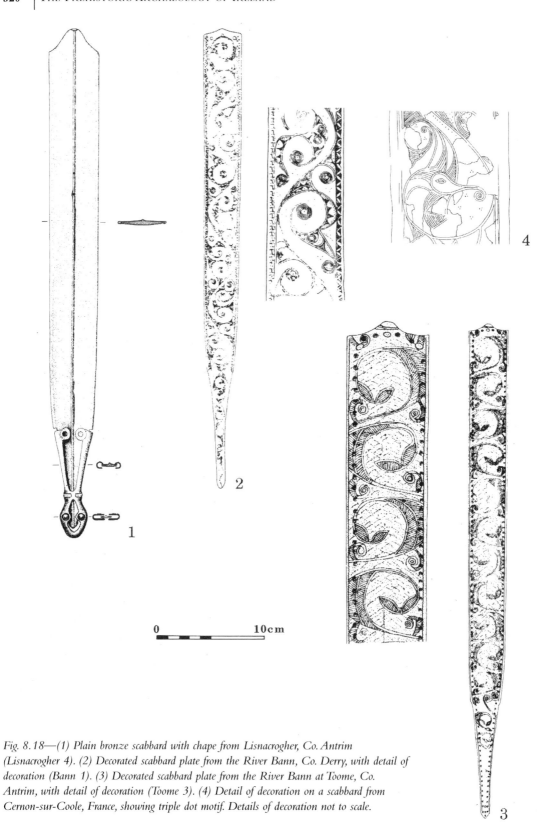

Fig. 8.18—(1) Plain bronze scabbard with chape from Lisnacrogher, Co. Antrim
(Lisnacrogher 4). (2) Decorated scabbard plate from the River Bann, Co. Derry, with detail of
decoration (Bann 1). (3) Decorated scabbard plate from the River Bann at Toome, Co.
Antrim, with detail of decoration (Toome 3). (4) Detail of decoration on a scabbard from
Cernon-sur-Coole, France, showing triple dot motif. Details of decoration not to scale.

Fig. 8.19—Decorated bronze scabbard plates with details of decoration. (1) Lisnacrogher 1. (2) Toome 1. (3) Lisnacrogher 2. (4) Lisnacrogher 3. Details of decoration not to scale.

with a circular or boss-like terminal. The junctions between the scrolls are filled with spirals and triangles and parts of the stems of the scrolls bear pairs of minute, almost lentoid motifs like eyes and are also emphasised with punched triangles. The scabbard edges are decorated with an engraved zigzag line. A broadly similar basic pattern occurs on the scabbard plate from the River Bann (Toome 1), which has three large S-scrolls touching one another, the junctions filled mostly with spirals (Fig. 8.19, 2). The stems of the major S-scrolls expand and contain tiny loose spirals, and the ends of these S-scrolls finish in smaller scrolls with spiral ends.

Lisnacrogher 2 is a scabbard plate that has retained its chape and that has an elegant and cleverly composed symmetrical pattern, arranged about a midrib and consisting of opposed S-scrolls forming a series of lyres in tiers—or, if viewed horizontally, a pair of opposed attenuated running waves with double pelta-shaped offshoots filled with parallel hatching or other designs (Fig. 8.19, 3). As on Lisnacrogher 1, parts of the stems of the S-scrolls are accentuated by punched triangles. The overall decorative scheme has a further ambiguity: this is one of those compositions that can be viewed in either its positive (engraved motifs) or negative (background) design. Lisnacrogher 3 is a scabbard plate with chape and a hammered midrib (Fig. 8.19, 4). The principal design is a series of large loose spirals touching one another, their junctions filled with small spiral motifs. This design is interrupted by the midrib and the motifs do not always precisely join each other. Near the top, the midrib has been used effectively to symmetrically divide the curvilinear ornament, which includes a pair of pelta shapes with spiral ends. The larger motifs on the scabbard are filled with a few spirals, some parallel hatching and some so-called basketry work—in which small rectangular fields of parallel hatching are placed at right angles to each other. This is the only Irish scabbard with this sort of basketry motif.

The art of these scabbards has inspired considerable comment and discussion, much of it concerned with stylistic affinities, origins and chronology. Though each one is different, they have a number of features in common, including the accomplished use of the rocked-graver technique (Lowery *et al.* 1971). Lines were engraved using a hand-held, pointed metal implement which, when moved backwards or forwards with a rocking motion, could produce deep fine lines cut with varied and slightly zigzag effects, depending on whether the point was round or chisel-shaped, for example. Overall ornament is another shared characteristic and the principal designs are based on sequences of S-scrolls and spirals. There is a noteworthy preference for quite a range of minor motifs used to fill the main figures and the spaces between them. Barry Raftery suggests that this Irish scabbard style contains two groups, each the product of different craft centres. A Bann group consists of scabbards, usually of slender proportions, without midribs and with tongues that are slightly concave. Each of the decorated scabbards in this group also has pairs of small leaf shapes sometimes forming zigzag ornament. A Lisnacrogher group has midribs on three of the four examples and a sharp distinction between plate and tongue. The tops are usually of prominent bell shape and the mouths of the decorated examples are outlined by punched zigzag decoration.

These Irish swords and scabbards are clearly related to a series of British examples (Stead 2006). Four British scabbards have overall curvilinear ornament extending the full length of the scabbard plate in the Irish fashion, a trait rarely found on the Continent. The presence of centrally placed suspension loops on the Yorkshire scabbards and on the plain scabbard from Lisnacrogher is another insular feature. A few decorative motifs are shared too: the basketry motif on Lisnacrogher 3 is found on the Bugthorpe, Yorkshire, scabbard, for instance, and the zigzag motif along the edges of Lisnacrogher 1 is found on two scabbards from Wetwang, Yorkshire. These similarities suggest that the Irish swords and scabbards are broadly contemporary with those in Yorkshire, but there are significant contrasts. The slender Irish chapes are different from their heavier and often decorated Scottish and northern English counterparts, and the profusion of ornament on the Irish scabbards and their propensity for employing a variety of minor filler motifs may be contrasted with the sparse, more open-textured style of the majority of the Yorkshire pieces.

Spear and shield

It is possible that spear and shield were the common attributes of the warrior at this time, but once again

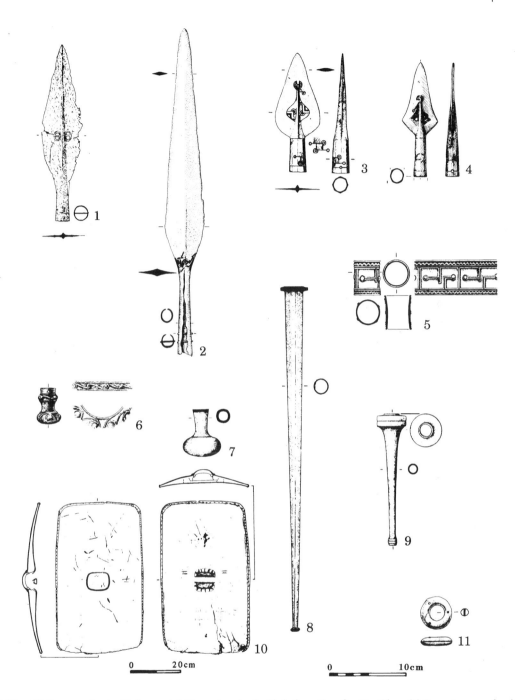

Fig. 8.20—(1) Iron spearhead with bronze inlaid openings in the blade from Corrofin, Co. Clare. (2) Large iron spearhead from Lisnacrogher, Co. Antrim. (3) Bronze spearhead from Boho, Co. Fermanagh. (4) Bronze spearhead from the River Blackwater, Moy, Co. Tyrone. (5) Decorated bronze ferrule from Lisnacrogher, Co. Antrim. (6) Type 1 spearbutt from Lisnacrogher, Co. Antrim. (7) Type 2 spearbutt from Derrymore Island, Lough Gara, Co. Sligo. (8) Type 3 spearbutt from the River Shannon at Carrick-on-Shannon, Co. Leitrim. (9) Type 4 spearbutt from the River Shannon at Banagher, Co. Offaly. (10) Shield of leather and wood from Clonoura, Co. Tipperary. (11) Hollow two-piece bronze ring from Lisnacrogher, Co. Antrim.

the archaeological record is disconcertingly deficient. Part of the problem is a familiar one: the simple socketed iron spear is a weapon that remained essentially unchanged over many centuries and cannot be easily dated unless clearly associated with other material or decorated in some distinctive way. An iron spearhead found in a river near Inchiquin Lake, Corrofin, Co. Clare (Fig. 8.20, 1), has a pair of openwork bronze settings in the blade and traces of a rectilinear step pattern on the socket. The perforations in the blade recall similar features in Dowris phase bronze spearheads. Two large iron spearheads from Lisnacrogher, Co. Antrim (Fig. 8.20, 2), are presumably broadly contemporary with the swords and scabbards from that site. These are impressive objects, about 41cm and 47cm in length respectively, and if they were ever mounted on the sort of wooden shafts also found at Lisnacrogher, which were about 2.4m in length, they would have been formidable weapons. In contrast, two quite small bronze spearheads, about 14–15cm in length, are known; one comes from a bog at Boho, Co. Fermanagh, the other from the River Blackwater at Moy, Co. Tyrone (Bourke 1993). Both have decoration (Fig. 8.20, 3–4) that recalls that on one of several cylindrical mounts from Lisnacrogher. These small weapons may have been for parade and display but could also have been throwing rather than thrusting spears.

Over 70 bronze spearbutts are recorded, no less than 25% of them coming from Lisnacrogher, Co. Antrim. These are bronze mounts of various shapes that are presumed to have been fitted as terminals to wooden spearshafts, and most are hollow-cast. Barry Raftery (1998) has divided them into four main groups. Type 1, the Lisnacrogher type, is a small waisted spearbutt with a convex base and a moulding below the mouth. One example from the eponymous site has La Tène ornament in relief on moulding and base (Fig. 8.20, 6). Type 2, the doorknob type, has a prominent rounded end and a slender cylindrical or funnel-shaped socket (Fig. 8.20, 7). Type 3, the tubular type, is a long, slender, tapering mount (Fig. 8.20, 8). A small number have mouldings at top and bottom; five stand apart from the rest, being made of hammered sheet bronze, and include the longest known examples, up to 43cm in length. Some bear La Tène decoration. Type 4, the conical type, is a short cast form with a prominent and usually grooved

moulding around the mouth (Fig. 8.20, 9). A number of types 1 and 2 have been found in rivers, and a significant number of types 3 and 4 have been recovered from the rivers Shannon and Bann. Not one of these mounts has yet been found with a spearhead, though some have been found with wooden shafts or retaining parts of these shafts. Some examples, notably of the type 2 doorknob form, have sockets of surprisingly narrow diameters, sometimes only a little more than 1cm. Wooden shafts of such slender dimensions must have been easily broken and it is questionable whether the bronze mounts were functional pieces; they could have been mounts for ceremonial staffs and, if they were spearbutts at all, they could conceivably have been primarily for display, like the small bronze spearheads. Whether all of these mounts were butts for spears must remain uncertain, but a couple of depictions of spears with bulbous ends to their shafts might be representations of spearbutts of this sort. A stone carving from Maryport, Cumberland, one of a collection of carvings of Romano-British date, shows a horned figure with a shield and a spear with a rounded butt. A silver plaque from Bewcastle, also in Cumberland, features a Roman deity holding a spear with a rounded extension to the end of the shaft. Type 1 seems to be a north-eastern Irish type while type 2 has a wider distribution, including a significant number of finds in Scotland and England, where they may have been in use as late as the fourth or fifth century AD in late and post-Roman times (Heald 2001). The tubular and conical forms (types 3 and 4) seem to be distinctively Irish types, with the former strongly represented in the west.

The Clonoura shield

Only one complete shield is known but it is an exceptionally interesting discovery. It was found in a nearly upright position in Littleton Bog in Clonoura townland, south-east of Thurles, Co. Tipperary. The shield is rectangular with rounded corners, 57cm by 35cm, and made of a slightly convex board of alderwood covered with a single piece of calf hide on both faces (Fig. 8.20, 10). These are fastened together with strips of leather stitched around the edges. There is a domed alderwood boss or umbo on the front, covered with stitched leather, with a bar of oak behind to provide a grip. On the back a pair of incisions cut in the leather on either side of this grip were probably for the attachment of carrying thongs. It is interesting to note that the front of the shield displays haphazardly distributed ancient cut-marks made either by sword blades or by spear thrusts, dramatic evidence of combat usage and an indication that warfare may have been a serious activity for some elements of society. Composite shields of leather and wood may have been common and of different shapes, with metal attachments of various sorts, as a series of miniature hide-shaped shields from Britain demonstrate. The closest parallels for the Clonoura shield are to be found in depictions of shields in stone and metal of the early centuries AD in northern Britain.

LISNACROGHER, CO. ANTRIM

The swords, scabbards and spearbutts from Lisnacrogher have been mentioned. These form a major part of a remarkable collection of objects recovered in the nineteenth century from a bog in or near the townland of that name in the valley of the Clogh River, some 7km north of Ballymena, Co. Antrim. Nothing remains of the site and even its precise location is disputed (Raftery 1983). Numerous finds were made in the years 1882 to 1888 and the site was visited in 1883 by W. F. Wakeman, whose published reports are not very informative. He noted timbers, encircling stakes and 'rough basket-like work' that may have been wattlework, and listed many of the artefacts acquired by northern collectors such as Canon J. Grainger of nearby Broughshane. Robert Munro, whose short description of his visit in 1886 is the best contemporary account, wrote that 'the bog in which these objects were found occupies the site of a former lake, which till recently, retained so much water as to prevent the working of the peat for fuel. To remedy this the outlet was deepened, and so new or undisturbed portions of the bog were brought within reach of the peat-cutters. The antiquities were found from time to time in a circumscribed area, within a small plot belonging to one of the neighbouring farmers. When attention was first directed to the locality, and the workers questioned as to the circumstances in which the relics came to light, it appears that some kind of wooden structure was encountered, which, however, had been entirely removed before being

seen by anyone competent to form an opinion as to its nature.' Munro questioned the farmer, who clearly recalled the existence of stakes and irregularly disposed oak beams and brushwood, and concluded, having seen the remnants of some oak timbers containing mortises, that there was 'little doubt that it was a crannog, but of no great dimensions'. He makes the important observation that 'as to the relics, there is no record of their association with the crannog beyond the fact of their being found in its vicinity'. These relics, as we have seen, included one complete bronze scabbard and three extraordinary decorated scabbard plates, as well as at least three bronze chapes, two iron spearheads, four bronze ferrules for spearshafts, and some eighteen bronze spearbutts, several still attached to long wooden shafts. Other finds included three enigmatic hollow bronze rings, two bronze ring-headed pins, a simple bronze torc, several bronze bracelets and rings, a number of decorative bronze mounts, and an iron axe, adze and sickle. Two cauldrons made of sheets of iron are said to have been found but are not preserved. A gold ribbon torc is also said to have come from Lisnacrogher but this may not be a genuine provenance. The three hollow two-piece bronze rings from the site (Fig. 8.20, 11) are rare Irish examples of a puzzling artefact widely distributed on the Continent (Raftery 1988). An example from a cemetery at Kirkburn, Yorkshire, was found near the skull of a young woman who had been buried with a newborn infant, but on the Continent they have often been found in male graves, although some have been found in female burials too. The Lisnacrogher rings belong to an early riveted variety and might date from the third century BC. They have been thought to be part of some mechanism for suspending a scabbard from a belt but seem too flimsy for this purpose; they may have been ornaments or amulets.

With so little information about the wooden structure or structures 'of no great dimensions' it is impossible to know whether Lisnacrogher actually was a settlement or crannog and whether, if there was a settlement there, it had any connection with all the material recovered. This material has been considered the stock of a metalworker and the site has been thought to be a chieftain's family armoury and workshop, containing equipment accumulated over several generations. The apparent absence of settlement debris may not be significant because mundane finds like saddle querns and metal fragments might well have held little or no interest for nineteenth-century scavengers and collectors. All that can reasonably be said is that such an assemblage of metalwork has never been found on a prehistoric settlement of any date in Ireland and, on present evidence, the balance of probability is that the original lake here was an important focus for votive offerings like Dowris, Co. Offaly, and Loughnashade, Co. Armagh.

PERSONAL ORNAMENTS

Torcs, fibulae and pins are the commonest personal ornaments. Most are stray finds. The fine gold torcs from Broighter, Co. Derry, and Knock, Co. Roscommon, and the gold ribbon torcs, if worn as personal ornaments, were probably the possessions of an aristocracy, but many of the simpler bronze fibulae and pins are also works of considerable craftsmanship and may have been status symbols too, albeit of a lesser nature. The fibula or brooch is a common type of dress-fastener on the Continent, where it is capable of subtle and chronologically significant typological subdivision, with variations assignable to different phases of the La Tène period there. To a lesser extent the same is true in Britain. In Ireland, however, the majority are local forms and are less easily datable. Three principal Irish types have been recognised: rod-bow and leaf-bow safety-pin fibulae and Navan-type brooches. Rod-bow fibulae have slender flat or arched bows formed of a rod of bronze; their foot curves back and touches or is attached to the bow and they usually have a double-coiled safety-pin-type spring with an external chord or loop (Fig. 8.21, 1–3). A decorated example found 3–4m deep in a bog at Lecarrow, Co. Sligo, has a typical spring with two coils and an external chord; the tip of the catchplate curves upwards to form an unusual ring from which the foot extends to the bow. At this point the foot forms a tiny bird's head. Another similar fibula, an old find from Clogher, Co. Tyrone, is decorated with cast trumpet curves and has three small settings that may once have held enamel. An iron example, much corroded, was found in the excavation of the ringfort at Feerwore, Co. Galway. The profile of most of these rod-bow fibulae, with an almost straight bow, is similar to that of the flattened-bow fibulae of southern England, and it is possible that their genesis may lie in contacts with the Wessex region as early as the third century BC.

Leaf-bow fibulae usually have slightly curved profiles and characteristic bows that are cast or hammered to a broad, flat, slender leaf shape (Fig. 8.21, 4–5). Double coils and external chords are common, but five-coiled springs are known, as are internal chords. Decoration on the bow may be no more than a simple central line but occasionally is a little more elaborate, with elegant elongated arcs. The most ornate example has an openwork bow, the oval opening flanked by cast trumpet curves in relief, and was found with a cremated burial and some glass beads at Kiltierney, Co. Fermanagh. A small number of fibulae, the Navan-type brooches, named after two old finds at Navan Fort, Co. Armagh, form a distinctively Irish group (Fig. 8.21, 6). They have elaborate openwork bows with finely cast decoration with trumpet curves and lentoid bosses. One of the Navan finds and examples from Lough Ree and from the Somerset hoard in County Galway (Fig. 8.10, 6) have circular settings for red enamel. The term 'brooch' is often preferred because the fibula's characteristic safety-pin spring is replaced by a pin with an unusual and innovative ball-and-socket mechanism, or in one instance by a skeuomorphic spring containing a spindle on which the pin swivels. It has been variously suggested that these brooches may have been influenced by late British fibulae, by openwork Roman brooches or clasps, or by larger openwork mirror handles known in southern England. Whatever their inspiration, a date in the late first century BC or the first century AD seems plausible.

Among the few miscellaneous fibulae recorded, one from near Donaghadee, Co. Down, was found at a place called Loughey in about 1850, along with two glass bracelets, 150 glass beads, bronze rings, bronze tweezers and a small bronze toggle (Jope and Wilson 1957; Henderson 1987). They were all found in a small pit and it is thought, on very slender evidence, that they had accompanied a female cremation. The fibula, with its solid catchplate, is a type well known in southern England and derived from a Continental Nauheim type. It and the other items are imports and probably date from the first century AD. A similar fibula was found on the shores of Lough Gara at

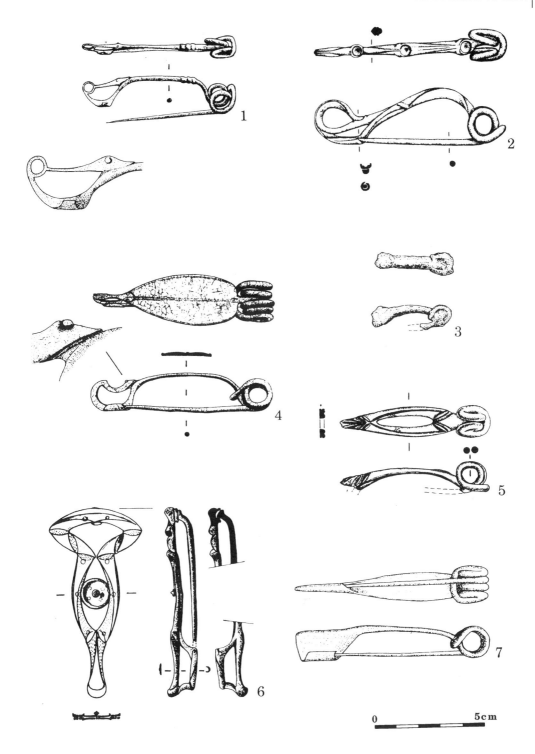

Fig. 8.21—Rod-bow fibulae: (1) Lecarrow, Co. Sligo; (2) Clogher, Co. Tyrone. (3) Iron fragment from Feerwore, Co. Galway. Leaf-bow fibulae: (4) unprovenanced; (5) Kiltierney, Co. Fermanagh. (6) Navan-type brooch from Navan Fort, Co. Armagh. (7) Nauheim-derivative fibula from Derrybeg, Co. Sligo.

Derrybeg, Co. Sligo (Fig. 8.21, 7), and one was reportedly found with a cremation in a ring-ditch at Ballydavis, Co. Laois.

Though there are a few finds of textiles, nothing is known about late prehistoric clothing. Christopher Hawkes (1982), prompted by the idea that novel dress-fasteners might be connected with novel dress, did speculate that the appearance of the La Tène fibula in Ireland could have coincided with the introduction, also from southern Britain, of a male fashion for wearing ankle-length trousers of chequered pattern, but so far, at least, evidence is lacking. It is interesting to note that dress pins were still popular and were evidently not displaced by the fibula. Indeed, if surviving numbers are any indication, they seem to have been marginally commoner, but whether they represent a continuation in pin fashion from earlier times is uncertain. Most of the Irish examples are stray finds and there is considerable variety. The basic form is a pin with a ring-shaped head immediately above an angular bent neck (Fig. 8.22). They are normally of cast bronze and some heads are annular, others penannular. A number have bosses on the ring and some have curvilinear ornament in relief. One distinctive type has a large decorative setting for imposing studs of red enamel; another has a prominently forward-curving head. Some of these pins have parallels in Britain but the precise chronology of the different types is unclear. There is

an occasional hint of regional preferences: ring-headed pins are well represented in County Antrim, for instance, where rod- and leaf-bow fibulae are virtually absent.

DISCS AND HORNS AND SOLAR SYMBOLS

A series of bronze discs and horns are further testimony of the proficiency of the bronzesmith and artist, and some are, in their own right, remarkable expressions of artistic excellence. They are usually dated on stylistic grounds to the early centuries AD (Jope 2000). The Bann disc, as it is generally called, is a small bronze disc, only 10.5cm in diameter, which was dredged from the River Bann at Loughan Island near Coleraine in 1939. It is very slightly convex with three perforations, one containing a small bronze ring (Fig. 8.23, 1). It was probably a decorative mount of some description, though it has been suggested that it might be a pan from a weighing scales, and its convex face has an elegant composition of fine lines forming what is essentially a swirling three-limbed figure, a triskele, within a circle. The design is initiated by three raised lines radiating from a central circle and swirling in a clockwise direction; these lines, which are slender trumpet curves, join with other trumpet curves which swirl in the reverse, anticlockwise, direction

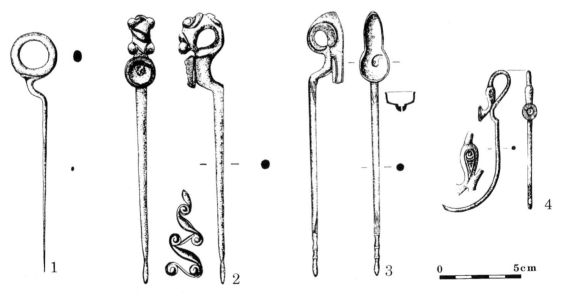

Fig. 8.22—Ring-headed pins. (1) No provenance. (2) Grange, Co. Sligo. (3) Roscavey, Co. Tyrone. (4) River Shannon.

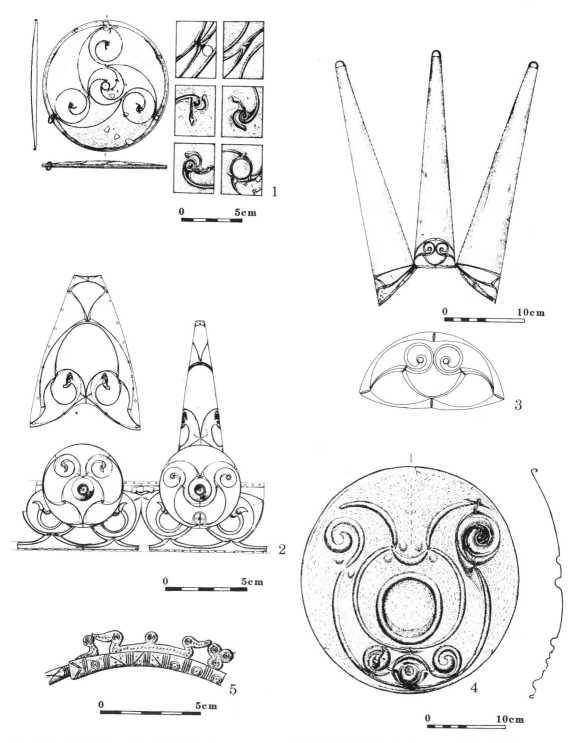

Fig. 8.23—(1) The Bann disc, with details of trumpet curves and birds' heads. (2) The Petrie crown, with detail of ornament on horn. (3) The Cork horns, with detail of ornament on the central horn consisting of a pair of triskeles formed by trumpet curves. (4) Unprovenanced bronze disc of Monasterevin type. (5) Detail of an early bronze torc from Attancourt (Haute-Marne), showing solar boat with birds' heads.

and terminate in stylised birds' heads. Based on compass-drawn curving lines, the overall design displays exceptional restraint and has a rhythmic quality suggesting 'an interplay of rotational forces caught in a moment of time'. The bronze object known as the Petrie crown is so called because it was once in the collection of the nineteenth-century antiquary George Petrie, who did not record—or never knew—its provenance. It is a fragmentary piece, now consisting of a band of openwork sheet bronze with a pair of slightly dished discs attached to the front (Fig. 8.23, 2). Each disc apparently supported a bronze horn, one of which survives. This horn is made of a sheet of hammered bronze folded to a conical shape. Each element of the fragment—the band, the discs and the horn—is very skilfully decorated with a symmetrical design of thin and elongated trumpet curves, some terminating in different sorts of birds' heads. The design on the disc below the surviving horn is particularly interesting because the bird's-head terminals flank a circle set in a crescent form. This, like the design on a series of other bronze discs, is probably a solar symbol. With a maximum height and length of only 15cm, this metal object seems too small to be worn itself, but a row of small holes at the top and bottom of the band indicate that it was meant to be attached to something, perhaps a leather backing, and this could have been worn as a headpiece, though whether for display on a human head or in a ritual context on an idol is obviously unknown. An equally fragile bronze helmet with short conical horns, and also not a functional item, was found in the River Thames near Waterloo Bridge. A pair of bronze conical horns, possibly part of a head-dress, was found in a bog at Runnabehy near Frenchpark, Co. Roscommon, and according to E. P. Kelly (2006a; 2006b) this is just one of many significant Iron Age deposits found at possible boundaries.

The object now called the Cork horns is another horned headpiece (Fig. 8.23, 3), though possessing three longer horns about 26–29cm in length. It was found near Cork in river mud at a location which was originally probably in a tidal salt-marsh, below the high-water mark, and which recalls the find-spot of the Broighter hoard in the north. This horned object is also incomplete: the three conical horns of sheet bronze were attached together by overlapping flanges and were once

attached to a lost portion, probably of leather. Each horn bears a symmetrical design in low relief mainly composed of a pair of triskeles formed by attenuated trumpet curves. A more complex version occurs on the central horn, where one limb of each triskele ends in a boss and spiral motif reminiscent of a bird's head. Triple horns are unusual and provide another useful reminder that some ornaments may not have been worn by human figures, animate or inanimate. Triple horns occur on images of bulls in England in Romano-British contexts and in Gallo-Roman France.

Several features demonstrate that these three objects are closely related. They share a symmetry of composition, motifs such as slender trumpet curves and triskeles, and an elaborate technique of decoration in which at least part of the background was cut away to produce the relief ornament. A variety of forms of stylised birds' heads link all three together as well: those on the Bann disc are quite abstract and mainly formed of tiny trumpet curves and lentoid bosses, three separate types are to be found on the Petrie crown, while the pair on the Cork horns are perhaps the least bird-like. The decoration on the discs of the Petrie crown is also similar to the designs on a puzzling series of larger bronze discs.

A pair of large bronze discs found together at Monasterevin, Co. Kildare, has given the name 'Monasterevin type' to a group of four complete and three fragmentary discs (Fig. 8.23, 4). Other pairs come from Lismore, Co. Waterford, and from Co. Armagh (Ó Floinn 2009). None have any details of their discovery recorded. Made of sheet bronze, these discs are usually slightly concave and range in diameter from about 25cm to just over 30cm; their purpose is unknown. Decoration is similar but not identical and consists of bold repoussé work up to 10mm high. The overall pattern is a fairly consistent one: a large central circle or roundel, which varies from a slight concavity to a deep bowl-shaped hollow, is placed within a symmetrical field of trumpet curves forming an approximately U-shaped or semicircular arrangement with spiral terminals which contains a prominent circle. Given the positioning of a pair of spirals above a circle, it is probably not surprising that this design has been described as a geometrical fantasy and compared to a grotesque face with large staring eyes. The bronze discs on the Petrie crown provide a clue to another more plausible explanation. The disc below the surviving horn shows a cross set in a crescentic shape that has spiral terminals with birds' heads and a circular device between them. This is a solar symbol, a stylised depiction of the boat of the sun drawn across the heavens by birds (Fig. 8.23, 5), the circular device representing the sun, which is also symbolised by the wheel below. The larger motif is repeated in a more stylised manner on the second disc of the crown and on the Monasterevin-type discs as well, and illustrates just how a series of stylised forms may have been imbued with a magical significance which we can only dimly perceive today (Waddell 2009).

9

ELUSIVE SETTLEMENTS AND RITUAL SITES

Although fine metalwork is eloquent testimony of a wealthy aristocracy and a proficient artisan class, and various ceremonial centres offer abundant evidence of constructional skills and organisational complexity, knowledge of domestic occupation sites and our understanding of settlement, economy and social structure in the period from 600 BC to the early centuries AD is still meagre in the extreme.

While ringforts are generally dated to the second half of the first millennium AD, to the early medieval period, excavation of a small number has revealed slight traces of earlier, pre-ringfort occupation of late prehistoric date. The simple iron socketed axehead, the fragmentary iron fibula, some occupation debris and other artefacts from Feerwore, Co. Galway, indicate settlement of some description on a gently sloping, low hill probably in the late second or early first century BC. No associated structures were found and a ringfort was built on the site several centuries later (Raftery 1944). Traces of occupation, including gullies and hearths, radiocarbon-dated to AD 90–320, have been discovered beneath a ringfort at Dunsilly, Co. Antrim (McNeill 1992), and some stake-holes with associated charcoal, well stratified beneath a ringfort bank at Lisdoo, Co. Fermanagh, provided a date of AD 250–530 (Warner et al. 1990). At Millockstown, Co. Louth, limited excavation of a sequence of enclosures of early medieval date revealed that the earliest phase, an approximately oval ditched enclosure some 60m across, may date from AD 250–610 (Manning 1986). A number of circular features, 3.6–4.6m in internal diameter, in a ringfort at Lislackagh, near Swinford, Co. Mayo, have been radiocarbon-dated to 200 BC–AD 140 (G. Walsh 1995) but these could be earlier ceremonial ring-ditches. Corn-drying kilns, a good indicator of settlement, have been identified at a number of locations, such as Tullyallen, Co. Louth (Linnane 2007), and Marshes Upper, Dundalk, Co. Louth (Mossop 2004).

More clearly defined structural remains have occasionally been identified. A series of post-holes have been interpreted as the foundations of an oblong house at Killoran 16, near Derryville Bog, and dated to 180 BC–AD 425 (Gowen et al. 2005). The foundation trench of a small circular timber structure 4m in diameter was found in Magheraboy, near Sligo, and radiocarbon-dated to 370–30 BC, but there were no associated finds to indicate its purpose (Danaher 2007). A U-shaped arrangement of post-holes at Muckridge, near Youghal, Co. Cork, surrounded a hearth and a pit; charcoal from a nearby pit was dated to AD 20–350 (Noonan 2003). Traces of other Iron Age circular structures (with a notable scarcity of artefacts) have been identified in Cork, Limerick and Tipperary (McLaughlin and Conran 2008; McQuade et al. 2009). It may be that simple circular wicker houses were the norm and have left little archaeological trace (Lynn 2003a). Significant regional differences are likely, however. Upland areas were evidently farmed; the stone foundations of a small subrectangular house, a small enclosure and several sections of pre-bog field wall have been dated to the Iron Age in the Barrees valley, Co. Cork, at altitudes ranging from about 180m to 300m OD (W. O'Brien 2009).

Wetland locations were undoubtedly settled as well but evidence for the use of substantial lake settlements or crannogs has yet to be revealed. If there was settlement at Lisnacrogher the nature of the site remains uncertain. But while some occupation at Rathtinaun, Lough Gara, Co. Sligo, dated from both the Dowris phase and the early medieval period, there was also activity there in the later centuries BC. The latter is attested by a series of radiocarbon dates for a deposit of charred cereals and a number of wattle-built and clay-lined hearths that have a date range of 490 BC–AD 230. The construction of substantial bog trackways may be another indication of settlement in these locations or nearby. Barry Raftery's excavations at Corlea, Co. Longford, established that a massive timber trackway, justifiably termed a road, in Corlea townland was in fact part of a system that extended for some 2km into the neighbouring townland of Derraghan. Dendrochronological analysis determined that the oak timbers were felled about 148 BC. This Corlea–Derraghan roadway was constructed of large oak planks laid transversely on parallel lines of timbers of birch or ash placed on the bog surface. Up to 25ha of woodland were cleared in this huge undertaking, and the whole process of felling, transport and construction was evidently a major coordinated effort by a local community or communities (Raftery 1996). The discovery of parts of two-piece tub-shaped wooden containers raises the possibility that feasting or drinking may have been a way in which work-parties were mobilised. In any event, these vessels and other pieces of finely crafted, slotted, mortised and tenoned timbers provide rare testimony of the carpenter's skill. The joiners and builders presumably lived in dispersed settlements in the general locality, but where is not known. There are few finds from the area and the only significant contemporary artefact is a matching pair of bronze bridle-bits found near Abbeyshrule, 12km to the east. In all probability most trackways of all dates were functional routeways but some may have had ritual associations and there is the intriguing possibility that some in Britain and Ireland were built at the time of midwinter lunar eclipses (Field and Parker Pearson 2003).

Coastal locations were occupied at this time too, though the evidence is limited: radiocarbon-dated charcoal from a shell midden at Poul Gorm,

Glengarriff, Co. Cork, suggests that the site was frequented in the period 370–20 BC (McCarthy 1986). Some animal bone from a shell midden at Ballymulholland, Co. Derry, indicated a date range of 385–176 BC and some iron slag demonstrated nearby iron-working (Mallory and McCormick 1988). The offerings of fish and shellfish placed in the wedge tomb at Altar near Schull, Co. Cork (Chapter 3), included periwinkle, limpet, wrasse and eel and were dated in the main to the first two centuries AD. Some Iron Age finds from coastal middens may come from beaching places where seagoing craft might easily make land (Warner 1998).

As we shall see, excavation at the royal sites of Tara, Navan and Knockaulin has produced abundant evidence for ritual activity, but evidence for mundane domestic settlement has yet to be clearly identified. None of the sites mentioned shed much light on the broader questions of settlement and economy but a majority of them illustrate one striking fact. Admittedly the sample is very small and very varied but, apart from a few iron artefacts and, even more rarely, some glass beads, for instance, these sites have not produced a consistent range of diagnostic artefacts. It is perhaps not surprising that prestigious bronze objects, like bridle-bits, scabbards or spearbutts, should be absent, but the scarcity of smaller metal objects and of pottery in any quantity is noteworthy. Most coarse pottery seems to date from the Dowris phase and earlier, and it is possible that pottery may simply have become an unfashionable and rare commodity, its domestic roles taken over by containers of iron, wood and leather (Raftery 1995). Wooden vessels were used, and if there was now a greater reliance on perishable materials, and if, as may be the case, few settlement sites were enclosed by substantial earthworks, then the elusive quality of later prehistoric settlement may be disconcerting but not surprising.

QUERN STONES

It would seem to be a reasonable belief that the distribution of domestic artefacts might provide a significant clue as to the whereabouts of the elusive settlement sites. Since quern stones are likely to be discarded close to their place of use, these objects

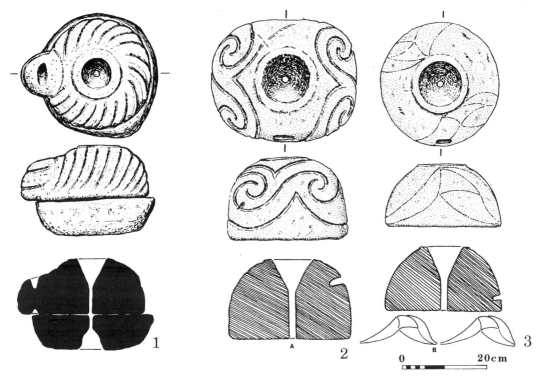

Fig. 9.1—Beehive querns. (1) From the north of Ireland, with decorated upper stone with socket for vertical handle set in a projecting lug. (2) Decorated upper stone with 'horizontal' handle socket from Ticooly-O'Kelly, Co. Galway. (3) Decorated upper stone with 'horizontal' handle socket from Clonmacnoise, Co. Offaly.

might be particularly informative. It is generally believed that the rotary quern was introduced to Britain in the fifth or fourth century BC (Heslop 1988). The earliest form is the beehive quern and the conventional assumption is that this type of quern appeared in Ireland in or about the first century BC, though the evidence for such a late arrival is slim. The appearance of this novel method of grinding cereals may have been an event of some significance: the new rotary method represented a considerable improvement on the saddle quern particularly because it crushed as well as ground the cereal and was therefore less onerous for the operator. Although it may have displaced the saddle quern for corn-grinding purposes, the complete replacement of the saddle quern may have been a gradual one, because these could still have been used for minor grinding tasks and for crushing nuts and suchlike. The rotary quern consists of two circular stones; the upper stone, rotated with a handle, has a central hole that serves as a chute for the corn, which is ground between the stones, working its way to the edge as it is ground (Fig.

9.1). The narrowness of the chute or feedpipe often implies the use of a metal spindle, this pivotal piece sitting in a socket in the centre of the lower stone. There are two basic forms of ancient rotary quern: those with thick grinding stones of relatively small diameter, the heavy upper one being slightly domed (hence the name beehive quern), and the flat disc quern, which in Ireland seems to have replaced the beehive form in the first millennium AD.

Irish beehive querns have been studied by Séamas Caulfield, who recorded over 200 examples in 1977, and more have been found since then. Most are 28–36cm in diameter and invariably have flat grinding surfaces and a funnel-shaped perforation in the upper stone. The position of the handle socket varies; some are horizontally placed, others are vertical with a large proportion of them set in a projecting lug. The position of the handle socket is the basis of an imprecise threefold subdivision in which querns with horizontal handle sockets, with vertical sockets and with sockets 'off the horizontal' are distinguished. There are some indications of regional trends: querns with

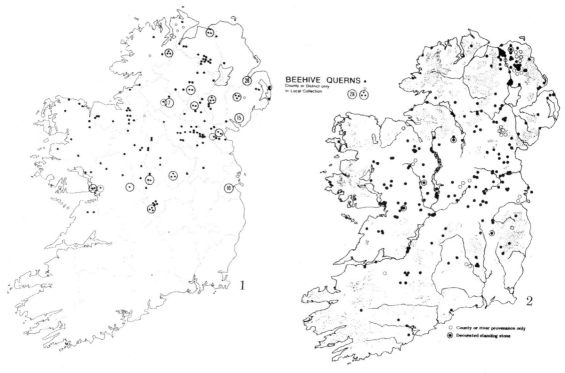

Fig. 9.2—General distribution maps. (1) Beehive querns. (2) Artefacts excluding querns.

horizontal sockets are concentrated in mid-Ulster, in the upper Shannon region and northern Connacht, while those with vertical sockets are found mainly in the north-east, in north Leinster and in Tyrone, Antrim and Down. The general distribution of beehive querns is mainly confined to the northern half of the island, with only a few examples found south of a Galway to Dublin line (Fig. 9.2, 1). The distribution is noteworthy in several respects. A number of concentrations of quern stones, around Belfast, Dublin, Draperstown, Co. Derry, and Bailieborough, Co. Cavan, for instance, reflect the activities of local collectors and antiquarians and do not represent clusters of possible settlements. The general northern bias of the beehive type is genuine, however, and may be contrasted with the island-wide distribution of saddle querns and the later disc querns. Caulfield was intrigued by the similarity between this pattern and the northern distribution of material such as bridle-bits, spearbutts and La Tène art (Fig. 9.2, 2). There is a broad similarity, but even more intriguing is the fact that in this northern half of the country there is also evidence of considerable mutual

exclusivity. This is apparent in the north-east, where most querns lie well to the west of the River Bann while the metalwork is concentrated in the Bann valley and to the east. Some metal finds and some concentrations of quern stones come from areas of relatively good soils in the midlands, but there appears to be a tendency for some quern stones to be associated with poorer soils. This divergent distributional pattern is also to be seen in north Connacht but the significance of all this is far from clear. Richard Warner (2002b) has argued that the metalwork-users were 'rancher-warriors' and that the quern-users, for the most part, were poorer corn-growers.

No beehive quern has been found in a datable context and the type is in effect undated. A small number were clearly special objects and are decorated with curvilinear La Tène ornament. For these at least the assumed date of between the second century BC and the fourth century AD may be appropriate, if not very precise. If their introduction occurred sometime in the earlier first millennium AD, it is difficult to see any connection between the appearance of rotary querns and an intensification of arable farming. A lull in farming activity reflected in woodland regeneration is a feature of a number of pollen diagrams at this time. It has been suggested that a significant increase in tree growth with a consequent decrease in farming land occurred in County Louth in the period 200 BC–AD 200 (Weir 1993), after which farming activity seems to have expanded considerably. A similar event in the pollen record indicating a reduction in arable farming has been detected elsewhere, but it seems to be a feature of the early centuries AD. In the Mooghaun region minimal farming activity occurs between *c.* AD 1 and AD 300 though the area was not abandoned (Molloy 2005), but in Derryville Bog, for instance, the regression begins *c.* AD 80 and continues for some 600 years until AD 700 (Caseldine, Hatton *et al.* 2005). A number of pollen diagrams from the west of Ireland suggest that this diminution in farming activity extended from AD 200 or 300 to the sixth or seventh century (Molloy and O'Connell 1993; 2004; Jeličić and O'Connell 1992). It has been suggested that this farming regression may have been due to climatic deterioration, but this is by no means certain and the socio-economic consequences of this development remain unclear.

There is little doubt that the beehive quern type originated in northern England and southern Scotland, where querns of similar shape, size and handle socket configuration are well represented. Caulfield believed that their appearance was one significant piece of evidence for an immigration of people, but given the superiority and specialised nature of the rotary quern its rapid adoption by farming communities would not be surprising, and this is apparently what happened in Scotland (Armit 1991). Since the introduction of the rotary quern is generally considered to be an important change in farming practice, one of the most puzzling features of the beehive quern in Ireland is its complete absence from settlement sites. Not one has been found in a ringfort, for example, which does suggest that the quern type had disappeared by the middle of the first millennium AD, when ringforts became common, but none have been found on earlier settlements either. They do show signs of use, apparently, but where circumstances of discovery have been recorded, the majority of these querns have been found in bogs. Inevitably this raises the question of ritual deposition and it is possible that

querns, like various metal types, were considered sufficiently valuable for this purpose. It is also possible, of course, that these querns were themselves special objects, used only in specific circumstances and not necessarily in a domestic context. If their primary role was an exceptional one, preparing grain for a special cereal-based alcoholic drink, for instance, the sort of drink that might have filled a fine wooden tankard found near Carrickfergus, Co. Antrim, then this might explain their distributional peculiarities and their eventual deposition in a particular way.

WOODEN AND BRONZE VESSELS

A small number of wooden and bronze vessels give merely a hint of the range of containers that were probably in regular use. Wooden vessels must have been very common, and platters, a trough and fragments of several tub-shaped vessels (hollowed from tree trunks with inserted circular bases) were found beneath the Corlea roadway. The tankard found in a bog at Carrickfergus, Co. Antrim (Fig. 9.3, 1), was stave-built. Its base is a lathe-turned wooden disc and its body is formed of nine staves now held in place by a broad band of bronze around the upper exterior. It has one sheet-bronze loop handle with a decorated D-shaped escutcheon above bearing engraved curvilinear ornament (Ó Néill 2002). It is very similar to a bronze-bound wooden tankard from a bog at Trawsfynydd, Merioneth, which has a bronze-decorated wooden base that was probably meant to be seen and to impress the happy user's drinking companions.

Two elegantly carved round-bottomed wooden bowls, each with one handle, are wooden versions of a type also known in bronze (Earwood 1989). One, from County Armagh (Fig. 9.3, 2), has been radiocarbon-dated to 213 BC–AD 61, and the other, from a bog near Cloughmills, Co. Antrim, has provided a broadly similar date of 174 BC–AD 134. A large alder trough found in Toar Bog, south of Tyrellspass, Co. Westmeath, measured 1.29m in length and had projecting handles at either end; it had been carefully repaired and secured in place in the bog by three long pegs, one of which was radiocarbon-dated to 197 BC–AD 68 (Murray 2002). The finest bronze bowl is one found in the river just north of Keshcarrigan, Co. Leitrim, which

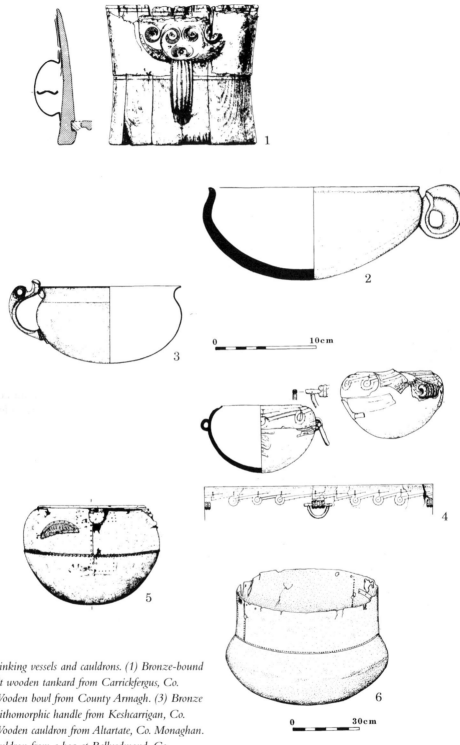

Fig. 9.3—Drinking vessels and cauldrons. (1) Bronze-bound and stave-built wooden tankard from Carrickfergus, Co. Antrim. (2) Wooden bowl from County Armagh. (3) Bronze bowl with ornithomorphic handle from Keshcarrigan, Co. Leitrim. (4) Wooden cauldron from Altartate, Co. Monaghan. (5) Bronze cauldron from a bog at Ballyedmond, Co. Galway. (6) Bronze cauldron of 'projecting-bellied' form from Ballymoney, Co. Antrim.

flows into Lough Scur (Fig. 9.3, 3). Only 14cm in diameter, this small bowl, perhaps a ceremonial drinking cup, was either cast or beaten into shape and then finished and polished by being spun on a lathe. A graceful bird's-head handle is soldered on. A similar handle was found in the Somerset hoard (Fig. 8.10, 2). A bronze bowl found in a hillfort at Fore, Co. Westmeath, contained a cremation burial and may be an import from southern England.

Cauldrons of iron, wood and bronze are known, though not all are securely dated. The Drumlane, Co. Cavan, iron cauldron has already been mentioned; its multi-sheet construction, recalling earlier bronze cauldrons, has prompted suggestions of an early date. Cauldrons made of sheets of iron are said to have been found at Lisnacrogher but have not survived. A wooden cauldron found in a bog at Altartate Glebe, near Clones, Co. Monaghan (Fig. 9.3, 4), is carved from a single piece of poplar and has two ribbed lugs, one still containing a D-shaped handle of yew wood. It is difficult to date on stylistic grounds, but the hemispherical shape of the body and the ribbed lugs have been compared to bronze Dowris phase cauldrons, and a frieze of incised parallel lines and dot and circle ornament below the rim has been compared to a motif on a British pottery vessel possibly of fourth-century BC date. A broadly similar but undecorated round-bottomed wooden cauldron from Clogh, Co. Fermanagh, has been radiocarbon-dated to 663–363 BC. A small group of bronze cauldrons with parallels in England and Scotland may date from the early centuries AD. These include a globular specimen found in a bog at Ballyedmond, near Tuam, Co. Galway, and several examples with bulbous bodies and vertical necks, sometimes called 'projecting-bellied cauldrons' (Fig. 9.3, 6). Like earlier bronze cauldrons, these could have served as containers for the preparation of either food or drink for special occasions. The uses to which the wooden cauldrons may have been put are unknown, but it is worth considering the possibility that they in particular had a part to play in alcohol-related rituals. Evidence for convivial drinking has been claimed in various places at various times since the third millennium BC, and special drinking vessels, such as drinking horns, sometimes suggest a ceremonial aspect. The Carrickfergus tankard and the Keshcarrigan cup might well have fulfilled such a role, and the recognition of drinking rituals remains 'a real challenge to archaeology' (Vencl 1994).

ROYAL SITES AND LARGE ENCLOSURES IN LATER PREHISTORY

Large monuments such as Haughey's Fort, Co. Armagh, demonstrate that hilltop enclosures and earthworks on a significant scale were constructed at least as early as 1100 BC. As we have seen, monuments such as this and sites like Rathgall, Co. Wicklow, may have been occupied by an aristocratic element, and they seemingly had a ritual component or a ceremonial role as well. The social developments first detected in the Bishopsland phase are still in evidence and, indeed, there is some suggestion that exotic artefacts, display and ritual may have become even more important. Presumably some élite elements of society continued to have both a political and a religious role, continuing to control long-distance exchange networks and to participate in ritual activities. It is still difficult to draw a line between the sacred and the secular, and nowhere is this more in evidence than on certain 'royal sites', where archaeology of ritual and of settlement, and mythology and early history are all intertwined.

A number of celebrated 'royal sites' figure prominently in early Irish literature, and four—Tara (Teamhair), Navan (Emhain Mhacha), Rathcroghan (Cruachain) and Knockaulin (Dún Ailinne)—are identified as pre-Christian centres in the calendar of saints known as *Félire Óengusso* ('The Martyrology of Oengus'), which dates from about AD 830. A much-quoted hyperbolic verse proclaims the triumph of Christianity and the abandonment of these pagan sites with the advent of the new religion in or about the fifth century. In a variety of early medieval sources these sites are variously remembered as royal settlements or forts, cemeteries and assembly places. The presence of large, approximately circular earthen enclosures with bank or rampart and internal ditch at three locations has long provided archaeological support for the idea that they are in some way related. Survey and excavation now show that these sites are related, at least in so far as each of them contains one or more large enclosures and has had a complex history of ceremonial and ritual activity in later prehistoric times. A possible prehistoric ceremonial enclosure, of penannular form and some 50m in diameter, exists at Uisneach, Co. Westmeath (Schot 2006), a royal and assembly site considered to be the centre of Ireland in medieval tradition. The convention of using Anglicised names (Tara, Navan, Rathcroghan, Knockaulin) is adopted here to distinguish between the physical or archaeological and the literary manifestations of these sites.

Tara, Co. Meath

The Hill of Tara is situated about midway between the towns of Dunshaughlin and Navan in south central Meath. The monuments lie on a low ridge some 2km long and about 155m above sea level. The ridge drops steeply to the west, with dramatic views over the central plain of the Irish midlands. The first recorded survey of the monuments at Tara is found in a collection of topographic texts known as *Dindshenchas* (the lore of placenames), the earliest version of which occurs in the Book of Leinster, dating from about AD 1160. Various monuments and natural features are named and tales about them recorded. The medieval names were reassigned to the monuments in the nineteenth century, notably by John O'Donovan and George Petrie as part of their work for the Ordnance Survey. Some of these names, ultimately the result of what was a medieval archaeological survey, are now in common usage and are applied to a variety of enclosures, burial mounds and linear earthworks. Here the Irish-language forms of the names of some of the major monuments are used in modernised spelling. Over 30 monuments are visible on the hill, and as many again have been identified through aerial photography or geophysical survey (Newman 1997b). The principal monuments extend over an area some 900m in length from south to north and include several enclosures and a large number of burial mounds (Fig. 9.4).

To the south is a partly destroyed enclosure named Ráth Laoghaire (Lóegaire's Fort, named after an early medieval king of Tara) with an overall diameter of about 130m. It seems to consist of a rampart with internal ditch but there may be slight traces of another bank within the ditch. The largest enclosure on the hill has been named Ráth na Rí (the Fort of the Kings). It is an earthwork of approximately oval plan measuring about 310m north–south and 210m east–west (Fig. 9.5). It encloses some 70,000m^2 of the summit and is one of those fairly rare hilltop enclosures characterised by an internal ditch and external bank, a type found at Navan and Knockaulin. At least five monuments are known to occur within Ráth na Rí: they include the Mound of the Hostages (Dumha na nGiall), Dumha na mBó (a mound noted on the first edition of the Ordnance Survey maps but destroyed by agriculture since then), the Forrad (An Forrad: the King's Seat or inauguration mound) and Teach Cormaic (Cormac's House). Part of the rampart of the enclosure has been incorporated into modern field boundaries and modified by the addition of a stone wall along the top. Examination of its ground-plan reveals that at various points the rampart deviates from its elliptical curve. These aberrations cannot all be explained by local topographic anomalies, and it seems that some were created intentionally. Two of these bulges correspond with known monuments, namely Dumha na mBó and the Mound of the Hostages, and a third with a very low circular feature (*c.* 40m in diameter) due west of the Forrad revealed by aerial photography. It seems likely that the bulges result from a deliberate attempt on the part of the builders to accommodate earlier monuments. That the rampart had to deviate to enclose earlier sites might suggest poor planning, but it seems likely that the deviations were intended to visibly proclaim the inclusion of these monuments by exaggerating the effect of their presence on the later enclosure. A section through the internal ditch was excavated in the 1950s and showed it to be a deep, V-shaped fosse dug to a depth of 3m into the bedrock; it had a deep, vertical-sided palisade trench several metres inside it. More recent limited excavation (Roche 2002) revealed extensive traces of iron- and bronze-working sealed beneath the bank and possibly dating from as early as the second century BC. This activity extended across the area where the ditch was later dug. The ditch fill contained few artefacts but animal bones were found at almost every level, representing a sequence of deposition spanning several centuries. These bones were mainly those of mature cattle, pig, sheep or goat, horse and dog, and the broken nature of the remains suggested that all of these animals were eaten. Human bones were also found and included skull fragments and the skeleton of an infant. The animal bones were interpreted as food debris, the remains of

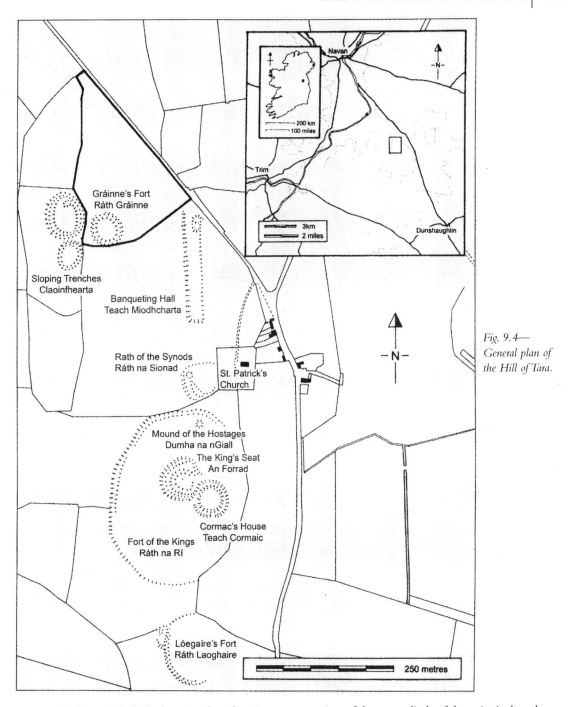

Fig. 9.4—
General plan of
the Hill of Tara.

ceremonial feasts. This fairly functional explanation, however, may underestimate the significance of this material and its context. The ancient name of Tara, *temair,* is cognate with words like the Greek *temenos,* meaning 'sacred enclosure', and the Latin *templum* or 'sacred precinct', its Indo-European root, **tem-,* meaning 'to cut' (Mac Giolla Easpaig 2005). The cutting of the great ditch of the principal enclosure on the hill in the first century BC may have been a seminal and profoundly important act, not just demarcating the hilltop sanctuary but also creating a liminal boundary that itself intersected with the paranormal and was infused with magico-religious significance (Dowling 2006).

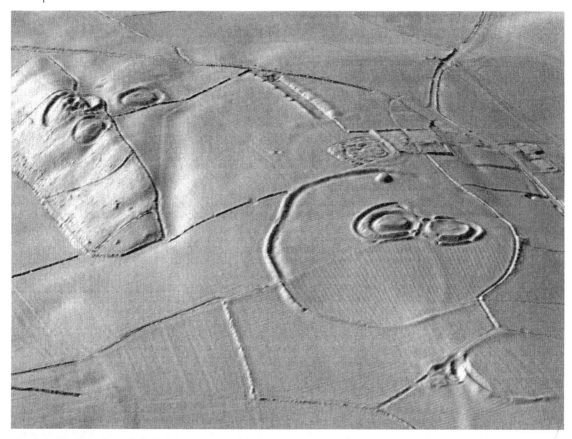

Fig. 9.5—High-resolution hill-shaded computer model of the Hill of Tara obtained by aerial LiDAR survey. The internal ditch of the large enclosure of Ráth na Rí is clearly visible in the centre of the image, and the ring-barrows known as Ráth Gráinne and the Claoinfhearta (the 'Sloping Trenches'—with vegetation digitally removed) are on the upper left.

There are three possible entrances, one on the north-west, another on the east, and geophysical survey has revealed a third on the south. The eastern entrance is just a gap in the very degraded rampart at this point but it seems to be aligned with the entrance to a ringfort known as Teach Cormaic (the supposed dwelling of the heroic king Cormac mac Airt). Geomagnetic survey here has revealed a puzzling funnel-shaped feature, possibly palisade trenches, widening from about 8m near the entrance gap to about 20m towards the ringfort. Geophysical prospection has also confirmed the existence of the entrance on the south and has shown that a linear positive magnetic feature just inside the internal ditch there is also interrupted by a gap approximately 3m wide. This feature may be a continuation of the palisade trench identified by Ó Ríordáin but there is no corresponding gap in the internal ditch. The same is true of the ditch at

the north-western entrance, where geophysical survey has also failed to record a gap in the fosse even though there are positive magnetic traces of the possible palisade trench. Conor Newman suggests that the ditch at both the north-western and southern entrances was backfilled in order to create causeways, events possibly contemporary with the erection of the palisade.

Two conjoined earthworks are the most visible monuments in Ráth na Rí. The circular earthwork now called Teach Cormaic is a bivallate ringfort; the enclosed area is flat, with a low, subrectangular mound (traces of a house?) just off-centre, and is surrounded by two earthen banks with an intervening ditch. The overall diameter is 73m and the entrance, with causeway through the ditch, is on the north-east (Fig. 9.6). The Forrad (or 'royal seat'), the inauguration mound, is a prominent flat-topped mound surrounded by a ditch and—for

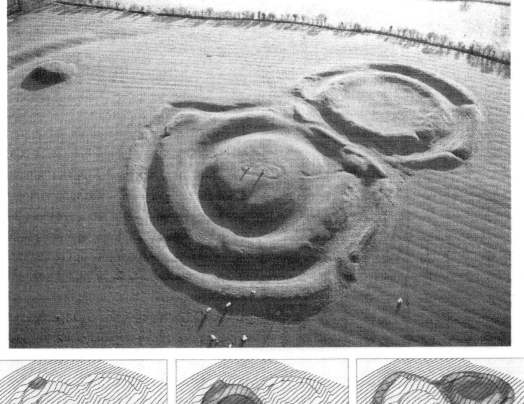

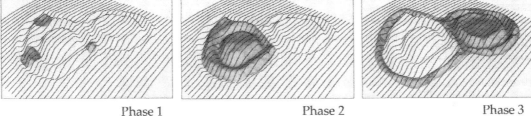

| Phase 1 | Phase 2 | Phase 3 |

Fig. 9.6—Above: the Forrad (centre) and Teach Cormaic (right), with the Mound of the Hostages (top left). Below: possible sequence of development of the Forrad and Teach Cormaic.

most of its circumference—by two banks with an intervening ditch. The internal arrangement of the ditches suggest that this is a large bivallate ring-barrow, an impression strengthened by the fact that three small, circular burial mounds have been deliberately incorporated into the larger inner bank (on the north-east, south-east and west). The outer bank is noticeably narrower and may be a later addition; since its size is similar to the outer bank of the adjacent ringfort, it is possible that it represents an attempt to physically link the later habitation site to the burial complex. A similar conjoined earthwork occurs at Carnfree near Rathcroghan. A pillar stone of Newry granite on the summit of the Forrad stands 1.55m high and is said to have been originally located near the Mound of the Hostages

to the north. For this reason it is today believed to be the Lia Fáil, the 'stone of destiny', a stone that uttered a cry at the inauguration of a legitimate king of Tara.

The medieval name Dumha na nGiall, 'the Mound of the Hostages', is applied to a large circular mound at the northern end of Ráth na Rí. Excavation has shown that it is an early prehistoric monument: a small, undifferentiated passage tomb, possibly built around 3000 BC (Chapter 3), was covered by a cairn, which was later enveloped in a mantle of earth containing numerous later burials of the late third and early second millennia BC. A curving segment of ditch was found beneath this monument and is the earliest identified feature on the hill. Conceivably part of a late fourth-

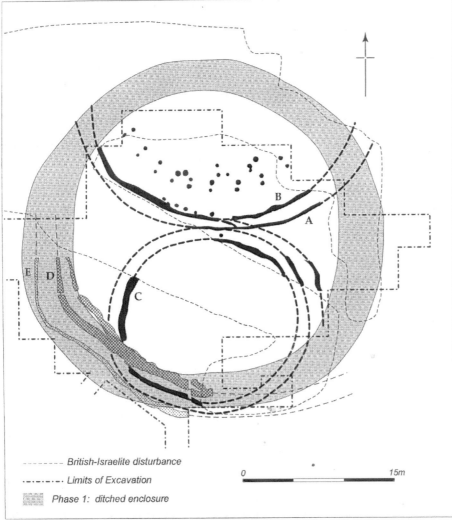

Fig. 9.7—Above: Rath of the Synods. Below: simplifed plan of Ó Ríordáin's excavations at the Rath of the Synods, showing the various possible timber circles of phase 2 and the phase 1 ditched enclosure.

British-Israelite disturbance

Limits of Excavation

Phase 1: ditched enclosure

0   15m

millennium BC enclosure, this ditch has been radiocarbon-dated to 3500–3000 BC. The huge oval circle composed of ditch and paired pits revealed by geophysical survey (Fig. 4.3; Chapter 4) enclosed the Mound of the Hostages.

The non-defensive internal ditch of Ráth na Rí, the presence of this complex prehistoric burial mound and of the ring-barrow known as the Forrad (and the smaller mounds it incorporates) all suggest that Ráth na Rí was a monument with a major ritual purpose. If Teach Cormaic is indeed a ringfort-type settlement of the first millennium AD, then a ritual role was superseded or augmented by settlement activity, a sequence of events that also seems to have occurred at the Rath of the Synods.

The name of the Rath of the Synods commemorates the ecclesiastical synods supposed to have been held at Tara in the early medieval period. The site suffered considerable damage between 1899 and 1902, when some lunatic diggings were undertaken by the British Israelites in an attempt to find the Ark of the Covenant (Carew 2003). Though the monument has the appearance of a much-disturbed multivallate ringfort, excavation by Seán P. Ó Ríordáin in 1952–3 demonstrated that it had a complicated history (Grogan 2008). The first phase was a ditched enclosure with maximum external diameters of 32m by 27.5m; of unknown date, it recalls the 45m-diameter ditched enclosure of phase 3i found beneath the great mound at Navan (below). The second phase at the Rath of the Synods consisted of a series of arcs of palisade trenches. Labelled A–E, they have been interpreted as parts of a series of larger circular timber enclosures that extended beyond the excavated area (Fig. 9.7). The trenches contained closely set but not contiguous posts, and the probable circles would have varied in diameter from about 16m to 30m. Only one of the elements of the possible multiple C circles can be claimed with any confidence to be a full circle, however, and the suggestion that some of the post-holes identified inside arc B (even though some of them appear to form pairs) are part of a circle of spaced timber posts is even more uncertain. Grogan suggests that the juxtapositioning of possible circles A and B to the north with the multiple circle C to the south recalls a series of figure-of-eight timber structures found at Navan (phase 3ii). This ceremonial phase was followed by a funerary phase,

when a small circular burial mound with a broad ditch was built; nine cremations and one unburnt burial were associated with it. Another cluster of later burials, mostly unburnt, occurred to the south near the centre of the site. The multivallate ringfort whose remains are visible today is the fourth and final phase and is dated to between the late second and early fourth centuries AD. It consists of four ramparts, each with external ditch, and the inner enclosure was placed on the site of the phase 1 ring-ditch, the burial mound being deliberately incorporated between the second and third banks. According to Grogan, the original monument was trivallate with a maximum diameter of some 88m, the fourth rampart being a later addition. He describes this monument as a residential enclosure, with various post-holes possibly representing a small subrectangular house and traces of fires, pits, animal bones, traces of iron-working and other material interpreted as habitation debris. The finds were unusual and for the most part consisted of fragments of imports from the Roman world or copies of Roman types perhaps made locally. They included a lead seal, glass beads, pieces of glass vessels, pottery sherds and an iron barrel padlock and bolt. The pottery included some Samian ware and many of the sherds, like the glassware, seem to be from fine drinking vessels. Cattle and pig bones, some from large animals, were common, but since they seem not to have been preserved no modern analysis has been possible. Given the complex ritual history of the site and the unusual nature of many of the finds, it does seem likely that the multivallate enclosure also had a ceremonial role.

Ráth Gráinne, the supposed fort of Gráinne, the legendary lover of Diarmaid, is a large ring-barrow with central circular mound surrounded by a ditch with external bank (Fig. 9.8, 41). The mound measures about 32m in diameter and has a circular depression 13.5m in diameter with an encircling ditch and a low external bank (a small ring-barrow) at its centre. The diameter of Ráth Gráinne's external bank is about 70m and it widens considerably in the north-east quadrant to incorporate a small mound. Geophysical and aerial survey has demonstrated an extraordinary sequence of ring-barrow construction here, the latter small mound being, in fact, the central mound of a larger ring-barrow (Fig. 9.8, 42) deliberately incorporated into Ráth Gráinne. This larger ring-barrow (42) is

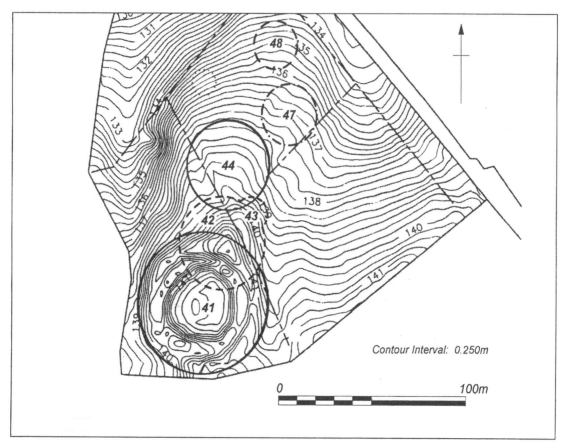

Fig. 9.8—Ráth Gráinne (41) and associated monuments. Geophysical survey has revealed a remarkable ritual sequence: burial mound 43 has been incorporated into the large ring-barrow 42, which is then partly overlapped by a later ring-barrow (44), with 42 in turn being partly incorporated by Ráth Gráinne (41). Full circles represent monuments visible on the ground or in aerial photographs; dotted circles represent geophysical signatures.

about 60m in diameter and it too has a small circular mound, *c.* 20m in diameter, with possible ditch (43) incorporated in its north-eastern quadrant. Geophysical survey suggests that the north-western quadrant of 42 has been overlapped by a larger ring-barrow (44) which has a central circular area (diameter about 26m) enclosed by a ditch with low external bank (44m diameter approximately). Thus a possible sequence consists of the small mound 43 being incorporated into the large ring-barrow 42, which is then partly erased by the later ring-barrow 44, with 42 in turn being subsumed in part by Ráth Gráinne (41). Several other low-profile circular sites are located to the north and north-east.

The so-called Sloping Trenches or Claoinfhearta lie north-west of the Banqueting Hall

on the steep western slope of the hill. One explanation—prompted by their location—considered the northern example to be the remains of a royal residence that slipped down the hill when a king of Tara gave a false judgement. Both the northern and the southern Claoinfhearta are large ring-barrows, 80m and 57m in diameter respectively. The northern monument has a small ring-barrow incorporated into its bank on the north, and a hole in the central mound indicates ancient disturbance. The southern has a small round mound on top of its central mound, and there are three other small mounds placed between the two large ring-barrows. Eight more small mounds lie in a line to the south along the ridge.

The practice of deliberately incorporating earlier monuments within the circuit of later ones has been noted at Ráth na Rí, at the Rath of the Synods, the Forrad and Ráth Gráinne (and in a different way at the Mound of the Hostages), and presumably means that earlier monuments were often considered important enough to warrant their inclusion in the new. The time-span between such different phases of activity may only be determined by excavation but, even if the chronology is not clear, these various monuments provide remarkable evidence of significant periods of carefully planned ritual continuity. At both the Forrad and Ráth Gráinne the earlier mound is incorporated in such a way that it protrudes not on the inside but on the outside of the bank and therefore does not interrupt the curve of the internal ditch. In contrast, at the northern Claoinfhearta, and possibly at the Rath of the Synods, the entire monument—bank, internal ditch and mound—seems to have been incorporated, but here too the central mound is on the line of the bank and protrudes on its outside. From the possible enclosure that pre-dates the passage tomb in the Mound of the Hostages to the late Roman contacts evinced in the Rath of the Synods, from before 3000 BC to at least AD 400, the Hill of Tara has been the focus of activity, much of it funerary and ritual, for over three millennia. While various monuments clearly succeeded one another over time, it has yet to be demonstrated that this impressive prehistoric continuum is an unbroken one. Continuous or not, the long sequence of activity is a good illustration of how monuments and landscapes are enhanced or remodelled by successive generations.

A long pair of parallel earthen banks just over 70m north of the Rath of the Synods is called the Teach Miodchuarta or Banqueting Hall and was the subject of much medieval speculation, even to the nature of the seating arrangements. The parallel banks are slightly curved and run downslope from south to north for some 203m with a width of about 30m. Both banks were seemingly raised from material dug from the interior, which is now below ground level; there are at least five gaps in the western bank and five or six in the eastern. Conor Newman (2007b) suggests that the Banqueting Hall is probably one of the later monuments on the celebrated hill (possibly dating from the fifth to the eighth century AD) and was a processional way designed to unite the remains on Tara into a formal, religious arena. A semi-subterranean space, this is the one monument on the hill where the views to the outside world are denied. Starting at the north (that is the lower) end, it offers a ceremonial routeway to the summit sanctuary of Ráth na Rí in which the visitor, in an almost literal sense, enters Tara. Proceeding along the avenue, glimpses of the tombs of the ancestral kings and queens of Tara are caught through the gaps on the right-hand side. Reflecting on the lives of the ancestors, the royal party is reminded of the burden of responsibility that comes with World Kingship, and of the fact that in re-enacting an inauguration ceremony they are about to take their place in history. The hill of Skreen is visible to the east; this is the limbo that awaits those who break the taboos of kingship or fail to live up to the principle of the ideal just ruler. Cormac mac Airt, the most famous of the legendary kings of Tara, in whose reign trees sagged under the weight of their fruit and rivers burst their banks with fish, lost his kingship and was banished to Skreen after being blinded, and thus physically blemished, by a bee sting. To the west lie the Claoinfhearta, one of which, according to legend, was the dwelling of Lugaid mac Conn that collapsed catastrophically when he delivered a false judgement against a simple herdswoman. He survived as king only for a year, for 'no grass came through the earth, or leaf on tree, nor grain in corn . . .'. Emerging from the Teach Miodhchuarta ten centuries ago, the way forward of a royal party would have been blocked by the ditch of the great ditch and pit enclosure built around 3,500 years earlier, forcing them to the right, in accordance with the rules for entering Tara righthandwise. Moving counter-clockwise around the ramparts of Ráth na Rí and into the inner sanctuary through its entrance in the east, the climax of the inauguration ceremony took place beside the Mound of the Hostages when the king placed his foot on the Lia Fáil, which according to tradition cried out to announce his rightful reign.

Navan, Co. Armagh

The name 'the Navan complex' has been given to a concentration of archaeological monuments in an area of intense late prehistoric activity stretching for just over 1km around Navan Fort in County Armagh. This complex is considered to be the archaeological manifestation of Emhain Mhacha, the capital of the Ulaid in early Irish literature.

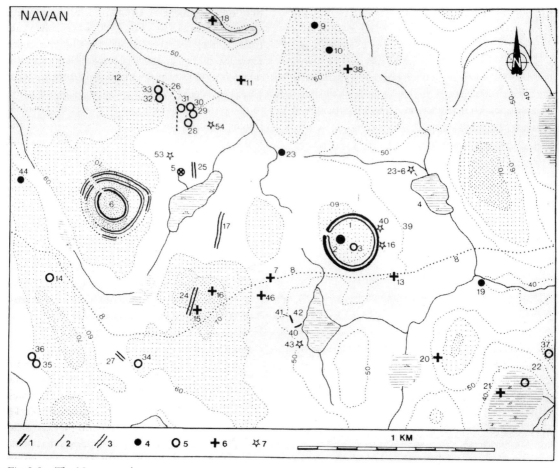

Fig. 9.9—The Navan complex.

Agricultural and other activities have damaged many of the sites but have also resulted in a large number of stray archaeological finds, many of them of late prehistoric date. Over 40 sites of possible prehistoric date have been identified, many of them by aerial photography. Some 46 actual or possible sites have been recorded (Fig. 9.9) and range from such substantial monuments as the enclosure known as Navan Fort to a number of more ephemeral crop marks. There are two zones of prehistoric activity: one comprises the Navan enclosure (Fig. 9.9, 1), which contains a mound (2) placed just off-centre and a ring-ditch (3). To the north are the sites of two mounds of possible fourth-millennium BC date thought to have been passage tombs (9 and 10), and to the north-east is a small natural lake (shown on the plan at its original, larger extent) now called Loughnashade (4). The focus of a western zone is the multivallate hillfort

now known as Haughey's Fort (6) and to its north-east is the artificial pond traditionally called the King's Stables (5), already described in Chapter 6, with groups of ring-ditches to the north and south. A double linear ditch system has been identified to the east and south, notably in Creeveroe townland (17 and 24). An eastern zone is represented by the ecclesiastical centre at Armagh, 2.6km to the east (Warner 1994a; 1994b). While the two possible passage tombs and a number of artefacts indicate early prehistoric activity, the Navan complex begins to develop around the thirteenth century BC with the construction of Haughey's Fort and the King's Stables. The excavations in the Navan enclosure in the central zone suggest that this became the focus of later activity, perhaps coinciding with the abandonment of Haughey's Fort in or about the tenth century BC. Some activity did continue there; it will be recalled that one pit, which contained a small iron object, possibly a strap handle, produced charcoal samples with radiocarbon dates that ranged from *c.* 400 to 200 BC.

The Navan enclosure

Excavations were undertaken in the Navan enclosure by D. M. Waterman between 1963 and 1972 (Lynn 1997; 2003b). This large earthwork encloses the summit of a drumlin ridge and, though only about 60m above sea level, has commanding views in all directions, especially to the north-west. It is this site that, in the past, has been specifically identified as the legendary capital of Ulster, the Emhain Mhacha of the tales of the Ulster Cycle.

The enclosure, 6ha in area, is a large circle surrounded by a wide, deep, V-shaped ditch with a very substantial external earthen bank, with an overall diameter of approximately 286m (Fig. 9.10). While there seems to be a possible entrance on the west, the eastern focus of the entrances to various structures in the interior suggest an eastern entrance to the enclosure. One of the oak timbers recovered from excavation of the lowest fill of the ditch has provided a dendrochronological estimated felling date of 94 ± 9 BC (Mallory *et al.* 1999; Mallory 2000). Thus the enclosure may be broadly contemporary with Ráth na Rí on Tara.

Waterman's excavations were conducted at two visible monuments in the interior: a ring-barrow (site A), much ploughed over and surviving mainly as a wide, shallow ditch with traces of an external bank south-east of the centre of the enclosure, and a large, circular, flat-topped mound (site B), 50m in diameter and 6m high, standing on the centre of the hilltop about 55m west of the centre. Site A was partially excavated in 1961 and proved to be a wide, annular ditch, 2m deep and 5.5m wide on average, with a V-shaped profile. The diameter of the ditch was approximately 30m centre to centre (Fig. 9.11). No entrance was found in the area excavated. There appeared to be a low, broad, external bank on the west. The excavation of the interior of the monument revealed two main phases. Features of phase A (which definitely pre-dated the digging of the ditch) included three concentric slots with diameters of about 16.5m, 18.5m and 20m respectively, and they were cut away by the later surrounding ditch. A sequence was established showing that the middle slot was dug

first, then the outer and finally the inner, and it seemed that each slot was used in turn independently of the others. A series of post-pipes, 1m apart on average, were located in the inner slot, indicating that some form of timber walling had been embedded in it, and it was suggested, therefore, that the three circles represent successive timber structures. Subsequent geophysical survey and limited excavation have demonstrated that these phase A circles at site A are part of a much larger figure-of-eight structure over 50m in overall length (now called site C: see below). The date of phase B is uncertain; this phase is represented by a structure formed by a pair of concentric ring-slots with diameters of about 12m and 16m, with a wide space of 2m between them. The slots were about 30cm in width and in depth and had an entrance on the east flanked by large post-holes. There was a large post-hole, 70cm in diameter and 61cm deep, in the centre of this phase B structure, as well as a number of scattered post-holes and a hearth. Waterman believed that this might represent a substantial house of the early medieval period because two east-facing extended unburnt burials (one of which had been in a nailed coffin) were found to the east of the entrance and more or less flanking the access. The only dating evidence for the ring-barrow (built on the southern part of site C) was provided by the terminal of a bronze penannular brooch of the early medieval period, found 90cm above the bottom of the ditch, and some animal bones radiocarbon-dated to *c.* AD 400 (Gault 2002).

The great mound

The great mound (site B) was excavated between 1963 and 1971. It was approximately 6m high and 50m in diameter at the base. About two thirds of the site were excavated and approximately one third of the lowest part of the mound, on the north, was left undisturbed for future investigation. After excavation the mound was restored to its original form. Five major phases were identified.

Phases 1–2: there was some activity on the hilltop in the fourth or third millennium BC (phase 1), marked by scatters of pottery and several hundred flaked flints, a number of flint implements (including a Bann flake) and three fragments of polished stone axes. The hilltop was ploughed sometime after this early activity, as shown by faint

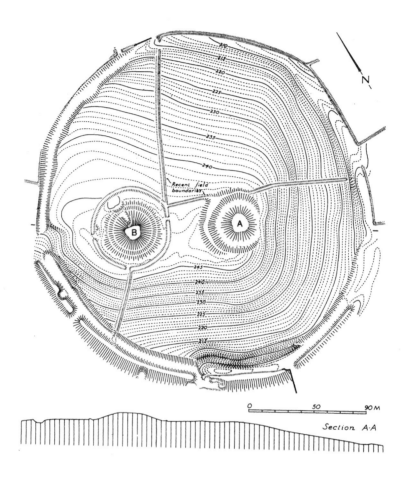

Fig. 9.10—Above: contour plan of Navan Fort, showing the large mound (site B) and the ring-barrow (site A). Below: an artist's impression of Navan Fort today; the mound, site B, is on the left.

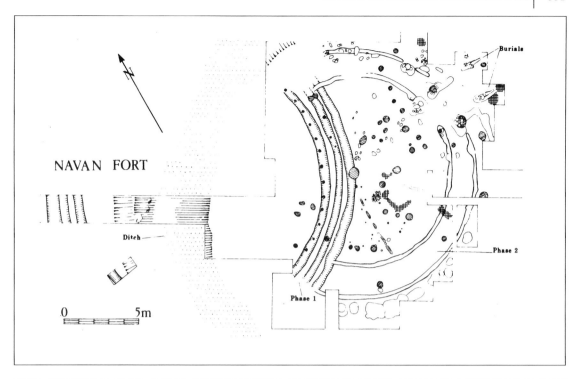

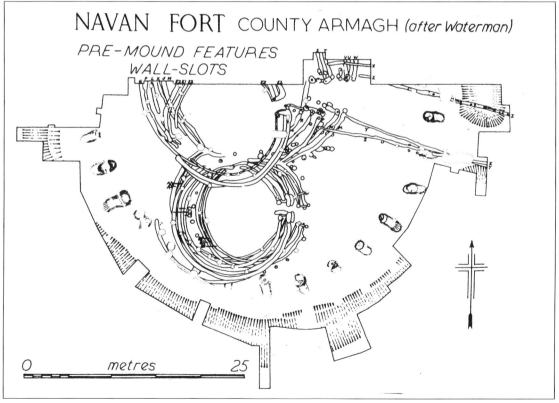

Fig. 9.11—Above: Navan site A: the ring-barrow. Below: Navan site B: simplified plan of the pre-mound features.

shallow gullies filled with a thin fossil ploughsoil (phase 2).

Phase 3 represents the major period of later prehistoric activity and is divided into three subphases (3i–3iii). Though the radiocarbon-dating evidence is ambiguous, the earliest activity of this phase (3i) is thought to have begun around the ninth century BC with the digging of a circular ditch, about 5m wide and 1m deep, enclosing a space approximately 45m in diameter (Fig. 9.11). Four or five metres inside this ditch, and apparently contemporary with it, was a ring of large pits a little over 4m apart centre to centre. The pits had been cut through the fossil soil and ranged in maximum diameter from 1.8m to 3.3m. They may have held the posts of a palisade standing within the ditch that was interrupted by a cobbled causeway 4.4m wide

on the east. Although the circular structure and the ditch would seem to have been contemporary, a radiocarbon date from one of the post-pits and two from the ditch do not overlap even at two standard deviations: the timber post date falls approximately into the period *c.* 1600–1200 BC, while the ditch has yielded two dates in the range *c.* 900–550 BC. It may have begun to silt up in the seventh century BC.

Phase 3ii–iii probably dates from the fourth to the second century BC. Phase 3ii is represented by a complex sequence of circular timber structures revealed as foundation trenches or ring-slots. A series of nine successive ring-slots overlay the line of the presumed palisade of phase 3i on the south (Fig. 9.12). The earliest of these may have been dug while the palisade was standing, but later examples

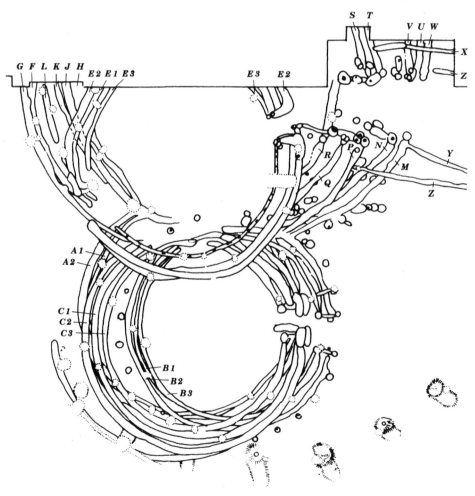

Fig. 9.12—Detail of successive ring-slots at Navan phase 3ii.

cut the line of the palisade. A layer of dark soil *c.* 30cm deep, which would normally be interpreted as an occupation layer (called 'fossil soil' in the excavation report), accumulated during the period represented by the construction and use of the slots. The earliest slots were cut into subsoil but the latest examples barely reached subsoil and were filled with material identical to that into which they were cut. While two slots (D and R) could not be fitted into any sequence, the ring-slots more or less occurred in three groups of three concentric circles (A–C), and the sequence in each group was middle, outer and inner (as in the group of ring-slots observed beneath the ring-barrow at site A). The diameters of the slots ranged from 13.5m to 10m, and gaps on the east, 1–2m wide, sometimes in-turned and flanked by post-pits, were presumably entrances. Lumps of burnt clay were found in the loose fill of some slots, which may have held vertical plank or post-and-wattle walls, and some post-holes seemed to suggest the provision of additional support on occasion. Small burnt areas and groups of flat stones indicated the presence of hearths at the centres of the A–C structures. Attached to or touching the northern side of the southern A–C slots was a series of six further ring-slots of greater diameter, *c.* 20–25m. Their full extent was not revealed so that it is not possible to suggest exactly which of the five or six slots on the east (S–W) were linked with which of the six on the west (F–H, J–L).

It is clear that the individual elements of the northern and southern ring-slot groups were attached and formed figure-of-eight units that communicated by means of narrow gaps on the northern sides of the southern ring-slots. Which circle was connected with which is again not clear, but it seems that the rebuilding of the northern structures did not follow the same sequence as those on the south. It is possible that the construction sequences of the two groups were to some extent independent, or that some of the southern slots, perhaps at the beginning, were not matched by northern ring-slots. Chris Lynn has suggested that one reason for the consistent repositioning of the southern ring-slots could be that each structure, or group of three structures, had to be placed so that it could be joined to a northern structure already in existence and which was not renewed at the same time. The northern ring-slots had wide gaps on the

east approached by parallel entrance palisade slots 5.5m apart, later replaced by a second pair 7.8m apart. Some of the slots retained impressions of the sockets for stout upright posts *c.* 50cm apart.

It was thought that the southern ring-slots of these figure-of-eight structures represented the wall-trenches of eight or nine successive round houses with doors on the east, most of them communicating with open-air enclosures on the north, these in turn being approached by fenced avenues. With the presence of hearths and what seemed to be occupation debris including animal bone, it was reasonable to consider these to have been domestic dwellings with attached stockyards approached by droveways. The recognition, however, of much larger figure-of-eight structures that could never have been roofed (like site C below) has prompted suggestions that these site B circles may have been non-utilitarian. Some ritual explanation certainly seems very likely, particularly given the extraordinary repetitive constructional sequence of middle and outer and inner ring-slots observed in circles A–C, although Lynn has suggested that this sequence could be due to careful wall replacement, a new wall being built while most of an earlier one was still standing. It is generally believed, however, that diameters of 10m to 13.5m are beyond the acceptable limits for roofing a timber building without internal supports, so the site B figure-of-eight structures may have been unroofed. The question is unresolved because it is also possible that the smaller circular components could still have been roofed with dome-shaped or conical wickerwork. Since there is a certain amount of evidence for burning, it is also conceivable that these may have been relatively temporary structures built with the intention of eventually burning them (Lynn 2006).

In phase 3iii another series of three ring-slots to the north (E1–3) replace the southern and northern figure-of-eight structures and seemingly display the same construction sequence—middle, outer, inner. They range in diameter from about 11m to 13.5m but now have two opposed entrances on east and west. If they were attached to larger enclosures, these lie in the unexcavated area to the north. The latest ring-slot, the inner one, is narrower than the others and it retained clear traces at intervals of the sockets of small, elongated timbers (stakes with timbering between them?). This

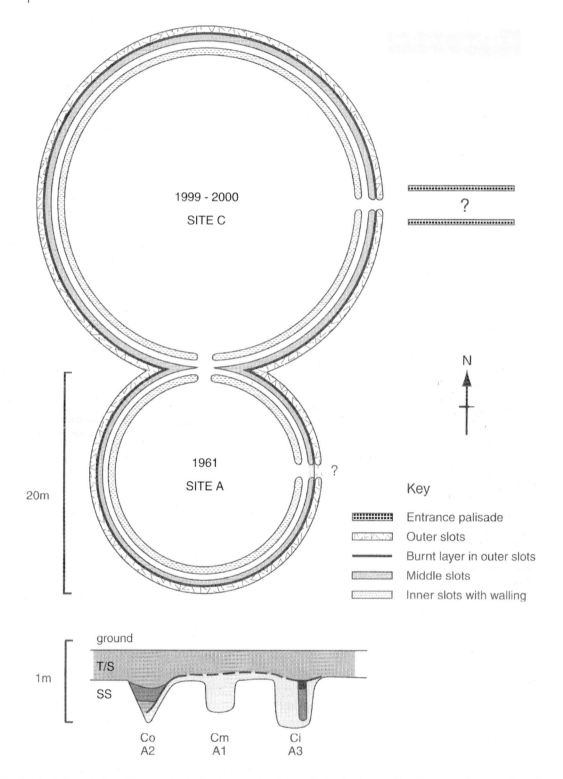

Fig. 9.13—Schematic plan of Navan site C: the ring-slots found beneath the ring-barrow (site A) are now known to form the one figure-of-eight structure.

structure may have been removed to make way for the phase 4 building.

A range of finds were recovered, including several hundred sherds of coarse bucket-shaped pots (almost all from the fossil soil of phase 3), shale armlets, glass beads, a bronze bar toggle, a fragment of a winged chape, part of a socketed bronze sickle, a tiny socketed bronze axe, a bronze pin with a spiral-ribbed head, small iron objects and a bronze ring-headed pin. Though a few small fragments of clay moulds (for a pin and a blade) were found, there was no evidence of metalworking on site. The discovery of a skull and jaw of a Barbary ape (*Macaca sylvana*) was an exceptional find. This animal must have been a prestigious import from North Africa and is an important indication that far-flung contacts existed and included not just metalwork but perishable goods as well. The skull, which was found in ring-slot C2 (phase 3ii), has been radiocarbon-dated to 390–20 BC. The bones of other animal species were present in unusual proportions; there were twice as many pigs as cattle, and nine times as many pigs as sheep or goat. This has prompted the suggestion that the bones might represent a ritual rather than a domestic assemblage.

As already mentioned, the discovery of site C raised questions about the nature of the phase 3ii figure-of-eight structures beneath the great mound. A combination of geophysical survey and limited excavation has shown that the three ring-slots found beneath the ring-barrow at site A (phase 1: Fig. 9.11) are part of a large figure-of-eight structure (Lynn 2000; 2002). The conjoined circles have general diameters of approximately 20m and 30m respectively, with probable entrances on the east (Fig. 9.13). Unlike the structures at site B, it is evident that even the smaller of the two could not have been roofed and they were also burnt. The inner and outer slots contained burnt material, including burnt animal bone. The middle slot—the first to be dug—contained a clean fill with no trace of timber posts. The other two, however, did contain traces of successive timber structures, which were probably burnt down in a process that also involved the cremation of pig, cattle and sheep or goat, the same range and relative quantities of animals found at site B.

The 'forty-metre structure'

The subsequent history of the site, which was undoubtedly ceremonial in quite an exceptional way, would tend to confirm that there was already a significant ritual or religious dimension to phases 3ii and 3iii. Phase 4 is represented by the construction of a huge, multi-ring timber structure (Fig. 9.14), which seems to have been positioned to fit neatly inside and concentric with the phase 3i ditch. In many excavated areas the surface of the fossil soil that accumulated during phase 3iii remained the ground surface, with no further deposition during phase 4. The timber structure was circular and consisted of five major concentric rings of posts and a large central post, some 280 in all. The outer wall of the building (37.3m in diameter) comprised 34 large post-pits, 1.25m in diameter and depth and approximately 3.5m apart. Each pit originally contained a single post (in every case supplemented later by the insertion of a second, identical, contiguous post) linked by horizontal split timbers in a trench. Outside this was a narrow, deeper, discontinuous slot, 40.5m in diameter. This slot and the light walling it contained were quickly abandoned, being cut away by the sloping pits dug to insert the secondary posts in the main wall, suggesting that it may have served as a fence-slot during the construction phase, or even as some sort of external lean-to against the main wall. The post-pits of the internal rings measured about 36–46cm in diameter and were dug to an average depth of about 91cm through the fossil soil into the subsoil; the oak butts of many of these large posts were preserved in the damp ground. The entrance was on the west, and here the internal post-ring system was interrupted by four roughly parallel rows of posts forming three aisles leading to the centre of the structure. At the centre was a timber post so large that it had to be dragged at an angle into its post-pit on a sloping ramp 6m long cut into subsoil. The axe-dressed stump of this great post, about 50cm in diameter, was found in the central pit, which was 2.3m deep. This central post (perhaps a carved timber pillar) could have been 13m or more in height.

Large patches of the area inside this structure were covered with spreads of relatively clean clay, material that could not be packed back into the post-pits. This often sealed the packing around individual posts as well as undisturbed phase 3iii fossil soil, and was in turn directly covered by phase 5 material. There were no hearths or other evidence

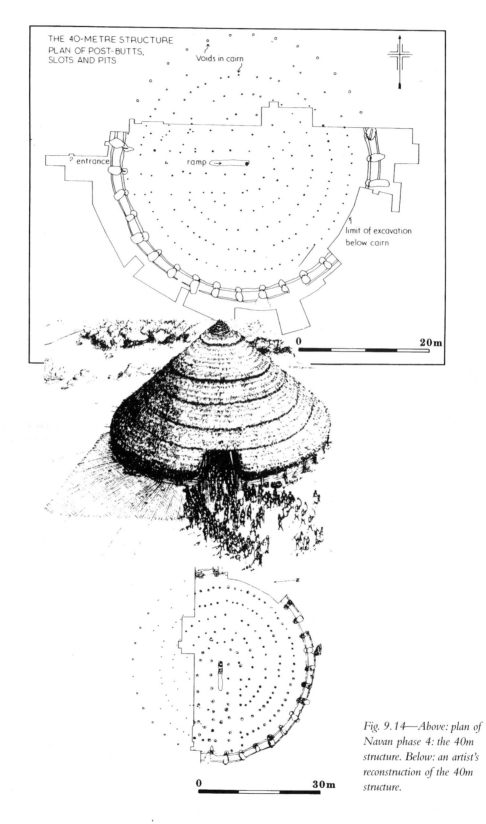

THE 40-METRE STRUCTURE
PLAN OF POST-BUTTS,
SLOTS AND PITS

Voids in cairn

? entrance

ramp

limit of excavation
below cairn

0   20m

0   30m

Fig. 9.14—Above: plan of Navan phase 4: the 40m structure. Below: an artist's reconstruction of the 40m structure.

for occupation in this phase 4 structure. Furthermore, surplus clay spread out from the very large central post-pit sealed the clay spreads and packing of neighbouring posts, showing that the central post was inserted later than these and perhaps last of all. This huge monument was carefully built to a predetermined radial plan and it may have been temporarily roofed; a number of posts (and all of the paired examples on the perimeter) were pushed 10–15cm into the soil below the bases of the sockets dug for them, and this suggests that they were probably load-bearing. Dendrochronological analysis has determined that the large central post was felled in late 95 BC or early 94 BC, and this dates the completion of the great timber structure.

Phase 5 followed quickly, and the multi-ring timber structure evidently had a relatively short period of use. While it was still standing, its interior was filled with a cairn of limestone boulders. That the wooden structure still stood was demonstrated by the survival of roughly cylindrical vertical voids left by its rotted oak posts at a high level in the cairn (and continuing down into the post-pits) and by the fact that the wall of the structure also served as an external revetment for the cairn. The cairn was 37.5m in diameter with a maximum height of 2.8m at the centre. Its surface was divided into clearly defined but somewhat irregular radial sectors by the use of different sizes of stones, by various arrangements of stones and by varying admixtures of soil, clay or turf in the sectors. The radial divisions visible in the top of the cairn did not apparently extend downwards through the cairn, and they do not appear to be related in any significant way to the radial alignments in the timber structure that it entombed. The next step, in what appears to have been a continuous process, was the burning of the outer wall and the exposed upper timbers of the forty-metre structure. This burning, around and over the cairn, was probably deliberate, as plentiful remains of brushwood survived as charred twigs around the excavated perimeter of the building against the base of the timber wall. The cairn was finally covered by a mound of turves, 2.5m high at the centre, and much of this material must have been obtained by stripping the turf and topsoil from a large area.

The great timber building of phase 4 was not used for occupation, and the size and plan of the undertaking suggest that it may have been a communal effort under the supervision of a technically competent person or group. The free-standing post at the centre would seem to confirm the suggestion that it was used for a ritual or ceremonial purpose early in the first century BC,

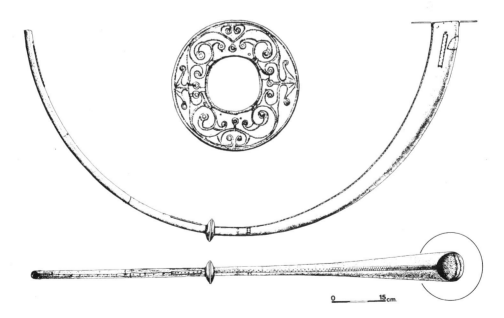

Fig. 9.15—The Loughnashade horn: the decorated disc at the mouth is shown enlarged.

and the construction of the building, its use, the building of the cairn, the burning and the addition of the sod mound may well have been planned from the start as parts of a more or less continuous series of ritual acts.

During drainage works in nearby Loughnashade in or about the early nineteenth century four large bronze horns were found, along with a number of human skulls and other bones. No precise details have been recorded and three of the horns have disappeared. One survives and is a great curving horn, about 1.86m in length, made of riveted sheet bronze with a decorative disc at the bell end bearing La Tène repoussé ornament (Fig.

9.15). The discovery of fine bronzework and human bones suggests that the site was the focus of ritual depositions, some possibly contemporary with the ceremonial activity at the Navan enclosure (Raftery 1987).

Knockaulin, Co. Kildare

Knockaulin is a rounded hill, rising to 180m above sea level, south-west of Kilcullen, Co. Kildare. Its summit is crowned by a great earthwork: an oval area of some 13ha is enclosed by a substantial rampart with internal ditch (Fig. 9.16). The monument has been identified since the nineteenth century as the Dún Ailinne of early Irish literature,

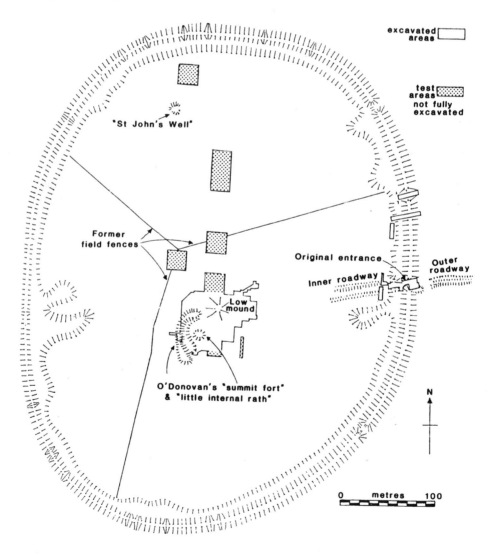

Fig. 9.16—Plan of Knockaulin, Co. Kildare.

the seat of the kings of Leinster. The only visible features in the enclosure were a small earthwork noted by John O'Donovan, a low mound on the summit of the hill (approximately circular with a diameter of about 20m and a height of some 80cm) and a well called St John's Well. From 1968 to 1975, apart from limited test excavation in the northern half of the enclosure and some trenches across the rampart and at the entrance on the east, excavation concentrated on the summit area (Johnston and Wailes 2007). Geophysical prospection consisted of a magnetometer survey of the whole area within the enclosing bank and ditch, with more intensive survey on the summit, where resistivity survey was also undertaken; the only substantial anomalies detected were in the area of the low mound and correlated with areas of intense burning.

The external bank and internal ditch have been damaged in numerous places by small, recent quarries to extract bedrock. The ditch is interrupted by a causeway on the east, and this seems to be the original entrance. Though this area had also been damaged by quarrying, excavation confirmed the existence of an 8m-wide roadway with the remains of a low drystone revetment or kerb on either side; it did not have a prepared surface nor did it show any wheel ruts. Its axis was aligned on the summit of the hill. This and the fact that the causeway proved to be undug bedrock confirmed the impression that this was an original entrance. The entrance appeared quite simple: the ends of the bank terminated without trace of revetting in either timber or stone, and no evidence of a timber gate was found. The bank was of simple dump construction and the ditch was filled with natural silting. One radiocarbon date obtained from the humus beneath the rampart gives a terminal date for its construction—probably sometime after the fifth century BC. Excavation revealed some slight traces of early prehistoric activity in the summit area. The earliest is attested by an irregular circular ditch (Fig. 9.17: 281) with a diameter of about 20m which contained a hollow scraper and part of a leaf-shaped flint arrowhead, a pit (293) containing sherds of a decorated pot of the type found in Linkardstown burials of the fourth millennium BC, several hundred stray fragments of other pottery vessels as well as pieces of flint and chert and a cup-marked stone. Some sherds of a Bowl Tradition pot found in a pit (2790) are the only late third-millennium BC evidence.

Late prehistoric structures

Three major phases of late prehistoric activity from 390 BC were identified on the summit in the area of the low mound: these were labelled the 'white', 'rose' and 'mauve' phases. A thin and compressed ginger-coloured sod was identified where protected by undisturbed late prehistoric levels, and a circular trench approximately 22m in diameter to support close-set timber uprights (a palisade or fence) was cut through this sod (Fig. 9.17: trench 512, 'white' phase). The entrance may have been on the northeast. There was no dating evidence in what remained of the primary fill of this trench, but since the succeeding structure ('rose' phase) appeared to have been built immediately or shortly after the extraction of the posts in trench 512, and since the 'rose' phase is late, a similar late prehistoric date is inferred for the 'white' phase.

The remarkable structures of the 'rose' phase were on a more ambitious scale. The three concentric trenches set about 1m apart (60, 513, 514) enclosed an inner area of 28.5m; the entrance to this circle was flanked by substantial fences (278, 314) forming a sort of 'funnel' that contained an avenue of posts, which in turn enclosed two short trenches (2231, 2232). On the southern side of the large 'rose' enclosure were smaller conjoined timber circles (519, 520 etc.), with a narrow 1m-wide entrance to the larger circles. No structures, or even isolated posts, could be shown to have stood within the main 'rose' phase circle, which was apparently an open space. Bernard Wailes believes that these concentric trenches and the timbers they contained supported some superstructure. The graded size of the posts in the three concentric trenches, the inner one (60) containing the smallest, the middle trench (513) containing timbers of middle size and the outer trench up to 1m deep (514) holding the largest timbers, suggests that this putative superstructure was raked, with the inner side being lower than the outer. According to Wailes, this would be consistent with a two-tier standing (or seating) arrangement for persons viewing or participating in ceremonial events or displays conducted in the open interior space. There are obvious architectural parallels with the configuration at Navan 3ii, where, however, there was a sequence of construction of smaller circular

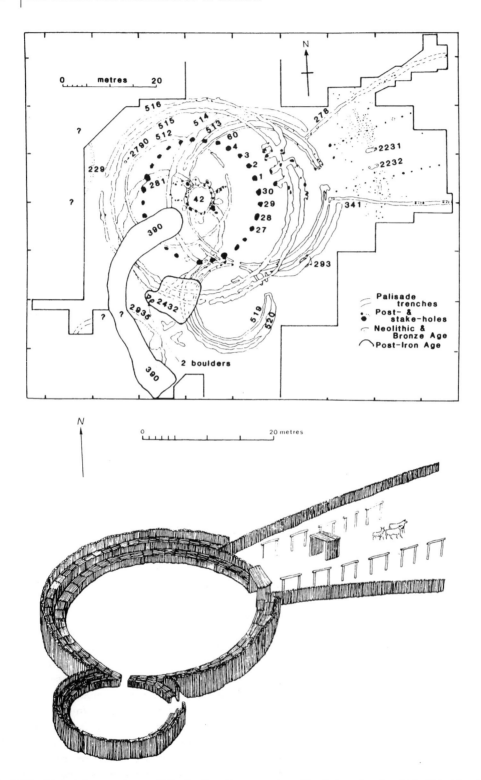

Fig. 9.17—Plan of the summit area of Knockaulin with construction of 'rose' phase (trenches 519, 520, 514, 513, 60, 278, 341, etc.).

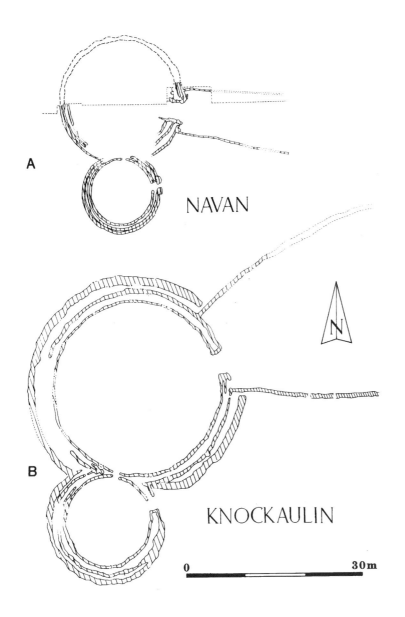

A

NAVAN

B

KNOCKAULIN

N

Fig. 9.18—A comparison of Navan phase 3ii and the Knockaulin 'rose' phase.

0   **30m**

conjoined structures with associated occupation material (Fig. 9.18).

The 'rose' phase structures were dismantled (except for a few posts in trench 314 which were burnt in place) and a slightly larger but different structure built in the following 'mauve' phase. Two concentric timber circles were constructed (515, 516) with an overall diameter of some 42m and with a substantial entrance to the east-north-east. A 20m-diameter circle of large, free-standing posts was erected in the centre of this enclosure: where sufficient primary fill remained in place, it was estimated that these posts were on average about 50cm in diameter. In the centre of this circle was a circular trench, 6m in diameter (42), in which several well-defined post-holes (most at least 25cm in diameter) could be identified. There was no obvious entrance and no occupation debris. Around the perimeter of this structure was a series of holes of uncertain purpose—it was not possible to determine whether they once held timbers. Wailes has tentatively reconstructed these features (Fig.

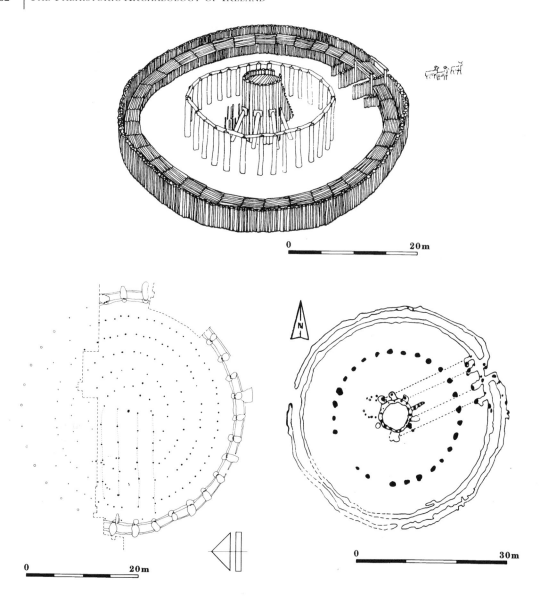

Fig. 9.19—Above: a reconstruction of the Knockaulin 'mauve' phase structure. Below: Navan phase 4, showing ambulatory (on left) and (on right) the Knockaulin 'mauve' phase for comparison.

9.19) as a timber tower with supporting timber buttresses (rather than a hut, given the small diameter, the size of the posts and the absence of a hearth or entrance). The outermost timber circles (515 and 516) and the 20m circle of free-standing timbers were contemporary. While the presumed tower cannot be stratigraphically linked to the circles, given that they are all stratigraphically post-'rose' and share the same geometric centre Wailes believes that they all formed part of the same

design, and since the minimum distance between the outer wall (516) and the 20m timber circle, or between the latter and the tower, is 9m, a roofed structure is considered implausible. A tentative reconstruction shows a buttressed central wooden tower about 9m high surrounded by a circle of free-standing timber posts, with the 42m-diameter timber double palisade around the outside. The latter may have supported a platform as in the 'rose' phase circle. Again Chris Lynn has drawn attention to parallels with the Navan 40m structure: the dimensions are similar and both have a central timber feature, and if the four in-turned entrance elements of trench 515 are extended inwards, they align with posts in the 20m circle and produce three aisles running from the entrance to the centre, as at Navan (Fig. 9.19). He has also noted the possibility that the ring of large free-standing posts could conceivably have supported some sort of superstructure.

The 'mauve' phase structure was dismantled in its turn, but not all at once. The posts in trenches 515 and 516 were extracted while the 20m timber circle remained standing, for some later material overlies the fill of 515 but not the fill of the post-holes of the circle. Eventually these were extracted and the tower dismantled, though it is not certain whether this all happened at the one time. Thus the 'white', 'rose' and 'mauve' structures were all deliberately dismantled. Wailes remarked that not one post had decayed in its socket, but almost everywhere the packing of the post-holes had been disturbed by rocking the timbers in the course of extraction. The absence of any sterile humus may imply that the phases followed one another immediately, the whole sequence perhaps lasting only a few decades, at most a century or two.

Later material deliberately deposited on the site included redeposited glacial till with a small area of rough paving, followed by numerous thin lenses of humus containing animal bone, burnt stone, charcoal, and ash—perhaps the remains of periodic feasting. Cattle and pig make up the bulk of the animal bones, with a little horse, dog and sheep represented. Many of the cattle were killed as very young calves in spring shortly after birth, while others were killed at about six months of age, probably in autumn—possible evidence of periodic ritual feasting during the warmer months of the year. This and the structural evidence would support the excavator's belief that late prehistoric Knockaulin was one very large ceremonial site. It is presumably connected with the concentration of ring-barrows, enclosures and linear earthworks on the Curragh some 5km to the north-west, which should be considered part of a larger Knockaulin complex (Clancy 2005). An irregular quarry ditch (390) cut through all the late prehistoric levels on the hill, its upcast forming the irregular earthwork noted by O'Donovan and clearly a feature much

later than the abandonment of the site. A late prehistoric date for the ritual activity is indicated by a range of artefacts including an iron sword found in the fill of the 'mauve' phase palisade trench 516 and possibly of the second or third century BC. Also found were an iron spearhead, several iron needles, fragments of bronze fibulae and glass beads. A number of radiocarbon dates suggest that much of the ceremonial activity recorded took place between 165 BC and AD 530.

Rathcroghan, Co. Roscommon

Rathcroghan is probably best known as the royal seat of the legendary Queen Maeve and her consort Ailill, king of Connacht, and the place where that great Cattle Raid of Cooley, the *Táin Bó Cúailnge*, was initiated. The general area was known as Cruachain in early literature and it also figures, like Navan and Tara, as a major royal settlement. It is sometimes described as the location of a great cemetery where many warriors are buried, as well as an assembly place and the inauguration site of kings; it also had an entrance to the Otherworld. Rathcroghan today is a complex of earthworks and other monuments about 5km north-west of the village of Tulsk, Co. Roscommon (Fig. 9.20). The monuments are scattered across the eastern end of a broad, elevated plateau with commanding views, particularly to the east and south, over part of the rolling pastureland of Mag nAí ('the plain of the sheep'). They form a significant concentration above the 100–110m contour. Over 60 sites are known, and this number includes at least 27 prehistoric burial mounds, a number of enclosures of uncertain date, standing stones (including a fallen stone named Miosgán Meabha or 'Maeve's heap'), linear earthworks (some possible droveways for livestock), some dozen ringforts dating from medieval times and miscellaneous—if not unclassifiable—sites such as the cave known as Oweynagat (Uaimh na gCat, the 'cave of the cats' or the cave of Cruachain), fabled as that entrance to the Otherworld (Waddell *et al.* 2009).

At the approximate centre of the complex stands the great circular mound called Rathcroghan Mound, Ráth Crúachan. It is broad, low and approximately circular, with an average diameter of some 88m and 6m in height. From its base it slopes fairly steeply at first and then more gently to an almost flat summit about 30m across. There is a low,

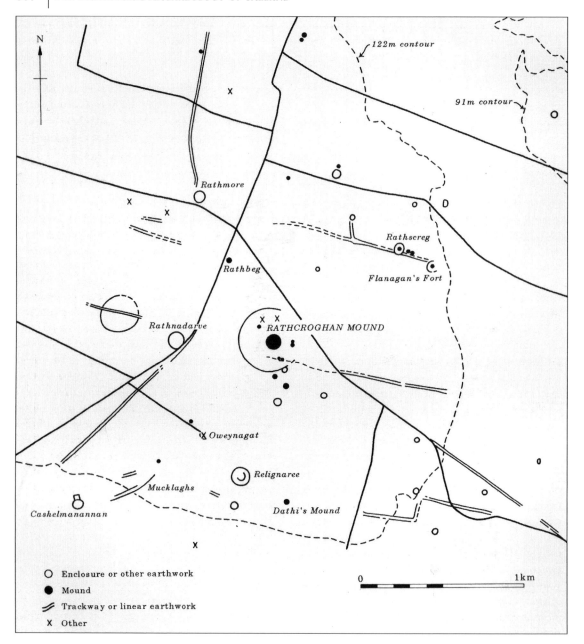

Fig. 9.20—General plan of Rathcroghan, Co. Roscommon.

irregular mound measuring about 4m across eccentrically placed on the flat summit; an eighteenth-century watercolour shows this mound standing to a height of about 1m at that time. Two sloping ramps occur on the west and east respectively (Fig. 9.21). Geophysical survey using magnetic gradiometry on and in the vicinity of the great mound has presented a very complex picture. With the exception of the mound at the centre of the image, the most striking feature is a very large circular enclosure, 360m in diameter, formed by a substantial ditch (Fig. 9.22). Monuments within this enclosure include a pair of annular ring-barrows 65m to the east, a pair of parallel, straight ditches to the south-east, set 8m apart and extending for at least 90m, that may have represented a formal approach to the area of the great mound, and a northern enclosure approximately 26m in diameter

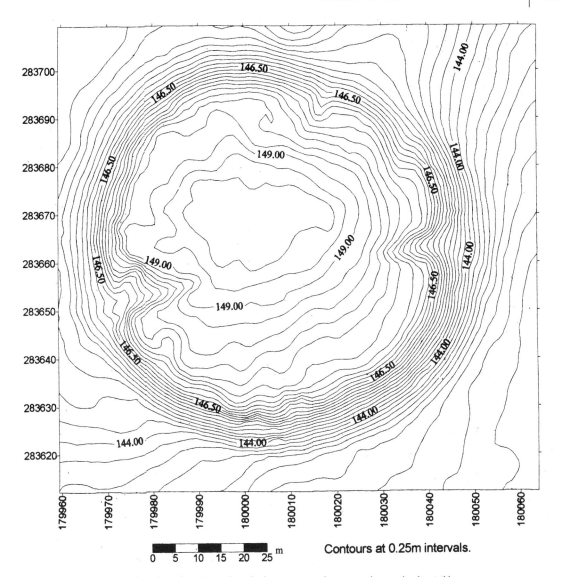

Fig. 9.21—Contour plan of Rathcroghan Mound, with the ramps on the east and west clearly visible.

with an eastern avenue possibly of timber palisades that extend for a distance of over 100m and beyond the eastern limits of the geophysical survey. Whatever its form, this avenue, like the avenue to the south approaching the mound, recalls the similar though smaller eastern avenues leading to the circular enclosures at Navan and Knockaulin, which have been dated to the later centuries BC (Fig. 9.23). This configuration of a ceremonial avenue approaching an Iron Age circular enclosure from the east has also been identified at Lismullin, near Tara (O'Connell 2009a; 2009b).

Geophysical survey using a range of

techniques has also demonstrated that Rathcroghan Mound is a monument of exceptional internal complexity and is the product of an elaborate and calculated series of constructional phases over time. Buried deep within its core are the remains of two substantial concentric stone walls, *c.* 22m and 35m in diameter, possibly the remains of a large bivallate enclosure deliberately entombed within the body of the mound and lying 1–2m below its summit. The 22m wall is probably the penannular enclosure so clearly visible in the magnetic gradiometry (Fig. 9.24). This sort of action obviously recalls the burial of the forty-metre structure beneath the cairn of

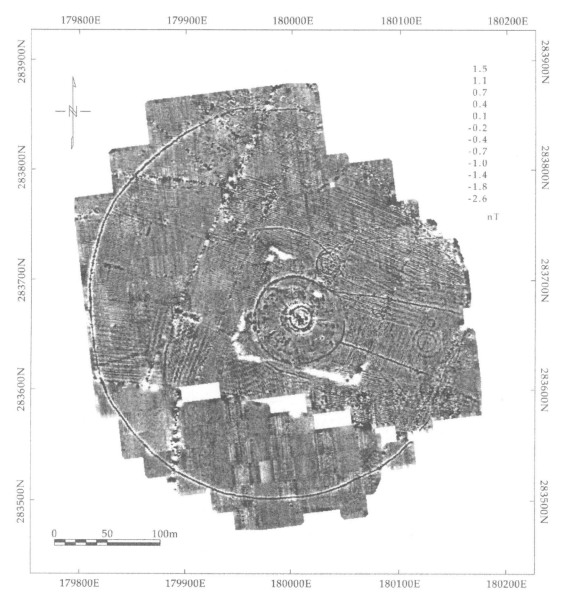

Fig. 9.22—Magnetic gradiometry survey of Rathcroghan Mound and its vicinity. The large circular enclosure, 360m in diameter, is clearly visible.

the great mound at Navan. It seems likely, too, that the mound perimeter at Rathcroghan, when newly constructed, was defined by a vertical or steeply sloping façade, perhaps retained by a timber palisade. A double pit circle clearly visible in the magnetic gradiometry may represent one of the later major episodes of building on the mound and is likely to represent the foundations of a substantial timber-built structure. At 32m in diameter, such an

elaborate construction would have been an imposing monument elevated above the surrounding landscape on the mound's summit. There is also geophysical (magnetic susceptibility) survey evidence that a number of other features once occupied the summit; a bewildering pattern of various arcs and circles (some with possible diameters up to 30m or so) perhaps represent timber structures built and replaced over time (Fig.

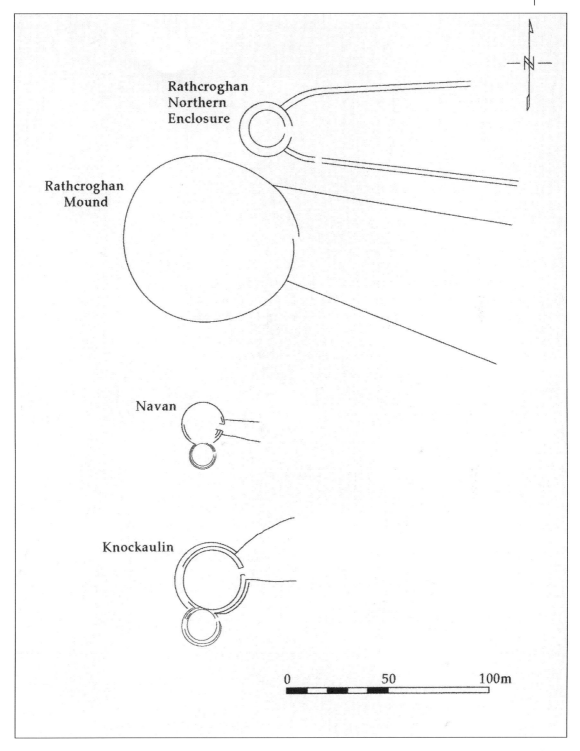

Fig. 9.23—Eastern avenues approaching the Rathcroghan northern enclosure and Rathcroghan Mound, compared with the smaller eastern approaches to the figure-of-eight structures at Navan and Knockaulin.

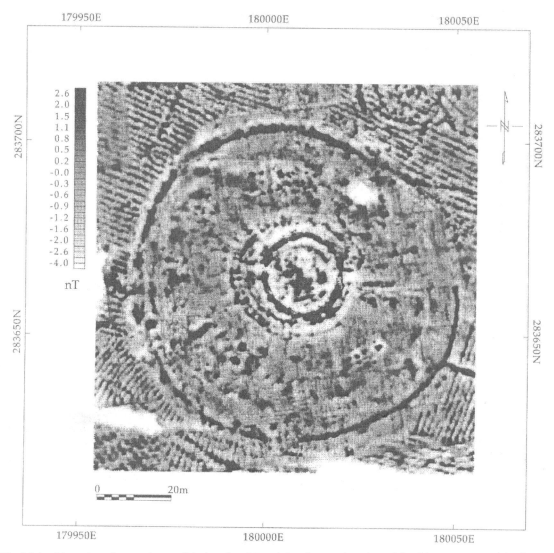

Fig. 9.24—Magnetic gradiometry image of Rathcroghan Mound. Its edge may have been defined by a near-vertical façade, perhaps retained by a timber palisade; the central penannular signature probably represents one of two stone structures buried within the mound, and a double ring of pits may be the foundations of a large timber structure built on the mound's summit.

9.25). The enhanced magnetic susceptibility associated with a central group of these structures suggests that intensive burning was associated with one or more of these phases. The very last monument to be superimposed on the summit may have been the small earthen mound mentioned above.

The monument variously called Dathí's Stone or Dathí's Mound has the appearance of an embanked burial mound. The encircling bank has opposed entrances on east and west and an overall

diameter of about 40m; there is a prominent pillar stone on the summit of the mound. Dathí was, supposedly, the last pagan king of Ireland; according to legend, he died about AD 429 and was buried at Rathcroghan. Limited excavation in 1981 confirmed that the circular mound was natural and carved out of a small gravel ridge (Waddell 1988). A considerable amount of the mound's surface was exposed and no graves were found. The enclosing bank proved to be roughly built of small stones and earth, and some charcoal from its base provided a

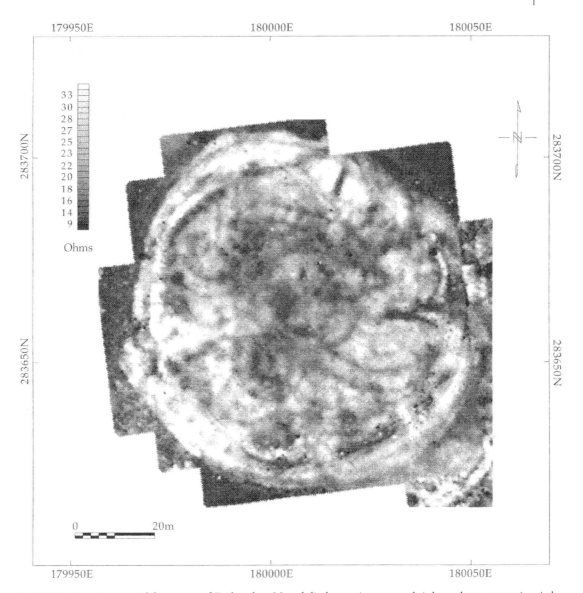

Fig. 9.25—Magnetic susceptibility survey of Rathcroghan Mound displays various arcs and circles, perhaps representing timber structures built and replaced on its summit over time.

series of radiocarbon dates suggesting that it was built either in the last two centuries BC or the early centuries AD. While the radiocarbon determinations did not offer a more precise chronology, they did at least contradict the traditional fifth-century AD date. Excavation demonstrated that there was a substantial ditch inside the bank that was filled with a fairly homogeneous and possibly deliberate clay deposit. This internal ditch indicates that the site has affinities with the ring-barrow type, but the large

pillar stone does set it apart from the rest of the mounds in the area and it could have had a ceremonial rather than a funerary purpose.

A number of other mounds seem to be variants on the ring-barrow type too. Rathbeg, near Rathcroghan crossroads, is a prominent site. Despite its name, it is not a rath or ringfort but a burial mound situated on a hillock. The mound is surrounded by two concentric banks situated on the steep sides of the hillock and there may be internal ditches. Flanagan's Fort (which acquired its name from a man who lived nearby) seems to have consisted of a bank with internal ditch enclosing an area of rising ground with a low oval artificial mound on the summit. But not all mounds are ring-barrows with mound, ditch and external bank; a number of simple circular mounds occur (and could well be of early prehistoric date). Rathscreg is a round mound on a low hill apparently enclosed by two widely spaced banks.

Enclosures include sites such as Cashelmanannan (Manannan's Fort), near the Mucklaghs, which is a much-ruined monument with two small fields attached. Rathnadarve, to the north, is a fine ringfort with bank and external ditch. There is a large enclosure, about 250m across, some 200m to the north-west. It is barely detectable on the ground but, for the most part, clearly visible from the air in the right conditions. Further to the north is the imposing earthwork called Rathmore, which is a medieval monument perhaps built on top of a natural hillock to give some additional height. The base of the steep-sided mound is surrounded by a broad ditch, and geophysical survey has shown that a substantial circular timber structure once stood on its summit. The large enclosure called Relignaree to the south of Rathcroghan Mound is another complex medieval monument; of circular plan with an internal diameter of 100m, it may have had a long and complicated history. The name, 'the cemetery of the kings', is a fanciful one, and those references to a great cemetery in the early literature may well refer to the mounds of the Rathcroghan complex as a whole. An interesting group of earthworks is situated on and just below the 120m contour about 600m west of Relignaree. Two linear earthworks known as the Mucklaghs are among the most imposing of the Rathcroghan monuments; they are so called because legend has it they are the results of the rootings of a magical boar. The northern example is the shorter and more massive of the two and consists of a relatively closely set pair of large earthen banks which curve very slightly and run roughly east to west down a gentle slope for a distance of about 100m; the banks, which are set 2.5–3m apart, average 3m in height and are 5–7m in width. The southern Mucklagh is a more or less straight pair of earthen banks, some 200m long and set about 6m apart, which measure up to 2m in height and up to 4m in width. At the north-eastern

end, one bank with traces of a ditch on its north-western side continues on for over 150m. At the other end, the parallel banks terminate not far from a pool of water. Leaving porcine explanations aside, it is difficult to suggest anything other than a ceremonial purpose for these large embankments. A smaller pair of earthworks known as the Knockans at Teltown, Co. Meath, are similar.

Oweynagat ('the cave of the cats') is a particularly noteworthy site; this is the cave of Cruachain, an entrance to the Otherworld and the focus of much magical activity in early legend. The Morrigan, an ancient war goddess, had temporary residence here, and a host of fearsome animals, birds and monsters are associated with it. It is a long, narrow, natural limestone cave, entered via part of a stone-built early medieval souterrain with ogham inscriptions on two roof stones, one of which contains the name 'Maeve' and reads VRAICCI MAQI MEDVVI ('[the stone of] Fraoch son of Medf'). Aside even from the intriguing inscription, the mere presence of an ogham stone at Oweynagat is noteworthy: such stones are very rare in Connacht, the majority being found in the south of Ireland. Rathnadarve, Rathmore, Oweynagat and other ringforts all testify to the continued importance of Rathcroghan in medieval times.

Kingship rituals

In medieval sources Tara, Navan, Knockaulin and Rathcroghan were perceived to have similar status and were portrayed in epic literature as royal settlements, the seats of kings, hence the term 'royal site'. The similarities they share might suggest that they served similar purposes in later prehistoric times at least, but there is archaeological evidence that they were important places with evidence of remarkable ritual persistence over a longer period of time, even from early prehistory in the case of Tara and well into the historic era at Rathcroghan. To date it is fair to say that unambiguous evidence for prehistoric settlement as such has not been forthcoming, but ritual and ceremonial activity is well attested. The medieval accounts would seem to be the stuff of fiction, and some of the descriptions of a royal house are clearly variations on a stock storyteller's formula. The account in the eighth-century *Táin Bó Fraich* of the great round house of Ailill and Medb in the rath of Cruachain—'This was the arrangement of the house: seven partitions in it, seven beds from the fire to the wall in the house all around. There was a fronting of bronze on each bed, carved red yew all covered with fair varied ornament . . .'—is very similar to other fanciful descriptions, including that of Conchobar's house at Emhain Mhacha. Thus the extent to which such literary descriptions are constructs of an imaginary past (perhaps with the aim of legitimising royal status and political power) has been a part of that debate on the value of these texts as a possible window on the Iron Age (Chapter 8).

The large enclosures, some with banks and internal ditches, have a non-defensive symbolic character. They enclose abundant evidence for cult practices, and while the structures from Navan phase 3ii (the smaller figure-of-eight structures) present interpretative difficulties, the weight of present evidence suggests that this too was primarily a ritual site in a sacred enclosure. Navan, like Knockaulin, may have been an assembly place—and the evidence for feasting is pertinent here. The literary evidence may offer some clues as to the nature of the rituals that sometimes accompanied these festivals. Chris Lynn (2003b) has considered the possible cosmological significance of the ceremonial architecture at Navan and has suggested that the practice of burying circular structures beneath a mound may have been an attempt to reconstruct an example of a mythical Otherworld hostel of the type then believed to exist underneath ancient mounds. The possibility that some form of solar worship may have taken place there has also been explored (Warner 1996). Both the ritual and the royal aspects are reflected in the strong literary association of sites like Tara and Rathcroghan with inauguration rites and a goddess of sovereignty. For instance, in the epic *Táin Bó Cúailnge*, at Cruachain, Ailill was king of Connacht because of his marriage to Maeve or Medb, who had previously been the wife of Conchobar, king of Ulster, and two other Connacht kings. The original Medb was not a historical person but a goddess who personified the kingship of Tara and of Connacht. Her name is cognate with words in Irish and other languages signifying drunkenness (like the English word 'mead'); her name means 'the drunken one' or 'she who intoxicates'. The kings of Cruachain may be described as quasi-divine or sacred individuals and their reign was inaugurated by a mystic marriage with the goddess. The

marriage may have taken the form of a ceremony that induced a 'divine' intoxication of the new king. To gain possession of Medb of Cruachain was to gain possession of the kingship, a fact that explains the unusual number of her husbands. She had a counterpart in Medb Lethderg of Tara, who, it is said, mated with nine of the kings of Ireland. Here we do have 'a window on the Iron Age' when we glimpse that original Medb, the goddess-queen who weds each king in turn. The prehistoric 'kingship marriage' with Medb in her guise as a goddess of sovereignty may have been an exercise both in the legitimisation of a theocratic leader and in the control of the forces of that other supernatural world of gods, goddesses and ancestors.

We can only surmise what forms of prehistoric ritual may have been practised at places like Rathcroghan. It has been suggested that the major components of a prehistoric inauguration rite involved an alcoholic drink, an equine ritual and a feast, all a part of a wider, older and ultimately Indo-European institution, ideology and mythology of sacral kingship (McCone 1990). There are echoes of this in the twelfth-century account of the inauguration rite involving horse sacrifice of the Cenél Conaill, one of the northern septs of the Uí Néill in Donegal, as recorded by Giraldus Cambrensis in his *Topography of Ireland*: 'When the whole people of that land has been gathered together in one place, a white mare is brought forward into the middle of the assembly. He who is to be inaugurated, not as a chief, but as a beast, not as a king, but as an outlaw, embraces the animal before all, professing himself to be a beast also. The mare is then killed immediately, cut up in pieces, and boiled in water. A bath is prepared for the man afterwards in the same water. He sits in the bath surrounded by all his people, and all, he and they, eat of the meat of the mare which is brought to them. He quaffs and drinks of the broth in which he is bathed, not in any cup, or using his hand, but just dipping his mouth into it about him. When this unrighteous rite has been carried out, his kingship and dominion has been conferred' (O'Meara 1951). As various writers have pointed out, this ritual has extraordinary parallels with the Hindu *asva-medha* or horse sacrifice, in which the principal spouse of the king submits to a symbolic union with a dead stallion (Doherty 2005). Another rite possibly associated with prehistoric kingship is the *tairb-feis* or bull feast, in which a future king of Tara is foretold in a vision induced in a ritual trance after a bull sacrifice (Koch and Carey 1995). Other elements of early Irish inauguration rituals have Indo-European analogies too and may be echoes of prehistoric practices. These include a mock chariot race, the giving of a rod to the king, ritual steps in five directions and the chanting of praise-poems (Dillon 1973). The difficulties that many people have in accepting the concept of sacral kingship probably lies in the fact that ancient Irish (and Indo-European) kingship was based on service to a free community (Jaski 2000) in contrast to the more familiar form of anointed absolute monarch ruling by divine right.

There is a celebrated description in the Annals of Connacht of the inauguration of Feidhlim Ó Conchobhair as king of Connacht in AD 1310. He was proclaimed king on a mound conceivably containing the bones of his O'Conor ancestors at Carnfree, just over 6km to the south-south-east of Rathcroghan: '. . . in a style as royal, as lordly and as public as any of his race from the time of Brian son of Eochu Muigmedoin till that day. And when Fedlimid mac Aeda meic Eogain had married the Province of Connacht his foster-father waited upon him during the night in the manner remembered by the old men and recorded in the old books; and this was the most splendid king-ship marriage ever celebrated in Connacht down to that day'. This seems to have been an extraordinary medieval re-enactment of an archaic rite intended to ensure the fertility of man and beast and earth throughout the kingdom. Carnfree is a reminder that smaller ceremonial sites of possible prehistoric date also exist and present some of the features of their larger and better-known counterparts, notably mounds and enclosures located in prominent positions. Here, the prehistoric burial cairn known as Carnfree (Carn Fraoigh—the cairn of Fraoch) stands at just over 110m above sea level on a broad ridge known as Ard Chaoin ('the smooth height'). Nearby is a large circular tumulus and several ring-barrows. Other monuments on the ridge include other ring-barrows, a tall pillar stone in an embanked circle, and a conjoined earthwork very similar to the Forrad and Teach Cormaic at Tara. While the monuments here may reflect some two millennia of ritual activity, Elizabeth FitzPatrick (2004) has cautioned that documented medieval inauguration practices do not prove the prehistoric enactment of such kingship rituals at Carnfree or anywhere else.

Other rituals may have occurred, of course, and some may be more readily identified in the archaeological record. For instance, there is abundant evidence in early Irish literature that wood and trees were culturally charged phenomena and invested with ritual significance. Sacred trees are documented, and that trees had totemic significance is clear from personal names such as Mac Cuill, 'son of hazel', and Macc Cairthin, 'son of rowan' (Lucas 1963). The name of the major medieval Munster dynasty the Éoganacht is associated with the yew tree, eó in Middle Irish, and according to F. J. Byrne (1973) this implies descent from a divine or human personage connected with the sacred yew, suggesting a parallel with the Gaulish 'yew people', the Eburones. Wood remains from archaeological contexts may tell us much more than details of woodland composition. There may be some patterning, for instance, in the selection of wood species for anthropomorphic carvings (Coles 1998). Different woods may have been carefully chosen for ritual fires. Excavation at Raffin, Co. Meath, has yielded traces of activity from Neolithic to Iron Age times (Newman et al. 2007). The Iron Age monument was a circular enclosure some 65m in diameter formed by a bank with internal ditch, a miniature (and later) version of the great internally ditched ceremonial enclosures at Tara and Navan (Fig. 9.26). At its centre was a circular structure surrounded by a ring of timber posts, and a small ogham-inscribed stone was found in its ditch. A small pit marked by a pillar stone was found in the northern part of the enclosure. It contained successive layers of charcoal and soil, and the reddish colour of its sides indicated a series of burning incidents. A fragment of the frontal cranium of an adult human lay on the uppermost layer. The skull portion was worn smooth, suggesting frequent handling. Differences in the charcoal assemblages in the pit layers implied five distinct and sequential burning episodes; a series of radiocarbon dates, three from the layers and one from the skull fragment, demonstrated that the burnings were contemporary and took place between the third and fifth centuries AD. The skull fragment was dated to 110–140 BC and was at least a century old when placed on the uppermost layer beneath the pillar

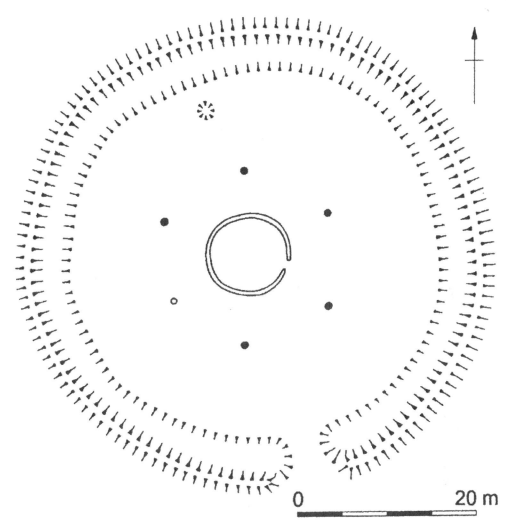

Fig. 9.26—Raffin, Co. Meath: a small circular enclosure formed by a bank with internal ditch (with a circular structure surrounded by a ring of timber posts in its centre) is a miniature version of the great internally ditched ceremonial enclosures at Tara and Navan.

stone. Eight charcoal types were identified: hazel was the main wood used but oak was well represented in the upper layers, while willow or aspen were the main charcoal types in the lower layers. Ash was found only in the two uppermost layers, and birch and holly (noted in a nearby pollen profile) did not occur. Alder, not a readily combustible wood, was identified, as were twig-like branches of fruit-bearing species such as rowan and crab-apple. A process of selection clearly took place. Bearing in mind the ogham stone found in the ditch and the fact that many of the letters of this stroke script are named after trees, Newman asked

the intriguing question of whether the wood-burning episodes could have any correlation with the wood lore of an ogham scribe.

The small hillfort at Freestone Hill, Co. Kilkenny, with a single stony bank and external ditch enclosing an area of about 2ha, was excavated in the late 1940s. As already mentioned (Chapter 7), some coarse pottery, glass beads and a radiocarbon date now indicate Dowris phase occupation on the site. The excavations also revealed that there had been a prehistoric cemetery mound of about 2000 BC on the hill, with later activity there attested by some provincial Roman bronzes, including toilet implements and bracelet fragments, and a coin of Constantine II of the fourth century AD. These finds, unusual in an Irish context and all from within a small oval enclosure on the summit, have been reinterpreted as votive offerings at a sanctuary or shrine in the late Roman period in the fourth or fifth century AD (Ó Floinn 2000).

THE HILLFORT PROBLEM

As we have seen, when considering Haughey's Fort and other contemporary sites, the appearance of numbers of enclosed settlements, particularly those of large size occupying naturally defensible locations, may be considered as indicators of social change in later prehistory (Chapter 6). These hillforts, as they are often called, lend support to the idea that society was becoming increasingly hierarchical and complex, and their emergence may even reflect tribal formation. If defence was a primary consideration, then they at the very least suggest the emergence of powerful local individuals and the adoption of heroic pastimes such as persistent raiding. The term 'hillfort', of course, implies a defensive capability and is widely used of large hilltop enclosures that seem to deliberately exploit the natural terrain for this purpose. As we have also seen, those investigated so far have proven to be Bronze Age monuments, but the dates of many others have yet to be determined and, given the Iron Age date for many such sites in Britain, some may well belong to this later phase. The lack of trial excavation and our consequent ignorance of even the approximate date of most of these monuments make assessment particularly difficult. Barry Raftery (1994a), who first studied these at a time when they were considered to be a characteristic feature of the Iron Age, identified three classes. A common type is the univallate monument, with a single line of defence (class 1). One of the largest known is Knocknashee, near Ballymote, Co. Sligo, where the denuded remains of a rampart enclose an entire hilltop at a height of about 270m above sea level, an approximately oval area of some 22ha. A stretch of outer bank exists on the east. Two fairly intact prehistoric cairns lie within the enclosure towards its northern end. There are over 30 hut circles or small enclosures also visible within it, mainly on the sheltered

eastern side, but their chronological relationship to the defences is unknown. Most univallate enclosures are much smaller, usually less than 3.5ha in extent. Carn Tigherna, near Fermoy, Co. Cork, is one example and is a prominent landmark. It is an irregular oval enclosure with a large stone dump rampart—approximately 250m in maximum dimensions—enclosing 2.9ha (Fig. 9.27). A series of outer low banks and ditches appear to be an attempt to enhance the approach to a north-western entrance. In the centre is a cairn which produced one or two prehistoric burials in the nineteenth century and was further disturbed by being robbed for material to construct a high cross in 1933 (to commemorate the nineteenth centenary of the death of Christ) and to build a Second World War lookout post at a later date (Doody 2008).

Class 2 hillforts are multivallate, and examples like Haughey's Fort, Cashel, Co. Cork, and Mooghaun, Co. Clare, with widely spaced banks have been assigned to the later Bronze Age. Multivallate sites are commoner in Munster than in the rest of the country. Size is important: there is a distinction to be made between hillforts and hilltop enclosures, the latter having an internal diameter of less than 50m (Grogan 2005). The famous Grianán of Aileach in County Donegal, overlooking both Lough Swilly and Lough Foyle, is a multivallate site with a long and complex history (Fig. 9.28). A central stone fort, restored in the late nineteenth century, may be of medieval date, and its relationship to the remains of two pairs of enclosing and very denuded earthen banks is uncertain; these are usually considered to be the remains of a prehistoric hillfort, though it has been suggested that they are no more than token ramparts contemporary with the inner stone fort. A well is dedicated to St Patrick (Lacy 1983). Examples of prehistoric monuments with closely spaced multivallate defences are rare but include the Rath of the Synods on Tara and the larger hillfort at Belmont, north of Tuam, Co. Galway, which consists of a bank with external ditch, measuring about 160m by 135m, enclosing an area of about 1.5ha. There is a slight counterscarp bank (surmounted by a modern stone wall) outside this ditch, with traces of another external ditch in places. The only visible feature in the interior is a small modern graveyard (Raftery 1976b). Ballinkillen, Co. Carlow, with maximum dimensions of 267m by 225m, is

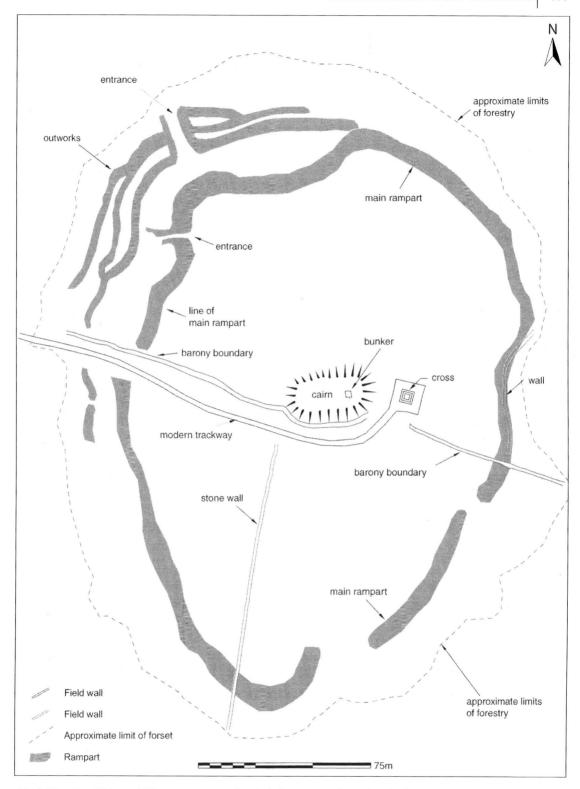

Fig. 9.27—Carn Tigherna hillfort, near Fermoy, Co. Cork, has a series of outer low banks and ditches enhancing the approach to a north-western entrance.

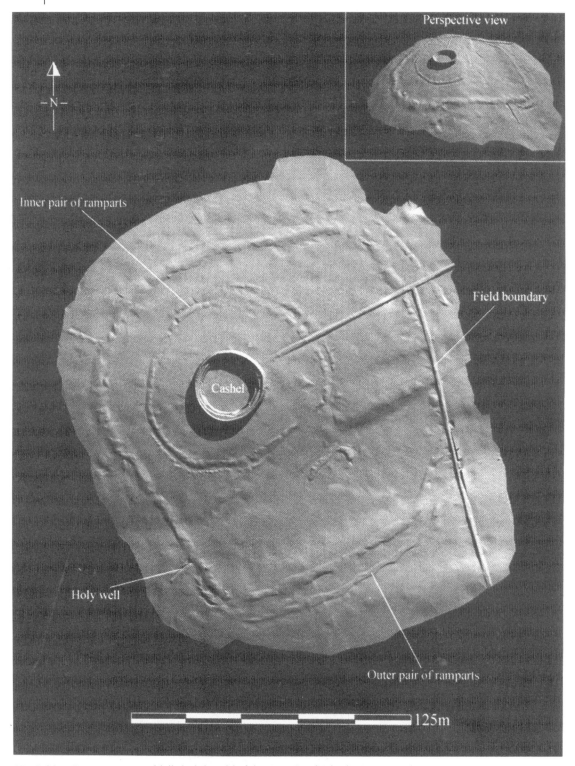

Perspective view

Inner pair of ramparts

Field boundary

Cashel

Holy well

Outer pair of ramparts

125m

Fig. 9.28—Computer-generated hill-shaded model of the Grianán of Aileach, Co. Donegal.

enclosed by a double bank with intervening ditch. The banks are close together, with a maximum overall width of 13m (Brindley and Kilfeather 1993). Laghtea, Co. Tipperary, also consists of a double bank with intervening ditch surrounding three sides of a hilltop; on the east a series of crags and bluffs may have offered some natural protection (Condit and O'Sullivan 1999).

There is a remarkable concentration of multivallate hillforts in an area of some 30km² near Baltinglass, Co. Wicklow (Fig. 9.29). Two occur on Baltinglass Hill itself: Rathcoran on the summit, at an elevation of about 360m, appears to be an unfinished bivallate monument with traces of quarry hollows between the two incomplete ramparts, which enclose 10.5ha. A passage tomb surrounded by a modern wall lies on the highest point in its southern part. Rathnagree, on Tuckmill Hill, a lower ridge 500m to the north, is a small trivallate monument about 270m in diameter. Across the River Slaney, no more than 5km away, the 300m-high hills at Tinoranhill, Co. Wicklow, and Hughstown, Co. Kildare, both have denuded enclosures on their summits. Tinoran is a bivallate or trivallate enclosure over 500m across and Hughstown is bivallate. Just over 3km north-east of Baltinglass Hill, on the long ridge of Spinan's Hill, at a height of about 400m, is a bivallate enclosure

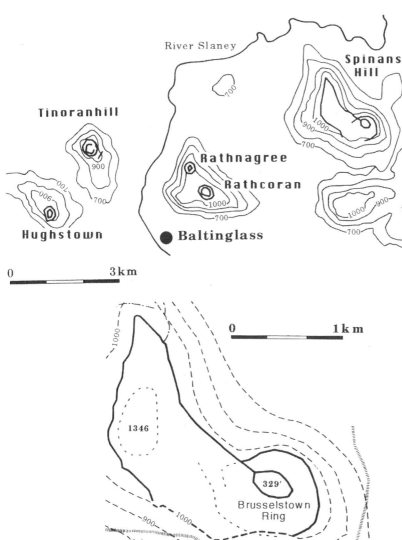

Fig. 9.29—Above: schematic plans of a hillfort complex at Baltinglass, Co. Wicklow (above), and at nearby Spinan's Hill, Co. Wicklow (below).

known as Brusselstown Ring. This monument has two widely spaced ramparts encompassing more than 17ha and occupies the south-eastern end of the ridge. Attached to it on the west and north-west is another huge outer enclosure of irregular plan, formed for most of its visible length by a double rampart with intervening ditch averaging 15m in overall width. This rampart has been traced for about 4km and runs just above the 300m contour; it may originally have enclosed an area of 132ha. Several cairns, possibly a passage tomb cemetery, and another possible enclosure have been traced on Spinan's Hill itself in the north-western section of the great enclosure. It is quite possible that the Spinan's Hill complex, and indeed various hillforts in the Blessington cluster as a whole, represent a sequence of activity over a long period of time. The huge enclosure, however, seems to have been conceived as a unit and may have been a major late prehistoric undertaking like the Dorsey enclosure in County Armagh.

Class 3 hillforts in Raftery's classification are inland promontory forts and fewer than a dozen are recorded. Lurigethan, Co. Antrim, is a large and steep-sided promontory of some 13ha defended by a series of closely set ramparts and ditches some 300m in length. The number of ditches and banks varies in places from three to six. Knockdhu, Co. Antrim, is about 8ha in extent and defended by two closely set banks and ditches. Other examples, like several in counties Kerry, Louth and Meath, are generally much smaller. Castle Gale, Co. Limerick, has an enclosed area of only 1.4ha and is defended on its southern side by a pair of banks with an intervening ditch. An additional stretch of rampart defends part of the northern slope. A possible cairn crowns the summit of the hill.

As already noted, in the absence of excavation, the date and purpose of these hilltop enclosures can only be guessed at, and, at present, surface morphology—neither size nor rampart form—or elevation provide few clues. The evidence from a very small number of excavations, from Haughey's Fort, Dún Aonghasa, Cashel and Mooghaun in particular, demonstrates the construction of multivallate enclosures in the late second and first millennia BC. Sites such as Lyles Hill and Donegore, Co. Antrim, of course, show that hilltop palisaded enclosures may be as old as the Neolithic, and while most large hilltop enclosures may well

belong to the later prehistoric period, it would be unwise to assume that all are of this date. Dún Aonghasa was evidently a multi-period monument, and given the evidence from Haughey's Fort for some activity there around *c.* 400–200 BC and the evidence for iron-working at Rathgall, Co. Wicklow, sometime in the period AD 180–540, it is clear that some sites were the focus of later activity too. In general the practice of hilltop enclosure on a substantial scale may have spanned more than a millennium.

Though the term hillfort is commonly used, it is by no means certain that all these hilltop sites served the same function and not all may have been defensive sites. The widely spaced dump stone ramparts at Mooghaun, with no carefully constructed vertical faces, seem a less than effective impediment to an attacking force, and the defence of such a long perimeter here and at Spinan's Hill, for instance, in the face of a determined onslaught would demand an impossibly large body of defenders. Closely spaced ramparts would have had a defensive capability, and the denuded ramparts and silted-up ditches at many sites may still prove, on excavation, to have been imposing defences, perhaps with timber breastworks. It is unlikely that there is a single explanation for hilltop enclosures: it is possible that some were hillforts and built primarily as defended settlements or as intermittently occupied refuge places, but others may have been stock compounds, perhaps associated with seasonal upland grazing. Those multivallate sites with widely spaced ramparts, 10m to more than 50m apart, could well have served this purpose. The consistent association of a number of sites with prehistoric cairns may be more than just a coincidental preference for a hilltop location. At many sites the burial monument seems not to have been disturbed and may have conferred a special status on the enclosure. It is possible that the cairns, or the social activities that were associated with them, sanctified the hilltop in some way. If some enclosures were not defensive and used only for periodic communal gatherings or ceremonial with associated intermittent settlement, periodic refurbishment or aggrandisement of the ramparts may still have been just an occasional occurrence.

Whatever the uses of these large enclosures, their construction represented a considerable investment in time and labour, and this alone is testimony of their importance. Their strategic role in the organisation of the wider landscape, perhaps as focal points in a pattern of smaller dispersed and possibly undefended homesteads, remains unclear. Some may have demarcated territories or territorial boundaries. Their distribution is puzzling too, with large multivallate enclosures a noteworthy feature in the southern half of the island and a general scarcity of hillforts in the north. The contrast between this pattern and the distribution of supposedly contemporary artefacts such as beehive querns and metalwork has prompted the suggestion that the multivallate enclosures are unrelated to and possibly earlier than this material. Some caution is necessary here; survey will undoubtedly augment present distribution maps and, of course, the date of the great majority of hillforts is unknown. Comparisons with the loosely dated artefactual evidence, broadly assigned to the period 300 BC–AD 300, are therefore premature and, in any event, beehive querns apart, this material is represented, albeit slightly, in the southern half of the island. Since much of it has been recovered from bogs, it is possible that the Munster scarcity could be due to the absence of, or to the limited commercial or agricultural exploitation of, certain types of contexts such as lowland bogs. There are many intriguing questions to be answered, of course, not least about the distribution of beehive querns and multivallate enclosures, but it is not certain that these questions are related.

LINEAR EARTHWORKS

The term 'linear earthwork' is loosely applied to a varied group of bank or bank and ditch systems and has included such earthworks as the parallel pairs of banks at Tara, the so-called Banqueting Hall, the Mucklaghs at Rathcroghan, and much longer earthworks as well. Some pairs of parallel banks, like some of the other examples at Rathcroghan, may have been droveways for animals, but others are on such a scale that they probably had another purpose. Some may have served to demarcate sections of the landscape, as with the 700m-long stretch of parallel banks in Riverstown townland to the west of Tara. Others may have been ceremonial roadways. The system of parallel ditches in Creeveroe townland in the Navan complex may extend for some 1.7km

and excavation has shown it to be contemporary with Haughey's Fort and the King's Stables (Conway 2006). The Friar's Walk, Kiltierney, Co. Fermanagh, is a long linear earthwork of L-shaped plan which has been traced for some 1,100m in an area rich in prehistoric remains, including a passage tomb and a stone circle. Excavation demonstrated that it consisted of a pair of parallel earthen banks 15m apart with internal rock-cut ditches, with a strip of level ground between. No dating evidence was found but the association with a complex of ritual or burial monuments is noteworthy (Daniells and Williams 1977). This is the case at sites like Tara and Rathcroghan. One of two linear earthworks on the Curragh in County Kildare consists of a pair of low banks with an intervening ditch and is called 'the race of the Black Pig'.

While it must be stressed that both date and purpose remain matters of speculation, some particularly long linear systems may mark major territorial divisions and may be associated in some way with hilltop enclosures. At Shankill, Co. Kilkenny, a limited excavation at part of a 2km-long stretch of low earthen bank with a ditch on its southern side failed to produce any clues as to its date; local information suggested that it was part of an earthwork known as the Rathduff dyke or trench recorded near Paulstown on the borders between Kilkenny and Carlow and about 8km north-east of Freestone Hill (O'Flaherty 1987). Aerial photography has revealed a system of four parallel ditches, 14m apart, running for some 500m at Grevine West, south of Kilkenny, and about 1.5km north-east of a probable hillfort. At Woodsgift, in north-western County Kilkenny, another system of two pairs of ditches with an overall width of 40m runs for over 800m about 3km south of Clomantagh Hill, which has a hillfort on its summit (Gibbons 1990). A pair of parallel banks known as Rian Bó Phádraig ('the track of St Patrick's cow') is said to connect the ecclesiastical centres of Cashel, Co. Tipperary, and Ardmore, Co. Waterford, a distance of over 90km; limited excavation at a section near Ardfinnan, Co. Tipperary, proved inconclusive but it is considered a medieval roadway by some (O'Donnell 1999; Nugent 2005). The Knockans at Teltown, at least in their final form, appear to be medieval linear earthworks as well.

Teltown, Co. Meath (ancient Tailtiu), is

celebrated in early Irish literature as the site of Óenach Tailten, the principal assembly of the Uí Néill kings of Tara, held at the festival of Lughnasa at least as early as the sixth century AD. In medieval literature it, along with Rathcroghan and the Boyne Valley, are named as the chief cemeteries of pagan Ireland. The Tripartite Life of St Patrick, compiled some time prior to the early tenth century, records the saint's visit to the location of the royal assembly, his founding of a church at Donaghpatrick, and his blessing of the royal fort called Rath Aithir (Swift 2000). The monuments at Teltown include a substantial multivallate enclosure believed to be the Rath Aithir of old; Rath Dubh, a large, more or less flat-topped and slightly oval mound with an average basal diameter of about 100m; and, in a large 2km-wide loop of the Blackwater that may have been the location of the ancient fair, several marshy hollows that are thought to be artificial ponds (Swan 1998). A linear earthwork known as the Knockans was situated on rising ground to the north of the loop in the river. The greater part of this monument with its two parallel and slightly curving earthen banks was destroyed in 1997, but the available evidence suggests that the northern bank was a broad, low, gently sloping earthwork with a length of about 80–100m, a height of about 2.5m and a width of about 12m; the southern bank, the more massive and steeper of the two, was about 72m long and 3.5m high with a maximum basal width of about 30m. There was a marshy hollow, a possible former pond, at the monument's eastern end.

Limited excavation revealed that the construction of the southern bank seems to have begun with the deposition on the old ground surface of layers of silts and silty sand retained on their southern side by a loosely built stone revetment. These were followed over a period of time by numerous layers (up to 60cm thick) of fine, water-laid sediments and moss along the northern slope of the silt and stone embankment. No artefacts or bone were found and this deposit may have been formed by seasonal water-level changes in the adjacent pond. The next phase in the development of the southern bank occurred when further layers of silt were deposited along its top and a stake and wattle structure was erected on its north-facing slope. Some additional layers of silt and turves were

added and a row of four small stakes was then driven into the southern side of the embankment. This feature was sealed by a black layer containing wood fragments. Some hazel from this context produced a very general late prehistoric radiocarbon determination with calibrated date ranges of 810–482 BC and 440–412 BC. There then followed a distinct change in the type of material deposited. Layers of ash and charcoal were seemingly transported to the site and carefully laid to a depth of about 60cm along the length of the top of the embankment and eventually sealed by several layers of turves. Some additional lenses of sediment caused by pond encroachment on the northern slope of the embankment produced some hazel charcoal that provided an early medieval radiocarbon date of AD 640–770. A further change in the nature of deposition on the bank then took place: a series of layers of material were deposited over the mainly organic core, and a sample of hazel charcoal from one of these produced another somewhat later early medieval radiocarbon date of AD 790–978. The main phase of bank construction, with the addition of up to 2m of earth, seems to have occurred shortly thereafter and there was no evidence in the various machine-exposed sections to suggest that any significant period of time had elapsed or that the process of augmentation was a particularly lengthy one. The construction or modification of parts of this linear earthwork in or about the eighth century and again in the ninth or tenth century AD indicates the deliberate reuse of a prehistoric monument or possibly the deliberate construction of a prehistoric form in medieval times.

The Claidh Dubh or Black Dyke is a well-known earthwork in County Cork, where it has been traced in several discontinuous sections for some 24km from the Limerick–Cork boundary, north-west of Charleville, to east Cork near Carrigtohill. The longest stretch extends across the valley of the River Blackwater between the Ballyhoura Hills and the Nagles Mountains for approximately 14km. Excavation of a section which forms the townland boundary between Castleblagh and Ballydague, near the village of Ballyhooley, revealed an earthen bank with a shallow ditch on either side and a well-made trackway running parallel to it. There may have been a palisade on top of the bank. No direct dating evidence was found, but peat, which sealed the ditch and partly covered the bank, had apparently commenced to form about AD 100 and thus indicated a date sometime prior to this for this section of the earthwork (Doody 2008).

The Black Pig's Dyke

The best-known linear earthwork is the Black Pig's Dyke in Ulster, named after a folk-tale about a magical black pig which—when chased across several counties—rooted up large tracts of land. It is just one of several northern linear earthworks with various names identified in counties Leitrim, Cavan, Monaghan, Armagh and Down. The Black Pig's Dyke has been claimed by earlier writers to have been a single defensive earthwork stretching from Bundoran in the west to Dundalk in the east. In County Leitrim it is a discontinuous section of ditch some 2.5m wide traced for some 9km in the Kiltyclogher area between Lough Melvin and Lough Macnean Upper and variously called the Black Pig's Race or the Worm Ditch. Another ditch has been noted between Dowra and Lough Allen to the south. A 2km length of the earthwork occurs in County Cavan, east of Bellananagh. In County Monaghan similarly named discontinuous segments of one or two banks and ditches have been recorded in over a dozen townlands south of Scotshouse, running from the Fermanagh lake system, north of Redhills, Co. Cavan, south-eastwards to Drumcor Lough, then eastwards to Ballinageeragh, near Drum, a total distance of some 9km (Lynn 1989b). A limited excavation of a section of the dyke in Aghareagh West, near Scotshouse, demonstrated that the monument there had consisted of a timber palisade and external ditch with a double bank with intervening ditch beyond. The overall width was about 24m and the ramparts were of dump construction, surviving to a maximum height of about 1.5m. The palisade trench contained the burnt remains of oak timbers, which provided a radiocarbon determination of 390–70 BC (Walsh 1987).

A small section of linear earthwork occurs in east Monaghan, just west of Lough Ross near Crossmaglen, Co. Armagh. Sections of linear earthwork in Armagh include a stretch north-east of the village of Meigh, running northwards towards Camlough west of Newry, and, further north, a segment 6km south of Armagh city called the Dane's Cast. This is the name given to half a

dozen lengths of earthwork in western County Down extending southwards for some 10km on the eastern side of the Newry Canal from north of Scarva to near Goraghwood Station. Survey has shown that the various sections of this earthwork are all located on land about 30m above sea level and link natural obstacles such as Lough Shark and areas of bogland. It consists mostly of a bank and ditch, though in places there are two banks with an intervening ditch. In the early nineteenth century it was said to have continued southwards in the area of Bessbrook, Co. Armagh, but now cannot be traced. A short length of earthwork south of Goraghwood on the western side of the canal suggests that the dyke did run south-westwards into County Armagh.

The Dorsey in County Armagh, 5km north-east of Crossmaglen, is a series of earthworks and timber palisades that appear to form a large and irregularly rectangular enclosure of some 68ha (Lynn 1989a; 1992b). The name, from *dóirse*, 'the doors', reflects the tradition that this earthwork was believed to be a gateway to the north. On the south, facing north Louth, there are two separate lengths of earthworks to the west and to the east about 800m apart and separated from one another by an area of bogland along the Dorsy River, a name that has a different spelling (Fig. 9.30). The discovery of oak timbers in this bog in the nineteenth century suggests the presence of a palisade at this point. Both southern earthworks consist of an impressive rampart, up to 6m high in places, between two large ditches with a second outer bank in places. The overall width is about 40m. On the west and east the ends of these earthworks turn northwards, the western element becoming a palisade of roughly squared oak posts, traced for over 70m, with external ditch on the edge of a bog, the eastern consisting of a substantial bank and ditch running northwards more or less parallel to the Ummeracam River. On the north, discontinuous lengths of a smaller bank and ditch have been identified, some of it only traceable from the air. Some oak timbers were unearthed on the north-west in 1988 and may have come from the ditch. The northern elements appear to continue to both west and east, and this has led to suggestions that these extensions were part of the Black Pig's Dyke. It is not certain whether all the parts of the Dorsey complex are contemporary and it has been

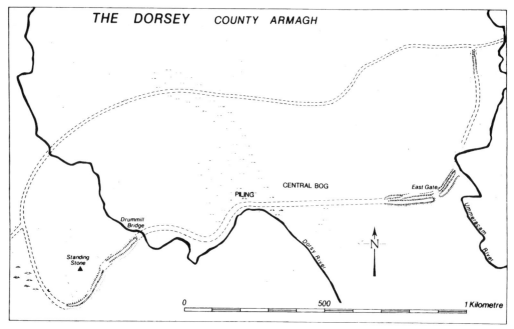

Fig. 9.30—The Dorsey, Co. Armagh.

suggested that it is not an enclosure but two separate linear earthworks of different dates, the northernmost being possibly the earlier. It may have been a multi-phase monument: oak timbers from the south-western palisade were dendrochronologically dated to about 100–90 BC, and the oak timbers found in 1988 at the northern rampart were felled around 140 BC; some radiocarbon determinations are consistent with these general dates.

Various writers have interpreted the Dorsey as a stronghold on the Black Pig's Dyke and part of the boundary defences of late prehistoric Ulster, the discontinuous nature of the dyke being explained by the fact that it was mainly intended to augment the natural obstacles offered by high ground, lake or bog, and to be an impediment to cattle-raiders. Since the regeneration of woodland *c.* 200 BC detected in pollen analyses from Loughnashade, Co. Armagh, could mean a reduction in the available winter grazing, it is possible that boundary markers or defences would have become more important in such times of stress. If it is a single contemporary construction, the Black Pig's Dyke is an impressive boundary marker. If it is not, it is equally significant that different communities may have felt the need to monumentally demarcate sections of their territories. The theory of monumental frontier

defences has been inspired in part by the supposed contemporaneity of the whole linear earthwork complex with Navan Fort and the perception, encouraged by the much later tales of the Ulster Cycle such as the *Táin Bó Cúailnge*, that cattle-raiding was a major preoccupation of a heroic society in the last few centuries BC. An alternative interpretation for the Dorsey earthworks has been offered by Aitchison (1993), who suggests that this monument was neither stronghold nor cattle compound but a focus of ritual activity with familiar wetland and watery associations. The location has no particular defensive advantage and much of the interior is bog, with the Dorsey and Ummercam rivers on either side. A 1.5m-high pillar stone stands in its south-western quarter. Its boundaries, which may have been redefined and even increased from time to time, may have served, like the circular boundary of Navan Fort, to restrict access, the impressive nature of the southern earthworks being an indication of status. Rather than a frontier defence of the people who built Navan Fort, the Dorsey may have been the ritual centre of a different socio-political group.

Another irregular enclosure, created by a huge earthen embankment about 6m high and 30m wide, which cuts off a large promontory on the River Shannon at Drumsna in north-east

Roscommon, has been considered a frontier fortification (Condit and Buckley 1989; 1998) but it may have served a similar ceremonial purpose. It too seems non-defensive in character, with two out-turned entranceways, one with a minimum width of no less than 16m.

CULT, SACRIFICE AND BURIAL

Almost a thousand years after the roughly carved wooden idol was placed in a bog at Ralaghan, Co. Cavan (Fig. 7.8), the first clear evidence for anthropomorphic carving in stone is found. The most remarkable example of early iconic stone-carving is probably the Corleck head, found about 1855 some 7km to the south-east of Ralaghan, near Shercock (Fig. 9.31, 2). It is carved from a block of local sandstone and has three stylised faces, each slightly different. All share closely set round eyes, a spatulate nose and a simply grooved mouth. A hole in the base of the head was probably a mortise for attaching it to a base, possibly a timber pillar. If this was the case, it may be compared to a 1.8m-high wooden carving found in the 1790s in a bog at Ballybritain, just north of Aghadowey, Co. Derry (Fig. 9.31, 1). Sadly, this 'heathen image', which was carved from a tree trunk and had four heads or faces with hair depicted, was allowed to fall to pieces and is only known from a minute sketch (Day and McWilliams 1993). These primitive carvings are very difficult to date, but since three-faced or three-headed carvings are known in Roman Britain and Gallo-Roman France, the Irish examples may well be pre-Christian and belong to the early centuries AD; nevertheless, since pagan practices are unlikely to have expired with the alacrity implied in early historical sources, a somewhat later date is quite possible too.

Numerous other stone heads of various sorts are also claimed to be pre-Christian, and groups of them have been identified in counties Donegal, Armagh, Cavan and Fermanagh, with scattered examples elsewhere (Rynne 1972a; Hickey 1976; Lanigan Wood and Verling 1995). None are precisely dated; some may be prehistoric, others are probably of medieval or post-medieval date, and some are probably folk-art of the seventeenth or eighteenth century. A crude, three-faced stone bust from Woodlands, near Raphoe, Co. Donegal, once

believed to be pre-Christian, may have been carved in the nineteenth century. A stone head from Beltany, Co. Donegal (Fig. 9.31, 3), is a good illustration of the dating problems posed by carvings of this sort. The circumstances of its discovery are vague; it was reputedly found near a stone circle but, in effect, where it came from originally and its archaeological context are unknown. There are faint traces of what may be a collar on the neck and this has been compared to a torc; the eyes and mouth have been compared to these features on the two faces of a stone idol on Boa Island, Co. Fermanagh, itself of uncertain date but, judging from other carvings in the region, probably assignable to sometime in the first millennium AD. The Beltany head is also comparable to various human heads on other stonework and metalwork of the early medieval period and attempts to date it are inevitably a subjective exercise.

An intriguing group of stone carvings comes from the Armagh area, but once again the picture is complicated by the presence of carvings and fragments of likely medieval date and by the vigorous local production of primitive stone heads and possibly other sculpture in the nineteenth century. One carving that may be of early date is the striking Tandragee idol, as it is now called (Fig. 9.31, 4). This is a bust of a ferocious-looking human figure with a horned helmet and with its right arm in what is usually considered a ritual pose comparable to that of some prehistoric carvings of the later first millennium BC in Germany. There are some points of comparison with other unprovenanced stone carvings from the Armagh area, but this unique piece, which may have been found near St Patrick's (Church of Ireland) Cathedral in Armagh, remains an enigma (Warner 2003a; Lanigan Wood 2000). Equally puzzling are stone carvings of three animals variously described as bears or dogs which may also have been found in the church precincts on Cathedral Hill during rebuilding work in the nineteenth century; these and some other undated carvings have led to the suggestion that the hill was the site of a pre-Christian cult centre. Excavation has uncovered traces of a substantial ditch of possible late prehistoric date on the hill and two radiocarbon dates provide terminal dates for its construction: *c.* AD 220–560 and 30 BC–AD 390 (Gaskell Brown and Harper 1984).

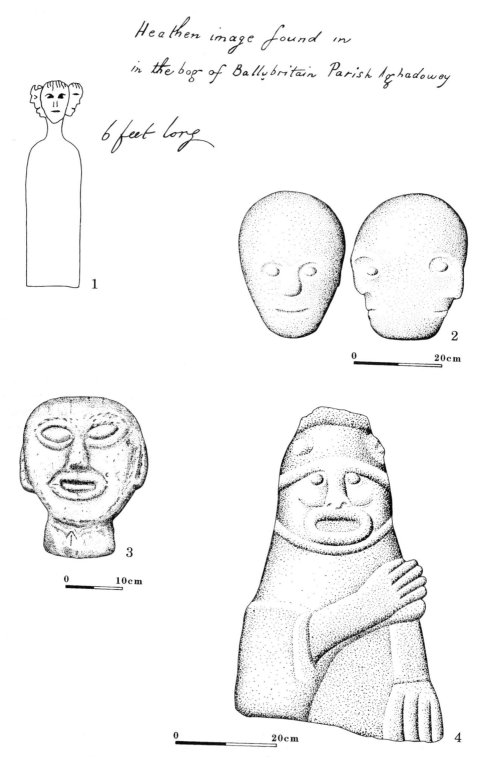

Heathen image found in
in the bog of Ballybritain Parish Aghadowey

6 feet long

Fig. 9.31—(1) A nineteenth-century sketch of a wooden idol with four heads or faces found in a bog at Ballybritain, Co. Derry. (2) Stone three-faced head from Corleck, Co. Cavan. (3) Stone head said to come from Beltany, Co. Donegal. (4) The Tandragee idol, Co. Armagh.

Aniconic carvings

It is possible that carvings like the Ballybritain pillar and the Corleck head once stood in small shrines or cult centres, and the same may have been true of a number of more elaborate, non-representational, carved stones. Five are known but again nothing is recorded about their original archaeological context. The decoration on a sixth, a pillar stone on Cape Clear, Co. Cork, is indecipherable, so its status is uncertain (O'Leary and Shee Twohig 1993). The finest of these aniconic carvings is the Turoe stone, a pillar stone profusely decorated with a superbly executed La Tène design (Fig. 9.32, 1). It is a glacial erratic of fine-grained granite, 1.68m in maximum length, dressed to a cylindrical shape with a rounded top. The upper part of the stone, for some 68cm, is decorated with a finely carved curvilinear pattern, delimited below by a rather irregularly executed step pattern. Set in the ground, it stands about 1.2m high and it may well have been painted originally. Its shape has led some commentators to suggest that it is a phallic symbol, but it should be noted that rounded and elongated glacial erratics occur naturally in the locality. At first glance, the freehand curvilinear pattern appears to cover the stone in a seamless fashion, but a detailed analysis by Michael Duignan (1976) revealed that the decorative scheme constituted four separate unitary compositions in two broad D-shaped and two narrower triangular panels, a quadripartite arrangement appropriate to a panelled or four-sided pillar. Any attempt to analyse the motifs employed demonstrates the imprecise and often ambiguous terminology common in La Tène art studies, but such detailed examination is necessary if the art of the stone is to be placed in its proper context. Some motifs are readily recognisable and include roundels, a symmetrical triskele, a bird's head, trumpet curves and comma leaves, motifs already encountered on various pieces of metalwork. Comma leaf shapes and trumpet curves are placed at the bottom corners of each panel. Curving-sided triangular shapes are a feature of the background or negative pattern, and in two prominent cases these triangular voids contain a floating comma leaf. More complex curvilinear forms include pelta shapes with one or two spiral ends, and asymmetrical triskeles or swirling shapes whose limbs sometimes terminate in other motifs such as pelta shapes or comma leaves and trumpet curves.

Re-erected in the townland of Bullaun, near Loughrea, Co. Galway, the Turoe stone was discovered at the foot of a low hill in nearby Feerwore townland in the 1850s and taken as a garden ornament to Turoe House, now no more. It may have been displaced from the summit of the hill, where it would have stood not far from the site of the ringfort of Feerwore, which did have a number of other low, rounded and undecorated boulders in its vicinity to the north and north-west. Unfortunately, in the excavation of the ringfort in 1938 no attempt was made to identify the former location of the decorated stone, or to try and determine the relationship of the various stones to the earthwork or to one another. The possibility that this stone once stood on a low hill along with some other undecorated stones is worth bearing in mind, because this was the case at Killycluggin.

The Killycluggin stone (Fig. 9.32, 2) once stood on a low drumlin near Ballyconnell, Co. Cavan, though where precisely is uncertain (Raftery 1978). It had been deliberately broken in the past and only two decorated fragments have been located; the larger had been partly buried on the upper slope of the hill, and the smaller had found its way to the bottom of the drumlin. The larger fragment lay about 10m east of a small circle of at least sixteen stones with a diameter of about 20m. While limited excavation determined that this large fragment was not in primary position, its original location was not identified but, given its size, it probably had not been moved very far. A small excavation in the stone circle was unproductive and the relationship between it and the decorated stone is not clear. The two fragments do not allow an accurate estimate of height to be made but it seems as if the stone was originally cylindrical in shape with a rounded top, the same general shape as the Turoe stone. The carved decoration on the lower part was seemingly in four rectangular panels framed by engraved lines and consisted of tightly coiled spirals linked by curving lines. The rounded top was partly covered by a zone of parallel lines.

The original location of the Castlestrange stone (Fig. 9.32, 3) is unknown. Like the Turoe stone, it too was moved to serve as an estate ornament and now lies near Athleague, Co. Roscommon. It is a squat granite boulder about 90cm high; oval in plan, it has a more or less flat top,

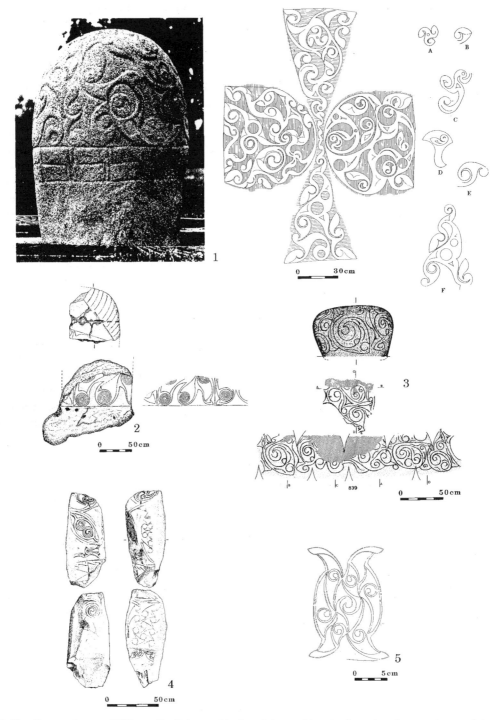

Fig. 9.32—Decorated stones. (1) Turoe, Co. Galway, with plan of the quadripartite decorative scheme and some of the principal motifs employed: (A) symmetrical triskele, (B) trumpet curve with comma leaf, (C) bird's head and asymmetrical triskele, (D) curving-sided triangular shape or void with floating comma leaf, (E) pelta shape with spiral ends, and (F) complex triskele terminating in a pelta shape and comma leaves. (2) Killycluggin, Co. Cavan. (3) Castlestrange, Co. Roscommon. (4) Mullaghmast, Co. Kildare. (5) Derrykeighan, Co. Antrim.

damaged in part, and straight but slightly sloping sides. The flat base is plain and the carved asymmetrical curvilinear decoration appears to cover the rest of the stone without a significant break. Motifs include two triskeles, loose spirals and shallow C-shaped curves.

The Mullaghmast stone (Fig. 9.32, 4) is a fragment of a slender, four-sided schist pillar with a sloping flat top. All surfaces have been damaged; the lower part is missing and what survives is about 90cm in length. It was found built into a castle wall on Mullaghmast hill, Co. Kildare. Decoration is either engraved or carved in relief. The principal motifs include, on the sloping top, a triskele within a circle partly framed by a trumpet curve that springs from a large lentoid motif on one of the sides, which in turn contains two plump spirals with lobed terminals. Another similar spiral survives on the much-damaged opposing side. The two other opposing sides each have similar decoration consisting of a pattern of interlocking C-shaped curves. At least two narrow horizontal panels of mainly rectilinear ornament occurred on the lower parts of the stone. The pattern of interlocking C-shaped curves and the motif of two spirals in a lentoid field are designs found on some artwork of the fifth century AD and later, and though the Mullaghmast stone is not precisely dated it is usually considered a late expression of La Tène art, foreshadowing the more rigid and symmetrical representation of some of its motifs in the repertoire of artists of the early medieval period.

The fifth decorated stone is a fragmentary piece of basalt of rectangular shape found incorporated as a quoin stone in a ruined church at Derrykeighan, Co. Antrim (Fig. 9.32, 5). One of two decorated faces has an engraved curvilinear design, based on a pattern of compass-drawn curves, which has been described as a 'pattern of recurved spirals and broken-back curves . . . symmetrical about the diagonal axes' and which finds a particularly good parallel on one of a number of decorated bone flakes from Loughcrew, Co. Meath. Curving-sided triangular voids, of course, are also a feature of the decorative scheme on the Turoe stone.

Analysis of the decorative motifs on the Turoe stone indicated that its sculptor was familiar with late insular styles of La Tène art on decorated metalwork in Wales, such as a plaque and a shield boss from the votive deposit at Llyn Cerrig Bach, Anglesea, and on several engraved bronze mirrors in southern England, such as Old Warden, Bedfordshire, and Great Chesterford, Essex, dating from the first centuries BC and AD. The recognition that the Turoe stone represents an advanced stage of insular La Tène art was a significant conclusion because the stone was generally considered to have been inspired by some simpler decorated stones on the Continent, notably a number of pillar stones in Brittany, and since large decorated stones of this sort were unknown in Britain, a direct Irish connection with north-western France was a common assumption. It may be that the idea of decorating pillar stones was a Breton fashion, and one that was copied in Ireland, but it seems much more likely that the Turoe stone and various other decorated pillar stones wherever they occur are the scattered lithic survivors of a more widespread timber form. It is unlikely that the intricate symbolism of La Tène art, where some motifs must have been charged with magical meaning, was only expressed in stone and bronze. It is unfortunate that so little is known about the original context of these monuments, but the fact that some of them were probably the targets of early Christian iconoclasts may be another indication of their former significance.

Human sacrifice

Human sacrifice that included the deposition of the body in a watery location, perhaps in a bog pool, seems to have been an Iron Age custom. The young man whose body was found naked in Lindow Moss near Manchester, and who had been killed by a blow to his head, strangled and had his throat cut all in quick succession, is the best-known British example. While the majority of bodies found in Irish bogs are of medieval or later times and are usually clothed (Ó Floinn 1995), a number of naked or near-naked corpses, some showing signs of a violent death, appear to be ritual sacrifices of Iron Age date. A male found in 1821 at Gallagh, near Castleblakeney, Co. Galway, was buried wearing a short leather cloak but was otherwise naked (Fig. 9.33). A pointed wooden stake had been placed on each side of the body; it is reported that there was a 'band of sally rods' around his neck, and these willow rods may have been either the means by which he was strangled or a symbolic torc.

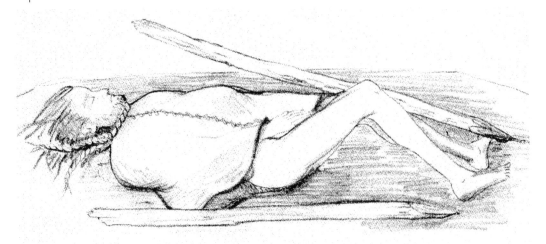

Fig. 9.33—Artist's reconstruction of the sacrificial bog body deposited at Gallagh, near Castleblakeney, Co. Galway. The body was naked but for a short leather cloak, and pointed wooden stakes had been placed on either side.

Radiocarbon dates suggest this deposition occurred in the last few centuries BC.

Part of a body recovered from a bog south-east of Tyrellspass at Oldcroghan, Co. Offaly, represented the arms and torso of a tall adult male whose hands (like those of Lindow Man) showed no sign of manual labour, suggesting special or aristocratic status; he may have been tortured and decapitated before being placed in the bog. Another male body, found in a bog at Clonycavan, near Ballivor, Co. Meath, may also be a person of rank; his hair was bound together in a topknot held in place by a gel made of a pine resin that may have come from northern Spain or southern France. He too had been killed *c.* 200 BC, this time by several blows to the head. It has been argued that deposits such as Gallagh, Oldcroghan and Clonycavan are part of a widespread pattern of metal deposition and ritual sacrifice at boundary locations (Kelly 2006a; 2006b). A distinction should be made, however, between artefact deposits, even of gold, and bloody sacrifices that—in the annihilation of an individual—probably had a more profound significance.

Other sorts of ritual deposits may have been common too. The sixth-century BC deposits of three different kinds of cereals (barley, rye and oats) in the boulder circle at Carrowmore no. 26, Co. Sligo, of animal bones in the passage tomb at Carrowmore no. 3, dated to AD 230–520, or the deposits of charcoal, shellfish and fish remains in the wedge tomb at Altar, Co. Cork, dated to the last few

centuries BC and the early centuries AD, have all provided revealing evidence of organic offerings. The significance of the numerous bone flakes, some decorated with La Tène art, a number of finely made bone combs and other objects found in a passage tomb (cairn H) at Loughcrew, Co. Meath, is uncertain, but they could also have been votive offerings. A series of exotic objects including a hoard of five gold objects comprising two bracelets, two rings and a chain necklace, numerous Roman coins, two Roman disc brooches, a fragment of a torc with some inscribed Roman lettering, and glass beads, all found in front of the passage tomb at Newgrange, are not only evidence of contacts with Roman Britain but have also been considered offerings made to 'the gods of Newgrange' in the early centuries AD (Swift 2003).

Ring-barrow, embanked ring-ditch, ring-ditch

Our limited understanding of the burial customs of late prehistory may be blamed, in part, on limited excavation, but the custom of depositing token cremations and a limited range of grave-goods and the fact, as in earlier times, that only a minority of the population had the privilege of formal burial are also contributing factors. There is good evidence that quite a variety of burial customs were practised, some representing a continuity of funerary tradition from at least the second millennium BC. It is possible to identify half a dozen different types of burial, with various sorts of mound or other

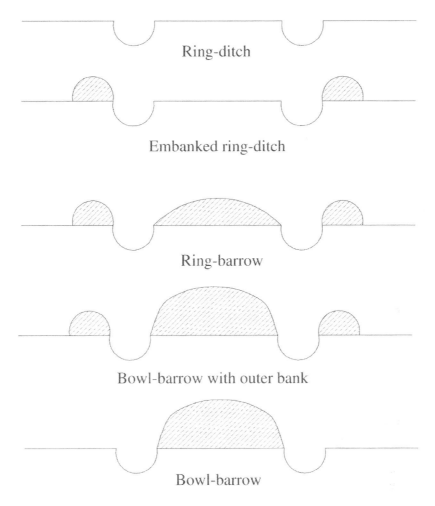

Fig. 9.34—Types of Iron Age burial monuments.

earthwork being used, earlier monuments occasionally reused, and both cremation and unburnt burial being practised; the excavated evidence to the 1970s has been reviewed by Barry Raftery (1981). The five types of funerary monument identified by Conor Newman (1997b) on the Hill of Tara are good illustrations of one aspect of the monumental variety that occurs (Fig. 9.34).

Ring-barrows are circular mounds of earth surrounded by a ditch with an external bank. Mounds are usually quite low and frequently no higher than the surrounding bank. In many cases mounds are so slight as to be almost imperceptible, if there at all, and some monuments appear to consist of ditch and bank enclosing a level area. Here it is questionable whether the term 'barrow' is

appropriate, and a name such as 'embanked ring-ditch' would be more accurate. The principal distinguishing feature of both ring-barrow and embanked ring-ditch is a bank and inner ditch, and in many cases these are annular. Some have an entrance through the bank and a corresponding causeway across the ditch, often on the eastern side; examples with two opposed entrances are also known. A small number of elaborate ring-barrows have multiple banks and ditches (Fig. 9.35). These monuments are widely distributed, but both numbers and distribution are difficult to assess since classification is sometimes problematic and many ring-ditches revealed by aerial photography may be ring-barrows or embanked ring-ditches degraded by ploughing.

They vary in size: a few are very large,

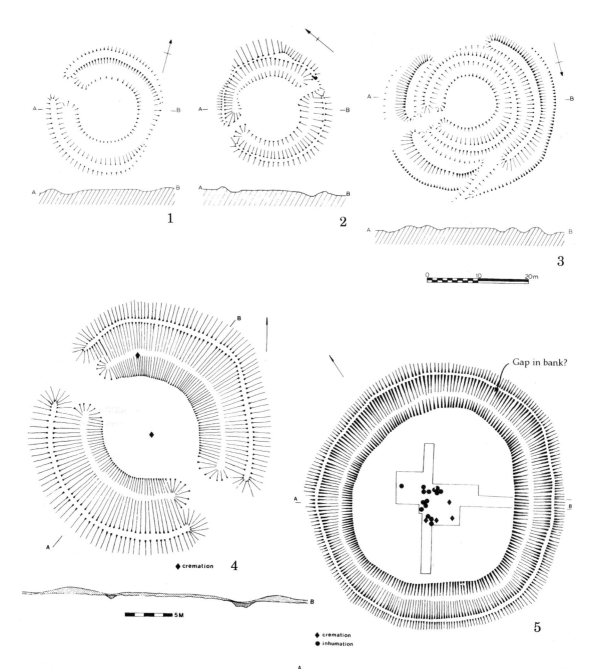

Fig. 9.35—Ring-barrows and embanked ring-ditches. (1) Ring-barrow with an entrance on the west, Tullymore, Co. Donegal. (2) Ring-barrow with opposed entrances, Coumgagh, Co. Kerry. (3) Multivallate ring-barrow with three ditches and two banks, Creevy, Co. Donegal. (4–5) Embanked ring-ditches on Carbury Hill, Co. Kildare.

exceeding 30m in overall diameter. Both the northern and southern Claoinfhearta or 'Sloping Trenches' on the western slopes of the Hill of Tara are exceptionally large examples, 80m and 57m in diameter respectively, and the northern one is the largest mound in that celebrated complex. Most ring-barrows seem to range in overall diameter from about 15m to 25m. A number occur in groups or cemeteries, often along with other monuments; those at Tara, Rathcroghan, Carnfree and the Curragh have already been mentioned. Slieve Breagh, on a hill north-west of Slane, Co. Meath, is another example where an extensive series of earthworks includes at least a dozen ring-barrows (de Paor and Ó h-Eochaidhe 1956).

Ring-barrow excavation has revealed a complicated picture in which cremation is the predominant ritual. Mounds with encircling banks and internal ditches are known from the second millennium BC, if not earlier: Lissard, Co. Limerick, yielded a vase urn and cremation; Carrowlisdooaun, Co. Mayo, contained a cremation, and a flat bronze axehead was found in the ditch; Lemonstown, Co. Wicklow, produced a vessel of the Bowl Tradition; and a pit filled with sand and turves contained a token cremation in a mound at Pubble, Co. Derry (Waddell 1990; Corlett 2005). A ring-barrow at Mullaghmore, Co. Down, probably dates from the Dowris phase, as do some small deposits of cremated bone and fragments of a human skull in a burial mound at Kilmahuddrick, Co. Dublin (Chapter 4). The upper fills of the Kilmahuddrick ditch contained some small deposits of cremated bone radiocarbon-dated to the Iron Age (fourth to second century BC), demonstrating a significant pattern of ritual continuity.

Some other excavated ring-barrows probably date from the end of the first millennium BC or the early centuries AD. A small annular ring-barrow, just over 15m in overall diameter, at Grannagh, near Ardrahan, Co. Galway, was partly investigated in 1916 and completely excavated in 1969. A scattered deposit of cremated human bone, a bead of green glass and the top of a small bone pin were found at the centre, and the deep internal ditch contained several more pockets of cremated bone at various points. Finds included bronze fibulae, multicoloured glass beads, a dumb-bell-shaped glass bead, bone beads, bone pins and iron fragments, mostly from the ditch. A date in the first century BC or the first

century AD seems probable. A smaller ring-barrow at Oran Beg, near Oranmore, Co. Galway, measured 11m in overall diameter with a low bank and shallow internal ditch. A token deposit of cremated bone was found near the centre of the mound and an even smaller deposit of burnt bone was found in the ditch in the north-eastern quadrant. This was accompanied by over 80 tiny glass beads, mainly blue but some yellow, evidently fused together in the cremation pyre, a small fragmentary bronze ring and a small bronze toggle. Excavation of a number of mounds in a barrow cemetery at Carrowjames, south-west of Balla, Co. Mayo, demonstrated that while several were of second-millennium BC date and contained pottery and other finds of the Cordoned Urn Tradition, two of the others, tumuli 4 and 8, the largest in the cemetery, were later ring-barrows. Tumulus 4 had an overall diameter of 21.35m and the very low mound, a thin layer of material from the surrounding ditch, covered three scattered cremations and two small pockets of cremated bone; an earlier burial, which consisted of a token cremation in a bucket-shaped urn, was found beneath the bank. Nothing was found to securely date the burials. Tumulus 8 was a smaller ring-barrow of similar construction with an overall diameter of 15.5m. Some 25 small cremations were found and ten of them were accompanied by small objects such as glass beads, bronze dumb-bell-shaped beads or toggles, and a small bronze ring. One cremation, a substantial deposit in a pit, was accompanied by two small bronze rings and three small bronze studs.

A series of earthworks on the Curragh, Co. Kildare, were excavated in 1944, and one of them, a small ring-barrow 14m across, yielded no finds; only part of the ditch was investigated, however, and it is now clear from more recent excavations that ditches were important locations for burial and other deposits. One possible multivallate ring-barrow was also excavated on the Curragh: a long pit containing the extended skeleton of an adult and covered by a small mound was surrounded by a pair of concentric ditches with diameters of about 12m and 18m respectively, each possibly having an external bank. Unfortunately the burial is undated and the history of this partially excavated site was complicated by the presence of later unburnt burials, which the excavator thought medieval in date. A minimal mound, consisting of no more than a thin spread of redeposited material in the central area, is a feature of some ring-barrows with low profiles such as tumulus 8 at Carrowjames, Co. Mayo, and this tendency finds its most extreme expression in the related embanked ring-ditches, which have internal ditches but no trace of a central raised area at all. Two were excavated on Carbury Hill, Co. Kildare (Fig. 9.35). One, 26m in overall diameter, had opposed entrances with causeways on the north-west and south-east. The central area and the ditch were fully excavated; a small pocket of cremated bone was found in the centre in a small hollow in the bedrock below the humus, a fragment of fused blue glass was found nearby, and a second deposit of burnt bone was found in the ditch on the north just 10cm above its base. A small handled spoon made of jet was an intriguing find on the site, though exactly where it was discovered is not recorded; it has been compared to late Roman silver spoons of about AD 400. The second was exceptionally large, with an overall diameter of over 51m. It was only partially excavated and a mix of burials was revealed in the central area. Four cremations were found, two of them apparently disturbed by later unburnt burials. One of the cremated deposits was accompanied by two small iron rings and a pin-shaped fragment. There were also fifteen unburnt burials, three disturbed by other later interments. All the undisturbed burials were extended with heads to the south-west, and one, an adult male, was accompanied by iron shears, an implement not easily dated.

Three embanked ring-ditches were partly excavated on the Curragh. One, situated on the highest point in the area, was about 45m in overall diameter with an entrance on the west; a second, about 35m in overall diameter with entrances on the east and west, enclosed the unburnt burial of an adult female in a central pit which was believed to be an instance of burial alive; and the third, over 28m in diameter, had one entrance on the south-west. None produced any dating evidence.

A number of ring-ditches are late prehistoric in date and, whether they once had low external banks or not, they are evidently a related phenomenon. A small penannular example with an external diameter of 7m at Ballybronoge South, near Patrickswell, Co. Limerick, contained fourteen deposits of burnt human bone and some animal bone in the ditch; a spiral bronze ring and a fragment of decorated bone

were also found (Eogan and Finn 2000). At the Rath of the Synods at Tara, the first phase of funerary activity included an oval ring-ditch and a low ring-barrow to the north-west; the latter contained five primary cremations, and several more burials were added later. A small cemetery of four ring-ditches was excavated by Valerie Keeley (1996; 1999) during the construction of a bypass at Ballydavis, near Portlaoise, Co. Laois. The largest (site 1) was 16m in diameter with an entrance on the east. A central burial deposit consisted of a cremation, a small cylindrical bronze box with an iron mount on the lid decorated with red enamel, a bronze fibula of Nauheim type, bronze wire and over 80 stone and glass beads. The ditch produced an iron blade, nails, part of a bronze bracelet and pin, evidence of iron-working and cremated bone, all of which seemed to represent several phases of activity. A smaller ring-ditch (site 2) some 40m to the east measured 8m in diameter and had one entrance on the south-east; an iron blade and a fragment of bronze were found in the ditch, and one of a number of shallow pits nearby contained a bronze fibula. Two further ring-ditches (sites 3 and 4) were each 6m in diameter; one was annular and its ditch contained charcoal, burnt bones, four glass beads and some decorated pieces of bone, while the other had an entrance on the north-west and the ditch fill contained charcoal. The bronze box is a particularly interesting discovery because it recalls a small decorated bronze box found in a chariot grave at Wetwang Slack, Yorkshire, and since the burial of a dismantled chariot is a relatively rare indication of high status in north-eastern England, it suggests that a small cremation in a modest ring-ditch might nonetheless be a high-status burial. This may also be the case at Rath, near Ashbourne, Co. Meath, where a small cemetery of three ring-ditches has been excavated (Schweitzer 2005). In one, several deposits of cremated bone in the ditch were followed by the insertion of a crouched unburnt skeleton (possibly female) into the backfilled ditch; three bronze toe-rings were found at the feet and, judging from finds in Britain, such items may be Iron Age status symbols too.

The evidence, limited though it is, from circular ring-barrow and embanked ring-ditch indicates one funerary pattern in the later centuries BC and early centuries AD that involved cremation and the occasional deposition of small or token deposits of bone, sometimes accompanied by small but significant items of glass or bronze. Burial mounds with ditch or with ditch and outer bank and of a more substantial nature than low-profile ring-barrows were also built: a 2m-high circular mound with ditch at Cush, Co. Limerick, covered a central pit containing a cremation and a decorated bone plaque, and a large example of one of these barrows at Rathdoony Beg, near Ballymote, Co. Sligo, had an encircling ditch with external bank; partial excavation dated it to the Iron Age (Mount 1999).

The occasional use of earlier monuments occurs. The mound of a passage tomb at Kiltierney, Co. Fermanagh, was modified in the first century BC or the first century AD, when a shallow ditch was dug around it, the mound was enlarged and nineteen small mounds, each about 3m in diameter and 1m high, were built around the edge of the monument just outside the ditch, forming, in effect, a discontinuous outer bank in ring-barrow fashion. Some cremated burials were placed in shallow pits in the augmented original mound, and one was accompanied by a fine leaf-bow fibula (Fig. 8.21, 5) and four glass beads. Some cremated bone was also found beneath some of the small satellite mounds, and one produced a cremation, an iron fibula and burnt fragments of decorated bronze, possibly part of a mirror handle. This cremation, like the deposit of burnt bone found in a bronze bowl in a pit at Fore, Co. Westmeath, was presumably the burial of someone of importance. The presence of small deposits of cremated bone without grave-goods at Kiltierney, for instance, also raises the question of whether such a simple ritual was a widespread fashion in later prehistory and hitherto unrecognised in the absence of radiocarbon dating. Some simple deposits of cremated bone in a cairn-like structure at Ballymacaward, near Ballyshannon, Co. Donegal, have been dated to the Iron Age (E. O'Brien 1999). An earlier mound was reused at Carrowbeg North, Co. Galway, where a small mound of earth and stone covering a cremation and bronze razor of the early second millennium was surrounded by a broad ditch about 1.2m deep. Four unburnt burials, of three adult females and one adult male, were inserted into the northern part of the ditch. Three were extended and one was flexed. One of the female burials, the flexed skeleton, was accompanied by eleven bone beads, a small bone toggle and a small bronze locket-like object, probably an amulet; none of these objects are

precisely datable but the excavator cited Roman parallels for the amulet.

As we have seen, both crouched and extended unburnt burial is recorded. It is believed that the reappearance of the rite of crouched burial reflects the influence of contacts with Roman Britain from the first century BC onwards (E. O'Brien 2003). Crouched burials at sites such as the Rath of the Synods and on Lambay Island, Co. Dublin, are amongst the earliest manifestations of this particular ritual. One of two crouched unburnt burials in a cemetery of extended burials at Betaghstown, Co. Meath, was accompanied by two iron penannular brooches of the first century BC or slightly later, an iron belt buckle and a bronze disc. A series of unburnt burials, most of them crouched or flexed, have been found in the vicinity of the great mound at Knowth, Co. Meath, and a number of them were accompanied by necklaces or armlets of glass beads. Extended unburnt burials with varying orientations probably emulate the custom in Roman Britain from the second century AD. This form of burial with an east–west orientation has been dated to between the fourth and sixth centuries AD, and the practice of using 'long stone cists' or—more precisely—long, parallel-sided, slab-lined graves containing extended skeletons without grave-goods emerges in the fifth century.

There is also significant evidence for funerary continuity from Iron Age to early medieval times. Continuity of burial practice has been identified, for instance, at Glebe South, near Balrothery in north Co. Dublin, where Iron Age cremations in two ring-ditches (some cremations dated to the period 300 BC to AD 400) were followed by unburnt extended burials, one radiocarbon-dated to AD 430–640 (Carroll *et al.* 2008). A small ring-ditch at Ardsallagh, near Navan, Co. Meath, produced some cremated bone of the first to third centuries AD and this activity was followed by the interment of some 30 extended unburnt burials of the fourth to seventh centuries (Clarke and Carlin 2009). Elizabeth O'Brien (2009) suggests that while extended burials at sites such as these may have been those of Christians, religious affiliation may have been of secondary importance in the face of a need to assert a connection with the past and to make a political statement giving emphasis to dynastic continuity, whether real or contrived.

10

PROTOHISTORY

'THE PEOPLE OF THE FERTILE EARTH'

The literate world encroaches slowly on late prehistoric Ireland. It would be agreeable if early historical sources added a new dimension to our understanding of the later centuries BC and the early first millennium AD, but this is not the case. The earliest references to places and people are tantalisingly brief (Freeman 2001). Fragments of an account of a voyage to the Atlantic from the Greek colony of Massalia are preserved. Known as the Massaliote Periplus, this was a sea journey from present day Marseilles, through the straits of Gibraltar into the 'Outer Sea' and along the coasts of western Europe; it may have been written shortly before 500 BC but survives only in part in the *Ora Maritima* of Rufius Festus Avienus of the late fourth century AD. This Periplus or manual for navigators recorded the existence of the islands of *Ierne* and *Albion*, Greek forms of the earliest known names of Ireland and Britain. The name *Ierne* (or *Iverni*) may be an ethnic name meaning the 'people of the fertile earth' (Koch 1986).

About 325 BC, another voyager, Pytheas of Massalia, whose account is also known only at second hand in later works, simply refers to both islands as the *Pretanic* islands, a name later rendered as *Britanni* and the earliest usage of the term 'the British isles'. Early in the first century AD, Philemon recorded from merchants that the length of the island of Ireland was twenty days' journey, a reasonably accurate estimation if an average daily journey of 21 miles (33km) is accepted. Philemon was probably one of the sources for Ptolemy's

Geography, compiled in Alexandria in the second century AD. This is a list of placenames (including settlement, headland, island and river names) and tribal names, given with their longitude and latitude. From this information it is possible to reconstruct Ptolemy's map, which is the oldest documentary account of this island (Fig. 10.1). Some names are inaccurate, a few are readily identifiable and scholars disagree about many others. In fact there is a measure of scholarly agreement on the identification of only nine of the 47 names recorded by Ptolemy (Toner 2000). *Buvinda* is the River Boyne, *Senos* the Shannon, *Oboca* may be the River Liffey, and the name *Regia*, which occurs twice, may refer to royal sites. It has been suggested that *Isamnion*, though shown as a promontory, may be a reference to Emhain Mhacha or Navan Fort, but it may refer to the Cooley peninsula. Some tribal names, such as the *Manapii* and the *Brigantes*, are also found in Britain.

References by Roman writers are for the most part less than helpful, as they almost invariably reflect the common view of the barbarian world as a savage and inhospitable place. Tacitus is an exception; in the late first century AD he wrote that Ireland 'is small in comparison with Britain, but larger than the islands of the Mediterranean. In soil and climate, and in the character and civilization of its inhabitants, it is much like Britain; and its approaches and harbours have now become better known from merchants who trade there. An Irish prince, expelled from his home by a rebellion, was welcomed by Agricola, who detained him, nominally as a friend, in the hope of being able to

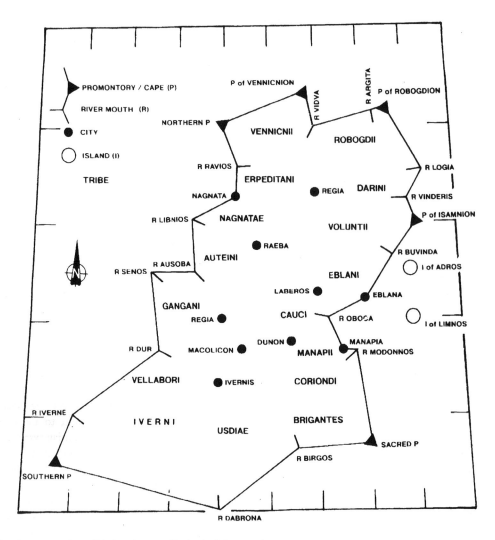

Fig. 10.1—A reconstruction of Ptolemy's map of Ireland of the second century AD.

make use of him. I have often heard Agricola say that Ireland could be reduced and held by a single legion with a fair-sized force of auxiliaries . . .'. Freeman points out that the nameless *regulus* (petty king or chieftain) noted by Tacitus in the retinue of Agricola is the first Irish individual mentioned in classical literature.

Though the first-century AD references to merchants and traders are interesting, they are not very illuminating, and the nature and degree of Ireland's contact with the Roman world at this time are obscure and the subject of continuing debate. In the nineteenth and early twentieth centuries it was claimed that there may have been a Roman invasion of Ireland, and various finds of Roman

material seemed to lend some support to this hypothesis (Raftery 1994a). Not all Roman objects, however, are ancient imports and this material spans several centuries in date. Coins are the commonest item reported; these and other finds have been reviewed by Donal Bateson (1973; 1976), who has concluded that most Roman coins found in Ireland (some 80%) were probably imported in relatively recent times, in the eighteenth or nineteenth century or even later. A number of coin finds and other discoveries may be accepted as genuine when the circumstances of their discovery seem plausible or when they have been found with other objects or unearthed in an archaeological excavation. This authentic material seems to fall into two major groups, one belonging to the first and second centuries AD, and the other mainly to the fourth and early fifth centuries AD. The acceptable numismatic evidence also includes two large hoards of silver coins of the second century AD. One, found in 1827 at Flower Hill, near Bushmills, Co. Antrim, comprised 300 silver coins; the other, found on Feigh Mountain, near the Giant's Causeway, may have contained 500 silver coins.

Other genuine finds of material of Roman date include the objects found at Freestone Hill and Newgrange. The excavations at Freestone Hill (Chapter 7) produced a fourth-century copper coin of Constantine the Great, two late Roman toilet implements (variously described as nail cleaners or ear scoops) and bracelet fragments. These objects have been interpreted as cult offerings at a small rural shrine set within an earlier late Bronze Age hillfort and using an older burial mound as its focus. The numerous items from Newgrange included disc brooches, rings, gold coins and a hoard of five gold objects found in 1842 that consisted of two finger-rings, two spiral-twisted bracelets and a gold chain. The coins range in date from the first to the late fourth century AD, but most of the objects belong to the latter century. Because of its location near the entrance to the passage tomb, the hoard and the significant number of other finds may be votive deposits perhaps connected with a cult of the Celtic god Nodens or Nuadu, as Ó Floinn has argued (2000; 2001). An oculist's stamp found in 1842 in Golden, Co. Tipperary, may be another offering, this time associated with a well with curative powers; the small slate tablet bears a Latin inscription about an eye ointment, and these stamps were used to impress details of the concoction on sticks of eye salve (Daffy 2002). A tiny sherd of Roman pottery found near a holy well at Randalstown, Co. Meath, and a bronze bracelet from another well at nearby Phoenixtown may represent similar offerings at a sacred spring (Kelly 2002).

A large hoard of Roman silver found in 1854 west of Coleraine at Ballinrees, Co. Derry, contained over 1,500 coins and over 5kg of silver bars, ingots, fragments of plate, a bowl, a mount, scabbard bridge, buckle and two spoons. The coin evidence indicated that this hoard probably dates from AD 407–11. A smaller hoard of broadly similar date was found in a gravel pit at Balline, near

Knocklong, Co. Limerick, in 1940; it comprised four silver ingots and three pieces of cut silver plate and was presumed to have been looted in Britain in the early fifth century (Ó Ríordáin 1947). What precipitated the concealment of other deposits of Roman material elsewhere is not clear, but most have usually been considered the property of traders or the booty of raiders or pirates, hidden for safekeeping and never recovered. Stray finds are even more difficult to interpret: the Roman fibula found with the Annesborough, Co. Armagh, hoard of late second-millennium BC bronzes (Fig. 6.8) may be a casual loss and an accidental association with earlier material, or it may be a late dedicatory offering when that find was reburied. Small objects like this, though not common, are widely distributed. Roman fibulae have been found in sandhills at Ballyness and Dunfanaghy, Co. Donegal, 'near Galway' and near Bantry, Co. Cork. Toilet implements, such as nail cleaners and probes, also come from Ballyness and from Dooey, Co. Donegal, and a bronze patera or ladle has been found on Rathlin Island. Coastal finds of this sort could well denote the use of local landing or beaching spots as part of a network of coastal trading places. At first glance, this might also seem to be a reasonable explanation for a sherd of Samian ware excavated at a site in the Dundrum sandhills, Co. Down, but numerous fragments of souterrain pottery of the early medieval period were also found there; this Roman potsherd and a number of others from various locations in Ireland may be imports of the late first millennium AD or later, acquired as relics, for grinding down for pigments, for medicinal usage or for some other purpose. Indeed, the Dundrum fragment seemed to have been neatly squared as if it had been shaped as a decorative inlay (Collins 1959a). Roman pottery fragments from demonstrably early archaeological contexts are, however, probably genuine imports. Fragments of Roman pottery from Knowth, a bronze toilet implement and the unburnt burials there attributed to Roman influence may all be related. Clogher, Co. Tyrone, occupied in the Dowris phase and a major royal settlement in the early medieval period, was also a defended enclosure at some time prior to AD 400, this occupation perhaps associated with a first-century AD Romano-British brooch and potsherds. Some Roman material, including pottery, a lead seal, glass ware and an iron barrel

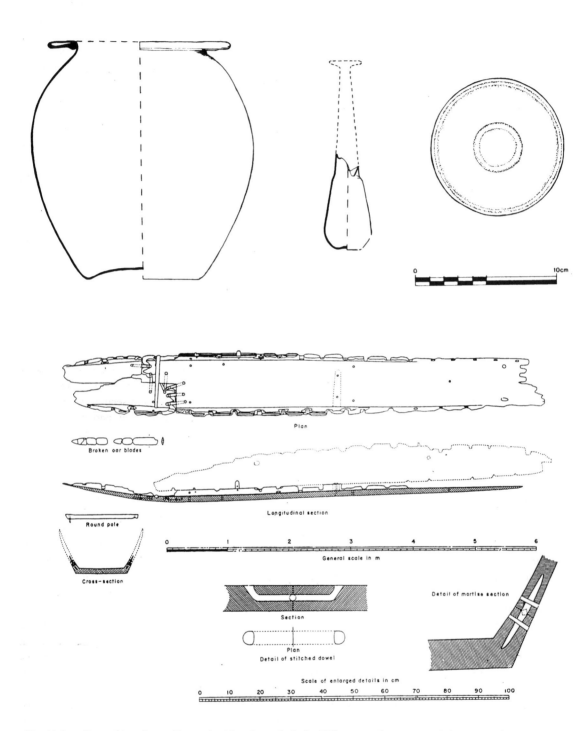

Fig. 10.2—Above: objects from a Roman burial at Stoneyford, Co. Kilkenny; a glass urn containing a cremation was accompanied by a circular bronze mirror and a small glass phial. Below: the remains of a carvel-built wooden boat from Lough Lene, Co. Westmeath.

padlock, come from the Rath of the Synods at Tara, and bronze fibulae were found at Knockaulin, Co. Kildare. The so-called doorknob-type spearbutts (Chapter 7) also imply contact with Scotland and England in the fourth or fifth century AD.

A number of discoveries suggest especially close contact with Roman Britain, and the most important of these is a remarkable cremation found at Stoneyford, Co. Kilkenny, in the nineteenth century (Bourke 1989). It was reportedly found in a 'rath' (a term which could have been applied at the time to either a ringfort or a mound) and protected by stones. It consisted of a cremation in a glass urn accompanied by a small bronze mirror and a glass phial, perhaps for cosmetics (Fig. 10.2). This sort of burial was typical of the Roman middle class in the first century AD and suggests the presence of a Roman individual, possibly a woman, or even a Roman community in the valley of the King's River, a tributary of the Nore, just west of Thomastown. It may be noteworthy that the Nore was possibly navigable from Waterford to this point. The identification of the remains of a wooden boat in Lough Lene, Co. Westmeath, is an important indication of the role inland waterways played in trade and communications (Fig. 10.2). This was a slender, flat-bottomed craft over 8m long, in part constructed in a Roman technique in which each oak plank or strake is carvel-built, with timbers placed edge to edge, joined with mortise and tenon and held together with wooden pegs; the tenons were of yew and the oak parts of the 1m-wide bottom portion were stitched together by wooden withies inserted into drilled holes. Fragments of two oar blades were also found (Brindley and Lanting 1990b; 1991; Ó hEailidhe 1992).

If the Stoneyford burial was that of a woman, it must recall the possible female cremation and glass beads and other objects found at Loughey, near Donaghadee, Co. Down. The evidence here is less than satisfactory, and whether possible Roman women mean possible Roman communities is difficult to know. A series of burials found in 1835 on Bray Head, Co. Wicklow, are also poorly documented, but it has been suggested that they too could have been the remains of such a community. A small cemetery consisted of a number of extended unburnt skeletons, each with a stone at their head and feet; copper coins of Trajan (AD 97–117) and Hadrian (AD 117–138) were found,

and had perhaps been placed in the mouths of the corpses in the Roman manner as payment for the ferryman Charon on the final journey across the River Acheron to the land of the dead. Finally, another group of burials was found on Lambay Island off the north Dublin coast in 1927 and, unfortunately, was equally poorly recorded. A number of crouched unburnt skeletons were apparently accompanied by a range of grave-goods. Five Romano-British brooches of first- and second-century AD date are preserved, and one grave contained the remains of an iron sword and a cup-shaped bronze object of uncertain purpose, possibly a shield boss. Other objects included bronze scabbard mounts, a bronze bracelet, a bronze finger-ring, an iron mirror, a beaded collar or torc, a decorated bronze disc and a triangular bronze mount. The collar is a well-known northern British type and the triangular mount has close parallels in Wales, and it is evident that the Lambay folk had close contacts with these parts of Britain. There is, of course, nothing to confirm the often-expressed belief that these people were refugees. The Lambay material is part of a larger body of evidence testifying to a pattern of significant contact across the Irish Sea in the first and second centuries AD, and the people buried there and at Bray may equally well have been members of settled coastal communities.

The discovery of Roman pottery, coins and other material in a large coastal promontory fort at Drumanagh, near the village of Loughshinny in north County Dublin, suggests that this site may have been an important settlement of the period and one which figured prominently in the trading networks of the time. But the economic significance of a site like this is impossible to gauge without excavation. Some of the finds from Lambay Island, just 6km south-east of Drumanagh, are a useful reminder that contacts across the Irish Sea were also contacts with native, non-Roman, communities in Britain who, in some instances, may have been intermediaries in the transmission of Roman goods. There may well have been Romano-British traders in Ireland, and some Irish people may have travelled to late Roman Britain. Richard Warner (1995) has speculated that some of the Roman material found in Ireland may be best explained by one or more military intrusions, perhaps on occasion by mixed forces of Romanised

Irish and Romano-British adventurers, in the first or second century AD. This is by no means impossible; there were, after all, Irish raids on Britain a century or two later. The implications of Roman finds in Ireland will continue to be debated, and they will no doubt be variously attributed to settlers, traders, invaders, refugees, freebooters and others. Indeed, a single explanation is unlikely, and many or all of these factors may have been involved. While some of the later material of the fourth and fifth centuries (such as the Balline hoard) may have been the ill-gotten gains of looters, some objects may reflect trading contacts and others might even be attributable to early Christian missionaries. Located as it was beyond the limits of the western Empire, Ireland's relationship with the Roman world was undoubtedly complex and the surviving evidence presents real interpretative difficulties. There is, however, a growing body of evidence to suggest that a process of 'Romanisation' was under way in some eastern parts of the island at least. While this is a term that is much debated, it has come to have a particular meaning in an Irish context. Coined at a time when a colonialist perspective dominated Roman studies, it reflects a belief in the civilising role of Rome and casts indigenous peoples as passive recipients of Roman influences. Now there is a growing understanding of the complexity of the interaction between the two (Scott 2003). In Ireland, post-colonial theory is an especially blunt and problematic tool in most areas of study of the intricate interrelationship between this island and Britain. In these crucial early centuries AD, the Hiberno-Roman engagement was much more than a one-sided process of acculturation involving the adoption by local élites of various Roman fashions, for instance.

A body of evidence, including the material from the Rath of the Synods on Tara and the promontory fort at Drumanagh, suggests that Meath and north Dublin may be a particularly good illustration of a region where the nature of this process of engagement can be clarified. Raffin, Co. Meath, lies about 20km north of Tara and, as we have seen, its Iron Age circular enclosure, some 65m in diameter with its bank and internal ditch, was a miniature version of the great internally ditched ceremonial enclosures at Tara and Navan (Chapter 9). In use between the third and fifth centuries AD, at a time when the roles of some of the great royal

centres were in decline, it may represent not just a miniature local version of that phenomenon but an alternative new order. Conor Newman (1998) has argued that the wealth of Roman Britain offered new opportunities for the acquisition of wealth and status through commerce or theft. The emergence of a new wealthy stratum in society may then have altered the established power structures and produced a multiplicity of smaller élite centres like Raffin that mimicked older architectural forms. These new élites may have had other interests as well. Raffin is situated in the catchment of the River Blackwater, a tributary of the Boyne, an area with a significant concentration of Roman material and fringed on the north-east by a number of ogham stones (Newman 2005). In imitation of Roman memorial stones, these ogham-inscribed monuments probably served a dual purpose, commemorating the dead and demarcating boundaries associated with them. The origins of the ogham script lie in the Roman grammatical tradition, and while it may have been invented by an Irish person training with a Roman grammarian in Britain or Gaul, Newman suggests that the coincidence in distribution of Roman and Hiberno-Roman material culture in the Meath area raises the possibility that it originated here in the fourth and fifth centuries.

The phrase 'Hiberno-Roman material culture', like the word 'engagement' used here, encapsulates an intriguing and imperfectly understood problem. The Hiberno-Roman encounter was reciprocal, and there is a range of material in both Ireland and England that testifies to this and to the likelihood of complementary schools of metal-workers on either side of the Irish Sea. The earliest form of a well-known early medieval brooch is derived from a smaller Roman type; this penannular brooch type dates from approximately AD 450–550 and is found in Britain, where some 30 examples are known, and some twenty are recorded in Ireland (Fig. 10.3). There is an eastern distributional bias in the Irish finds and there are two concentrations in Britain, one in Scotland, the other in the lower Severn region. This general pattern is also to be seen in the distribution of certain dress-pin types. Raghnall Ó Floinn (2001) believes that this indicates the adoption in Ireland of Romano-British forms of dress and—since the brooches were probably items of female wear—

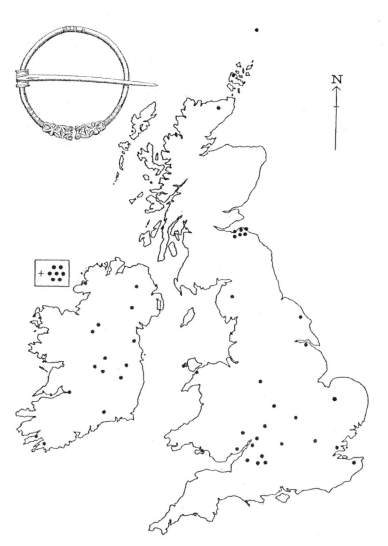

Fig. 10.3—General distribution of Hiberno-Roman penannular brooches.

perhaps intermarriage with southern British women. A small series of silver disc-headed and other pins are finely decorated with a range of geometric motifs, including spirals, triangles and star-shaped motifs with echoes of vegetal ornament, and are examples of a 'Military Style' of decoration transmitted along the borders of the provincial Roman north-west by the movement of soldiers. This distinctive style is to be found on some of the silver objects in the Ballinrees hoard, and these high-status pins are another example of the emulation of late Roman fashion by insular élites in the later fourth and fifth centuries (Gavin and Newman 2007).

The fourth- and fifth-century evidence in particular implies significant interplay with Britain and, as Richard Warner (1995) has said, 'the changes of the 4th century were altogether too pervasive and too long-lasting to be explained by trivial contacts'. Modern scholarship demonstrates that the claim that Ireland was different and remained aloof from significant contact with the Roman world can no longer be sustained. The innovations at this time in material culture, social custom and language are the precursors of other more profound and long-lasting changes that would reshape landscape and people.

Bibliography

Addyman, P.V. 1965 Coney Island, Lough Neagh: prehistoric settlement, Anglo-Norman castle and Elizabethan fortress. *Ulster Journal of Archaeology* **28**, 78–101.

Addyman, P.V. and Vernon, P.D. 1966 A beach pebble industry from Dunaff Bay, Inishowen, Co. Donegal. *Ulster Journal of Archaeology* **29**, 6–15.

Aitchison, N.B. 1987 The Ulster Cycle: heroic image and historical reality. *Journal of Medieval History* **13**, 87–116.

Aitchison, N.B. 1993 The Dorsey: a reinterpretation of an Iron Age enclosure in south Armagh. *Proceedings of the Prehistoric Society* **59**, 285–301.

Almagro, M. 1966 *Las estelas decoradas del suroeste peninsular.* Madrid.

ApSimon, A. 1969a An earlier Neolithic house in Co. Tyrone. *Journal of the Royal Society of Antiquaries of Ireland* **99**, 165–8.

ApSimon, A. 1969b The earlier Bronze Age in the north of Ireland. *Ulster Journal of Archaeology* **32**, 28–72.

ApSimon, A. 1976 Ballynagilly and the beginning and end of the Irish Neolithic. In S. J. de Laet (ed.), *Acculturation and continuity in Atlantic Europe mainly during the Neolithic period and the Bronze Age*, 15–30. Dissertationes Archaeologicae Gandensis. Bruges.

ApSimon, A. 1997 Wood into stone: origins for Irish megalithic tombs? In A. Rodríguez Casal (ed.), *O Neolítico Atlántico e as orixes do megalitismo. Actas do Coloquio Internacional (Santiago de Compostela, 1–6 de Abril de 1996),* 129–40. Santiago de Compostela.

Armit, I. 1991 The Atlantic Scottish Iron Age: five levels of chronology. *Proceedings of the Society of Antiquaries of Scotland* **121**, 181–214.

Armit, I. 2007 Social landscapes and identities in the Irish Iron Age. In C. Haselgrove and T. Moore (eds), *The later Iron Age in Britain and beyond*, 130–9. Oxford.

Armstrong, E.C.R. 1917 Some associated finds of bronze celts discovered in Ireland. *Proceedings of the Royal Irish Academy* **33**C, 511–26.

Armstrong, E.C.R. 1933 *Guide to the collection of Irish antiquities. Catalogue of Irish gold ornaments in the collection of the Royal Irish Academy* (2nd edn). Dublin.

Avery, M. 1997 The patterns of the Broighter torc. *Journal of Irish Archaeology* **8**, 73–89.

Baillie, M.G.L. 1982 *Tree-ring dating and archaeology.* Chicago.

Baillie, M.G.L. and Brown, D.M. 2002 Oak dendrochronology: some recent archaeological developments from an Irish perspective. *Antiquity* **76**, 497–505.

Bamforth, D.B. 2006 A microwear analysis of selected artifacts. In P. C. Woodman, N. Finlay and E. Anderson, *The archaeology of a collection: the Keiller–Knowles collection of the National Museum of Ireland*, 221–38. Dublin.

Barber, M. 2003 *Bronze and the Bronze Age. Metalwork and society in Britain c. 2500–800 BC.* Stroud.

Barrett, J.C. 1981 Aspects of the Iron Age in Atlantic Scotland. A case study in the problems of archaeological interpretation. *Proceedings of the*

Society of Antiquaries of Scotland **111**, 205–19.

Barry, T.B. 1981 Archaeological excavations at Dunbeg promontory fort, County Kerry. *Proceedings of the Royal Irish Academy* **81**C, 295–329.

Bateson, J.D. 1973 Roman material from Ireland: a re-consideration. *Proceedings of the Royal Irish Academy* **73**C, 21–97.

Bateson, J.D. 1976 Further finds of Roman material from Ireland. Colloquium on Hiberno-Roman relations and material remains. *Proceedings of the Royal Irish Academy* **76**C, 171–80.

Bayley, D. 2006 Newtownbalregan. In I. Bennett (ed.), *Excavations 2003*, 342. Bray.

Bayliss, A. and Woodman, P. 2009 A new Bayesian chronology for Mesolithic occupation at Mount Sandel, Northern Ireland. *Proceedings of the Prehistoric Society* **75**, 101–23.

Beckett, J. 2005 Selective burial in Irish megalithic tombs: burial practice, age, sex and representation in the Neolithic. In S. R. Zakrzewski and M. Clegg (eds), *Proceedings of the Fifth Annual Conference of the British Association for Biological Anthropology and Osteoarchaeology*, 31–9. British Archaeological Reports, International Series 1383. Oxford.

Beckett, J. and Robb, J. 2006 Neolithic burial taphonomy, ritual, and interpretation in Britain and Ireland. In R. Gowland and C. Knüsel (eds), *Social archaeology of funerary remains*, 57–80. Oxford.

Bengtsson, H. and Bergh, S. 1984 The hut sites at Knocknarea North, Co. Sligo. In G. Burenhult (ed.), *The archaeology of Carrowmore*, 216–318. Stockholm.

Bergh, S. 1995 *Landscape of the monuments. A study of the passage tombs in the Cúil Irra region, Co. Sligo, Ireland.* Stockholm.

Bergh, S. 1997 Design as message. Role and symbolism of Irish passage tombs. In A. Rodríguez Casal (ed.), *O Neolítico Atlántico e as orixes do megalitismo. Actas do Coloquio Internacional (Santiago de Compostela, 1–6 de Abril de 1996)*, 141–50. Santiago de Compostela.

Bergh, S. 2000 Transforming Knocknarea—the archaeology of a mountain. *Archaeology Ireland* **52** (2),14–18.

Bergh, S. 2002 Knocknarea: the ultimate monument. Megaliths and mountains in Neolithic Cúil Irra, north-west Ireland. In C. Scarre (ed.), *Monuments and landscape in Atlantic Europe. Perception and society during the Neolithic and Bronze Age*, 139–51. London.

Bergh, S. 2006 Mullaghfarna. In I. Bennett (ed.), *Excavations 2003*, 445–6. Bray.

Bhreathnach, E. (ed.) 2005 *The kingship and landscape of Tara.* Dublin.

Bhreathnach, E. and Newman, C. 1995 *Tara.* Dublin.

Bolger, T. 2003 Site 12, Rathmullan. In I. Bennett (ed.), *Excavations 2001*, 326–7. Bray.

Boreland, D. 1996 Late Bronze Age pottery from Haughey's Fort. *Emania* **14**, 21–8.

Borlase, W.C. 1897 *The dolmens of Ireland.* London.

Bourke, C. 1993 Antiquities from the River Blackwater II: Iron Age metalwork. *Ulster Journal of Archaeology* **56**, 109–13.

Bourke, E. 1989 Stoneyford: a first-century Roman burial from Ireland. *Archaeology Ireland* **3** (2), 56–7.

Bourke, L. 2001 *Crossing the Rubicon. Bronze Age metalwork from Irish rivers.* Galway.

Bowman, S. and Needham, S. 2007 The Dunaverney and Little Thetford flesh-hooks: history, technology and their position within the later Bronze Age Atlantic zone feasting complex. *Antiquaries Journal* **87**, 53–108.

Bradley, J. 1999 Excavations at Moynagh Lough, Co. Meath, 1997–98. *Ríocht na Midhe* **10**, 1–17.

Bradley, J. 2004 Moynagh Lough, Co. Meath, in the late Bronze Age. In H. Roche, E. Grogan, J. Bradley, J. Coles and B. Raftery (eds), *From megaliths to metals. Essays in honour of George Eogan*, 91–8. Oxford.

Bradley, R. 1990 *The passage of arms. An archaeological analysis of prehistoric hoards and votive deposits.* Cambridge.

Bradley, R. 1993 *Altering the earth. The origins of monuments in Britain and Continental Europe.* Edinburgh.

Bradley, R. 1997 *Rock art and the prehistory of Atlantic Europe.* London.

Bradley, R. 1998a *The significance of monuments: on the shaping of human experience in Neolithic and Bronze Age Europe.* London.

Bradley, R. 1998b Stone circles and passage graves—a contested relationship. In A. Gibson and D. Simpson (eds), *Prehistoric ritual and religion. Essays in honour of Aubrey Burl*, 2–13.

Stroud.

Brennan, J., Briggs, C.S. and ApSimon, A.M. 1978 A giant beaker from Cluntyganny townland, County Tyrone. *Ulster Journal of Archaeology* **41**, 33–6.

Bridgford, S.D. 1997 Mightier than the pen? (an edgewise look at Irish Bronze Age swords). In J. Carman (ed.), *Material harm. Archaeological studies of war and violence*, 95–115. Glasgow.

Briggs, C.S. 1987 Buckets and cauldrons in the late Bronze Age of north-west Europe: a review. In J. C. Blanchet (ed.), *Les relations entre le Continent et les Iles Britanniques à l'Age du Bronze*, 161–87. Amiens.

Briggs, C.S. 2001 The past and future of Irish implement petrography. *Ulster Journal of Archaeology* **60**, 32–46.

Briggs, C.S. 2009 Erratics and re-cycled stone: scholarly irrelevancies or fundamental utilities to lithic studies in prehistoric Britain and beyond? *Internet Archaeology* **26** (http://intarch.ac.uk/journal/issue26/briggs_index.html).

Brindley, A.L. 1999 Irish Grooved Ware. In R. Cleal and A. MacSween (eds), *Grooved Ware in Britain and Ireland*, 23–35. Oxford.

Brindley, A.L. 2001 Tomorrow is another date: some radiocarbon dates for Irish bronze artefacts. In W. H. Metz, B. L. van Beek and H. Steegstra (eds), *Patina. Essays presented to Jay Jordan Butler on the occasion of his 80th birthday*, 146–60. Groningen.

Brindley, A.L. 2004 Prehistoric pottery. In W. O'Brien, *Ross Island. Mining, metal and society in early Ireland*, 316–38. Galway.

Brindley, A.L. 2007 *The dating of food vessels and urns in Ireland*. Galway.

Brindley, A.L. and Kilfeather, A. 1993 *Archaeological inventory of County Carlow*. Dublin.

Brindley, A.L. and Lanting, J.N. 1990a Radiocarbon dates for Neolithic single burials. *Journal of Irish Archaeology* **5**, 1–7.

Brindley, A.L. and Lanting, J.N. 1990b A Roman boat in Ireland. *Archaeology Ireland* **4** (3), 10–11.

Brindley, A.L. and Lanting, J.N. 1991 A boat of the Mediterranean tradition in Ireland: preliminary note. *Nautical Archaeology* **20**, 69–70.

Brindley, A.L. and Lanting, J.N. 1992a Radiocarbon dates from the cemetery at Poulawack, Co. Clare. *Journal of Irish Archaeology* **6**, 13–17.

Brindley, A.L. and Lanting, J.N. 1992b Radiocarbon dates from wedge tombs. *Journal of Irish Archaeology* **6**, 19–26.

Brindley, A.L. and Lanting, J. 1998 Radiocarbon dates for Irish trackways. *Journal of Irish Archaeology* **9**, 45–67.

Brindley, A.L., Lanting, J.N. and Mook, W.G. 1983 Radiocarbon dates from the Neolithic burials at Ballintruer More, Co. Wicklow, and Ardcrony, Co. Tipperary. *Journal of Irish Archaeology* **1**, 1–9.

Brindley, A.L., Lanting, J.N. and Mook, W.G. 1988 Radiocarbon dates from Moneen and Labbacallee, County Cork. *Journal of Irish Archaeology* **4**, 13–20.

Brindley, A.L., Lanting, J.N. and Mook, W.G. 1990 Radiocarbon dates from Irish *fulachta fiadh* and other burnt mounds. *Journal of Irish Archaeology* **5**, 25–33.

Brodie, N. 1994 *The Neolithic–Bronze Age transition in Britain*. British Archaeological Reports, British Series 238. Oxford.

Brück, J. 1999 What's in a settlement? Domestic practice and residential mobility in early Bronze Age southern England. In J. Brück and M. Goodman (eds), *Making places in the prehistoric world: themes in settlement archaeology*, 52–75. London.

Brück, J. 2006 Death, exchange and reproduction in the British Bronze Age. *European Journal of Archaeology* **9**, 73–101.

Budd, P., Gale, D. and Thomas, R.G. 1997 Cornish copper and the origins of extractive metallurgy in the British Isles: some scientific considerations. In P. Budd and D. Gale (eds), *Prehistoric extractive metallurgy in Cornwall*, 15–17. Truro.

Burenhult, G. 1980 *The archaeological excavation at Carrowmore, Co. Sligo, Ireland. Excavation seasons 1977–1979*. Theses and Papers in North European Archaeology, no. 9. Stockholm.

Burenhult, G. 1984 *The archaeology of Carrowmore. Environmental archaeology and the megalithic tradition at Carrowmore, Co. Sligo, Ireland*. Theses and Papers in North European Archaeology, no. 14. Stockholm.

Burenhult, G. 2000 Carrowmore megalithic tombs. In I. Bennett (ed.), *Excavations 1998*, 180–3. Bray.

Burgess, C.B. 1974. The bronze age. In C. Renfrew (ed.), *British prehistory. A new outline*, 165–232.

London.

Burgess, C.B. 1980 *The age of Stonehenge*. London.

Burgess, C.B. 1982 The Cartington knife and the double-edged knives of the late Bronze Age. *Northern Archaeology* **3**, 32–45.

Burgess, C.B. and Cowen, J.D. 1972 The Ebnal hoard and early Bronze Age metalworking traditions. In F. Lynch and C. B. Burgess (eds), *Prehistoric man in Wales and the west: essays in honour of Lily F. Chitty*, 167–82. Bath.

Burgess, C.B. and Gerloff, S. 1981 *The dirks and rapiers of Great Britain and Ireland*. Prähistorische Bronzefunde IV:7. Munich.

Butler, J.J. 1963 Bronze Age connections across the North Sea. *Palaeohistoria* **9**, 1–286.

Byrne, F.J. 1973 *Irish kings and high-kings*. London.

Byrne, G. 1991 Rathlackan. Court tomb with associated pre-bog settlement. In I. Bennett (ed.), *Excavations 1990*, 46. Bray.

Byrne, G. 1994 Rathlackan. Court tomb with associated pre-bog settlement. In I. Bennett (ed.), *Excavations 1993*, 61–2. Bray.

Cahill, M. 1995 Later Bronze Age goldwork from Ireland—form, function and formality. In J. Waddell and E. S. Twohig (eds), *Ireland in the Bronze Age. Proceedings of the Dublin Conference, April 1995*, 63–72. Dublin.

Cahill, M. 1998a Mooghaun bracelet rediscovered. *Archaeology Ireland* **12** (1), 8–9.

Cahill, M. 1998b A gold dress-fastener from Clohernagh, Co. Tipperary, and a catalogue of related material. In M. Ryan (ed.), *Irish antiquities. Essays in memory of Joseph Raftery*, 27–78. Bray.

Cahill, M. 2001 Unspooling the mystery. *Archaeology Ireland* **15** (3), 8–15.

Cahill, M. 2002 The Dooyork hoard. *Irish Arts Review* **19**, 118–21.

Cahill, M. 2004a The gold beads from Tumna, Co. Roscommon. In H. Roche, E. Grogan, J. Bradley, J. Coles and B. Raftery (eds), *From megaliths to metals. Essays in honour of George Eogan*, 99–108. Oxford.

Cahill, M. 2004b Finding function in the Irish late Bronze Age. In A. Perea, I. Montero and Ó. García-Vuelta (eds), *Tecnología del oro antiguo: Europa y América. Ancient gold technology: America and Europe*, 349–58. Madrid.

Cahill, M. 2005 Cuirass to gorget? An interpretation of the structure and decorative elements of some gold ornaments from the Irish late Bronze Age. *Archaeology Ireland* **19** (4), 26–30.

Cahill, M. 2006 John Windle's golden legacy—prehistoric and later gold ornaments from Co. Cork and Co. Waterford. *Proceedings of the Royal Irish Academy* **106**C, 219–337.

Carew, M. 2003 *Tara and the Ark of the Covenant*. Dublin.

Carey, A. 2002 Excavations at Knockacarrigeen Hill, Tuam, Co. Galway. *Journal of the Galway Archaeological and Historical Society* **54**, 55–71.

Carlin, N., Clarke, L. and Walsh, F. 2008 *The archaeology of life and death in the Boyne floodplain: the linear landscape of the M4, Kinnegad–Enfield–Kilcock motorway*. Dublin.

Carroll, J., Ryan, F. and Wiggins, K. 2008 *Archaeological excavations at Glebe South and Darcystown, Balrothery, Co. Dublin*. Dublin.

Carroll, M. 2006 Site C, Kilmurry. In I. Bennett (ed.), *Excavations 2003*, 276. Bray.

Case, H. 1961 Irish Neolithic pottery: distribution and sequence. *Proceedings of the Prehistoric Society* **27**, 174–233.

Case, H. 1973 A ritual site in north-east Ireland. In G. Daniel and P. Kjaerum (eds), *Megalithic graves and ritual*, 173–96. Jutland Archaeological Society Publications 11. Copenhagen.

Case, H. 1977 An early accession to the Ashmolean Museum. In V. Markotic (ed.), *Ancient Europe and the Mediterranean*, 19–34. Warminster.

Case, H. 1993 Beakers: deconstruction and after. *Proceedings of the Prehistoric Society* **59**, 241–68.

Case, H. 1995a Irish Beakers in their European context. In J. Waddell and E. S. Twohig (eds), *Ireland in the Bronze Age. Proceedings of the Dublin Conference, April 1995*, 14–29. Dublin.

Case, H. 1995b Beakers: loosening a stereotype. In I. Kinnes and G. Varndell (eds), *'Unbaked Urns of Rudely Shape'. Essays on British and Irish pottery for Ian Longworth*, 55–67. Oxford.

Case, H. 2001 The Beaker culture in Britain and Ireland: groups, European contacts and chronology. In F. Nicolis (ed.), *Bell Beakers today: pottery, people, culture, symbols in prehistoric Europe, International Colloquium, Trento, Italy, May 1998*, 361–77. Trento.

Caseldine, C., Hatton, J. and Gearey, B. 2005 Pollen and palaeohydrological analyses. In M. Gowen, J. Ó Néill and M. Phillips (eds), *The Lisheen Mine*

Archaeological Project 1996–8, 83–136. Bray.

Caseldine, C., Thompson, G., Langdon, C. and Hendon, D. 2005 Evidence for an extreme climatic event on Achill Island, Co. Mayo, Ireland, around 5200–5100 cal. yr BP. *Journal of Quaternary Science* **20**, 169–78.

Caulfield, S. 1977 The beehive quern in Ireland. *Journal of the Royal Society of Antiquaries of Ireland* **107**, 104–38.

Caulfield, S. 1978 Neolithic fields: the Irish evidence. In H. C. Bowen and P. J. Fowler (eds), *Early land allotment in the British Isles: a survey of recent work*, 137–43. British Archaeological Reports, British Series 48. Oxford.

Caulfield, S. 1983 The Neolithic settlement of north Connaught. In T. Reeves-Smyth and F. Hamond (eds), *Landscape archaeology in Ireland*, 195–216. British Archaeological Reports, British Series 116. Oxford.

Caulfield, S. [1988] *Céide Fields and Belderrig. A guide to two prehistoric farms in north Mayo.* Killala [pamphlet: no date].

Caulfield, S. [1992] *Ceide Fields, Ballycastle, Co. Mayo* [15pp guidebook: no date or place of publication].

Caulfield, S., O'Donnell, R.G. and Mitchell, P.I. 1998 14C dating of a Neolithic field system at Céide Fields, County Mayo, Ireland. *Radiocarbon* **40**, 629–40.

Chapman, M. 1992 *The Celts: the construction of a myth.* Basingstoke.

Chapple, R.M., Dunlop, C., Gilmore, S. and Heaney, L. 2009 *Archaeological investigations along the A1 Dualling Scheme, Loughbrickland to Beech Hill, Co. Down, N. Ireland (2005)*, British Archaeological Reports, British Series 479. Oxford.

Clancy, P. 2005 *The Curragh, Co. Kildare—the archaeology of an ancient grassland.* Archaeology Ireland Heritage Guide No. 31. Bray.

Clark, G. 1975 *The earlier Stone Age settlement of Scandinavia.* Cambridge.

Clarke, D.L. 1970 *Beaker pottery of Great Britain and Ireland.* Cambridge.

Clarke, D.L. 1976 Mesolithic Europe: the economic basis. In G. de G. Sieveking, I. H. Longworth and K. E. Wilson (eds), *Problems in economic and social archaeology*, 449–82. London.

Clarke, L. and Carlin, N. 2009 From focus to locus: a window upon the development of a funerary landscape. In M. B. Deevy and D. Murphy (eds), *Places along the way. First findings on the M3*, 1–20. Dublin.

Cleary, K. 2005 Skeletons in the closet: the dead among the living on Irish Bronze Age settlements. *Journal of Irish Archaeology* **14**, 23–42.

Cleary, R.M. 1995 Later Bronze Age settlement and prehistoric burials, Lough Gur, Co. Limerick. *Proceedings of the Royal Irish Academy* **95**C, 1–92.

Cleary, R.M. 2003 Enclosed Late Bronze Age habitation site and boundary wall at Lough Gur, Co. Limerick. *Proceedings of the Royal Irish Academy* **103**C, 97–189.

Clodoré, T. and LeClerc, A.-S. 2002 *Préhistoire de la musique. Sons et instruments de musique des âges du Bronze et du Fer en France.* Nemours.

Cody, E. 2002 *Survey of the megalithic tombs of Ireland, Vol. VI. County Donegal.* Dublin.

Coffey, G. 1894 Notes on the classification of spear-heads of the Bronze Age found in Ireland. *Proceedings of the Royal Irish Academy* **19**, 486–510.

Coffey, G. 1906 Early iron sword found in Ireland. *Proceedings of the Royal Irish Academy* **26**C, 42–3.

Coffey, G. 1909 The distribution of gold lunulae in Ireland and north-western Europe. *Proceedings of the Royal Irish Academy* **27**C, 251–8.

Coffey, G. 1911 Stone with cup-and-ring markings at Ryfad, County Fermanagh. *Journal of the Royal Society of Antiquaries of Ireland* **41**, 25.

Coffey, G. 1913 Ornamented bronze spear-heads with apertures in the blades. *Proceedings of the Royal Irish Academy* **30**C, 445–8.

Coghlan, H.H. and Raftery, J. 1961 Irish prehistoric casting moulds. *Sibrium* **6**, 223–44.

Coles, B. 1998 Wood species for wooden figures: a glimpse of a pattern. In A. Gibson and D. Simpson (eds), *Essays in honour of Aubrey Burl. Prehistoric ritual and religion*, 163–73. Stroud.

Coles, B. and Coles, J. 1989 *People of the wetlands. Bogs, bodies and lake-dwellers.* London.

Coles, J.M. 1962 European Bronze Age shields. *Proceedings of the Prehistoric Society* **28**, 156–90.

Coles, J.M. 1963 Irish Bronze Age horns and their relations with northern Europe. *Proceedings of the Prehistoric Society* **29**, 326–56.

Coles, J.M. 1965 The archaeological evidence for a 'bull cult' in late Bronze Age Europe. *Antiquity* **39**, 217–19.

Coles, J.M. 1967 Some Irish horns of the late Bronze Age. *Journal of the Royal Society of Antiquaries of Ireland* **97**, 113–17.

Coles, J.M. 1971 Bronze Age spearheads with gold decoration. *Antiquaries Journal* **51**, 94–5.

Coles, J.M., Heal, S.V.E. and Orme, B.J. 1978 The use and character of wood in prehistoric Britain and Ireland. *Proceedings of the Prehistoric Society* **44**, 1–45.

Collard, M. 2005 Hartshill Quarry. The oldest ironworking site in Britain? *Current Archaeology* **195**, 134–9.

Collins, A.E.P. 1952 Excavations in the sandhills at Dundrum, Co. Down, 1950–51. *Ulster Journal of Archaeology* **15**, 2–26.

Collins, A.E.P. 1954 The excavation of a double horned cairn at Audleystown, Co. Down. *Ulster Journal of Archaeology* **17**, 7–56.

Collins, A.E.P. 1956 A stone circle on Castle Mahon mountain, Co. Down. *Ulster Journal of Archaeology* **19**, 1–10.

Collins, A.E.P. 1957a Trial excavations in a round cairn on Knockiveagh, Co. Down. *Ulster Journal of Archaeology* **20**, 8–28.

Collins, A.E.P. 1957b Excavations at the Giant's Ring, Ballynahatty. *Ulster Journal of Archaeology* **20**, 44–50.

Collins, A.E.P. 1959a Further investigations in the Dundrum sandhills. *Ulster Journal of Archaeology* **22**, 5–20.

Collins, A.E.P. 1959b Further work at Audleystown long cairn, Co. Down. *Ulster Journal of Archaeology* **22**, 21–7.

Collins, A.E.P. 1965 Ballykeel dolmen and cairn, Co. Armagh. *Ulster Journal of Archaeology* **28**, 47–70.

Collins, A.E.P. 1966 Barnes Lower court cairn, Co. Tyrone. *Ulster Journal of Archaeology* **29**, 43–75.

Collins, A.E.P. 1970 Bronze Age moulds in Ulster. *Ulster Journal of Archaeology* **33**, 23–36.

Collins, A.E.P. 1976 Dooeys Cairn, Ballymacaldrack, County Antrim. *Ulster Journal of Archaeology* **39**, 1–7.

Collins, A.E.P. 1977 A sand-dune site at the White Rocks, County Antrim. *Ulster Journal of Archaeology* **40**, 21–6.

Collins, A.E.P. 1978 Excavations on Ballygalley Hill, County Antrim. *Ulster Journal of Archaeology* **41**, 15–32.

Collins, A.E.P. and Seaby, W.A. 1960 A crannog at Lough Eskragh, Co. Tyrone. *Ulster Journal of Archaeology* **23**, 25–37.

Collins, A.E.P. and Waterman, D.M. 1955 *Millin Bay. A late Neolithic cairn in Co. Down*. Belfast.

Collins, A.E.P. and Wilson, B. 1963 The Slieve Gullion cairns. *Ulster Journal of Archaeology* **26**, 19–40.

Collins, A.E.P. and Wilson, B. 1964 The excavation of a court cairn at Ballymacdermot, Co. Armagh. *Ulster Journal of Archaeology* **27**, 3–22.

Collins, T. 2009 Hermitage, Ireland: life and death on the western edge of Europe. In S. McCartan, R. Schulting, G. Warren and P. Woodman (eds), *Mesolithic horizons. Papers presented at the Seventh International Conference on the Mesolithic, Belfast 2005*, 876–9. Oxford.

Collins, T. and Coyne, F. 2003 Fire and water . . . early Mesolithic cremations at Castleconnell, Co. Limerick. *Archaeology Ireland* **17** (2), 24–7.

Collins, T. and Coyne, F. 2006 As old as we felt . . . *Archaeology Ireland* **20** (4), 2.

Collins, T. and Lynch, L. 2001 Prehistoric burial and ritual, in southwest Ireland. *Antiquity* **75**, 493–4.

Collis, J. 2003 *The Celts: origins, myths and inventions*. Stroud.

Colquhoun, I. and Burgess, C.B. 1988 *The swords of Britain*. Prähistorische Bronzefunde IV:5. Munich.

Condit, T. 1992 Ireland's hillfort capital— Baltinglass, Co. Wicklow. *Archaeology Ireland* **6** (3), 16–20.

Condit, T. and Buckley, V.M. 1989 The 'Doon' of Drumsna—gateway to Connacht. *Emania* **6**, 12–28.

Condit, T. and Buckley, V.M. 1998 *The Doon of Drumsna. An Iron Age frontier fortification in Connacht*. Archaeology Ireland Heritage Guide No. 1. Bray.

Condit, T. and O'Sullivan, A. 1999 Landscapes of movement and control: interpreting prehistoric hillforts and fording-places on the River Shannon. *Discovery Programme Reports* **5**, 25–39.

Conneller, C. 2006 Death. In C. Conneller and G. Warren (eds), *Mesolithic Britain and Ireland. New approaches*, 139–64. Stroud.

Connolly, A. 1994 Saddle querns in Ireland. *Ulster Journal of Archaeology* **57**, 26–36.

Connolly, M. 1999 *Discovering the Neolithic in County Kerry: a passage tomb at Ballycarty*. Bray.

Conway, M. 2005 Corrstown: a large middle Bronze Age village. *Current Archaeology* **195**, 120–3.

Conway, M. 2006 Survey and excavation in the Navan environs with 'Time Team'. Creeveroe, Haughey's Fort and Ballydoo. *Emania* **20**, 29–52.

Coombs, D. 1975 Bronze Age weapon hoards in Britain. *Archaeologia Atlantica* **1**, 49–81.

Cooney, G. 1992a Body politics and grave messages: Irish Neolithic mortuary practices. In N. Sharples and A. Sheridan (eds), *Vessels for the ancestors*, 128–42. Edinburgh.

Cooney, G. 1992b Irish prehistoric mortuary practice: Baurnadomeeny reconsidered. *Tipperary Historical Journal* (1992), 223–9.

Cooney, G. 1997 Excavation of the portal tomb site at Melkagh, Co. Longford. *Proceedings of the Royal Irish Academy* **97**C, 195–244.

Cooney, G. 2000 *Landscapes of Neolithic Ireland.* London.

Cooney, G. 2003 Lambay Island. In I. Bennett (ed.), *Excavations 2001*, 126–8. Bray.

Cooney, G. 2006 Newgrange—a view from the platform. *Antiquity* **80**, 697–710.

Cooney, G. 2007 *The Bremore promontory.* Archaeology Ireland Heritage Guide No. 39. Bray.

Cooney, G. and Grogan, E. 1999 *Irish prehistory: a social perspective* (2nd edn). Bray.

Cooney, G. and Mandal, S. 1998 *The Irish Stone Axe Project. Monograph I.* Bray.

Cooney, G., O'Sullivan, M. and Downey, L. 2006 *Archaeology 2020. Repositioning Irish archaeology in the knowledge society. A realistically achievable perspective.* Dublin.

Copley, M.S., Berstan, R., Dudd, S.N., Docherty, G., Mukherjee, A.J., Straker, V., Payne, S. and Evershed, R. P. 2003 Direct chemical evidence for widespread dairying in prehistoric Britain. *Proceedings of the National Academy of Science* **100**, 1524–9.

Corcoran, J.X.W.P. 1964 Excavation of two chambered cairns at Kilnagarns Lower, Co. Leitrim. *Journal of the Royal Society of Antiquaries of Ireland* **94**, 177–98.

Corcoran, J.X.W.P. 1965 A bronze bucket in the Hunterian Museum, University of Glasgow. *Antiquaries Journal* **45**, 12–17.

Corlett, C. 1997 The prehistoric archaeology of the parish of Kilgeever, south-west County Mayo. *Journal of the Galway Archaeological and Historical Society* **49**, 65–103.

Corlett, C. 2005 Ring-barrows—a circular argument with a ring of truth? In T. Condit and C. Corlett (eds), *Above and beyond. Essays in memory of Leo Swan*, 63–71. Bray.

Corns, A., Fenwick, J. and Shaw, R. 2008 More than meets the eye . . . the Discovery Programme's high-resolution LiDAR survey of Tara. *Archaeology Ireland* **22** (3), 34–8.

Costa, L.J., Sternke, F. and Woodman, P.C. 2005 Microlith to macrolith: the reasons behind the transformation of production in the Irish Mesolithic. *Antiquity* **79**, 19–33.

Cotter, C. 1993 Western Stone Fort Project. Interim report. *Discovery Programme Reports* **1**, 1–19.

Cotter, C. 1995 Western Stone Fort Project. Interim report. *Discovery Programme Reports* **2**, 1–11.

Cotter, C. 1996 Western Stone Fort Project. Interim report. *Discovery Programme Reports* **4**, 1–14.

Cotter, E. 2005 Bronze Age Ballybrowney, Co. Cork. In J. O'Sullivan and M. Stanley (eds), *Recent archaeological discoveries on national road schemes 2004*, 37–43. Archaeology and the National Roads Authority Monograph Series No. 2. Dublin.

Cotter, E. 2008 Clonbaul/Kilbride. In I. Bennett (ed.), *Excavations 2005*, 273. Dublin.

Cowen, J.D. 1967 The Hallstatt sword of bronze: on the Continent and in Britain. *Proceedings of the Prehistoric Society* **33**, 377–454.

Crew, P. and Rehren, T. 2002 High-temperature workshop residues from Tara: iron, bronze and glass. *Discovery Programme Reports* **6**, 83–102.

Cross, S. 2003 Irish Neolithic settlement architecture—a reappraisal. In I. Armit, E. Murphy, E. Nelis and D. Simpson (eds), *Neolithic settlement in Ireland and western Britain*, 195–202. Oxford.

Cunliffe, B. 1984 *Danebury: an Iron Age hillfort in Hampshire. Vol. 1: the excavations, 1969–1978.* London.

Cunliffe, B. 1997 *The ancient Celts.* Oxford.

Cunliffe, B. 2001 *Facing the ocean. The Atlantic and its peoples 8000 BC–AD 1500.* Oxford.

Cunliffe, B. 2003 *The Celts: a very short introduction.*

Oxford.

Cunliffe, B. 2005 *Iron Age communities in Britain* (4th edn). London.

Cunliffe, B. 2009 A race apart: insularity and connectivity. *Proceedings of the Prehistoric Society* **75**, 55–64.

Cuppage, J. 1986 *Archaeological survey of the Dingle peninsula*. Ballyferriter.

Curran-Mulligan, P. 1994 Yes, but it *is* art! *Archaeology Ireland* **8** (1), 14–15.

Daffy, S. 2002 A site for sore eyes: a Hiberno-Roman curative cult at Golden, Co. Tipperary. *Archaeology Ireland* **16** (2), 8–9.

Daly, A. and Grogan, E. 1993 Excavation of four barrows in Mitchelstowndown West, Knocklong, County Limerick. *Discovery Programme Reports* **1**, 44–60.

Danaher, E. 2004 Curraheen 1. In I. Bennett (ed.), *Excavations 2002*, 74–6. Bray.

Danaher, E. 2007 *Monumental beginnings: the archaeology of the N4 Sligo Inner Relief Road*. Dublin.

Daniells, M.J. and Williams, B.B. 1977 Excavations at Kiltierney Deerpark, County Fermanagh. *Ulster Journal of Archaeology* **40**, 32–41.

Davies, O. 1937 Excavations at Ballyrenan, Co. Tyrone. *Journal of the Royal Society of Antiquaries of Ireland* **67**, 89–100.

Davies, O. 1938 Castledamph stone circle. *Journal of the Royal Society of Antiquaries of Ireland* **68**, 106–12.

Davies, O. 1939a Excavation of a horned cairn at Aghanaglack, Co. Fermanagh. *Journal of the Royal Society of Antiquaries of Ireland* **69**, 21–38.

Davies, O. 1939b Excavations at Clogherny. *Ulster Journal of Archaeology* **2**, 36–43.

Davies, O. 1939c Excavation at the Giant's Grave, Loughash. *Ulster Journal of Archaeology* **2**, 254–68.

Davies, O. 1949 Excavations at the horned cairn of Ballymarlagh, Co. Antrim. *Ulster Journal of Archaeology* **12**, 26–42.

Davies, O. and Evans, E.E. 1933 Excavations at Goward, near Hilltown, Co. Down. *Proceedings of the Belfast Natural History and Philosophical Society* (1932–3), 90–105.

Davies, O. and Mullin, J.B. 1940 Excavation of Cashelbane cairn, Loughash, Co. Tyrone. *Journal of the Royal Society of Antiquaries of Ireland* **70**, 143–63.

Davies, O. and Radford, C.A.R. 1936 Excavation of the horned cairn of Clady Halliday. *Proceedings of the Belfast Natural History and Philosophical Society* (1935–6), 76–85.

Davis, R. 2006 *Basal-looped spearheads. Typology, chronology, context and use*. British Archaeological Reports, International Series 1497. Oxford.

Day, A. and McWilliams, P. 1993 *Ordnance Survey Memoirs of Ireland*, Vol. 22. Belfast.

De Paor, L. and Ó h-Eochaidhe, M. 1956 Unusual group of earthworks at Slieve Breagh, Co. Meath. *Journal of the Royal Society of Antiquaries of Ireland* **86**, 97–101.

De Valera, R. 1960 The court cairns of Ireland. *Proceedings of the Royal Irish Academy* **60**C, 9–140.

De Valera, R. 1965 Transeptal court cairns. *Journal of the Royal Society of Antiquaries of Ireland* **35**, 5–37.

Demakopoulou, K., Eluère, C., Jensen, J., Jockenhövel, A. and Mohen, J.-P. (eds) 1999 *Gods and heroes of the European Bronze Age*. London.

Desnoyers, F.E. 1876 Nouveaux objets trouvés dans la Loire pendant les années 1872, 1873 et une partie de 1874. *Mémoires de la société archéologique et historique de l'Orléanais* **15**, 113–96.

Devereux, P. and Jahn, R.G. 1996 Preliminary investigations and cognitive considerations of the acoustical resonances of selected archaeological sites. *Antiquity* **70**, 665–6.

Dickson, J.H. 1978 Bronze Age mead. *Antiquity* **52**, 108–13.

Dillon, M. 1973 The consecration of Irish kings. *Celtica* **10**, 1–8.

Doherty, C. 2005 Kingship in early Ireland. In E. Bhreathnach (ed.), *The kingship and landscape of Tara*, 3–31. Dublin.

Doody, M. 1987 Ballyveelish, Co. Tipperary. In R. M. Cleary, M. F. Hurley and E. A. Twohig (eds), *Archaeological excavations on the Cork–Dublin gas pipeline (1981–82)*, 8–35. Cork.

Doody, M. 2007 *Excavations at Curraghatoor, Co. Tipperary*. Cork.

Doody, M. 2008 *The Ballyhoura Hills Project*. Discovery Programme Monograph 7. Bray.

Dowd, M. 2002 Kilgreany, Co. Waterford: biography of a cave. *Journal of Irish Archaeology* **11**, 77–97.

Dowd, M. 2008 The use of caves for funerary and ritual practices in Ireland. *Antiquity* **82**, 305–17.

Dowling, G. 2006 The liminal boundary: an analysis of the sacral potency of the ditch at Ráith na Ríg, Tara, Co. Meath. *Journal of Irish Archaeology* **15**, 15–37.

Doyle, I.W. 2005 Excavation of a prehistoric ringbarrow at Kilmahuddrick, Clondalkin, Dublin. *Journal of Irish Archaeology* **14**, 43–75.

Dronfield, J. 1995a Subjective vision and the source of Irish megalithic art. *Antiquity* **69**, 539–49.

Dronfield, J. 1995b Migraine, light and hallucinogens: the neurocognitive basis of Irish megalithic art. *Oxford Journal of Archaeology* **14**, 261–75.

Dronfield, J. 1996 Entering alternative realities: cognition, art and architecture in Irish passage-tombs. *Cambridge Archaeological Journal* **6**, 37–72.

Duignan, M. 1976 The Turoe stone: its place in insular La Tène art. In P.-M. Duval and C. Hawkes (eds), *Celtic art in ancient Europe, five protohistoric centuries*, 201–17. London.

Earwood, C. 1989 Radiocarbon dating of late prehistoric wooden vessels. *Journal of Irish Archaeology* **5**, 37–44.

Earwood, C. 1992 A radiocarbon date for early Bronze Age wooden polypod bowls. *Journal of Irish Archaeology* **6**, 27–8.

Earwood, C. 1993 *Domestic wooden artefacts in Britain and Ireland from Neolithic to Viking times.* Exeter.

Edmonds, M. 1995 *Stone tools and society. Working stone in Neolithic and Bronze Age Britain.* London.

Edwards, R. and Brooks, A. 2008 The island of Ireland: drowning the myth of an Irish landbridge? In J. L. Davenport, D. P. Sleeman and P. C. Woodman (eds), *Mind the gap. Postglacial colonization of Ireland. Supplement to The Irish Naturalists' Journal*, 19–34.

Ehrenberg, M. 1977 *Bronze Age spearheads from Berkshire, Buckinghamshire and Oxfordshire.* British Archaeological Reports, British Series 144. Oxford.

Ehrenberg, M. 1989a *Women in prehistory.* London.

Ehrenberg, M. 1989b The interpretation of regional variability in British and Irish Bronze Age metalwork. In H.-Å. Nordström and A. Knape (eds), *Bronze Age studies. Transactions of the British–Scandinavian colloquium in Stockholm, May 10–11, 1985*, 77–88. Stockholm.

Eogan, G. 1963 A Neolithic habitation-site and megalithic tomb in Townleyhall townland, Co. Louth. *Journal of the Royal Society of Antiquaries of Ireland* **93**, 37–81.

Eogan, G. 1964 The later Bronze Age in Ireland in the light of recent research. *Proceedings of the Prehistoric Society* **30**, 268–351.

Eogan, G. 1965 *Catalogue of Irish bronze swords.* Dublin.

Eogan, G. 1969 'Lock-rings' of the late Bronze Age. *Proceedings of the Royal Irish Academy* **67**C, 93–148.

Eogan, G. 1972 'Sleeve-fasteners' of the Late Bronze Age. In F. Lynch and C. B. Burgess (eds), *Prehistoric man in Wales and the west: essays in honour of Lily F. Chitty*, 189–209. Bath.

Eogan, G. 1974 Pins of the Irish late Bronze Age. *Journal of the Royal Society of Antiquaries of Ireland* **104**, 74–119.

Eogan, G. 1981 The gold vessels of the Bronze Age in Ireland and beyond. *Proceedings of the Royal Irish Academy* **81**C, 345–82.

Eogan, G. 1983 *The hoards of the Irish Later Bronze Age.* Dublin.

Eogan, G. 1984 *Excavations at Knowth, I.* Dublin.

Eogan, G. 1986 *Knowth and the passage tombs of Ireland.* London.

Eogan, G. 1990 Irish megalithic tombs and Iberia: comparisons and contrasts. In *Probleme der Megalithgräberforschung. Vorträge zum 100 Geburtstag von Vera Leisner*, 113–37. Berlin.

Eogan, G. 1991 Prehistoric and early historic cultural change at Brugh na Bóinne. *Proceedings of the Royal Irish Academy* **91**C, 105–32.

Eogan, G. 1993a Aspects of metal production and manufacturing systems during the Irish Bronze Age. *Acta Praehistorica et Archaeologica* **25**, 87–110.

Eogan, G. 1993b The late Bronze Age: customs, crafts and cults. In E. S. Twohig and M. Ronayne (eds), *Past perceptions. The prehistoric archaeology of south-west Ireland*, 121–33. Cork.

Eogan, G. 1994 *The accomplished art. Gold and goldworking in Britain and Ireland during the Bronze Age (c. 2300–650 BC).* Oxford.

Eogan, G. 1996 Pattern and place: a preliminary study of the decorated kerbstones at site 1, Knowth, Co. Meath, and their comparative setting. In *Actes du 2ème Colloque Interrégional d'Art Mégalithique, Vannes, 1995. Revue archéologique de l'Ouest, Supplément* 8, 97–104.

Eogan, G. 1997 'Hair-rings' and European late

Bronze Age society. *Antiquity* **71**, 308–20.

Eogan, G. 1998a Knowth before Knowth. *Antiquity* **72**, 162–72.

Eogan, G. 1998b Heart-shaped bullae of the Irish late Bronze Age. In M. Ryan (ed.), *Irish antiquities. Essays in memory of Joseph Raftery*, 17–26. Bray.

Eogan, G. 1999a Megalithic art and society. *Proceedings of the Prehistoric Society* **65**, 415–46.

Eogan, G. 1999b *The socketed bronze axes in Ireland.* Prähistorische Bronzefunde IX:22. Stuttgart.

Eogan, G. 1999c From Skåne to Scotstown: some notes on amber in Bronze Age Ireland. In A. F. Harding (ed.), *Experiment and design. Archaeological studies in honour of John Coles*, 75–86. Oxford.

Eogan, G. 2001 A composite late Bronze Age object from Roscommon, Ireland. In W. H. Metz, B. L. van Beek and H. Steegstra (eds), *Patina. Essays presented to Jay Jordan Butler on the occasion of his 80th birthday*, 231–40. Groningen.

Eogan, G. 2007 The tool kit of a late Bronze Age wood-worker from Loughbown, County Galway, Ireland. In C. Burgess, P. Topping and F. Lynch (eds), *Beyond Stonehenge. Essays on the Bronze Age in honour of Colin Burgess*, 354–60. Oxford.

Eogan, G. 2008a Decorated thick penannular rings of the Irish late Bronze Age. In F. Verse *et al.* (eds), *Durch die Zeiten . . . Festschrift für Albrecht Jockenhövel zum 65. Geburtstag*, 177–83. Rahden.

Eogan, G. 2008b A cupmarked stone at Bobsville (Clonabreany), Co. Meath. *Ríocht na Midhe* **19**, 1–14.

Eogan, G. and Richardson, H. 1982 Two maceheads from Knowth, County Meath. *Journal of the Royal Society of Antiquaries of Ireland* **112**, 123–38.

Eogan, G. and Roche, H. 1997 *Excavations at Knowth, 2.* Dublin.

Eogan, G. and Roche, H. 1998 Further evidence for Neolithic habitation at Knowth, Co. Meath. *Ríocht na Midhe* **9**, 1–9.

Eogan, J. 2007 Cleansing body and soul? *Seanda: National Roads Authority Archaeology Magazine* **2**, 38–9.

Eogan, J. and Finn, D. 2000 New light on late prehistoric ritual and burial in County Limerick. *Archaeology Ireland* **14** (1), 8–10.

Eriksen, P. 2006 The rolling stones of Newgrange.

Antiquity **80**, 709–10.

Eriksen, P. 2008 The great mound of Newgrange. An Irish multi-period mound spanning from the megalithic tomb period to the early Bronze Age. *Acta Archaeologica* **79**, 250–73.

Evans, E.E. 1935 Excavations at Aghnaskeagh, Co. Louth. *County Louth Archaeological Journal* **8**, 235–55.

Evans, E.E. 1938 Doeys Cairn, Dunloy, Co. Antrim. *Ulster Journal of Archaeology* **1**, 59–78.

Evans, E.E. 1939 Excavations at Carnanbane, County Londonderry. A double horned cairn. *Proceedings of the Royal Irish Academy* **45**C, 1–12.

Evans, E.E. and Davies, O. 1934 Excavation of a chambered horned cairn at Ballyalton, Co. Down. *Proceedings of the Belfast Natural History and Philosophical Society* (1933–4), 79–103.

Evans, E.E. and Davies, O. 1935 Excavation of a chambered horned cairn, Browndod, Co. Antrim. *Proceedings of the Belfast Natural History and Philosophical Society* (1934–5), 70–87.

Evans, E.E. and Mitchell, G.F. 1954 Three bronze spear-heads from Tattenamona, near Brookborough, Co. Fermanagh. *Ulster Journal of Archaeology* **17**, 57–61.

Evans, J. 1881 *The ancient bronze implements, weapons and ornaments of Great Britain and Ireland.* London.

Fahy, E. 1960 A hut and cooking-place at Drombeg, Co. Cork. *Journal of the Cork Historical and Archaeological Society* **65**, 1–17.

Fahy, E. 1961 A stone circle, hut and dolmen at Bohonagh, Co. Cork. *Journal of the Cork Historical and Archaeological Society* **66**, 93–104.

Fahy, E. 1962 A recumbent stone circle at Reanascreena South, Co. Cork. *Journal of the Cork Historical and Archaeological Society* **67**, 59–69.

Fenwick, J. 1995 The manufacture of the decorated macehead from Knowth, County Meath. *Journal of the Royal Society of Antiquaries of Ireland* **125**, 51–60.

Fenwick, J. and Newman, C. 2002 Geomagnetic survey on the Hill of Tara, Co. Meath, 1998–9. *Discovery Programme Reports* **6**, 1–17.

Field, N. and Parker Pearson, M. 2003 *Fiskerton. An Iron Age timber causeway with Iron Age and Roman votive offerings: the 1981 excavations.* Oxford.

Finlay, N. 2003 Cache and carry: defining moments in the Irish later Mesolithic. In L.

Bevan and J. Moore (eds), *Peopling the Mesolithic in a northern environment*, 87–94. British Archaeological Reports, International Series 1157. Oxford.

Finney, J.B. 2006 *Middle Iron Age warfare of the hillfort dominated zone c. 400 BC to c. 150 BC.* British Archaeological Reports, British Series 423. Oxford.

FitzGerald, M. 2006 Archaeological discoveries on a new section of the N2 in counties Meath and Dublin. In J. O'Sullivan and M. Stanley (eds), *Settlement, industry and ritual*, 29–42. Archaeology and the National Roads Authority Monograph Series No. 3. Dublin.

FitzGerald, M. 2007a Catch of the day at Clowanstown, Co. Meath. *Archaeology Ireland* **21** (4), 12–15.

FitzGerald, M. 2007b Revolutionising our understanding of prehistoric basketry. *Seanda: National Roads Authority Archaeology Magazine* **2**, 49–51.

FitzPatrick, E. 2004 *Royal inauguration in Gaelic Ireland c. 1100–1600. A cultural landscape study.* Woodbridge.

Flanagan, L.N.W. 1966 An unpublished flint hoard from the Braid Valley, Co. Antrim. *Ulster Journal of Archaeology* **29**, 82–90.

Flanagan, L.N.W. 1970 A flint hoard from Ballyclare, Co. Antrim. *Ulster Journal of Archaeology* **33**, 15–22.

Flanagan, L.N.W. and Flanagan, D.E. 1966 The excavation of a court cairn at Bavan, Co. Donegal. *Ulster Journal of Archaeology* **29**, 16–38.

Fokkens, H., Achterkamp, Y. and Kuijpers, M. 2008 Bracers or bracelets? About the functionality and meaning of bell beaker wrist-guards. *Proceedings of the Prehistoric Society* **74**, 109–40.

Foley, C. 1988 Only an old pile of stones. Creggandevesky court tomb, Co. Tyrone. In A. Hamlin and C. Lynn (eds), *Pieces of the past*, 3–5. Belfast.

Foley, C. 1998 Copney stone circles—a County Tyrone enigma. *Archaeology Ireland* **43**, 24–8.

Forsythe, W. and Gregory, N. 2007 A Neolithic logboat from Greyabbey, County Down. *Ulster Journal of Archaeology* **66**, 6–13.

Fox, C. 1939 The socketed bronze sickles of the British Isles. *Proceedings of the Prehistoric Society* **5**, 222–48.

Fraser, S.M. 1998 The public forum and the space between: the materiality of social strategy in the Irish Neolithic. *Proceedings of the Prehistoric Society* **64**, 203–24.

Fredengren, C. 2002 *Crannogs. A study of people's interaction with lakes, with particular reference to Lough Gara in the north-west of Ireland.* Bray.

Freeman, P. 2001 *Ireland and the Classical world.* Austin.

Fry, M.F. 2000 *Coití. Logboats from Northern Ireland.* Belfast.

Garwood, P. 1991 Ritual tradition and the reconstitution of society. In P. Garwood, D. Jennings, R. Skeates and J. Toms (eds), *Sacred and profane: proceedings of a conference on archaeology, ritual and religion*, 10–32. Oxford.

Gaskell Brown, C. and Harper, A.E.T. 1984 Excavations on Cathedral Hill, Armagh, 1968. *Ulster Journal of Archaeology* **47**, 109–61.

Gault, A. 2002 Applying Bayesian mathematics to the Navan Fort radiocarbon chronology. *Emania* **19**, 25–34.

Gavin, F. and Newman, C. 2007 Notes on insular silver in the 'Military Style'. *Journal of Irish Archaeology* **16**, 1–10.

Gerloff, S. 1986 Bronze Age Class A cauldrons: typology, origins and chronology. *Journal of the Royal Society of Antiquaries of Ireland* **116**, 84–115.

Gerloff, S. 1995 Bronzezeitliche goldblechkronen aus Westeuropa. In A. Jockenhövel (ed.), *Festschrift für Hermann Müller-Karpe zum 70 Geburtstag*, 153–94. Bonn.

Gerloff, S. 2004 Hallstatt fascination: 'Hallstatt' buckets, swords and chapes from Britain and Ireland. In H. Roche, E. Grogan, J. Bradley, J. Coles and B. Raftery (eds), *From megaliths to metals. Essays in honour of George Eogan*, 125–54. Oxford.

Gibbons, M. 1990 The archaeology of early settlement in County Kilkenny. In W. Nolan and K. Whelan (eds), *Kilkenny: history and society. Interdisciplinary essays on the history of an Irish county*, 1–32. Dublin.

Gibson, A. 2002a *Prehistoric pottery in Britain and Ireland.* Stroud.

Gibson, A. 2002b The later Neolithic palisaded enclosures of the United Kingdom. In A. Gibson (ed.), *Behind wooden walls: Neolithic palisaded enclosures in Europe*, 5–23. British Archaeological Reports, International Series

1013. Oxford.

Gibson, A.M. and Simpson, D.D.A. 1987 Lyles Hill, Co. Antrim. *Archaeology Ireland* **1** (2), 72–5.

Giles, M. 2007 Making metal and forging relations: ironworking in the British Iron Age. *Oxford Journal of Archaeology* **26**, 395–413.

Glob, P.V. 1951 *Ard og Plov i Nordens oldtid.* Aarhus.

Gooder, J. 2007 Excavation of a Mesolithic house at East Barns, East Lothian, Scotland: an interim report. In K. Pedersen and C. Waddington (eds), *Mesolithic studies in the North Sea basin and beyond.* 49-59. Oxford.

Gosling, P. 1993 *Archaeological inventory of County Galway. Vol. 1: West Galway.* Dublin.

Gowen, M. 1988 *Three Irish gas pipelines: new archaeological evidence in Munster.* Dublin.

Gowen, M. 2007 Quality management and Irish commercial sector archaeology. In W. J. H. Willems and M. H. van den Dries (eds), *Quality management in archaeology*, 22–34. Oxford.

Gowen, M. and Halpin, E. 1992 A Neolithic house at Newtown. *Archaeology Ireland* **6** (2), 25–7.

Gowen, M. and Tarbett, C. 1988 A third season at Tankardstown. *Archaeology Ireland* **2** (4), 156.

Gowen, M. and Tarbett, C. 1990 Tankardstown South Neolithic house sites. In I. Bennett (ed.), *Excavations 1989*, 38–9. Dublin.

Gowen, M., Ó Néill, J. and Phillips, M. (eds) 2005 *The Lisheen Mine Archaeological Project 1996–8.* Bray.

Green, H.S. 1980 *The flint arrowheads of the British Isles.* British Archaeological Reports, British Series 75. Oxford.

Green, M. 1998 Vessels of death: sacred cauldrons in archaeology and myth. *Antiquaries Journal* **78**, 63–84.

Green, S.W. and Zvelebil, M. 1990 The Mesolithic colonization and agricultural transition of south-east Ireland. *Proceedings of the Prehistoric Society* **56**, 57–88.

Green, S.W. and Zvelebil, M. 1993 Interpreting Ireland's prehistoric landscape: the Bally Lough Archaeological Project. In P. Bogucki (ed.), *Case studies in European prehistory*, 1–29. Boca Raton.

Groenman-van Waateringe, W. and Butler, J.J. 1976 The Ballynoe stone circle. Excavations by A.E. van Giffin, 1937–1938. *Palaeohistoria* **18**, 73–104.

Groenman-van Waateringe, W., Kilian, M. and van Londen, H. 1999 The curing of hides and skins in European prehistory. *Antiquity* **73**, 884–90.

Grogan, E. 1990 Bronze Age cemetery at Carrig, Co. Wicklow. *Archaeology Ireland* **4** (4), 12–14.

Grogan, E. 1993 North Munster Project. Interim report. *Discovery Programme Reports* **1**, 39–68.

Grogan, E. 1996 Neolithic houses in Ireland. In T. Darvill and J. Thomas (eds), *Neolithic houses in northwest Europe and beyond*, 41–60. Oxford.

Grogan, E. 2002 Neolithic houses in Ireland: a broader perspective. *Antiquity* **76**, 517–25.

Grogan, E. 2004 The implications of Irish Neolithic houses. In I. A. G. Shepherd and G. J. Barclay, *Scotland in ancient Europe. The Neolithic and early Bronze Age of Scotland in their European context*, 103–14. Edinburgh.

Grogan, E. 2005 *The North Munster Project. Vol. 1: The later prehistoric landscape of south-east Clare. Vol. 2: The prehistoric landscape of North Munster.* Bray.

Grogan, E. 2008 *The Rath of the Synods, Tara, Co. Meath: excavations by Seán P. Ó Ríordáin.* Dublin.

Grogan, E., O'Donnell, L. and Johnston, P. 2007 *The Bronze Age landscapes of the Pipeline to the West.* Bray.

Grogan, E., O'Sullivan, A., O'Carroll, F. and Hagen, I. 1999 Knocknalappa, Co. Clare: a reappraisal. *Discovery Programme Reports* **5**, 111–23.

Guerra-Doce, E. 2006 Exploring the significance of Beaker pottery through residue analysis. *Oxford Journal of Archaeology* **25**, 247–59.

Gwilt, A., Kucharski, K., Silvester, R. and Davis, M. 2005 A late Bronze Age hoard from Trevalyn Farm, Rossett, Wrexham. *Studia Celtica* **39**, 27–61.

Halpin, A. and Newman, C. 2006 *Ireland. An Oxford archaeological guide.* Oxford.

Harbison, P. 1968 Catalogue of Irish early Bronze Age associated finds containing copper or bronze. *Proceedings of the Royal Irish Academy* **67**C, 35–91.

Harbison, P. 1969a *The daggers and halberds of the early Bronze Age in Ireland.* Prähistorische Bronzefunde VI:1. Munich.

Harbison, P. 1969b *The axes of the early Bronze Age in Ireland.* Prähistorische Bronzefunde IX:1. Munich.

Harbison, P. 1970 Two prehistoric bronze weapons from Ireland in the Hunt collection. *Journal of the Royal Society of Antiquaries of Ireland* **100**, 191–9.

Harbison, P. 1973 The earlier Bronze Age in

Ireland. *Journal of the Royal Society of Antiquaries of Ireland* **103**, 93–152.

Harbison, P. 1976 *Bracers and V-perforated buttons in the Beaker and Food Vessel cultures of Ireland.* Archaeologia Atlantica Research Report I. Bad Bramstedt.

Harbison, P. 1978 A flat tanged dagger from Co. Tyrone now in the Monaghan County Museum. *Clogher Record* **9**, 333–5.

Harding, A.F. 1993 British amber spacer-plate necklaces and their relatives in gold and stone. In C. W. Beck and J. Bouzek (eds), *Amber in archaeology. Proceedings of the second international conference on amber in archaeology, Liblice 1990*, 53–8. Prague.

Harding, A.F. 2000 *European societies in the Bronze Age.* Cambridge.

Harding, D.W. 2007 *The archaeology of Celtic art.* London.

Härke, H. 1997 The nature of burial data. In C. K. Jensen and K. H. Nielsen (eds), *Burial and society. The chronological and social analysis of archaeological burial data*, 19–27. Aarhus.

Harrison, R.J. 1980 *The Beaker Folk. Copper Age archaeology in western Europe.* London.

Harrison, R.J. 2004 *Symbols and warriors. Images of the European Bronze Age.* Bristol.

Hartnett, P.J. 1957 Excavations of a passage grave at Fourknocks, Co. Meath. *Proceedings of the Royal Irish Academy* **58**C, 197–277.

Hartnett, P.J. 1971 The excavation of two tumuli at Fourknocks (sites II and III), Co. Meath. *Proceedings of the Royal Irish Academy* **71**C, 35–89.

Hartwell, B. 1994 Late Neolithic ceremonies. *Archaeology Ireland* **8** (4), 10–13.

Hartwell, B. 1998 The Ballynahatty complex. In A. Gibson and D. Simpson (eds), *Prehistoric ritual and religion. Essays in honour of Aubrey Burl*, 32–44. Stroud.

Hartwell, B. 2002 A Neolithic ceremonial timber complex at Ballynahatty, Co. Down. *Antiquity* **76**, 526–32.

Hawkes, C.F.C. 1971 The Sintra gold collar. In G. de G. Sieveking (ed.), *Prehistoric and Roman studies*, 38–50. London. [*British Museum Quarterly 35.*]

Hawkes, C.F.C. 1982 The wearing of the brooch: early Iron Age dress among the Irish. In B. G. Scott (ed.), *Studies on early Ireland. Essays in honour of M. V. Duignan*, 51–73. Belfast.

Hawkes, C.F.C. and Clarke, R.R. 1963 Gahlstorf and Caister-on-Sea. Two finds of late Bronze Age Irish gold. In I. Ll. Foster and L. Alcock (eds), *Culture and environment. Essays in honour of Sir Cyril Fox*, 193–250. London.

Haworth, R. 1971 The horse harness of the Irish early Iron Age. *Ulster Journal of Archaeology* **34**, 26–49.

Heald, A. 2001 Knobbed spearbutts of the British and Irish Iron Age: new examples and new thoughts. *Antiquity* **75**, 689–96.

Hedges, R.E.M., Housley, R.A., Ramsey, C.B. and van Klinken, G.J. 1991 Radiocarbon dates from the Oxford AMS system: *Archaeometry* datelist 12. *Archaeometry* **33**, 121–34.

Hedges, R.E.M., Housley, R.A., Ramsey, C.B. and van Klinken, G.J. 1993 Radiocarbon dates from the Oxford AMS system: *Archaeometry* datelist 17. *Archaeometry* **35**, 305–26.

Hencken, H. O'N. 1935 A cairn at Poulawack, County Clare. *Journal of the Royal Society of Antiquaries of Ireland* **65**, 191–222.

Hencken, H. O'N. 1939 A long cairn at Creevykeel, Co. Sligo. *Journal of the Royal Society of Antiquaries of Ireland* **69**, 53–98.

Hencken, H. O'N. 1942 Ballinderry crannog no. 2. *Proceedings of the Royal Irish Academy* **47**C, 1–76.

Hencken, H. O'N. and Movius, H.L. 1934 The cemetery-cairn of Knockast. *Proceedings of the Royal Irish Academy* **41**C, 232–84.

Henderson, J. 1987 The Iron Age of 'Loughey' and Meare: some inferences from glass analyses. *Antiquaries Journal* **67**, 29–42.

Henderson, J. 1988 Glass production and Bronze Age Europe. *Antiquity* **62**, 435–51.

Henderson, J.C. 2007 *The Atlantic Iron Age. Settlement and identity in the first millennium BC.* London.

Hensey, R. 2008 The observance of light: a ritualistic perspective on 'imperfectly' aligned passage tombs. *Time and Mind: The Journal of Archaeology, Consciousness and Culture* **1**, 319–30.

Herity, M. 1974 *Irish passage graves.* Dublin.

Herity, M. 1982 Irish decorated Neolithic pottery. *Proceedings of the Royal Irish Academy* **82**C, 247–404.

Herity, M. 1987 The finds from Irish court tombs. *Proceedings of the Royal Irish Academy* **87**C, 5–281.

Herity, M. and Eogan, G. 1977 *Ireland in prehistory.*

London.

Herring, I.J. 1938 The cairn excavation at Well Glass Spring, Largantea, Co. Londonderry. *Ulster Journal of Archaeology* **1**, 164–88.

Herring, I.J. and May, A. McL. 1937 The Giant's Grave, Kilhoyle, Co. Londonderry. *Proceedings of the Belfast Natural History and Philosophical Society* (1936–7), 34–48.

Herring, I.J. and May, A. McL. 1940 Cloghnagalla cairn, Boviel, Co. Londonderry. *Ulster Journal of Archaeology* **3**, 41–55.

Heslop, D.H. 1988 The study of beehive querns. *Scottish Archaeological Review* **5**, 59–65.

Hickey, H. 1976 *Images of stone*. Belfast.

Hill, J.D. 1995 How should we understand Iron Age societies and hillforts? A contextual study from southern Britain. In J. D. Hill and C. G. Cumberpatch (eds), *Different Iron Ages: studies on the Iron Age in temperate Europe*, 45–66. British Archaeological Reports, International Series 602. Oxford.

Hodges, H.W.M. 1958 A hunting camp at Cullyhanna Lough, near Newtown Hamilton, County Armagh. *Ulster Journal of Archaeology* **21**, 7–13.

Hughes, J. 2005 Two Neolithic structures in Granny townland, County Kilkenny. In J. O'Sullivan and M. Stanley (eds), *Recent archaeological discoveries on national road schemes 2004*, 25–35. Archaeology and the National Roads Authority Monograph Series 2. Dublin.

Hull, G. 2006 Excavation of a Bronze Age round-house at Knockdomny, Co. Westmeath. *Journal of Irish Archaeology* **15**, 1–14.

Hurl, D. 2001 The excavation of a wedge tomb at Ballybriest, County Londonderry. *Ulster Journal of Archaeology* **60**, 9–31.

Ireland, A. 1992 The finding of the 'Clonmacnoise' gold torcs. *Proceedings of the Royal Irish Academy* **92**C, 123–46.

Jackson, J.S. 1979 Metallic ores in Irish prehistory: copper and tin. In M. Ryan (ed.), *The origins of metallurgy in Atlantic Europe. Proceedings of the Fifth Atlantic Colloquium*, 107–25. Dublin.

Jackson, K.H. 1964 *The oldest Irish tradition: a window on the Iron Age*. Oxford.

James, S. 1999 *The Atlantic Celts: ancient people or modern invention?* London.

Janik, L. 2005 Redefining social relations—tradition, complementarity and internal tension.

In N. Milnar and P. Woodman (eds), *Mesolithic studies at the beginning of the 21st century*, 176–93. Oxford.

Jaski, B. 2000 *Early Irish kingship and succession*. Dublin.

Jelčić, L. and O'Connell, M. 1992 History of vegetation and land use from 3200 B.P. to the present in the north-west Burren, a karstic region of western Ireland. *Vegetation History and Archaeobotany* **1**, 119–40.

Johnston, P., Kiely, J. and Tierney, J. (eds) 2008 *Near the bend of the river. The archaeology of the N25 Kilmacthomas realignment*. Dublin.

Johnston, S. 1991 Distributional aspects of prehistoric Irish petroglyphs. In P. Bahn and A. Rosenfeld (eds), *Rock art and prehistory. Papers presented to symposium G of the AURA Congress, Darwin 1988*, 86–95. Oxford.

Johnston, S. 1993 The relationship between prehistoric Irish rock art and Irish passage tomb art. *Oxford Journal of Archaeology* **12**, 257–79.

Johnston, S.A. and Wailes, B. 2007 *Dún Ailinne. Excavations at an Irish royal site, 1968–1975*. Philadelphia.

Jones, C. 1998 The discovery and dating of the prehistoric landscape of Roughan Hill in Co. Clare. *Journal of Irish Archaeology* **9**, 27–43.

Jones, C. 2004 *The Burren and the Aran Islands. Exploring the archaeology*. Cork.

Jones, C. 2007 *Temples of stone. Exploring the megalithic tombs of Ireland*. Cork.

Jope, E.M. 1958 A heavy bronze ring of Italian type from Co. Derry. *Ulster Journal of Archaeology* **21**, 14–16.

Jope, E.M. 1962 Iron Age brooches in Ireland: a summary. *Ulster Journal of Archaeology* **24–5**, 25–38.

Jope, E.M. 2000 *Early Celtic art in the British Isles*. Oxford.

Jope, E.M. and Wilson, B.C.S. 1957 A burial group of the first century A.D. near Donaghadee, Co. Down. *Ulster Journal of Archaeology* **20**, 73–95.

Karl, R. 2003 Iron Age chariots and medieval texts: a step too far in 'breaking down boundaries'? *E-Keltoi. Journal of Interdisciplinary Celtic Studies* **5** (http://www.uwm.edu/Dept/celtic/ekeltoi/index.html).

Kavanagh, R. 1973 The Encrusted Urn in Ireland. *Proceedings of the Royal Irish Academy* **73**C, 507–617.

Kavanagh, R. 1976 Collared and cordoned cinerary urns in Ireland. *Proceedings of the Royal Irish Academy* **76**C, 293–403.

Kavanagh, R. 1991 A reconsideration of razors in the Irish earlier Bronze Age. *Journal of the Royal Society of Antiquaries of Ireland* **121**, 77–104.

Keeley, V. 1996 Ballydavis early Iron Age complex. In I. Bennett (ed.), *Excavations 1995*, 51–2. Bray.

Keeley, V. 1999 Iron Age discoveries at Ballydavis. In P. G. Lane and W. Nolan (eds), *Laois: history and society. Interdisciplinary essays on the history of an Irish county*, 25–34. Dublin.

Kelly, E.P. 1974 Aughinish Island. In T. G. Delaney (ed.), *Excavations 1974*, 20–1. Belfast.

Kelly, E.P. 2002 Antiquities from Irish holy wells and their wider context. *Archaeology Ireland* **16** (2), 24–8.

Kelly, E.P. 2006a Secrets of the bog bodies: the enigma of the Iron Age explained. *Archaeology Ireland* **20** (1), 26–30.

Kelly, E.P. 2006b *Kingship and sacrifice: Iron Age bog bodies and boundaries.* Archaeology Ireland Heritage Guide No. 35. Bray.

Kelly, F. 1988 *A guide to early Irish law.* Dublin.

Kelly, S. 1995 Artefact decomposition in peatlands. *Irish Archaeological Wetland Unit Transactions* **4**, 141–54.

Kiely, J. 2003 A Neolithic house at Cloghers, Co. Kerry. In I. Armit, E. Murphy, E. Nelis and D. Simpson (eds), *Neolithic settlement in Ireland and western Britain*, 182–7. Oxford.

Kiely, J. 2006 Prehistoric settlement on the M8 Rathcormac/Fermoy bypass. *Seanda: National Roads Authority Archaeology Magazine* **1**, 54–7.

Kiely, J. and Sutton, B. 2007 The new face of Bronze Age pottery. In J. O'Sullivan and M. Stanley (eds), *New routes to the past*, 25–33. Archaeology and the National Roads Authority Monograph Series No. 4. Dublin.

Kilbride-Jones, H.E. 1939 The excavation of a composite tumulus at Drimnagh, Co. Dublin. *Journal of the Royal Society of Antiquaries of Ireland* **69**, 190–220.

Kilbride-Jones, H.E. 1951 Double horned cairn at Cohaw, County Cavan. *Proceedings of the Royal Irish Academy* **54**C, 75–88.

Kilbride-Jones, H.E. 1980 *Zoomorphic penannular brooches.* London.

Kimball, M.J. 2000a Variation and context: ecology and social evolution in Ireland's later Mesolithic.

In A. Desmond, G. Johnson, M. McCarthy, J. Sheehan and E. Shee Twohig (eds), *New agendas in Irish prehistory. Papers in commemoration of Liz Anderson*, 31–47. Bray.

Kimball, M.J. 2000b *Human ecology and Neolithic transition in eastern County Donegal, Ireland. The Lough Swilly Archaeological Survey.* British Archaeological Reports, British Series 300. Oxford.

King, H. 1999 Excavation on the Fourknocks Ridge, Co. Meath. *Proceedings of the Royal Irish Academy* **99**C, 157–98.

Kirk, S.M. 1974 High altitude cereal growing in County Down, Northern Ireland? A note. *Ulster Journal of Archaeology* **36–7**, 99–100.

Knight, J., Coxon, P., Marshall McCabe, A. and McCarron, S.G. 2004 Pleistocene glaciations in Ireland. In J. Ehlers and P. L. Gibbard (eds), *Quaternary glaciations—extent and chronology 2*, 183–91. Amsterdam.

Knowles, W.J. 1886 A flint arrowhead with portion of shaft . . . *Journal of the Royal Society of Antiquaries of Ireland* **17**, 126–8.

Knowles, W.J. 1909 On the mounting of leaf-shaped arrowheads of flint. *Proceedings of the Society of Antiquaries of Scotland* **43**, 278–83.

Koch, J.T. 1986 New thoughts on *Albion, Ierne*, and the Pretanic Isles. *Proceedings of the Harvard Celtic Colloquium* **6**, 1–28.

Koch, J.T. 1991 Ériu, Alba and Letha: when was a language ancestral to Gaelic first spoken in Ireland? *Emania* **9**, 17–27.

Koch, J.T. 1994 Windows on the Iron Age: 1964–1994. In J. P. Mallory and G. Stockman (eds), *Ulidia. Proceedings of the First International Conference on the Ulster Cycle of Tales,* 229–42. Belfast.

Koch, J.T. 2007 *An atlas for Celtic studies.* Oxford.

Koch, J.T. and Carey, J. (eds) 1995 *The Celtic heroic age. Literary sources for ancient Celtic Europe and early Ireland and Wales.* Malden.

Kytlicová, O. 1991 *Die Bronzegefasse in Böhmen.* Prähistorische Bronzefunde II:12. Stuttgart.

Kytmannow, T. 2008 *Portal tombs in the landscape. The chronology, morphology and landscape setting of portal tombs of Ireland, Wales and Cornwall.* British Archaeological Reports, British Series 455. Oxford.

Lacy, B. 1983 *Archaeological survey of County Donegal.* Lifford.

Laidlaw, G. 2008 Cleansing body and soul? Part 2. *Seanda: National Roads Authority Archaeology Magazine* **3**, 26–7.

Lalonde, S. 2008 Trade routes and grave goods: a unique Bronze Age burial in County Offaly. *Seanda: National Roads Authority Archaeology Magazine* **3**, 46–8.

Lanigan Wood, H. 2000 Dogs and Celtic deities. Pre-Christian stone carvings in Armagh. *Irish Arts Review* **16**, 26–33.

Lanigan Wood, H. and Verling, E. 1995 Stone sculpture in Donegal. In W. Nolan, L. Ronayne and M. Dunlevy (eds), *Donegal: history and society. Interdisciplinary essays on the history of an Irish county*, 51–83. Dublin.

Lanting, J.N. and Brindley, A.L. 1998 Dating cremated bone: the dawn of a new era. *Journal of Irish Archaeology* **9**, 1–8.

Lanting, J.N., Aerts-Bijma, A.T. and van der Plicht, J. 2001 Dating of cremated bones. *Radiocarbon* **43**, 249–54.

Leask, H.G. and Price, L. 1936 The Labbacallee megalith, Co. Cork. *Proceedings of the Royal Irish Academy* **43**C, 77–101.

Leon, B.C. 2005 Mesolithic and Neolithic activity on Dalkey Island—a reassessment. *Journal of Irish Archaeology* **14**, 1–21.

Lewis-Williams, D. and Pearce, D. 2005 *Inside the Neolithic mind. Consciousness, cosmos and the realm of the gods.* London.

Linnane, S.J. 2007 Tullyallen. In I. Bennett (ed.), *Excavations 2007*, 269–70. Bray.

Liversage, G.D. 1958 An island site at Lough Gur. *Journal of the Royal Society of Antiquaries of Ireland* **88**, 67–81.

Liversage, G.D. 1960 A Neolithic site at Townleyhall, Co. Louth. *Journal of the Royal Society of Antiquaries of Ireland* **90**, 49–60.

Liversage, G.D. 1968 Excavations at Dalkey Island, Co. Dublin, 1956–1959. *Proceedings of the Royal Irish Academy* **60**C, 53–233.

Logan, E. 2007 Uncovering Carlow's oldest farmstead. *Seanda: National Roads Authority Archaeology Magazine* **2**, 67–8.

Logue, P. 2003 Excavations at Thornhill, Co. Londonderry. In I. Armit, E. Murphy, E. Nelis and D. Simpson (eds), *Neolithic settlement in Ireland and western Britain*, 149–55. Oxford.

Lohan, M. 1999 Ceremonial monuments in Moytura, Co. Mayo. *Journal of the Galway Archaeological and Historical Society* **51**, 77–108.

Longworth, I.H. 1984 *Collared urns of the Bronze Age in Great Britain and Ireland.* Cambridge.

Lowery, P.R., Savage, R.D.A. and Wilkins, R.L. 1971 Scriber, graver, scorper: notes on experiments in bronzeworking technique. *Proceedings of the Prehistoric Society* **37**, 167–82.

Lucas, A.T. 1960 National Museum of Ireland: archaeological acquisitions in the year 1958. *Journal of the Royal Society of Antiquaries of Ireland* **90**, 1–40.

Lucas, A.T. 1961 National Museum of Ireland: archaeological acquisitions in the year 1959. *Journal of the Royal Society of Antiquaries of Ireland* **91**, 43–107.

Lucas, A.T. 1963 The sacred trees of Ireland. *Journal of the Cork Historical and Archaeological Society* **68**, 16–54.

Lucas, A.T. 1964 National Museum of Ireland: archaeological acquisitions in the year 1962. *Journal of the Royal Society of Antiquaries of Ireland* **94**, 85–104.

Lucas, A.T. 1966 National Museum of Ireland: archaeological acquisitions in the year 1963. *Journal of the Royal Society of Antiquaries of Ireland* **96**, 7–27.

Lucas, A.T. 1967 National Museum of Ireland: archaeological acquisitions in the year 1964. *Journal of the Royal Society of Antiquaries of Ireland* **97**, 1–28.

Lucas, A.T. 1968 National Museum of Ireland: archaeological acquisitions in the year 1965. *Journal of the Royal Society of Antiquaries of Ireland* **98**, 93–159.

Lucas, A.T. 1970 National Museum of Ireland: archaeological acquisitions in the year 1967. *Journal of the Royal Society of Antiquaries of Ireland* **100**, 145–66.

Lucas, A.T. 1971 National Museum of Ireland: archaeological acquisitions in the year 1968. *Journal of the Royal Society of Antiquaries of Ireland* **101**, 184–244.

Lucas, A.T. 1972 Prehistoric block-wheels from Doogarymore, Co. Roscommon, and Timahoe East, Co. Kildare. *Journal of the Royal Society of Antiquaries of Ireland* **102**, 19–48.

Lynch, A. 1981 *Man and environment in south-west Ireland.* British Archaeological Reports, British Series 85. Oxford.

Lynch, A. 1988 Poulnabrone—a stone in time.

Archaeology Ireland **2** (3), 105–7.

Lynch, A. and Ó Donnabháin, B. 1994 Poulnabrone, Co. Clare. *The Other Clare* **18**, 5–7.

Lynch, F. 2001 Axes or skeumorphic cushion stones: the purpose of certain 'blunt' axes. In W. H. Metz, B. L. van Beek and H. Steegstra (eds), *Patina. Essays in honour of Jay Jordan Butler on the occasion of his 80th birthday*, 400–4. Groningen.

Lynn, C.J. 1977 Trial excavations at the King's Stables, Tray townland, Co. Armagh. *Ulster Journal of Archaeology* **40**, 42–62.

Lynn, C.J. 1986 Navan Fort: a draft summary of D. M. Waterman's excavations. *Emania* **1**, 11–19.

Lynn, C.J. 1988 Armagh in 3000 BC. In A. Hamlin and C. Lynn (eds), *Pieces of the past*, 8–10. Belfast.

Lynn, C.J. 1989a An interpretation of 'The Dorsey'. *Emania* **6**, 5–14.

Lynn, C.J. 1989b A bibliography of northern linear earthworks. *Emania* **6**, 18–21.

Lynn, C.J. 1991 Knockaulin (Dún Ailinne) and Navan: some architectural comparisons. *Emania* **8**, 51–6.

Lynn, C.J. 1992a The Iron Age mound in Navan Fort: a physical realization of Celtic religious beliefs? *Emania* **10**, 33–57.

Lynn, C.J. 1992b Excavations at the Dorsey, County Armagh, 1977. *Ulster Journal of Archaeology* **54–5**, 61–77.

Lynn, C.J. (ed.) 1997 *Excavations at Navan Fort 1961–71 by D. M. Waterman*. Belfast.

Lynn, C.J. 2000 Navan Fort site C excavations, June 1999, interim report. *Emania* **18**, 5–16.

Lynn, C.J. 2002 Navan Fort site C excavations, May 2000, interim report no. 2. *Emania* **19**, 5–18.

Lynn, C.J. 2003a Ireland in the Iron Age—a basket case? *Archaeology Ireland* **17** (2), 20–3.

Lynn, C.J. 2003b *Navan Fort. Archaeology and myth*. Bray.

Lynn, C.J. 2006 Some Iron Age figure-of-eight plan structures in Ireland. Problems of interpretation with particular reference to the examples from Navan Fort, Co. Armagh. *Emania* **20**, 5–19.

Macalister, R.A.S. 1928 *The archaeology of Ireland* (1st edn). Dublin.

McCartan, S.B. 2003 Mesolithic hunter-gatherers in the Isle of Man: adaptions to an island environment? In L. Larsson, H. Kindgren, K. Knutsson, D. Leoffler and A. Åkerlund (eds), *Mesolithic on the move. Papers presented at the Sixth International Conference on the Mesolithic in Europe, Stockholm 2000*, 331–9. Oxford.

McCarthy, A. 1986 'Poul Gorm', Glengarriff. In C. Cotter (ed.), *Excavations 1986*, 15. Dublin.

McCarthy, M. 2003 Moneyreague. In I. Bennett (ed.), *Excavations 2001*, 50–2. Bray.

McComb, A.M.G. and Simpson, D. 1999 The wild bunch: exploitation of hazel in prehistoric Ireland. *Ulster Journal of Archaeology* **58**, 1–16.

McCone, K. 1990 *Pagan past and Christian present in early Irish literature*. Maynooth.

McConway, C. and Donnelly, E. 2006 Daggers at dawn. *Archaeology Ireland* **20** (2), 5.

McCormick, F. 2004 Hunting wild pig in the late Mesolithic. In H. Roche, E. Grogan, J. Bradley, J. Coles and B. Raftery (eds), *From megaliths to metals. Essays in honour of George Eogan*, 1–5. Oxford.

McCormick, F. 2007 Mammal bone studies from Irish prehistoric sites. In E. Murphy and N. J. Whitehouse (eds), *Environmental archaeology in Ireland*, 77–101. Oxford.

McCormick, F. and Murray, E. 2007 *Excavations at Knowth 3—Knowth and the zooarchaeology of Early Christian Ireland*. Dublin.

McCormick, F., Gibbons, M., McCormac, F.G. and Moore, J. 1996 Bronze Age to medieval shell middens near Ballyconneely, Co. Galway. *Journal of Irish Archaeology* **7**, 77–84.

Macdonald, P. and Ó Néill, J. 2009 Investigation of the find-spot of the Tamlaght hoard, Co. Armagh. In G. Cooney, K. Becker, J. Coles, M. Ryan and S. Sievers (eds), *Relics of Old Decency. Archaeological studies in later prehistory. A Festschrift for Barry Raftery*, 167–79. Dublin.

McErlean, T., McConkey, R. and Forsythe, W. 2002 *Strangford Lough. An archaeological survey of the maritime cultural landscape*. Belfast.

McEvoy, B., Richards, M., Forster, P. and Bradley, D.G. 2004 The *longue durée* of genetic ancestry: genetic marker systems and Celtic origins on the Atlantic façade of Europe. *American Journal of Human Genetics* **75**, 693–702.

Mac Giolla Easpaig, D. 2005 The significance and etymology of the placename *Temair*. In E. Bhreathnach (ed.), *The kingship and landscape of Tara*, 423–49. Dublin.

McLaughlin, M. and Conran, S. 2008 The emerging Iron Age of south Munster. *Seanda:*

National Roads Authority Archaeology Magazine **3**, 51–3.

MacLean, R. 1993 Eat your greens: an examination of the potential diet available in Ireland during the Mesolithic. *Ulster Journal of Archaeology* **56**, 1–8.

McMann, J. 1994 Forms of power: dimensions of an Irish megalithic landscape. *Antiquity* **68**, 525–44.

McNeill, T.E. 1992 Excavations at Dunsilly, County Antrim. *Ulster Journal of Archaeology* **54–5**, 78–112.

McQuade, M. 2008 Gone fishin'. *Archaeology Ireland* **22** (1), 8–11.

McQuade, M. and O'Donnell, L. 2006 Late Mesolithic fish traps from the Liffey estuary, Dublin, Ireland. *Antiquity* **81**, 569–84.

McQuade, M., Molloy, B. and Moriarty, C. (eds) 2009 *In the shadow of the Galtees: archaeological excavations along the N8 Cashel to Mitchelstown road scheme*. Archaeology and the National Roads Authority Monograph Series No. 4. Dublin.

McSparron, C. 2003 The excavation of a Neolithic house and other structures at Enagh, County Derry. *Ulster Journal of Archaeology* **62**, 1–15.

McSparron, C. 2008 'Have you no homes to go to?' *Archaeology Ireland* **22** (3), 18–25.

Madden, A.C. 1969 The Beaker wedge tomb at Moytirra, Co. Sligo. *Journal of the Royal Society of Antiquaries of Ireland* **99**, 151–9.

Mallory, J.P. 1982 The sword of the Ulster Cycle. In B. G. Scott (ed.), *Studies on early Ireland. Essays in honour of M. V. Duignan*, 99–114. Belfast.

Mallory, J.P. 1984 The Long Stone, Ballybeen, Dundonald, County Down. *Ulster Journal of Archaeology* **47**, 1–4.

Mallory, J.P. [1985] *Navan Fort. The ancient capital of Ulster*. Belfast.

Mallory, J.P. 1986 Donegore Hill. In C. Cotter (ed.), *Excavations 1985*, 11. Dublin.

Mallory, J.P. 1992a A Neolithic settlement at Bay Farm II, Carnlough, Co. Antrim. *Ulster Journal of Archaeology* **54–5**, 3–12.

Mallory, J.P. 1992b Migration and language change. In E. Straume and E. Skar (eds), *Peregrinatio Gothica III*, 145–53. Universitetets Oldsaksamlings Skrifter, Ny rekke, no. 14. Oslo.

Mallory, J.P. 1992c The world of Cú Chulainn: the archaeology of *Táin Bó Cúailnge*. In J. P. Mallory (ed.), *Aspects of the Táin*, 103–59. Belfast.

Mallory, J.P. 1995 Haughey's Fort and the Navan Complex in the late Bronze Age. In J. Waddell and E. S. Twohig (eds), *Ireland in the Bronze Age. Proceedings of the Dublin Conference, April 1995*, 73–86. Dublin.

Mallory, J.P. 2000 Excavations of the Navan ditch. *Emania* **18**, 21–35.

Mallory, J.P. and Hartwell, B. 1984 Donegore. *Current Archaeology* **92**, 271–5.

Mallory, J.P. and McCormick, F. 1988 Excavations at Ballymulholland, Magilligan Foreland, Co. Londonderry. *Ulster Journal of Archaeology* **51**, 103–14.

Mallory, J.P., Brown, D.M. and Baillie, M.G.L. 1999 Dating Navan Fort. *Antiquity* **73**, 427–31.

Mallory, J.P., Moore, D.G. and Canning, L.J. 1996 Excavations at Haughey's Fort 1991 and 1995. *Emania* **14**, 5–20.

Mandal, S. 1997 Striking the balance: the roles of petrography and geochemistry in stone axe studies in Ireland. *Archaeometry* **39**, 289–308.

Mandal, S., Cooney, G., Meighan, I.G. and Jamieson, D.D. 1997 Using geochemistry to interpret porcellanite stone axe production in Ireland. *Journal of Archaeological Science* **24**, 757–63.

Manning, C. 1985 A Neolithic burial mound at Ashleypark, Co. Tipperary. *Proceedings of the Royal Irish Academy* **85C**, 61–100.

Manning, C. 1986 Archaeological excavations of a succession of enclosures at Millockstown, Co. Louth. *Proceedings of the Royal Irish Academy* **86C**, 135–81.

Manning, C. 1988 A note on sacred trees. *Emania* **5**, 34–5.

Masterson, B. 1999 Archaeological applications of modern survey techniques. *Discovery Programme Reports* **5**, 131–46.

May, A. McL. 1942 Cornaclery round cairn, townland of Ballydullaghan, County of Londonderry. *Journal of the Royal Society of Antiquaries of Ireland* **72**, 81–97.

May, A. McL. 1953 Neolithic habitation site, stone circles and alignments at Beaghmore, Co. Tyrone. *Journal of the Royal Society of Antiquaries of Ireland* **83**, 174–97.

Meeks, N.D., Craddock, P.T. and Needham, S.P. 2008 Bronze Age penannular gold rings from the British Isles: technology and composition. *Jewellery Studies* **11**, 13–30.

Megaw, R. and Megaw, V. 2001 *Celtic art. From its beginnings to the Book of Kells*. London.

Meighan, I.G., Simpson, D. and Hartwell, B. 2002 Newgrange—sourcing of its granitic cobbles. *Archaeology Ireland* **16** (1), 32–5.

Meighan, I.G., Simpson, D.D.A., Hartwell, B.N., Fallick, A.E. and Kennan, P.S. 2003 Sourcing the quartz at Newgrange, Brú na Bóinne, Ireland. In G. Burenhult and S. Westergaard (eds), *Stones and bones. Formal disposal of the dead in Atlantic Europe during the Mesolithic–Neolithic interface 6000–3000 BC*, 247–51. British Archaeological Reports, International Series 1201. Oxford.

Mitchell, G.F. 1947 An early kitchen-midden in County Louth. *County Louth Archaeological Journal* **11**, 169–74.

Mitchell, G.F. 1949 Further early kitchen-middens in County Louth. *County Louth Archaeological Journal* **12**, 14–20.

Mitchell, G.F. 1955 The Mesolithic site at Toome Bay, Co. Londonderry. *Ulster Journal of Archaeology* **18**, 1–16.

Mitchell, G.F. 1956 An early kitchen-midden at Sutton, Co. Dublin. *Journal of the Royal Society of Antiquaries of Ireland* **86**, 1–26.

Mitchell, G.F. 1971 The Larnian culture: a minimal view. *Proceedings of the Prehistoric Society* **37**, 274–83.

Mitchell, G.F. 1972 Further excavation of the early kitchen-midden at Sutton, Co. Dublin. *Journal of the Royal Society of Antiquaries of Ireland* **102**, 151–9.

Mitchell, G.F. 1989 *Man and environment in Valencia Island*. Dublin.

Mitchell, G.F. and de G. Sieveking, G. 1972 Flint flake, probably of Palaeolithic age, from Mell townland, near Drogheda, Co. Louth, Ireland. *Journal of the Royal Society of Antiquaries of Ireland* **102**, 174–7.

Mitchell, G.F. and Ryan, M. 1997 *Reading the Irish landscape*. Dublin.

Mogey, J.M. and Thompson, G.B. 1956 Excavation of two ring-barrows in Mullaghmore townland, Co. Down. *Ulster Journal of Archaeology* **19**, 11–28.

Molloy, K. 2005 Holocene vegetation and land-use history at Mooghaun, south-east Clare, with particular reference to the Bronze Age. In E. Grogan, *The North Munster Project. Vol. 1: The later prehistoric landscape of south-east Clare*, 255–87. Discovery Programme Monograph 6. Bray.

Molloy, K. and O'Connell, M. 1993 Early land use and vegetation history at Derryinver Hill, Renvyle peninsula, Co. Galway, Ireland. In F. M. Chambers (ed.), *Climate change and human impact on the landscape*, 185–283. London.

Molloy, K. and O'Connell, M. 1995 Palaeoecological investigations towards the reconstruction of environment and land-use changes during prehistory at Céide Fields, western Ireland. *Probleme der Küstenforschung im südlichen Nordseegebiet* **23**, 187–225.

Molloy, K. and O'Connell, M. 2004 Holocene vegetation and land-use dynamics in the karstic environment of Inis Oírr, Aran Islands, western Ireland: pollen analytical evidence evaluated in the light of the archaeological record. *Quaternary International* **113**, 41–64.

Molloy, K. and O'Connell, M. 2007 Fresh insights into long-term environmental change on the Aran Islands based on palaeoecological investigations of lake sediments from Inis Oírr. *Journal of the Galway Archaeological and Historical Society* **59**, 1–17.

Moloney, A. 1993 *Excavations at Clonfinlough, Co. Offaly*. Irish Archaeological Wetland Unit Transactions 2. Dublin.

Monk, M.A. 1986 Evidence from macroscopic plant remains for crop husbandry in prehistoric and early historic Ireland: a review. *Journal of Irish Archaeology* **3**, 31–6.

Monk, M.A. 1988 Archaeobotanical study of samples from pipeline sites. In M. Gowen (ed.), *Three Irish gas pipelines: new archaeological evidence from Munster*, 185–91. Dublin.

Monk, M.A. 1993 People and environment: in search of the farmers. In E. S. Twohig and M. Ronayne (eds), *Past perceptions. The prehistoric archaeology of south-west Ireland*, 35–52. Cork.

Monk, M.A. 2000 Seeds and soils of discontent: an environmental archaeological contribution to the nature of the early Neolithic. In A. Desmond, G. Johnson, M. McCarthy, J. Sheehan and E. Shee Twohig (eds), *New agendas in Irish prehistory. Papers in commemoration of Liz Anderson*, 67–87. Bray.

Moore, D.G. 2003 Neolithic houses in Ballyharry townland, Islandmagee, Co. Antrim. In I. Armit,

E. Murphy, E. Nelis and D. Simpson (eds), *Neolithic settlement in Ireland and western Britain*, 156–63. Oxford.

Moore, D.G. 2004 Hostilities in early Ireland: trouble with the new neighbours—the evidence from Ballyharry, County Antrim. In A. Gibson and A. Sheridan (eds), *From sickles to circles. Britain and Ireland at the time of Stonehenge*, 142–54. Stroud.

Moore, J. 2003 Beyond hazelnuts and into the forest. In L. Bevan and J. Moore (eds), *Peopling the Mesolithic in a northern environment*, 53–8. British Archaeological Reports, International Series 1157. Oxford.

Moore, M.J. 1995 A Bronze Age settlement and ritual centre in the Monavullagh Mountains, County Waterford, Ireland. *Proceedings of the Prehistoric Society* **61**, 191–243.

Moroney, A. 1999 Winter sunsets at Dowth. *Archaeology Ireland* **13** (4), 29–31.

Mossop, M. 2004 Area 17, Marshes Upper, Dundalk. In I. Bennett (ed.), *Excavations 2002*, 380. Bray.

Mossop, M. 2009 Lakeside developments in County Meath, Ireland: a late Mesolithic fishing platform and possible mooring at Clowanstown 1. In S. McCartan, R. Schulting, G. Warren and P. Woodman (eds), *Mesolithic horizons. Papers presented at the Seventh International Conference on the Mesolithic, Belfast 2005*, 895–9. Oxford.

Mount, C. 1994 Aspects of ritual deposition in the late Neolithic and Beaker periods at Newgrange, Co. Meath. *Proceedings of the Prehistoric Society* **60**, 433–43.

Mount, C. 1995 New research on Irish early Bronze Age cemeteries. In J. Waddell and E. Shee Twohig (eds), *Ireland in the Bronze Age. Proceedings of the Dublin Conference, April 1995*, 97–112. Dublin.

Mount, C. 1997a Adolf Mahr's excavations of an early Bronze Age cemetery at Keenoge, County Meath. *Proceedings of the Royal Irish Academy* **97**C, 1–68.

Mount, C. 1997b Early Bronze Age burial in south-east Ireland in the light of recent research. *Proceedings of the Royal Irish Academy* **97**C, 101–93.

Mount, C. 1998 Five early Bronze Age cemeteries at Brownstown, Graney West, Oldtown and Ploopluck, County Kildare, and Strawhall, County Carlow. *Proceedings of the Royal Irish Academy* **98**C, 25–99.

Mount, C. 1999 Excavation and environmental analysis of a Neolithic mound and Iron Age barrow cemetery at Rathdoony Beg, County Sligo, Ireland. *Proceedings of the Prehistoric Society* **65**, 337–71.

Mount, C. and Hartnett, P.J. 1993 Early Bronze Age cemetery at Edmondstown, County Dublin. *Proceedings of the Royal Irish Academy* **93**C, 21–79.

Movius, H.L. 1937 A Stone Age site at Glenarm, Co. Antrim. *Journal of the Royal Society of Antiquaries of Ireland* **67**, 181–220.

Movius, H.L. 1940a An early postglacial archaeological site at Cushendun, Co. Antrim. *Proceedings of the Royal Irish Academy* **46**C, 1–48.

Movius, H.L. 1940b Report on a Stone Age excavation at Rough Island, Strangford Lough, Co. Down. *Journal of the Royal Society of Antiquaries of Ireland* **70**, 111–42.

Movius, H.L. 1942 *The Irish Stone Age*. Cambridge.

Movius, H.L. 1953 Curran Point, Larne, Co. Antrim: the type-site of the Irish Mesolithic. *Proceedings of the Royal Irish Academy* **56**C, 1–195.

Müller-Karpe, H. 1980 *Handbuch der Vorgeschichte*. Band IV.3. Munich.

Murphy, B. 1977 A handaxe from Dun Aenghus, Inishmore, Aran Islands, Co. Galway. *Proceedings of the Royal Irish Academy* **77**C, 257–9.

Murphy, D. and Clarke, L. 2003 Lagavooreen. In I. Bennett (ed.), *Excavations 2001*, 309–11. Bray.

Murphy, E. 2003 Funerary processing of the dead in prehistoric Ireland. *Archaeology Ireland* **17** (2), 13–15.

Murphy, E. and McCormick, F. 1996 The faunal remains from the inner ditch of Haughey's Fort. Third report: 1991 excavation. *Emania* **14**, 47–50.

Murphy, E. and Whitehouse, N.J. (eds) 2007 *Environmental archaeology in Ireland*. Oxford.

Murray, C. 2002 Pallasboy. In I. Bennett (ed.), *Excavations 2000*, 349. Bray.

Needham, S. 1979a A pair of early Bronze Age spearheads from Lightwater, Surrey. In C. B. Burgess and D. Coombs (eds), *Bronze Age hoards*, 1–40. British Archaeological Reports, British Series 67. Oxford.

Needham, S. 1979b Two recent shield finds and

their Continental parallels. *Proceedings of the Prehistoric Society* **45**, 111–34.

Needham, S. 1996 Chronology and periodisation in the British Bronze Age. *Acta Archaeologica* **67**, 121–40.

Needham, S. 2000a The gold and copper metalwork. In G. Hughes (ed.), *The Lockington gold hoard: an early Bronze Age barrow cemetery at Lockington, Leicestershire*, 23–47. Oxford.

Needham, S. 2000b The development of embossed goldwork in Bronze Age Europe. *Antiquaries Journal* **80**, 27–65.

Needham, S. 2001 When expediency broaches ritual intention: the flow of metal between systemic and buried domains. *Journal of the Royal Anthropological Institute* **7**, 275–98.

Needham, S. 2005 Transforming Beaker culture in north-west Europe; processes of fusion and fission. *Proceedings of the Prehistoric Society* **71**, 171–217.

Neill, M. 1996 Haughey's Fort excavation 1991: analysis of wood remains. *Emania* **14**, 29–46.

Nelis, E. 2003 Donegore and Lyles Hill, Neolithic enclosed sites in Co. Antrim: the lithic assemblages. In I. Armit, E. Murphy, E. Nelis and D. Simpson (eds), *Neolithic settlement in Ireland and western Britain*, 203–17. Oxford.

Newman, C. 1993 The Tara survey. Interim report. *Discovery Programme Reports* **1**, 69–89.

Newman, C. 1995 The Iron Age to Early Christian transition: the evidence from dress fasteners. In C. Bourke (ed.), *From the isles of the north. Early medieval art in Ireland and Britain*, 17–25. Belfast.

Newman, C. 1997a Ballinderry crannog no. 2, Co. Offaly: the later Bronze Age. *Journal of Irish Archaeology* **8**, 91–100.

Newman, C. 1997b *Tara: an archaeological survey.* Discovery Programme Monograph 2. Dublin.

Newman, C. 1998 Reflections on the making of a 'royal site' in early Ireland. *World Archaeology* **30**, 127–41.

Newman, C. 2005 Re-composing the archaeological landscape of Tara. In E. Bhreathnach (ed.), *The kingship and landscape of Tara*, 361–409. Dublin.

Newman, C. 2007a Misinformation, disinformation and downright distortion: the battle to save Tara, 1999–2005. In C. Newman and U. Strohmayer, *Uninhabited Ireland. Tara, the M3 and public spaces in Galway*, 61–101. Galway.

Newman, C. 2007b Procession and symbolism at Tara: analysis of Tech Midhchúarta (the 'Banqueting Hall') in the context of the sacral campus. *Oxford Journal of Archaeology* **26**, 415–38.

Newman, C., O'Connell, M., Dillon, M. and Molloy, K. 2007 Interpretation of charcoal and pollen data relating to an Iron Age ritual site in eastern Ireland: a holistic approach. *Vegetation History and Archaeobotany* **16**, 349–65.

Noonan, D. 2003 Muckridge 1. In I. Bennett (ed.), *Excavations 2001*, 53. Bray.

Northover, J.P. 1989 The gold torc from Saint Helier, Jersey. *Annual Bulletin of the Société Jersiaise* **25**, 112–37.

Nugent, L. 2005 The Rian Bó Phádraig—fact or fiction: problems facing medieval roads in the twentieth century. *Tipperary Historical Journal* (2005), 1–8.

O'Brien, E. 1999 Excavation of a multi-period burial site at Ballymacaward, Ballyshannon, Co. Donegal. *Donegal Annual* **51**, 56–61.

O'Brien, E. 2003 Burial practices in Ireland: first to seventh centuries BC. In J. Downes and A. Ritchie (eds), *Sea change: Orkney and northern Europe in the later Iron Age AD 300–800*, 63–72. Balgavies.

O'Brien, E. 2009 Pagan or Christian? Burial in Ireland during the 5th to 8th centuries AD. In N. Edwards (ed.), *The archaeology of the early medieval Celtic churches*, 135–54. London.

O'Brien, W. 1992 Boulder-burials: a Later Bronze Age megalith tradition in south-west Ireland. *Journal of the Cork Historical and Archaeological Society* **97**, 11–35.

O'Brien, W. 1994 *Mount Gabriel. Bronze Age mining in Ireland.* Galway.

O'Brien, W. 1999 *Sacred ground. Megalithic tombs in coastal south-west Ireland.* Galway.

O'Brien, W. 2003 The Bronze Age copper mines of the Goleen area, Co. Cork. *Proceedings of the Royal Irish Academy* **103**C, 13–59.

O'Brien, W. 2004a *Ross Island. Mining, metal and society in early Ireland.* Galway.

O'Brien, W. 2004b (Con)Fusion of tradition: the circle henge in Ireland. In A. Gibson and A. Sheridan (eds), *From sickles to circles. Britain and Ireland at the time of Stonehenge*, 323–38. Stroud.

O'Brien, W. 2008 Cashel hillfort, Clashanimud. In I. Bennett (ed.), *Excavations 2005*, 49. Dublin.

O'Brien, W. 2009 *Local worlds. Early settlement*

landscapes and upland farming in south-west Ireland. Cork.

O'Connell, A. 2009a Director's first findings from excavations at Lismullin 1. In M. B. Deevy and D. Murphy (eds), *Places along the way. First findings on the M3*, 21–42. Archaeology and the National Roads Authority Monograph Series No. 5, Dublin.

O'Connell, A. 2009b M3 Clonee–North of Kells Contract 2, Dunshaughlin–Navan. Report on the archaeological excavation of Lismullin 1, Co. Meath. http://www.m3motorway.ie/Archaeology/Section2/Lismullin1/file, 1627, en.pdf

O'Connell, M. 1980 Pollen analysis of fen peat from a Mesolithic site at Lough Boora, Co. Offaly, Ireland. *Journal of Life Sciences (Royal Dublin Society)* **2**, 45–9.

O'Connell, M. 1986 Reconstruction of local landscape development in the post-Atlantic based on palaeoecological investigations at Carrownaglogh prehistoric field system, County Mayo, Ireland. *Review of Palaeobotany and Palynology* **49**, 117–76.

O'Connell, M. 1990 Origins of Irish lowland blanket bog. In G. J. Doyle (ed.), *Ecology and conservation of Irish peatlands*, 49–71. Dublin.

O'Connell, M. 1994 *Connemara. Vegetation and land use since the last Ice Age*. Dublin.

O'Connell, M. and Molloy, K. 2001 Farming and woodland dynamics in Ireland during the Neolithic. *Proceedings of the Royal Irish Academy* **101**B, 99–128.

O'Connell, M. and Molloy, K. 2005 Native woodland composition and dynamics: a long-term perspective based on a Holocene pollen profile from Inis Oírr, Aran Islands, western Ireland. In C. Doyle and D. Little (eds), *Ireland's native woodlands. Conference proceedings, Galway, 8th–11th September 2004*, 20–47 [CD-ROM]. Galway.

O'Connor, Bl. 2003 Recent excavations in a rock art landscape. *Archaeology Ireland* **17** (4), 14–16.

O'Connor, Bl. 2006 Drumirril. In I. Bennett (ed.), *Excavations 2003*, 397–8.

O'Connor, Br. 1980 *Cross-channel relations in the late Bronze Age*. British Archaeological Reports, International Series 91. Oxford.

O'Connor, Br. 2004 The earliest Scottish metalwork since Coles. In I. A. G. Shepherd and

G. J. Barclay (eds), *Scotland in ancient Europe. The Neolithic and early Bronze Age of Scotland in their European context*, 205–16. Edinburgh.

Ó Donnabháin, B. and Brindley, A.L. 1990 The status of children in a sample of Bronze Age burials containing pygmy cups. *Journal of Irish Archaeology* **5**, 19–24.

O'Donnell, M.G. 1999 Excavation of a section of the Rian Bó Phádraig near Ardfinnan. *Tipperary Historical Journal* (1999), 183–9.

O'Donovan, E. 2004 A Neolithic house at Kishoge, Co. Dublin. *Journal of Irish Archaeology* **12–13**, 1–27.

Ó Drisceoil, D. 1988 Burnt mounds: cooking or bathing? *Antiquity* **62**, 671–80.

O'Dwyer, S. 2004 *Prehistoric music of Ireland*. Stroud.

O'Flaherty, B. 1987 A linear earthwork at Shankill, Co. Kilkenny. In R. M. Cleary, M. F. Hurley and E. A. Twohig (eds), *Archaeological excavations on the Cork–Dublin gas pipeline (1981–82)*, 53–4. Cork.

O'Flaherty, R. 1995 An analysis of Irish early Bronze Age hoards containing copper or bronze objects. *Journal of the Royal Society of Antiquaries of Ireland* **125**, 10–45.

O'Flaherty, R. 1998 The early Bronze Age halberd: a history of research and a brief guide to the sources. *Journal of the Royal Society of Antiquaries of Ireland* **128**, 74–94.

O'Flaherty, R. 2007 A weapon of choice—experiments with a replica Irish early Bronze Age halberd. *Antiquity* **81**, 423–34.

O'Flaherty, R., Bright, P., Gahan, J. and Gilchrist, M.D. 2008 Up close and personal . . . the evidence for impact damage on Irish halberds. *Archaeology Ireland* **22** (4), 22–5.

Ó Floinn, R. 1995 Recent research into Irish bog bodies. In R. C. Turner and R. G. Scaife (eds), *Bog bodies. New discoveries and new perspectives*, 137–45. London.

Ó Floinn, R. 2000 Freestone Hill, Co. Kilkenny: a reassessment. In A. P. Smyth (ed.), *Seanchas. Studies in early and medieval Irish archaeology, history and literature in honour of Francis J. Byrne*, 12–29. Dublin.

Ó Floinn, R. 2001 Patrons and politics: art, artefact and methodology. In M. Redknap, N. Edwards, S. Youngs, A. Lane and J. Knight (eds), *Pattern and purpose in Insular art*, 1–14. Oxford.

Ó Floinn, R. 2009 Notes on some Iron Age finds from Ireland. In G. Cooney, K. Becker, J. Coles, M. Ryan and S. Sievers (eds), *Relics of Old Decency. Archaeological studies in later prehistory. A Festschrift for Barry Raftery*, 199–208. Dublin.

O'Hara, R. 2006 Grange Rath, Colp West. In I. Bennett (ed.), *Excavations 2003*, 365–6. Bray.

Ó hEailidhe, P. 1992 'The Monk's Boat'—a Roman-period relic from Lough Lene, Co. Westmeath, Eire. *International Journal of Nautical Archaeology* 21, 185–90.

O'Kelly, C. 1971 *Illustrated guide to Newgrange.* Wexford.

O'Kelly, M.J. 1951 An early Bronze Age ringfort at Carrigillihy, Co. Cork. *Journal of the Cork Historical and Archaeological Society* 56, 69–86.

O'Kelly, M.J. 1954 Excavations and experiments in ancient Irish cooking-places. *Journal of the Royal Society of Antiquaries of Ireland* 84, 105–55.

O'Kelly, M.J. 1958a A horned cairn at Shanballyedmond, Co. Tipperary. *Journal of the Cork Historical and Archaeological Society* 63, 37–72.

O'Kelly, M.J. 1958b A wedge-shaped gallery grave at Island, Co. Cork. *Journal of the Royal Society of Antiquaries of Ireland* 88, 1–23.

O'Kelly, M.J. 1960 A wedge-shaped gallery grave at Baurnadomeeny, Co. Tipperary. *Journal of the Cork Historical and Archaeological Society* 65, 85–115.

O'Kelly, M.J. 1970 An axe mould from Lyre, Co. Cork. *Journal of the Cork Historical and Archaeological Society* 75, 25–8.

O'Kelly, M.J. 1982 *Newgrange. Archaeology, art and legend.* London.

O'Kelly, M.J. 1989 *Early Ireland. An introduction to Irish prehistory.* Cambridge.

O'Kelly, M.J. and O'Kelly, C. 1983 The tumulus of Dowth, County Meath. *Proceedings of the Royal Irish Academy* 83C, 135–90.

O'Kelly, M.J. and Shee, E. 1974 Bronze Age burials at Coolnahane and Ballinvoher, Co. Cork. *Journal of the Cork Historical and Archaeological Society* 80, 71–85.

O'Kelly, M.J. and Shell, C.A. 1979 Stone objects and a bronze axe from Newgrange, Co. Meath. In M. Ryan (ed.), *The origins of metallurgy in Atlantic Europe. Proceedings of the fifth Atlantic colloquium*, 127–44. Dublin.

O'Kelly, M.J., Cleary, R.M. and Lehane, D. 1983 *Newgrange, Co. Meath, Ireland. The late Neolithic/Beaker period settlement.* British Archaeological Reports, International Series 190. Oxford.

O'Kelly, M.J., Lynch, F. and O'Kelly, C. 1978 Three passage-graves at Newgrange, Co. Meath. *Proceedings of the Royal Irish Academy* 78C, 249–352.

O'Leary, P. and Shee Twohig, E. 1993 A possible Iron Age pillar stone on Cape Clear, Co. Cork. *Journal of the Cork Historical and Archaeological Society* 98, 133–40.

O'Meara, J.J. 1951 *The first version of the Topography of Ireland by Giraldus Cambrensis.* Dundalk.

Ó Néill, J. 2001 A glimpse of Wicklow's past. *Archaeology Ireland* 15 (4), 30–1.

Ó Néill, J. 2002 Reconstructing the Carrickfergus tankard. *Ulster Journal of Archaeology* 61, 8–16.

Ó Néill, J. 2003 Kilmurry North. In I. Bennett (ed.), *Excavations 2001*, 424–5.

Ó Néill, J. 2004 *Lapidibus in igne calefactis coquebatur:* the historical burnt mound tradition. *Journal of Irish Archaeology* 12–13, 79–85.

Ó Néill, J. 2005 Worked wood. In M. Gowen, J. Ó Néill and M. Phillips (eds), *The Lisheen Mine Archaeological Project 1996–8*, 329–40. Bray.

Ó Néill, J. and Plunkett, G. 2007 A middle Bronze Age occupation site at Ballyarnet Lake, County Derry: the site in its wider context. In J. Barber, C. Clark, M. Cressy *et al.* (eds), *Archaeology from the wetlands: recent perspectives*, 175–81. Edinburgh.

Ó Néill, J., Plunkett, G. and Whitehouse, N. 2007 The archaeological and palaeoecological investigation of a middle Bronze Age settlement at Ballyarnet Lake, County Derry. *Ulster Journal of Archaeology* 66, 39–49.

O'Neill, L., Donnelly, C., Mallory, J. and McNeill, T. 2003 Rough Island. In I. Bennett (ed.), *Excavations 2001*, 76–7. Bray.

Ó Nualláin, S. 1972 A Neolithic house at Ballyglass, near Ballycastle, Co. Mayo. *Journal of the Royal Society of Antiquaries of Ireland* 102, 49–57.

Ó Nualláin, S. 1976 The central court tombs of the north-west of Ireland. *Journal of the Royal Society of Antiquaries of Ireland* 106, 92–117.

Ó Nualláin, S. 1977 A dual court-tomb at Garran townland, County Monaghan. *Journal of the Royal Society of Antiquaries of Ireland* 107, 52–60.

Ó Nualláin, S. 1978 Boulder-burials. *Proceedings of the Royal Irish Academy* **78**C, 75–114.

Ó Nualláin, S. 1983 Irish portal tombs: topography, siting and distribution. *Journal of the Royal Society of Antiquaries of Ireland* **113**, 75–105.

Ó Nualláin, S. 1984 A survey of stone circles in Cork and Kerry. *Proceedings of the Royal Irish Academy* **84**C, 1–77.

Ó Nualláin, S. 1989 *Survey of the megalithic tombs of Ireland. Vol. V: County Sligo.* Dublin.

Ó Nualláin, S. 1994 Stone rows in the south of Ireland. *Proceedings of the Royal Irish Academy* **94**C, 179–256.

Ó Nualláin, S. 1998 Excavation of the smaller court-tomb and associated hut sites at Ballyglass, Co. Mayo. *Proceedings of the Royal Irish Academy* **98**C, 125–75.

Ó Ríordáin, B. 1967 Cordoned urn burial at Laheen, Co. Donegal. *Journal of the Royal Society of Antiquaries of Ireland* **97**, 39–44.

Ó Ríordáin, B. 1997 A Bronze Age cemetery mound at Grange, Co. Roscommon. *Journal of Irish Archaeology* **8**, 43–72.

Ó Ríordáin, B. and Waddell, J. 1993 *The funerary Bowls and Vases of the Irish Bronze Age.* Galway.

Ó Ríordáin, S.P. 1936 Excavations at Lissard, Co. Limerick, and other sites in the locality. *Journal of the Royal Society of Antiquaries of Ireland* **66**, 173–85.

Ó Ríordáin, S.P. 1939 Excavation of a stone circle and cairn at Kealkil, Co. Cork. *Journal of the Cork Historical and Archaeological Society* **44**, 46–9.

Ó Ríordáin, S.P. 1947 Roman material in Ireland. *Proceedings of the Royal Irish Academy* **51**C, 35–82.

Ó Ríordáin, S.P. 1951 Lough Gur excavations: the great stone circle (B) in Grange townland. *Proceedings of the Royal Irish Academy* **54**C, 37–74.

Ó Ríordáin, S.P. 1954 Lough Gur excavations: Neolithic and Bronze Age houses on Knockadoon. *Proceedings of the Royal Irish Academy* **56**C, 297–459.

Ó Ríordáin, S.P. and de Valera, R. 1952 Excavation of a megalithic tomb at Ballyedmonduff, Co. Dublin. *Proceedings of the Royal Irish Academy* **55**C, 61–81.

Ó Ríordáin, S.P. and Ó h-Iceadha, G. 1955 Lough Gur excavations: the megalithic tomb. *Journal of the Royal Society of Antiquaries of Ireland* **85**, 34–50.

O'Sullivan, A. 1996 Neolithic, Bronze Age and Iron Age woodworking techniques. In B. Raftery, *Trackway excavations in the Mountdillon bogs, Co. Longford, 1985–1991*, 291–342. Irish Archaeological Wetland Unit Transactions 3. Dublin.

O'Sullivan, A. 1997 Last foragers or first farmers? *Archaeology Ireland* **11** (2), 14–16.

O'Sullivan, A. 1998 *The archaeology of lake settlement in Ireland.* Dublin.

O'Sullivan, A. 2001 *Foragers, farmers and fishers in a coastal landscape. An intertidal archaeological survey of the Shannon estuary.* Dublin.

O'Sullivan, A., Little, A. and Parkes, M. 2007 The power of stone. *Archaeology Ireland* **21** (3), 36–9.

O'Sullivan, Ann and Sheehan, J. 1996 *The Iveragh peninsula. An archaeological survey of south Kerry.* Cork.

O'Sullivan, J. 2007 The quiet landscape: archaeological discoveries on a road scheme in east Galway. In J. O'Sullivan and M. Stanley (eds), *New routes to the past*, 81–100. Archaeology and the National Roads Authority Monograph Series No. 4. Dublin.

O'Sullivan, M. 1986 Approaches to passage tomb art. *Journal of the Royal Society of Antiquaries of Ireland* **116**, 68–83.

O'Sullivan, M. 1993 *Megalithic art in Ireland.* Dublin.

O'Sullivan, M. 1996 Megalithic art in Ireland and Brittany: divergence or convergence? In *Actes du 2ème Colloque Interrégional d'Art Mégalithique, Vannes, 1995. Revue archéologique de l'Ouest, Supplément* 8, 81–96.

O'Sullivan, M. 2005 *Duma na nGiall. The Mound of the Hostages, Tara.* Bray.

Palk, N.A. 1984 *Iron Age bridle-bits from Britain.* Edinburgh.

Parkes, P. 2004 Fosterage, kinship, and legend: when milk was thicker than blood? *Comparative Studies in Society and History* **46**, 587–615.

Patay, P. 1990 *Die Bronzegefässe in Ungarn.* Prähistorische Bronzefunde II:10. Munich.

Pedersen, L. 1995 7000 years of fishing: stationary fishing structures in the Mesolithic and afterwards. In A. Fischer (ed.), *Man and sea in the Mesolithic. Coastal settlement above and below present sea level. Proceedings of the International Symposium, Kalundborg, Denmark 1993*, 75–86. Oxford.

Pétrequin, P., Cassen, S., Croutsch, C. and Weller, O. 1997 Haches alpines et haches carnacéennes dans l'Europe du Ve millénaire. *Notae Praehistoricae* **17**, 135–50.

Piggott, S. 1983 *The earliest wheeled transport from the Atlantic coast to the Caspian Sea*. London.

Pilcher, J.R. 1969 Archaeology, palaeoecology, and 14C dating of the Beaghmore stone circle site. *Ulster Journal of Archaeology* **32**, 73–91.

Pilcher, J.R. and Smith, A.G. 1979 Palaeological investigations at Ballynagilly, a Neolithic and Bronze Age settlement in County Tyrone, Northern Ireland. *Philosophical Transactions of the Royal Society of London* **286**, 345–69.

Pitts, M. and Roberts, M. 1998 *Fairweather Eden*. London.

Plunkett, G. 2006 Hekla 3, environmental downturn and Irish late Bronze Age hillfort connections revisited. *Emania* **20**, 62–7.

Pollock, A.J. and Waterman, D.M. 1964 A Bronze Age habitation site at Downpatrick. *Ulster Journal of Archaeology* **27**, 31–58.

Powell, A.B. 2005 The language of lineage: reading Irish court tomb design. *European Journal of Archaeology* **8**, 9–28.

Powell, T.G.E. 1974 The Sintra collar and the Shannongrove gorget: aspects of late Bronze Age goldwork in the west of Europe. *North Munster Antiquarian Journal* **16**, 3–13.

Prendergast, F. 2008 'In the eye of the beholder': symbolism and meaning in Irish passage tomb alignment and height. In F. Coimbra and G. Dimitriadis (eds), *Cognitive archaeology as symbolic archaeology*, 3–12. British Archaeological Reports, International Series 1737. Oxford.

Pryor, F. 1980 *A catalogue of British and Irish prehistoric bronzes in the Royal Ontario Museum*. Toronto.

Purcell, A. 2002a Excavation of three Neolithic houses at Corbally, Kilcullen, Co. Kildare. *Journal of Irish Archaeology* **11**, 31–75.

Purcell, A. 2002b The rock-art landscape of the Iveragh peninsula in County Kerry, south-west Ireland. In C. Chippendale and G. Nash (eds), *European landscapes of rock art*, 71–92. London.

Raftery, B. 1974 A prehistoric burial mound at Baunogenasraid, Co. Carlow. *Proceedings of the Royal Irish Academy* **74**C, 277–312.

Raftery, B. 1975 A late Bronze Age bar toggle from Ireland. *Archaeologia Atlantica* **1**, 83–9.

Raftery, B. 1976a Rathgall and Irish hillfort problems. In D. W. Harding (ed.), *Hillforts. Later prehistoric earthworks in Britain and Ireland*, 339–57. London.

Raftery, B. 1976b The hillfort at Belmont in Co. Galway. *Journal of the Galway Archaeological and Historical Society* **35**, 89–95.

Raftery, B. 1978 Excavations at Killycluggin, County Cavan. *Ulster Journal of Archaeology* **41**, 49–54.

Raftery, B. 1981 Iron Age burials in Ireland. In D. Ó Corráin (ed.), *Irish antiquity. Essays and studies presented to Professor M. J. O'Kelly*, 173–204. Cork.

Raftery, B. 1982 Two recently discovered bronze shields from the Shannon basin. *Journal of the Royal Society of Antiquaries of Ireland* **112**, 5–17.

Raftery, B. 1983 *A catalogue of Irish Iron Age antiquities*. Marburg.

Raftery, B. 1984 *La Tène in Ireland. Problems of origin and chronology*. Marburg.

Raftery, B. 1987 The Loughnashade horns. *Emania* **2**, 21–4.

Raftery, B. 1988 *Hollow two-piece metal rings in La Tène Europe*. Marburger Studien zur Vor- und Frühgeschichte 11. Marburg.

Raftery, B. 1994a *Pagan Celtic Ireland. The enigma of the Irish Iron Age*. London.

Raftery, B. 1994b Reflections on the Irish Scabbard Style. In C. Dobiat (ed.), *Festschrift für Otto-Hermann Frey zum 65. Geburtstag*, 475–92. Marburger Studien zur Vor- und Frühgeschichte 16. Marburg.

Raftery, B. 1995 The conundrum of Irish Iron Age pottery. In B. Raftery, V. Megaw and V. Rigby (eds), *Sites and sights of the Iron Age. Essays on fieldwork and museum research presented to Ian Matheson Stead*, 149–56. Oxford.

Raftery, B. 1996 *Trackway excavations in the Mountdillon bogs, Co. Longford, 1985–1991*. Irish Archaeological Wetland Unit Transactions 3. Dublin.

Raftery, B. 1998 Knobbed spearbutts revisited. In M. Ryan (ed.), *Irish antiquities. Essays in memory of Joseph Raftery*, 97–110. Bray.

Raftery, B. 2000 A bit too far: Ireland's Transylvanian link in the later Iron Age. In A. P. Smyth (ed.), *Seanchas. Studies in early and medieval Irish archaeology, history and literature in honour of Francis J. Byrne*, 1–11. Dublin.

Raftery, B. 2004 Pit 119: Rathgall, Co. Wicklow. In H. Roche, E. Grogan, J. Bradley, J. Coles and B. Raftery (eds), *From megaliths to metals. Essays in honour of George Eogan*, 83–90. Oxford.

Raftery, B., Jennings, D. and Moloney, A. 1995 Annaghcorrib 1, Garryduff Bog, Co. Galway. *Irish Archaeological Wetland Unit Transactions* **4**, 39–53.

Raftery, J. 1944 The Turoe stone and the rath of Feerwore. *Journal of the Royal Society of Antiquaries of Ireland* **74**, 23–52.

Raftery, J. 1951 *Prehistoric Ireland*. London.

Raftery, J. 1960 A Bronze Age tumulus at Corrower, Co. Mayo. *Proceedings of the Royal Irish Academy* **61**C, 79–93.

Raftery, J. 1967 The Gorteenreagh hoard. In E. Rynne (ed.), *North Munster studies. Essays in commemoration of Monsignor Michael Moloney*, 61–71. Limerick.

Raftery, J. 1970 Prehistoric coiled basketry bags. *Journal of the Royal Society of Antiquaries of Ireland* **100**, 167–8.

Raftery, J. 1971 A Bronze Age hoard from Ballytegan, County Laois. *Journal of the Royal Society of Antiquaries of Ireland* **101**, 85–100.

Raftery, J. 1973 A Neolithic burial mound at Ballintruer More, Co. Wicklow. *Journal of the Royal Society of Antiquaries of Ireland* **103**, 214–19.

Ramsey, G. 1995 Middle Bronze Age metalwork: are artefact studies dead and buried? In J. Waddell and E. S. Twohig (eds), *Ireland in the Bronze Age. Proceedings of the Dublin Conference, April 1995*, 49–62. Dublin.

Ramsey, G., Bourke, C. and Crone, D. 1992 Antiquities from the River Blackwater I, Bronze Age metalwork. *Ulster Journal of Archaeology* **54–5**, 138–49.

Renfrew, C. 1987 *Archaeology and language. The puzzle of the Indo-Europeans*. London.

Richards, C. 2004 Labouring with monuments: constructing the dolmen at Carreg Samson, south-west Wales. In V. Cummings and C. Fowler (eds), *The Neolithic of the Irish Sea. Materiality and traditions of practice*, 72–80. Oxford.

Richardson, Á. and Johnston, P. 2007 Excavation of a Middle Bronze Age settlement site at Knockhouse Lower, Co. Waterford (03E1033). *Decies. Journal of the Waterford Archaeological and Historical Society* **63**, 1–17.

Robb, J. 1993 A social prehistory of European languages. *Antiquity* **67**, 747–60.

Roberts, M.B. and Parfitt, S.A. 1999 *Boxgrove. A Middle Pleistocene hominid site at Eartham Quarry, Boxgrove, West Sussex*. London.

Roche, H. 2002 Excavations at Ráith na Ríg, Tara, Co. Meath, 1997. *Discovery Programme Reports* **6**, 19–165.

Roche, H. 2004 The dating of the embanked stone circle at Grange, Co. Limerick. In H. Roche, E. Grogan, J. Bradley, J. Coles and B. Raftery (eds), *From megaliths to metals. Essays in honour of George Eogan*, 109–16. Oxford.

Roche, H. and Eogan, G. 2007 A re-assessment of the enclosure at Lugg, County Dublin, Ireland. In C. Gosden, H. Hamerow, P. de Jersey and G. Lock (eds), *Communities and connections: essays in honour of Barry Cunliffe*, 154–68. Oxford.

Ronayne, M. 2001 The political economy of landscape: conflict and value in a prehistoric landscape in the Republic of Ireland—ways of telling. In B. Bender and M. Winer (eds), *Contested landscapes: movement, exile and place*, 149–64. Oxford.

Ronayne, M. 2008 The state we're in on the eve of the World Archaeological Congress (WAC) 6. Archaeology in Ireland vs corporate takeover. *Public Archaeology* **7**, 114–29.

Ruggles, C. 1999 *Astronomy in prehistoric Britain and Ireland*. London.

Ruiz-Gálvez Priego, M. 1995 *Ritos de paso y puntos de pasa. La ría de Huelva en el mundo del Bronce final europeo*. Madrid.

Russell, I.R. and Corcoran, E. 2002 Excavation of a possible Bronze Age enclosure at Kilsharvan townland, Co. Meath. *Ríocht na Midhe* **13**, 32–4.

Ryan, M. 1975 Urn burial in Killeenaghmountain townland, near Kilwatermoy, Tallow, County Waterford. *Journal of the Royal Society of Antiquaries of Ireland* **105**, 147–9.

Ryan, M. 1980 An early Mesolithic site in the Irish midlands. *Antiquity* **54**, 46–7.

Ryan, M. 1981 Poulawack, Co. Clare: the affinities of the central burial structure. In D. Ó Corráin (ed.), *Irish antiquity. Essays and studies presented to Professor M. J. O'Kelly*, 134–46. Cork.

Ryan, M. (ed.) 1983 *Treasures of Ireland. Irish art 3000 B.C.–1500 A.D.* Dublin.

Rynne, E. 1962 Late Bronze Age rattle-pendants

from Ireland. *Proceedings of the Prehistoric Society* **28**, 383–5.

Rynne, E. 1963 Notes on some antiquities in Co. Kildare. *Journal of the Kildare Archaeological Society* **13**, 458–62.

Rynne, E. 1964 Middle Bronze Age burial at Knockboy, Co. Antrim. *Ulster Journal of Archaeology* **27**, 62–6.

Rynne, E. 1972a Celtic stone idols in Ireland. In C. Thomas (ed.), *The Iron Age in the Irish Sea Province*, 79–98. London.

Rynne, E. 1972b Tanged dagger from Derrynamanagh, Co. Galway. *Journal of the Royal Society of Antiquaries of Ireland* **102**, 240–3.

Rynne, E. 1982 A classification of pre-Viking Irish iron swords. In B. G. Scott (ed.), *Studies on early Ireland. Essays in honour of M. V. Duignan*, 93–7. Belfast.

Rynne, E. 1983 Some early Iron Age sword-hilts from Ireland and Scotland. In A. O'Connor and D.V. Clarke (eds), *From the Stone Age to the 'Forty-Five. Studies presented to R. B. K. Stevenson*, 188–96. Edinburgh.

Rynne, E. and Ó hÉailidhe, P. 1965 A group of prehistoric sites at Piperstown, Co. Dublin. *Proceedings of the Royal Irish Academy* **64**C, 61–84.

Saville, A. 2003 Indications of regionalisation in Mesolithic Scotland. In L. Larsson, H. Kindgren, K. Knutsson, D. Leoffler and A. Åkerlund (eds), *Mesolithic on the move. Papers presented at the sixth international conference on the Mesolithic in Europe, Stockholm 2000*, 340–50. Oxford.

Scarre, C. 2004 Displaying the stones: the materiality of 'megalithic' monuments. In E. DeMarrais, C. Gosden and C. Renfrew (eds), *Rethinking materiality. The engagement of mind with the material world*, 141–52. Cambridge.

Scarre, C. 2006 Consolidation, reconstruction and the interpretation of megalithic monuments. *ARKEOS—perspectivas em diálogo* **16**, 13–43.

Schmidt, P.K. and Burgess, C.B. 1981 *The axes of Scotland and northern England*. Prähistorische Bronzefunde IX:7. Munich.

Schot, R. 2006 *Uisneach Midi a medón Érenn*: a prehistoric 'cult' centre and 'royal site' in Co. Westmeath. *Journal of Irish Archaeology* **15**, 39–71.

Schulting, R.J. and Richards, M.P. 2002 The wet, the wild and the domesticated: the Mesolithic–Neolithic transition on the west

coast of Scotland. *European Journal of Archaeology* **5**, 147–89.

Schulting, R.J. and Wysocki, M. 2005 'In this chambered tumulus were found cleft skulls . . .': an assessment of the evidence for cranial trauma in the British Neolithic. *Proceedings of the Prehistoric Society* **71**, 107–38.

Schweitzer, H. 2005 Iron Age toe-rings from Rath, County Meath, on the N2 Finglas–Ashbourne Road scheme. In J. O'Sullivan and M. Stanley (eds), *Recent archaeological discoveries on national road schemes 2004*, 93–8. Archaeology and the National Roads Authority Monograph Series No. 2. Dublin.

Scott, B.G. 1974 Some notes on the transition from bronze to iron in Ireland. *Irish Archaeological Research Forum* **1** (1), 9–24.

Scott, B.G. 1977 Metallographic study of some early iron tools and weapons from Ireland. *Proceedings of the Royal Irish Academy* **77**C, 301–17.

Scott, B.G. 1990 *Early Irish ironworking*. Belfast.

Scott, S. 2003 Provincial art and Roman imperialism: an overview. In S. Scott and J. Webster (eds), *Roman imperialism and provincial art*, 1–7. Cambridge.

Shee, E. and Evans, D.M. 1965 A standing stone in the townland of Newgrange, Co. Meath. *Journal of the Cork Historical and Archaeological Society* **70**, 124–30.

Shee Twohig, E. 1981 *The megalithic art of western Europe*. Oxford.

Shee Twohig, E. 1996 Context and content of Irish passage tomb art. In *Actes du 2ème Colloque Interrégional d'Art Mégalithique, Vannes, 1995. Revue archéologique de l'Ouest, Supplément 8*, 67–80.

Shee Twohig, E. 1998 A 'Mother Goddess' in north-west Europe *c.* 4200–2500 BC? In L. Goodison and C. Morris (eds), *Ancient goddesses. The myths and the evidence*, 164–79. London.

Shee Twohig, E. 2000 Frameworks for the megalithic art of the Boyne Valley. In A. Desmond, G. Johnson, M. McCarthy, J. Sheehan and E. Shee Twohig (eds), *New agendas in Irish prehistory. Papers in commemoration of Liz Anderson* 89–105. Bray.

Shee Twohig, E. 2001 Change and continuity: post passage tomb ceremonial near Loughcrew, Co.

Meath. *Revue archéologique de l'Ouest, Supplément* 9, 113–24.

Shee Twohig, E. 2004 *Irish megalithic tombs* (2nd edn). Princes Risborough.

Shepherd, I.A.G. 2009 The V-bored buttons of Great Britain. *Proceedings of the Prehistoric Society* **75**, 335–69.

Sheridan, A. 1986 Megaliths and megalithomania: an account and interpretation of the development of passage tombs in Ireland. *Journal of Irish Archaeology* **3**, 17–30.

Sheridan, A. 1987 Nappan Neolithic site. In C. Cotter (ed.), *Excavations 1986*, 11. Dublin.

Sheridan, A. 1995 Irish Neolithic pottery: the story in 1995. In I. Kinnes and G. Varndell (eds), *'Unbaked Urns of Rudely Shape'. Essays on British and Irish pottery for Ian Longworth*, 3–21. Oxford.

Sheridan, A. 2003a French connections I: spreading the *marmites* thinly. In I. Armit, E. Murphy, E. Nelis and D. Simpson (eds), *Neolithic settlement in Ireland and western Britain*, 3–17. Oxford.

Sheridan, A. 2003b Ireland's earliest 'passage' tombs: a French connection? In G. Burenhult and S. Westergaard (eds), *Stones and bones. Formal disposal of the dead in Atlantic Europe during the Mesolithic–Neolithic interface, 6000–3000 BC*, 9–25. British Archaeological Reports, International Series 1201. Oxford.

Sheridan, A. 2003c The chronology of Irish megalithic tombs. In G. Burenhult and S. Westergaard (eds), *Stones and bones. Formal disposal of the dead in Atlantic Europe during the Mesolithic–Neolithic interface, 6000–3000 BC*, 69–73. British Archaeological Reports, International Series 1201. Oxford.

Sheridan, A. 2004 Going round in circles? Understanding the Irish Grooved Ware 'complex' in its wider context. In H. Roche, E. Grogan, J. Bradley, J. Coles and B. Raftery (eds), *From megaliths to metals. Essays in honour of George Eogan*, 26–37. Oxford.

Sheridan, A. 2006 A non-megalithic funerary tradition in early Neolithic Ireland. In M. Meek (ed.), *The modern traveller to our past. Festschrift in honour of Ann Hamlin*, 24–31. Belfast.

Sheridan, A. and Northover, P. 1993 A Beaker period copper dagger blade from the Sillees River near Ross Lough, Co. Fermanagh. *Ulster Journal of Archaeology* **56**, 61–9.

Sheridan, A. and Shortland, A. 2004 '. . . beads which have given rise to so much dogmatism, controversy and rash speculation': faience in early Bronze Age Britain and Ireland. In I. A. G. Shepherd and G. J. Barclay (eds), *Scotland in ancient Europe. The Neolithic and early Bronze Age of Scotland in their European context*, 263–79. Edinburgh.

Sheridan, A., Cooney, G. and Grogan, E. 1992 Stone axe studies in Ireland. *Proceedings of the Prehistoric Society* **58**, 389–416.

Sherratt, A. 1986 The Radley 'earrings' revised. *Oxford Journal of Archaeology* **5**, 61–6.

Sherratt, A. 1987 'Earrings' again. *Oxford Journal of Archaeology* **6**, 119.

Sikora, M. and Buckley, L. 2003 Casting new light on old excavations. *Archaeology Ireland* **17** (1), 16–19.

Simpson, D.D.A. 1986 A late Bronze Age sword from Island MacHugh, Co. Tyrone. *Ulster Journal of Archaeology* **49**, 103–4.

Simpson, D.D.A. 1990 The stone battle axes of Ireland. *Journal of the Royal Society of Antiquaries of Ireland* **120**, 5–40.

Simpson, D.D.A. 1995 The Neolithic settlement site at Ballygalley, Co. Antrim. In E. Grogan and C. Mount (eds), *Annus archaeologiae. Archaeological research 1992*, 37–44. Dublin.

Simpson, D.D.A. 1996a Irish perforated stone implements in context. *Journal of Irish Archaeology* **7**, 65–76.

Simpson, D.D.A. 1996b The Ballygalley houses, Co. Antrim, Ireland. In T. Darvill and J. Thomas (eds), *Neolithic houses in northwest Europe and beyond*, 123–32. Oxford.

Simpson, D.D.A. and Gibson, A. 1989 Lyles Hill. *Current Archaeology* **114**, 214–15.

Sims-Williams, P. 1998 Celtomania and Celtoscepticism. *Cambrian Medieval Celtic Studies* **36**, 1–35.

Skak-Nielsen, N.V. 2009 Flint and metal daggers in Scandinavia and other parts of Europe. A re-interpretation of their function in the Late Neolithic and Early Copper and Bronze Age. *Antiquity* **83**, 349–58.

Smart, D. 2000 Design and function in fishing gear: shell mounds, bait and fishing practices. In R. Young (ed.), *Mesolithic lifeways. Current research from Britain and Ireland*, 15–22. Leicester.

Smith, A.G. 1975 Neolithic and Bronze Age

landscape changes in northern Ireland. In J. G. Evans, S. Limbrey and H. Cleere (eds), *The effect of man on the landscape: the highland zone*, 64–74. London.

Smith, A.G. and Willis, E.H. 1962 Radiocarbon dating of the Fallahogy Landnam phase. *Ulster Journal of Archaeology* 24–5, 16–24.

Smith, R.A. 1920 *British Museum. A guide to the antiquities of the Bronze Age in the Department of British and Medieval Antiquities.* London.

Smyth, J. 2006 The role of the house in early Neolithic Ireland. *European Journal of Archaeology* 9, 229–57.

Spratling, M.G. 1980 Weighing of gold in prehistoric Europe. In W. A. Oddy (ed.), *Aspects of early metallurgy*, 179–83. London.

Sprockhoff, E. 1955 Central European Urnfield Culture and Celtic La Tène: an outline. *Proceedings of the Prehistoric Society* 21, 257–81.

Stanley, M. 2007 Anthropomorphic wooden figures: recent Irish discoveries. In J. Barber, C. Clark, M. Cressy *et al.* (eds), *Archaeology from the wetlands: recent perspectives. Proceedings of the 11th WARP conference, Edinburgh 2005*, 183–90. Edinburgh.

Stanley, M., McDermott, C., Moore, C. and Murray, C. 2003 Throwing off the yoke. *Archaeology Ireland* 17 (2), 6–8.

Stead, I.M. 2006 *British Iron Age swords and scabbards.* London.

Stephens, N. and Collins, A.E.P. 1960 The Quaternary deposits at Ringneill Quay and Ardmillan, Co. Down. *Proceedings of the Royal Irish Academy* 61C, 41–77.

Stirland, J. 2008 200,000-year-old flint from County Down. *Archaeology Ireland* 22 (1), 23–4.

Stout, G. 1991 Embanked enclosures of the Boyne region. *Proceedings of the Royal Irish Academy* 91C, 245–84.

Stout, G. 2002 *Newgrange and the Bend of the Boyne.* Cork.

Stout, G. and Stout, M. 2008 *Newgrange.* Cork.

Swan, L. 1998 *Teltown. An ancient assembly site in County Meath.* Archaeology Ireland Heritage Guide No. 3. Bray.

Sweetman, P.D. 1976 An earthen enclosure at Monknewtown, Slane, Co. Meath. *Proceedings of the Royal Irish Academy* 76C, 25–72.

Sweetman, P.D. 1985 A late Neolithic/early Bronze Age pit circle at Newgrange, Co. Meath.

Proceedings of the Royal Irish Academy 85C, 195–221.

Sweetman, P.D. 1987 Excavation of a late Neolithic/early Bronze Age site at Newgrange, Co. Meath. *Proceedings of the Royal Irish Academy* 87C, 283–98.

Swift, C. 2000 *Óenach Tailten*, the Blackwater Valley and the Uí Néill kings of Tara. In A. P. Smyth (ed.), *Seanchas. Studies in early and medieval Irish archaeology, history and literature in honour of Francis J. Byrne*, 109–20. Dublin.

Swift, C. 2003 The gods of Newgrange in Irish literature and Romano-Celtic tradition. In G. Burenhult and S. Westergaard (eds), *Stones and bones. Formal disposal of the dead in Atlantic Europe during the Mesolithic–Neolithic interface, 6000–3000 BC*, 53–63. British Archaeological Reports, International Series 1201. Oxford.

Taylor, J.J. 1970 Lunulae reconsidered. *Proceedings of the Prehistoric Society* 36, 38–81.

Taylor, J.J. 1980 *Bronze Age goldwork of the British Isles.* Cambridge.

Taylor, J.J. 1999 Gold reflections. In A. F. Harding (ed.), *Experiment and design. Archaeological studies in honour of John Coles*, 108–15. Oxford.

Thomas, J. 1996 The cultural context of the first use of domesticates in continental central and northwest Europe. In D. R. Harris (ed.), *The origins and spread of agriculture and pastoralism in Eurasia*, 310–22. London.

Thomas, J. 1999 *Understanding the Neolithic.* London.

Thrane, H. 1995 Penultima Thule: the Bronze Age in the western Baltic region as an analogy to the Irish Bronze Age. In J. Waddell and E. S. Twohig (eds), *Ireland in the Bronze Age. Proceedings of the Dublin Conference, April 1995*, 149–57. Dublin.

Tierney, J., Ryan, M. and Richardson, Á. 2008 Beaker settlement: area 2, Graigueshoneen td licence no. 98E0575. In P. Johnston, J. Kiely and J. Tierney (eds), *Near the bend of the river. The archaeology of the N25 Kilmacthomas realignment*, 33–43. Dublin.

Tierney, M. 2002 Ballymaley. In I. Bennett (ed.), *Excavations 2000*, 17. Bray.

Tilley, C. 2007 Architectural order and the ordering of imagery in Malta and Ireland: a comparative perspective. In D. A. Barrowclough and C. Malone (eds), *Cult in context. Reconsidering ritual in archaeology*, 118–33.

Oxford.

Tipping, R. 2002 Climatic variability and 'marginal' settlement in upland British landscapes: a re-evaluation. *Landscapes* **3**, 10–29.

Tobin, R. 2003 Corbally Neolithic houses. In I. Bennett (ed.), *Excavations 2001*, 185–7. Bray.

Toner, G. 2000 Identifying Ptolemy's Irish places and tribes. In D. N. Parsons and P. Sims-Williams (eds), *Ptolemy. Towards a linguistic atlas of the earliest Celtic place-names of Europe*, 73–82. Aberystwyth.

Topp, C. 1962 The portal dolmen of Drumanone, Co. Roscommon. *Bulletin of the University of London Institute of Archaeology* **3**, 38–46.

Topping, P. 1996 Structure and ritual in the Neolithic house: some examples from Britain and Ireland. In T. Darvill and J. Thomas (eds), *Neolithic houses in northwest Europe and beyond*, 157–70. Oxford.

Tourunen, A. 2008 Fauna and *fulachta fiadh*: animal bones from burnt mounds on the N9/N10 Carlow bypass. In J. O'Sullivan and M. Stanley (eds), *Roads, rediscovery and research*, 37–43. Archaeology and the National Roads Authority Monograph Series No. 5. Dublin.

Treherne, P. 1995 The warrior's beauty: the masculine body and self-identity in Bronze-Age Europe. *Journal of European Archaeology* **3**, 105–44.

Uckelmann, M. 2008 Irland oder Iberien— Überlegungen zum Ursprung einer Ornamentform der Bronzezeit. In F. Verse and B. Knoche (eds), *Durch die Zeiten . . . Festschrift für Albrecht Jockenhövel zum 65. Geburtstag*, 259–68. Rahden.

Van Wijngaarden-Bakker, L.H. 1985 Faunal remains and the Irish Mesolithic. In C. Bonsall (ed.), *The Mesolithic in Europe*, 125–33. Edinburgh.

Van Wijngaarden-Bakker, L.H. 1986 The animal remains from the Beaker settlement at Newgrange, Co. Meath: final report. *Proceedings of the Royal Irish Academy* **86**C, 17–111.

Vander Linden, M. 2007 What linked the Bell Beakers in third millennium Europe? *Antiquity* **81**, 343–52.

Vencl, S. 1994 The archaeology of thirst. *Journal of European Archaeology* **2**, 299–326.

Waddell, J. 1978 The invasion hypothesis in Irish prehistory. *Antiquity* **52**, 121–8.

Waddell, J. 1988 Excavation at 'Dathi's Mound',

Rathcroghan, Co. Roscommon. *Journal of Irish Archaeology* **4**, 23–36.

Waddell, J. 1990 *The Bronze Age burials of Ireland*. Galway.

Waddell, J. 1992 The Irish Sea in prehistory. *Journal of Irish Archaeology* **6**, 29–40.

Waddell, J. 1995a The Cordoned Urn tradition. In I. Kinnes and G. Varndell (eds), *'Unbaked Urns of Rudely Shape'. Essays on British and Irish pottery for Ian Longworth*, 113–22. Oxford.

Waddell, J. 1995b Celts, Celticisation and the Irish Bronze Age. In J. Waddell and E. S. Twohig (eds), *Ireland in the Bronze Age. Proceedings of the Dublin Conference, April 1995*, 158–69. Dublin.

Waddell, J. 2005a Cheques and balances. *Archaeology Ireland* **19** (1), 7–8.

Waddell, J. 2005b *Foundation myths. The beginnings of Irish archaeology*. Bray.

Waddell, J. 2009 The elusive image. In G. Cooney, K. Becker, J. Coles, M. Ryan and S. Sievers (eds), *Relics of Old Decency. Archaeological studies in later prehistory. A Festschrift for Barry Raftery*, 339–47. Dublin.

Waddell, J. and Conroy, J. 1999 Celts and others: maritime contacts and linguistic change. In R. Blench and M. Spriggs (eds), *Archaeology and language IV. Language change and cultural transformation*, 125–37. London.

Waddell, J., Fenwick, J. and Barton, K. 2009 *Rathcroghan. Archaeological and geophysical survey in a ritual landscape*. Dublin.

Waddington, C. 1998 Cup and ring marks in context. *Cambridge Archaeological Journal* **8**, 29–54.

Waddington, C. (ed.) 2007 *Mesolithic settlement in the North Sea basin: a case study from north-east England*. Oxford.

Wallace, P.F. and Ó Floinn, R. 2002 *Treasures of the National Museum of Ireland. Irish Antiquities*. Dublin.

Walsh, A. 1987 Excavating the Black Pig's Dyke. *Emania* **3**, 5–11.

Walsh, F. 2006 Neolithic Monanny, County Monaghan. In J. O'Sullivan and M. Stanley (eds), *Settlement, industry and ritual*, 7–17. Archaeology and the National Roads Authority Monograph Series No. 3. Dublin.

Walsh, F. 2007 Tracing the Bronze Age in Tober. *Seanda: National Roads Authority Archaeology Magazine* **2**, 14–15.

Walsh, G. 1995 Iron Age settlement in Co. Mayo. *Archaeology Ireland* **9** (2), 7–8.

Walsh, P. 1995 Structure and deposition in Irish wedge tombs: an open and shut case? In J. Waddell and E. S. Twohig (eds), *Ireland in the Bronze Age. Proceedings of the Dublin Conference, April 1995*, 113–27. Dublin.

Walshe, P.T. 1941 The excavation of a burial cairn on Baltinglass Hill, Co. Wicklow. *Proceedings of the Royal Irish Academy* **46**C, 221–36.

Warner, R.B. 1982 The Broighter hoard: a reappraisal, and the iconography of the collar. In B. G. Scott (ed.), *Studies on early Ireland. Essays in honour of M. V. Duignan*, 29–38. Belfast.

Warner, R.B. 1987 Ireland and the origins of escutcheon art. In M. Ryan (ed.), *Ireland and Insular art A.D. 500–1200*, 19–22. Dublin.

Warner, R.B. 1991 Cultural intrusions in the early Iron Age: some notes. *Emania* **9**, 44–52.

Warner, R.B. 1994a The Navan archaeological complex: a summary. In J. P. Mallory and G. Stockman (eds), *Ulidia. Proceedings of the First International Conference on the Ulster Cycle of Tales*, 165–70. Belfast.

Warner, R.B. 1994b The Navan complex: a new schedule of sites and finds. *Emania* **12**, 39–44.

Warner, R.B. 1995 Tuathal Techtmar: a myth or ancient literary evidence for a Roman invasion? *Emania* **13**, 22–32.

Warner, R.B. 1996 Navan and Apollo. *Emania* **14**, 77–81.

Warner, R.B. 1998 An Iron Age lead pin from County Donegal. In M. Ryan (ed.), *Irish antiquities. Essays in memory of Joseph Raftery*, 111–22. Bray.

Warner, R.B. 2002a A newly discovered Iron-Age 'pendant' from Navan. *Emania* **19**, 37–42.

Warner, R.B. 2002b Beehive querns and Irish 'La Tène' artefacts: a statistical test of their cultural relatedness. *Journal of Irish Archaeology* **11**, 125–30.

Warner, R.B. 2003a Two pagan idols—remarkable new discoveries. *Archaeology Ireland* **17** (1), 24–7.

Warner, R.B. 2003b Old letters and new technology—the Ballyrashane gold hoard. In J. Fenwick (ed.), *Lost and found. Discovering Ireland's past*, 151–64. Bray.

Warner, R.B. 2004 Irish gold artefacts: observations on Hartmann's analytical data. In H. Roche, E. Grogan, J. Bradley, J. Coles and B. Raftery (eds), *From megaliths to metals. Essays in honour of George Eogan*, 72–82. Oxford.

Warner, R.B. 2006 The Tamlaght hoard and the Creeveroe axe. *Emania* **20**, 20–8.

Warner, R.B. 2009 Clogher in late prehistory. In G. Cooney, K. Becker, J. Coles, M. Ryan and S. Sievers (eds), *Relics of Old Decency. Archaeological studies in later prehistory. A Festschrift for Barry Raftery*, 505–16. Dublin.

Warner, R. [B.], Chapman, R., Cahill, M. and Moles, N. 2009 The gold source found at last? *Archaeology Ireland* **23** (2), 22–5.

Warner, R.B., Mallory, J.P. and Baillie, M.G.L. 1990 Irish early Iron Age sites: a provisional map of absolutely dated sites. *Emania* **7**, 46–50.

Warren, G. 2003 Life in the trees: Mesolithic people and the woods of Ireland. *Archaeology Ireland* **17** (3), 21–2.

Waterman, D.M. 1964 The stone circle, cairn and alignment at Drumskinny, Co. Fermanagh. *Ulster Journal of Archaeology* **27**, 23–30.

Waterman, D.M. 1965 The court cairn at Annaghmare, Co. Armagh. *Ulster Journal of Archaeology* **28**, 3–46.

Waterman, D.M. 1968 Cordoned Urn burials and ring-ditch at Urbalreagh, Co. Antrim. *Ulster Journal of Archaeology* **31**, 25–32.

Waterman, D.M. 1978 The excavation of a court cairn at Tully, County Fermanagh. *Ulster Journal of Archaeology* **41**, 3–14.

Watson, A. and Keating, D. 1999 Architecture and sound: an acoustic analysis of megalithic monuments in prehistoric Britain. *Antiquity* **73**, 325–36.

Weir, D.A. 1993 Dark Ages and the pollen record. *Emania* **11**, 21–30.

Weir, D.A. 1994 The environment of Emain Macha. In J. P. Mallory and G. Stockman (eds), *Ulidia: Proceedings of the First International Conference on the Ulster Cycle of Tales*, 171–80. Belfast.

Weir, D.A. 1995 A palynological study of landscape and agricultural development in County Louth from the second millennium BC to the first millennium AD. *Discovery Programme Reports* **2**, 77–126.

Whelan, C.B. 1952 *A bone industry from the Lower Bann*. Belfast.

Whittle, A. 2003 *The archaeology of people. Dimensions of Neolithic life*. London.

Wilde, W.R. 1861 *Catalogue of the antiquities of animal materials and bronze in the museum of the Royal Irish Academy.* Dublin.

Wilde, W.R. 1862 *Catalogue of the antiquities of gold in the museum of the Royal Irish Academy.* Dublin.

Williams, B.B. 1978 Excavations at Lough Eskragh, County Tyrone. *Ulster Journal of Archaeology* **41**, 37–48.

Williams, B.B., Wilkinson, J.L. and Magee, R.W. 1992 Bronze Age burials at Kilcroagh, County Antrim, and faience beads in Ireland. *Ulster Journal of Archaeology* **54–5**, 48–60.

Williams, D.M. 2004 Marine erosion and archaeological landscapes: a case study of stone forts at cliff-top locations in the Aran Islands, Ireland. *Geoarchaeology* **19**, 167–75.

Wood, J. 2000 Food and drink in European prehistory. *European Journal of Archaeology* **3**, 89–111.

Woodman, P.C. 1967 A flint hoard from Killybeg. *Ulster Journal of Archaeology* **30**, 8–14.

Woodman, P.C. 1977 Recent excavations at Newferry, Co. Antrim. *Proceedings of the Prehistoric Society* **43**, 155–99.

Woodman, P.C. 1978a The chronology and economy of the Irish Mesolithic: some working hypotheses. In P. Mellars (ed.), *The early postglacial settlement of northern Europe*, 333–69. London.

Woodman, P.C. 1978b *The Mesolithic in Ireland.* British Archaeological Reports, British Series 58. Oxford.

Woodman, P.C. 1985 *Excavations at Mount Sandel 1973–77.* Belfast.

Woodman, P.C. 1992 Excavations at Mad Man's Window, Glenarm, Co. Antrim: problems of flint exploitation in east Antrim. *Proceedings of the Prehistoric Society* **58**, 77–106.

Woodman, P.C. 1997 Killuragh. In I. Bennett (ed.), *Excavations 1996*, 67–8. Bray.

Woodman, P.C. 1998 Pushing out the boat for an Irish Palaeolithic. In N. Ashton, F. Healy and P. Pettitt (eds), *Stone Age archaeology. Essays in honour of John Wymer*, 146–57. Oxford.

Woodman, P.C. 2000 Getting back to basics: transitions to farming in Ireland and Britain. In T. D. Price (ed.), *Europe's first farmers*, 219–59. Cambridge.

Woodman, P.C. 2003a *Pushing back the boundaries.* John Jackson Lecture 2003. Occasional Papers in Irish Science and Technology 27. Royal Dublin Society.

Woodman, P.C. 2003b Colonising the edge of Europe: Ireland as a case study. In L. Larsson, H. Kindgren, K. Knutsson, D. Leoffler and A. Akerlund (eds), *Mesolithic on the move. Papers presented at the Sixth International Conference on the Mesolithic in Europe, Stockholm 2000*, 57–61. Oxford.

Woodman, P.C. 2004a Some problems and perspectives: reviewing aspects of the Mesolithic period in Ireland. In A. Saville (ed.), *Mesolithic Scotland and its neighbours*, 285–97. Edinburgh.

Woodman, P.C. 2004b The exploitation of Ireland's coastal resources—a marginal resource through time? In M. González Morales and G. A. Clark (eds), *The Mesolithic of the Atlantic façade: proceedings of the Santander symposium*, 37–55. Tempe.

Woodman, P.C. and Anderson, E. 1990 The Irish Later Mesolithic: a partial picture. In P. M. Vermeersch and P. van Peer (eds), *Contributions to the Mesolithic in Europe*, 377–87. Louvain.

Woodman, P.C. and Johnson, G. 1996 Excavations at Bay Farm 1, Carnlough, Co. Antrim, and the study of the 'Larnian' technology. *Proceedings of the Royal Irish Academy* **96**C, 137–235.

Woodman, P.C. and McCarthy, M. 2003 Contemplating some awful(ly interesting) vistas: importing cattle and red deer into prehistoric Ireland. In I. Armit, E. Murphy, E. Nelis and D. Simpson (eds), *Neolithic settlement in Ireland and western Britain*, 31–9. Oxford.

Woodman, P.C., Anderson, E. and Finley, N. 1999 *Excavations at Ferriter's Cove, 1983–95: last foragers, first farmers in the Dingle Peninsula.* Bray.

Woodman, P.C., Doggart, R. and Mallory, J.P. 1992 Excavations at Windy Ridge, Co. Antrim, 1981–82. *Ulster Journal of Archaeology* **54–5**, 18–35.

Woodman, P.C., Finlay, N. and Anderson, E. 2006 *The archaeology of a collection: the Keiller–Knowles collection of the National Museum of Ireland.* Dublin.

Woodman, P.C., McCarthy, M. and Monaghan, N. 1997 The Irish Quaternary Fauna Project. *Quaternary Science Reviews* **16**, 129–59.

Woodward, A., Hunter, J., Ixer, R. *et al.* 2006 Beaker age bracers in England: sources, function and use. *Antiquity* **80**, 530–43.

Yates, M.J. 1985 Restoration of the Cuilbane stone circle, Garvagh, County Londonderry, and the discovery of a cache of flints. *Ulster Journal of Archaeology* **48**, 41–50.

Zvelebil, M. 1994 Plant use in the Mesolithic and its role in the transition to farming. *Proceedings of the Prehistoric Society* **60**, 35–74.

Zvelebil, M. 2003 People behind the lithics. Social life and social conditions of Mesolithic communities in temperate Europe. In L. Bevan and J. Moore (eds), *Peopling the Mesolithic in a northern environment*, 1–26. British Archaeological Reports, International Series 1157. Oxford.

Zvelebil, M., Macklin, M.G., Passmore, D.G. and Ramsden, P. 1996 Alluvial archaeology in the Barrow valley, southeast Ireland: the 'Riverford Culture' re-visited. *Journal of Irish Archaeology* **7**, 13–40.

Zvelebil, M., Moore, J.A., Green, S.W. and Henson, D. 1987 Regional survey and the analysis of lithic scatters: a case study from southeast Ireland. In P. Rowley-Conwy, M. Zvelebil and H. P. Blankholm (eds), *Mesolithic north-west Europe: recent trends*, 9–32. Sheffield.

Index

A

Abbeyshrule, Co. Longford, 251, 334
Achill, Co. Mayo, 45
adzes, *10*, 56, 217
Aghanaglack, Co. Fermanagh, 92
Aghintemple, Co. Longford, 62
Aghnaskeagh, Co. Louth, 102
Agricola, 395, 396
agriculture, 25–62, 175, 179, 281
    arable farming, 27, 29, 227, 228, 281, 337
    dairying, 125, 217
    Dowris phase, 283
    and megalithic tombs, 87
Albania, 273
Albion, 395
alder (*Alnus*), 3, 28, 53, 129, 226, 251, 277, 324, 337, 373
alder shovel, *149*
Altanagh, Co. Tyrone, 277
Altar, Co. Cork, 108, 150, 179, 334, 388
Altartate Glebe, Co. Monaghan, wooden cauldron, *338*, 339
amber, 257, 271–3, 286
    beads, 119, 185, 218, 222, *223*, 232, 262, *263*, 279, 280, 281, 306
    buttons, 128
    necklaces, *146*, 147, 163, 167
    Nordic influence, 271–3
    rings, 218
Ambleside, Cumbria, 191
    sword type, 213
anchor, *308*, 309
aniconic carvings, 385–7
animal bones, 16, 22, 26, 30, 33, 34, 49, 81, 104, 125, 126, 185
    Annaghmare, Co. Armagh, 93
    Ashleypark, Co. Tipperary, 113
    Ballinderry, Co. Westmeath, 279
    Ballybronoge South, Co. Limerick, 392
    Ballymulholland, Co. Derry, 334
    Ballyveelish, Co. Tipperary, 217
    Baunogenasraid, Co. Carlow, 111
    burnt mounds, 184
    Carrowmore, Co. Sligo, 80
    Clonfinlough, Co. Offaly, 222
    Dalkey Island, Co. Dublin, 13
    dating, 26
    Dún Aonghasa, Inis Mór, Aran, Co. Galway, 229, 231
    Ferriter's Cove, Co. Kerry, 14
    Fourknocks I, Co. Meath, 75
    Geroid Island, Lough Gur, 43
    Grange, Co. Limerick, 119
    Kilshane, Co. Dublin, 48
    King's Stables, 228
    Knockaulin, Co. Kildare, 363
    Knockroe, Co. Tyrone, 158
    Knowth, Co. Meath, 41, 72
    Lough Gur, Co. Limerick, 108
    Mooghaun, Co. Clare, 282
    Navan Fort, Co. Armagh, 353, 355
    Newgrange, Co. Meath, 117
    Poulnabrone, Co. Clare, 101
    radiocarbon dating, 2
    Rahally, Co. Galway, 285
    ritual deposits, 388
    Ross Island, Co. Kerry, 131, 132
    Tara, Co. Meath, 340, 345, 349
animals, 18
Annadale, Co. Leitrim, 251
Annagh, Co. Limerick, 114
Annaghbeg, Co. Longford, 136
Annaghcorrib, Co. Galway, 222
Annaghkeen, Co. Galway, 156
Annaghmare, Co. Armagh, *89*, 91, 93–4, 95, 96
Annals of Connacht, 372
Annesborough, Co. Armagh, hoard, 198–9, 397
antler artefacts, 72, 74
    hafts, 142
    hilt plates, *247*, 248
    pins, 71, 76, 79, 80, 82, 83
    pommels, 316
    rods, 74, 83
    toggle, 280
antler points, 18
antler sleeves, for adzes, *10*

antlers, 185
Antrim, County, 84, 272, 295, 301
    axes, 58
    bowls, 152
    bracers (wrist-guards), 128
    bronze knives, *275*
    bronze terret, *315*
    collared urns, 161
    cordoned urns, 162
    flaked axe rough-outs, 56
    iron ore, 301
    porcellanite, 56, 58, 96, 102
    ring-headed pins, *315*
    wedge tombs, 107
anvils, 125, 132, 201, 211, 279
    bronze, 274
    miniature, 197
ape skull, 306, 355
Appleby, Lincolnshire, 193–4
apples, 30
Arboe, Co. Tyrone
    cup-headed pin, *269*, 270
    gold bulla, 262
Ardcrony, Co. Tipperary, 111, 255
Ardmayle, Co. Tipperary, 206
Ardmore, Co. Tipperary, 379
Ardnaglug bog, Co. Roscommon, 305
Ardsallagh, Co. Meath, 393
Armagh, County, 383
    bronze discs, 330
    bronze socketed axehead, *276*
    court tombs, 92
    linear earthworks, 381
    passage tombs, 65, 84
    stone carvings, 383
    stone heads, 383
    wooden bowl, 337, *338*
armlets
    glass, 393
    gold, 203, 208, *256*
    shale, 355
Arran, Scotland, 162
    pitchstone, 35
arrowheads
    flint, 38, 58–9, 96, 119, 125, 129
        barbed and tanged, 109, 121, *127*, 129
        leaf-shaped, 102, 154
        lozenge-shaped, 95
art
    Celtic La Tène art style, 302
    court tombs, 95
    motifs, 84–5, 147, 196, 197, 251, 262, 306, 319, 322, 387
        Fourknocks I, Co. Meath, 75
        lunulae, 145
    passage tombs, 69, 70, 73, 75, 76, 83–7, 119
    pillar stones, 385
    rock carvings, 173–5
    stone circles, 385
artefacts, distribution of, *336*
Arctic fox, 2

ash, 41, 60, 179, 222, 226, 227, 277, 373
Ashgrove, Fife, Scotland, 130
Ashleypark, Co. Tipperary, 113, 115
Askillaun, Co. Mayo, 178
Athenry, Co. Galway, bronze shield, 253
Athleague, Co. Roscommon, 385
Athlone, Co. Westmeath
    bronze shield, 253–4
    bronze sickle, *275*
    sword, *292*, 298
    torcs, 201, *202*
Atlantic cauldrons, 239
The Atlantic Celts: ancient people or modern invention?
    (James), 303
Atlantic period, 27, 29
Atlantic seaways, 270–1, 303
Attancourt, France, bronze torc, *329*
Attymon, Co. Galway, horse-bits and pendants, 312, 313, *314*
Audleystown, Co. Down, *90*, 91, 92, 93, 152
Aughinish, Co. Limerick, 281, 311
Avebury, Wiltshire, 177
Avery, Michael, 309
axeheads, 248
    bronze, 391
        socketed, *210*, *234*, 245, *268*, 272, 274, *276*, 277, *294*, *295*
    iron, 295, 296, 297, 333
    limestone, 62
    mudstone, 61
    Scandinavian-type socketed, 272
    stone, 16, 22, 38, *54*, *55*, 58, 60, 277, *278*, 280
axes, 9, 10, 132, 139, 141, 195–7, 208, 274
    bronze, 132, 134, 136, *137*, 139, 141, 150, 221, *263*
        Ballyvally phase, 138
        Derryniggin phase, 138–9
        socketed, 198, 235, *263*, 274–7
    copper, 129, 130, 132, 133, 134, *135*, 136, 139
    core, 8, 9, 17
    flake, 8, 10, 17
    flat, 138–9
    flint, 9, 56
    hoards, 139
    iron, 294, *296*, 297
        shaft-hole, 297, *298*
        socketed, *296*
    jadeite, 58
    porcellanite, 55, 56, *57*, 58
    short-flanged, 195
    socketed, 197, 248
    stone, 8, *9*, 10, 11, 13, 15, 17, 33, 35, 53–8, 154
        battleaxes, *127*, 129, 130, *160*, 161, 163, 167, 286
        court tombs, 95, 96
        distribution of, 54–6
    stone moulds, 148
    trading or exchanging of, 58
    tranchet, 9
axial pits, 95

B
Bailieborough, Co. Cavan, 336

Ball, Dr Robert, 244
Ballina, Co. Mayo, 145
Ballinasloe, Co. Galway, 249, 271
Ballinchalla, Co. Mayo, pottery, *155*
Ballinclemesig, Co. Kerry, 266
Ballinderry, Co. Offaly, 242, 279–80
Ballinderry, Co. Westmeath, 274, 316
    iron sword, *317*
    tools, *273*
Balline, Co. Limerick, 397
Ballinesker, Co. Wexford, 266–7
Ballinkillen, Co. Carlow, 374–7
Ballinrees, Co. Derry, 397
Ballintaggart, Co. Down, 35
    cemetery, 172
Ballintober, Co. Mayo, 211
Ballintruer More, Co. Wicklow, 111, *112*
Ballintubbrid, Co. Wexford, 163
Ballinvoher, Co. Cork, 157
balls
    chalk, 70, 74, 80, 83
    limestone, 83
    stone, 69, 77, 78, 82, 83, 117
Ballyalton bowls, 53
Ballyalton, Co. Down, 56, 62, 92, 96
Ballyarnet Lake, Co. Derry, 162
Ballybeg, Co. Cork, copper axe, 134, *135*
Ballybriest, Co. Derry, 43, *51*, 96, 107, 109
Ballybritain, Co. Derry, wooden idol, 383, *384*
Ballybronoge South, Co. Limerick, 392
Ballybrowney, Co. Cork, 219
Ballycarty, Co. Kerry, 83
Ballyclare, Co. Antrim, flint hoard, *127*, 129
Ballycommane, Co. Cork, 178, 179
Ballyconnell, Co. Cavan, 385
Ballycroghan, Co. Down, 248
Ballycullen, Co. Armagh, dagger, *140*
Ballycullen, Co. Down, 2
Ballycurrin Demesne, Co. Galway, 271
Ballydavis, Co. Laois, 328, 392
Ballyduff, Co. Wexford, 156, 163
Ballyedmond, Co. Galway, bronze cauldron, *338*, 339
Ballyedmonduff, Co. Dublin, *103*, 104, 106, 107, 109
Ballygalley, Co. Antrim, 35, *36*, 57, 58
Ballygawley, Co. Tyrone, sickle, *275*
Ballyglass, Co. Mayo, 35, 43, 87, 91, 96
    court tomb, *89*
    settlements, *36*, 44
Ballygowan, Co. Kilkenny, bronze sickle, 274, *275*
Ballyharry, Co. Antrim, 30, 31, 37, 38, 40, 46
Ballyhoura Hills Project, 213
Ballykeaghra, Co. Galway, 265
Ballykeel, Co. Armagh, 99, 100
Ballykeoghan, Co. Kilkenny, 185
Ballykilleen, Co. Offaly, 129
Ballykilmurry, Co. Wicklow, wooden model of a sword,
    316, *317*
Ballylin, Co. Offaly, 271
Ballylumford, Co. Antrim, 306
Ballymacaldrack, Co. Antrim, *90*, 92, 95, 96, 156, 161
Ballymacaward, Co. Donegal, 393

Ballymacdermot, Co. Armagh, 92, 95, 96
Ballymaley, Co. Clare, 185
Ballymarlagh, Co. Antrim, 94, 96
Ballymena, Co. Antrim, spearhead, *140*
Ballymoney, Co. Antrim, bronze cauldron, *338*
Ballymulholland, Co. Derry, 334
Ballynagilly, Co. Tyrone, 26, 27, 29, 33, *34*, 38, 46, 122,
    124
Ballynahow, Co. Cork, 156
    pottery, *155*
Ballyness, Co. Donegal, 397
Ballynoe, Co. Down, 119
Ballyrenan, Co. Tyrone, 96, 99, 100, 102, 162
Ballyrisode Hill, Co. Cork, 56
Ballyscullion, Co. Antrim, 27
Ballyshannon Bay, Co. Donegal, bronze sword hilt, 316,
    317
Ballyshannon, Co. Donegal, 144, 189, 316
Ballytegan, Co. Laois, *268*, 269, 272
Ballyvally, Co. Down, *137*, 138
Ballyvally phase, 138–9
Ballyveelish, Co. Tipperary, 158, 164, 216–17
Ballyvourney, Co. Cork, *182*, 183
Baltic amber, 271
Baltinglass, Co. Wicklow, 43, 82, 87, 377
Baltinglass Hill, Co. Wicklow, 30, *64*, 65, 377
Banagher, Co. Offaly, spearbutt, *323*
Banemore, Co. Kerry, 145
Bann disc, 328, *329*, 330
Bann flakes, 16, 17
Bann River, 7, 17, 55, 262, 319, *320*, 322, 324, 336
    scabbard plates, *320*
    spearhead, *190*
bar-form, 17
Barbary ape skull, 306, 355
barge poles, *308*
barley, 27, 30, 45, 48, 125, 162, 172, 217, 219, 227
Barnacurragh, Co. Galway, 240
Barnes Lower, Co. Tyrone, *60*, 92, 95, 96
Barrees valley, Co. Cork, 178, 333
Barrow River, Co. Kildare, rapier, *192*
barrows, 31, 172, 217, 219
    see also ring-barrows
basketry bags, 61–2
baskets, wooden, 19
Bateson, Donal, 396
Baunogenasraid, Co. Carlow, 111, 113, 167–8
Baurnadomeeny, Co. Tipperary, 109
Bavan, Co. Donegal, 92, 96, 102
Bay Farm, Co. Antrim, 13, 161
Bay Farm II, Co. Antrim, 42
beads, 61, 73, 82, 96, 163, 286
    amber, 119, 185, 218, 271, 272, 279, 280, 281, 306
        Clonfinlough, Co. Offaly, 222, *223*, 232
        Mount Rivers, Co. Cork, *263*
    necklaces, 163, 167
        Rathtinaun, Co. Sligo, 262
    bronze, 163, 167
    faience, 156, *159*, *160*, 162, 163–4, 167, 286
    glass, 172, 226, 285, 334, 345, 355, 373, 388, 391,
        392, 399

Knockaulin, Co. Kildare, 363
Loughey, Co. Down, 326
necklaces, 393
Rathgall, Co. Wicklow, 286, *287*
gold, 267, 272, 286
jet, 128, 147, 167
pottery, 72
schist, 96, 102
stone, 96, 102, 128, *160*, 392, 393
court tombs, 62, 96
passage tombs, 69, 71, 73, 77, 80
portal tombs, 101, 102
Beaghmore, Co. Tyrone, 28, *176*, 179, 180–1
'Beaker Folk', 121, 128, 129, 130, 302
Beaker period
burial rituals, 126–32
goldwork, 144
Beaker pottery, 53, 115, 117, 119, 121–4, 125, 128, 129, 130, 132, 133
all-over-cord (AOC) style, 122, *123*
all-over ornament, *123*
cemetery mounds, 170
copper mines, 131
decoration, 147
European Beakers, 122
styles of, *123*
wedge tombs, 104, 108, 109, 126, 152
beehive querns, 335–7, 379
Beenateevaun, Co. Kerry, dirk, *192*
beetles, 184, 226
Behy, Co. Mayo, 44, *90*, 91
Belderg Beg, Co. Mayo, 45
Belfast, 56, 336
Belleek, Co. Fermanagh, 191
Bellville, Co. Cavan, gold plaques, *144*, 145
Belmont, Co. Galway, 374
Beltany, Co. Donegal, stone head, 383, *384*
Belturbet, Co. Cavan, 250
Benraw, Co. Down, 143–4
Betaghstown, Co. Meath, 393
Bewcastle, Cumberland, 324
biconical cups, *159*, 163
Bipartite Bowl pottery, *51*, 53, 95–6, 100, 102, 111, *112*, 113, 152, 154
bipartite vases, 154, 156, 157
bipartite vessels, 156
birch (*Betula*), 2, 3, 10, 19, 27, 28, 53, 183, 277, 334, 373
birds, 1, 4, 6, 8, 13, 14, 19, 21, 101
Bishopsland, Co. Kildare, hoard, 197–8, 274
Bishopsland phase, 187
deposition of hoards, 208
goldwork, 199, 204, 206, 208, 306
metalwork, 188–211
weapons, 247, 248
Black Dyke (Claidh Dubh), Co. Cork, 380
Black Mountain, Belfast, 58
Black Pig's Dyke, 381–3
Blackhills, Co. Laois, weapon hoard, 248, *249*, 250
Blacklands, Co. Tyrone, 136
copper knife, *127*
Blackwater River, 194, 380

Blackwater River, Co. Armagh, dagger, *140*
Blackwater River, Co. Tyrone, bronze spearhead, *323*, 324
blades, 8, 10
backed, 9
bronze, 136, 162, 163
copper, 136
flint, 16, 21, 124
Blessington, Co. Wicklow, lunula, *146*
Boa Island, Co. Fermanagh, 383
boars, 22, 78
boats
gold, *308*, 309
log boats, 18, 32, 222, 277
wooden, *398*, 399
Bog of Allen, Co. Kildare, gold bulla, 262
Bog of Cullen, Co. Tipperary, 244, 265, 294
bog ores, 301
bog trackways, 334
Boho, Co. Fermanagh, bronze spearhead, *323*, 324
Bohonagh, Co. Cork, 177–8, 179
bone artefacts
belt hook, 154
pins, 61, 82, 83, 156, *160*, 163
bone points, 17
Boolybrien, Co. Clare, 245
Boreal period, forest cover, 3–4
borers, 17
Borrisnoe, Co. Tipperary, gold gorget, *254*, 255
boulder-burials, 179
boulder monuments, 179
Boviel, Co. Derry, 109
bowl food vessels, 151
Bowl Tradition, 119, 128, 151–4
artefacts, 154, 158, 168, 359, 391
burial rite, 152
distribution of, 152, *153*
bowls, 61
Ballyalton, 53
Bipartite, 53, 100, 111
bronze, *238*, 337–9
Decorated, 49, 52
gold, 257, 268
Goodland, 49, 52
Lyles Hill, *51*
miniature, 154
polypod, *123*, 124, 125
regional groups, *265*
wooden, 61, *123*, 337
bows, 59–60
boxes
bronze, 392
gold, 266–8
wooden, 281, 305
Boxgrove, west Sussex, 1
Boyne River, 277
bronze pendant, *312*
socketed axehead, *276*
Boyne Valley, 115
cemetery, *66*
passage tombs, 65–73

bracelets, 206–8, *257*, *268*, *295*
    bronze, 199, 231, 270, 306, 325
    distribution of, *264*
    glass, 326
    gold, 199, 206, 207, 208, 255, *257*, 262–4, 265, 388
    jet, 286
    knobbed, 294, *295*
    lignite, *278*, 279, 280, 286
    penannular, 199, *266*, 294
        distribution of, *264*, 265
    ribbon-like, 263–4
    shale, 280
bracers (wrist-guards), 121, *127*, 128, 143
Braid River valley, Co. Antrim, 61
Bray, Co. Wicklow, 4
Bray Head, Co. Wicklow, 399
Breaghwy, Co. Mayo, halberd, *140*, 141
breastplates
    bronze, 250
    gold, *256*
Breeny More, Co. Cork, 179
bridle-bits, 311–13
    bronze, 311, 334
    iron, 281, 294
Britain
    bar torcs, 201
    Beaker pottery, 122
    cauldrons, 239
    transitional palstaves, 197
Brittany
    Beaker pottery, 122
    haches armoricaines, 277
    megalithic tombs, 109
Brockagh, Co. Kildare, *137*, 139
Brockley, Rathlin Island, 56
Broighter, Co. Derry, hoard, 306–9
bronze, 132–4
Bronze Age, 187–232
    Bishopsland phase metalwork, 188–211
    Killymaddy phase metalwork, 172, 187, 188–211
    metalwork, 188–213
    Roscommon phase metalwork, 211
    settlements and economy, 213–32
The Bronze Age landscapes of the Pipeline to the West, 184
bronze artefacts, 154, 294
    cauldrons, 296, *338*, 339
    conical horns, 330
    cuirasse, *256*
    discs, 289, 328, *329*, 330
    figurines, 294
    helmets, 250
    horse-bits, *310*
    ingot, *307*
    linchpin, *315*, 316
    mirrors, 387
    mounts, *307*
    replacement with iron, 291
    statuettes, 294
    tools and implements, 273–7
    wetland depositions, 194
bronzesmiths, 211

bronze-working, 285, 340
brooches, 326
    bronze, 349
    early medieval, 319, 400
    Hiberno-Roman, 401
    iron, 393
    Italic safety-pin, 294, *295*
    La Tène, 304
    medieval, 400
    Navan-type, *327*
    Romano-British, 397, 399
Broughter, Co. Derry, 326
Browndod, Co. Antrim, 92, 94
Brozas, Spain, decorated slab, 251, *252*
Brück, Joanna, 172
Brusselstown Ring, Co. Wicklow, 378
buckets
    bronze, *237*
    distribution in Ireland and Britain, *236*
    Dowris hoard, *234*, 235–9
    regional groups, *265*
buckles, 393, 397
Bugthorpe, Yorkshire, 322
buildings, rectilinear, 40, 41
Bulgaria, 273
bull cult, 246–7
bull feast, 372
bullae, gold, 260–2
Bullaun, Co. Galway, 385
Burgess, Colin, 191
burial customs, 150–64
burial mounds, 164, 393
burial pits, *22*
burial rituals, 81–3
burials
    cremated, 286
    crouched, 393, 399
    extended, 393
    unburnt, 393
burnt mounds, 181–5
Bush Barrow, Wiltshire, 154
buttons, Beaker period, 128–9
Byrne, F.J., 372

C
Cahericon, Co. Clare, 184
Cahill, Mary, 257, 258, 267, 272, 306
cairns, 87
cake, bronze, *307*
Calheme, Co. Antrim, 246
Caltragh, Co. Sligo, 185
Cambrensis, Giraldus, 371
Canrawer, Co. Galway, 56
Cape Castle, Co. Antrim, bronze bucket, *237*, 238
Cape Clear, Co. Cork, 385
Cappagh, Co. Kerry, wooden sword, *292*, 294
caprovines (sheep or goat), 217
Carbury Hill, Co. Kildare, *390*, 392
Carhan, Co. Kerry, 136
Carinated Bowl pottery, 50, *51*, 52, 95–6
Carlow, County, 185

Carn, Co. Mayo, halberd, 139, *140*
Carn Tigherna, Co. Cork, 374, *375*
Carnbane East, Co. Meath, 78
Carnbane West, Co. Meath, 77
Carndonagh, Co. Donegal, rapier, *192*
Carnfree, Co. Roscommon, 343, 372
Carrick-on-Shannon, Co. Leitrim, spearbutt, *323*
Carrickfergus, Co. Antrim, wooden tankard, 337, *338*
Carrickinab, Co. Down, 153, 154
Carrickshedoge, Co. Wexford, 134
Carrig, Co. Wicklow, 163, *165*, 167
Carrigdirty Rock, Co. Limerick, 61
Carrigillihy, Co. Cork, oval enclosure, 219–20
Carrowbeg North, Co. Galway, 393
Carrowdore, Co. Down, 201
Carrowjames, Co. Mayo, 391, 392
Carrowkeel cemetery, 78, 87
Carrowkeel, Co. Sligo, 50
Carrowkeel pottery, *51*, 52, 82, 83, 116
Carrowlisdooaun, Co. Mayo, 391
Carrowmore, Co. Sligo, 26, 65, 78–81, 388
Carrownaglogh, Co. Mayo, 281
Carrowntreila, Co. Mayo, 53
Carrowreagh, Co. Sligo, 87
carts, 289
    fitments, 313–16
Cashel, Co. Cork, 232, 283, 374, 378
Cashel, Co. Sligo, iron sword, *317*
Cashel, Co. Tipperary, 267, 379
Cashelkeelty, Co. Kerry, 26, 178
cassiterite, 150
Castle Gale, Co. Limerick, 378
Castle Treasure, Co. Cork, 144
Castledamph, Co. Tyrone, 180
Castlederg, Co. Tyrone, cauldron, 241
Castlemahon, Co. Down, 179
Castlerea, Co. Roscommon, gold earrings, *205*, 206
Castlestrange, Co. Roscommon, carved stone, 385–6
Castletownroche, Co. Cork, 132
    copper axes, 134, *135*
cattle, 35, 43, 125, 217, 219, 224, 226, 232, 363
Cattle Raid of Cooley, 318
cauldrons, 339
    distribution in Ireland and Britain, *236*
    Dowris hoard, 239–41
    iron, 296, 339
    method of construction, *240*
    model, *308*
    regional groups, *265*
    uses of, 242–4
    wooden, 238
Caulfield, Séamas, 335
Cavan, County, 383
Céide Fields, Co. Mayo, 29, 43, *44*, 44–5
Celtic Iron Age, 305
Celtic La Tène art style, 302
Celtic languages, 302–3
Celts, 300, 302–5
The Celts: origins, myths and inventions (Collis), 304
The Celts: the construction of a myth (Chapman), 303–4
cemeteries, 65, 164–72

cemetery mounds, 165, 167–72
Cenél Conaill, 371
cereals, 28, 30, 31, 35, 217
    ritual deposits, 388
ceremonial feasting, 289
Cernon-sur-Coole, France, *320*
Chancellorsland, Co. Tipperary, 172, 217–19
chapes, 247–8
    boat-shaped, *292*, 294
    bronze, 294
    tongue-shaped, *210*, 211
    winged, *292*, 294
Chapman, Malcolm, 303
charcoal, 29, 33, 35, 42
chariots, 289
    fitments, 313–16
chert, 8, 9, 21, 58
chevaux-de-frise, 228
chisels, 56, 197, 274, 286, 289
    bronze, 197
    stone, 217
Churchfield, Co. Mayo, 251
Chute Hall, Co. Kerry, 245
circular buildings, 40, 42
circular enclosures, 115–72
cist burials, 152–3, *153*, 157, 164, *165*
Claidh Dubh, Co. Cork, 380
Clane, Co. Kildare, 114
Clare, County, 257
    gold gorgets, *254*
Clashbredane, Co. Cork, 139
Clogh, Co. Fermanagh, 339
Clogh River, Co. Antrim, 325
Clogher, Co. Tyrone, 281, 397
    fibula, 326, *327*
Clogherclemin, Co. Kerry, bronze horn, *245*
Clogherny, Co. Tyrone, 107
Cloghers, Co. Kerry, 35
Cloghskelt, Co. Down, 156, 164, 166
Clonaddadoran, Co. Laois, 59
Clonard, Co. Meath, halberd, *140*, 141
Clondalkin, Co. Dublin, *137*
Clones, Co. Monaghan, 258
Clonfinlough, Co. Offaly, 220–4, 232
Clongill, Co. Meath, bronze pendant, *312*
Clonlum, Co. Armagh, 102
Clonmacnoise, Co. Offaly, decorated stone, *335*
Clonmantagh Hill, Co. Kilkenny, 379
Clonoura, Co. Tipperary, shield, *323*, 324–5
Clonshannon, Co. Wicklow, 156
Clontygora, Co. Armagh, 156, 158
Clonycavan, Co. Meath, 388
Cloonbaul, Co. Mayo, 117
Cloonbony, Co. Longford, 53
Cloonbrin, Co. Longford, leather shield, 251, *252*
Clooneenbaun, Co. Roscommon, 199
Cloonlara, Co. Mayo, 251
Cloonta, Co. Mayo, rapier, *192*
clothing, 328
Cloughmills, Co. Antrim, 337
Clowanstown, Co. Meath, 19

Cloyne, Co. Cork, gold discs, *144*
Cluntyganny, Co. Tyrone, Beaker pottery, *123*, 124
coastal sites, 42, 283, 334
coastline, changes in, 4
Cohaw, Co. Cavan, *90*, 91, 92, 94
coins
    copper, 399
    gold, 397
    Roman, 388, 396, 399
    silver, 397
Colchester, Essex, 239
Coles, John, 244, 246, 251
Collared Urn Tradition, 158–61, 179
collared urns
    artefacts associated with, 161
    Killeenaghmountain, Co. Waterford, *159*
collars, gold, 265, *266*
Collis, John, 304
Colp West, Co. Meath, 216
Coney Island, Lough Neagh, 154
Cong, Co. Mayo, 181
Coolcronaun, Co. Mayo, 293
Coolmanagh, Co. Carlow, 201
Coolnahane, Co. Cork, pottery, *157*
Cooltrain, Co. Fermanagh, 147
Coombs, David, 242
Cooney, Gabriel, 306
Cooradarrigan, Co. Cork, 179
Copney Hill, Co. Tyrone, 180
copper axes, 129, 130, 132, 133, 134, *135*, 136, 139
copper knives, *127*, 129, 130, 136, 142
copper mines, 131
    Mount Gabriel, Co. Cork, *149*
Corbally, Co. Kildare, 37–8
Cordoned Urn Tradition, 161–2
    distribution of, *160*, 161
cores, *9*, 16
Cork, County, 177, 179, 191
    Claidh Dubh/Black Dyke, 380
Cork horns, *329*, 330
Corkey, Co. Antrim, bowl and bronze dagger, *151*, 154
Corlea, Co. Longford, 53, 136, 334, 337
Corleck, Co. Cavan, stone head, 383, *384*
Cornaclery, Co. Derry, 171
Corran, Co. Armagh, *127*, 128
    gold disc, *144*
Corrofin, Co. Clare, iron spearhead, *323*, 324
Corrower, Co. Mayo, 153, 171
Corrstown, Co. Derry, 213, *214*
Cotton, Co. Down, halberd, *140*
Coumagh, Co. Kerry, ring-barrow, *390*
Coura Lough, 233
court tombs, 63, 87–97, 110
    Annaghmare, Co. Armagh, *89*
    art, 95
    beads, 96
    burial rituals, 92
    distribution of, 87, *88*
    dual court tombs, 93
    flint artefacts, 96
    plans, *90*

    pottery, 95–6
    radiocarbon dating, 96
    relationship with megalithic tombs in England, Wales
      and Scotland, 96–7
    stone axes, 96
    Tully, Co. Fermanagh, *88*
    unburnt bones, 92
    varieties of, 87
    vase urns, 158
    vases, 156
Creevy, Co. Donegal, ring-barrow, *390*
Creevykeel, Co. Sligo, *90*, 91, 92, 95, 96
Creggan, Co. Antrim, 161
Creggandevesky, Co. Tyrone, 92, 94, 96
cremations, 22, 92, 391, 399
Crevilly, Co. Antrim, ribbed axehead, *276*
Croghaun Mountain, Co. Sligo, 26, 81
Cromaghs, Co. Antrim, 274
crook-ards, 31
Crossna, Co. Roscommon, bronze tools, *273*, 274
crotals, 246
crucibles, 148, 218, 224, 228, 279
Crumlin, Co. Dublin, pottery, *151*
Cú Chulainn, 318
cuff-fasteners, 257
Culleenamore, Co. Sligo, 42, 283
Cullen, Co. Tipperary, 254, 268
Cullyhanna, Co. Armagh, 224
Cunliffe, Barry, 305, 318
cup-marked stones, 76, 83, 85, 104, 113
cups, 163
    bronze, 227, 237, *238*, 306
    handle, *307*
    pottery, 164
Curragh, Co. Kildare, 363, 379
    earthworks, 391
    ring-barrows, 391
    ring-ditches, 392
Curraghatoor, Co. Tipperary, 33, 217
Curraheen, Co. Cork, 124
Cush, Co. Limerick, 393
Cushendun, Co. Antrim, 4, 13

D
daggers, *140*, 141–2
    bronze, *151*, 154, 158, 161, 167
    classification, 142
    copper, 130, 136
    flat riveted (type Corkey), 142
Dalkey Island, Co. Dublin, 13, 26, 124, 130
Dane's Cast, Co. Armagh, 381
Danesfort, Belfast, 55–6
Day, Robert, 209
dead
    cult of the, 63–114
      burial rituals, 81–3
      court tombs, 87–97
      grave-goods, 81–3
      passage tomb art, 83–7
      passage tombs, 63–81
    disposal of the, 22

Decorated Bowl pottery, *51*, 52, 53, 95–6
Denhead, Scotland, 249
Denmark, 239, 269, 270
deposition
    of material, 38
    of rapiers, 194–5
Derreen, Co. Roscommon, 239
Derrinboy, Co. Offaly, hoard, *205*, 206
Derry, County, 179
Derrybeg, Co. Sligo, fibula, *327*, 328
Derrybrien, Co. Galway, 271
Derryinver, Co. Galway, 281
Derrykeighan, Co. Antrim, decorated stone, *386*, 387
Derrymore Island, Co. Sligo, spearbutt, *323*
Derrynablaha, Co. Kerry, 173, *174*
Derrynamanagh, Co. Galway, *127*, 136
Derrynane, Co. Kerry, bronze horn, *245*
Derryniggin, Co. Leitrim, 138
Derryniggin phase, 138–9
Derryville Bog, Co. Tipperary, 294, 337
Derryvony, Co. Cavan, 306
Devilsbit Mountain, Co. Tipperary, gold hat or crown,
    267, 268
Dingle peninsula, Co. Kerry, 181
dirks, 191–4
discs
    bronze, 289, 328, *329*, 330
    gold, 129, 143, *144*, 144–5, *257*, 262
    wooden, 222, 337
Doagh Glebe, Co. Fermanagh, 195
dock (*Rumex*), 2
dog, 217, 226
Donegal, County, 301, 383
Donegore Hill, Co. Antrim, 46, 378
Doody, Martin, 213
Dooey, Co. Donegal, 397
Doogarymore, Co. Roscommon, block wheels, *288*, 289
Dooyork, Co. Mayo, 306
Dorsey, Co. Armagh, earthworks, 381–2
Dorsy River, 382
Downpatrick, Co. Down, 162, 270
    gold hoard, 206–8
Dowris, Co. Offaly, hoard, 233–47
    axehead, *234*
    axes, 235, 277
    buckets, *234*, 235–9
    cauldrons, *234*, 235, 239–41
    gouges, *234*, 235
    hammer, *234*, 235
    horns, *234*, 235, 244–6
    knives, *234*, 235, *275*
    pendants, *234*, 235, 246
    razors, *234*, 235
    scabbard chape, *234*, 235
    spearheads, 235
    swords, *234*, 235
Dowris phase, 187, 334
    amber, 271
    end of, 291
    goldwork, 254–64
    metalwork, 233, *265*

Dowth, Co. Meath, 65, *66*, 73, 115
Draperstown, Co. Derry, 336
dress-fasteners, 254, 257–60
dress pins, 328
Drimnagh, Co. Dublin, 53, 113
drinking horns, 339
drinking vessels, *338*, 339
Drissoge, Co. Meath, 269
    gold hoard, 263
Dromatouk, Co. Kerry, 178
Drombeg, Co. Cork, *176*, 177, 184
'Druid Stone', Ballintoy, Co. Antrim, *64*, 65
Drumanagh, Co. Dublin, 313, 399, 400
Drumanone, Co. Roscommon, *98*, 99, 101
Drumbest, Co. Antrim, bronze horn, *245*, 245
Drumeague, Co. Cavan, *127*
Drumirril, Co. Monaghan, 175
Drumlane, Co. Cavan, iron cauldron, 296, 339
Drumman More Lake, Co. Armagh, 274
Drumnahare, Co. Down, 181
Drumskinny, Co. Fermanagh, 179
Drumwhinny, Co. Fermanagh, 59
Drunkendult, Co. Antrim, 246
Dublin, 336
Duignan, Michael, 385
Dumha na nGiall, *see* Mound of the Hostages, Tara, Co.
    Meath
Dún Aonghasa, Inis Mór, Aran, Co. Galway, 2, 224,
    228–31, *230*, 378
Dunaverney, Co. Antrim, flesh-hook, 242, 270
Dunbeg, Co. Kerry, 283
Dunboyne, Co. Meath, 258
Dundrum, Co. Down, 397
Dunfanaghy, Co. Donegal, 397
Dunfierth, Co. Kildare, 145
    lunulae, *146*
dung beetles, 226
Dungannon, Co. Tyrone, 246
Dunmore, Co. Galway, bronze linchpin, *315*, 316
Dunsilly, Co. Antrim, 333
Dysart, Co. Westmeath, 206

E
ear-spools, *256*, 267
early Bronze Age, metalwork phases of, *133*
early medieval period, 334
earrings, *144*, 204–6
    basket, 143, 144, 147
    gold, 143
earthworks, 370
East Anglia, torcs, 203
economy, 124–6
    in 1600–1000 BC, 213–32
Edenderry, Co. Offaly, iron sword, 316, *317*
Edenvale, Co. Antrim, spearhead, *190*
Edmondstown, Co. Dublin, 153
    flat cemetery, *165*, 166
eel migration, 7
elm (*Ulmus*), 3, 27, 29
embanked ring-ditches, 389, *390*
Enagh, Co. Derry, 38

Enagh East, Co. Clare, 274
enclosures, 43, 339–74
   hilltop, 374
Enfield, Co. Meath, 299
England, 399
engraved slabs, Brozas, Spain, *252*
Enniscorthy, Co. Wexford, 201, 267
Eogan, George, 233, 257, 291
Erbenheim-type swords, 247, 248
Essexford Lough, Co. Louth, 62
Ewart Park swords, 293
exchange, and production, 148–58
extraction sites, 56

F
Fahee South, Co. Clare, 185
faience beads, 156, *159*, *160*, 162, 163–4, 167, 286
Fallahogy, Co. Derry, 27, 28
False Bay, Co. Galway, 156
farming, *see* agriculture
Feerwore, Co. Galway, 295, 326, 333
   iron axe, *297*
   iron fragment, *327*
Feigh Mountain, Co. Antrim, 397
Félire Óengusso, 339
Feltwell, Norfolk, 242
Fenagh, Co. Leitrim, 111
Fergus River, 283
Fermanagh, County, 179, 383
Ferriter's Cove, Co. Kerry, 14–15, 22, 26
   stone assemblage, 16–17
ferrules, bronze, *288*, *323*, 325
fibulae, 199, 258, 294, *295*, 326
   bronze, 363, 391, 392, 399
   iron, 333, 393
   leaf-bow, 326, *327*, 393
   Nauheim-derivative, 326, *327*
   Navan-type, *307*, 326
   rod-bow, 326, *327*
   Roman, 397
field systems, 44–5, 281
figurines, bronze, 294
Fir Bolg, 270
fish, 8, 14
fish-traps, 18–19
Fisherstreet, Co. Clare, 56
Fitzpatrick, Elizabeth, 372
flake axes, 8, 10
flakes, *9*, 16–17, 21
   backed, 17
   tanged, 16
Flanagan's Fort, 369
flat cemeteries, 165, 166–7
flat graves, 164
flax, 62
flesh-hooks, 197, 270
   bronze, 242, *243*
flint, *9*, 42, 49, 58
flint arrowheads, 46, 59, 96
   concave-based, *59*
   leaf-shaped, *59*

lozenge-shaped, *59*
   transverse, *60*
flint artefacts, 8, 13, *60*, 61, 163
   axes, 56
   cores, 8
   flakes, 2
   javelin-head, *60*
   knives, *60*, 154, 156, 163
   maceheads, *72*
   petit tranchet, *60*
   scrapers, *60*, 83, 96, 154
flint-knapping, 30, 49
Flower Hill, Co. Antrim, 397
food vessel urns, 157
food vessels, 156
   enlarged, 157
Fore, Co. Westmeath, 339, 393
foundation trenches, 38
founder's hoards, 211
Fourknocks, Co. Meath, 116
Fourknocks I, Co. Meath, 65, 73–7, 81, 83, 168
   burial rituals, 74–5
   decorated stones, 74, *75*
   grave-goods, 73
   plan of, *74*
Fourknocks II, Co. Meath, 75
fox, 4, 18, 226
France, 133, 201, 239, 270
   torcs, 203
Frankford, Co. Offaly, 134, 141
Fredengren, Christina, 281
Freestone Hill, Co. Kilkenny, 283, 373–4, 397
Friar's Walk, Co. Fermanagh, 379
fulachta fiadh, 181–5

G
Gahlstorf, Germany, 263
Galicia, Spain, 175
Gallagh, Co. Galway, 387–8
Gerloff, Sabine, 191, 239
Germany, 269, 270
   Beaker pottery, 122
Geroid Island, Lough Gur, 43
giant Irish deer, 3
Giant's Ring, Co. Down, 116–17, *118*
gifts to the gods, 208–11
glass beads, *see* beads, glass
glass bracelets, 326
Glebe South, Co. Dublin, 393
Glenavy, Co. Antrim, pottery, *155*
Gleninagh, Co. Galway, 178
Gleninsheen, Co. Clare, 255
Glenstal, Co. Limerick, axehead, *276*
Glenulra, Co. Mayo, 43
goat, 224, 226
Goidelic Celts, 270
gold, 132–4, 142, 143–5
gold artefacts, *267*
gold ornaments, uses of, *256*
Golden, Co. Tipperary, 397
goldwork, 199–208

bracelets, 206–8, 262–4
  distribution in Ireland, *259*
  Dowris phase, 254–64
  earrings, 204–6
  torcs, 199–204
Goodland bowls, 49, *51*, 52, 100, 109
Goodland, Co. Antrim, 30, 48–9, 94
gorgets, gold, *254*, 254–5, *256*, 257
  distribution of, *259*, *265*
Gortaclare, Co. Clare, 142
  dagger, *140*
Gorteenreagh, Co. Clare, gold hoard, 255, 257
Gortrea, Co. Galway, 129
gouges, 274
Goward, Co. Down, 95
Graigueshoneen, Co. Waterford, 124
Grainger, Canon J., 325
Grange, Co. Limerick, stone circle, 61, 119, 122, *123*, 181
Grange, Co. Roscommon, 142, 158
  circular mound, 168
  dagger, *140*
Grange, Co. Sligo, ring-headed pin, *328*
Grannagh, Co. Galway, 391
Granny, Co. Kilkenny, 38
grappling iron, *308*
grave-goods, 73, 81–3, 170, 171
Great Chesterford, Essex, 387
great Clare find, 265, *266*, 283
Greece, 191, 270, 271
greenstone, 14–15
Grevine West, Co. Kilkenny, 379
Grianán of Aileach, Co. Donegal, 374, *376*
Griffinrath, Co. Kildare, 245
Grogan, Eoin, 306
Grooved Ware, *51*, 53
Growtown, Co. Meath, copper axe, 134, *135*
Gündlingen swords, 291–5
  distribution of, *293*

H
haches armoricaines, 277
Hagenau, Kr Regensburg, 251
hair-rings, 260–2, 280
halberds, 134, 139–41, *140*, 208
  bronze, 141
  carn type, 139–41
  copper, 129, 133, 136, 141
  Cotton type, 141
Hallstatt, Austria, 304
hammer stones, 13
hammers, 234, 235, 274
  bronze, 197
  metal, 148
  stone, 8, 10, 16, 125, 131, 132, 148, *149*, 150
Harding, Anthony, 248
Härke, Heinrich, 171
Harristown, Co. Waterford, *160*, 163
Hart, Bavaria, 237
Haughey's Fort, Co. Armagh, 224–7, 232, 237, 277, 283, 339, 348, 374, 378

Hawkes, Christopher, 328
hazel (*Corylus*), 3, 28
hazel picks, *149*
hazelnuts, 6–7, 30
helmets
  bronze, 250
  leather, 250
Hemigkofen-type swords, 247
Hencken, Hugh, 279
Hermitage, Co. Limerick, 10, 22
Herzprung, Germany, 251
Hiberno-Roman material, 400, 401
Hill of Tara, *see* Tara, Co. Meath
hillforts, 373, 374–9
  inland promontory forts, 378
  multivallate, *284*, 285–6, 374, 377, 379
  univallate, 374
Hillswood, Co. Galway, 141
hilltop settlements, 45–6, 232, 285
hilt-guards, 316
hoards, 139
  Annesborough, Co. Armagh, 198–9, 397
  axes, 139
  depositing of, 208–11, 289
  Dowris, 233–47
  flint, *127*, 129
  founder's, 211
  Roscommon, 209–11
  tools, *273*
  weaponry, *249*
Holocene period, 2
horns, 244–6
  bronze, *245*, 264
  Loughnashade, Co. Armagh, *357*, 358
  regional groups, *265*
horse harness, 309–16
  side links, *310*
horse pendants, 297, 313
horse sacrifice, 371
horse trappings, 289
horses, 31, 125, 217
Hosszúpályi, Hungary, buckets, 237, 273
Huelva, Spain, 249, 271
Hughstown, Co. Kildare, 377
human remains, 22–3, 101, 218, 372
human sacrifice, 387–8
hunters and foragers
  6500–4000 BC, 10–16
  8000–6500 BC, 4–8

I
Iberia, 133, 251, 270
iconic stone-carving, 383
idols, wooden, 242, *243*
Ierne, 395
inauguration rites, 371–2
incense cups, 164
Inch Island, Co. Donegal, 143
Inchnagree, Co. Cork, 193
Inis Cealtra, Co. Clare, 289
Inis Oírr, Aran, Co. Galway, 27

Innermessan, Wigtownshire, 245
insects, 226
Inver, Co. Donegal, 95
Irish La Tène horizon, 305
Irish medieval literature, 318
Irish Stone Axe Project, 54
iron, 294–5
    production of, 299
Iron Age, 291
    burial monuments, *389*
    burial rituals, 393
    Celtic Iron Age, 305
    circular structures, 333
    human sacrifice, 387
iron artefacts, 295–6
iron ores, distribution in Ireland, *301*, 301
iron slag, 295
iron-smelting furnace, *299*
Island, Co. Cork, wedge tomb, *105*, 106
Island MacHugh, Co. Tyrone, 281
Islandmagrath, Co. Clare, 283
Isleham, Cambridgeshire, 239
Iveragh peninsula, Co. Kerry, 173, 178, 181

J
Jackson, K.H., 318
jadeite, 58
James, Simon, 303
Jarlshof, Shetland Islands, 231
javelin-heads, flint, 60, 93, 94, 96, 100
Jerpoint West, Co. Kilkenny, 111
jet
    beads, 128
    buttons, *127*, 128
    necklaces, *146*, 147
juniper, 3

K
Kanturk, Co. Cork, 191
Kealkil, Co. Cork, 177, 178
Keating, Geoffrey, 183
Keeley, Valerie, 392
Keelogue, Co. Galway, 193
    chape, *292*
    rapier, *192*
Keenoge, Co. Meath, 153, 154, 166–7
Kelly, E.P., 330
keltoi, 304
Kernanstown, Co. Carlow, 99
Kerry, County, 177, 179
Keshcarrigan, Co. Leitrim, bronze bowl, 337, *338*
Kilbeg, Co. Westmeath, shaft-hole axe, 297, *298*
Kilbride, Co. Mayo, 274
Kilcrea Castle, Co. Cork, 136
Kilcroagh, Co. Antrim, *160*, 163
Kildare, County, 185
Kilgreany Cave, Co. Waterford, 2
Kilhoyle, Co. Derry, *103*, 104, 107, 109, 152, 158
Killaha East, Co. Kerry, dagger, 136, *137*
Killarney, Co. Kerry, lunula, *146*
Killeenaghmountain, Co. Waterford, collared urns, *159*,

161
Killoran, Co. Tipperary, 215, 333
Killukin, Co. Roscommon, rapier, *192*, 194
Killuragh cave, Co. Limerick, 22
Killycarney, Co. Cavan, 154
    pottery, *151*
Killycluggin, Co. Cavan, carved stone, 385, *386*
Killymaddy, Co. Antrim, 187, *188*, 274
Killymaddy phase, 172, 187, 188–211
Kilmahamogue, Co. Antrim, 251
Kilmahuddrick, Co. Dublin, 172, 391
Kilmashogue, Co. Dublin, 158
Kilmore, Co. Galway, bronze knife, *275*
Kilmuckridge, Co. Wexford, 144
Kilmurry, Co. Kerry, bronze hoard, 294, *295*
Kilmurry, Co. Kilkenny, 181
Kilmurry North, Co. Kilkenny, 215
Kilnamanagh, Co. Sligo, 195
kilns, 333
    corn-drying, 333
Kilshane, Co. Dublin, 48
Kilsharvan, Co. Meath, 219
Kiltale, Co. Meath, dagger, *140*, 142
Kiltenan South, Co. Limerick, 172
Kiltiernan, Co. Dublin, 102
Kiltierney, Co. Fermanagh, 119, 128, 175, 393
    leaf-bow fibula, 326, *327*
King's Stables, Co. Armagh, 224, 227–8, 232, 348
kingship rituals, 370–4
Kinnegad, Co. Westmeath, 294, 299
Kintyre, Scotland, 162
Kirkburn, Yorkshire, 325
Kish, Co. Wicklow, 189, 248–9
    axehead, *276*
Kishoge, Co. Dublin, 38
    rectangular house, *39*
knives, 162
    bronze, 274, *275*
    copper, *127*, 129, 130, 136, 142
Knock, Co. Roscommon, 326
    hoard, 305–6
Knockacarrigeen, Co. Galway, 285
Knockadoon, Co. Limerick, 33, 219
    see also Lough Gur, Co. Limerick
Knockanbaun, Co. Sligo, 189, 249
Knockans, Co. Meath, 370, 379–80
Knockast, Co. Westmeath, *160*, 161, 162
    cemetery mounds, 166, 167, *169*, 170
Knockaulin, Co. Kildare, 316, 334, 339, 358–63, 399
    late prehistoric structures, 359–63
    mauve phase, 361, *362*
    plan of, *360*
    rose phase, 359, 361
    white phase, 359
Knockboy, Co. Antrim, 163
    pottery, *159*
Knockcommane, Co. Limerick, 300
Knockdhu, Co. Antrim, 378
Knockdomny, Co. Westmeath, 215
Knockeyon hill, Co. Westmeath, 21
Knockhouse Lower, Co. Waterford, 162, 219

Knockiveagh, Co. Down, 43
Knocknagur, Co. Galway, 129, 132
    hoard, *135*
Knocknagur phase, 134–6
Knocknalappa, Co. Clare, 248, 269, 280
Knocknarea, Co. Sligo, 49–50, 78, *79*
Knocknashee, Co. Sligo, 374
Knockroe, Co. Tyrone, 158
Knowth, Co. Meath, 40–1, 43, 65, *66*, 117, 130
    Beaker pottery, 124
    burial rituals, 81
    description, 70–3
    flint macehead, *72*
    orientation of, 71
    passage tomb art, 84–5, *86*
    plan of, *71*
    pottery, *123*
    Roman material, 397
    unburnt burials, 393
Koch, John, 318
Kurd buckets, 237, 273
Kurin, Co. Derry, 271

L
La Tène
    art, 309, 319, 385, 387
    period, 306
    swords, 316
La Tène, Switzerland, 304
Labbacallee, Co. Cork, 102–4, 108
Lacklevera, Co. Monaghan, 124
ladles, 61
    bronze, 397
Lagavooreen, Co. Meath, 219
Laghtea, Co. Tipperary, 377
Lagore, Co. Meath, wooden figure, 244
Laheen, Co. Donegal, pottery, *160*, 161, 163
lakeside settlements, 162
Lambay Island, Co. Dublin, 56, 57
    burials, 393, 399
Largantea, Co. Derry, 107, 109, 152, 158
    Beaker pottery, *123*
Largatreany, Co. Donegal, 306
Larkfield, Co. Leitrim, spearhead, *190*
Larne, Co. Antrim, 13
lateritic ores, 301
Lattoon, Co. Cavan, 272
    gold hoard, *257*, 258
Lawrencetown, Co. Meath, sickle, *275*
lead, 184, 196, 239, 260, 262, 277, 345, 397
leather artefacts
    body armour, 250
    clothing, 62
    helmets, 250
    shields, 250, 251, *252*, *323*
Lecarrow, Co. Sligo, fibula, 326, *327*
Lemonstown, Co. Wicklow, 391
Lia Fáil, 343
Liffey River, 4, 17, 18–19, 395
lignite bracelets, *278*, 279, 280, 286
Limerick, County, 257

Limerick-style bowl pottery, *51*, 52
linchpins, *315*, 316
Lindow Moss, near Manchester, 387
linear earthworks, 379–83
    Black Pig's Dyke, 381–3
Linkardstown, Co. Carlow, 60, 111
Linkardstown Graves, 111–14
Lisdoo, Co. Fermanagh, 333
Lisdrumturk, Co. Monaghan, cauldron, 241, 296
Lisheen Mine Archaeological Project, 184, 215
Lisheen Mine, Co. Tipperary, 184
Lislackagh, Co. Mayo, 333
Lismore, Co. Waterford, 330
Lisnacrogher, Co. Antrim, 319, *320*, 325–6, 334, 339
    bracelets, 325
    chapes, 325
    ferrules, *323*, 325
    iron spearheads, *323*, 324, 325
    ring-headed pins, 325
    rings, *323*, 325
    scabbard, 319, *320*, 325
    scabbard plates, *321*, *322*, 325
    spearbutts, *323*, 324, 325
    torc, 325
Lissan, Co. Derry, rapier, *192*, 193
Lissanode, Co. Westmeath, 289
    rattle-pendants, *288*
Lissard, Co. Limerick, 164, 172, 391
Lissyviggeen, Co. Kerry, 177
Littleton Bog, Co. Tipperary, 324
Llyn Cerig Bach, Wales, 311, 387
Llyn Fawr, Glamorgan, 274, 291, 298
lock-rings, 254, *255*, 258–9
    distribution of, *259*
    regional groups, *265*
log boats, 18, 43, 222, 277
Loire River, pieces of Irish trumpets, 245
Longstone, Co. Kildare, 128
Longstone, Co. Tipperary, 163
Longworth, Ian, 158
looms, 62
Lough Allen, Co. Leitrim, 301
Lough Beg, Co. Antrim, horse-bits, *310*
Lough Boora, Co. Offaly, 8
Lough Eskragh, Co. Tyrone, 224, 277–9
Lough Gara, Co. Sligo, 21, 253
Lough Gur, Co. Limerick, 38, 40, 43, 61, 108, 109, 130, 152, 224, 250, 313
    bronze shields, 253
    bronze yoke mounts, *315*
    settlement, *32*, *33*
    see also Knockadoon, Co. Limerick
Lough Lene, Co. Westmeath, wooden boat, *398*, 399
Lough Mourne, 295, 296
Lough Nahanagan, Co. Wicklow, 3
Lough Ravel, Co. Antrim, hoard, 132, 134, *135*
Lough Ree, 326
Lough Sheeauns, Co. Galway, 28–9
Loughash (Cashelbane), Co. Tyrone, 107, 152
Loughash (Giant's Grave), Co. Tyrone, *103*, 104, 107
Loughcrew, Co. Meath, 387, 388

cemetery, 65, 77–8, 85
Loughey, Co. Down, 326, 399
Loughnashade, Co. Armagh, 348
    bronze horns, *357*, 358
    pollen analysis, 227, 382
Loughran's Island, Co. Derry, horse-bits, *310*
Lugaid mac Conn, 347
Lugg, Co. Dublin, 181
Lullymore Bog, Co. Kildare, 21
lunulae
    gold, 129, 143, 145–7, *148*, 258
        classical, 145, *146*, 147
        distribution of, *146*, 147
        provincial, 145, 147
        unaccomplished, 145, *146*, 147
Lurgan, Co. Armagh, 198
Lurigethan, Co. Antrim, 378
Lyles Hill, Co. Antrim, 45–6, 378
Lyles Hill pottery, 33, 45, 46, *51*, 52, 180, 181
Lynch, Ann, 101, 178
Lynn, Chris, 353, 362, 371
Lyre, Co. Cork, 148
    mould for flat axes, *135*

M
mac Airt, Cormac, 347
Macalister, R.A.S., 270, 300
maceheads, 83, 86, 110
    flint, 71, *72*
Macroom, Co. Cork, 206, 246
Magheraboy, Co. Sligo, 46–8, 333
Magheragallen, Co. Donegal, 154
Magilligan, Co. Derry, bronze bucket, *237*, 238–9
Maguire's Bridge, Co. Fermanagh, 53
Malin More, Co. Donegal, 95
Mallow, Co. Cork, 132
mammals, native species, 3
Manannán mac Lir, 309
Marshes Upper, Dundalk, Co. Louth, 333
Martinstown, Co. Meath, 113
Maryport, Cumberland, 324
Massaliote Periplus, 395
Maughanasilly, Co. Cork, 178
Mayo, County, 201
mead, 130
Meenwaun, Co. Offaly, 271
megalithic tombs, 40, 45, 63, 79, 81, 119, 181, 183, 272, 301
    arrowheads, 59
    Ballyalton, Co. Down, 56
    Ballyglass, Co. Mayo, 35, 43
    Beaker pottery, 122
    Bowl Tradition, 152
    burial rituals, 150
    County Sligo, 26
    encrusted urns, 158
    Poulnabrone, Co. Clare, 46
    ritual activity, 115
    Townleyhall, Co. Louth, 42
    unburnt burials, 93
    Vase Tradition, 156

    in Western Europe, 86
        see also court tombs; passage tombs; wedge tombs
Melkagh, Co. Longford, 99
Mell, Co. Louth, 2
Mesolithic
    burial, 10
    distribution map of discovery of material, *20*
    early, 10, 16
    hunting, 26
    late, 10, 13, 14, 15, 25
metal artefacts, 130–1, 232
metallurgy, 131
metalwork, 232, 286–7
    Bishopsland phase, 188–211
    deposition, 311
    dirks, 191–4
    Dowris phase, 233
    Killymaddy phase, 188–211
    Knocknagur phase, 134–6
    rapiers, 191–4
    regional traditions, 264–70
    Roscommon phase, 211
    spearheads, 188–91
microliths, 8
Midlandian glaciation, 2
Milavče, Bohemia, 251
milk, 125, 217, 219
Millin Bay, Co. Down, 72, 119
Millockstown, Co. Louth, 333
miniature pottery cups (Pygmy cups), 164
mirrors, bronze, 387
Mitchelstown, Co. Cork, 163
Mitchelstowndown East, Co. Limerick, 21
Mitchelstowndown West, Co. Limerick, 172
Monasterevin, Co. Kildare, bronze discs, 330
Monavullagh mountains, Co. Waterford, 181
Moneen, Co. Cork, 168
Moneyreague, Co. Cork, 181
Monknewtown, Co. Meath, 115, 116, 124, 130
monuments, 173–85
Mooghaun, Co. Clare, 281–5, 337, 374, 378
Mooghaun North, Co. Clare, 265
    hoard, *266*
mould gates, *210*
moulds, stone, 148
Mound of the Hostages, Tara, Co. Meath, 76, *127*, 129, 163, 167, 171, 340, 343
Mount, Charles, 164
Mount Gabriel, Co. Cork, 131–2
    copper mines, 148–50
Mount Hekla, Iceland, 228
Mount Rivers, Co. Cork, 271
    axehead, *276*
    gold hoard, 263
Mount Sandel (Upper), Co. Derry, 4–8, 22, 42
    hut sites and reconstruction, *5*
    stone assemblage, 8–10
    territory, 7
Mount Stuart, Scotland, jet necklace, *146*
Moy, Co. Tyrone, spearhead, 324
Moy River, Co. Mayo, 293

Moylough, Co. Sligo, 141, 175
Moynagh Lough, Co. Meath, 15, 17, 26, 162, 280, 289
Moynalty Lough, Co. Monaghan, 289
    bronze ferrule, *288*
Moytirra, Co. Sligo, 108, 109
    Beaker pottery, *123*
Muckridge, Co. Cork, 333
Mullagh, Co. Cork, 289
Mullaghfarna, Co. Sligo, 50, 78
Mullaghmast, Co. Kildare, carved stone, *386*, 387
Mullaghmore, Co. Down, 172, 391
Mullyleggan, Co. Armagh, bronze sword, *247*, 248
Munro, Robert, 325
Munsterian glaciation, 2
Murlough peninsula, Co. Down, 42
Mycenae, *256*, 257
Mycenaean swords, 273

N
Nahanagan stadial, 3
Nannau, south Wales, bucket, 235, 237, 273
Nappan Mountain, Co. Antrim, 30
Navan, Co. Armagh, 250, 272, 283, 334, 371
Navan Fort, Co. Armagh, 227, 326, 339, 347–58
    Barbary ape skull, 271, 306, 355
    contour plan, *350*
    'forty-metre structure', 355–8
    great mound (site B), 349–55
    Navan enclosure, 349
    Navan-type brooch from, *327*
    parallel ditches, 379
    plan of, *354*
    pre-mound features, *351*
    ring-barrow, *351*
    ring-slots, *352*
    zones of prehistoric activity, 348
neck-rings, 199–204
    bronze, 199, 265
    gold, 199, 206, 207, 265, *266*, 270, 305, 309
    see also torcs
necklaces
    amber, *146*, 147
    glass, 393
    gold, *308*, 309
    gold wire, 309
    jet, *146*, 147
necklets, 206
needle points, 8, 21
needles, iron, 363
Neolithic, 25–62, 114, 119, 121, 125, 217, 219, 286, 372,
    378
    burnt mounds, 185
    monuments, 65, 78
    mortuary house, 95
    pottery, 11, 48, 52, 109
    settlements, 41, 42, 50
Newferry, Co. Antrim, 10–11
    flint assemblage, *12*
    organic remains, 17
Newgrange, Co. Meath, 31, 41, 43, 61, 65, 66–70, 117,
    130, 175, 181, 199, 397

    art, 85, 86
    Beaker pottery, *123*
    entrance stone, *68*, 85
    passage tomb, *67*, 125
    Roman material, 388
    'roof-box', 68
    standing stones, 68–9
Newman, Conor, 279, 342, 347, 389, 400
Newtown, Co. Cavan, 145
Newtown, Co. Meath, 35
Newtownbalregan, Co. Meath, Beaker pottery, 124
Norrismount, Co. Wexford, 113

O
Ó Conchobhair, Feidhlim, 372
Ó Nualláin, Seán, 179
Ó Ríordáin, Seán P., 172
    Lough Gur, 40, 224
    Tara, 342, 345
oak (*Quercus*), 3
O'Brien, Elizabeth, 393
oculist's stamp, 397
O'Donovan, John, 340, 359
ogham script, 400
ogham stone, 373
O'Kelly, M.J., 183
Old Warden, Bedfordshire, 387
Oldcroghan, Co. Offaly, 388
Omagh, Co. Tyrone, moulds, *140*, 143
Ora Maritima, 395
Oran Beg, Co. Galway, 391
organic materials, 61–2
organic remains, 17–23

P
paddles, wooden, 222, *223*
palstaves, 187, 195–7, 199, 211, 224
Parknabinnia, Co. Clare, 92–3, *103*
passage tombs, 63–81, 110, 393
    art, 83–7
    Baltinglass Hill, Co. Wicklow, *64*
    Boyne Valley, 65–73
    Carrowkeel cemetery, 78, 87
    Carrowmore cemetery, 26, 65, 78–81, 388
    distribution of, *64*
    'Druid Stone', Ballintoy, Co. Antrim, *64*, 65
    finds from, *82*
    Fourknocks I, Co. Meath, 65, 73–7, 81, 83, 168
    Loughcrew (Slieve na Caillighe) cemetery, 65, 77–8,
        85
    Mound of the Hostages, Tara, *see* Mound of the
        Hostages, Tara, Co. Meath
    Newgrange, Co. Meath, *see* Newgrange, Co. Meath
    numbers of, 63
    orientation of, 65
    with three cells, 65
Patrickstown, Co. Meath, 78
Penard, Glamorgan, 213
pendants, 82, *234*, 262, 286, 313
    bone, 72, 73, 77, 78, 101
    bronze, 235, 246, *312*, *314*

clay, 119
   pottery?, 70
   stone, 69, 71, 73, 82, 119
Pepperhill, Co. Cork, 35
personal ornaments, 326–8
petit tranchet derivative arrowheads, 61
Petrie crown, *329*, 330–1
Petrie, George, 330, 340
petroglyphs, *see* rock art
phalera, bronze, 289
Philemon, 395
Phoenixtown, Co. Meath, 397
picks, 17
pigs, 43, 125, 217, 219, 224, 226, 231
pillar stones, 385
   see also standing stones
pine, 3
pins, 268–70, 326
   antler, 71, 76, 79, 80, 82, 83
   bone, 61, 78, 83, 156, 163, 229, 391
      passage tombs, 69, 70, 73, 74, 76, 77
   bronze, 145, 231, 268–70, 280, 325
   cup-headed, 269, 270
   disc-headed, 269
   gold, 272, 309, 326
   mushroom-headed, *82*, 83
   ring-headed, *328*
   silver, 401
   sunflower, *268*, 269, 270
   wooden, 61
Piperstown, Co. Dublin, 30
pit graves, 164
pits, 38, 41, 285
plaques, gold, *144*, 145
Pleistocene period, 1, 2
ploughs, 31
Point of Sleat, Isle of Skye, 270
points, 8, 17
Pollacorragune, Co. Galway, *160*, 162, 164
pollen analysis, 26–7, *28*
polypod bowls, *123*, 124, 125
porcellanite, 30, 56, 57, 102
   axes, 35, 55, 56, 96, 180
      distribution of, *57*, 58
   bracers (wrist-guards), 128
portal tombs, 63, 97–102
   distribution of, *98*
   Drumanone, Co. Roscommon, *98*
   human remains, 101–2
   Kernanstown, Brownshill, Co. Carlow, *99*
Portglenone, Co. Derry, cauldron, 239, *240*
Portlaoise, Co. Laois, 271
Portugal, 175, 270
post-holes, 38
pottery, 33, 35, 49, 50–3, 83, 94, 95–6, 100, 119
   Bowl Tradition, *151*
   coarse, 217, 232
   found in wedge tombs, 108–9
   vessel, *278*
   see also Beaker pottery
Poul Gorm, Co. Cork, 334

Poulawack, Co. Clare, 113, 168, *169*
Poulnabrone, Co. Clare, 46, 60, 101, 102
Powell, Terence, 270
Pretanic islands, 395
Proleek, Co. Louth, 99
protohistory, 395–401
Ptolemy's *Geography*, 395, *396*
Pubble, Co. Derry, 391
punches
   bronze, 274, 302
   wooden, 251
pygmy cups, 154, 164
pyrites, 301
Pytheas of Massalia, 395

Q
querns, 126, 226, 334–7
   beehive, 335–7, 379
   saddle, 31, 216, 222, *223*, 226, 277, 279, 280, 281, 286, 326
      Ballygalley, Co. Antrim, 35
      Ballyharry, Co. Antrim, 37
      Corbally, Co. Kildare, 38
      Lisheen Mine area, 184
      Moynagh Lough, Co. Meath, 162

R
'race of the Black Pig', 379
radiocarbon dating, 27, 33
Raffin, Co. Meath, 372, *373*, 400
Raftery, Barry, 297, 313, 322, 324, 334, 374, 389
Rahally, Co. Galway, 285
Ralaghan, Co. Cavan, 242, *243*, 383
Randalstown, Co. Meath, 397
rapiers, 191–5
Rath Aithir, 380
Rath, Co. Meath, 392
Rath Dubh, 380
Ráth Laoghaire, Co. Meath, 340
Rath of the Synods, Tara, *see* Tara, Co. Meath
Rathbeg, Co. Roscommon, 369
Rathcannon, Co. Limerick, 172
Rathcoran, Co. Wicklow, 377
Rathcroghan, Co. Roscommon, 339, 363–70
   Cashelmananan (Manannan's Fort), 370
   Cave of Cruachain, 363
   Dathí's Stone/Dathí's Mound, 368
   eastern avenues approaching, *367*
   Flanagan's Fort, 369
   magnetic gradiometry survey, *366*, *368*
   magnetic susceptibility survey, *369*
   Miosgan Meabha, 363
   Mound, 363, 365
   Mucklaghs, 370, 379
   Oweynagat, 363, 370
   plan of, *364*
   Rathbeg, 369
   Rathmore, 370
   Rathnadarve, 370
   Relignaree, 370
   ring-barrows, 364, 369

Rathdoony Beg, Co. Sligo, 393
Rathgall, Co. Wicklow, 260, 272, *284*, 285, *287*, 339, 378
Rathlin Island, 397
Rathmullan, Co. Meath, Beaker pottery, 124
Rathnagree, Co. Wicklow, 377
Rathpatrick, Co. Kilkenny, 185
Rathroeen, Co. Mayo, 145
Rathscreg, Co. Roscommon, 370
Rathtinaun, Co. Sligo, 262, 271, 280, 289, 334
    iron artefacts, 297
rattle-pendants, 289
    from Lissanode, Co. Westmeath, *288*
rattles, bronze, 246–7
razors, 162, 163, 274
    bronze, *160*
Reanascreena South, Co. Cork, 177, 178
recumbent stones, 177
red deer, 3, 8, 18, 31, 217
Redbog, Co. Louth, 29
reed basket, 61
reels, 267
reindeer, 3
Renfrew, Colin, 303
Reyfad, Co. Fermanagh, rock art, 173, *174*
Rian Bó Phádraig, 379
Rianxo, Spain, gold hat or crown, *267*
ribbon torcs, 204, *204*
ribwort plantain (*Plantago lanceolata*), 27
ring-barrows, 172, 389–91
    see also barrows
ring-ditches, *165*, 172, 392
    penannular, 167
        Scotch Street, Armagh, 115, *116*
ring-money, 260–2
ringforts, 219, 227, 297, 326, 333, 342, 343, 345, 370,
    385
rings
    bronze, 227, *230*, 239, 262, 271, 274, 280, 286, 289,
        294, *323*, 326
        Ballytegan, Co. Laois, *268*
        hollow, 229, *323*
    gold, 185, 206
    iron, 311, 392
    regional groups, *265*
ritual deposits, 388
ritual sites, *48*, 49
rituals, 109–11
rivers, depositions of rapiers, 194
rock art, 173–5
Rockfield, Co. Kerry, 172
Rockmarshall, Co. Louth, 13, 22
Roddansport, Co. Down, 4
rods, 9
Roman Britain, cremation, 399
Roman material, 388, 396, 397–400
    fibula, 397
    Freestone Hill, Co. Kilkenny, 373–4
    pottery, 397
    silver, 397
    Stoneyford, Co. Kilkenny, *398*
    Tara, Co. Meath, 345, 397–9

Roosky, Co. Longford, 53
Roscavey, Co. Tyrone, ring-headed pin, *328*
Roscommon, County, 301
Roscommon hoard, 209–11, *210*
Roscommon phase, 187
Rosnoën swords, 213
Ross Island, Co. Kerry, 131, 136, 148
Rossan, Co. Westmeath, 295, 299
Rossconor, Co. Down, axehead, *276*
rotary querns, 335, 337
Rough Island, Co. Down, 43
Roughan Hill, Co. Clare, 125, *126*, 130
royal sites, 339–74
    see also Knockaulin, Co. Kildare; Navan Fort, Co.
        Armagh; Rathcroghan, Co. Roscommon; Tara, Co.
        Meath
Rubane, Co. Down, pottery, *151*
Runnabehy, Co. Roscommon, 330
Runnymede, Berkshire, 272
Rush, Co. Dublin, pottery, *151*
Russellstown, Co. Carlow, 43
rye, 227, 388

S
sacred trees, 372
saddle querns, 35, 184, 277–8, 335
Saint-Germain-du-Plain, France, *256*
St John's Well, Co. Kildare, 359
St Patrick, 380
Saintjohns, Co. Kildare, gold hoard, 208
salmon, 7
Samian ware, 397
sandhills, 154, 156, 158, 283
saws, double-edged, 197
scabbard plates, *320*, *321*, 322, 325
scabbards
    bronze, 319–22, 325
    wooden, 194
scalene triangle, 8–9
Scandinavia, 272
schist beads, 96, 102
Scotch Street, Armagh, 115
Scotland, 158, 270, 272, 337, 399
    Beaker pottery, 130
    Cordoned Urn Tradition, 162
Scots pine (*Pinus sylvestris*), 3
Scragh Bog, Co. Westmeath, 29
scrapers, 10, 42, 49–50, 61
    concave, 49–50, 61, 96
    convex, 61, 96
    hollow, 61
settlements, 124–6
    in 1600–1000 BC, 213–32
    fourth and third millennia, 31–50
    hierarchy of, 231–2
    and society 1000–600 BC, 277–89
    upland, 50
    see also royal sites
Shanaclogh, Co. Limerick, 172
Shanballyedmond, Co. Tipperary, 95, 96
Shankill, Co. Kilkenny, 379

Shanmullagh, Co. Armagh, dagger, *140*
Shannon River, 194, 253, 283
   iron sword, *292*, 298
   ring-headed pin, *328*
Shannongrove, Co. Limerick, 255
sheep, 62, 184, 219, 224, 231
Sheepland, Co. Down, 162
shell middens, 13–14, 42–3, 283, 334
shellfish, 13, 14, 15, 22, 42, 43, 81, 108, 334, 388
shells, 81
shield boss, bronze, 399
shields, 197, 250–4, 257, 270, 272, 273, 322–4
   bronze, 209, 238, 250, 251, *252*, 253, 254, 289
   Clonoura, Co. Tipperary, 324–5
   leather, 250, 251, *252*, *323*, 325
   wooden, 251, *252*, *323*, 325
Shipton-on-Cherwell, Oxfordshire, 239
sickles, 187, 197, 274
   bronze, 274, *275*, 291, 355
   iron, 325
siderite, 301
Sillees River, Co. Fermanagh, 136
Sintra, Portugal, gold collar, 270
Skrene, Co. Sligo, 206
skulls
   ape, 306, 355
   human, 279–80
sleeve-fasteners, *255*, 257, 258
   distribution of, *260*
   regional groups, *265*
Slieve Anierin ('Iron Mountain'), Co. Leitrim, 301
Slieve Breagh, Co. Meath, 40, *41*, 391
Slieve na Caillighe, *see* Loughcrew, Co. Meath
Slieve na Caillighe cemetery, *see* Loughcrew, Co. Meath
smiths, 211
Somerset, Co. Galway, 326
   hoard, 306, *307*, 339
Sonnagh Demesne, Co. Westmeath, 189
Spain, 201
spearbutts, 399
   bronze, *323*, 324, 325, 336
spearheads, *140*, 148, 188–91, 194, 211, 249–50, 264, 271, 274, 286, 294
   basal-looped, 189
   bronze, 142–3, 198, 235, 265, 271, 280, 289, *295*, *323*, 324
      Dowris hoard, *234*
      moulds, *230*, 231
      protected-looped, 191
   end-looped, 143
   iron, 300, *323*, 324, 325, 363
   kite-shaped, 187, 188, *189*
   leaf-shaped, 189, 213, 294, *295*
   with lunate openings in the blade, *250*
   moulds, 143, 187, 224
   protected-looped, 191
   side-looped, 189, *190*
   slate, 33, 38
spears, 322–4
   iron, socketed, 324
Spinan's Hill, Co. Wicklow, 377, 378

spindle-whorls
   bone, 280
   stone, 62, 217, 279
spokeshaves, 11, 17
spoons
   bone, 154
   ceramic, 154, 163
   jet, 392
   silver, 392, 397
   wooden, 154
standing stones, 68–9, 94, 119, 175–81
   see also pillar stones
statuettes, bronze, 294
stone alignments, 175–81
stone artefacts, 8, 154
stone axeheads, 38
stone axes, 8, *9*, 11, 17, 53–4, *55*, 96, 129
   ceremonial axeheads, 58
   flint axehead, *55*
   parallel-sided axehead, *55*
   rock types used in, 56
   straight-sided axehead, *55*
   symmetrical oval, *55*
stone basins, 82
stone battleaxes, *127*, 129, 130, *160*, 161, 163, 167, 286
stone circles, 175–81
stone heads, 383
stone idols, 383
stone implements, 53–61
   found in portal tombs, 102
stone moulds, for flat axes, 148
stone walls, 45
stones, decorated, *386*
Stoneyford, Co. Kilkenny, 399
Strangford Lough, Co. Down, 43
Streamstown, Co. Westmeath, 312
sunflower pins, *268*, 269, 270
sword blades, *210*
swords, 194, 209, 227, 235, 247–8, 250, 251, 264, 273
   Ballintober-type, 211–13, 247, 248
   bronze, 231, 232, 238, 244, *247*, 249, 254, 279, 280, 283, 302
      Dowris hoard, *234*
      leaf-shaped, 209
      moulds, 228, *230*
   examples of, *292*
   flange-hilted, 211
   Gündlingen-type, 291–5
   iron, *292*, 298, 306, 316, *317*, 363
   leaf-shaped, 209
   wooden, 294
   wooden model, *292*, 316, *317*

T
Tacitus, 395
Táin Bó Cúailnge, 318, 371
Táin Bó Fraich, 370
tairb-feis, 371
Tamlaght, Co. Armagh, hoard, 227, 237, *238*
Tandragee, Co. Armagh, stone idol, 383, *384*
Tankardstown, Co. Limerick, 33–4, 35, 129, 171

Tara, Co. Meath, 44, 119, 167, 334, 340–7, 379
  Banqueting Hall, 347, 379
  Claoinfhearta (Sloping Trenches), *342*, 346, 347, 391
  Dumha na mBó, 340
  the Forrad, 340, 342, *343*, 343, 345
  general plan of, *341*
  gold earrings, *205*, 206
  great ditch and pit circle, *120*
  hill-shaded computer model of, *342*
  incorporation of earlier monuments in later ones, 346–7
  Mound of the Hostages, Tara, Co. Meath, 76, *127*, 129, 163, 167, 171, 340, 343
  Ráth Gráinne, 345–6
  Ráth na Rí, 297, 299, 340, 342, 345
  Rath of the Synods, *344*, 345, 347, 374, 392, 400
  Sloping Trenches, *342*, 346, 391
  Teach Cormaic, 340, 342, *343*, 345
  Teach Miodchuarta, 347
Tattenamona, Co. Fermanagh, spearheads, 188, *189*
Taylor, Joan, 145, 147, 201, 257
Tedavnet, Co. Monaghan, 144
Teltown, Co. Meath, 379–80
Tempo, Co. Fermanagh, weapon hoard, 189, 248, *249*
temporary occupation sites, 43
terrets, bronze, *315*, 316
textiles, 62
Thames River, 330
Thames valley, 212–13, 247
Thornhill, Co. Derry, 43, 46
Ticooly-O'Kelly, Co. Galway, beehive quern, *335*
Tievebulliagh, Co. Antrim, porcellanite axes, 35, 56, 162
Timoney, Co. Tipperary, 61
tin, 136, 138, 148, 150, 163, 204, 260, 302, 306
Tinoranhill, Co. Wicklow, 377
Tipperary, County, 257
Tirkernaghan, Co. Tyrone, 124
  wooden bowl, *123*
Toar Bog, Co. Westmeath, 337
Tober, Co. Offaly, 216
toggles
  antler, 280
  bronze, *287*, 326
toilet implements, Roman, 397
token deposits, 162–4, 171–2
tools, hoards, *273*
Toome, Co. Antrim, 295–6, 319
  iron axe, *296*
  spearhead, *190*
Tooradoo, Co. Limerick, 262, 271
Toormore, Co. Cork, 108, 138, 179
Topography of Ireland (Cambrensis), 371
Topped Mountain, Co. Fermanagh, 156
  dagger, 142, 156
torcs, 199–204, 326
  bar, 199, 201
  bar-twisted, 201, *202*
  bronze, 199, 325, *329*
  buffer, 305–6, 309
  from Coolmanagh, Co. Carlow, *204*
  distribution of, *200*

  flange-twisted, 201–3, 306
  gold, 199–204, 326
  gold bar, *202*
  gold buffer, *308*
  gold ribbon, *307*, 326
  gold twisted, *308*
  Rath of the Synods, Tara, 201–3
  ribbon, 305, 306
  twisted, 306, 309
  untwisted triple-flanged, *204*
  see also neck-rings
Tormarton, Gloucestershire, 189
Townleyhall, Co. Louth, 42, 72
trackway, wooden, 21, 53, 136, 145, 222, 242, 334
transhumance, 42
Trawsfynydd, Merioneth, 337
tress-rings, gold, 199, 208
trumpet pieces, bronze, 271
Tully, Co. Fermanagh, 87, *88*, 92, 96
Tullyallen, Co. Louth, 333
Tullymore, Co. Donegal, ring-barrow, *390*
Tulnacross, Co. Tyrone, cauldron, 239, *240*
Tulsk, Co. Roscommon, 363
  horse-bits, *310*
Tumna, Co. Roscommon, 272
Turoe, Co. Galway, carved stone, 385, *386*, 387
tweezers, bronze, 274, 280, 326
Twyford, Co. Westmeath, 61
Tyrone, County, 179, 301

U
Uckelmann, Marion, 251
Uisneach, Co. Westmeath, 340
Ulster, 179
Ummercam River, 382
Urbalreagh, Co. Antrim, *160*, 161, *165*, 167
urns
  cinerary, 154
  collared, 158–61, 179
  cordoned, *160*, 161–2
  encrusted, 154, 156, 158, 164, 166, 167, 170
  see also Vase Tradition

V
Valencia Island, Co. Kerry, 21
vase food vessels, 154
Vase Tradition, 154–8
  encrusted urns, 154, 156, 158, 164, 166, 167, 170
  urns, *157*, 179
vase urns, 157
vases, *155*
  artefacts found with, 156
  distribution of, 156
  tripartite, 154, 156, 157
vegetation, development of, 3
Vénat, France, 240
Vesnoy, Co. Roscommon, 264
vessels
  bronze, 209, 337–9
  gold, *308*, 309
vices, 197

votive deposits, 136, 242, 272, 311, 387, 397

W
Wailes, Bernard, 359
Wakeman, W.F., 325
Wales, torcs, 203
Wardhouse, Co. Leitrim, 110
warfare, 46, 232, 316, 318, 325
Warner, Richard, 309, 336, 399, 401
water-lily seeds, 6, 7
Waterman, D.M., 349
weaponry, 247–54, 264
    chapes, 247–8
    engraved slabs, *252*
    hoards, *249*
    Iron Age, 316–25
    shields, 250–4
    spears, 248–50
    swords, 247–8
wedge tombs, 63, 102–9, 158, 179, 334
    distribution of, *103*, 106–7
    funerary rituals, 107–8
    orientation of, 106
    plans, *103*
    Toormore Bay, Co. Cork, 138
    unburnt burials, 108
Weir, David, 227
West Row, Mildenhall, 194
wetland depositions, 194
wetland sites, 162, 213, 280, 283, 334
Wetwang Slack, Yorkshire, 322, 392
wheat, 25, 26, 27, 30, 34, 42, 45, 69, 162, 215, 217, 282
wheels, wooden, *288*, 289

White Rocks, Co. Antrim, 42
Whitepark Bay, Co. Antrim, 42, 122, 154, 283
Whitespots, Co. Down, 129, 134
Wicklow, County, 301
wild animals, 4, 125
wild boar, 125
wild cat, 1, 3, 18, 125
wild pig, 3, 4, 6, 8, 13, 14, 16, 18, 22, 226
Williamstown, Co. Westmeath, 172
willow (*Salix*), 3
wooden artefacts
    bowls, *62*, 124, *338*
    cauldrons, *338*, 339
    idol, 383, *384*
    mould for shields, *252*
    pins, 61
    shields, 251, *323*
    tankard, *338*
    vessels, *278*, 337–9
    yokes, 289, *315*, 316
Woodgrange, Co. Down, 2
Woodgrange interstadial, 2
woodland management, 4, 222
Woodlands, Co. Donegal, 383
Woodman, Peter, 4, 10, 14
Woodsgift, Co. Kilkenny, 379
wrist-guards, 121, *127*, 128, 143

Y
yew, 59–60
yoke mounts, 313, *315*
yokes, wooden, 289, *315*, 316